Fodor's 2015

ARIZONA
THE GRAND
CANYON

WELCOME TO ARIZONA

From the vastness of the Grand Canyon to Sedona's red rocks and the living Sonoran Desert, Arizona's landscapes are awe-inspiring. The state's spectacular canyons, blooming deserts, raging rivers, petrified forests, and scenic mountains enthrall lovers of the outdoors in pursuit of hiking, rafting, golf, or picturesque spots to watch the sunset. But there is more to Arizona than beautiful vistas. World-renowned spas in Phoenix provide plenty of pampering, while Native American cultures thrive throughout the state.

TOP REASONS TO GO

★ **Grand Canyon:** Whether you hike, raft, or drive it, you shouldn't miss it.

★ **Native American Heritage:** There's no better place to experience these thriving cultures.

★ **Flavorful Food:** Blending Native American and Southwestern spices, Arizona's cuisine pops.

★ **Road Trips:** The wide-open spaces of Arizona dazzle anew with every curve of the road.

★ **Stunning Landscapes:** From Sedona's red rocks to Monument Valley, beauty reigns.

★ **Outdoor Experiences:** Canyons, deserts, and mountains offer adventures aplenty.

Fodor's ARIZONA & THE GRAND CANYON 2015

Publisher: Amanda D'Acierno, *Senior Vice President*

Editorial: Arabella Bowen, *Editor in Chief*; Linda Cabasin, *Editorial Director*

Design: Fabrizio La Rocca, *Vice President, Creative Director*; Tina Malaney, *Associate Art Director*; Chie Ushio, *Senior Designer*; Ann McBride, *Production Designer*

Photography: Melanie Marin, *Associate Director of Photography*; Jessica Parkhill and Jennifer Romains, *Researchers*

Maps: Rebecca Baer, *Senior Map Editor*; Mark Stroud (Moon Street Cartography), David Lindroth, *Cartographers*

Production: Linda Schmidt, *Managing Editor*; Evangelos Vasilakis, *Associate Managing Editor*; Angela L. McLean, *Senior Production Manager*

Sales: Jacqueline Lebow, *Sales Director*

Marketing & Publicity: Heather Dalton, *Marketing Director*; Katherine Punia, *Senior Publicist*

Business & Operations: Susan Livingston, *Vice President, Strategic Business Planning*; Sue Daulton, *Vice President, Operations*

Fodors.com: Megan Bell, *Executive Director, Revenue & Business Development*; Yasmin Marinaro, *Senior Director, Marketing & Partnerships*

Copyright © 2015 by Fodor's Travel, a division of Random House LLC

Writers: Andrew Collins, Mara Levin, Elise Riley, Michael Weatherford

Editor: Luke Epplin

Editorial Contributor: Debbie Harmsen

Production Editor: Carrie Parker

ISBN 978-0-8041-4276-2

ISSN 1559–6230

All details in this book are based on information supplied to us at press time. Always confirm information when it matters, especially if you're making a detour to visit a specific place. Fodor's expressly disclaims any liability, loss, or risk, personal or otherwise, that is incurred as a consequence of the use of any of the contents of this book.

SPECIAL SALES

This book is available at special discounts for bulk purchases for sales promotions or premiums. For more information, e-mail specialmarkets@randomhouse.com

PRINTED IN THE UNITED STATES OF AMERICA

10 9 8 7 6 5 4 3 2 1

CONTENTS

Fodor's Features

MAPS

ABOUT
THIS GUIDE

Fodor's Recommendations

Everything in this guide is worth doing—we don't cover what isn't—but exceptional sights, hotels, and restaurants are recognized with additional accolades. **Fodor's**Choice★ indicates our top recommendations; and **Best Bets** call attention to notable hotels and restaurants in various categories. Care to nominate a new place? Visit ⊕ *Fodors.com/contact-us.*

Trip Costs

We list prices wherever possible to help you budget well. Hotel and restaurant price categories from **$** to **$$$$** are noted alongside each recommendation. For hotels, we include the lowest cost of a standard double room in high season. For restaurants, we cite the average price of a main course at dinner or, if dinner isn't served, at lunch. For attractions, we always list adult admission fees; discounts are usually available for children, students, and senior citizens.

Hotels

Our local writers vet every hotel to recommend the best overnights in each price category, from budget to expensive. Unless otherwise specified, you can expect private bath, phone, and TV in your room. For expanded hotel reviews, facilities, and deals visit ⊕ *Fodors.com.*

Top Picks	Hotels &
★ **Fodor's**Choice	Restaurants
	🛏 Hotel
Listings	⚐ Number of
✉ Address	rooms
✉ Branch address	⍾ Meal plans
☎ Telephone	✗ Restaurant
🖷 Fax	⌔ Reservations
⊕ Website	👗 Dress code
✉ E-mail	🖮 No credit cards
🎟 Admission fee	$ Price
⊙ Open/closed times	
Ⓜ Subway	**Other**
✛ Directions or Map coordinates	⇨ See also
	☞ Take note
	⛳ Golf facilities

Restaurants

Unless we state otherwise, restaurants are open for lunch and dinner daily. We mention dress code only when there's a specific requirement and reservations only when they're essential or not accepted. To make restaurant reservations, visit ⊕ *Fodors.com.*

Credit Cards

The hotels and restaurants in this guide typically accept credit cards. If not, we'll say so.

EXPERIENCE ARIZONA

WHAT'S WHERE

The following numbers refer to chapters.

2 Phoenix, Scottsdale, and Tempe. Rising where the Sonoran Desert meets the Superstition Mountains, the Valley of the Sun is filled with resorts and spas, shops and restaurants, and more than 200 golf courses.

3 Grand Canyon National Park. One of nature's longest-running works in progress, the canyon exalts and humbles the human spirit. Whether you select the popular South Rim or the remote North Rim, don't just peer over the edge—take the plunge into the canyon on a mule train, on foot, or on a raft trip.

4 North-Central Arizona. Cool, laid-back towns here are as bewitching as the high-country landscape they inhabit. There are quaint escapes such as Prescott and Jerome, Sedona with its red-rock buttes, and the vibrant university town of Flagstaff.

5 Northeast Arizona. This remote area includes the stunning surroundings of Monument Valley. Alongside today's Navajo and Hopi communities, the breathtaking Canyon de Chelly and Navajo National Monument are reminders of how ancient peoples lived with the land.

6 Eastern Arizona. Summer visitors flock to the lush, green White Mountains and the warm colors of the Painted Desert. Petrified Forest National Park protects trees that stood when dinosaurs walked Earth.

7 Tucson. The modern history of Arizona begins here, where Hispanic, Anglo, and Native American cultures became intertwined in the 17th century and still are today. Farther out, city slickers enjoy horseback rides at some of the region's many guest ranches, or luxury pampering at world-class spas.

8 Southern Arizona. Splendid mountain and desert scenery evokes the romanticized spirit of the Wild West. Enduring pockets of westward expansion are the largest draw today: notorious Tombstone and the mining boomtown Bisbee.

9 Northwest Arizona and Southeast Nevada. This underexplored corner of Arizona includes Lake Havasu City and its bit of Britannia in the form of London Bridge; old-fashioned Americana around Kingman on legendary Route 66; and Hoover Dam and Laughlin's casinos, a short jaunt away in Nevada.

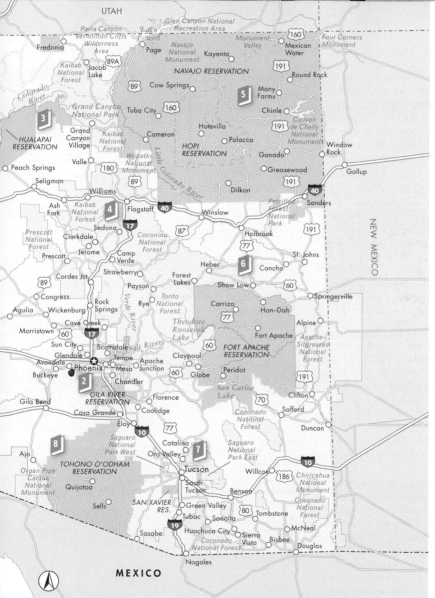

UTAH

Paria Canyon
Vermilion Cliffs
Wilderness
Area

Glen Canyon National
Recreation Area

Lake
Powell

Monument
Valley

Four Corners
Monument

Fredonia

Page

160

Mexican
Water

Kaibab
National
Forest

89A

Jacob
Lake

Navajo
National
Monument

Kayenta

191

Cow Springs

89

Round Rock

Grand Canyon
National Park

NAVAJO RESERVATION

5

Many
Farms

Colorado River

Tuba City

160

Chinle

191

Grand
Canyon
Village

Kaibab
National
Forest

Hotevilla

Canyon
de Chelly
National
Monument

3

Cameron

Polacca

Window
Rock

HUALAPAI
RESERVATION

Valle

Wupatki
National
Monument

HOPI
RESERVATION

Ganado

Peach Springs

180

Little Colorado River

Greasewood

Gallup

Seligman

89

Dilkon

Ash
Fork

Williams

Petrified
Forest
National
Park

40

Sanders

Kaibab
National
Forest

4

Flagstaff

40

Winslow

Holbrook

191

NEW MEXICO

Prescott
National
Forest

Clarkdale

Sedona

17

Coconino
National
Forest

87

77

St. Johns

191

U.S.
89

Jerome

Camp
Verde

Heber

6

Concho

Cordes Jct

Strawberry

Forest
Lakes

Show Low

60

Springerville

Congress

Payson

Rye

Tonto
National
Forest

Carrizo

77

Hon-Dah

Alpine

Agulia

Wickenburg

Rock
Springs

Fort Apache

Apache-
Sitgreaves
National
Forest

Morristown

Cave Creek

17

Theodore
Roosevelt
Lake

FORT APACHE
RESERVATION

Sun City

Salt River

Glendale

Scottsdale

Tempe

Apache
Junction

Claypool

60

Peridot

191

Avondale

Phoenix

Mesa

Globe

Buckeye

2

Chandler

San Carlos
Lake

Clifton

Gila Bend

GILA RIVER
RESERVATION

Florence

70

Safford

Coolidge

Coronado
National
Forest

Duncan

Casa Grande

Eloy

10

77

8

Saguaro
National
Park West

Catalina

Saguaro
National
Park East

Ajo

Oro Valley

7

Willcox

186

Chiricahua
National
Monument

Organ Pipe
Cactus
National
Monument

TOHONO O'ODHAM
RESERVATION

Quijotoa

Tucson

Coronado
National
Forest

Sells

South
Tucson

Benson

80

Tombstone

McNeal

SAN XAVIER
RES.

Green Valley

Sonoita

19

Tubac

Huachuca City

Sierra
Vista

Bisbee

Sasabe

Coronado
National Forest

Douglas

Nogales

MEXICO

ARIZONA PLANNER

When to Go

High season at the resorts of Phoenix and Tucson is winter, when the snowbirds fly south. Expect the best temperatures—and the highest prices—November through March, when nearly every weekend is filled with outdoor festivals. Spring wildflowers are best from March until May. If you're on a budget, the posh desert resorts drop their prices—sometimes by more than half—June through September. The South Rim of the Grand Canyon and Sedona are busy year-round, but least busy during the winter months.

When Not to Go

For a statewide excursion, keep in mind that Arizona's climate is extreme. Although a winter visit might be most comfortable in Phoenix, remember that the Grand Canyon, Flagstaff, and Sedona—Arizona's high country—will be quite cold then. Also take note that areas such as eastern Arizona are most popular with summer travelers, so many shops and restaurants are closed in the winter months. Remember that the North Rim of the Grand Canyon is closed in winter, from mid-October to mid-May.

Getting Here and Around

Getting Here: Phoenix and Tucson have international airports. Amtrak lines service Flagstaff and Tucson. Car rental is available at airports in Phoenix, Tucson, and Flagstaff.

Getting Around: You'll need a car to properly explore Arizona. Deceptively vast, Arizona is the nation's sixth-largest state at nearly 114,000 square miles. No matter where you start your journey, expect to spend a good portion of your time in the car. Fortunately, Arizona offers an attractive canvas that ranges from desert to forest. It surprises some visitors that the drive from Phoenix to the Grand Canyon takes at least a half day—and that's without stopping or taking side roads. *See more driving times below.*

Road conditions vary by season and location, so expect anything: you can start your day in 100°F heat in Phoenix and end it in near-freezing temperatures in the Grand Canyon. Be sure to plan accordingly for the weather: if driving in the desert in summer, keep bottled water in the car; in winter in the high country, be prepared for icy roads. And remember that violent flash floods and dust storms can pepper the desert during the summer monsoons. Storms usually pass quickly. For road information, the Arizona Department of Transportation has a travelers' assistance line. Just dial 📞 *511* from any phone.

TYPICAL TRAVEL TIMES		
	Hours by Car	Distance
Phoenix–Flagstaff	2½	145 miles
Phoenix–Grand Canyon South Rim	4½	175 miles
Phoenix–Lake Mead/Hoover Dam	4½	260 miles
Phoenix–Monument Valley	6	275 miles
Phoenix–Yuma	3	185 miles
Tucson–Phoenix	2	120 miles

What to Pack

Thanks to extreme climates and Western informality, you can go almost anywhere in Arizona in a pair of jeans.

Bring layers for trips north or east, particularly when temperatures dip after the sun sets.

For formal dining, call ahead for attire requirements. In most places, a shirt and dress slacks will be sufficient.

Depending on your desired level of activity, you'll need to pack different gear: golf shoes, hiking boots, or flip-flops. Most golf courses offer club and golf-cart rentals, but plan on bringing your own shoes. If the slopes are your destination, you can rent all your ski or snowboard gear before hitting the lifts.

No matter your plans, be prepared with water, and hats and sunscreen for sun protection. The desert heat can be intense and quite deceptive.

Tribal Lands

Arizona has 22 Native American tribes, each with its own government and culture. Most tribes have websites or phone-information lines, and it's best to contact them for information before a trip. Many require a permit for hiking or biking in scenic areas. Always be respectful of individual cultures and traditions.

How's the Weather?

Phoenix averages 325 sunny days and 7 inches of precipitation annually. The high mountains see about 25 inches of rain. The Grand Canyon is usually cool at the rim and about 20°F warmer on the floor. The North Rim is generally about 10°F cooler than the South Rim, which is open year-round. Temperatures in valley areas like Phoenix and Tucson average about 60°F to 70°F in the daytime in winter and between 100°F and 115°F in summer. Flagstaff and Sedona stay much cooler, dropping into the 30s and 40s in winter and leveling off at 80°F to 90°F in summer.

Did You Know . . .

With the exception of the Navajo Nation in the northeast corner of the state, Arizona doesn't observe daylight saving time. Arizona is in the Mountain Standard Time zone.

Avg. High/ Low Temps.

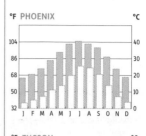

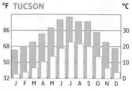

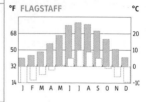

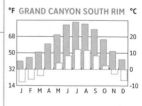

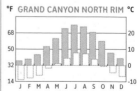

ARIZONA & THE GRAND CANYON TOP ATTRACTIONS

The Grand Canyon

(A) When it comes to visiting Grand Canyon National Park, there are statistics and there are sights, and both are sure to leave you in awe. With an average width of 10 miles, a length of 277 miles, and a depth of 1 mile, the enormity of the canyon is nearly impossible to fathom. Most choose to view the spectacle from the South Rim, although the North Rim also offers an amazing perspective. Whether exploring the area on foot, by mule, by raft, or by plane, the journey is one worth savoring.

Petrified Forest and the Painted Desert

(B) The Painted Desert takes on hues that range from blood-red to the purest pink throughout the day. View a forest of trees that stood with dinosaurs at the Petrified Forest, as well as ancient dwellings and fossils. The pieces of petrified logs look deceptively like driftwood cast on an oceanless beach. You can enjoy the entire national park in less than a day and take in a bit of nostalgia with Route 66's vestiges in nearby Holbrook along the way.

Sedona

(C) Loved for its majestic red rocks, its spiritual energy, and its fantastic resorts and spas, Sedona is unlike any other town in America. The fracturing of the western edge of the Colorado Plateau created the red-rock buttes that loom over Sedona, and this landscape has attracted artists, entrepreneurs, and New Age followers from all over who believe the area contains some of Earth's most important vortexes of energy. Take the active route and explore Oak Creek Canyon and the surrounding area on foot or by bike or jeep, or indulge in the luxe life at a world-class spa or restaurant.

Scottsdale

(D) The West's most Western town, modern Scottsdale is equal parts kitsch and overt opulence. Resorts, spas, and golf

can easily absorb an entire vacation. Stroll through art galleries and Western boutiques in Old Town during the day, and discover chic nightlife and fine cuisine at night. The weekly Art Walk and Frank Lloyd Wright's Taliesin West are a great introduction to the local artistic scene. Scottsdale is part of the Valley of the Sun, along with Phoenix, Tempe, and some 20 other communities.

The Heard Museum

(E) One of Phoenix's cultural treasures, the Heard proudly features one of the most comprehensive collections of Native American art in the world. Interactive exhibits are alongside a staggering amount of Southwestern pottery, jewelry, kachinas, and textiles. Plus, the museum gift shop is one of the best places in town to find authentic souvenirs worth cherishing.

Monument Valley

(F) One of the most familiar sights of Arizona—thanks to dozens of Hollywood productions and the keen eye of Ansel Adams—the fantastic sculpted red-sandstone buttes, mesas, and rock formations of Monument Valley Navajo Tribal Park are yet another reminder of the abundance of nature's handiwork in the Grand Canyon state. Take a Navajo-guided tour to appreciate the nuances of the area.

Desert Botanical Garden

(G) Although there are stellar museums and preserves across Arizona, none is like the Desert Botanical Garden, 150 acres just outside Downtown Phoenix dedicated to the diversity of the desert. With more than 4,000 species of cacti, succulents, trees, and flowers, visitors discover the variety and breadth of this mysterious landscape—all in the comfort of America's sixth-largest city.

QUINTESSENTIAL ARIZONA & THE GRAND CANYON

Road Trips

Arizona is *the* place to take a road trip. Get in the car, pick a destination, and go take a look at the Western landscape on historic roads like Route 66. For optimal enjoyment, avoid the interstate highways and take these smaller routes instead. It's there you'll see Arizona's most beautiful landscapes, taste its spicy cuisine, and make memories worth cherishing.

Go to Bisbee. Go to Jerome. Go to Oatman. Go to Greer. Travel AZ 260 from Payson to Show Low or historic Route 66 from Ash Fork to Topock; take AZ 60 through the Salt River Canyon, or U.S. 191 from Springerville to Clifton; and take AZ 88, the Apache Trail, from Apache Junction to Roosevelt Dam.

Wherever you go, roll down the windows, turn up the radio, and enjoy the ride. Regardless of your destination, the wide-open spaces of Arizona entice and amaze anew with every bend in the road.

Salsa and Margaritas

You're in Arizona, so join the quest to find your favorite salsa and margaritas. No two salsas are the same, and every city and town boasts its own local favorite. Spicy and chunky? Tangy and juicy? Tear-inducing? They run the gamut.

You'll find that salsa flavors change regionally, from mesquite-imbued concoctions in the east, inspired by Tex-Mex cuisine, to fresh-from-the-garden medleys in southern Arizona that are authentically Mexican. In Tucson, check out Café Poca Cosa's salsa, a deep-red blend of garlic, chiles, and tomatoes that's almost decadent. In Phoenix the brave go to Los Dos Molinos, where powerful hatch chiles punctuate every dish.

Perfectly salty-and-sour margaritas can take the sting away from a particularly robust salsa, all while washing down a delightful Mexican feast.

Arizona is known for its magnificent natural landmarks, its rich history, and its captivating cuisine. Here are some easy ways to get to know the lay of the land and start thinking like an Arizonan.

The Night Sky

Away from the metropolitan areas of the Valley of the Sun (Phoenix, Tempe, Scottsdale, and surrounds) and Tucson, where the by-products of urban life obscure the firmament, the night sky is clear and unpolluted by lights or smog. In December in the desert, the Milky Way stretches like a chiffon scarf across the celestial sphere. Lie on your back on the hood of your car at night, allow your eyes time to adjust to the darkness, and you'll see more stars than you could have possibly imagined.

For a closer look, you can visit Lowell Observatory and Northern Arizona University (both in Flagstaff), or the Kitt Peak National Observatory in southwest Arizona (outside Tucson) and look at celestial objects through large telescopes.

Rodeo

People take rodeo seriously in Arizona, whether it's a holiday extravaganza like those in Prescott or Payson (which draw top cowboys from around the country), a bull-riding competition at Camp Verde, or a bunch of working cowboys gathered for a team-roping contest in Williams.

Particularly with the emergence of bull riding as a stand-alone event—and the crowds often cheer as much for the bulls as for the cowboys—rodeos these days are no longer the hayseed and cowpokey events Arizona grandpas might have enjoyed. Rock-and-roll rodeo has arrived and there's frequently live music as well as roping. And other cowboy experiences, like horseback riding and dude ranch stays, are as popular as ever. So, if you see a rodeo advertisement posted in a shop window, take a walk on the wild side and check out the fine arts of riding and roping.

IF YOU LIKE

Hiking

Arizona has a wealth of awe-inspiring natural landmarks. So you can hike in and out, up and down, or around beautiful and varied landscapes, into canyons, to a mountain summit, or just along a meandering trail through a desert or a forest.

Wherever you go, make sure you're well prepared with water, food, sunscreen, a good hat, and a camera to capture your achievement. Be sure you have a decent pair of hiking shoes, and check the weather report first. Storms can roll into the desert quickly (particularly during monsoon season), and you don't want to get caught in a flash flood or dust storm.

From the long-heralded trails such as **Bright Angel** in the Grand Canyon to iconic **Camelback Mountain** in Phoenix, there's a summit or path in every corner of the state waiting for you.

If waterfalls are your thing, check out the Grand Canyon's **Havasu Falls,** a fairly strenuous 10-mile hike that descends 3,000 feet to splashing pools of turquoise water.

The highest of the four peaks that make up San Francisco Peaks is **Mount Humphreys,** the ultimate goal for hikers seeking the best view in the state. Timing an ascent can be tricky, though, as the snow in Flagstaff sometimes doesn't melt until mid-July, and by then the summer rains and lightning come almost daily in the afternoon. Go early in the morning and pay attention to the sky.

For some archaeology, **Walnut Canyon National Monument,** just a few minutes east of Flagstaff, has a paved and stepped trail descending 185 feet into an island of stone where you can explore prehistoric cliff dwellings. The climb out is strenuous.

Water Sports

You don't miss the water until it's not there, but Arizonans do their best to ensure that the well doesn't go completely dry. Dams and canal systems help to fill vast reservoirs, and the resulting rivers and lakes provide all manner of water-sport recreation. Of course, this is a state that considers floating in a pool or soaking in a hot tub "water-sport recreation." You can have it "easy," you can have it "rough," or you can have it "fast."

Easy is a week on a **houseboat** on a lake. Houseboats are available for rent on major lakes along the Colorado River, as well as on Lake Powell, Lake Mead, and Lake Havasu. On smaller lakes motorized boats are prohibited, but **kayaks** and **canoes** make for an enjoyable excursion along the pine-covered shorelines. You can even take a rowboat out on Tempe Town Lake, or bake in the sun while taking a lazy float down the Salt River just east of Phoenix

Rough is a **river raft trip.** There are nearly two dozen commercial rafting companies offering trips as short as three days or as long as three weeks through the Grand Canyon. Options include motorized rafts or dories rowed by Arizona's version of the California surfer—the Colorado River boatman. The Hualapai tribe, through the Hualapai River Runners, offers one-day river trips. Don't let the short duration fool you: Boatmen take you through several rapids, and thrills abound.

Fast involves a **speedboat** and water skis or Jet Skis. Both are popular on major lakes and along the Colorado River. You can go from dam to dam along the Colorado, and on lakes the size of Powell and Mead you can ski until your legs give out.

Desert

Arizona has a desert for you; actually, it has more than one. The trouble is, any desert is inhospitable to life forms unaccustomed to its harsh realities. People die in the desert here every year, from thirst, exposure, and one inexplicable trait—stupidity. Using good sense, you can explore any stretch of desert in April and May and experience a landscape festooned with flowers and blooming cacti.

To experience the desert without running the risk of leaving your bones to bleach in the sun, there are two exceptional alternatives: the **Desert Botanical Garden** in Phoenix is a showcase of the ecology of the desert with more than 4,000 different species of desert flora sustained on 150 acres. A walk through here is wonderfully soothing and extremely educational. You'll be stunned by the variety of color and texture in native desert plants. It's much more than saguaro cacti. Be sure to check out the butterfly exhibit.

There's also the **Arizona-Sonora Desert Museum** in Tucson, which isn't really a museum but a zoo and a botanical garden featuring the animals and plants of the Sonoran Desert. If you want to see a diamondback rattlesnake without jumping out of your shoes, this is the place.

And, of course, there are long drives in which you can see wide expanses from the comfort of your car. Early spring brings the flaming-red blossoms of the ocotillo and the soft yellow-green branches of the palo verde, and the desert will be carpeted with ephemeral flowers of pink, blue, and yellow.

Along U.S. 93, south of Wikieup in northwest Arizona, you can see the desert in its most abundant display, but there are countless other places, as well.

Native American Culture

John Ford Westerns and the enduring myths of the Wild West pale in comparison to the experience of seeing firsthand the Native American cultures that thrive in Arizona. You can stop at a trading post and see artisans demonstrating their crafts, visit one of Arizona's spectacular Native American museums, or explore an ancient Native American dwelling.

Hubbell Trading Post and **Cameron Trading Post** are on Navajo reservations, while **Keam's Canyon Trading Post** is on the Hopi Reservation.

The **Heard Museum**, in Phoenix, houses an impressive array of Native American cultural exhibits and has, quite possibly, the best gift shop in town if you're looking for something truly special and authentic. The **Museum of Northern Arizona**, in Flagstaff, has collections related to the natural and cultural history of the Colorado Plateau, an extensive collection of Navajo rugs, and an authentic Hopi *kiva* (men's ceremonial chamber). The **Colorado River Museum**, in Bullhead City, focuses on the history of the area and includes information and artifacts pertaining to the Mojave tribe. **Chiricahua Regional Museum and Research Center,** in Willcox, focuses on Apache culture.

The **Montezuma Castle National Monument** is one of the best-preserved prehistoric ruins in North America. **Tuzigoot National Monument** is not as well preserved as Montezuma Castle, but is more impressive in scope. The **Casa Grande Ruins National Monument** is a 35-foot-tall structure built by the Hohokam Indians who lived in the area.

TOP EXPERIENCES

Grand Canyon Hiking

You could spend the rest of your life hiking the Grand Canyon and never cover all the trails. There are hiking and walking trails aplenty, for all levels of fitness; we suggest you go with a guide or consult a ranger to find the best trail for you. Bright Angel Trail is the most famous, but it's tough: with an elevation change of more than 5,000 feet, don't try to hike to the Colorado River and back in one day. Less strenuous is part of the 12-mile Rim Trail, a paved, generally horizontal walk. Other outstanding choices are the South Kaibab Trail and the Hermit Trail. Many short routes lead to epic views, like the Cape Royal and Roosevelt Point trails on the North Rim.

Jeep Tours

Why drive yourself when open-air four-wheeling is available, complete with guide? Jeep tours abound in the Grand Canyon state, whether it's a rough ride on a Pink Jeep tour in the red rocks of Sedona or a Lavender Jeep tour in historic Bisbee, a weeklong excursion or an afternoon adventure. Some of these companies have special permits that provide access to national forests and an up-close view of Native American communities.

Colorado River–Rafting

Hiking too boring? Jeep tours not enough? True thrill-seekers take the plunge when they visit Arizona. There are nearly two dozen commercial river-rafting companies in Arizona that offer trips as short as a day or as long as three weeks through the Grand Canyon on the Colorado River. These rough-riding trips are popular with travelers, so be sure to make reservations very early, up to a year in advance.

Personal Pampering

If roughing it in the great outdoors isn't your vacation style, head to one of Arizona's world-class spas. Enjoy a standard mani-and-pedi afternoon, or further indulge in a specialty treatment, such as a creekside massage at L'Auberge de Sedona, or a Native American–inspired session at the Waldorf Astoria Spa at the Boulders Resort in Carefree. Between sessions be sure to take advantage of relaxation rooms, saunas, and pools. Finish the day with a decadent meal at your resort's restaurant.

Biltmore Golfing

One of Phoenix's most historic hotels is also home to some of the Valley's most heralded golf courses. The Arizona Biltmore, Arizona's first resort, set the standard in 1929. The Biltmore has two 18-hole PGA championship courses, Adobe and Links. Arizona's climate is particularly hospitable to golfers, so greens fees are especially pricey in winter and spring. Early risers can find slightly more affordable fees in the wee hours of the morning in summer.

Native American Traditions

Westerns and the enduring myths of the Wild West don't compare to the experience of seeing firsthand the Native American cultures that thrive in Arizona. In northeast Arizona, you can visit Navajo and Hopi reservations; there are nearly two dozen tribes in the state. Stop at a trading post on a reservation to see artisans demonstrating their crafts. Visit one of Arizona's fantastic Native American museums, such as the Heard Museum in Phoenix or the Museum of Northern Arizona in Flagstaff. At spectacular national monuments, such as Montezuma Castle near Camp Verde, visitors can see 600-year-old preserved dwellings.

ARIZONA WITH KIDS

Places that are especially appealing to children are indicated throughout this guide by a family icon in the margin.

Choosing a Destination

You can make your trip one for adventure, education, or good ol' American play. Stay close to the urban areas surrounding Phoenix or Tucson if you want to revel in **water parks,** swimming pools, and resort children's programs. Travel north to Sedona, where you can see **Snoopy Rock,** before exploring the wonder that is the **Grand Canyon.** If you're looking for an educational journey, don't forget to stop by Phoenix's **Heard Museum** for an introduction to Native American cultures, or spend some quality time in northeast Arizona at **Monument Valley** or **Canyon de Chelly,** two geological marvels.

Choosing a Place to Stay

This is the Old West, after all, and there's a great deal of "roughing it" that you could experience if you're staying at **campsites, dude ranches,** or **motels** near the Grand Canyon or northeast Arizona. Don't expect to always have great mobile phone reception or cable TV. The cities of Arizona, however, have some of the most heralded **resorts** in the world. In Phoenix, check out the **Arizona Grand Resort,** which has an extensive water park. Posh resorts like the **JW Marriott Desert Ridge** and the **Westin Kierland Resort & Spa** have special kids-only programs that include evening "dive-in" movies and daytime sports and recreation instruction.

Outdoor Activities

With its majestic landscapes and sites that are right out of a Hollywood script, you're going to be spending a lot of your time in Arizona outside. Be sure to take advantage of the national parks' **Junior Ranger Programs.** Of course, there's nothing quite as up close and personal as a mule ride down the **Grand Canyon,** an adventurous rafting trip down the **Colorado River,** or a walk back in time through **Kartchner Caverns State Park.** Let your kids make the most of their digital cameras while they document your journey. If you prefer something slightly less adventurous, be sure to check out **Oak Creek Canyon** in Sedona, and cool off at **Slide Rock State Park.** On one of your nights away from the city, take advantage of your location and search for constellations and stargaze.

Indoor Activities

On hot summer days, choose indoor activities for the afternoon, when the sun is at its most intense, and your kids are likely to be their most impatient. This might be a good time to head to Downtown Phoenix and check out the **Heard Museum,** the **Phoenix Art Museum,** and the **Arizona Science Center,** all of which are steps away from the city's light-rail system. If you're in the cooler country, take advantage of nighttime programs and events at **Lowell Observatory in Flagstaff,** where you can watch the stars in relative comfort.

Road Trip Tips

Chances are, you'll be exploring most of Arizona by car. There are kid-friendly stops along the way from Phoenix to Sedona or the Grand Canyon, including **Meteor Crater** and **Montezuma Castle,** that can help break up your hours in the car. Children and adults alike can be quite stunned by how quickly Arizona's landscape changes. Your child could start the day in the desert, and wake up from a nap driving through a ponderosa pine winter wonderland in eastern Arizona.

OH STARRY NIGHT
TIPS FOR STARGAZING IN ARIZONA

If your typical view of the night sky consists of a handful of stars dimly twinkling through a hazy, light-polluted sky, get ready for a treat. In most of Arizona, the night sky blazes with starlight—and with a little practice, you can give your family a memorable astronomical tour.

Constellations

Constellations are stories in the sky—many depict animals or figures from Greek mythology. Brush up on a few of these tales before your trip, and you'll be an instant source of nighttime entertainment.

The stars in the Northern Hemisphere appear to rotate around Polaris, the North Star, in fixed positions relative to one another. To get your celestial bearings, first find the bright stars of the Big Dipper. An imaginary line drawn through the two stars that form the outside edge of the cup (away from the handle) will point straight to Polaris (which also serves as the last star in the handle of the Little Dipper). Once you've identified Polaris, you should be able to find the other stars on our chart. Myriad astronomy books and Web sites have additional star charts; *National Geographic* has a cool interactive version with images from the Hubble Space Telescope (⊕ *www.nationalgeographic.com/stars*).

Planets

Stars twinkle, planets don't (because they're so much closer to Earth, the atmosphere doesn't distort their light as much). Planets are also bright, which makes them fairly easy to spot. Unfortunately, we can't show their positions on this star chart, because planets orbit the sun and move in relation to the stars.

The easiest planet to spot is Venus, the brightest object in the night sky besides the moon and the Earth's closest planetary neighbor. Look for it just before sunrise or just after sunset; it'll be near the point where the sun is rising or setting. (Venus and Earth orbit the sun at different speeds; when Venus is moving away from Earth, we see it in the morning, and when it's moving toward us, we see it in the evening.) Like the moon, Venus goes through phases—check it out through a pair of binoculars. You can also spot Mars, Jupiter, Saturn, and Mercury—with or without the aid of binoculars.

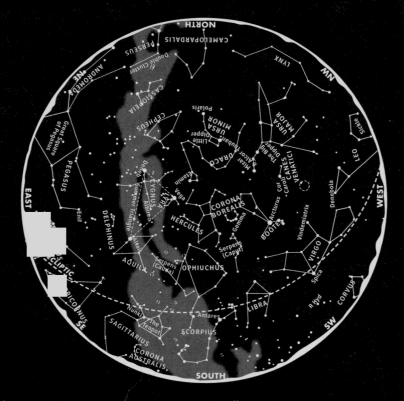

Meteors

It's hard to match the magic of a meteor shower—the natural fireworks display that occurs as Earth passes through a cloud of debris called meteoroids. These pieces of space junk—most the size of a pebble—hit our atmosphere at high speeds, and the intense friction produces brief but brilliant streaks of light. Single meteors are often called "shooting stars" or "falling stars."

Because our planet passes through the same patches of interstellar refuse each year, it's easy to roughly predict when the major meteor showers will occur. Notable ones include the Perseids (mid-August), the Orionids (late October), the Leonids (mid-November), and the Geminids (mid-December). Each shower is named after the point in the sky where meteors appear to originate. If you're not visiting during a shower, don't worry—you can spot individual meteors any time of the year.

Satellites

Right now, according to NASA, there are about 3,000 operative man-made satellites (along with 6,000 pieces of space junk) orbiting the Earth—and you can catch a glimpse of one with a little practice. Satellites look like fast-moving, non-blinking points of light; the best way to spot one is to lie on your back and scan the sky for movement. Be on the lookout for satellites an hour or two before or after sunset (though you may see them at other times as well).

You can take the guesswork out of the search with a few cool online tools (⊕ *www.nasa. gov* or *www.heavens-above.com*). Select your location, and these Web sites will help you predict—down to the minute—when certain objects will be streaking overhead. It's especially worthwhile to use these sites to look for the two brightest satellites: the International Space Station and the space shuttle.

FLAVORS OF ARIZONA

Despite the fact that it's become a culinary melting pot, Arizona has long been lumped into the spicy Southwest category of cuisine. But by pairing global influences with diverse Native American cultures, regional history, and local agriculture, chefs and entrepreneurs have earned Arizona a star on the food walk of fame.

The Native Palate

From flash-flood farming in the south and sustained agriculture in the Verde Valley to livestock ranching in the state's northernmost reaches, Native American food customs are becoming customary off the reservations. Gourds, desert beans, mesquite pods, tree nuts, cactus fruit, agave nectar, and local game like quail and elk are buzzwords on award-winning menus. And Navajo fry bread, a tradition born from the worst of times, is one of the state's most sought-after treats.

Don't be surprised to find ingredients such as agave, prickly pear, or hatch chiles punctuating your meal. These native flavors provide spice and, yes, sweetness to seemingly commonplace dishes. Better yet, most gift shops and locally owned grocery stores sell these native ingredients, which make excellent souvenirs.

Spice of Life

Arizona has long been defined by its heat. With a natural affection for everything from Mexican jalapeños to New Mexican hatch chiles, food artists give recipes ranging from chips and salsa to chicken mole and chilaquiles a memorable flair.

Spicy food is plentiful in the desert, but locals know that there's a difference between spice and heat—you might say it's a matter of degree. Some of the area's finest chefs have crafted menus that give a nod to a variety of peppers or chiles, but that doesn't mean your palate will suffer.

When prepared properly, habaneros, hatch chiles, and a host of other peppers can please even the pickiest diner. Try an entrée, or even a drink, that has a hint of chile flavor, and discover that spice isn't just for daredevils.

The Chimichanga

To get a real taste of Sonoran Mexican food, be sure to order a chimichanga. Kind of like a burrito on steroids, chimichangas are deep-fried concoctions generally filled with sautéed meat, peppers, and onions; garnished with sour cream or guacamole; and topped with either a red or green chile sauce. For true local flavor, order *machaca* (tender, shredded beef) and bring your appetite.

Fruits of the Desert

Arizona's local wine industry is not to be overlooked. Vineyards in Southern Arizona's Santa Cruz Valley, as well as those in North-Central Arizona near Sedona, have steadily grown in popularity since the first opened in 1973. Now, there are more than five-dozen wineries across the state, crafting cabernet, chardonnay, zinfandel, and more.

A Dip to Die For

Salsa is neither simple nor a garnish. It's almost its own food group in Arizona. From garden-fresh pico de gallo to chile-infused purees that make their impact with just a drop, salsas are incredibly diverse in the desert.

Every Mexican restaurant seems to have its own recipe, typically offered in mild and hot varieties—it's OK to try both. Styles vary by chef, from julienned pico de gallo that's tortilla chip–friendly to complex, saucelike salsas that have layers of heat. New concoctions show up on menus constantly, including fruit-based salsas that garnish breakfast burritos.

GREAT ITINERARIES

1

HIGHLIGHTS OF ARIZONA

Arizona is full of history, culture, and awe-inspiring natural landmarks. Here are some suggestions for mixing a road trip with some of the state's top attractions.

Phoenix and the Valley of the Sun: 1–2 Days

The metropolitan Phoenix area is the best place to begin your trip to Arizona, with a wealth of hotels and resorts. Reserve a day in the Valley and visit the Heard Museum and Desert Botanical Garden. Select one of the area's popular Mexican restaurants for dinner. If time permits, stroll through Old Town Scottsdale's tempting art galleries. Depending on your remaining time in the Valley, you can escape to a spa for a day of pampering, get out your clubs and hit the links, or—if the season is right—catch a Major League Baseball spring-training game.

Logistics: Sky Harbor International Airport is located at the center of the city and is 20 minutes away from most of the Valley's major resorts. Plan on driving everywhere in the greater Phoenix area, as public transportation is nearly nonexistent. The Valley of the Sun is a large area, but Phoenix itself is remarkably simple to navigate. Designed on a grid, numbered streets run north–south and named streets (Camelback Road, Glendale Avenue) run east–west. Grand Avenue, running about 20 miles from Downtown to Sun City, is the only diagonal. If you need to know which direction you're facing, you can see South Mountain, conveniently looming in the south, from nearly any point in the city.

Grand Canyon South Rim: 1–2 Days

The sight of the Grand Canyon's immense beauty has taken many a visitor's breath away. Whatever you do, though, make sure you catch a sunset or sunrise view of the canyon. A night, or even just dinner, at grand El Tovar Hotel won't disappoint, but book your reservation early (up to six months ahead). Outdoors enthusiasts will want to reserve several days to hike and explore the canyon; less ambitious travelers can comfortably see the area in one or two days.

Logistics: Arizona is a large state; the drive north from Phoenix to the South Rim of the Grand Canyon will take several hours, so budget at least a half day to make the 225-mile trip. Take Interstate 17 north from Phoenix into Flagstaff. The best way to reach the South Rim of the canyon is via U.S. 180 northwest from Flagstaff. It's best to travel to the canyon from the city during the week—Interstate 17 fills with locals looking to escape the heat on Friday and Saturday. If you have specific plans, whether it's a mule ride and rafting trip or dining and lodging, be sure to book very early for the canyon—reservations are necessary.

Red Rocks and Spectacular Sights: 3–4 Days

Option 1: Sedona and Surrounding Area

The unusual red-rock formations in Sedona are a key destination for most visitors to Arizona, and it's no wonder. Spend at least a day exploring the town and its beauty, whether on a calm stroll or a thrilling jeep tour. The surrounding area includes Flagstaff, a college town with a love for the outdoors and the stars; Prescott, with its Whiskey Row and Victorian homes; and Jerome, a charming artists' community that thrives more with every passing year.

Logistics: If possible, visit Sedona midweek, before the city folk fill the streets on the weekend. If Sedona is too pricey for your stay, consider the nearby towns of Flagstaff or Prescott, which have ample motels and budget hotels.

Option 2: Landmarks of Indian Country

The majestic landscapes in Monument Valley and Canyon de Chelly are among the biggest draws to Arizona. Made famous by countless Western movies and famous photographs, the scenes are even more astounding firsthand. This northeast corner of the state is worth several days of exploration. The famous Four Corners, where Arizona, New Mexico, Colorado, and Utah meet, are within a short drive but there isn't much to see. For a brief trip, make Monument Valley and Canyon de Chelly the priorities. With added days, you can visit a Native American trading post, Lake Powell and Glen Canyon, and the Four Corners. On your drive, be sure to spend an hour or two at Petrified Forest National Park, where you'll see the remains of a prehistoric forest.

Logistics: Approximately 100 miles from Sedona, the fascinating sites of northeast Arizona are a destination unto themselves. Don't be fooled: this is a remote area and will take hours to reach, whether you're coming from Phoenix, Sedona, or the Grand Canyon. Most travelers view this corner of the state as a road trip heaven, as the highways offer one scenic drive after the other. Plan on making one of the main towns—Tuba City, Page, Window Rock—your base, and take day trips from there. No matter what your itinerary, plan ahead and make reservations early: the best way to see these popular sites is via guided tour.

Scenic Drives and Historic Towns: 2–4 Days

Option 1: Tucson, the Old West, and Historic Sites

If culture and history are a bit more attractive, consider spending time in Tucson and visiting its neighboring historic communities. Spend at least a day in Tucson proper, visiting Mission San Xavier del Bac, Saguaro National Park, and the Arizona-Sonora Desert Museum. If hiking is your game, don't miss Sabino Canyon, which offers gorgeous views of the area. With Tucson as your hub, take a day trip just a bit farther south to historic Tombstone and Bisbee. On the way back to the interstate, stop by Kartchner Caverns State Park for a view of the series of spectacular wet caves. Hour-long guided tours are available by reservation; book several months in advance to guarantee entry.

Logistics: Phoenix is two hours away via Interstate 10, a relatively unscenic drive. Casa Grande is the midway point between the two cities, and is a good place to stop for a rest. History buffs might want to stop at Picacho Peak, site of the westernmost battle of the Civil War.

Option 2: The White Mountains of Eastern Arizona

If nature walks and hiking are tops on your itinerary, consider spending a few days in the White Mountains before returning to Phoenix. The breathtaking White Mountains area of eastern Arizona is a favorite for anglers and cross-country skiers. The White Mountains Trails System near Pinetop-Lakeside is considered one of the best in the nation, and can accommodate all fitness levels. Eastern Arizona is primarily a summer

destination. Creekside resorts with private cabins are common in the area, but many properties close from November to April, except for a few ski resorts.

Logistics: The most scenic route back to Phoenix is via the Salt River Canyon on U.S. 60 to Globe. The landscape transforms from ponderosa pine forests to high desert along the journey, marking an ideal transition from one extreme to the other. Or you can travel to Tucson from the White Mountains on one of the most scenic routes in the United States (if a bumpy and wild ride is your style). The Coronado Trail, U.S. 191 from Springerville to Clifton, is one of the world's curviest roads. The trip, which includes steep stretches and plenty of turns, will take at least four hours. Once in Clifton, you can continue south to Willcox, where Interstate 10 will take you to Tucson.

ROAD TRIP TIPS

■ If your budget permits, renting a four-wheel-drive vehicle will allow you to take advantage of side trips to remote areas.

■ Climate extremes, both heat and cold, make Arizona traveling hazardous, so heed the advice of locals. If somebody tells you it's a "little warm" to be poking around in those hills, they're probably correct.

■ Carry plenty of water, and if your vehicle should break down, put the hood up and stay with the vehicle.

■ Arizona's distances can be surprisingly vast. The drive from Phoenix to the Grand Canyon takes at least a half day.

ARIZONA LANDSCAPE ADVENTURES

Arizona's spectacular landscape dominates the eye and floods the senses. No place else in the world has so many unique and bizarre geological features—and the canyons, deserts, and mountains are more than just a backdrop for your journey. To understand and experience the land, you must get outdoors and be willing to accept nature on its own terms.

written by Melissa Kim
updated by Cara LaBrie

ARIZONA'S NATURAL FEATURES

Oak Creek Canyon, near Sedona

The diversity that these regions contain, not just in terrain but in flora and fauna, is unparalleled in the Lower 48. Resourceful plants and animals teach us so much about adapting to our surroundings and learning from nature. Some humans have also learned to survive in these harsh environments, but for most of us even a brief foray into Arizona's landscapes can be an adventure.

Canyons, mountains, and deserts are all closely related in the state's basic regions:

■ The northern section is part of the **Colorado Plateau**, a high-elevation region characterized by glowing red rocks and impossibly graceful slot canyons. It is also home to the Grand Canyon.

■ Along the state's southwestern corridor is the **Basin and Range Province**, where cactus-littered deserts and scrubby valleys rise abruptly to the San Francisco Peaks and Chiracahua Mountains.

■ In between, the **Central Highlands** contain mountain ranges where peaks drop away to canyons and desert grasslands, such as the easily accessible Saguaro National Park and the Arizona-Sonora Desert Museum.

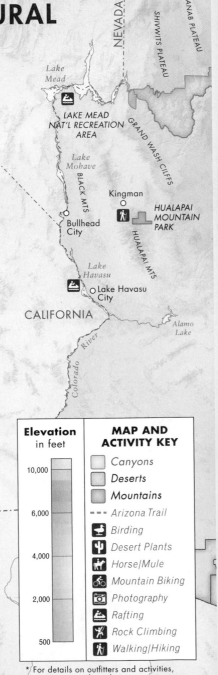

Elevation
in feet

10,000

6,000

4,000

2,000

500

MAP AND ACTIVITY KEY

☐ Canyons
☐ Deserts
☐ Mountains
- - - Arizona Trail
🦆 Birding
🌵 Desert Plants
🐎 Horse/Mule
🚵 Mountain Biking
📷 Photography
🚣 Rafting
🧗 Rock Climbing
🚶 Walking/Hiking

*/ For details on outfitters and activities, see corresponding chapters.

Lake Powell

Page

Four Corners
Monument

Antelope
Canyon

MONUMENT VALLEY
NAVAJO TRIBAL PARK

KAIBAB PLATEAU

MONUMENT VALLEY

MARBLE CANYON

ECHO CLIFFS

BLACK MESA

CHUSKA MTS.

GRAND CANYON
NATIONAL PARK

NORTH RIM

Colorado River

Grand Canyon

SOUTH RIM

Tusayan
Museum

HAVASU CYN.

CANYON DE CHELLY
NATIONAL MONUMENT

NEW MEXICO

COCONINO PLATEAU

PAINTED DESERT

Wupatki
Nat'l Monument

San Francisco Peaks

SUNSET CRATER VOLCANO
NAT'L MONUMENT

Humphreys Peak ▲
12,633ft

Flagstaff

• Meteor Crater

Oak Creek Canyon

Sedona

COCONINO
NATIONAL FOREST

PETRIFIED FOREST
NATIONAL PARK

MOGOLLON PLATEAU

Prescott

VERDE VALLEY

MOGOLLON RIM

Payson

Springerville

Casa
Malpais

WHITE MOUNTAINS

SUPERSTITION MOUNTAINS

Arizona Trail

Mt. Baldy
11,404ft ▲

APACHE-SITGREAVES
NATIONAL FOREST

Scottsdale

Phoenix

Avondale

Mesa

Desert Botanical
Garden

Tempe

Boyce Thompson
Southwestern
Arboretum

Casa Grande

SANTA CATALINA MTS

GALIURO MTS

CABEZA PRIETA
NATIONAL WILDLIFE
RESERVE

Arizona–Sonora
Desert Museum

Tucson

▲ Mount Lemmon

CHIRICAHUA NATIONAL
MOUNTAINS

ORGAN PIPE CACTUS
NATIONAL MONUMENT

Kitt Peak ▲

SAGUARO
NATIONAL PARK

CHIRICAHUA NATIONAL
MONUMENT

Tohono O'odham
National Cultural
Center

Madera
Canyon

Cochise
Stronghold ▲

SULPHUR SPRINGS VALLEY

SONORA

CORONADO
NATIONAL FOREST

HUACHUCA MTS

Ramsey Canyon

MEXICO

Nogales

Douglas

CANYONS

 While the Grand Canyon lives up to its impressive reputation, it is one of many such precious places in Arizona. Each canyon is a unique classroom of geology, where you can see the results of millions of years of shifts in the land.

More than 500 million years ago, a vast sea covered what is now Arizona. Sediments formed in thick layers as the sea rose and fell. Subsequent movement in the earth's crust created mountain ranges and lifted up entire sections of northern Arizona. Erosion and downcutting by rivers created deep canyons, uncovering layers of sandstone, shale, and limestone.

Forces of water and wind work to create some of Arizona's signature landscapes. High-elevation plateaus are continually eroded by rain, ice, rivers and groundwater, chipping and cracking the soft rock to form mesas and buttes, isolated hills or formations with steep sides and flat tops. What's the difference? One general rule of thumb is that a mesa is wider than it is high, while a butte is taller than it is high.

Some Grand Canyon excursions, such as mule tours (top) and rafting (opposite), are so popular they are booked up to a year in advance.

You can get your ecology credits here, too. As elevation changes from canyon floor to rim, so do the plants and animals. You can easily pass through four different biomes in a day's hike. Riparian communities on the canyon floor give way to a desert scrub, then to pinyon and Ponderosa pine forests. Where elevation exceeds 8,000 feet, spruce-fir forests make you feel as if you've somehow been transported to Canada.

ANCIENT PEOPLE AND THE LAND

Archaeologists have uncovered artifacts that show that people have lived in the Grand Canyon for at least 4,000 years. Tools, fire pits, cave paintings, and other remains indicate the presence of hunter-gatherers called the Archaic people, descendants of Paleoindians. You can see some "Archaic origami" stick figures on display at the Tusayan Museum at the South Rim.

TOP CANYON EXPERIENCES

WHITEWATER RAFTING
It's the rivers that helped create the canyons, after all, so spending time on the water is to spend time imagining the steady flow that carved out these works of natural art. About two dozen outfitters offer trips on the Colorado River through or near the Grand Canyon. Some sections are quiet and gentle, others rage and roil.

HORSE AND MULE TOURS
The best way to get a sense of the sheer scale of canyons is to be humbled by them—which means that you have to get to the bottom and look up. Hiking can be arduous, so many tour operators and parks offer horse or mule expeditions.

BIRDING
The entire state offers magnificent birding, but two extremes stand out. In the Grand Canyon, you can spot the enormous California condor's nine-foot wingspan since it was re-introduced in the 1990s. In the canyons of southeast Arizona, birders congregate in summer time to search for tiny hummingbirds.

BEYOND THE GRAND CANYON

In the northeast corner of Arizona, **Canyon de Chelly National Monument**, a National Park on Navajo Tribal Trust Land, rivals the Grand Canyon in natural splendor and can't be beat for cultural significance. People have been in residence here continuously since prehistoric times.

Antelope Canyon, called the world's most photographed slot canyon, is near Page in northern Arizona. You'll need an authorized guide to hike into this narrow sandstone canyon, which is inside the Navajo Reservation.

Just north of Sedona in north-central Arizona, you can drive through **Oak Creek Canyon**. Stop along the way to take a closer look at the red sandstone cliffs and buttes.

WORTH NOTING
- Canyon X, northeast Arizona
- Havasu Canyon, Grand Canyon
- Ramsey Canyon, southern Arizona
- Madera Canyon, southern Arizona

DESERTS

Deserts are full of mystery, surprises, and stories of plants, animals, and people overcoming odds to survive and flourish. Track down a rare desert bloom, listen to the screech of an owl, or hear the hiss of a rattlesnake and you'll get a sense of the unique beauty and power of the landscape.

Just one of Arizona's claims to nature's hall of fame is as the only state to have all four of the major deserts in the United States within its borders. The Great Basin, the nation's largest cold desert, spills down to touch the northernmost areas of Arizona. In northwest Arizona, low shrubs such as yucca and the Joshua Tree dominate the small Mojave Desert, a hot desert, which has the nation's lowest elevation and highest temperatures. Only a few skinny fingers of the Chihuahan Desert grasslands stretch into the state's southeast corner. Arizona's largest desert, the Sonoran, is unusual with its biseasonal rainfall, mild winters, and subtropical climate that give rise to a diversity rarely seen in a desert environment.

Although deserts may look barren from a distance, a closer look reveals classic saguaros (top) and blooming prickly pear cacti (opposite).

And then there's the Painted Desert, not actually a true desert. In this high, dry region of the Colorado Plateau, colorful layers of sedimentary rocks are buckled and pitched up in grand steps, and carved into canyons and other-worldly rock formations.

ANCIENT PEOPLE AND THE LAND
Thousands of years ago, native people learned to live and thrive in the Sono-ran Desert, creating canals to irrigate crops, migrating with the seasons from low valleys to cooler mountains, and harvesting desert plants. Today, the 20,000-plus members of the Tohono O'odham Nation live on more than 2.8 million acres in southwestern Arizona. To see handicrafts by tribal members and sample local food, stop by San Xavier Plaza in Tucson.

TOP DESERT EXPERIENCES

WALKING AND HIKING
Whether you're on a gentle nature stroll or a challenging scramble up a mountain, take the time for a scavenger hunt. Seek out a blooming teddy bear cholla, find a whiptail lizard sunning on a rock, or listen for the howl of a coyote at dusk.

PHOTOGRAPHY
The desert has a singular beauty that changes as the light shifts from scorching midday to shadowy dusk to evocative moonshine. With practice you can learn how to capture the best images of sweeping horizons, wildflowers, horses, cowboys, and even the wings of a hummingbird.

VIEWING DESERT PLANTS
Throughout the dry desert landscape, hardy succulents—water-retaining plants including cactus—are well-adapted to the extreme conditions. In wild parks and botanical gardens, you can observe bizzare-looking forms like the Joshua Tree as well as the more familiar saguaro, prickly pear, and barrel cactus.

TOP DESTINATIONS

Part zoo, part botanical garden, part natural history museum, the popular **Arizona-Sonora Desert Museum** allows you to sample the wildlife of the Sonoran Desert in downtown Tucson.

If you've got a little more time and energy, head for **Saguaro National Park** near Tucson. Its two districts have wonderful outdoor opportunities. For vistas of abundant cacti, try the Valley View Overlook.

For a true desert wilderness experience, head southwest to **Organ Pipe Cactus National Monument**, where organ pipe, saguaro, chollo, ocotillo, creosote, and other succulent plants flourish. Hike a trail, bike the 21-mile Ajo Mountain Drive, or camp here for pure serenity.

WORTH NOTING
- Desert Botanical Garden, Phoenix
- Boyce Thompson Arboretum, east of Phoenix
- Cabeza Prieta National Wildlife Refuge, southern Arizona
- Petrified Forest National Park, eastern Arizona

MOUNTAINS

What goes down, must come up. As Arizona's deserts and canyons were formed, so were mountain ranges. Mountain peaks reaching above 4,000 feet in elevation can be found in all parts of the state except the southwest corner.

Ancient rocky ranges with high meadows and cool alpine lakes, cratered volcanic peaks, and desert mountains that fall away to river gorges in deep canyons—Arizona has it all. The diversity of wildlife is immense and you really can travel from a cactus-covered desert to a snow-covered mountain peak in a day. The same geologic forces that created canyons—tectonic to volcanic to glacial activity—have left the state with mountains both old and young.

The rising and falling of the land created not just ranges but also isolated high-elevation areas in southern Arizona. Dubbed "sky islands," a collection of 40 forested mountain groups with lush vegetation at the top and their accompanying canyons below is surrounded by deserts or grasslands. The confluence of desert and forest communities has created habitats for rare and endemic

In warm weather, mountains can be cool escapes. Multi-use trails for bikers and hikers criss-cross the area near Sedona (top) and Flagstaff (opposite).

species, and wildlife-watching opportunities are truly unparalleled. And in eastern Arizona, the pine-covered White Mountains are a cool respite for many outdoor adventures.

ANCIENT PEOPLE AND THE LAND
As Arizona's prehistoric inhabitants evolved from hunting and gathering to agriculture, one group made its home in the forested mountain ranges and nearby valleys: the Mogollon. About 2,000 years ago, early Mogollon people hunted mountain game and gathered fruits, berries, and seeds from alpine meadows and forests to supplement what crops they could grow in the lower valleys. At Casa Malpais, in Springerville, remains of a 16-acre pueblo complex include what is thought to be a Mogollon solstice observatory, built around AD 1200.

TOP MOUNTAIN EXPERIENCES

MOUNTAIN BIKING
You can join a group ride with one of many biking clubs, take a guided tour, or venture out on your own. Recommended spots include: the Elephant Head Trail in Coronado National Forest, and trails in the Coconino National Forest, between Sedona and Flagstaff.

HIKING THE ARIZONA TRAIL
One of the eleven National Scenic Trails, this long-distance route covers about 800 miles from Mexico to Utah. People commonly take one section at a time. The trail takes you through major mountain ranges, from the Huachucas and Santa Rita in the south, through the Superstition Wilderness and over the San Francisco Peaks.

ROCK CLIMBING
Southern Arizona rock formations and towering cliffs are a great place to learn the basics of climbing. Take a course and start with basic bouldering, then learn how to rope up for multi-pitch climbs. Mount Lemmon and Cochise Stronghold, both near Tucson, are popular climbing spots.

TOP DESTINATIONS

Just north of Flagstaff, the volcanic **San Francisco Peaks** can be experienced by foot, mountain bike, horse, or even ski lift. Humphrey's Peak, the state's highest spot at 12,633 feet, is a rewarding trek for experienced hikers.

Erosion has carved out a "Wonderland of Rocks" at **Chiricahua National Monument** in the southeastern section of the state. A perfect example of a sky island, this is considered one of the most ecologically diverse regions in the entire country.

About 1,000 years ago, a series of violent erruptions formed **Sunset Crater Volcano National Monument** and destroyed plants for five miles. Now, you can hike on a lava flow, climb a cinder cone, and see signs of life regenerating.

WORTH NOTING
- Apache-Sitgreaves National Forest, eastern Arizona
- White Mountains, eastern Arizona
- Superstition Wilderness, Phoenix
- Hualapai Mountain Park, northwest Arizona
- Santa Catalina Mountains, Tucson

DISTINCTIVE ANIMALS OF ARIZONA

❶ Coatimundi

These high-energy mammals combine a long ringed tail like a monkey's, a snout like an anteater's, the lumbering walk of a bear, and the mask of a raccoon. Members of the raccoon family, they live in large social groups. Normally tree dwellers, in mountainous southeastern Arizona these nonstop foragers can make dens in caves and crevices.

❷ Desert bighorn sheep

Found primarily in the mountains of the Sonoran and Mojave Deserts, the sheep favor steep slopes and canyon walls. Unique padded hooves allow them to grab the surface of the rock. Males use their large curved horns for fighting and to break open cactus, a common food for the large grazers.

❸ Elegant trogon

This rare, distinctive bird migrates from Mexico to southeast Arizona's mountains and canyons in the summer. The foot-long birds make their nests in dead or dying sycamore trees in cavities created by woodpeckers. The colorful male has an emerald green back and throat, with a bright red breast and a white breast band.

❹ Gila woodpecker

One of the Sonoran Desert's signature species, this woodpecker works away at the saguaro cactus, creating cavities that serve as homes for itself and other animals, including owls, rats, lizards purple martins, and other birds. The very common birds don't hammer just to make holes; they also use sound to mark their territory.

❺ Western diamondback rattlesnake

Reptiles are plentiful in all of Arizona's deserts, and while most are fascinating and beautiful, the rattlesnakes can also be very dangerous. The Western Diamondback, with its triangular-shaped head and black and white ringed tail, is active late afternoon and at night, and will strike if it's disturbed. Tread carefully!

DISTINCTIVE PLANTS OF ARIZONA

❻ Ocotillo

Common in both the Sonoran and Chihuahan Deserts, this tall woody shrub has long, thin, spiny stems that rise up out of a short trunk. Reddish orange flowers bloom at the tips of these stems in spring, providing nectar—and energy—to migrating hummingbirds.

❼ Ponderosa pine

Forests of these tall stately pines cover high-elevation areas on the Colorado Plateau, and in some cases pure stands stretch for thousands of acres—such as the one from Flagstaff along the Mogollon Rim to the White Mountains. Growing more than 100 feet tall, this tree provides food and shelter to many animals and birds.

❽ Rocky Mountain iris

There's nothing quite like a mountain meadow in May, when blooming alpine wildflowers herald the season. Among the lupines, paintbrushes, lilies, and poppies, look for the Rocky Mountain iris between 6,000 and 9,000 feet ele-

vation. Growing one or two feet high, the stems produce one to four delicate purple flowers with accents of yellow and white.

❾ Saguaro cactus

This iconic plant plays such a vital role in the Sonoran Desert, providing food and shelter to bats, bees, and birds. A giant, columnar cactus, with short stout arms that point to the sky, it can grow to be 40 feet tall or higher, with an average life span of 150 years. Its large, creamy white flowers bloom by night in late April and May, harbingers of the red juicy fruit.

❿ Yellow palo verde (foothill palo verde)

Look for this twiggy, thorny shrub on rocky hillsides. Its green bark contains chlorophyll, so it can still carry on with photosynthesis even when the shrub's leaves drop off during the dry season. The palo verde is the primary nurse plant for the saguaro cactus, providing shade for its seedlings.

A GEOLOGY PRIMER

Left: dramatic spires at the Chiracahuas. Top right: Rainbow Bridge, the world's longest natural bridge. Lower right: Monument Valley's Mittens and Merrick Butte.

ARCH This type of opening in a rock wall forms either through erosion, when wind and sand wear away the rock face, or through the freezing action of water. When water enters spaces or joints in a rock and freezes, the expansion of the ice can crack off chunks of rock.

BRIDGE If an opening through a rock is created by water flowing beneath it, it is called a bridge. You can see many natural bridges in Arizona, such as Rainbow Bridge near Lake Powell and Devil's Bridge near Sedona.

BUTTE A butte is what remains when a mesa erodes. You can see good examples of this formation in Monument Valley in northeast Arizona.

CAVES Natural underground chambers that open to the surface give you an opportunity to descend below the Earth's surface and learn about the forces of heat and water upon rocks and minerals. Kartchner Caverns, south of Tucson, is a living cave where water still flows, dissolving minerals and creating beautiful formations.

MESA A mesa, or hill with a smooth, flat, tablelike top (mesa means "table" in Spanish), is a clear example of how hard rock stands higher and protects the soft rock beneath. A single mesa may cover hundreds of square miles of land. There are many mesas in the Hopi Reservation, including the villages of First, Second, and Third Mesa.

MONUMENT This general term applies to geologic formations that are much taller than they are wide, or to formations that resemble man-made structures. These are what give Monument Valley its name.

PETRIFIED WOOD If you want to know what the desert of the Southwest used to look like, picture the Florida Everglades populated with giant dragonflies and smaller species of dinosaurs. Arizona's Petrified Forest offers a glimpse of the once lush, tropical world. Stumps and logs from the ancient woodland are now turned to rock because they were immersed in water and sealed away from the air, so normal decay did not occur. Instead, the preserved wood gradually hardened as silica, or sand, filtered into its porous spaces, almost like cement. Erosion was among the geological processes that exposed the wood.

SPIRE As a butte erodes, it may become one or more spires. You can see wonderful examples of these rock formations in southern Arizona's Chiricahua National Monument.

PHOENIX, SCOTTSDALE, AND TEMPE

WELCOME TO PHOENIX, SCOTTSDALE, AND TEMPE

TOP REASONS TO GO

★ **Resort spas:** With dozens of outstanding desert spas, Phoenix has massaged and wrapped its way to the top of the relaxation destinations list.

★ **Shops and restaurants:** Retail centers Old Town Scottsdale and Fashion Square are another way to retreat and relax in the Valley of the Sun, as are a melting pot of fine and funky dining establishments.

★ **The Heard Museum:** This small but world-renowned museum elegantly celebrates Native American people, culture, art, and history.

★ **The great outdoors:** Sure there's urban sprawl, but Phoenix also has cool and accessible places to get away from it all, like the Desert Botanical Garden, Papago Park, Tempe Town Lake, and mountain and desert preserves.

★ **Golf:** All year long, links lovers can take their pick of top-rated public and private courses—many with incredibly spectacular views.

1 Downtown Phoenix. As the site of Arizona's government operations and the state's largest concentration of skyscrapers, this area used to be strictly business. Nowadays it's home to some of the Valley's major museums, performance venues, and sports arenas, plenty of high-rise homeowners, and a light-rail system that's changing the face of the city.

2 Greater Phoenix. Here's an unusual mix of attractions ranging from hip, historic neighborhoods to acres of mountain preserves, cultural and ethnic centers, and corridors of modern commercial enterprise. Hike a couple of peaks, peek at the animals in the Phoenix Zoo, zoom on over to the Phoenix Art and Heard museums, and then relax at a luxury mountainside resort—all in one day.

GETTING ORIENTED

It can be useful to think of Phoenix as a flower with petals (other communities) growing in every direction from the bud of Sky Harbor Airport. The East Valley includes Scottsdale, Paradise Valley, Ahwatukee, Tempe, Mesa, Fountain Hills, and Apache Junction. To the southeast are Chandler and Gilbert. The West Valley includes Glendale, Sun City, Peoria, and Litchfield Park. Central Avenue, which runs north and south through the heart of Downtown Phoenix, is the city's east–west dividing line. Everything east of Central is considered the East Valley and everything west of Central is the West Valley.

3 **Scottsdale.** Once an upscale Phoenix sibling, it now flies solo as a top American destination. A bastion of high-end and specialty shopping, historic sites, elite resorts, restaurants, spas, and golf greens next to desert views, Scottsdale can easily absorb an entire vacation.

4 **Tempe and Around.** The home of Arizona State University and a creative melting pot of residents, Tempe is equal parts party and performance, especially along its main artery, Mill Avenue, where commerce and culture collide.

SPA TIME IN ARIZONA: SAY AHHH

OK, so you came, you saw, you shopped, you dined, you recreated. Now it's time for some rest and relaxation at one, or even several, of the *many* area spas. Arizona's own approach to pampered repose is world-renowned and worth exploring with all of your senses.

Above: Royal Palms's couples massage. Upper right: A water retreat at Sanctuary on Camelback Mountain. Lower right: Moroccan-inspired treatment room in Joya Spa at Montelucia Resort

Whether you're looking for a simple massage or an entire lifestyle change, Arizona rubs just about everyone the right way—from exclusive "immersion environments" of remote destination spas, to more accessible and affordable resort and day spas around the state. Each has its own signature style and blend of services, including purely local luxury at Sanctuary Spa on Camelback Mountain. In the midst of the Southwest's deserts and cities, you're sure to find spa menus boasting treatments and treats from around the world: Swedish and Japanese massages, French manicures and Vichy showers, Turkish-style baths, ayurvedic practices from India, California cuisine, and mood music from the Middle East and New Mexico.

A HISTORY OF HEALING

Arizona's hot, arid climate was considered a cure-all for respiratory ailments and joint pain. The East Coast power elite (Astors, Vanderbilts, and Rockefellers, to name a few) who grew sick of brutal winters and humid summers made a second home out of local resorts and spas. The hospitality industry has been striving to meet high standards for rejuvenation and health ever since.

RULES TO RELAX BY

Observing simple spa rules can ensure ultimate spa satisfaction versus an uncomfortable experience. First, decide on a budget beforehand and research spa menus; many are available online. Plan on a 15%–20% gratuity (cash preferred) for each treatment, though some spas include gratuity in their pricing. Second, book at least a week ahead, longer for the most popular spas like Sanctuary on Camelback Mountain in Paradise Valley. Third, check in at least 20 minutes prior to your first treatment. The earlier you arrive, the longer you can enjoy the spa's gratis amenities, such as pools and steam rooms.

DAY OR DESTINATION?

Day spas are just that. They keep daytime hours and offer luxury treatments, but not long-term wellness programs. Destination spas, like Mii amo at Sedona's Enchantment Resort *(⇨ See Chapter 4)* and Tucson's exclusive Canyon Ranch *(⇨ See Chapter 7)*, have "immersion environments" with on-site accommodations and curricula designed for an inner- and outer-body overhaul. Most resort spas operate like day spas and don't require an overnight stay; however, hotel guests take precedence when it comes to booking.

LOCAL LURE AND LORE

A few spas are sanctioned to offer the innovative treatments and environments

inspired by the traditions of local Native American tribes. Just south of Phoenix, Aji Spa at the Sheraton Wild Horse Pass Resort draws on the surrounding Pima and Maricopa communities to create unique experiences. Many of their treatments employ time-honored healing methods, approved by tribal elders.

A TOUCH OF ROMANCE

If an indulgent spa visit is your ideal romantic getaway, pick a place that truly specializes in making it special. Most spa menus include a couples' massage, but some focus on creating an entire experience for pairs. Alvadora Spa at the Royal Palms in Phoenix offers romance packages (and discounted rates during the hot summer months) along with twosome-oriented treatments and amenities, while Joya at Paradise Valley's Montelucia offers a specially outfitted couples' day suite.

TASTE TREATMENT

If you're focusing on a detoxifying spa experience, the last thing you want to do is replenish with unsavory elements. Camelback Inn in Scottsdale and The Boulders in Carefree have restaurants or cafés that specialize in "spa cuisine," often surprisingly delicious, health-conscious dishes made with locally grown ingredients—good for you and the planet.

VALLEY OF THE SUN GOLF: DRIVING AMBITION

Itching to get into the swing of things? Hoping to partake in some coursework? Looking to get linked in? In other words, would you rather be golfing? You're in the right place. Despite the dry climate this place is a gold mine of lush greens and far-reaching fairways.

Above: It's easy to find greens in the Valley of the Sun. Upper right: Tournament Players Club (TPC) at the Fairmont Scottsdale Princess Resort. Lower right: The setting at The Boulders

Golf is one of Arizona's leading draws for locals and visitors from around the world. Big, professional courses mean big business in the Valley of the Sun, evidenced by the more than 200 courses that consume much of the area and surround some of its finest resorts, locally based golf companies such as Ping and Dixon, and by the Phoenix Open—an annual world-class tournament and weeklong party that takes place in North Scottsdale at the renowned Tournament Players Club (TPC). That might sound intimidating, but consider it an invitation. Whether you're an amateur or an ace, and whether you're looking out for pars, your pocketbook, or just a pretty place to play a round, there's something for all ranges here.

TEE-TIME TIP

Book online, up to weeks in advance during winter and spring. Get availability, pricing, and discounted tee-time information by visiting an individual course's website. For municipal courses, visit ⊕ *www.phoenix.gov/parks* or ⊕ *www.thegolfcourses. net* and search Phoenix or Scottsdale for links to all the Valley's links.

PLAN AHEAD

Call well ahead for tee times during the cooler months from January to April, especially for popular courses. In summer, it's not uncommon to schedule a round before dawn. If you're booking a room at a resort with a course, be sure to book your tee time then also. Last-minute tee times are sometimes available through online reservation services, depending on the season.

PERFECT YOUR GOLF SWING

Feel like you need to swing like a pro before you take on the Valley of the Sun's premier golf courses? Troon North has a solution: the **Callaway Golf Performance Center** (☎ *480/585–5300* ⊕ *www.troonnorthgolf.com*) is a state-of-the-art facility that analyzes your swing and fits your clubs with 3-D imagery and software designed by the experts at Callaway. Golf greats like Tiger Woods and Phil Mickelson use similar technologies to perfect their games—why shouldn't you? With only a handful of facilities like this in the country, it's definitely worth checking out.

SAVINGS TIPS

Encanto Park and Papago Golf Course are just two of the city and public courses that are a great value. Check course websites for discounts. Some golf courses offer a discounted twilight rate—and the weather is often much more amenable at this time of day.

Fees drop dramatically in summer but remember that afternoon heat can be sweltering.

"GREENER" GREENS

Short of creating sand and cactus courses, desert golf facilities are hard-pressed to answer the eco-friendly call, but some are making strides in chipping away their carbon cleat-print. Most courses now use reclaimed water and are experimenting with low-water grasses.

GROUPS TO GUIDE YOU

Package deals abound at resorts as well as through booking agencies like **Arizona Golf Adventures** (☎ *800/398–8100* ⊕ *www.arizonagolfadventures.com*), who will plan and schedule a nonstop golf holiday for you. If you're looking for a little more pampering, try **Scottsdale Swing** (☎ *888/807–9464* ⊕ *www.scottsdaleswing.com*), which will arrange a complete golf holiday, including access to the area's best nightclubs. For a copy of the *Arizona Golf Guide*, contact the **Arizona Golf Association** (☎ *602/944–3035 or 800/458–8484* ⊕ *www.azgolf.org*).

Updated by
Elise Riley

The Valley of the Sun, otherwise known as metro Phoenix (i.e., Phoenix and all its suburbs, including Tempe and Scottsdale), is named for its 325-plus days of sunshine each year. Although many come to Phoenix for the golf and the weather, the Valley has much to offer by way of shopping, outdoor activities, and nightlife. The best of the latter is in Scottsdale and the East Valley with their hip dance clubs, old-time saloons, and upscale wine bars.

The Valley marks the northern tip of the Sonoran Desert, a prehistoric seabed that extends into northwestern Mexico with a landscape offering much more than just cacti. Palo verde and mesquite trees, creosote bushes, brittle bush, and agave dot the land, which is accustomed to being scorched by temperatures in excess of 100°F for weeks at a time. Late summer brings precious rain as monsoon storms illuminate the sky with lightning shows and the desert exudes the scent of creosote. Spring sets the Valley blooming, and the giant saguaros are crowned in white flowers for a short time in May—in the evening and cool early mornings—and masses of vibrant wildflowers fill desert crevices and span mountain landscapes.

PHOENIX, SCOTTSDALE, AND TEMPE PLANNER

WHEN TO GO

It's a common misconception that Phoenix forever hovers around 100°F. That might hold true from May to October, but the winter months have been known to push the mercury down to 35°F. The city also has experienced consecutive days of nonstop rain. Such instances are rare, but it's good to be prepared and check weather reports before you pack.

Phoenix can get pretty darn hot in summer, so plan your outdoor activities for the cooler parts of the day and save the air-conditioned stuff for when it's needed: the Heard Museum is not only a must-see, it's also inside, as are the nearby Phoenix Art Museum and many other popular attractions.

FESTIVALS AND EVENTS

JANUARY **Barrett-Jackson.** This fabulous car auction attracts thousands every January. ☎ *480/421–6694* ⊕ *www.barrett-jackson.com.*

P. F. Chang's Rock 'n' Roll Marathon. Live bands line the marathon course and a concert follows the 26.2-mile race that attracts runners each January. ☎ *800/311–1255* ⊕ *runrocknroll.competitor.com/arizona.*

Russo and Steele. Every January, the Russo and Steele auction features some of the most sought-after vehicles in the world. ☎ *602/252–2697* ⊕ *www.russoandsteele.com.*

Waste Management Phoenix Open. Formerly the Phoenix Open, this golf tournament is the "Greatest Show on Grass." ☎ *602/870–0163* ⊕ *www. wmphoenixopen.com.*

FEBRUARY **The Heard Museum World Championship Hoop Dance Contest.** Every February, the Heard Museum hosts the spectacular Annual World Hoop Dance Championship, with traditional music and costumes. ☎ *602/252–8840* ⊕ *www.heard.org.*

The Parada del Sol Parade and Rodeo. This annual horse-drawn parade is an Arizona tradition featuring cowboys, cowgirls, horses, and floats. ☎ *480/990–3179* ⊕ *www.paradadelsol.us.*

MARCH **Indian Fair & Market.** Every March, more than 700 Native American artists and artisans are showcased at the Heard Museum. ☎ *602/252–8840* ⊕ *www.heard.org.*

Ostrich Festival. This is a weekend of music, entertainment, and (of course) ostrich races in Chandler every March. ☎ *480/963–4571* ⊕ *www.ostrichfestival.com.*

Scottsdale Arts Festival. This weekend event in March is jam-packed with arts and crafts—and music. ☎ *480/499–8587* ⊕ *www.scottsdaleartsfestival. org.*

APRIL **Scottsdale Culinary Festival.** Foodies from across the Valley mark their calendars for this week-long festival in April. Taste the creations from some of the best chefs in town at this outoor celebration of food. ☎ *480/945–7193* ⊕ *www.scottsdalefest.org.*

OCTOBER **Arizona State Fair.** Come for classic fair fun, including arm wrestling and calf roping every October. ☎ *602/252–6771* ⊕ *www.azstatefair.com.*

DECEMBER **Las Noches de las Luminarias.** Adjacent to the twinkling zoo, the Desert Botanical Garden lights up every night during Las Noches de las Luminarias, when thousands of luminarias (paper bags with lights inside) line the Garden's pathways. Stroll, listen to live music, and enjoy the beauty of the desert. Tickets sell out quickly, so be sure to make a reservation for this annual December event. ☎ *480/941–1225* ⊕ *www.dbg.org.*

PLANNING YOUR TIME

Three to five days is an optimal amount of time to spend in Phoenix if you want to relax, get outside to hike or golf, and see the main sites like the Heard Museum and Scottsdale. Extra time will allow you to make some interesting side trips to nearby places like Arcosanti, Wickenburg, Cave Creek, and Carefree.

Remember that the Valley of the Sun is sprawling, so planning ahead will help you save time and gas. If you're heading to the Heard Museum Downtown, for instance, you might want to visit the nearby Arizona Science Center and/or the Phoenix Art Museum, too, both of which are close to the light-rail line. If you're going to Taliesin West, do so before or after spending time in Scottsdale.

■TIP➜ If you're driving to the Grand Canyon from Phoenix, allow at least two full days, with a minimum drive time of four hours each way. You can always anticipate slow-moving traffic on Interstate 17, but in the afternoon and evening on Friday and Sunday lengthy standstills are almost guaranteed, something to remember if your plans involve getting back to Sky Harbor Airport to catch a flight out.

GETTING HERE AND AROUND

AIR TRAVEL

Phoenix Sky Harbor International Airport (PHX) is served by most major airlines. The airport is a 10-minute drive from Downtown Phoenix or Tempe, and 15 minutes to North Scottsdale. SuperShuttle vans each take up to seven passengers to different destinations. Fares are $14 to Downtown Phoenix and around $28 to Scottsdale.

Air Contacts Phoenix Sky Harbor International Airport (*PHX*). 🕾 *602/273–3300* ⊕ *www.phxskyharbor.com.* **SuperShuttle** 🕾 *602/244–9000, 800/258–3826* ⊕ *www.supershuttle.com.*

CAR TRAVEL

To get around Phoenix, *you will need a car.* Only the major downtown areas (Phoenix, Scottsdale, and Tempe) are pedestrian-friendly. Don't expect to nab a rental car without a reservation, especially from January to April.

Roads in Phoenix and its suburbs are laid out on an 800-square-mile grid. Grand Avenue, running 20 miles from Downtown to Sun City, is the only diagonal. Central Avenue is the main north–south grid axis: all roads parallel to and west of Central are numbered avenues; all roads parallel to and east of Central are numbered streets. The numbering begins at Central and increases in each direction.

PUBLIC TRANSPORTATION TRAVEL

The Valley's light-rail system is convenient for exploring the Downtown Phoenix museums or the area near Arizona State University. Fares are $3.50/day and multiday passes are available. Phoenix runs a free Downtown Area Shuttle (DASH), and Tempe operates the Free Local Area Shuttle (FLASH).

Public Transportation Contacts Valley Metro 🕾 *602/253–5000* ⊕ *www. valleymetro.org.*

TAXI TRAVEL

Taxi fares are unregulated in Phoenix, except at the airport. The 800-square-mile metro area is so large that one-way fares in excess of $50 are not uncommon. Except within a compact area, travel by taxi isn't recommended. Taxis charge about $3 for the first mile and $2 per mile thereafter, not including tips.

Taxi Contacts Checker/Yellow Cab ☎ *480/888-8888* ⊕ *www.aaayellowaz. com*. **Clean Air Cab** ☎ *480/777-9777* ⊕ *www.cleanaircab.com*. **Courier Cab** ☎ *602/232-2222.*

2

TOURS

If you'd like a break from driving, consider a tour to see the Valley's top attractions. Reservations are a must all year.

Open Road Tours. This operator offers excursions to Sedona and the Grand Canyon, Phoenix city tours, and Native American–culture trips to the Salt River Pima–Maricopa Indian Reservation. ☎ *602/997–6474, 855/553–8830* ⊕ *www.openroadtoursusa.com* ✉ *From $59.*

Vaughan's Southwest Tours. This 4½-hour city tour stops at the Pueblo Grande Museum, Mummy Mountain, and Old Town Scottsdale. Vaughan's tours use custom vans and accommodate groups of 11 or fewer passengers. The company will also take you east to the Apache Trail. ☎ *602/971–1381, 800/513–1381* ⊕ *www.southwesttours.com* ✉ *From $60.*

VISITOR INFORMATION

Most Valley cities have tourism centers where you can get maps or excursion suggestions.

Greater Phoenix Convention & Visitors Bureau ☎ *877/225-5749, 602/254-6500* ⊕ *www.visitphoenix.com* ═ *No credit cards*. **Scottsdale Convention & Visitors Bureau** ☎ *800/782-1117, 480/421-1004* ⊕ *www.experiencescottsdale. com* ═ *No credit cards.*

EXPLORING

DOWNTOWN PHOENIX

Changes in the Valley over the past two decades have meant the emergence of a real Downtown in Phoenix, where people hang out: there are apartments and loft spaces; cultural and sports facilities, including Jefferson Street's Chase Field and US Airways Center; and large areas for conventions and trade shows. It's retained a mix of past and present, too, as restored homes in Heritage Square, from the original townsite, give an idea of how far the city has come since its inception around the turn of the 20th century.

GETTING HERE AND AROUND

There are lots of parking options Downtown, and they're listed on the free map provided by Downtown Phoenix Partnership, available in many local restaurants (⊕ *www.downtownphoenix.com*). Many Downtown sites are served by the light-rail system or DASH (Downtown Area Shuttle), a free bus service.

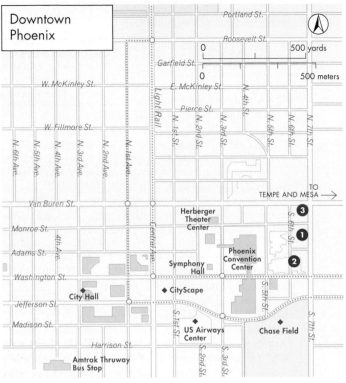

TIMING

Artlink Phoenix First Fridays. On the first Friday of every month galleries stay open late and crowds converge to view the work of emerging and established artists, listen to live music, and see impromptu street performances. It's an excellent way to check out the Phoenix arts scene. ☎ 602/256–7539 ⊕ *www.artlinkphoenix.com* ▭ *No credit cards.*

EXPLORING

FAMILY **Arizona Science Center.** With more than 300 hands-on exhibits, this is the venue for science-related exploration. You can pilot a simulated airplane flight, travel through the human body, navigate your way through the solar system in the Dorrance Planetarium, and watch a movie in a giant, five-story IMAX theater. ⊠ *600 E. Washington St., Downtown Phoenix* ☎ *602/716–2000* ⊕ *www.azscience.org* ⛿ *Museum $15; combination museum, IMAX, and planetarium $32* ⊙ *Daily 10–5.*

FAMILY **Children's Museum of Phoenix.** A playground for kids of all ages, this museum features hands-on exhibits where children learn by playing. Venture through the "noodle forest," relax in the book loft, or get a crash course in economics by role-playing at the on-site market. ⊠ *215 N. 7th St., Downtown Phoenix* ☎ *602/253–0501* ⊕ *www. childrensmuseumofphoenix.org* ⛿ *$11* ⊙ *Tues.–Sun. 9–4.*

Heritage Square. In a parklike setting from 5th to 7th Street between Monroe and Adams streets, this city-owned block contains the only remaining houses from the original Phoenix townsite. On the south side of the square, along Adams Street, stand several houses built between 1899 and 1901. The Bouvier Teeter House has a Victorian-style tearoom, and the Thomas House and Baird Machine Shop are now Pizzeria Bianco, one of the area's most popular eateries. ✉ *Downtown Phoenix* ⊕ *www.phoenix. gov/parks/parks/heritagepk.html* ▭ *No credit cards*

Arizona Doll and Toy Museum. The one-story brick Stevens House holds the Arizona Doll and Toy Museum. ✉ *602 E. Adams St., Downtown Phoenix* ☎ *602/253–9337* ▱ *$5* ☉ *Sept.–July, Tues.–Sat. 10–4, Sun. noon–4.*

Rosson House Museum. This 1895 Victorian in the Queen Anne style is the queen of Heritage Square. Built by a physician who served a brief term as mayor, it's the sole survivor among fewer than two dozen Victorians erected in Phoenix. It was bought and restored by the city in 1974. ✉ *113 N 6th St., Downtown Phoenix* ☎ *602/262–5070* ⊕ *www. rossonhousemuseum.org* ▱ *$7.50* ☉ *Wed.–Sat. 10–4, Sun. noon–4.*

> **QUICK BITES**
>
> **Switch.** One of Phoenix's coolest ways to beat the summer heat, Switch offers a unique menu. Choose from fresh sandwiches, healthful salads, a fabulous cheese platter, gourmet burgers, steaks, seafood, baked goods, and crêpes, all served in a sleek, modern setting with couch conversation pits and one of downtown's best patios. ✉ *2603 N. Central Ave., Downtown Phoenix* ☎ *602/264–2295* ⊕ *www.switchofarizona.com.*

> **WORD OF MOUTH**
>
> "I really enjoyed a visit to the Desert Botanical Garden in Phoenix when I visited Arizona. There is a special sculpture exhibit (separate admission) and they have concerts on Sundays."
> –dsgmi

GREATER PHOENIX

While suburban towns are popping up all around Phoenix, the city's core neighborhoods just outside Downtown Phoenix maintain the majority of their history and appeal. There are options aplenty to take you out hiking in the hills, or inside to some interesting cultural sites.

GETTING HERE AND AROUND

One of the largest metropolitan areas in the United States, Greater Phoenix is a sprawling mix of urban and suburban. Sky Harbor Airport is one of the busiest in the nation. Although Phoenix has some public transportation, it's best to explore the Valley by car.

TOP ATTRACTIONS

FAMILY
Fodor'sChoice
★

Desert Botanical Garden. Opened in 1939 to conserve and showcase the ecology of the desert, these 150 acres contain more than 4,000 different species of cacti, succulents, trees, and flowers. A stroll along the 0.5-mile-long "Plants and People of the Sonoran Desert" trail is a fascinating lesson in environmental adaptations; children enjoy playing the

CLOSE UP

Phoenix History: A City Grows in the Desert

As the Hohokam (the name comes from the Pima word for "people who have gone before") discovered 2,300 years ago, the miracle of water in the desert can be augmented by human hands. Having migrated from northwestern Mexico, Hohokam cultivated cotton, corn, and beans in tilled, rowed, and irrigated fields for about 1,700 years, establishing more than 300 miles of canals—an engineering phenomenon when you consider the limited technology available. They constructed a great town on whose ruins modern Phoenix is built, and then vanished. Drought, long winters, and other causes are suggested for their disappearance.

MODERN BEGINNINGS
From the time the Hohokam left until the Civil War, the once-fertile Salt River valley lay forgotten, used only by occasional small bands of Pima and Maricopa Indians. Then in 1865 the U.S. Army established Fort McDowell in the mountains to the east, where the Verde River flows into the Salt River. To feed the men and the horses stationed there, a former Confederate Army officer reopened the Hohokam canals in 1867. Within a year, fields bright with barley and pumpkins earned the area the name Pumpkinville. By 1870 the 300 residents had decided that their new city would arise from the ancient Hohokam site, just as the mythical phoenix rose from its own ashes.

A CITY ON THE RISE
Phoenix would grow indeed. Within 20 years it had become large enough—its population was about 3,000—to wrest the title of territorial capital from Prescott. By 1912, when Arizona was admitted as the 48th state, the area, irrigated by the brand-new Roosevelt Dam and Salt River Project, had a burgeoning cotton industry. Copper was mined elsewhere but traded in Phoenix, and cattle were raised elsewhere but slaughtered and packed here in the largest stockyards outside Chicago.

Meanwhile, the climate, so long a crippling liability, became an asset. Desert air was the prescribed therapy for the respiratory ills rampant in the sooty, factory-filled East; Scottsdale began in 1901 as "30-odd tents and a half-dozen adobe houses" put up by health seekers. By 1930 travelers looking for warm winter recreation as well as rejuvenating aridity filled the elegant Wigwam Resort and Arizona Biltmore, the first of the many luxury retreats for which the area is now known worldwide. The 1950s brought residential air-conditioning, an invention that made the summers bearable for the growing workforce of the burgeoning technology industry.

PHOENIX TODAY
The Valley is very much a work still in progress, and historians are quick to point out that never in the world's history has a metropolis grown from "nothing" to attain the status of Phoenix in such a short period of time. At the heart of all the bustle, though, is a way of life that keeps its own pace: Phoenix is one of the world's largest small towns—where people dress informally and where the rugged, Old West spirit lives on in many of the Valley's nooks and crannies despite the sprawling growth. And if summer heat can be overwhelming, at least it has the restorative effect of slowing things down to an enjoyable pace.

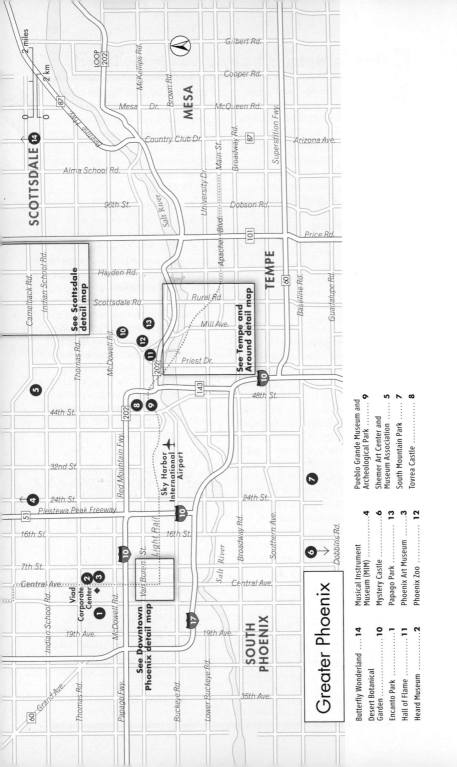

Greater Phoenix

self-guiding game "Desert Detective." Specialized tours are available at an extra cost; check online for times and prices. ■TIP➜ The Desert Botanical Garden stays open late, to 8 year-round, and it's particularly lovely when lighted by the setting sun or by moonlight. You can plan for a cool, late visit after a full day of activities. ✉ *1201 N. Galvin Pkwy.* ☎ *480/941–1225* ⊕ *www.dbg.org* 🎟 *$22* ⊘ *Daily 8–8.*

FAMILY **Hall of Flame.** Retired firefighters lead tours through nearly 100 restored fire engines and tell harrowing tales of the "world's most dangerous profession." The museum has the world's largest collection of firefighting equipment, and children can climb on a 1916 engine, operate alarm systems, and learn fire safety lessons from the pros. Helmets, badges, and other firefighting-related articles dating from as far back as 1725 are on display. ✉ *6101 E. Van Buren St.* ☎ *602/275–3473* ⊕ *www. hallofflame.org* 🎟 *$7* ⊘ *Mon.–Sat. 9–5, Sun. noon–4.*

FAMILY
Fodor's Choice
★
Heard Museum. Pioneer settlers Dwight and Maie Heard built a Spanish colonial–style building on their property to house their collection of Southwestern art. Today the staggering collection includes such exhibits as a Navajo hogan and rooms filled with art, pottery, jewelry, kachinas, and textiles. The Heard also actively supports contemporary Indian artists and displays their work. Their fabulous signature cultural exhibition is "Home: Native People in the Southwest." Annual events include the World Championship Hoop Dance Contest in February and the Guild Indian Fair & Market in March. Children enjoy the interactive art-making exhibits. ■TIP➜ The museum also has an incredible gift shop with authentic, high-quality goods purchased directly from Native American artists. There's a museum satellite branch in Scottsdale that has rotating exhibits. ✉ *2301 N. Central Ave., North Central Phoenix* ☎ *602/252–8840* ⊕ *www.heard.org* 🎟 *$18* ⊘ *Mon.–Sat. 9:30–5, Sun. 11–5.*

Musical Instrument Museum (MIM). A fun destination for even casual music fans, the museum offers a rare display of music and instruments going back hundreds of years—including more than 15,000 instruments and artifacts from across the globe. Special galleries highlight video demonstrations as well as audio tracks that showcase the sounds that instruments, both primitive and contemporary, create. Among the museum's dazzling array of instruments are the piano on which John Lennon composed "Imagine," and the first Steinway piano. ✉ *4725 E. Mayo Blvd.* ☎ *480/478–6000* ⊕ *www.mim.org* 🎟 *$18* ⊘ *Mon.–Sat. 9–5, Sun. 10–5.*

FAMILY **Mystery Castle.** At the foot of South Mountain lies a curious dwelling built from desert rocks by Boyce Gulley, who came to Arizona to cure his tuberculosis. Full of fascinating oddities, the castle has 18 rooms with 13 fireplaces, a downstairs grotto tavern, a roll-away bed with a mining railcar as its frame, and some original pieces of Frank Lloyd Wright–designed furniture. The pump organ belonged to Elsie, the "Widow of Tombstone," who buried six husbands under suspicious circumstances. ✉ *800 E. Mineral Rd., South Phoenix* ☎ *602/268–1581* 🎟 *$10* ⊘ *Oct.–June, Thurs.–Sun. 11–4. Call to confirm hrs.*

FAMILY **Phoenix Art Museum.** This museum is one of the most visually appealing pieces of architecture in the Southwest. Basking in natural light, the museum makes great use of its modern, open space by tastefully fitting more than 17,000 works of art from all over the world—including sculptures by Frederic Remington and paintings by Georgia O'Keeffe, Thomas Moran, and Maxfield Parrish—within its soaring concrete walls. The museum hosts more than 20 significant exhibitions annually and has one of the most acclaimed fashion collections in the country. Complete your tour with lunch at Arcadia Farms, the in-house café that serves some of the best homemade fare in town. ⊠ *1625 N. Central Ave., Central Phoenix* ☎ *602/257–1222* ⊕ *www.phxart.org* ⊠ *$15; donations only Wed. evening and 1st Fri. evening* ☉ *Wed. 10–9, Thurs.– Sat. 10–5, Sun. noon–5; 1st Friday evening 6–10.*

FAMILY
Fodor'sChoice
★
Pueblo Grande Museum and Archaeological Park. Phoenix's only national landmark, this park was once the site of a 500-acre Hohokam village supporting about 1,000 people and containing homes, storage rooms, cemeteries, and ball courts. Three exhibition galleries hold displays on the Hohokam culture and archaeological methods. View the 10-minute orientation video before heading out on the ½-mile Ruin Trail past excavated sites that give a hint of Hohokam savvy: there's a building whose corner doorway was perfectly placed for watching the summer-solstice sunrise. Children especially like the hands-on, interactive learning center. Guided tours by appointment only. ⊠ *4619 E. Washington St.* ☎ *602/495–0901* ⊠ *$6.*

Tovrea Castle. Get a glimpse of what Phoenix was like a century ago by touring the extensive grounds and the two floors of the castle, constructed in the 1920s and early 1930s. Unfortunately, the cupola— the castle's "crown"—doesn't meet fire codes, so visitors can't get the 360-degree views that cattle baron E. A. Tovrea enjoyed. A Phoenix landmark, this 44-acre site in central Phoenix is managed jointly by the city of Phoenix and a group of loyal preservationists. ⊠ *5041 E. Van Buren St.* ☎ *602/256–3221, 800/838–3006* ⊕ *www.tovreacastletours. com* ⊠ *$15* ☉ *Tours Sept.–June, Fri.–Sun.; call for reservations.*

🛢 **WORTH NOTING**
Butterfly Wonderland. The largest butterfly pavilion in the United States, Butterfly Wonderland gives kids (and their parents) a close-up view of these fluttering wonders. A temperature controlled rainforest environment is home to thousands of butterflies. You should also make time to check out the honeybee exhibit, the live ant colony, and the 3D theater. ⊠ *9500 E. Via De Ventura, North Scottsdale* ☎ *480/800–3000* ⊕ *butterflywonderland.com* ⊠ *Adults $19* ☉ *Daily 9–5.*

FAMILY
Encanto Park. Urban Encanto (Spanish for "enchanted") Park covers 222 acres at the heart of one of Phoenix's oldest residential neighborhoods. There are many attractions, including picnic areas, a lagoon where you can paddleboat and canoe, a municipal swimming pool, a nature trail, Enchanted Island amusement park (⊕ *www.enchantedisland.com*), fishing in the park's lake, and two public golf courses. ⊠ *1202 W. Encanto Blvd., North Central Phoenix* ☎ *602/261–8991* ⊕ *www.phoenix.gov/ parks/encanto.html* ⊠ *Park free, Enchanted Island rides $1.15 each* ☉ *Park daily 5:30 am–11 pm; Enchanted Island hrs vary by season and weather.*

FAMILY **Papago Park.** An amalgam of hilly desert terrain, streams, and lagoons, this park has picnic *ramadas* (shaded, open-air shelters), a golf course, a playground, hiking and biking trails, and even largemouth bass and trout fishing. (An urban fishing license is required for anglers age 15 and over. Visit ⊕ *www.azgfd.gov* for more information.) The hike up to landmark **Hole-in-the-Rock**—a natural observatory used by the native Hohokam to devise a calendar system—is steep and rocky, and a much easier climb up than down. **Governor Hunt's Tomb,** the white pyramid at the top of Ramada 16, commemorates the former Arizona leader and provides a lovely view. ⊠ *625 N. Galvin Pkwy.* ☎ *602/495–5458* ⊕ *www.phoenix.gov/parks/trails/locations/papago* ▢ *Free* ⊗ *Daily 5 am–11 pm.*

> ## PAPAGO SALADO
>
> The word *Papago*, meaning "bean eater," was a name given by 16th-century Spanish explorers to the Hohokam, a vanished native people of the Phoenix area. Farmers of the desert, the Hohokam lived in central Arizona from about 300 BC to AD 1450, when their civilization abandoned the Salt River (Rio Salado) valley, leaving behind the remnants of their villages and also a complex system of irrigation canals.

FAMILY **Phoenix Zoo.** Four designated trails wind through this 125-acre zoo, replicating such habitats as an African savanna and a tropical rain forest. Meerkats, warthogs, desert bighorn sheep, and the endangered Arabian oryx are among the unusual sights. The Forest of Uco is home to the endangered spectacled bear from South America. Harmony Farm introduces youngsters to small mammals, and a stop at the Big Red Barn petting zoo provides a chance to interact with goats, cows, and more. ■TIP→ In December the zoo stays open late (until 10 pm) for the popular "ZooLights" exhibit that transforms the area into an enchanted forest of more than 225 million twinkling lights, many in the shape of the zoo's residents. Starry Safari Friday Nights in summer are fun, too. ⊠ *455 N. Galvin Pkwy.* ☎ *602/273–1341* ⊕ *www.phoenixzoo.org* ▢ *$20* ⊗ *Hrs vary by month and weather. Check website for details. Generally Sept.–May, daily 9–4; June–Aug., daily 7–2. ZooLights extends holiday hrs until 10.*

Shemer Art Center and Museum Association. Near the Phoenician resort, the Shemer Art Center features revolving exhibits of current Arizona artists who have agreed to donate one of their pieces to the center's permanent collection. The collection is largely contemporary, and exhibits change every month or so in this former residence. ⊠ *5005 E. Camelback Rd., Camelback Corridor* ☎ *602/262–4727* ⊕ *www.shemerartcenter.org* ▢ *Free* ▭ *No credit cards* ⊗ *Tues.–Sat. 10–3, Thurs. 6:30–8:30.*

FAMILY **South Mountain Park.** This desert wonderland, the world's largest city park (almost 17,000 acres), offers a wilderness of mountain-desert trails for hikers, bikers, and horseback riders—and a great place to view sunsets. The Environmental Center has a model of the park as well as displays detailing its history, from the time of the ancient Hohokam people to gold seekers. Roads climb past picnic ramadas constructed by the Civilian Conservation Corps, winding through desert flora to the trailheads.

Look for ancient petroglyphs, try to spot a desert cottontail rabbit or chuckwalla lizard, or simply stroll among the desert vegetation. Maps of all scenic drives as well as hiking, mountain biking, and horseback trails are available at the Gatehouse Entrance just inside the park boundary. ⊠ *10919 S. Central Ave., South Phoenix* ☎ *602/262–7393* ⊕ *www.phoenix.gov/parks/trails/locations/south* 🖘 *Free* ▭ *No credit cards* ⊙ *Daily 5 am–7 pm.*

> **WORD OF MOUTH**
>
> "Don't miss Taliesin West! It's a large property, aside from the beautiful main house/studio. . . . Plan on a good half day so you don't have to rush." –Underhill

SCOTTSDALE

Nationally known art galleries, souvenir shops, and a funky Old Town fill downtown Scottsdale—the third-largest artist community in the United States. Fifth Avenue is known for shopping and Native American jewelry and crafts stores, while Main Street and Marshall Way are home to the international art set with galleries and interior-design shops.

GETTING HERE AND AROUND
Although your tour of downtown can easily be completed on foot, there's a regular free trolley service (☎ *480/421–1004* ⊕ *www.scottsdaleaz.gov/trolley*).

TIMING
If you have limited time in the area, spend a half day in Old Town Scottsdale and the rest of the day at Taliesin West.

Scottsdale ArtWalk. Every Thursday from 7 to 9 pm (except Thanksgiving), the galleries along Main Street and Marshall Way stay open for the Scottsdale ArtWalk, an indoor-outdoor celebration of the arts. Tour the galleries, watch street performers, and grab a bite to eat. ⊕ *www.scottsdalegalleries.com* ▭ *No credit cards.*

TOP ATTRACTIONS
Old Town Scottsdale. "The West's Most Western Town," this area has rustic storefronts and wooden sidewalks; it's touristy, but the closest you'll come to experiencing life here as it was 80 years ago. High-quality jewelry and Mexican imports are sold alongside kitschy souvenirs. ⊠ *Main St. from Scottsdale Rd. to Brown Ave., Old Town.*

Fodor's Choice ★   **Taliesin West.** Ten years after visiting Arizona in 1927 to consult on designs for the Biltmore hotel, architect Frank Lloyd Wright chose 600 acres of rugged Sonoran Desert at the foothills of the McDowell Mountains as the site for his permanent winter residence. Today the site is a National Historic Landmark and still an active community of students and architects. Wright and apprentices constructed a desert camp here using organic architecture to integrate the buildings with their natural surroundings. In addition to the living quarters, drafting studio, and small apartments of the Apprentice Court, Taliesin West has two theaters, a music pavilion, and the Sun Trap—sleeping spaces surrounding an open patio and fireplace. Six guided tours are offered, ranging from a one-hour "panorama" tour to a three-hour behind-the-scenes tour,

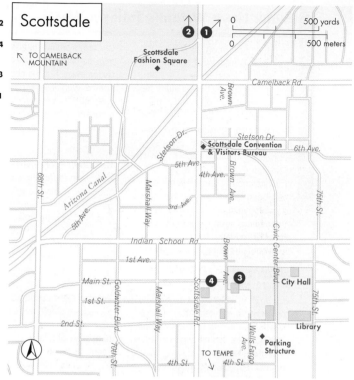

with other tours offered seasonally; all visitors must be accompanied by a guide. ■**TIP→** Wear comfortable shoes for walking.

To reach Taliesin West, drive north on the 101 Freeway to Frank Lloyd Wright Boulevard. Follow Frank Lloyd Wright Boulevard for a few miles to the entrance at the corner of Cactus Road. ✉ *12621 Frank Lloyd Wright Blvd., North Scottsdale* ☎ *888/516–0811, 480/860–2700* ⊕ *www.franklloydwright.org* ▤ *$28–$75* ⊘ *Daily 9–4, with evening tours most days. Call to confirm.*

WORTH NOTING

Heard Museum North Scottsdale. This satellite of the big Heard in Downtown Phoenix has one gallery with its own small, permanent collection of Native American art. The gift shop is well stocked with expensive, high-quality items. ✉ *32633 N. Scottsdale Rd., at Carefree Hwy., North Scottsdale* ☎ *480/488–9817* ⊕ *www.heard.org/north* ▤ *$5* ⊘ *Hrs vary by season; call ahead.*

Scottsdale Historical Museum. Scottsdale's first schoolhouse, this redbrick building houses a reconstruction of the 1910 schoolroom, as well as photographs, original furniture from the city's founding fathers, and displays of other treasures from Scottsdale's early days. ✉ *7333 E. Scottsdale Mall, Old Town* ☎ *480/945–4499* ⊕ *www.scottsdalemuseum.com*

CLOSE UP

Frank Lloyd Wright's Taliesin West

More than just an artist's retreat and workshop, Taliesin West and the surrounding desert still inspire both visitors and architects who study here. Frank Lloyd Wright once said, "The desert abhors the straight, hard line." Though much of Wright's most famed work is based on such lines, this sprawling compound takes its environment into consideration as few desert structures do. Taliesin West mirrors the jagged shapes and earthen colors of its mountain backdrop and desert surroundings. Even Wright's interior pieces of "origami" furniture assume the mountain's unpredictable shapes.

ARIZONA INSPIRATION

Wright first came to Phoenix from Wisconsin in 1927 to act as a consultant to architect Albert Chase McArthur on the now famed Arizona Biltmore. Later Wright was also hired to design a new hotel in what is currently Phoenix South Mountain Park. Wright and his working entourage returned to the Valley and, instead of residing in apartments, they built a camp of asymmetrical cabins with canvas roofs that maximized but pleasantly diffused light, and blended into the rugged mountain backdrop.

When the hotel project failed due to the stock market crash of 1929, Wright and his crew returned to Taliesin, his Wisconsin home and site of his architectural fellowship, and the camp was disassembled and carted away. But the concept of his humble worker village would remain in Wright's creative consciousness and a decade later the renowned architect found an appropriate plot of land north of Scottsdale.

NATURAL CONSTRUCTION

Built upon foundations of caliche, known as nature's own concrete, and painted in crimson and amber hues that highlight the "desert masonry," the buildings seem to adhere naturally to the landscape. The asymmetrical roofs resemble those of Wright's South Mountain camp and were covered with canvas for many years before Wright added glass. Supported by painted-steel-and-redwood beams, they face the sun-filled sky like the hard shell of a desert animal that seems to be comfortable here despite all the odds against its survival.

ARCHITECTURAL LEGACY

The more than 70-year-old property and its structures, which Wright envisioned as a "little fleet of ships," are perhaps some of the best nonnative examples of organic architecture. They also serve as desert building blocks for future generations of Wright protégés—some perhaps schooled on these very grounds—to balance man and Mother Nature.

Free ⊟ *No credit cards* ⊙ *Oct.–May, Wed.–Sat. 10–5; June and Sept., Wed.–Sat. 10–2.*

TEMPE AND AROUND

Tempe is the home of Arizona State University's main campus and a thriving student population. A 20-minute drive from Phoenix, the tree- and brick-lined Mill Avenue is the main drag, filled with student hangouts, bookstores, boutiques, eateries, and a repertory movie house.

Taliesin West was Frank Lloyd Wright's winter residence. The original Taliesin in Wisconsin was his summer home.

There are always things to do or see, and plenty of music venues and fun, casual dining spots. This is one part of town where the locals actually hang out, stroll, and sit at the outdoor cafés.

The inverted pyramid that is Tempe City Hall, on 5th Street, one block east of Mill Avenue, was constructed by local architects Rolf Osland and Michael Goodwin not just to win design awards (which they have), but also to shield city workers from the desert sun. The pyramid is built mainly of bronzed glass and stainless steel, and the point disappears in a sunken courtyard lushly landscaped with jacaranda, ivy, and flowers, out of which the pyramid widens to the sky: stand underneath and gaze up for a weird fish-eye perspective.

The banks of the Rio Salado in Tempe are the site of a new commercial and entertainment district, and Tempe Town Lake—a 2-mile-long waterway created by inflatable dams in a flood control channel—which is open for boating. There are biking and jogging paths on the perimeter.

GETTING HERE AND AROUND

Street parking is hard to find, especially amid all the construction, but you can park in the public garage at Hayden Square, just north of 5th Street and west of Mill Avenue. Get your ticket stamped by a local merchant to avoid paying parking fees. The Orbit free shuttle does a loop around Arizona State University, with stops at Mill Avenue and Sun Devil Stadium. Light-rail also stops at 3rd Street and Mill Avenue.

TIMING

Tempe Festival of the Arts. This free festival on Mill Avenue is held twice a year in early December and March–April; it has all sorts of interesting arts and crafts. ⊕ *www.tempefestivalofthearts.com* .

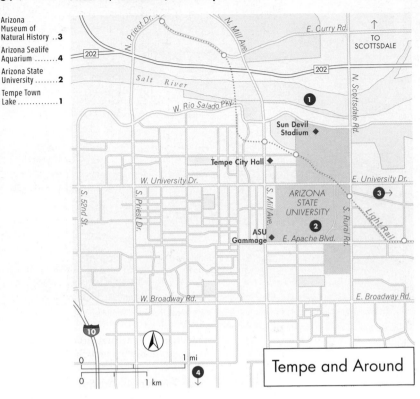

Tempe and Around

EXPLORING

FAMILY **Arizona Museum of Natural History.** Kids young and old get a thrill out of the largest collection of dinosaur fossils in the state at this large museum where you can also pan for gold and see changing exhibits from around the world. ⊠ *53 N. Macdonald St., Mesa* ☎ *480/644–2230* ⊕ *www. azmnh.org* ☑ *$10* ☻ *Tues.–Fri. 10–5, Sat. 11–5, Sun. 1–5.*

FAMILY **Arizona Sealife Aquarium.** For up-close views of some 5,000 creatures including sharks, stingrays, eels, and a giant octopus, head straight to this underwater menagerie in Tempe. You can walk through a 360-degree viewing tunnel in a 165,000-gallon tank that is the first of its kind. Who says there's no water in the desert? ⊠ *Arizona Mills, 5000 Arizona Mills Circle* ☎ *480/478–7600* ⊕ *www.visitsealife.com/arizona* ☑ *$18* ☻ *Mon.–Sat. 10–7:30, Sun. 10–6.*

Arizona State University. What began as the Tempe Normal School for Teachers—in 1886 a four-room redbrick building and 20-acre cow pasture—is now the 750-acre Tempe campus of ASU, the largest university in the Southwest. The university now has four campuses located across the Valley. As you walk around campus, you'll wind past public art and innovative architecture—including a music building that bears a strong resemblance to a wedding cake, designed by Taliesin students to echo Frank Lloyd Wright's Gammage Auditorium, and a law library shaped like an open book—and end up at the impressive 71,706-seat Sun Devil Stadium. ☎ 480/965–9011 ⊕ *www.asu.edu* ▭ *No credit cards.*

ASU Memorial Union. Stop here for maps of a self-guided walking tour of the Tempe campus. ⊠ *1290 S. Normal Ave.* ☎ *480/965–5728* ⊕ *eoss.asu.edu/mu.*

Sun Devil Stadium. Home to the Arizona State University's Sun Devils, this stadium is carved out of a mountain and cradled between the Tempe buttes. ⊠ *ASU Campus, 5th St.* ☎ *480/965-2100.*

FAMILY **Tempe Town Lake.** The human-made Town Lake has turned downtown Tempe into a commercial and urban-living hot spot, and attracts college students and Valley residents of all ages. Little ones enjoy the Splash Playground, and fishermen appreciate the rainbow trout–stocked lake. You also can rent a boat and tour the lake on your own. ⊠ *550 E. Tempe Town Lake* ☎ *480/350–5200.*

WHERE TO EAT

Phoenix and its surroundings have metamorphosed into a melting pot for every type of cuisine imaginable, from northern to Tuscan Italian; from mom-and-pop to Mexico City Mexican; from low-key Cuban to high-end French- and Greek-inspired Southwestern; from Japanese- and Spanish-style tapas to kosher food and American classics with subtle ethnic twists.

Just as the Valley of the Sun has attracted visitors from around the world, it has also been attracting a record number of worldly residents. Fortunately for everyone, many of those people are skilled chefs and/ or restaurateurs who have opted to share their gifts with the public.

Eateries like La Grande Orange grocery are revolutionizing Phoenix's "fast-food" concept with gourmet pay-and-take meals. Four-star cuisine, some concocted by celebrity chefs, also awaits all over the Valley, from Kai in Chandler to Scottsdale's Bourbon Steak, along with Binkley's and Café Bink in Carefree. Dotted with massive strip malls, Phoenix's outskirts are becoming a haven of corporate eateries, but don't worry, there's plenty of divine, independent dining for all tastes and all trends in between.

Many of the best restaurants in the Valley are in resorts, camouflaged behind courtyard walls, or tucked away in shopping malls. Newer, upscale eateries are clustered along Camelback Corridor—a veritable restaurant row, running west to east from Phoenix to Scottsdale—and in Scottsdale itself. Great Mexican food can be found throughout the Valley, but the most authentic spots are in the neighborhoods of North Central and South Phoenix.

Restaurants change hours, locations, chefs, prices, and menus frequently, so it's best to call ahead to confirm. Show up without a reservation during tourist season (October through mid-May), and you may have to head for a fast-food drive-through window to avoid a two-hour wait for a table.

Use the coordinate (✥ B2) at the end of each listing to locate a site on the corresponding map.

WHAT IT COSTS				
	$	**$$**	**$$$**	**$$$$**
At Dinner	under $13	$13–$20	$21–$30	over $30

Restaurant prices are the average cost of a main course at dinner of, if dinner is not served, at lunch, excluding sales tax of 8.3% in Phoenix, 7.95% in Scottsdale, and 8.1% in Tempe.

DOWNTOWN PHOENIX

$$$
MODERN
AMERICAN

✕ **The Arrogant Butcher.** The attention-grabbing name is intentional, as is the in-your-face décor and cuisine of this Downtown not-quite-bar, not-quite-restaurant. It's noisy, but that's part of the charm. You'll sit next to couples on their first date, bachelorette parties, families having a reunion, and concertgoers who are prepping their vocal cords for an upcoming show. Make a meal out of the charcuterie platters and to-die-for pretzel fondue. If you're craving home-cookin', order the chicken Stroganoff, and then call your mom. $ *Average main: $22* ✉ *2 E. Jefferson St., Downtown Phoenix* ☎ *602/324–8502* ⊕ *www.foxrc.com/restaurants/the-arrogant-butcher* ⚞ *Reservations essential* ⊗ *Closed Sun.* ✥ *B5.*

$$
MODERN
AMERICAN

✕ **Blue Hound Kitchen & Cocktails.** The menu at this quirky restaurant features concoctions worthy of Willy Wonka's palate, from gourmet tater tots to fire-hot ancho chile caramel corn. Located inside the Hotel Palomar Phoenix, Blue Hound is a great place to stop for cocktails or appetizers before a show and, if you have the time, a fantastic meal. Brunch is one of the best in the Downtown area; get a reservation if you plan on dining during the weekend. $ *Average main: $18* ✉ *Hotel Palomar Phoenix, 2 E. Jefferson St., Downtown Phoenix* ☎ *602/258–0231* ⊕ *www.bluehoundkitchen.com* ✥ *B5.*

$$
CHINESE

✕ **Gourmet House of Hong Kong.** Traditional Chinatown specialties like *chow fun* (thick rice noodles) are excellent at this simple, diner-style place: try the assorted-meat version, with chicken, shrimp, pork, and squid. Dishes with black-bean sauce are among the menu's best. Delights such as five-flavor frogs' legs, duck feet with greens, and beef tripe casserole are offered, if you're feeling adventurous. $ *Average main: $15* ✉ *1438 E. McDowell Rd., Downtown Phoenix* ☎ *602/253–4859* ⊕ *www.gourmethouseofhongkong.com* ✥ *C5.*

$
AMERICAN
Fodor'sChoice
★

✕ **Matt's Big Breakfast.** Fresh, filling, and simply fantastic, the food at this itty-bitty, retro hip diner is a great way to start any day, especially when you have time to walk or sleep it off afterward. Ingredients like hearty bacon strips, jams, and whole-grain breads come from local sources, and each one is of the highest quality. Try a cheesy omelet with a side of crispy hash browns or indulge in a Belgian waffle, but let it be known that Matt's fat pancakes are legendary. Lunch options include sandwiches and chili, or breakfast, again. Be prepared to wait, or call ahead for takeout. $ *Average main: $7* ✉ *825 N. 1st St., Downtown*

2

BEST BETS FOR PHOENIX, SCOTTSDALE, AND TEMPE DINING

With hundreds of restaurants to choose from, how will you decide where to eat? Fodor's writers and editors have selected their favorite restaurants by price, cuisine, and experience in the Best Bets lists *below*. In the first column, Fodor's Choice properties represent the "best of the best" in every price category.

Fodor$Choice ★

Binkley's Restaurant, $$$$, p. 120

Bourbon Steak, $$$$, p. 78

Chelsea's Kitchen, $$$, p. 70

Christopher's, $$$, p. 70

FEZ, $$, p. 73

House of Tricks, $$$, p. 81

J&G Steakhouse, $$$$, p. 71

Kai, $$$$, p. 80

La Grande Orange, $, p. 71

Matt's Big Breakfast, $, p. 66

Noca, $$$, p. 71

Pane Bianco, $, p. 74

Pepe's Taco Villa, $, p. 75

Rancho Pinot, $$$, p. 77

T. Cook's at the Royal Palms, $$$$, p. 72

Best by Price

$

Carolina's Mexican Food, p. 73

Fry Bread House, p. 73

La Grande Orange, p. 71

Pane Bianco, p. 74

Pepe's Taco Villa, p. 75

$$

Mrs. White's Golden Rule Café, p. 70

Via Delosantos, p. 75

$$$

Rancho Pinot, p. 77

$$$$

Binkley's Restaurant, p. 120

Bourbon Steak, p. 78

Kai, p. 80

Best by Cuisine

BEST LOCAL EATS

La Grande Orange, $, p. 71

Mrs. White's Golden Rule Café, $$, p. 70

Via Delosantos, $$, p. 75

BEST MARGARITAS

Los Dos Molinos, $$, p. 76

Pepe's Taco Villa, $, p. 75

Via Delosantos, $$, p. 75

Best by Experience

BEST BREAKFAST

La Grande Orange, $, p. 71

Matt's Big Breakfast, $, p. 66

BEST BRUNCH

Bourbon Steak, $$$$, p. 78

Lon's at the Hermosa, $$$, p. 76

The Mission, $$$, p. 79

BEST HOTEL DINING

Bourbon Steak, $$$$, p. 78

J&G Steakhouse, $$$$, p. 71

Kai, $$$$, p. 80

T. Cook's at the Royal Palms, $$$$, p. 72

BEST PATIO WINING AND DINING

Chelsea's Kitchen, $$$, p. 70

elements, $$$$, p. 76

House of Tricks, $$$, p. 81

Olive & Ivy, $$$, p. 80

BEST SPECIAL OCCASION

Binkley's Restaurant, $$$$, p. 120

Kai, $$$$, p. 80

T. Cook's at the Royal Palms, $$$$, p. 72

GREAT VIEW

elements, $$$$, p. 76

Lon's at the Hermosa, $$$, p. 76

T. Cook's at the Royal Palms, $$$$, p. 72

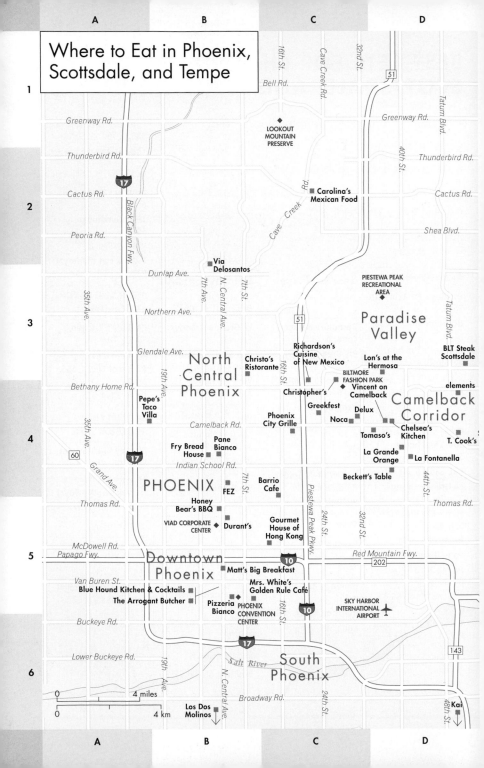

Where to Eat in Phoenix, Scottsdale, and Tempe

A   **B**   **C**   **D**

16th St.
Cave Creek Rd.
32nd St.
51

Bell Rd.

1

Greenway Rd.
LOOKOUT MOUNTAIN PRESERVE
Greenway Rd.
40th St.
Tatum Blvd.

Thunderbird Rd.
Thunderbird Rd.

17

Cactus Rd.
Cave Creek Rd.
Carolina's Mexican Food
Cactus Rd.

2

Peoria Rd.
Shea Blvd.

35th Ave.
Via Delosantos
7th Ave.
N. Central Ave.
7th St.
PIESTEWA PEAK RECREATIONAL AREA

Dunlap Ave.

Northern Ave.
51
Paradise Valley

3

Glendale Ave.
North Central Phoenix
Christo's Ristorante
16th St.
Richardson's Cuisine of New Mexico
Lon's at the Hermosa
BLT Steak Scottsdale
Tatum Blvd.

Bethany Home Rd.
19th Ave.
BILTMORE FASHION PARK
Vincent on Camelback
elements

35th Ave.
Pepe's Taco Villa
Christopher's
Greekfest
Delux
Camelback Corridor

Phoenix City Grille
Noca
Chelsea's Kitchen
T. Cook's

4

Grand Ave.
Camelback Rd.
Tomaso's
60
17
Fry Bread House
Pane Bianco
La Grande Orange
La Fontanella
44th St.

Indian School Rd.
Beckett's Table

PHOENIX
FEZ
Barrio Cafe

Thomas Rd.
Honey Bear's BBQ
7th St.
Piestewa Peak Pkwy.
24th St.
32nd St.
Thomas Rd.

VIAD CORPORATE CENTER
Durant's
Gourmet House of Hong Kong

McDowell Rd.
Papago Fwy.

5

Downtown Phoenix
10
Red Mountain Fwy.
202

Matt's Big Breakfast

Van Buren St.
Mrs. White's Golden Rule Café
SKY HARBOR INTERNATIONAL AIRPORT
Blue Hound Kitchen & Cocktails
The Arrogant Butcher
Pizzeria Bianco
PHOENIX CONVENTION CENTER
16th St.
10
143

Buckeye Rd.

17

Lower Buckeye Rd.
19th Ave.
Salt River
South Phoenix
24th St.
48th St.

6

0   4 miles
0   4 km
N. Central Ave.
Los Dos Molinos
Broadway Rd.
Kai

A   **B**   **C**   **D**

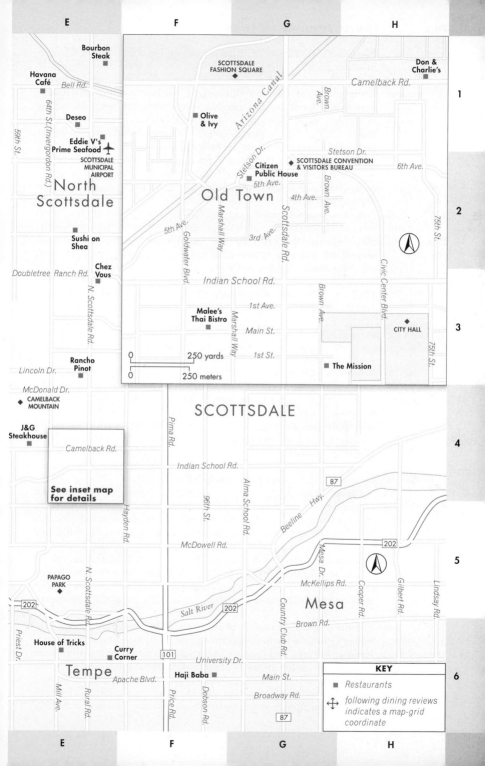

Phoenix ☎ *602/254–1074* 🌐 *www.mattsbigbreakfast.com* ✍ *Reservations not accepted* ⏲ *No dinner* ✥ *B5.*

$$ SOUTHERN 🍴 **Mrs. White's Golden Rule Café.** This plain yellow building downtown has been the best place in town for true Southern cooking for decades. The humble lunch counter and few surrounding tables are the setting in which to enjoy rich entrées—from fried chicken to catfish and pork chops. Each of the six entrées comes with corn bread and peach cobbler, all of which fill not just the belly but also the soul. Get there early: the restaurant closes nightly at 7 pm (except on Friday and Saturday, when it reopens from 9 pm to 3 am). [$] *Average main: $13* ✉ *808 E. Jefferson St., Downtown Phoenix* ☎ *602/262–9256* ✍ *Reservations not accepted* ✥ *B5.*

$$ PIZZA 🍴 **Pizzeria Bianco.** Brooklyn native Chris Bianco became famous for his pizza made with passion in this small establishment on Heritage Square. His wood-fired thin-crust creations incorporate the finest and freshest ingredients including house-made mozzarella cheese. The brick oven was imported from Italy. Bar Bianco next door is a good place to relax with a beverage while you wait for your table. [$] *Average main: $15* ✉ *623 E. Adams St., Downtown Phoenix* ☎ *602/258–8300* 🌐 *www.pizzeriabianco.com* ✍ *Reservations not accepted* ⏲ *Closed Sun.* ✥ *B5.*

GREATER PHOENIX

CAMELBACK CORRIDOR

$$ MODERN AMERICAN 🍴 **Beckett's Table.** With a menu full of comfort food far better than any mom could make, Beckett's Table combines elegance with tradition. The menu changes seasonally, but long-standing favorites include chicken 'n' dumplings made with saffron and kale, and tender shortribs with a red-wine deduction. No matter what you eat, make sure to order the bacon cheddar biscuits, and don't be shy about scraping the crumbs out of the basket. [$] *Average main: $18* ✉ *3737 E. Indian School Rd., Camelback Corridor* ☎ *602/954–1700* 🌐 *www.beckettstable.com* ✍ *Reservations essential* ⏲ *Closed Mon. No lunch* ✥ *D4*

$$$ AMERICAN Fodor's Choice ★ 🍴 **Chelsea's Kitchen.** With its hip, Pacific Northwest–chic interior and a patio that feels more like a secret garden, Chelsea's Kitchen can easily make you forget you're dining in the desert. This casually sophisticated establishment insists on the freshest ingredients (especially fish), used with equally fresh and flavorful ideas that complement the restaurant's cool but comfortable style. Specials change frequently, and are always worth steering away from the menu, but regulars love the shrimp ceviche, burgers, and mac 'n' cheese. [$] *Average main: $20* ✉ *5040 N. 40th St., Camelback Corridor* ☎ *602/957–2555* 🌐 *www.chelseaskitchenaz.com* ✥ *D4.*

$$$ FRENCH Fodor's Choice ★ 🍴 **Christopher's.** The creation of one of the Valley's premier chefs, Christopher Gross, the menu ranges from good-value wood-fired pizzas, outstanding burgers, and creative bar nosh to pricier French inspirations. Gross is famous for dishes like the smoked truffle-infused filet mignon, and the roasted red bell pepper soup is always on the menu. Don't forget the Gruyère mashed potatoes on the side, and the Grande Marnier soufflé to finish. [$] *Average main: $26* ✉ *Biltmore Fashion Park, 2502*

E. Camelback Rd., Suite 102, Camelback Corridor ☎ *602/522–2344* 🌐 *www.christophersaz.com* ✥ *C4.*

$ AMERICAN 🍴 **Delux.** Everything exudes "cool" in this hipster burger joint. Delux serves delicious salads, sandwiches, and burgers made with all-natural Harris Ranch beef—try the Delux Burger, with Maytag blue and Gruyère cheeses and caramelized onions. If you can't decide what kind of brew to wash it all down with, no worries: Order a flight of beers from their extensive bar. Open every night until 2 am, this is a great place to grab a late-night bite. Leave room for something cool and creamy at the Gelato Spot across the parking lot. [$] *Average main: $10* ✉ *3146 E. Camelback Rd., Camelback Corridor* ☎ *602/522–2288* 🌐 *www.deluxburger.com* ✍ *Reservations not accepted* ✥ *C4.*

$$$ GREEK 🍴 **Greekfest.** This informal but elegant restaurant is lovingly decorated with whitewashed walls, hardwood floors, and imported Greek artifacts. Search the menu's two pages of appetizers for *taramosalata* (caviar blended with lemon and olive oil) and *saganaki* (cheese flamed with brandy and extinguished with a squirt of lemon). The *moussaka* (lamb casserole) is wonderful, and don't forget dessert (try *galaktoboureko,* warm custard pie baked in phyllo). If all you seek is a sweet treat and some genuine Greek coffee, visit the adjoining Cafestia European dessert and coffeehouse. [$] *Average main: $21* ✉ *1940 E. Camelback Rd., Camelback Corridor* ☎ *602/265–2990* 🌐 *www.thegreekfest.com* 🕒 *Closed Sun.* ✥ *C4.*

$$$$ STEAKHOUSE Fodor's Choice ★ 🍴 **J&G Steakhouse.** This is more than a steakhouse; it's an experience. The menu changes seasonally, but if you're lucky enough to be there when the sweet corn ravioli is available, stop, order, and savor. The filet mignon is prepared to perfection, but you can spice it up with one of a half-dozen tableside sauces if you want. If you just want a drink—or start your meal a little early—the bar has one of the best views of the Valley. The wine list, which is more of a wine book, is one of the most extensive in town and features an entire page of wines available by the glass. [$] *Average main: $40* ✉ *The Phoenician, 6000 E. Camelback Rd., Camelback Corridor* ☎ *480/214–8000* 🌐 *www.jgsteakhousescottsdale.com* 🕒 *No lunch* ✥ *E4.*

$ AMERICAN Fodor's Choice ★ 🍴 **La Grande Orange.** This San Francisco–inspired store and eatery sells artisanal nosh and novelty items, along with a formidable selection of wines. Valley residents flock to LGO, as they call it, to see and be seen, and to feast on mouthwatering sandwiches, pizzas, salads, and decadent breads and desserts. The small tables inside fill up quickly at breakfast and lunch, but there's also seating on the patio. Try the Commuter Sandwich on a homemade English muffin, the open-faced croque-madame, or the delicious French pancakes with a sweet Spanish latte. [$] *Average main: $10* ✉ *4410 N. 40th St., Camelback Corridor* ☎ *602/840–7777* 🌐 *www.lagrandeorangegrocery.com* ✍ *Reservations not accepted* ✥ *D4.*

$$$ AMERICAN Fodor's Choice ★ 🍴 **Noca.** This small, hidden establishment is a Valley favorite. It's a fun place to see, be seen, and sample everything. The waitstaff are veteran fine-dining servers, and the chefs manage to turn even cotton candy into a culinary work of art. The menu changes daily—yes, daily—and features items such as Japanese Wagyu cheesesteak with Kobe beef or

braised lamb ragout with rosemary bread crumbs. The last Sunday of every month, the menu includes Noca's famous fried chicken. If you're hungry for a gourmet sandwich, stop by Nocawich, the restaurant's lunchtime conversion. $ *Average main: $24* ✉ *3118 E. Camelback Rd., Camelback Corridor* ☎ *602/956–6622* ⊕ *www.restaurantnoca. com* ⊘ *Closed Mon. in summer* ✛ *C4.*

$$$$

MEDITERRANEAN

Fodor's Choice

★

✕ **T. Cook's at the Royal Palms.** One of the finest restaurants in the Valley, T. Cook's oozes romance, from the floor-to-ceiling windows with dramatic views of Camelback Mountain to its 1930s-style Spanish-colonial architecture and décor. The menu is a foodie's delight, featuring Mediterranean-inspired creations ranging from venison tartare and duck confit salad to antelope or Colorado lamb, all prepared with precision. The charcuterie plate is one of the best in town, too. $ *Average main: $37* ✉ *Royal Palms Resort & Spa, 5200 E. Camelback Rd., Camelback Corridor* ☎ *602/808–0766* ⊕ *www.royalpalmshotel.com* ⌂ *Reservations essential* ✛ *D4.*

$$$$

ITALIAN

✕ **Tomaso's.** In a town where restaurants can come and go almost overnight, Tomaso's has been a favorite since 1977, and for good reason. Chef Tomaso Maggiore learned to cook at the family's restaurant in Palermo, Sicily, and honed his skills at the Culinary Institute of Rome. The result is authentic Italian cuisine that's consistently well prepared and delicious. The house specialty, herb-crusted rack of lamb, is outstanding. Other notables include risotto and osso buco. Enjoy lunch next door at Tommy V's. $ *Average main: $31* ✉ *3225 E. Camelback Rd., Camelback Corridor* ☎ *602/956–0836* ⊕ *www.tomasos.com* ⊘ *No lunch weekends* ✛ *D4.*

$$$$

ECLECTIC

✕ **Vincent on Camelback.** Chef Vincent Guerithault is best known for creating French food with a Southwestern touch. The menu changes daily, but it's all delicious. You can make a meal of his famous appetizers, such as corn ravioli with white-truffle oil, or macadamia crusted scallops with basil beurre blanc. The dessert menu overflows with intoxicating soufflés. The multiroom interior is intimate and elegant, but the service can be gruff. A favorite among locals is the market held in the parking lot on Saturday during cooler months. $ *Average main: $31* ✉ *3930 E. Camelback Rd., Camelback Corridor* ☎ *602/224–0225* ⊕ *www.vincentsoncamelback.com* ⌂ *Reservations essential* ⊘ *Closed Sun. No lunch.* ✛ *D4.*

NORTH CENTRAL PHOENIX

$$

MEXICAN

✕ **Barrio Cafe.** Owners Wendy Gruber and Silvana Salcido Esparza have taken Mexican cuisine to a new level. Expect guacamole made to order at your table and modern Mexican specialties such as *cochinita pibil*, 12-hour slow-roasted pork with red achiote and sour orange, and *chiles en nogada*, a delicious traditional dish from central Mexico featuring a spicy poblano pepper stuffed with fruit, chicken, and raisins. The flavor-packed food consistently draws packs of people, but you can drink in the intimate atmosphere—and a specialty margarita or *aqua fresca* (fruit water)—while you wait for a table. $ *Average main: $19* ✉ *2814 N. 16th St., North Central Phoenix* ☎ *602/636–0240* ⊕ *www.barriocafe. com* ⌂ *Reservations not accepted* ⊘ *Closed Mon.* ✛ *C4.*

$ MEXICAN 🍴 **Carolina's Mexican Food.** This small, nondescript restaurant in north Phoenix makes the most delicious, thin-as-air flour tortillas imaginable. In-the-know locals have been lining up at Carolina's for years to partake of the homey, inexpensive Mexican food, so it makes sense that she expanded from the original downtown location to let a little more of the Valley in on the action. The tacos, tamales, burritos, flautas, and enchiladas are served on paper plates. You can buy tortillas to take away, but good luck getting home with a full bag. There is also a branch in south Phoenix at 1202 East Mohave Street (the original location) and one in Peoria. [$] *Average main: $4* ✉ *2126 E. Cactus Rd., North Central Phoenix* ☎ *602/275–8231* 🌐 *www.carolinasmexicanfood.com* 🕒 *Closed Sun.* ✣ *C2.*

$$ ITALIAN 🍴 **Christo's Ristorante.** Don't judge this book by its cover. Cozy and unassuming in a Phoenix strip mall, Christo's keeps its tables filled with loyal customers who enjoy fine Italian cuisine. Attentive servers ensure that your water glass never empties, and folks rave about the fresh seafood dishes, the roasted rack of lamb, the veal, and the delicious pasta dishes. Start with the delicious, panfried calamari. Dinner's main courses come with soup and salad. Before or after dinner, enjoy a cocktail in the piano bar or spend your evening snacking to the music from the bar menu. [$] *Average main: $17* ✉ *6327 N. 7th St., North Central Phoenix* ☎ *602/264–1784* 🌐 *www.christos1.com* 🕒 *Closed Sun.* ✣ *B3.*

$$$$ STEAKHOUSE 🍴 **Durant's.** Durant's has endured since 1950 in the same location with the same menu and waiters who've been on staff almost as long, making it one of Phoenix's legendary eating establishments. Supreme steaks, chops, and fresh seafood, including Florida stone crab and oysters Rockefeller, dominate here; when the restaurant once tried to update its menu, regulars protested so furiously the idea was shelved. Durant's is not à la carte, like many Valley steakhouses, which means their entrée prices include soup or salad and a side dish. Those in the know enter through the kitchen door and frequent the Rat Pack–style bar for jumbo martinis fit for Ol' Blue Eyes himself. [$] *Average main: $34* ✉ *2611 N. Central Ave., at Virginia, North Central Phoenix* ☎ *602/264–5967* 🌐 *www.durantsaz.com* 🕒 *No lunch weekends* ✣ *B5.*

$$ ECLECTIC Fodor's Choice ★ 🍴 **FEZ.** From its sleek interior to its central location and diverse clientele, right down to its affordable lunch, happy hour, dinner, Sunday brunch, and late-night menus, FEZ covers everything. "American fare with a Moroccan flair" means bold culinary leaps, with choices like the half-pound grilled angus FEZ Burger, *kisras* (flat-bread pizza), and the signature crispy rosemary-pomegranate chicken—but it all lands safely on the taste buds. Drinks include specialty martinis and margaritas and a formidable wine list. [$] *Average main: $16* ✉ *3815 N. Central Ave., North Central Phoenix* ☎ *602/287–8700* 🌐 *www.fezoncentral.com* ✣ *B4.*

$ SOUTHWESTERN 🍴 **Fry Bread House.** Indian fry bread, a specialty of the Native American culture, is a delicious treat—pillows of deep-fried dough topped with sweet or savory toppings and folded in half. Choose from culture-crossing combinations like savory shredded chili beef with cheese, beans, green chiles, veggies, and sour cream, or try the sweeter synthesis of honey and sugar, or chocolate with butter. [$] *Average main: $7*

The Phoenix-area dining scene is hot, and not just because of the many spicy Southwestern and Mexican ingredients.

✉ *1003 E. Indian School Rd., North Central Phoenix* ☎ *602/351–2345* ⏲ *Closed Sun.* ⊕ *B4.*

$$ SOUTHERN

🍴 **Honey Bear's BBQ.** Honey Bear's motto—"You don't need no teeth to eat our meat"—may fall short on grammar, but this place isn't packed with folks looking to improve their language skills. In 1986 childhood friends Mark Smith and Gary Clark expanded from a catering business to their first wildly successful Honey Bear's restaurant on East Van Buren Street; today they are in demand all across the Valley. This is Tennessee-style barbecue, which means smoky baby back ribs basted in a tangy sauce. The sausage-enhanced "cowbro" beans and scallion-studded potato salad are great sides, and, teeth or no teeth, finishing off with a no-frills but tasty piece of sweet-potato pie will put a smile on your face. [$] *Average main: $12* ✉ *2824 N. Central., North Central Phoenix* ☎ *602/702–3060* 🌐 *www.honeybearsbbq.com* ✍ *Reservations not accepted* ⊕ *B5.*

$ ITALIAN Fodor's Choice ★

🍴 **Pane Bianco.** Chef-owner Chris Bianco spends his afternoons creating to-die-for sandwiches and his evenings serving his trademark pizza and pasta dishes. Order at the counter and pick up your brown-bagged meal (which always includes a piece of candy), or stay for dinner and enjoy a meatball hero, lasagna, or, of course, one of Bianco's fabulous pizzas (the Wiseguy—onion, mozzarella, fennel, and sausage—is a favorite). [$] *Average main: $12* ✉ *4404 N. Central Ave., North Central Phoenix* ☎ *602/234–2100* 🌐 *www.pizzeriabianco.com* ⏲ *No dinner weekends* ⊕ *B4.*

$ ✕ **Pepe's Taco Villa.** The neighbor-
MEXICAN hood's not fancy, and neither is
Fodor'sChoice this restaurant, but in a town with
★ a lot of gringo-ized south-of-the-
border fare, this is the real friendly,
real deal. Tacos *rancheros*—spicy,
shredded pork pungently lathered
with adobo paste—are a dream,
as are the green-corn tamales and
authentic imported *machacado*
(air-dried beef). The chiles rellenos
may be the best in the state. All are

perfect with a margarita from the
full bar. Don't leave without trying the sensational mole, a rich sauce
fashioned from chiles and chocolate. $ *Average main: $8* ✉ *2108 W.
Camelback Rd., North Central Phoenix* ☎ *602/242–0379* ⊕ *www.
pepestacovilla.com* ✛ *B4.*

$$$ ✕ **Phoenix City Grille.** If you've never tasted a green chile properly pre-
AMERICAN pared, head to Phoenix City Grille. From burgers to pasta, all of the
quintessentially American fare served here is infused with a hint of the
Southwest. For dinner, the pot roast can't be beat. If brunch is more
your thing, try the griddled corn cakes with bacon—the green chiles give
them just a bit of kick. $ *Average main: $22* ✉ *5816 N. 16th St., North
Central Phoenix* ☎ *602/266–3001* ⊕ *www.phoenixcitygrille.com* ✛ *C4.*

$$ ✕ **Richardson's Cuisine of New Mexico.** There are two types of spicy food:
SOUTHWESTERN dishes that you eat on a dare, and dishes that make you savor every mor-
sel and wish for more. Richardson's has the second option mastered,
and lures back locals with heat-filled dishes that test the limits of your
palate—but not in a threatening way. This is fine New Mexican cuisine, which means everything (including heat and quality) is ratcheted
up about three notches. The beef tenderloin chile relleno is the star of
the menu, which incorporates New Mexican hatch chiles in just about
every dish. If you're feeling adventurous, order a platter or a combination. You won't be disappointed. $ *Average main: $20* ✉ *6335 N.
16th St., North Central Phoenix* ☎ *602/287–8900* ⊕ *richardsonsnm.
com* ⌚ *Reservations essential* ✛ *C4.*

$$ ✕ **Via Delosantos.** The family-owned restaurant looks a little rough
MEXICAN around the edges outside, but it's what's inside that counts—an accom-
modating staff, an enormous and authentic Mexican menu, and one of
the best-tasting and best-priced house margaritas in town. Entrées are
ample, and include more than just tired combinations of beef, beans,
and cheese. Try the fajitas *calabacitas* with a yellow- and green-squash
succotash; or the delicious chicken *delosantos,* a cheesy chicken breast
and tortilla concoction. Expect to wait on weekends, either at the bar
or outside, but the experience will be worth it. $ *Average main: $13*
✉ *9120 N. Central Ave., North Central Phoenix* ☎ *602/997–6239*
⊕ *www.viadelosantos.net* ⌚ *Reservations not accepted* ✛ *B3.*

PARADISE VALLEY

$$$$ STEAKHOUSE 🍴 **BLT Steak Scottsdale.** Chef Laurent Tourondel's mini-empire includes this stylish dining room at the JW Marriott Camelback Inn Resort & Spa. A knowledgeable waitstaff offer suggestions for pairing sizzling steaks with sauces (including red wine and mustard), picking sides (including stuffed mushroom caps and poached green beans), and deciding on a potato dish (a favorite: Parmesan gnocchi). Everything goes well with Gruyère popovers, which are likely to disappear from your plate within seconds (they'll bring you more if you ask). Choose from inspired desserts with deceptively modest names such as bittersweet chocolate tart. [$] *Average main: $33* ✉ *JW Marriott Camelback Inn Resort & Spa, 5402 E. Lincoln Dr., Paradise Valley* ☎ *480/905-7979* 🌐 *www.bltscottsdale.com* 🕒 *No lunch* ✥ *D3.*

$$$$ ECLECTIC 🍴 **elements.** Perched on the side of Camelback Mountain at the Sanctuary resort, this stylish modern restaurant offers breathtaking desert-sunset and city-light views. They're the perfect complement to the culinary delights that fuse hearty American traditions and Asian flavors. Order such Asian-infused appetizers as the sake-braised mussels, pork belly with water chestnuts and snap peas, and carrot millet pot stickers. Seasonal specials and entrées are excellent; among the best is the filet mignon peppersteak with blue cheese fondue and potato fritter. [$] *Average main: $37* ✉ *Sanctuary on Camelback Mountin, 5700 E. McDonald Dr., Paradise Valley* ☎ *480/948–2100* 🌐 *www.elementsrestaurant.com* ✍ *Reservations essential* ✥ *D4.*

$$$ AMERICAN 🍴 **Lon's at the Hermosa.** In an adobe hacienda hand-built by cowboy artist Lon Megargee, this romantic spot has sweeping vistas of Camelback Mountain and the perfect patio for after-dinner drinks under the stars. Megargee's art and cowboy memorabilia decorate the dining room. The menu changes seasonally and includes appetizers like Kobe beef carpaccio and foie gras. Wood-grilled Kobe New York strip, and more-exotic dishes like roasted duck breast with duck confit and gnocchi, are main-course options. Phoenicians love the weekend brunch. [$] *Average main: $27* ✉ *Hermosa Inn, 5532 N. Palo Cristi Dr., Paradise Valley* ☎ *602/955–7878* 🌐 *www.hermosainn.com/lons* ✥ *D3.*

SOUTH PHOENIX

$$ MEXICAN 🍴 **Los Dos Molinos.** In a hacienda that belonged to silent-era movie star Tom Mix, this fun restaurant focuses on New Mexican–style Mexican food. That means *hot.* New Mexico chiles form the backbone and fiery breath of the dishes, and the green-chile enchilada and beef taco are potentially lethal. The red salsa and enchiladas with egg on top are excellent, as is the popular shrimp Veracruz with red-chile sauce. Don't even bother asking for your dish to be prepared mild. There's no such thing at "Los Dos," and that's part of the fun. This is a must-do dining experience if you want true New Mexican–style food, but be prepared to swig lots of water. There are other locations across the Valley, but this is considered the original. [$] *Average main: $13* ✉ *8646 S. Central Ave., South Phoenix* ☎ *602/243–9113* 🌐 *www.losdosmolinosphoenix.com* ✍ *Reservations not accepted* 🕒 *Closed Sun. and Mon.* ✥ *B6.*

WHERE TO REFUEL AROUND TOWN

Here are the most popular reliable chain restaurants, particularly for large groups (and large portions):

Elephant Bar. The predominantly Pacific Rim, elephant-size menu at this large chain offers some pleasant Cajun (catfish and jambalaya) and plain old American (New York steak, lemon herb chicken) entrées. Pacific Rim specialties include Miso Yaki fire-grilled salmon and the delicious pan-Asian vegetable-and-noodle soup with teriyaki chicken skewers. 🌐 *www.elephantbar.com.*

Garduño's. This gargantuan Mexican restaurant has several equally ample locations in the area. Try the unusually good green-chile clam chowder or the fresh guacamole made tableside for starters, and experience a grilled chimichanga or fajitas for a main course. 🌐 *www.gardunosrestaurants.com.*

Morton's of Chicago. The Windy City chain is famous for exceptional service, immense steaks, and entertaining presentations. Its business-formal atmosphere, menus, and operations are replicated at the North Scottsdale location. The monstrous 24-ounce porterhouse or 14-ounce double-cut filet can satisfy the hungriest cowpoke. 🌐 *www.mortons.com.*

Nello's. Leave it to two brothers from Chicago to come up with the motto "In Crust We Trust," and Nello's excels in both thin-crust and deep-dish pies. Try traditional varieties heaped with homemade sausage and mushrooms, or go vegetarian with the spinach pie. Pasta entrées are very good, too, and the family-style salads are inventive and fresh. 🌐 *www.nellosscottsdale.com.*

Oregano's. Huge portions are an understatement at this nine-branch casual Chicago-theme eatery. Come hungry and feast on tasty baked sandwiches, pizza (deep-dish, thin-crust, or stuffed), and pasta dishes. The young, friendly staff and kitschy 1950s décor create a fun and comfortable, family-friendly vibe. 🌐 *www.oreganos.com.*

Zoë's Kitchen. Cool, clean, fast, inexpensive, and nutritious, this national chain is great for a light but filling, Greek-inspired meal without the guilt. Each location is uniform in its bright, modern cafeteria-like setting, where first you order, then you sit. Make sure to try the Greek chicken pita or Greek salad, and the coleslaw with feta cheese. 🌐 *www.zoeskitchen.com.*

SCOTTSDALE

$$$ ECLECTIC Fodor's Choice ★

🍴 **Rancho Pinot.** The attention to quality here makes this one of the town's most lauded dining spots. The minimalist cowboy décor and almost secret-handshake location are forgotten upon the first bite of food and replaced with tastebud heaven. The inventive menu changes daily, depending on what's fresh. If you're lucky, you'll get a crack at the flatiron steak with pancetta and chimichurri sauce, the handmade pasta with fennel and chicken meatballs, or chicken with toasted polenta. Organic and locally grown and raised ingredients are used whenever possible, which is just another reason why you'll want to return as many times as possible. [$] *Average main: $21* ✉ *6208 N. Scottsdale*

Rd., northwest of Trader Joe's in Lincoln Village Shops, Scottsdale ☎ *480/367–8030* 🌐 *www.ranchopinot.com* ⏲ *Closed Sun., and Mon. May–Oct. No lunch* ✥ *E3.*

$$$ JAPANESE 🍴 **Sushi on Shea.** You may be in the middle of the desert, but the sushi here will make you think you're at the ocean's edge. Fresh yellowtail, toro, shrimp, scallops, freshwater eel, and even monkfish liver pâté are among the long list of delights. The best dish? Maybe it's the *una-jyu* (broiled freshwater eel with a sublime smoky scent) served over sweet rice. The fact that some people believe eel is an aphrodisiac only adds to its charm. The bento box is a good way to sample a variety of menu offerings. [$] *Average main: $24* ✉ *7000 E. Shea Blvd., Scottsdale* ☎ *480/483–7799* 🌐 *www.sushionshea.com* ⏲ *Closed Mon.* ✥ *E2.*

NORTH SCOTTSDALE

$$$$ STEAKHOUSE Fodor's Choice ★ 🍴 **Bourbon Steak.** This upscale steak restaurant run by top-rated chef Michael Mina has been living up to the royal reputation of the Fairmont Scottsdale Princess. Its severe but stunning stone-and-glass entry lets people know that they are in for something serious—seriously good. Its modern elegance is as sumptuous to the eyes as the food is to the palate. Select from American-grade or Japanese Kobe beef, but be prepared for steep prices. Even the fries are luxurious here. If you're on a budget, head to the adjacent burger bar. You won't be disappointed. [$] *Average main: $58* ✉ *Fairmont Scottsdale Princess, 7575 E. Princess Dr., North Scottsdale* ☎ *480/513–6002* 🌐 *www.scottsdaleprincess.com/dining/bourbon-steak* ✍ *Reservations essential* ⏲ *Closed Sun. No lunch.* ✥ *E1.*

$$$$ LATIN AMERICAN 🍴 **Deseo.** Seemingly surrounded by fine restaurants in North Scottsdale, this gem is discreetly tucked away in the Westin Kierland Resort. Designed and inspired by Douglas Rodriguez, the founder of Nuevo Latin cuisine, Deseo serves the best ceviche in town. Start with the muddle bar, where you can sip an assortment of creative mojitos that go beyond a hint of mint. The menu changes seasonally, and if fish isn't your thing, you can't go wrong with the Kobe beef flatbread or the skirt steak. [$] *Average main: $32* ✉ *Westin Kierland Resort & Spa, 6902 E. Greenway Pkwy., North Scottsdale* ☎ *480/624–1202* 🌐 *www.kierlandresort.com* ⏲ *No lunch* ✥ *E1.*

$$$$ AMERICAN 🍴 **Eddie V's Prime Seafood.** Specializing in fresh seafood done right (try the Hong Kong–style Chilean sea bass or the citrus-sautéed scallops), grilled meats, and fine wines, Eddie V's is great for fine dining. But with its inviting bar and lounge area and succulent appetizers like kung pao–style calamari and a variety of fresh oysters, Eddie's is also enormously popular (and slightly more affordable) as a happy-hour spot. [$] *Average main: $34* ✉ *Scottsdale Quarter, 15323 N. Scottsdale Rd., North Scottsdale* ☎ *480/730–4800* 🌐 *www.eddiev.com* ⏲ *No lunch* ✥ *E1.*

$$$ LATIN AMERICAN 🍴 **Havana Café.** Tapas are marvelous at this cozy Cuban-style cantina. While sampling authentic Cuban creations like shrimp pancakes, ham and chicken croquettes, Cuban tamales, and paella heaped with a whole Maine lobster, diners can shed the stresses of an arid metropolis. New Puerto Rican menu items include stuffed green plantains and plantains with pork cracklings. There's something special for vegetarians, too: *cho cho,* a fresh chayote squash stuffed with loads of veggies and

topped with a Jamaican curry sauce, and rice with pigeon peas. $ *Average main: $23* ✉ *6245 E. Bell Rd., North Scottsdale* ☎ *480/991–1496* ⊕ *www.havanacafe-az.com* ◷ *Closed Sun.* ✛ *E1.*

OLD TOWN

$ ✗ **Chez Vous.** An authentic French crêperie tucked into a Scottsdale shop-
BISTRO ping center, Chez Vous imports just enough of Paris to make diners say "merci" instead of "thank you" throughout the meal. Owners Richard and Isabelle Horvath make and serve the food, and their accents are undeniably legit. Crepes, clearly, are the specialty—the savory Brie crepe with roast chicken, apples and Brie is the most popular—but daily specials like quiche Lorraine are just as delightful. Desserts are a must, whether in the form of a crêpe or a specialty tarte. $ *Average main: $11* ✉ *8787 N. Scottsdale Rd., Old Town* ☎ *480/433–2575* ⊕ *www.chezvous-az.com* ⌸ *Reservations not accepted* ◷ *Closed Mon.* ✛ *E3*

$$ ✗ **Citizen Public House.** Everything about Citizen Public House exudes
MODERN "cool," from its hip Scottsdale address to its central see-and-be-seen
AMERICAN bar, to (most importantly) its menu of modern twists on traditional favorites. While the entrées here are finger-licking good—most notably the buttermilk chicken with corn-butter bean succotash—you can enjoy one of the best meals of your life by simply ordering a series of appetizers and sharing them with friends. Don't-miss items include the pork belly spaetzle and the mac 'n' cheese with Gorgonzola and Emmental. If you're looking for a taste of Phoenix culinary history, order the "original" chopped salad, and have your server explain all the elements as it's tossed tableside. $ *Average main: $21* ✉ *711 E. 5th Ave., Old Town* ☎ *480/398–4208* ⊕ *www.citizenpublichouse.com* ⌸ *Reservations essential* ✛ *G2.*

$$$ ✗ **Don & Charlie's.** Attention, sports fans! This hangout is a favorite
STEAKHOUSE with major-leaguers in town for spring training, college football Bowl games, or the Super Bowl. A venerable chophouse, D&C specializes in "American comforts" with prime-grade steak and sports memorabilia—the walls are covered with pictures, autographs, and uniforms. The spacious and Cheers-like interior; friendly staff; and New York sirloin, prime rib, and double-thick lamb chops are a hit. Sides include au gratin potatoes and creamed spinach. $ *Average main: $29* ✉ *7501 E. Camelback Rd., Old Town* ☎ *480/990–0900* ⊕ *www.donandcharlies.com* ◷ *No lunch* ✛ *H1.*

$$ ✗ **Malee's Thai Bistro.** This cozy but fashionable eatery in the heart of
THAI Scottsdale's Main Street Arts District serves sophisticated, Thai-inspired fare. Try the crispy *pla*: flash-fried whitefish fillets with fresh cilantro and sweet jalapeño garlic sauce. The vegetarian Arizona heatwave red curry is a must, along with curries made to order with tofu, chicken, beef, pork, or seafood. You specify the spiciness—from mild to flaming—but even "mild" dishes have a bite. $ *Average main: $15* ✉ *7131 E. Main St., Old Town* ☎ *480/947–6042* ⊕ *www.maleesthaibistro.com* ✛ *F3.*

$$$ ✗ **The Mission.** The food will take your taste buds to new levels at this
SOUTHWESTERN dark and sophisticated space adjacent to a historic Catholic mission. Sit at the elegant bar or fireside on the patio and enjoy an avocado margarita with supreme starters or sides like tableside guacamole; Mission fries with lemon, chile, and cumin; or grits with chipotle and honey. House

favorites include the pecan- and mesquite-grilled pork shoulder, and the homemade chorizo porchetta. The weekend brunch menu alone could keep this place afloat. [$] *Average main: $23* ✉ *3815 N. Brown Ave., Old Town* ☎ *480/636–5005* 🌐 *www.themissionaz.com* ✍ *Reservations essential* ✥ *G3.*

WORD OF MOUTH

"Treat yourself to some different cuisine and get a reservation at Kai at the Sheraton Wild Horse Pass Resort." –patandhank

$$$ MEDITERRANEAN 🍴 **Olive & Ivy.** Tucked into the south side of the high-traffic, high-priced Scottsdale waterfront complex, Olive & Ivy is a pleasant surprise. By day the light comes from the wall of windows that look out onto the ample patio with cozy couches and fire pits. By night the giant space becomes intimate with dim, designer lighting. A full dinner menu, featuring a mix of fish and meat creations with Italian and Mediterranean twists like veal and spinach ravioli, is available, but the delicious variety of appetizers, like bacon-wrapped dates, beet salad with goat-cheese and pistachio, and flatbreads make for a good meal. Wash them down with something from their ample wine list or one of their unique signature cocktails. [$] *Average main: $26* ✉ *7135 E. Camelback Rd., Ste. 195, Old Town* ☎ *480/751–2200* 🌐 *www.oliveandivyrestaurant.com* ✍ *Reservations essential* ✥ *F1.*

TEMPE AND NEARBY

CHANDLER

$$$$ SOUTHWESTERN Fodor's Choice ★ 🍴 **Kai.** Innovative Southwestern cuisine at the prestigious Kai ("seed" in the Pima language) uses indigenous ingredients from local tribal farms. The always-changing seasonal menu reflects the restaurant's natural setting on the Gila River Indian Community. Standout appetizers include a duo of Hudson Valley duck and citrus-and-chile-glazed sea trout. Entrées like loin of pecan-crusted Colorado lamb, and the Cheyenne River buffalo tenderloin are excellent. Try to dine at sunset: the restaurant has huge windows that showcase gorgeous mountain and desert views. [$] *Average main: $49* ✉ *Sheraton Wild Horse Pass Resort & Spa, 5594 W. Wild Horse Pass Blvd., Chandler* ☎ *602/225–0100* 🌐 *www.wildhorsepassresort.com* ✍ *Reservations essential* ⏲ *Closed Sun. and Mon. No lunch.* ✥ *D6.*

TEMPE

❻ $ INDIAN 🍴 **Curry Corner.** In the shadow of Arizona State University, Curry Corner serves up some of the best Indian food in town. The naan is plentiful at this mom-and-pop eatery, and the chicken tikka masala is the house specialty. Don't worry if the spice gets to you—there are pitchers of water nearby to cool your palate. [$] *Average main: $11* ✉ *1212 E. Apache Blvd., Tempe* ☎ *480/894–1276* ✥ *E6.*

$ MIDDLE EASTERN 🍴 **Haji Baba.** This casual Tempe treasure is a hole-in-the-wall Middle Eastern favorite that gets consistent rave reviews. The reasonably priced menu includes hummus, *labni* (fresh cheese made from yogurt), fabulous falafel gyros, shawarma, and kebab plates, all served up by a friendly and efficient staff. The adjoining store stocks an ample selection of imported Middle Eastern, Mediterranean, Indian, and European foods, including everything from delicious cured olives, fava beans, and grape leaves to chocolate-covered halvah bars, rose water, and countless other hard-to-find specialties. $ *Average main: $9* ✉ *1513 E. Apache Blvd., Tempe* ☎ *480/894–1905* ⌂ *Reservations not accepted* ☼ *No dinner Sun.* ✛ *F6.*

$$$

ECLECTIC

Fodor's Choice

★

✕ **House of Tricks.** There's nothing up the sleeves of Robert and Robin Trick, who work magic on the ever-changing eclectic menu that emphasizes the freshest available seafood, poultry, and fine meats, as well as vegetarian selections. One of the Valley's most unusual dining venues, the restaurant encompasses a completely charming 1920s home and a separate brick- and adobe-style house originally built in 1903, adjoined by an intimate wooden deck and outdoor patio shaded by a canopy of grapevines and trees. The ever-changing dinner menu serves up entrées like grilled Scottish salmon with smoked corn succotash. At lunch you can't go wrong with the quiche of the day. $ *Average main: $28* ✉ *114 E. 7th St., Tempe* ☎ *480/968–1114* ⊕ *www.houseoftricks.com* ☼ *Closed Sun.* ✛ *E6.*

WHERE TO STAY

The Valley of the Sun now offers locals and visitors some of the country's best choices when it comes to funky, high-fashion accommodations.

Developers and hoteliers have taken advantage of the Valley's wide-open spaces to introduce super-size, luxury resorts like the Westin Kierland and the JW Marriott Desert Ridge, offering everything from their own golf courses and water parks to four-star restaurants and shopping villages. Places like the retro-hip Hotel Valley Ho and the sleek, mountainside Sanctuary on Camelback Mountain have brought Arizona to the forefront of luxury-hotel style. Regal resorts like The Phoenician, the Four Seasons, the romantic Royal Palms Resort, and the Moroccan-inspired Montelucia keep lodging grounded in traditional, unsurpassed elegance, while plenty of boutique and business hotels keep it grounded in price.

Downtown Phoenix properties tend to be the business hotels, close to the heart of the city and the convention centers—and often closer to the average vacationer's budget. Many properties here cater to corporate travelers during the week but lower their rates on weekends to entice leisure travelers, so ask about weekend specials when making reservations. With more than 60,000 hotel rooms in the metro area, you can take your pick of anything from a luxurious resort to a guest ranch to an extended-stay hotel. For a true Western experience, guest-ranch territory is 70 miles northwest, in the town of Wickenburg.

Many people flee snow and ice to bask in the warmth of the Valley, so winter is the high season, peaking from January through March. Summer season—mid-May through the end of September—is giveaway time, when a night at a resort often goes for half the winter price, but be forewarned: in the height of summer it can be too hot to do anything outside your air-conditioned room.

Don't be surprised if you see a "Resort Fee" on your checkout statement. Most Valley hotels charge these fees, which range from $20 to $30 and cover such amenities as parking, in-room Wi-Fi, daily newspapers, in-room coffee/tea, fitness centers, pools, and more. Ask your hotel for a complete description of what the resort fee covers. *Hotel reviews have been shortened. For full information, visit Fodors.com. Use the coordinate (⊕ B2) at the end of each listing to locate a site on the corresponding map.*

WHAT IT COSTS			
	$	$$	$$$	$$$$
For 2 people	Under $151	$151–$225	$226–$350	over $350

Hotel prices are the lowest cost of a standard double room in high season.

DOWNTOWN PHOENIX

$$$
HOTEL
Fodor'sChoice
★

Hotel Palomar Phoenix. Hip and unabashedly quirky, this Downtown Phoenix boutique hotel has kicked up Phoenix's urban street cred a few notches and offers a compelling reason to stay Downtown. **Pros:** modern and luxurious furnishings; great Downtown views; attentive staff; evening wine reception; pets welcome. **Cons:** parking is costly; rowdy atmosphere could be tiresome. Ⓢ *Rooms from: $249* ⊠ *2 E. Jefferson St., Downtown Phoenix* ☎ *602/253–6633, 877/488–1908* ⊕ *www.hotelpalomar-phoenix.com* ⥎ *226 rooms, 16 suites* ⥐ *No meals* ⊕ *B5.*

$$$$
HOTEL

Hyatt Regency Phoenix. The convenience of downtown Phoenix's light rail makes the Hyatt Regency an attractive destination for vacationers, not just a hotel for conventiongoers. **Pros:** business amenities; light-rail access; views from restaurant. **Cons:** atrium blocks view on floors 8 to 10; parking gets pricey. Ⓢ *Rooms from: $399* ⊠ *122 N. 2nd St., Downtown Phoenix* ☎ *602/252–1234* ⊕ *www.phoenix.hyatt.com* ⥎ *688 rooms, 5 suites* ⥐ *No meals* ⊕ *B5.*

$$$
HOTEL

Renaissance Phoenix Downtown. One of the city's architectural marvels, this Downtown Phoenix destination has an appealing mix of classic comfort and modern accommodations. **Pros:** prime location for light-rail travel; great lobby bar. **Cons:** primarily oriented to business travelers, ongoing renovations are sometimes noticeable. Ⓢ *Rooms from: $299* ⊠ *50 E. Adams St., Downtown Phoenix* ☎ *602/333–0000, 800/309–8138* ⊕ *www.renaissancephoenixdowntown.com* ⥎ *447 rooms, 80 suites* ⥐ *No meals* ⊕ *B6.*

$$$$
HOTEL

Sheraton Downtown Phoenix Hotel. The grande dame of Downtown Phoenix hotels has positioned itself as the go-to residence of conventiongoers, but its service and the District restaurant make it desirable for leisure travelers as well. **Pros:** restaurant has one of the best happy-hour deals in town; great lobby for lounging or meeting people. **Cons:** hallways are long and impersonal; parking is expensive. Ⓢ *Rooms from: $579* ⊠ *340 N. 3rd St., Downtown Phoenix* ☎ *602/262–2500, 866/837–4213* ⊕ *www.sheratonphoenixdowntown.com* ⥎ *953 rooms, 47 suites* ⥐ *No meals* ⊕ *B5.*

BEST BETS FOR PHOENIX, SCOTTSDALE, AND TEMPE LODGING

Fodor's offers a selective listing of lodging at every price range, from the city's best budget motel to its most sophisticated luxury hotel. Here we've compiled our top picks by price and experience. The very best properties—those that provide a particularly remarkable experience in their price range—are designated with the Fodor's Choice logo.

Fodor'sChoice ★

FireSky Resort & Spa, $$$$, p. 89

Four Seasons Resort Scottsdale at Troon North, $$$$, p. 90

Hotel Palomar Phoenix, $$$, p. 82

Hyatt Regency Scottsdale Resort and Spa at Gainey Ranch, $$$$, p. 90

JW Marriott Desert Ridge Resort & Spa, $$$$, p. 88

The Phoenician, $$$$, p. 87

Pointe Hilton Squaw Peak Resort, $$$, p. 88

Rancho de los Caballeros, $$$$, p. 123

Royal Palms Resort and Spa, $$$$, p. 87

Sanctuary on Camelback Mountain, $$$$, p. 89

Westin Kierland Resort & Spa, $$$$, p. 90

Best by Price

$

Best Western Plus Inn Suites, p. 87

$$

aloft Tempe, p. 92

Hampton Inn Phoenix-Biltmore, p. 87

Wingate by Wyndham Scottsdale, p. 91

$$$

Hermosa Inn, p. 88

Hotel Indigo, p. 91

Pointe Hilton Squaw Peak Resort, p. 88

$$$$

Four Seasons Resort Scottsdale at Troon North, p. 90

JW Marriott Camelback Inn Resort & Spa, p. 88

The Phoenician, p. 87

Royal Palms Resort and Spa, p. 87

Best by Experience

BEST LARGE RESORTS

Arizona Biltmore Resort & Spa, $$$, p. 86

Omni Scottsdale Resort & Spa at Montelucia, $$$, p. 88

JW Marriott Desert Ridge Resort & Spa, $$$$, p. 88

The Phoenician, $$$$, p. 87

Westin Kierland Resort & Spa, $$$$, p. 90

BEST GOLF RESORTS

Fairmont Scottsdale Princess, $$$$, p. 90

Four Seasons Resort Scottsdale at Troon North, $$$$, p. 90

The Phoenician, $$$$, p. 87

BEST REMOTE RETREATS

Four Seasons Resort Scottsdale at Troon North, $$$$, p. 90

Rancho de los Caballeros, $$$$, p. 123

BEST SMALL RESORTS

Hermosa Inn, $$$, p. 88

Sanctuary on Camelback Mountain, $$$$, p. 89

Wigwam Resort, $$$$, p. 89

BEST URBAN HOT-SPOT HOTELS

FireSky Resort & Spa, $$$$, p. 89

Hotel Palomar Phoenix, $$$, p. 82

Hotel Valley Ho, $$$, p. 91

W Scottsdale, $$$$, p. 91

GREAT VIEW

JW Marriott Camelback Inn Resort & Spa, $$$$, p. 88

Sanctuary on Camelback Mountain, $$$$, p. 89

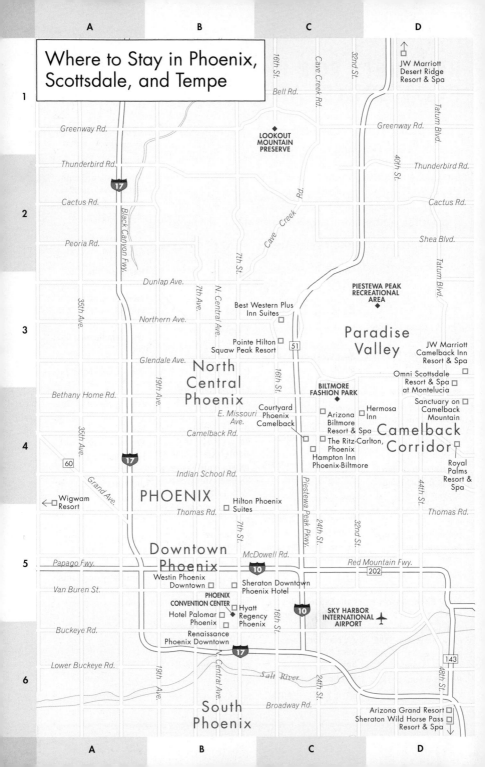

WHERE SHOULD I STAY?

	NEIGHBORHOOD VIBE	PROS	CONS
Downtown Phoenix	Big-name hotel chains in an urban setting; good nightlife.	Close to major venues for sports and entertainment.	Expensive parking; heavy convention crowd.
Camelback Corridor	Luxurious resorts perfect for a getaway.	Fantastic service and amenities; great dining nearby.	Costly resorts; you need a car.
North Central Phoenix	Intimate, nontouristy feel.	Good access to museums, attractions, and freeways.	Some properties lack amenities.
Paradise Valley	The ultimate in luxury getaways.	Five-star service, spas, and dining.	You'll pay for all that luxury.
Scottsdale/ North Scotts-dale/Old Town	Where West meets Chic; a haven for pleasure-seekers.	Beautiful desert views; hip.	Minimum 30-minute drive from the airport.
Tempe and Around	Great for younger travel-ers or families visiting college students nearby.	Less expensive; only a few minutes from downtown.	Few resorts offer luxury amenities.

$$$$ HOTEL **Westin Phoenix Downtown.** This Downtown Phoenix gem offers some of the largest rooms in the city, which give you a feeling of seclusion amid the urban hustle and bustle. **Pros:** large rooms with sitting areas; fantastic views; elegant furnishings and fixtures. **Cons:** tiny lobby and awkward process of getting to the hotel elevator; you have to walk through the lobby to get to the pool. [$] *Rooms from: $599* ✉ *333 N. Central Ave., Downtown Phoenix* ☎ *602/429–3500, 866/961–3775* 🌐 *www.westinphoenixdowntown.com* 🛏 *214 rooms, 28 suites* 🍴 *No meals* ✥ *B5.*

GREATER PHOENIX

CAMELBACK CORRIDOR

$$$ RESORT **Arizona Biltmore Resort & Spa.** Designed by Frank Lloyd Wright's colleague Albert Chase McArthur, the Biltmore has been Phoenix's premier resort since it opened in 1929. **Pros:** centrally located; stately; historic charm. **Cons:** finding a parking spot near your room can be a headache; hard to find lounge chairs at some pools. [$] *Rooms from: $329* ✉ *2400 E. Missouri Ave., Camelback Corridor* ☎ *602/955–6600, 800/950–0086* 🌐 *www.arizonabiltmore.com* 🛏 *648 rooms, 90 suites* 🍴 *No meals* ✥ *C4.*

$$ HOTEL **Courtyard Phoenix Camelback.** Public areas in this four-story hotel are mostly glass and tile, while rooms are tastefully done with light-colored walls and accents like plush down bedding, cherrywood armoires, and large, pullout desks to accommodate business travelers. **Pros:** great value; within walking distance of great shopping and dining. **Cons:** few frills; business-oriented. [$] *Rooms from: $219* ✉ *2101 E. Camelback Rd., Camelback Corridor* ☎ *602/955–5200, 800/321–2211* 🌐 *www.marriott.com/hotels/travel/phxcc-courtyard-phoenix-camelback* 🛏 *155 rooms, 12 suites* 🍴 *No meals* ✥ *C4.*

$$ HOTEL

Hampton Inn Phoenix-Biltmore. Conveniently located one block off Camelback Road, this four-story hotel is great for business travelers, with spacious and accommodating rooms appointed with comfortable yet modern furnishings. **Pros:** great value; central location; modern conveniences. **Cons:** though gated, the pool area is exposed to the parking lot and street. [$] *Rooms from: $225 ✉ 2310 E. Highland Ave., Camelback Corridor ☎ 602/956–5221 🌐 www.phoenixbiltmorearea.hamptoninn.com 🛏 112 rooms, 8 suites 🍴 Breakfast ✥ C4.*

WORD OF MOUTH

"I would HIGHLY recommend staying at The Royal Palms—it is heaven on earth. Such a tranquil oasis, yet near everything. It is small enough to feel very personal, yet private enough to relax and enjoy the lush grounds and wonderful service." –DebitNM

$$$$ RESORT FAMILY Fodor's Choice ★

The Phoenician. In a town where luxurious, expensive resorts are the rule, the Phoenician still stands apart, primarily in the realm of service. **Pros:** luxurious; highest industry standards. **Cons:** high prices, even in the off-season. [$] *Rooms from: $599 ✉ 6000 E. Camelback Rd., Camelback Corridor ☎ 480/941–8200, 800/888–8234 🌐 www.thephoenician.com 🛏 577 rooms, 66 suites 🍴 No meals ✥ E4.*

$$$ HOTEL

The Ritz-Carlton, Phoenix. Known for impeccable service, this graceful luxury hotel doesn't disappoint the interior decorator lurking inside you. **Pros:** impeccable service; a walkway (under Camelback Road) gives guests easy access to Biltmore Fashion Park. **Cons:** lacks the golf and spa amenities of other luxury resorts in town; can be business traveler–focused. [$] *Rooms from: $349 ✉ 2401 E. Camelback Rd., Camelback Corridor ☎ 602/468–0700 🌐 www.ritzcarlton.com/Phoenix 🛏 267 rooms, 14 suites 🍴 No meals ✥ C4.*

$$$$ RESORT Fodor's Choice ★

Royal Palms Resort and Spa. Once the home of Cunard Steamship executive Delos T. Cooke, this Mediterranean-style resort has a stately row of the namesake palms at its entrance, courtyards with fountains, and individually designed rooms. **Pros:** great for romantic getaways; houses a cozy cigar lounge; impeccable service. **Cons:** expensive; only one pool, and it's small. [$] *Rooms from: $550 ✉ 5200 E. Camelback Rd., Camelback Corridor ☎ 602/840–3610, 800/672–6011 🌐 www.royalpalmshotel.com 🛏 44 rooms, 26 suites, 46 casitas, 3 villas 🍴 No meals ✥ D4.*

NORTH CENTRAL PHOENIX

$ HOTEL

Best Western Plus Inn Suites. A comfortable base for travel, this affordable hotel is within a short drive of great recreation areas (Piestewa Peak) and great dining options, and is less than 1 mile from AZ 51, which offers quick and easy access to major freeways, Valley shopping, and Sky Harbor Airport. **Pros:** the price is right, especially for the area; pet-friendly. **Cons:** amenities aren't on par with nearby resorts; on a busy corner that can be a challenge during rush hour. [$] *Rooms from: $149 ✉ 1615 E. Northern Ave., North Central Phoenix ☎ 602/997–6285 🌐 www.bestwestern.com 🛏 77 rooms, 32 2-room suites 🍴 Breakfast ✥ C3.*

$$$ HOTEL

Hilton Phoenix Suites. This practical hotel is a model of excellent design within tight limits. **Pros:** spacious rooms with microwaves, refrigerators, and large desks; close to light rail. **Cons:** expensive parking; business-oriented. [$] *Rooms from: $259* ✉ *10 E. Thomas Rd., North Central Phoenix* ☎ *602/222–1111* 🌐 *www.phoenixsuites.hilton.com* 🛏 *226 suites* 🍴 *No meals* ✥ *B5.*

$$$$ RESORT FAMILY Fodor's Choice ★ 🏨 **JW Marriott Desert Ridge Resort & Spa.** Arizona's largest resort has an immense entryway with floor-to-ceiling windows that allow the sandstone lobby, the Sonoran Desert, and the resort's amazing water features to meld together perfectly. **Pros:** perfect for luxuriating with family or groups; close to north Valley restaurants, entertainmnent, and attractions. **Cons:** large size makes it a bit impersonal for the price tag; lots of walking and stairs required to get anywhere. [$] *Rooms from: $599* ✉ *5350 E. Marriott Dr., North Central Phoenix* ☎ *480/293–5000, 800/835–6206* 🌐 *www.jwdesertridgeresort.com* 🛏 *869 rooms, 81 suites* 🍴 *No meals* ✥ *D1.*

$$$ RESORT FAMILY Fodor's Choice ★ 🏨 **Pointe Hilton Squaw Peak Resort.** The highlight of this family-oriented Hilton is the 9-acre Hole-in-the-Wall River Ranch; it has swimming pools with waterfalls, a 130-foot waterslide, and a 1,000-foot "river" that winds past a miniature golf course, tennis courts, and artificial buttes. **Pros:** adjacent to the Phoenix Mountain Preserve, making it an ideal base for hiking and biking trips; affordable alternative to luxury resorts nearby. **Cons:** finding a parking spot can be a challenge; rooms near lobby are noisy. [$] *Rooms from: $259* ✉ *7677 N. 16th St., North Central Phoenix* ☎ *602/997–2626, 800/947–9784* 🌐 *www.pointehilton.com* 🛏 *563 suites, 80 casitas* 🍴 *No meals* ✥ *C3.*

PARADISE VALLEY

$$$ HOTEL 🏨 **Hermosa Inn.** The Hermosa, on 6 acres of lushly landscaped desert, is a blessedly peaceful alternative to some of the larger resorts nearby. **Pros:** luxurious but cozy; pet-friendly; fantastic restaurant. **Cons:** neighborhood location means you'll have to drive to get anywhere; lacks some luxury amenities of larger resorts nearby. [$] *Rooms from: $289* ✉ *5532 N. Palo Cristi Rd., Paradise Valley* ☎ *602/955–8614, 800/241–1210* 🌐 *www.hermosainn.com* 🛏 *34 casitas* 🍴 *No meals* ✥ *D4.*

$$$$ RESORT 🏨 **JW Marriott Camelback Inn Resort & Spa.** Built on 125 acres in the mid-1930s and gorgeously renovated to keep the cowboy character, this hacienda-style resort remains top-notch and was the first JW Marriott ever established. **Pros:** a specialty restaurant (BLT Steak); a world-class spa and golf course; stunning place to catch a sunset. **Cons:** noisy neighbors are easily heard at night; pool is small for a resort of this stature. [$] *Rooms from: $399* ✉ *5402 E. Lincoln Dr., Paradise Valley* ☎ *480/948–1700, 800/242–2635* 🌐 *www.camelbackinn.com* 🛏 *427 rooms, 26 suites* 🍴 *No meals* ✥ *D3.*

$$$ RESORT 🏨 **Omni Scottsdale Resort & Spa at Montelucia.** This luxury resort brings a touch of the Mediterranean to Paradise Valley with its exquisite dark furnishings and light stonework, its impeccable Joya Spa, its pool pavilion, and a Spanish-inspired wedding chapel. **Pros:** inner-city getaway with stellar sunset views. **Cons:** while the grounds are beautiful, the layout is boxy, awkward, and confusing. [$] *Rooms from: $299* ✉ *4949 E. Lincoln Dr., Paradise Valley* ☎ *480/627–3200, 888/627–3010* 🌐 *www.montelucia.com* 🛏 *251 guest rooms, 40 suites, 2 villas* 🍴 *No meals* ✥ *D3.*

$$$$ HOTEL Fodor's Choice ★ **Sanctuary on Camelback Mountain.** This luxurious boutique hotel is the only resort on the north slope of Camelback Mountain; secluded mountain casitas are painted in desert hues and feature breathtaking views of Paradise Valley. **Pros:** inner-city getaway with mountain seclusion; unparalleled views of Camelback's Praying Monk rock. **Cons:** it can be hard to find your room on the sprawling property; walking between buildings can mean conquering slopes or flights of stairs; not kid-friendly. [$] *Rooms from: $529* ✉ *5700 E. McDonald Dr., Paradise Valley* ☎ *480/948–2100, 800/245–2051* 🌐 *www.sanctuaryaz.com* 🛏 *105 casitas* 🍴 *No meals* ✥ *D4.*

SOUTH PHOENIX

$$$$ RESORT FAMILY **Arizona Grand Resort.** This beautiful all-suites resort next to South Mountain Park is home to Oasis, one of the largest water parks in the country, and one of the Valley's more challenging golf courses. **Pros:** great family or large-group location; all rooms are suites. **Cons:** huge property can overwhelm; freeway noise could be a problem in some rooms. [$] *Rooms from: $369* ✉ *8000 S. Arizona Grand Pkwy., South Phoenix* ☎ *602/438–9000, 866/267–1321* 🌐 *www.arizonagrandresort.com* 🛏 *740 suites* 🍴 *No meals* ✥ *D6.*

LITCHFIELD PARK

$$$$ RESORT **Wigwam Resort.** Built in 1918 as a retreat for executives of the Goodyear Company, the grand Wigwam Resort maintains its historical character while delivering a modern-day, luxury experience. **Pros:** although only a few minutes from downtown Phoenix, this resort feels away from it all; great service. **Cons:** odd resort layout makes it difficult to find anything; rooms can teeter on old historic charm and just plain "old." [$] *Rooms from: $359* ✉ *300 E. Wigwam Blvd., Litchfield Park* ☎ *623/935–3811* 🌐 *www.wigwamresort.com* 🛏 *259 rooms, 72 suites* 🍴 *No meals* ✥ *A4.*

SCOTTSDALE

$$$$ HOTEL FAMILY Fodor's Choice ★ **FireSky Resort & Spa.** This Scottsdale escape provides an elegant, intimate, eco- and family-friendly environment. **Pros:** the lavish pool and lounge area are considered among the area's nicest; pet-friendly; special rooms for tall people. **Cons:** no elevator; interior hallways can be noisy. [$] *Rooms from: $409* ✉ *4925 N. Scottsdale Rd., Scottsdale* ☎ *480/945–7666, 800/528–7867* 🌐 *www.fireskyresort.com* 🛏 *196 rooms, 8 suites* 🍴 *No meals* ✥ *E4.*

$$$ HOTEL FAMILY **Gainey Suites Hotel.** This independently owned boutique hotel is a rare find for both amenities and price. **Pros:** hotel layout, price, and inclusive breakfast buffet are ideal for families and groups. **Cons:** comfortable but fairly generic décor; have to leave property to enjoy recreation amenities. [$] *Rooms from: $289* ✉ *7300 E. Gainey Suites Dr., Scottsdale* ☎ *480/922–6969, 800/970–4666* 🌐 *www.gaineysuiteshotel.com* 🛏 *162 suites* 🍴 *Breakfast* ✥ *E3.*

$$ HOTEL **Holiday Inn Express Scottsdale North.** This hotel has a great location along the Scottsdale Road corridor, with trendy restaurants and shopping opportunities within easy walking distance, making this a comfortable, affordable, and family-friendly option. **Pros:** quiet; excellent

for the price in this area. **Cons:** these affordable rooms can't meet the high-scale standards of nearby hotels and resorts. [$] *Rooms from: $189* ✉ *7350 E. Gold Dust Rd., at Scottsdale Rd., Scottsdale* ☎ *480/596–6559, 888/465–4329* 🌐 *www.hiexpress.com* 🛏 *121 rooms, 1 suite* 🍴 *Breakfast* ✥ *E2.*

$$$$ RESORT FAMILY Fodor'sChoice ★ 🏨 **Hyatt Regency Scottsdale Resort and Spa at Gainey Ranch.** While staying here, it's easy to imagine that you're relaxing at an oceanside resort instead of in the desert; shaded by towering palms and with manicured gardens and paths, the property has water everywhere—a large pool area has a beach, a three-story waterslide, waterfalls, and a lagoon. **Pros:** lots of pools for all; oasis atmosphere; best Sunday brunch in town. **Cons:** if you're early to bed, avoid a room near the lobby. [$] *Rooms from: $539* ✉ *7500 E. Doubletree Ranch Rd., Scottsdale* ☎ *480/444–1234* 🌐 *www.scottsdale.hyatt.com* 🛏 *462 rooms, 7 casitas, 24 suites* 🍴 *No meals* ✥ *F2.*

$$$ HOTEL 🏨 **The Saguaro.** Surrounded by lush landscaping, this urban resort features two pools that are among the hottest hangouts in all of Scottsdale, and rooms that juxtapose old and new, with flat-screen TVs and retro furnishings that bring you back to the '60s. **Pros:** great location for shopping, entertainment, and Valley activities; part of the happening Scottsdale scene. **Cons:** very noisy; no elevator; furnishings are new but fixtures are old. [$] *Rooms from: $329* ✉ *4000 N. Drinkwater Blvd., Scottsdale* ☎ *480/308–1100, 877/808–2440* 🌐 *www.thesaguaro.com* 🛏 *194 rooms* 🍴 *No meals* ✥ *E4.*

NORTH SCOTTSDALE

$$$$ RESORT FAMILY 🏨 **Fairmont Scottsdale Princess.** Home of the Tournament Players Club Stadium golf course and the Phoenix Open, this resort covers 450 breathtakingly landscaped acres of desert. **Pros:** upscale favorite, especially for families; extras like in-room espresso machines; close to shopping. **Cons:** sprawling campus can be difficult to navigate; there is a parking charge. [$] *Rooms from: $499* ✉ *7575 E. Princess Dr., North Scottsdale* ☎ *480/585–4848* 🌐 *www.scottsdaleprincess.com* 🛏 *505 rooms, 69 casitas, 74 suites* 🍴 *No meals* ✥ *E1.*

$$$$ RESORT Fodor'sChoice ★ 🏨 **Four Seasons Resort Scottsdale at Troon North.** A resort in every sense of the word, Four Seasons Scottsdale is tucked in the shadows of Pinnacle Peak, near the popular hiking trail, and features large, casita-style rooms with separate sitting and sleeping areas as well as fireplaces, and balconies or patios. **Pros:** amazing service; breathtaking views. **Cons:** far from everything. [$] *Rooms from: $529* ✉ *10600 E. Crescent Moon Dr., North Scottsdale* ☎ *480/515–5700, 866/207–9696* 🌐 *www.fourseasons.com/scottsdale* 🛏 *188 rooms, 22 suites* 🍴 *No meals* ✥ *F1.*

$$$$ RESORT FAMILY Fodor'sChoice ★ 🏨 **Westin Kierland Resort & Spa.** Original artwork by Arizona artists is displayed throughout the Westin Kierland, and the spacious rooms all have balconies or patios with views of the mountains or the resort's water park and tubing river, where kids can enjoy programs organized by age group. **Pros:** bagpipers stroll around the courtyard at sunset; amazing beds and bedding; organic superfood menu; programs for kids' photography and scuba certification. **Cons:** bagpipers can be noisy; adults' pool very close to kids' area. [$] *Rooms from: $449* ✉ *6902 E. Greenway Pkwy., North Scottsdale* ☎ *480/624–1000, 800/354–5892*

🌐 *www.kierlandresort.com* 🛏 *732 rooms, 55 suites, 32 casitas* 🍴 *No meals* ✣ *E1.*

$$ HOTEL 🏨 **Wingate by Wyndham Scottsdale.** Located right off the 101 freeway, this affordable hotel is a convenient base of operations; cool and modern throughout, it has clean, large, simply decorated rooms. **Pros:** clean and spacious rooms; comfortable beds; good price for location. **Cons:** more practical than perfect, primarily for business clientele. [$] *Rooms from: $219* ✉ *14255 N. 87th St., North Scottsdale* ☎ *480/922–6500, 877/570–6500* 🌐 *www.wingatehotels.com* 🛏 *82 rooms, 35 suites* 🍴 *Breakfast* ✣ *F2.*

2

OLD TOWN

$$$ HOTEL 🏨 **Hotel Indigo.** This Scottsdale spot is simple, modern, and, most of all, centrally located to Scottsdale's best bars, nightclubs, and venues where people flock to see and be seen. **Pros:** great value; convenient Scottsdale location; pet-friendly. **Cons:** noise—whether it's from music in the lobby, people in the room next door, or the bar down the street—can be annoying. [$] *Rooms from: $261* ✉ *4415 N. Civic Center Plaza, Old Town* ☎ *480/941–9400* 🌐 *www.scottsdalehiphotel.com* 🛏 *117 rooms, 9 suites* 🍴 *No meals* ✣ *F4.*

$$$ HOTEL 🏨 **Hotel Valley Ho.** This Scottsdale hot-spot hotel was recently restored to its former '50s fabulousness, and the rooms don't disappoint with retro furnishings and styling. **Pros:** retro décor; great history; hip, youthful style. **Cons:** busy location; occasionally rowdy weekend crowd. [$] *Rooms from: $229* ✉ *6850 E. Main St., Old Town* ☎ *480/248–2000, 866/882–4484* 🌐 *www.hotelvalleyho.com* 🛏 *185 rooms, 6 suites* 🍴 *No meals* ✣ *E4.*

$$$$ HOTEL 🏨 **W Scottsdale.** A taste of youthful but sophisticated New York elegance, this hot-spot hotel in the heart of Scottsdale's shopping and social scene caters to the wants and needs of the fashionable but fickle traveler with "whatever, whenever" service that provides guests with anything they want ("as long as it's legal!"). **Pros:** unpretentious elegance right across from Scottsdale Fashion Square. **Cons:** the youthful exuberance that makes the hotel so much fun during the day can get a little noisy at night. [$] *Rooms from: $709* ✉ *7277 E. Camelback Rd., Old Town* ☎ *480/970–2100* 🌐 *www.wscottsdalehotel.com* 🛏 *230 rooms, 33 suites* 🍴 *No meals* ✣ *E4.*

TEMPE AND AROUND

CHANDLER

$$$$ RESORT FAMILY 🏨 **Sheraton Wild Horse Pass Resort & Spa.** The culture and heritage of the Pima and Maricopa tribes are reflected in every aspect of this tranquil property on the grounds of the Gila River Indian community, 11 miles south of Sky Harbor Airport. **Pros:** great views and service; peaceful; good for families and older travelers looking to escape urban chaos. **Cons:** conferences can sometimes overrun the place; beautiful handhewn guest room doors are loud when they slam shut; long hallways. [$] *Rooms from: $549* ✉ *5594 W. Wild Horse Pass Blvd., Chandler* ☎ *602/225–0100* 🌐 *www.wildhorsepassresort.com* 🛏 *500 rooms, 26 suites* 🍴 *No meals* ✣ *D6.*

TEMPE

$$ HOTEL **aloft Tempe.** True to its name, this hip hotel, located right on Tempe's Rio Salado waterfront, features loft-inspired design, with modern, minimalist décor. **Pros:** flat-screen TVs; eco-friendly; highly social; adjacent to Town Lake and ASU action. **Cons:** social lodging experience not for everyone. [$] *Rooms from: $179* ✉ *951 E. Playa Del Norte Dr., Tempe* ☎ *480/621–3300, 888/867–7492* 🌐 *www.alofthotels.com/tempe* 🛏 *136 rooms* 🍴 *No meals* ✥ *E6.*

$$$ HOTEL **Tempe Mission Palms.** A handsome, casual lobby and an energetic young staff set the tone at this three-story courtyard hotel. **Pros:** nice hotel with friendly service and a rooftop pool; right at the center of ASU and Mill Avenue activity. **Cons:** all that activity can be bad for light sleepers. [$] *Rooms from: $299* ✉ *60 E. 5th St., Tempe* ☎ *480/894–1400, 800/547–8705* 🌐 *www.missionpalms.com* 🛏 *291 rooms, 12 suites* 🍴 *No meals* ✥ *E6.*

NIGHTLIFE AND PERFORMING ARTS

Over the past decade the Valley of the Sun has gone from a "cow town" to "now town," and the nightlife and culture options are no exception. Downtown Phoenix and Scottsdale are especially packed with entertainment choices.

NIGHTLIFE

From brewpubs, sports bars, and coffeehouses to dance clubs, megaconcerts, and country venues, the Valley of the Sun offers nightlife of all types. Nightclubs, comedy clubs, upscale lounges, and wine bars abound in Downtown Phoenix, along Camelback Road in North Central Phoenix, and in Scottsdale and Tempe, as well as the other suburbs.

Among music and dancing styles, country-and-western has the longest tradition here. Jazz venues, rock clubs, and hotel lounges are also numerous and varied. Phoenix continues to get hipper and more cosmopolitan, so behind the bar you're just as likely to find a mixologist as a bartender. There are also more than 30 gay and lesbian bars, primarily on 7th Avenue, 7th Street, and the stretch of Camelback Road between the two.

You can find listings and reviews in the *New Times* free weekly newspaper, distributed Wednesday, or in the *Arizona Republic,* also online at 🌐 *www.azcentral.com,* the paper's website. The local gay scene is covered in *Echo Magazine,* which you can pick up all over town.

DOWNTOWN PHOENIX

BARS AND LOUNGES

CityScape. The best place to take part in Downtown Phoenix's thriving nightlife, CityScape offers a mix of clubs, entertainment, restaurants, and shopping, all within steps of downtown's hotels and sports arenas. ✉ *1 E. Washington St., Downtown Phoenix* 🌐 *www.cityscapephoenix.com.*

Majerle's Sports Grill. Operated by former Phoenix Suns basketball player Dan Majerle, this sports bar offers a comprehensive menu for pre- and postgame celebrations as well as some of the best people-watching potential in town. ✉ *24 N. 2nd St., Downtown Phoenix* ☎ *602/253–0118* ⊕ *www.majerles.com.*

The Rose & Crown. Next to two of the Valley's major sports complexes and inside a historic home, The Rose & Crown serves hearty, traditional, English pub grub—fish-and-chips, bangers and mash, and shepherd's pie—with equally hearty beers to wash it down. Expect a wait on game and special-event nights. ✉ *628 E. Adams St., at 7th St., Downtown Phoenix* ☎ *602/256–0223* ⊕ *www.theroseandcrownaz.com.*

Seamus McCaffrey's Irish Pub. Enjoy one of the dozen European brews on draft at this fun and friendly place. It also has the largest scotch collection in Arizona. A small kitchen turns out traditional Irish fare. ✉ *18 W. Monroe St., Downtown Phoenix* ☎ *602/253–6081* ⊕ *www.seamusmccaffreys.com.*

COFFEEHOUSES

Lux Central. Decorated with local art and retro furniture, Lux is an eclectic gathering place where artists, architects, and downtown businesspeople enjoy excellent classic European espresso drinks. ✉ *4402 N. Central Ave., Downtown Phoenix* ☎ *602/327–1396* ⊕ *www.luxcoffee.com.*

COMEDY CLUBS

Stand Up Live. This downtown comedy club features national acts on Thursday, Friday, Saturday, and Sunday nights. ✉ *CityScape, 50 W. Jefferson St., Downtown Phoenix* ☎ *480/719–6100* ⊕ *standuplive.com.*

GREATER PHOENIX
BARS AND LOUNGES

FEZ on Central. This place is a stylish restaurant by day and a gay-friendly hot spot by night. The sleek interior and fancy drinks make you feel uptown, while the happy-hour prices and location keep this place grounded. ✉ *3815 N. Central Ave., North Central Phoenix* ☎ *602/287–8700* ⊕ *www.fezoncentral.com.*

Fodor'sChoice
★
Jade Bar. This spot has spectacular views of Paradise Valley and Camelback Mountain; an upscale, modern bar lined with windows; and a relaxing fireplace-lighted patio. ✉ *Sanctuary on Camelback Mountain, 5700 E. McDonald Dr., Paradise Valley* ☎ *480/948–2100* ⊕ *www.sanctuaryoncamelback.com.*

Postino Wine Cafe. Postino has grown from a small neighborhood haunt into three separate destinations throughout the Valley. More than 40 wines are poured by the glass. Order a few grazing items off the menu (the bruschetta is unmatched by any in the Valley) and settle in, or carry out a bottle of wine, hunk of cheese, and loaf of bread for a twilight picnic. ✉ *3939 E. Campbell Ave., Camelback Corridor* ☎ *602/852–3939* ⊕ *www.postinowinecafe.com.*

BLUES, JAZZ, AND ROCK

Fodor'sChoice
★
Char's Has the Blues. This is one of the Valley's top blues clubs, with nightly bands. ✉ *4631 N. 7th Ave., North Central Phoenix* ☎ *602/230–0205* ⊕ *www.charshastheblues.com.*

Rhythm Room. Excellent local and national rock and blues artists perform here seven nights a week. ✉ *1019 E. Indian School Rd., North Central Phoenix* ☎ *602/265–4842* ⊕ *www.rhythmroom.com.*

CASINOS

Fort McDowell Casino. This casino is popular with the resort crowd. In addition to 150,000 square feet of slot machines, bingo, and keno games, the casino is one of the favorites in town for poker players. Take advantage of the free Valley-wide shuttle. ✉ *AZ 87 at Fort McDowell Rd., Fountain Hills* ☎ *800/843–3678* ⊕ *www.fortmcdowellcasino.com.*

GAY AND LESBIAN BARS

Cash Inn Country. This bar has an eclectic clientele of women and features music just as diverse, from Latin to country. ✉ *2140 E. McDowell Rd., North Central Phoenix* ☎ *602/244–9943* ⊕ *www.cashinncountry.net.*

Charlie's. A longtime favorite of local gay men, Charlie's has a country-western look (cowboy hats are the accessory of choice) and friendly staff. ✉ *727 W. Camelback Rd., North Central Phoenix* ☎ *602/265–0224* ⊕ *www.charliesphoenix.com.*

SCOTTSDALE

BARS AND LOUNGES

AZ88. This spot is great for feasting on huge portions of food and lavish quantities of liquor, but also for feasting your eyes on the fabulous people who flock here on weekend nights. It's a great stop before and after an Old Town event or a night of partying. ✉ *7353 Scottsdale Mall, Scottsdale Civic Center, Old Town* ☎ *480/994–5576* ⊕ *www.az88.com.*

Dos Gringos. A kitschy indoor-outdoor cantina, Dos Gringos will remind you of trips over the Mexican border, or at least spring break. Crowds (mostly college students and twentysomethings) swig margaritas and beer in a multilevel courtyard surrounded by TVs and limestone fountains. ✉ *4209 N. Craftsman Ct., Old Town* ☎ *480/423–3800* ⊕ *www.dosgringosaz.com.*

Kazimierz World Wine Bar. Enter this bar through a door marked "The Truth Is Inside," beyond which lies a dark, cavelike wine bar with comfy chairs and good music. ✉ *7137 E. Stetson Dr., Old Town* ☎ *480/946–3004* ⊕ *www.kazbar.net.*

Salty Senorita. This spot is known more for its extensive margarita selection and lively patio crowd than for its food. The restaurant-bar touts 51 different margaritas—with some recipes so secret they won't tell you what goes in them. Try the El Presidente or the Chupacabra. ✉ *3748 N. Scottsdale Rd., Old Town* ☎ *480/946–7258* ⊕ *www.saltysenorita.com.*

CASINOS

Casino Arizona at Salt River. This is the largest casino in the area, with five restaurants, four lounges, a sports bar, a 250-seat theater featuring live performances, two large blackjack rooms, and a keno parlor. There's live music and dancing most nights. ✉ *524 N. 92nd St., Scottsdale* ☎ *480/850–7777* ⊕ *www.casinoarizona.com.*

Casino Arizona at Talking Stick Resort. Locals come here for blackjack, poker, keno, more than 200 slot machines, and a dash of Las Vegas–like nightlife. ✉ *9800 E. Indian Bend Rd., Scottsdale* ☎ *480/850–7777* ⊕ *www.talkingstickresort.com.*

COMEDY CLUBS

The Comedy Spot. Catch local and national stand-up talent at this venue. They also offer classes for wannabe comedians on Sunday. ✉ *7117 E. 3rd Ave., Old Town* ☎ *480/945–4422* ⊕ *www. thecomedyspot.net.*

Jester'Z Improv Comedy. The improv troupe performs family-friendly comedy shows for a youngish crowd on Friday and Saturday nights. ✉ *7117 E. McDowell Rd., Scottsdale* ☎ *480/423–0120* ⊕ *www.jesterzimprov.com.*

COUNTRY-AND-WESTERN

Fodor's Choice ★ **Greasewood Flat.** It's not fancy; in fact, it's downright ramshackle, but Greasewood Flat's burgers are delicious and the crowds friendly. There's a dance floor with live music Thursday through Sunday. In winter, wear jeans and a jacket, since everything is outside; to keep warm, folks congregate around fires burning in halved oil drums. ✉ *27375 N. Alma School Pkwy., North Scottsdale* ☎ *480/585–9430* ⊕ *www. greasewoodflat.net.*

Handlebar-J. This is a lively restaurant and bar with a Western line-dancing, 10-gallon-hat-wearing crowd. ✉ *7116 E. Becker La., Scottsdale* ☎ *480/948–0110* ⊕ *www.handlebarj.com.*

GAY AND LESBIAN BARS

B. S. West. Tucked behind a shopping center on Scottsdale's main shopping drag, B. S. West draws a stylish, well-heeled gay crowd. ✉ *7125 E. 5th Ave., Old Town* ☎ *480/945–9028* ⊕ *www.bswest.com.*

TEMPE AND AROUND

BARS AND LOUNGES

Casey Moore's Oyster House. A laid-back institution where students, hippies, and families come together, Casey Moore's is in a 1910 house rumored to be haunted by ghosts. Enjoy more than two dozen beers on tap and fresh oysters at this Irish pub–style favorite. ✉ *850 S. Ash Ave., Tempe* ☎ *480/968–9935* ⊕ *www.caseymoores.com.*

The Monastery. You grill your own burgers and nosh on picnic food at this casual beer and wine pub. You can also play horseshoes, chess, or volleyball. ✉ *4810 E. McKellips, Mesa* ☎ *480/474–4477* ⊕ *www. realfunbar.com.*

CASINOS

Gila River Casino Wild Horse Pass. Part of the Wild Horse Pass Hotel & Casino, this casino includes 500 slots, live poker, blackjack, and keno. ✉ *5040 Wild Horse Pass Blvd., Chandler* ☎ *800/946–4452* ⊕ *www. wingilariver.com.*

GAMBLING

There are casinos on Native American reservations around the Valley of the Sun. Compared with Las Vegas, they offer smaller venues and a low-key atmosphere. The casinos follow Arizona gaming laws, such as no betting cash—chips only.

2

COMEDY CLUBS

The Tempe Improv. Part of a national chain, The Tempe Improv showcases better-known headliners from Thursday to Sunday. Get there early for good seats. ✉ *930 E. University Dr., Tempe* ☎ *480/921–9877* ⊕ *www.tempeimprov.com.*

DANCE CLUBS

School of Rock. A favorite for Arizona State University students, this is one of the most boisterous places on Mill Avenue. Wind and grind to a mix of techno and rock until the wee hours of the morning. ✉ *411 S. Mill Ave., Tempe* ☎ *602/471–1841* ⊕ *www.schoolofrockmillave.com.*

MICROBREWERIES

Four Peaks Brewing Company. This beer spot is the former redbrick home of Bordens Creamery. Wash down an ample supply of house-made brews on tap (including some seasonal specialties) with pub grub—pizza, wings, and burgers fill the menu. There's also a location in Scottsdale. ✉ *1340 E. 8th St., Tempe* ☎ *480/303–9967* ⊕ *www.fourpeaks.com.*

SanTan Brewing Company. Come here for good food with great beer and an energetic pub atmosphere without the tired, hole-in-the-wall or overly commercial feel. Wash down some SanTan wings and a stuffed burger with a SanTan IPA. ✉ *8 San Marcos Pl., Chandler* ☎ *480/917–8700* ⊕ *www.santanbrewing.com.*

PERFORMING ARTS

For weekly listings of theater, arts, and music, check out Thursday's *Arizona Republic,* pick up a free issue of the independent weekly *New Times,* or check out *Where Phoenix/Scottsdale Magazine,* available free in most hotels. A good online source of information on events in the Valley is the *Arizona Republic*'s website (⊕ *www.azcentral.com*).

TICKETS **Ticketmaster.** You can buy tickets for nearly every event in the Valley through Ticketmaster. ☎ *800/745–3000* ⊕ *www.ticketmaster.com.*

MAJOR PERFORMANCE VENUES

To feed its growing tourism industry Phoenix has cooked up enticing entertainment venues that attract everything from major-league sporting events to the hottest music acts and the most raved-about theater productions.

DOWNTOWN AND GREATER PHOENIX

Ak-Chin Pavilion. This outdoor amphitheater books major live concerts. ✉ *2121 N. 83rd Ave.* ☎ *602/254–7200.*

Celebrity Theatre. This 2,600-seat theater-in-the-round hosts concerts and other live performances. ✉ *440 N. 32nd St.* ☎ *602/267–1600* ⊕ *www.celebritytheatre.com.*

Comerica Theatre. Phoenix's high-tech, state-of-the-art entertainment venue morphs from an intimate Broadway stage setup to a concert hall seating 5,000. There are great views from almost every seat. ✉ *400 W. Washington St., Downtown Phoenix* ☎ *602/379–2800* ⊕ *www.comericatheatre.com.*

Herberger Theater Center. The home of the Arizona Theatre Company and other local theater companies, this theater also hosts performances of visiting dance troupes, orchestras, and Broadway shows. ✉ *222 E. Monroe St., Downtown Phoenix* ☏ *602/252–8497* ⊕ *www. herbergertheater.org.*

Orpheum Theatre. The Spanish-colonial Orpheum Theatre, built in 1927 and renovated throughout the '90s, is a glamorous theater showcasing ballet, theater, and film festivals. The Phoenix Convention Center coordinates ticketing for the facility. ✉ *203 W. Adams St., Downtown Phoenix* ☏ *602/262–7272* ⊕ *www.phoenixconventioncenter.com/ venues/orpheum-theatre.*

Symphony Hall. The Phoenix Symphony and Arizona Opera perform at Symphony Hall. ✉ *75 N. 2nd St., Downtown Phoenix* ☏ *602/495–1999* ⊕ *www.phoenixsymphony.org.*

SCOTTSDALE

Kerr Cultural Center. Theater, dance, and jazz performances are showcased at this center. ✉ *6110 N. Scottsdale Rd.* ☏ *480/596–2660* ⊕ *www. asukerr.com.*

Scottsdale Center for the Performing Arts. Performances at this cultural and entertainment complex rotate exhibits frequently, but they typically emphasize contemporary art and artists. You might be able to catch a comical, interactive performance of the long-running "Late Night Catechism," or an installation of modern dance or music. The acclaimed Scottsdale Arts Festival is held annually here in March. ✉ *7380 E. 2nd St., Old Town* ☏ *480/499–8587* ⊕ *www.scottsdaleperformingarts.org.*

TEMPE AND AROUND

ASU Gammage. Frank Lloyd Wright designed the ASU Gammage Auditorium, which presents more Broadway shows outside the Big Apple than any other venue in the nation. ✉ *Arizona State University, Mill Ave. at Apache Blvd.* ☏ *480/965–3434* ⊕ *www.asugammage.com.*

Chandler Center for the Arts. To see some of the nation's most popular touring performances for families and children, check out the events schedule at the Chandler Center for the Arts. ✉ *250 N. Arizona Ave., Chandler* ☏ *480/782–2680* ⊕ *www.chandlercenter.org.*

Crescent Ballroom. This small music venue only accommodates 350 people, but has a loyal following for its eclectic calendar of indie acts. There is a lounge open nightly. ✉ *308 N. 2nd Ave., Downtown Phoenix* ☏ *602/716–2222* ⊕ *www.crescentphx.com.*

Marquee Theatre. This venue hosts mainly headlining rock-and-roll entertainers. ✉ *730 N. Mill Ave.* ☏ *480/829–0607* ⊕ *www. luckymanonline.com.*

Mesa Arts Center. This arts organization is fast becoming one of the Valley's top destinations for exhibits, visual-art performances, and A-list concerts. ✉ *1 E. Main St., Mesa* ☏ *480/644–6500* ⊕ *www. mesaartscenter.com.*

Frank Lloyd Wright's architectural legacy in the Valley of the Sun includes ASU Gammage Auditorium in Tempe.

CLASSICAL MUSIC

Arizona Opera. This company stages an opera season in both Tucson and Phoenix. The Phoenix season runs from October to March at Symphony Hall and the Orpheum Theatre. ☎ *602/266–7464* ⊕ *www.azopera.com.*

Phoenix Symphony Orchestra. The resident company at Symphony Hall, the Phoenix Symphony Orchestra features orchestral works from classical and contemporary composers, a chamber series, composer festivals, and outdoor pops concerts. The season runs September through May. ✉ *75 N. 2nd St., Downtown Phoenix* ☎ *602/495–1999, 800/776–9080* ⊕ *www.phoenixsymphony.org.*

DANCE

Ballet Arizona. The state's professional ballet company presents a full season of classical and contemporary works (including pieces commissioned for the company) in Tucson and Phoenix. The season runs October through May. ☎ *602/381–1096* ⊕ *www.balletaz.org.*

THEATER

Actors Theatre of Phoenix. The resident theater troupe at the Herberger Theater Center presents a full season of drama, comedy, and musical productions September through May. ☎ *602/888–0638* ⊕ *www. actorstheatrephx.org.*

Arizona Theatre Company. Based in Tuscon, the Arizona Theatre Company also performs at the Herberger Theater Center. Productions, held September through June, range from classic dramas to musicals and new works by emerging playwrights. ✉ *222 E. Monroe, Downtown Phoenix* ☎ *602/256–6995* ⊕ *www.arizonatheatre.org.*

The Black Theatre Troupe. This troupe presents original and contemporary dramas and musical revues, as well as adventurous adaptations, between September and May. ✉ *Helen K. Mason Performing Arts Center, 1333 E. Washington St., Downtown Phoenix* ☎ *602/258–8129* ⊕ *www.blacktheatretroupe.org.*

FAMILY **Childsplay.** The state's theater company for young audiences and families, Childsplay holds performances during the school year at Tempe Center for the Arts. ✉ *Tempe Center for the Arts, 700 W. Rio Salado Pkwy., Tempe* ☎ *480/921–5700* ⊕ *www.childsplayaz.org.*

EXPERIENCE THE WILD WEST

In addition to the state and county fairs, and some seasonal shows, there are several places in and around Phoenix to get a taste of what the West was like way back when. Rawhide and the Rockin' R Ranch, closer to town, are more kid-friendly, while Pioneer Living History Village and Goldfield Ghost Town (⇨ see Apache Trail) are more sedate, with a stronger emphasis on authentic historic buildings.

FAMILY **Great Arizona Puppet Theater.** With performances in a historic building featuring lots of theater and exhibit space, the Great Arizona Puppet Theatre mounts a yearlong cycle of inventive puppet productions that change frequently. ✉ *302 W. Latham St., Downtown Phoenix* ☎ *602/262–2050* ⊕ *www.azpuppets.org.*

Phoenix Theatre. Across the courtyard from the Phoenix Art Museum, Phoenix Theatre stages musical and dramatic performances. ✉ *100 E. McDowell Rd., Downtown Phoenix* ☎ *602/254–2151* ⊕ *www.phoenixtheatre.com.*

WILD WEST SHOWS

FAMILY
Fodor's Choice
★
Rawhide Western Town and Steakhouse at Wild Horse Pass. A Valley favorite for more than four decades, Rawhide Western Town calls the 2,400-acre master-planned Wild Horse Pass Development in the Gila River Indian Community home. Featuring its legendary steakhouse and saloon, Main Street and all of its retail shops, and the Six Gun Theater, Rawhide is the kitschiest place in town to experience the Old West. Enjoy canal rides along the Gila River Riverwalk, train rides, and a Native American village honoring the history and culture of the Akimel O'othom and Pee Posh tribes. Immerse yourself into the Wild West, where you can watch a stunt show featuring gunslingers, have a fellow guest arrested and tossed in jail, or watch trick roping performed by the pros. ✉ *5700 W. North Loop Rd., Gila River Indian Community, Chandler* ☎ *480/502–5600* ⊕ *www.rawhide.com.*

FAMILY **Rockin' R Ranch.** This ranch includes a petting zoo, a reenactment of a Wild West shoot-out, and—the main attraction—a nightly cookout with a Western stage show. Pan for gold or take a wagon ride until the "vittles" are served, followed by music and entertainment. ✉ *6136 E. Baseline Rd., Mesa* ☎ *480/832–1539* ⊕ *www.rockinr.net.*

Rawhide Western Town, or another Wild West show with dinner, is a great recipe for family fun.

SHOPPING

Since its resorts began multiplying in the 1930s and '40s, Phoenix has acquired many high-fashion clothiers and leisure-wear boutiques, but you can still find the Western clothes that in many parts of town still dominate the fashion. Jeans and boots, cotton shirts and dresses, 10-gallon hats, and bola ties (the state's official neckwear) are still the staples. On the scene as well are the arts of the Southwest's true natives—Navajo weavers, sand painters, and silversmiths; Hopi weavers and kachina-doll carvers; Pima and Tohono O'odham (Papago) basket makers and potters; and many more. Inspired by the region's rich cultural traditions, contemporary artists have flourished here, making Phoenix—particularly Scottsdale, a city with more art galleries than gas stations—one of the Southwest's largest art centers alongside Santa Fe, New Mexico.

Today's shoppers find the best of the old and the new—all presented with Southwestern style. Upscale stores, one-of-a-kind shops, and outlet malls sell the latest fashions, cowboy collectibles, handwoven rugs, traditional Mexican folk art, and contemporary turquoise jewelry.

Most of the Valley's power shopping is concentrated in central Phoenix, Old Town Scottsdale, and the Kierland area in North Scottsdale, but auctions and antiques shops cluster in odd places—and as treasure hunters know, you've always got to keep your eyes open.

GREATER PHOENIX

CAMELBACK CORRIDOR
GIFTS

Cornelia Park. If Alice in Wonderland decided to open a store, it'd be Cornelia Park. An eclectic mix of home furnishings, gifts, and touches of whimsy, this boutique in Biltmore Fashion Park is one of the best places in the Valley to find a treasure or a gift. ⊠ *2502 E. Camelback Rd., Camelback Corridor* ☏ *602/955–3195* ⊕ *www.corneliapark.com.*

FARMERS' MARKETS

To find the fresh wares of a Valley farmers' market, visit ⊕ *www.arizonafarmersmarkets. com,* a comprehensive calendar listing started and maintained by longtime market coordinators Dee and John Logan.

HOME FURNISHINGS

The French Bee. Michael Hansen made a name for himself as a designer of jaw-dropping silk floral arrangements. Those talents eventually turned into the French Bee, a wonderland of flowers, vases, and home furnishings. It's a visual delight. ⊠ *3150 E. Camelback Rd., Scottsdale* ☏ *602/955–4158* ⊕ *www.thefrenchbee.com.*

MARKETS

Camelback Market. On Saturday from 9 am to 1 pm, October through May, some of the Valley's tastiest creations, from crepes to paella to panini, can be found in the parking lot of Vincent on Camelback, at the Camelback Market. The market also features a wine vendor and sellers of independent culinary curios like fresh pesto, honey, and jam. ⊠ *3930 E. Camelback Rd., Camelback Corridor* ⊕ *www.vincentsoncamelback.com.*

SHOPPING CENTER

Biltmore Fashion Park. Macy's, Saks Fifth Avenue, and Ralph Lauren anchor more than 70 stores and upscale boutiques in this posh, park-like setting. It's accessible from the Camelback Esplanade and The Ritz-Carlton by a pedestrian tunnel that runs beneath Camelback Road. ⊠ *2502 E Camelback Rd., Camelback Corridor* ☏ *602/955–8400* ⊕ *www.shopbiltmore.com.*

NORTH CENTRAL PHOENIX
ANTIQUES

Antiques on Central. One of the oldest antiques stores in Phoenix, Antiques on Central is the go-to place to find rare fine china and serving pieces as well as original paintings and antique furnishings. ⊠ *5037 N. Central Ave., North Central Phoenix* ☏ *602/264–4525* ⊕ *www. antiquesoncentral.com.*

ARTS AND CRAFTS

Drumbeat Indian Arts. This small, interesting shop specializes in Native American music, movies, books, drums, and crafts supplies. If you're lucky, you might find authentic fry bread and Navajo tacos being cooked in the parking lot on weekends. ⊠ *4143 N. 16th St., North Central Phoenix* ☏ *602/266–4823* ⊕ *www.drumbeatindianarts.com.*

Fodor'sChoice ★ **The Heard Museum Shop.** The shop at the Heard Museum is hands-down the best place in town for Southwestern Native American and other crafts, both traditional and modern. Prices tend to be high, but quality is assured, with many one-of-a-kind items among the collection of rugs, kachina dolls, pottery, and other crafts; there's also a wide selection of lower-priced gifts. ⊠ *2301 N. Central Ave., North Central Phoenix* ☎ *602/252–8840* ⊕ *www.heard.org.*

FOOD AND WINE

AJ's Fine Foods. The Valley's grandest upscale grocery store, AJ's is a great place to fill your basket with exclusive local creations ranging from salsas and sauces to spice mixes. It's possible to spend hours at any of the 11 identical Valley locations. It's also possible to spend far more money than you would at an average grocery store, but the vast inventory of unusual products not found together anywhere else and the first-class, one-stop shopping experience make it all worthwhile. The wine selection is among the best in town, and the sommelier-quality staff will gladly offer suggestions. Be sure to partake of the fresh, chef-prepared food offerings, like homemade soups, salad, pizza, specialty sandwiches, and gourmet take-out entrées from the bistro. ⊠ *5017 N. Central Ave., North Central Phoenix* ☎ *602/230–7015* ⊕ *www. ajsfinefoods.com.*

VINTAGE CLOTHING AND FURNITURE

Melrose Vintage. The cheerful, dollhouselike yellow exterior at this store is not the only thing that makes it memorable. The no-nonsense staff know their stuff, which includes tasteful and fun low- to high-end shabby-chic furnishings. ⊠ *4238 N. 7th Ave., North Central Phoenix* ☎ *602/636–0300* ⊕ *www.shopmelrosevintage.com.*

PARADISE VALLEY

ARTS AND CRAFTS

Fodor's Choice ★ **Cosanti Originals.** This is the studio where architect Paolo Soleri's famous bronze and ceramic wind chimes are made and sold. You can watch the craftspeople at work, then pick out your own—prices are surprisingly reasonable. ⊠ *6433 Doubletree Ranch Rd., Paradise Valley* ☎ *800/752–3187, 480/948–6145* ⊕ *www.cosanti.com.*

SOUTH PHOENIX

SHOPPING CENTER

COFCO Chinese Cultural Center. Adorned with replicas of pagodas, statues, and traditional Chinese gardens, this shopping and dining facility is the place to find Asian restaurants, gift shops, and the Super L, a huge Asian grocery store. Take a stroll through the market's fish department—you'll

> ### VINTAGE FINDS
>
> In certain parts of the Valley "old" is the new "new." The Melrose District, on 7th Avenue between Indian School and Camelback roads in central Phoenix, is banking on its Old Phoenix charm in a slow but steady race to become the next hip historic neighborhood. New faces on old buildings are the perfect welcome mat for progress with forthcoming lofts, condos, eateries, and big plans for public art, but the overall charm is anchored by its variety of vintage stores. Hours are generally 10–5, and many stores are closed Monday and Tuesday.

forget you're in the desert. ⊠ *668 N. 44th St.* ☎ *602/273–7268* ⊕ *www.phxchinatown.com.*

GLENDALE

A surprise to many visitors is the Old Towne district of suburban Glendale, with more than 80 antiques and collectibles shops nestled around historic Old Towne and Catlin Court, which are listed on the National Register of Historic Places.

ANTIQUES

Glendale Old Towne & Catlin Court. This antiques district has a plethora of shops and restaurants in colorful, century-old bungalows. Stroll the pedestrian-friendly streets and window shop, or have lunch at one of the neighborhood eateries to fuel up for some retail therapy. ⊠ *59th and Glendale aves., Glendale.*

SCOTTSDALE

If you're looking for luxury, whether that's in the form of a priceless work of art or a perfectly fitting pair of jeans, head to Scottsdale. Filled with galleries, luxury boutiques, and more than enough sites to purchase a pair of cowboy boots, Scottsdale takes Western chic to a whole new level.

ANTIQUES

Scottsdale Marketplace. One of the largest antiques stores in the Valley, this marketplace has more than three-dozen privately run booths that feature Asian and French antiques, furnishings, housewares, and a large selection of Western goods. ⊠ *6310 N. Scottsdale Rd.* ☎ *480/368–5720* ⊕ *www.scottsdalemarketplace.com.*

CLOTHING

My Sister's Closet. What began as an idea in this Camelback Corridor space turned into a revolution of resale clothing and furnishings. My Sister's Closet offers upscale resale clothing, shoes, accessories, and, yes, furniture. There are locations across the Valley, but the primary store remains the one at Town & Country Marketplace in Phoenix. You could find a luxury handbag for a third of the price, or a designer suit for pennies on the dollar. All items are guaranteed authentic. ⊠ *2033 E. Camelback Rd.* ☎ *602/954–6080* ⊕ *www.mysisterscloset.com.*

SHOPPING CENTER

Scottsdale Fashion Square. This shopping complex is home to many luxury shops unique to Arizona. There are also Barney's, Nordstrom, Dillard's, Neiman Marcus, Macy's, Louis Vuitton, Tiffany, Cartier, and Gucci. A huge food court, restaurants, and a cineplex complete the picture. ⊠ *7014 E. Camelback Rd.* ☎ *480/941–2140* ⊕ *www.fashionsquare.com.*

NORTH SCOTTSDALE

SHOPPING CENTERS

Kierland Commons. Next to the Westin Kierland Resort is one of the city's most popular shopping areas. "Urban village" is the catchphrase for this outdoor pedestrian mall with restaurants and upscale chain retailers, among them J. Crew and Tommy Bahama. ⊠ *15205 N. Kierland Blvd.* ☎ *480/348–1577* ⊕ *www.kierlandcommons.com.*

Scottsdale Quarter. This outdoor mall creates a fantastic one-two punch for shoppers in search of fantastic food and dining. Stroll the largest Apple Store in the Valley, get bargain goods at H&M, and catch a luxury dine-in movie (you read that right) at iPic. ⊠ *15279 N. Scottsdale Rd., North Scottsdale* ☎ *480/270–8123* ⊕ *www. scottsdalequarter.com.*

> **GO ANTIQUING**
>
> The central-Phoenix corridor, between 7th Street and 7th Avenue, has many antiques stores. Most shops sit north of Thomas and south of Camelback. Prices, though reasonable, are firm at most shops.

SHOPPING DISTRICTS

5th Avenue. Whether you seek handmade Native American arts and crafts, casual clothing, or cacti, you'll find it here—at such landmark shops as Gilbert Ortega and Kactus Jock. ⊠ *5th Ave. between Civic Center Rd. and Stetson Dr., Old Town.*

Main Street Arts District. Gallery after gallery displays artwork in myriad styles—contemporary, Western realism, Native American, and traditional. Several antiques shops are also here; specialties include porcelain and china, jewelry, and Oriental rugs. ⊠ *Bounded by Main St. and 1st Ave., Scottsdale Rd. and 69th St., Old Town.*

Marshall Way Arts District. Galleries that exhibit predominantly contemporary art line the blocks of Marshall Way north of Indian School Road, and upscale gift and jewelry stores can be found here, too. Farther north on Marshall Way across 3rd Avenue are more art galleries and creative stores with a Southwestern flair. ⊠ *Marshall Way from Indian School Rd. to 5th Ave., Old Town.*

OLD TOWN

ARTS AND CRAFTS

Gilbert Ortega Indian Jewelry and Gallery. This retailer has many Native-American shops throughout Scottsdale. Prices are steep, but the products are authentic and the selection is among the best in town. ⊠ *7155 E. 5th Ave., Old Town* ☎ *480/941–9281.*

Saba's Western Wear. After a few hours of kickin' around Scottsdale, it's natural to want an authentic pair of cowboy boots. Saba's has been a Valley fixture for nearly 100 years, selling not only boots but authentic cowboy garb including jeans, shirts, and belts. If you can't find a boot here, you're just not made for boots. ⊠ *7254 Main St., Old Town* ☎ *480/949–7404* ⊕ *www.sabas.com.*

Fodor's Choice ★ **Wilde Meyer Galleries.** With two locations in Scottsdale and another in Tucson, this is the place to go for the true colors of the Southwest. In addition to one-of-a-kind paintings, the galleries also feature rustic, fine-art imports from around the state and the world, including furniture, sculptures, and jewelry. ⊠ *4142 N. Marshall Way, Old Town* ☎ *480/945–2323* ⊕ *www.wildemeyer.com.*

GIFTS

Kactus Jock. This somewhat kitschy Arizona souvenir store sells food, t-shirts, and some art. ⊠ *7233 E. Main St., Old Town* ☎ *480/945–3380* ⊕ *www.kactusjock.com.*

SHOPPING CENTER

Fodor's Choice ★ **Old Town Scottsdale.** This is the place to go for authentic Southwest-inspired gifts, clothing, art, and artifacts. Despite its massive modern neighbors, this area and its merchants have long respected and maintained the single-level brick storefronts that embody Scottsdale's upscale cow-town charm. More than 100 businesses meet just about any aesthetic want or need, including Gilbert Ortega, one of the premier places for fine Native American jewelry and art. Some of Scottsdale's best restaurants are also found in this pleasing maze of merchandizing. ⊠ *Between Scottsdale Rd. and Drinkwater Blvd. from Indian School Rd. to 2nd St., Old Town.*

TEMPE AND AROUND

The East Valley cities of Tempe and Chandler are Phoenix's version of suburbia, offering large shopping malls that cater to families and teens. But don't knock 'em until you've tried 'em. Chandler's primary mall rivals the one in Scottsdale, and Tempe's outlet mall offers some of the best bargains in town—and the city's only aquarium.

CHANDLER

SHOPPING CENTERS

Chandler Fashion Center. This mall features anchor stores Nordstrom, Dillard's, Macy's, and Sears, along with more than 180 other national retail chains such as Coach, Pottery Barn, and the Cheesecake Factory. ⊠ *3111 W. Chandler Blvd., Chandler* ☎ *480/812–8488* ⊕ *www.shopchandlerfashioncenter.com.*

TEMPE

BOOKS

Fodor's Choice ★ **Changing Hands Bookstore.** This bookstore has a large selection of new and used books and often features special book-signings and other events with authors. ⊠ *6428 S. McClintock Dr., Tempe* ☎ *480/730–0205* ⊕ *www.changinghands.com.*

SHOPPING CENTERS

Arizona Mills. This mammoth retail outlet and entertainment destination features more than 175 outlet stores and sideshows, including Off 5th–Saks Fifth Avenue, and Last Call from Neiman Marcus. When you tire of bargain hunting, relax in the food court, cinemas, aquarium, or faux rainforest. ⊠ *5000 S. Arizona Mills Circle, I–10 and Baseline Rd. , Tempe* ☎ *480/491–7300* ⊕ *www.simon.com/mall/arizona-mills.*

Mill Avenue Shops. Named for the landmark Hayden Flour Mill, this is one of the Valley's favorite walk-and-shop experiences. Directly west of the Arizona State University campus and just steps from a Light Rail stop, Mill Avenue is an active melting pot of students, artists, residents, and tourists. Shops include some locally owned stores, mid-range chains, and countless bars and restaurants. The Valley Art Theater is a Mill Avenue institution and Tempe's home of indie cinema. Twice a year (in early December and March–April), the Mill Avenue area is the place to find indie arts and crafts when it hosts the Tempe Festival of the Arts. ⊠ *Mill Ave. between Rio Salado Pkwy. and University Dr., Tempe* ☎ *480/355–6060* ⊕ *www.millavenue.com.*

SPAS

There's no better place for relaxation than at one of Phoenix's rejuvenating resort spas. Many feature Native American–inspired treatments and use indigenous ingredients such as agave and desert clay. In resort spas, you can indulge in such treats as private, rooftop pools, Swiss showers, eucalyptus-scented steam rooms, plunge pools, and more. Most also offer fitness classes and state-of-the-art workout facilities. Why book just a treatment when you could instead enjoy a whole day of pampering?

■TIP➜ Be sure to ask about gratuity when you book your spa treatment. Many resorts automatically add 20% gratuity to the bill. To save a little money, consider booking a multi-treatment package. Often, these packages include built-in discounts and include gratuity. You could save up to 20% on your total bill.

Aji Spa at the Sheraton Wild Horse Pass Resort & Spa. A gem on the grounds of the Gila River Indian community, Aji incorporates its Native American surroundings into every aspect of the spa, from the name ("Aji" is Pima for sanctuary) to its Sonoran design and treatments. A complete spa experience awaits, from the plunge pool to the steam room and exercise facilities. Therapists take extra care to explain the indigenous practices and philosophies behind your treatment, whether it's the luxurious Four Directions scrub or a soothing facial. Enjoy lunch at the always-healthy spa café, and relax poolside at the coed patio that overlooks the resort and surrounding desert. ⊠ *Sheraton Wild Horse Pass Resort & Spa, 5594 W. Wild Horse Pass Blvd., Chandler* ☎ *602/225–0100* ⊕ *www.wildhorsepassresort.com* ☞ *$135 50-minute massage or 50-minute facial; 6-hour spa day with body treatment, massage, lunch, facial, and hand and foot treatment from $530. Hair salon, hot tub (indoor), sauna, steam room. Gym with: cardiovascular machines, weight-training equipment. Services: aromatherapy, facials, hydrotherapy, massage, salon services, scrubs, Vichy shower, wraps. Classes and programs: personal training. Pilates.*

Alvadora at the Royal Palms Resort & Spa. It comes as no surprise that the on-site spa at a resort that has its own Director of Romance offers one of the most romantic spa experiences in Arizona. The full-service Alvadora Spa oozes intimacy; its couples' treatment rooms feature private patios as well as showers and tubs. Public areas include tranquil courtyards and retreat areas that offer repose under the warm desert sun or in air-conditioned comfort. Treatments incorporate herbs, flowers, oils, and minerals from the Mediterranean—a nod to the resort's architecture—as well as orange-infused massages and facials, which are fitting, as the property was an orange grove before the resort's construction. ⊠ *5200 E. Camelback Rd., Camelback Corridor* ☎ *602/977–6400* ⊕ *www.royalpalmshotel.com* ☞ *$150 50-minute massage or 50-minute facial; custom spa day packages available. Hair salon, hot tub (indoor), steam room. Gym with: cardiovascular machines, weight-training equipment. Services: aromatherapy, facials, hydrotherapy, massage, salon services, scrubs, wraps. Classes and programs: meditation, personal training, Pilates, tai chi, yoga.*

Four Seasons Troon North Spa. Although most think of the Four Seasons Troon North as an escape for golfers, its spa proves that there's relaxation to be had away from the links. There are treatments especially for golfers, including a massage that incorporates warm golf balls and stretching to relieve a subpar day. But there's plenty of pampering for those who enjoy life away from the greens. Massages and facials are administered with delicate precision, and body wraps nourish your skin after an exhilarating hike under the desert sun. Be sure to take advantage of the facility's full amenities, including the fitness center and steam room. ✉ *10600 E. Crescent Moon Dr., North Scottsdale* ☎ *480/515–5700* ⊕ *www.fourseasons.com/scottsdale* ☞ *$165 50-minute massage or 50-minute facial; 3-hour spa day with two 50-minute spa treatments, lunch, and a 25-minute spa treatment from $475. Hair salon, sauna, steam room. Gym with: cardiovascular machines, weight-training equipment. Services: aromatherapy, facials, massage, salon services, scrubs, wraps. Classes and programs: meditation, nature walk, personal training, Pilates, tai chi, yoga.*

Joya Spa at Omni Montelucia Resort. This two-story spa offers a stairway to the heavens. Everything here is meticulously handcrafted, hand-picked, or hand-placed to summon the healing spirits. Inspired by the resort's Spanish and Moroccan designs, the spa features plush seating areas, quiet lounges with privacy draping, and a public sun deck. Offering Arizona's only hammam bathing ritual, the spa encourages visitors to linger and absorb the tranquil surroundings—the location at the base of Camelback Mountain doesn't hurt. If you're traveling with a group or searching for a romantic couples' escape, Joya offers a series of poolside treatment rooms that offer the ultimate in luxury and privacy. ✉ *4949 E. Lincoln Dr., Paradise Valley* ☎ *480/627–3200, 888/691–5692* ⊕ *www.joyaspa.com* ☞ *$149 50-minute massage or 50-minute facial; 3-hour spa day with choice of three 50-minute treatments from $365. Hair salon, sauna, pool (outdoor). Gym with: cardiovascular machines, weight-training equipment. Services: aquatherapy, aromatherapy, facials, massage, reflexology, salon services, scrubs, wraps. Classes and programs: guided hikes, personal training, Pilates, yoga.*

Jurlique Spa at FireSky Resort and Spa. With its relaxing interior, Jurlique focuses on repairing and restoring from within by relying on plant science and a combination of Eastern and Western spa philosophies. Keeping with the boutique FireSky Resort's green efforts, spa treatments incorporate natural products that are hypoallergenic and are not animal-tested. Your wallet will get some relaxation, too. Although Jurlique is one of the smallest resort spas in town, it offers some of the most affordable treatments around. ✉ *4925 N. Scottsdale Rd., Scottsdale* ☎ *480/424–6072* ⊕ *www.fireskyresort.com* ☞ *$125 60-minute massage or 60-minute facial; 2-hour spa day with 60-minute massage and facial from $240. Pool (outdoor). Gym with: cardiovascular machines, weight-training equipment. Services: aquatherapy, aromatherapy, facials, massage, scrubs.*

Fodor's Choice ★ **Sanctuary Spa at Sanctuary Camelback Mountain.** Savvy spagoers continue to select Sanctuary as their destination of choice, and with good reason. This sleek spa has 12 Asian-inspired indoor-outdoor treatment rooms nestled at the base of Camelback Mountain. For a more intimate experience, indulge in the privacy of the couple's suite or the stone-walled Sanctum hideaway (only available in the winter and spring). A meditation garden is the perfect place to reflect and relax before or after your treatment; for a longer experience consider a four-day Satori Wellness retreat. ✉ *5700 E. McDonald Dr., Paradise Valley* ☎ *480/607–2326, 800/245–2051* ⊕ *www.sanctuaryoncamelback.com* ☞ *$150 60-minute massage or 60-minute facial; 4-hour spa day with 60-minute massage, 60-minute facial, 60-minute body treatment, manicure, and pedicure from $605. Hair salon, hot tub (indoor), pool (outdoor), steam room. Gym with: cardiovascular machines, weight-training equipment. Services: acupuncture, aquatherapy, aromatherapy, facials, hypnotherapy, massage, reflexology, salon services, scrubs, wraps. Classes and programs: aquaerobics, guided hikes, guided walks, meditation, nutritional counseling, personal training, Pilates, stretching, swim instruction, tai chi, yoga.*

The Spa at JW Marriott Camelback Inn. One of the Valley's most popular spas blends Mediterranean and desert themes. Trained therapists will scrub, wrap, and polish your body to perfection, and use the finest products to massage your muscles and cleanse your pores. You'll want all the pampering after a one-on-one fitness session with one of the resort's trainers who specialize in Pilates and gyrokinesis. Refuel at Sprouts, the on-site café, and finish your day at the outdoor heated lap pool. ✉ *5402 E. Lincoln Dr., Scottsdale* ☎ *480/596–7040, 800/922–2635* ⊕ *www.camelbackspa.com* ☞ *$135 60-minute massage, $155 60-minute facial; 4-hour spa day with 60-minute massage, 60-minute facial, manicure, and pedicure from $360. Hair salon, pool (outdoor), sauna, steam room. Gym with: cardiovascular machines, weight-training equipment. Services: aquatherapy, aromatherapy, facials, massage, reflexology, salon services, scrubs, Vichy shower, wraps. Classes and programs: guided walks, meditation, personal training, Pilates, stretching, yoga.*

Fodor'sChoice
★ **Spa Avania at the Hyatt Regency Scottsdale at Gainey Ranch.** The spa experience here is designed to match your internal clock; every treatment, meal, beverage, and moment is timed to be in tune with your body's natural rhythm. The gorgeous stone-tiled facility seeks to cleanse the body of unnatural stimuli and give equilibrium through the senses, the way nature intended. Don't feel like that standard spa music during your treatment? No worries. Choose the soothing tunes you want on your in–treatment room iPod. Conclude your day with a dip in the mineral pool, and inhale your worries away in the eucalyptus steam room. By day's end, you will indeed feel rejuvenated and back in rhythm. ✉ *7500 E. Doubletree Ranch Rd., Scottsdale* ☎ *480/444–1234* ⊕ *www.scottsdale.hyatt.com* ☞ *$165 60-minute massage or 60-minute facial; 3-hour spa day with 60-minute massage, 60-minute facial, and 60-minute wrap from $490. Hair salon, hot tub (outdoor), pools (outdoor), sauna, steam room. Gym with: cardiovascular machines, weight-training equipment. Services: aquatherapy, facials, massage, salon services, scrubs, Vichy shower, wraps. Classes and programs: guided walks, meditation, personal training, Pilates, stretching, yoga.*

VH Spa at the Hotel Valley Ho. At the always hip Hotel Valley Ho, guests should feel comfortable entrusting renovation of the body and soul to the mod, colorful glass VH (Vitality Health) Spa. You can boost your treatments with a "flight" of antioxidants—what other people might call a glass of wine—because, hey, this is a vacation after all. If you don't feel like venturing south to the spa, you can get in-room treatments. Or, grab a cabana at the pool and get the five-star treatment there. ✉ *6850 E. Main St., Old Town* ☎ *480/248–2000* ⊕ *www.hotelvalleyho. com* ☞ *$125 60-minute massage or 60-minute facial. Hair salon, hot tub (outdoor), pool (outdoor), steam room. Gym with: cardiovascular machines, weight-training equipment. Services: acupuncture, aquatherapy, aromatherapy, facials, massage, reflexology, salon services. Classes and programs: guided hikes, Pilates, yoga.*

Fodor's Choice ★ **Well & Being at Willow Stream Spa, Fairmont Scottsdale Princess.** Perhaps one of the most romantic spa settings in the Valley, Well & Being at Willow Stream Spa is an ideal retreat for couples. A three-story experience, the spa offers more water than seems possible in a desert. Enjoy an afternoon at the rooftop pool—which also includes private cabanas—or cuddle with your loved one under the powerful waterfall that connects the men's and women's locker facilities. Inside, the locker rooms feature plunge pools and hot tubs, aromatherapy rooms, saunas, and steam rooms. After all that relaxation, you're sure to build up an appetite. Good thing the spa café serves fantastic (and healthy) cuisine to enjoy indoors, or in the quaint outdoor atrium. ✉ *Fairmont Scottsdale Princess Resort, 7575 E. Princess Dr., North Scottsdale* ☎ *480/585–4848* ⊕ *www.willowstream.com/scottsdale* ☞ *$169 60-minute massage or 60-minute facial. Hair salon, hot tub (outdoor), pool (outdoor), sauna, steam room. Gym with: cardiovascular machines, weight-training equipment. Services: aquatherapy, aromatherapy, facials, massage, reflexology, salon services, scrubs, wraps. Classes and programs: personal training, Pilates, tennis, yoga.*

SPORTS AND THE OUTDOORS

The mountains surrounding the Valley of the Sun are among its greatest assets, and outdoors enthusiasts have plenty of options within the city limits to pursue hiking, bird-watching, or mountain-biking passions. Piestewa Peak, north of Downtown Phoenix, is popular with hikers, and Camelback Mountain and the Papago Peaks are landmarks between Phoenix and Scottsdale. South of Downtown are the much less lofty peaks of South Mountain Park, which separates the Valley from the rest of the Sonoran Desert. East of the city, beyond Tempe and Mesa, the peaks of the Superstition Mountains—named for their eerie way of seeming just a few miles away—are the first of a range that stretches all the way into New Mexico.

Central Arizona's dry desert heat imposes particular restraints on outdoor endeavors—even in winter hikers and cyclists should wear lightweight opaque clothing, a hat or visor, and high-UV-rated sunglasses, and should carry a quart of water for each hour of activity. The intensity of the sun makes strong sunscreen (SPF 30 or higher) a must, and don't forget to apply it to your hands and feet. ⚠ From May 1 to October 1 you shouldn't jog or hike from one hour after sunrise until a half hour before sunset. During these times the air is so hot and dry that your body will lose moisture at a dangerous, potentially lethal rate. And keep your eyes peeled in natural desert areas; rattlesnakes and scorpions could be on the prowl.

MULTISPORT OUTFITTERS

Arizona Outback Adventures. The knowledgeable and personable staff at AOA lead half-day, full-day, and multiple-day adventures for hikers, bikers, rafters, and kayakers. The guides are extremely knowledgeable about local flora and fauna. Or, you can rent a road bike or a mountain bike to explore the area's mountain regions, parks, and canal paths. ⊠ *16447 N. 91st St., Scottsdale* ☎ *480/945–2881, 866/455–1601* ⊕ *www.aoa-adventures.com.*

BALLOONING

A sunrise or sunset hot-air-balloon ascent is a remarkable desert sightseeing experience. The average fee—there are more than three dozen Valley companies to choose from—is $200 per person, and hotel pickup is usually included. Since flight paths and landing sites vary with wind speeds and directions, a roving land crew follows each balloon in flight. Time in the air is generally between 1 and 1½ hours, but allow 3 hours for the total excursion.

Fodor's Choice ★ **Hot Air Expeditions.** This is the best ballooning in Phoenix. Flights are long, the staff is charming, and the gourmet snacks, catered by the acclaimed Vincent restaurant, are out of this world. ⊠ *Phoenix* ☎ *480/502–6999, 800/831–7610* ⊕ *www.hotairexpeditions.com.*

BICYCLING

There are plenty of gorgeous areas for biking in the Phoenix area, but riding in the streets isn't recommended, as there are few adequate bike lanes in the city. Popular parks such as South Mountain Park and the Tempe Town Lake have miles of trails. ⚠ Note that the desert climate can be tough on cyclists, so make sure you're prepared with lots of water.

Phoenix Parks and Recreation. The Parks and Recreation department has detailed maps of Valley bike paths. ☎ *602/262–6862* ⊕ *www.phoenix. gov/parks* ⊟ *No credit cards.*

Pinnacle Peak. This is a popular place to take bikes for the ride north to Carefree and Cave Creek, or east and south over the mountain pass and down to the Verde River, toward Fountain Hills. ⊠ *26802 N. 102nd Way, 25 miles northeast of Downtown Phoenix, North Scottsdale* ☎ *480/312–0990* ⊕ *www.scottsdaleaz.gov/parks/pinnacle* ⊟ *No credit cards.*

Scottsdale's Indian Bend Wash. This multiuse park system has paths suitable for bikes winding among its golf courses and ponds. ⊠ *Along*

BASEBALL'S SPRING TRAINING

For dyed-in-the-wool baseball fans there's no better place than the Valley of the Sun. Baseball has become nearly a year-round activity in the Phoenix area, beginning with spring training in late February and continuing through the Arizona Fall League championships in mid-November.

SPRING

Today the Cactus League consists of 15 Major League teams that play at stadiums across the Valley. Ticket prices are reasonable, around $7 to $8 for bleacher seats and $15 to $30 for reserved seats. Many stadiums have lawn-seating areas in the outfield, where you can spread a blanket and bring a picnic. Cactus League stadiums are more intimate than big-league parks, and players often come right up to the stands to say hello and to sign autographs.

Tickets for some teams go on sale as early as December. Brochures listing game schedules and ticket information are available from the **Cactus League**'s website (⊕ *www. cactusleague.com*).

SUMMER

During the regular Major League season the hometown Arizona Diamondbacks (⊕ *www. azdiamondbacks.com*) play on natural grass at Chase Field in the heart of Downtown Phoenix. The stadium is a technological wonder; if the weather's a little too warm outside, they close the roof, turn on the gigantic air-conditioners, and keep you cool while you enjoy the game. You can tour the stadium except on afternoon-game days and holidays.

FALL

At the conclusion of the regular season the Arizona Fall League runs until the week before Thanksgiving. Each major-league team sends six of its most talented young prospects to compete with other young promising players—180 players in all. There are six teams in the league, broken down into two divisions. It's a great way to see future Hall of Famers in their early years. Tickets for Fall League games are $6.

Call **Scottsdale Stadium** (☏ *480/312-2586*), one of the league's host sites, for ticket information.

Hayden Rd., from Shea Blvd. south to Indian School Rd., Scottsdale ☏ *480/312-7275* ⊕ *www.scottsdaleaz.gov/parks/greenbelt* ▭ *No credit cards.*

Trail 100. This trail runs throughout the Phoenix Mountain preserve; it's just the thing for mountain bikers. ⊠ *Enter at Dreamy Draw Park, just east of the intersection of Northern Ave. and 16th St., North Central Phoenix* ☏ *602/262-6862* ⊕ *www.phoenix.gov/parks* ▭ *No credit cards.*

FOUR-WHEELING

Taking a jeep through the backcountry has become a popular way to experience the desert's saguaro-covered mountains and curious rock formations. Prices start at around $100 per person.

Desert Dog Hummer Adventures. This operator heads out on half- and full-day Humvee tours to the Four Peaks Wilderness Area in Tonto National Forest and the Sonoran Desert. U-Drive desert cars and ATV tours are also available. ☎ 480/837–3966 ⊕ www.azadventures.com.

Wayward Wind Tours. This operator ventures down to the Verde River on its own trail and offers wilderness cookouts for large groups. ☎ 602/867–7825, 800/804–0480 ⊕ www.waywardwindtours.com.

Wild West Jeep Tours. Special permits allow Wild West Jeep Tours to conduct four-wheeler excursions in the Tonto National Forest, which, in addition to a wild ride, lets you also visit thousand-year-old Indian sites. ☎ 480/922–0144 ⊕ www.wildwestjeeptours.com.

GOLF

Arizona has more golf courses per capita than any other state west of the Mississippi River, making it one of the most popular golf destinations in the United States. The sport is also one of Arizona's major industries, and greens fees can run from $35 at a public course to more than $500 at some of Arizona's premier golfing spots. New courses seem to pop up routinely: there are more than 200 in the Valley (some lighted at night), and the PGA's Southwest section has its headquarters here.

MUNICIPAL COURSES

Fodor'sChoice
★ **ASU Karsten Golf Course.** NCAA champions train at this Arizona State University 18-hole golf course. ✉ 1125 E. Rio Salado Pkwy. ☎ 480/921–8070 ⊕ www.asukarsten.com ⛳ $110 weekdays, $130 weekends ⚑ 18 holes, 4765 yards, par 70.

Encanto Park. There are attractive, affordable public 9- and 18-hole courses at Encanto Park. ✉ 2775 N. 15th Ave., Phoenix ☎ 602/253–3963 ⊕ phoenix.gov/parks ⛳ $35 weekdays, $43 weekends ⚑ 18 holes, 6386 yards, par 70.

Papago Golf Course. Phoenix's best municipal course, Papago Golf Course is low-priced and has 18 holes. ✉ 5595 E. Moreland St., Phoenix ☎ 602/275–8428 ⊕ papagogolfcourse.net ⛳ $74 weekdays, $80 weekends ⚑ 18 holes, 7333 yards, par 72.

PUBLIC COURSES

Fodor'sChoice
★ **Gold Canyon Golf Club.** Near Apache Junction in the East Valley, Gold Canyon Golf Club offers fantastic views of the Superstition Mountains and challenging golf. ✉ 6100 S. King's Ranch Rd., Gold Canyon ☎ 480/982–9090, 800/827–5281 ⊕ www.gcgr.com ⛳ Dinosaur Mountain: $179 weekdays, $195 weekends. Sidewinder: $89 weekdays, $110 weekends ⚑ Dinosaur Mountain: 18 holes, 6653 yards, par 72. Sidewinder: 18 holes, 6533 yds, par 72.

Grayhawk. This 36-hole course has beautiful mountain views. In summer the greens fee is much lower. ✉ 8620 E. Thompson Peak Pkwy.,

North Scottsdale ☎ *480/502–1800* ⊕ *www.grayhawkgolf.com* ✉ *$215 weekdays, $245 weekends* 🏌 *Talon: 18 holes, 6973 yards, par 72. Raptor: 18 holes, 7135 yards, par 72.*

Hillcrest Golf Club. With 18 holes on 179 acres of well-designed turf, Hillcrest Golf Club is the best course in the Sun Cities development. ✉ *20002 Star Ridge Dr., Sun City West* ☎ *623/584–1500* ⊕ *www. hillcrestgolfclub.com* ✉ *$50 weekdays, $55 weekends* 🏌 *18 holes, 7002 yards, par 70.*

Raven Golf Club—Phoenix. Thousands of Aleppo pines and Lombardy poplars at this course make it a cool, shady 18-hole haven for summertime golfers. ✉ *3636 E. Baseline Rd., South Phoenix* ☎ *602/243–3636* ⊕ *www.ravenphx.com* ✉ *$135 weekdays, $150 weekends* 🏌 *18 holes, 7078 yards, par 72.*

SunRidge Canyon. East of Scottsdale, SunRidge Canyon is a great 18-hole course for both the low handicapper and those who score above 100. The incredible mountain views are almost distracting. ✉ *13100 N. SunRidge Dr., Fountain Hills* ☎ *480/837–5100* ⊕ *www.sunridgegolf.com* ✉ *$190* 🏌 *18 holes, 6823 yds. Par 71.*

Fodor's Choice **Troon North.** This course is a challenge for the length alone (7,070 yards).
★ The million-dollar views add to the experience at this perfectly maintained 36-hole course. ✉ *10320 E. Dynamite Blvd., North Scottsdale* ☎ *480/585–7700* ⊕ *www.troonnorthgolf.com* ✉ *$175 weekdays, $259 weekends* 🏌 *Monument: 18 holes, 7070 yards, par 72. Pinnacle: 18 holes, 7025 yards, par 71.*

RESORT COURSES

Arizona Biltmore Country Club. The granddaddy of Valley golf courses, Arizona Biltmore Country Club has two 18-hole PGA championship courses, lessons, and clinics. ✉ *Arizona Biltmore Resort & Spa, 24th St. and Missouri Ave., Camelback Corridor, Phoenix* ☎ *602/955–9655* ⊕ *www.arizonabiltmore.com* ✉ *$129* 🏌 *Adobe: 18 holes, 6430 yards, par 71/72. Links: 18 holes, 6300 yards, par 71.*

Camelback Golf Club. Challenging water holes and layouts make the two 18-hole courses at the JW Marriott's Camelback Golf Club one of the best in the area. ✉ *JW Marriott Camelback Inn, 7847 N. Mockingbird Lane, Paradise Valley* ☎ *480/948–1700* ⊕ *www.camelbackinn. com* ✉ *Padre $169, Ambiente $199* 🏌 *Padre: 18 holes, 6903 yards, par 72. Ambiente: 18 holes. 7225 yards, par 72.*

Lookout Mountain Golf Club. This property at the Pointe Hilton Tapatio Cliffs has pristine greens, beautiful mountain views, and one 18-hole, par-71 course. ✉ *Pointe Hilton at Tapatio Cliffs, 11111 N. 7th St., North Central Phoenix* ☎ *602/866–6356* ⊕ *www.tapatiocliffshilton. com* ✉ *$109* 🏌 *18 holes, 6515 yds. Par 72.*

Ocotillo Golf Resort. There's water in play on nearly all 27 holes at Ocotillo Golf Resort, which was designed around 95 acres of man-made lakes. ✉ *3751 S. Clubhouse Dr., Chandler* ☎ *480/917–6660* ⊕ *www. ocotillogolf.com* ✉ *$129* 🏌 *Blue/Gold: 18 holes, 7016 yards, par 72. White/Gold: 18 holes, 6804 yards, par 70. Blue/White: 18 holes, 6782 yards, par 71.*

The Valley of the Sun is a popular destination for golfing with more than 200 courses in the area.

Fodor'sChoice
★
The Phoenician Golf Club. Set at the base of Camelback Mountain, the Phoenician offers three nine-hole courses in one of the most picturesque settings in the Valley. ✉ *The Phoenician, 6000 E. Camelback Rd., Camelback Corridor, Scottsdale* ☎ *480/941–8200* ⊕ *www.thephoenician. com* ✉ *$209* ⚑ *Desert: 9 holes, 3060 yards, par 35. Canyon: 9 holes, 3008 yards, par 35. Oasis: 9 holes, 3202 yards, par 35.*

Tournament Players Club of Scottsdale. This 36-hole course by Tom Weiskopf and Jay Morrish is the site of the PGA Waste Management Phoenix Open, which takes place in January–February. ✉ *Fairmont Scottsdale Princess Resort, 17020 N. Hayden Rd., North Scottsdale* ☎ *480/585–4334, 888/400–4001* ⊕ *www.tpc.com* ✉ *Stadium $299, Champions $146* ⚑ *Stadium: 18 holes, 7216 yards, par 71. Champions: 18 holes, 7115 yards, par 71.*

Wigwam Golf and Country Club. This country club is the home of the famous Gold Course, as well as two other 18-hole courses. ✉ *Wigwam Resort, 300 E. Wigwam Blvd., Litchfield Park* ☎ *623/935–3811* ⊕ *www.wigwamresort.com* ✉ *$99 weekdays, $109 weekends* ⚑ *Patriot: 18 holes, 6001 yards, par 70. Gold: 18 holes, 7430 yards, par 72. Heritage: 18 holes, 6852 yards, par 72.*

HIKING

One of the best ways to see the beauty of the Valley of the Sun is from above, so hikers of all calibers seek a vantage point in the mountains surrounding the flat Valley. A short drive from Downtown, South Mountain Park (⇨ *see Exploring*) is the jewel of the city's mountain park preserves, with more than 60 miles of marked trails for hikers, horseback riders, and mountain bikers. ■ **TIP→ No matter the season, be sure to bring sunscreen, a hat, plenty of water, and a camera to capture a dazzling sunset. It's always a good idea to tell someone where you'll be and when you plan to return.**

Phoenix Mountain Preserve System. Much of Phoenix's famous mountains and hiking trails are part of the Phoenix Mountain Preserve, a series of mountains that encircles the Valley. The city's park rangers can help plan your hikes. ☎ *602/262–6862* ⊕ *www.phoenix.gov/parks.*

BEST SPOTS

Camelback Mountain and Echo Canyon Recreation Area. This recreation area has intermediate to difficult hikes up the Valley's most outstanding central landmark. *Difficult.* ⊠ *Tatum Blvd. and McDonald Dr., Paradise Valley* ☎ *602/262–6862 for Phoenix Parks & Recreation Dept.* ⊕ *www.phoenix.gov/parks.*

Lost Dog Wash Trail. Part of the continually expanding McDowell-Sonoran Preserve (⊕ *www.mcdowellsonoran.org*), Lost Dog Wash Trail is a mostly gentle 4.5-mile round trip that will get you away from the bustle of the city in a hurry. The trailhead has restrooms and a map that shows a series of trails for varying skill levels. *Easy.* ⊠ *23015 N. 128th St., north of Shea Blvd., North Scottsdale* ☎ *480/312–7013* ⊕ *www.scottsdaleaz.gov/preserve.*

FAMILY **The Papago Peaks.** These peaks were sacred sites for the Tohono O'odham. The soft-sandstone peaks contain accessible caves, some petroglyphs, and splendid views of much of the Valley. This is a good spot for family hikes. *Easy.* ⊠ *625 N. Galvin Pkwy., Phoenix* ☎ *602/262–6862* ⊕ *www.phoenix.gov/parks.*

Piestewa Peak. Just north of Lincoln Drive, Piestewa Peak has a series of trails for all levels of hikers. It's a great place to get views of downtown. Allow about 1½ hours for each direction. *Moderate.* ⊠ *2701 E. Piestewa Peak Dr., North Central Phoenix* ☎ *602/262–6862* ⊕ *www.phoenix.gov/parks.*

Pinnacle Peak Trail. This is a well-maintained trail offering a moderately challenging 3.5-mile round-trip hike—or a horseback experience for those who care to round up a horse at the local stables. Interpretive programs and trail signs along the way describe the geology, flora, fauna, and cultural history of the area. *Moderate.* ⊠ *26802 N. 102nd Way, 1 mile south of Dynamite and Alma School Rds., North Scottsdale* ☎ *480/312–0990* ⊕ *www.scottsdaleaz.gov/parks/pinnacle.*

FAMILY
Fodor'sChoice
★
Waterfall Trail. Part of the 25 miles of trails available at the White Tank Mountian Regional Park, this short and easy trail is kid-friendly. Strollers and wheelchairs roll along easily to Petroglyph Plaza, which boasts 1,500-year-old boulder carvings—dozens are in clear view from the trail. From there the trail takes a rockier but manageable course to a waterfall, which, depending on area rainfall, can be cascading, creeping, or completely dry. Stop at the visitor center to view desert reptiles such as the king snake and a gopher snake in the aquariums. *Easy.* ⊠ *20304 W. White Tank Mountain Rd., Waddell* ☎ *623/935–2505* ⊕ *www.maricopa.gov/parks/white_tank.*

HORSEBACK RIDING

More than two dozen stables and equestrian-tour outfitters in the Valley attest to the saddle's enduring importance in Arizona—even in this auto-dominated metropolis. Stables offer rides for an hour, a whole day, and even some overnight adventures. Some local resorts can arrange for lessons on-site or at nearby stables.

Arizona Cowboy College. The wranglers here will teach you everything you need to know about ridin', ropin', and ranchin'. ⊠ *30208 N. 152nd St., North Scottsdale* ☎ *480/471–3151* ⊕ *www.cowboycollege.com.*

MacDonald's Ranch. This ranch offers one- and two-hour trail rides and guided breakfast, lunch, and dinner rides through desert foothills above Scottsdale. ⊠ *26540 N. Scottsdale Rd., North Scottsdale* ☎ *480/585–0239* ⊕ *www.macdonaldsranch.com.*

Fodor'sChoice ★ **OK Corrals & Stable.** One-, two-, and four-hour horseback trail rides and steak cookouts are available from this company, which also runs one- to three-day horse-packing trips. They have the oldest pack station in the history of the Superstition Mountains, and all their guides are U.S. Forest Service–licensed. ⊠ *2655 E. Whiteley St., Apache Junction* ☎ *480/982–4040* ⊕ *www.okcorrals.com.*

Ponderosa Stables. You can enjoy your South Mountain experience from a higher perch. Consider renting horses at this nearby stable. This private company rents its land from the city of Phoenix, and will take you on an excursion, or send you on one of your own. ⊠ *10215 S. Central Ave., South Phoenix* ☎ *602/268–1261* ⊕ *www.arizona-horses.com.*

RAFTING

Desert Voyagers. This operator specializes in guided raft and kayak trips on the Verde and Salt rivers. ☎ *480/998–7238* ⊕ *www.desertvoyagers. com.*

SAILPLANING–SOARING

Turf Soaring School. Scenic sailplane rides from this company last from 20 to 30 minutes. Rates are from $109 per person. ⊠ *8700 W. Carefree Hwy., Peoria* ☎ *602/439–3621* ⊕ *www.turf-soaring.com.*

TENNIS

With all the blue sky and sunshine in the Valley, it's a perfect place to play tennis or watch the pros. Most major resorts, such as the Phoenician, Wigwam, Fairmont Scottsdale Princess, and JW Marriott Desert Ridge (and many smaller properties), have tennis courts. Granted, tennis plays second fiddle to golf here—but many of the larger resorts offer package tennis deals. If you're not staying at a resort, there are more than 60 public facilities in the area.

Kiwanis Park Recreation Center. This center has 15 lighted premier-surface courts (all for same-day or one-day-advance reserve). ⊠ *6111 S. All America Way, Tempe* ☎ *480/350–5201* ⊕ *www.tempe.gov/kiwanis.*

Scottsdale Ranch Park. Lessons are available at this city facility, which has 12 lighted courts. ⊠ *10400 E. Via Linda, North Scottsdale* ☎ *480/312–7774* ⊕ *www.scottsdaleaz.gov/parks/srp.*

TUBING

The Valley may not be known for its wealth of water, but locals manage to make the most of what there is. A popular summer stop is the northeast side of the Salt River, where sun worshippers can rent an inner tube and float down the river for an afternoon. Tubing season runs from May to September. Several Valley outfitters rent tubes. Make sure you bring lots of sunscreen, a hat, water—and a rope for attaching your cooler to a tube.

Salt River Recreation. This outfitter offers shuttle-bus service to and from your starting point and rents tubes for $17 (cash only) for the day. It's open during summer months only. ⊠ *Usery Pass and Power Rd., Mesa* ☎ *480/984–3305* ⊕ *www.saltrivertubing.com.*

SIDE TRIPS NEAR PHOENIX

There are a number of interesting sights within a 1- to 1½-hour drive of Phoenix. To the north, the thriving artist communities of Carefree and Cave Creek are popular Western attractions. Arcosanti and Wickenburg are half- or full-day trips from Phoenix. Stop along the way to visit the petroglyphs of Deer Valley Rock Art Center and the reenactments of Arizona territorial life at the Pioneer Living History Village. You also might consider Arcosanti and Wickenburg as stopovers on the way to or from Flagstaff, Prescott, or Sedona.

South of Phoenix, an hour's drive takes you back to prehistoric times and the site of Arizona's first known civilization at Casa Grande Ruins National Monument, a vivid reminder of the Hohokam who began farming this area more than 1,500 years ago.

DEER VALLEY ROCK ART CENTER

15 miles north of Downtown Phoenix.

Any visit to Arizona requires a viewing of petroglyphs, and the Deer Valley Rock Art Center is one of the best in the state. Its close location to the Valley makes it a no-brainer stop.

GETTING HERE AND AROUND
Take Interstate 17 north from Phoenix for 15 miles, exit at West Deer Valley Road, and drive 2 miles west.

EXPLORING
Deer Valley Rock Art Center. This is the largest concentration of ancient petroglyphs in the metropolitan Phoenix area. Some 1,500 of the cryptic symbols are here, left behind by Native American cultures that lived in the Valley (or passed through) during the last 1,000 years. After watching a video about the petroglyphs, pick up a pair of binoculars ($1) and an informative trail map and set out on the 0.25-mile

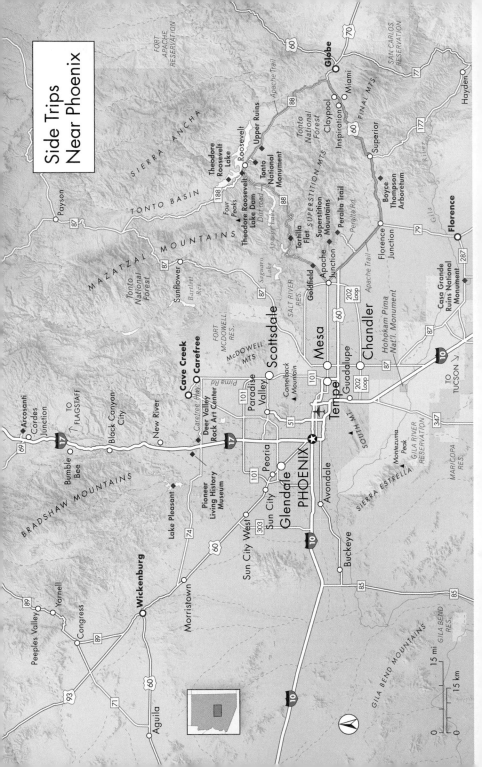

Side Trips Near Phoenix

path. Telescopes point to some of the most skillful petroglyphs; they range from human and animal forms to more abstract figures. ⇨ *Also see Petroglyphs CloseUp box in Chapter 6, Eastern Arizona.* ⊠ *3711 W. Deer Valley Rd., Phoenix* ☎ *623/582–8007* ⊕ *dvrac.asu.edu* ▱ *$7* ⊘ *Oct.–Apr., Tues.–Sat. 9–5.*

PIONEER LIVING HISTORY VILLAGE

25 miles north of Downtown Phoenix.

It's easy to wonder what places in Arizona were like 100 years ago or more. A trip to the Pioneer Living History Village provides an answer. Here you can get a glimpse at 19th-century living in the desert.

GETTING HERE AND AROUND

Take Interstate 17 north from Downtown Phoenix for 25 miles. Just north of Carefree Highway (AZ 74), take Exit 225, and turn left on Pioneer Road to get to the entrance.

EXPLORING

FAMILY **Pioneer Living History Museum.** This museum contains 28 original and reconstructed buildings from throughout territorial Arizona. Costumed guides filter through the bank, schoolhouse, and print shop, as well as the Pioneer Opera House, where classic melodramas are performed daily. It's popular with the grade-school field-trip set, and it's your lucky day if you can tag along for their tour of the site—particularly when John the Blacksmith forges, smelts, and answers questions that adults are too know-it-all to ask. ⊠ *3901 W. Pioneer Rd., Pioneer* ☎ *623/465–1052* ⊕ *www.pioneeraz.org* ▱ *$9* ⊘ *Sept.–May, Wed.–Sun. 9–4; June–Aug., Wed.–Sun. 7–11.*

CAVE CREEK AND CAREFREE

30 miles north of Downtown Phoenix.

Some 30 miles north of Phoenix, resting high in the Sonoran Desert at an elevation of 2,500 feet, the towns of Cave Creek and Carefree look back to a lifestyle far different from that of their more populous neighbors to the south.

Cave Creek got its start with the discovery of gold in the region. When the mines and claims "played out," the cattlemen arrived, and the sounds of horse hooves and lowing cattle replaced those of miners' picks. The area grew slowly and independently from Phoenix to the south, until a paved road connected the two in 1952. Today the mile-long main stretch of town on Cave Creek Road is a great spot to have some hot chili and cold beer, try on Western duds, or learn the two-step in a "cowboy" bar. You're likely to run into folks dressed in cowboy hats, boots, and bold belt buckles. Horseback riders and horse-drawn wagons have the right of way here, and the 25 mph speed limit is strictly enforced by county deputies. You can amble up the hill and rent a horse for a trip into the Tonto National Forest in search of some long-forgotten native petroglyphs or take a jeep tour out to the forest.

Just about the time the dirt-road era ended in Cave Creek, planners were sketching out a new community, which became neighboring Carefree. The world's largest sundial, at the town's center, is surrounded by crafts shops, galleries, artists' workshops, and cafés. Today Cave Creek and Carefree sit cheek by jowl—but the former has beans, beef, biscuits, and beer, while the latter discreetly orders up a notch or two.

GETTING HERE AND AROUND

Follow Interstate 17 north of Downtown Phoenix for 15 miles. Exit at Carefree Highway (AZ 74) and turn right, then go 12 miles. Turn left onto Cave Creek Road and go 3 miles to downtown Cave Creek, then another 4 miles on Cave Creek Road to Carefree. Pick up maps and information about the area at the Chamber of Commerce.

ESSENTIALS

Visitor Information Carefree–Cave Creek Chamber of Commerce ✉ *748 Easy St., No. 9* ☎ *480/488–3381* 🌐 *www.carefreecavecreek.org* 🕒 *Weekdays 8–4.*

EXPLORING

Cave Creek Museum. Exhibits at the Cave Creek Museum depict pioneer living, mining, and ranching. See the last original 1920s tuberculosis cabin and a collection of Indian artifacts from the Hohokam and Yavapai tribes. ✉ *6140 E. Skyline Dr., Cave Creek* ☎ *480/488–2764* 🌐 *www.cavecreekmuseum.org* 🎟 *$5* 🕒 *Oct.–May, Wed., Thurs., and weekends 1–4:30, Fri. 10–4:30.*

FAMILY **Frontier Town.** This pseudo-Western Frontier Town has wooden sidewalks, ramshackle buildings, and souvenir shops. ✉ *6245 E. Cave Creek Rd., Cave Creek* 🌐 *www.frontiertownaz.com.*

WHERE TO EAT

$$$$ MODERN AMERICAN Fodor's Choice ★

🍴 **Binkley's Restaurant.** This upscale restaurant is a diamond in the Valley's last bit of rough. In a town of cowboy bars and gut bombs, chef Kevin Binkley puts together world-class tasting menus that feature delicate portions of such dishes as black-truffle croque-madame, red-wine-braised octopus, and duck with bok choy and ginger. The menu changes daily, so be prepared for some delicious surprises. [$] *Average main: $45* ✉ *6920 E. Cave Creek Rd., Cave Creek* ☎ *480/437–1072* 🌐 *www.binkleysrestaurant.com* ✍ *Reservations essential* 🕒 *Closed Sun. and Mon. No lunch.*

$$ AMERICAN

🍴 **Cave Creek Smokehouse.** Some might remember this location as the Satisfied Frog, and while it keeps changing its name, locals still go here for a beer, some nachos and barbecue, and an authentic Cave Creek experience. [$] *Average main: $16* ✉ *6245 E. Cave Creek Rd., Cave Creek* ☎ *480/488–3317* 🌐 *www.cavecreeksmokehouse.net.*

$$ AMERICAN

🍴 **Horny Toad Restaurant.** Cave Creek's oldest restaurant is a rustic spot for barbecued pork ribs and steak, but the real star is the fried chicken. The quirky menu features a range of fare from soup "de joor" to Icelandic cod and carne asada. [$] *Average main: $17* ✉ *6738 E. Cave Creek Rd., Cave Creek* ☎ *480/488–9542* 🌐 *www.thehornytoad.com.*

$$$ AMERICAN

🍴 **Tonto Bar & Grill at Rancho Manana.** Old West ambience oozes from every corner of the Tonto Bar & Grill, from the hand-carved ceiling beams to the *latilla*-covered (stick-covered) patios with views of the pristine

Sonoran Desert. Try the cowboy Cobb salad or the Tonto burger piled with fried onions and cheddar for lunch; root beer–braised short ribs or onion-crusted walleye are good choices at dinner. $ *Average main: $25* ⊠ *5736 E. Rancho Manana Blvd., Cave Creek* ☎ *480/488–0698* ⊕ *www.tontobarandgrill.com.*

WHERE TO STAY

$$$
RESORT
Fodor'sChoice
★

The Boulders, a Waldorf Astoria Resort. One of the country's top resorts— and one of the few with an all-organic approach—hides amid hill-size, 12-million-year-old granite boulders and the lush Sonoran Desert. **Pros:** remote desert getaway; in the center of Cave Creek and Carefree shopping, events, and activities. **Cons:** on-site dining is priced above average; minimum 45-minute drive to Phoenix attractions. $ *Rooms from: $299* ⊠ *34631 N. Tom Darlington Dr., Cave Creek* ☎ *480/488–9009, 888/579–2631* ⊕ *www.theboulders.com* ⇗ *160 casitas, 61 villas and haciendas* �[Ⓞ] *No meals.*

$$
HOTEL

Cave Creek Tumbleweed Hotel. The 1950s flavor of this Western hotel fits perfectly with Cave Creek's style. **Pros:** a true Old West experience; quite affordable compared to the pricey area competition. **Cons:** sparse accommodations; no frills; far drive from Phoenix and Scottsdale activities. $ *Rooms from: $179* ⊠ *6333 E. Cave Creek Rd., Cave Creek* ☎ *480/488–3668* ⊕ *www.tumbleweedhotel.com* ⇗ *32 rooms, 8 casitas* ⏇ *No meals.*

NIGHTLIFE

Buffalo Chip Saloon. Watch real cowboys and cowgirls two-step to live music at this saloon, where you can also gorge on mesquite-grilled chicken and buffalo chips—hot, homemade potato chips. Reservations are suggested for the all-you-can-eat Friday-night fish fry that draws crowds. There's live music and dancing just about every night. ⊠ *6811 E. Cave Creek Rd., Cave Creek* ☎ *480/488–9118* ⊕ *www. buffalochipsaloon.com.*

Harold's Cave Creek Corral. Harold's has two full bars, a huge dance floor with live bands on weekends, a game room, 15 TVs, and a restaurant— serving some of the best ribs in the Valley. It's also the go-to place to watch Pittsburgh Steelers games during the NFL season. ⊠ *6895 E. Cave Creek Rd., Cave Creek* ☎ *480/488–1906* ⊕ *www.haroldscorral.com.*

SHOPPING

Cave Creek and Carefree have a thriving arts community, with hundreds of artists and dozens of galleries.

SHOPPING CENTERS

el Pedregal. Set at the foot of a 250-foot boulder formation, el Pedregal is a two-tier shopping plaza. In spring and summer there are open-air Thursday-night concerts in the courtyard amphitheater. In addition to its posh boutiques and specialty stores, el Pedregal is home to some of the finest art galleries in the area. ⊠ *34505 N. Scottsdale Rd., at Carefree Hwy.* ☎ *480/488–1072* ⊕ *www.elpedregal.com.*

Spanish Village. This outdoor shopping area includes a bell tower, fountains, courtyards, and winding alleyways. You can while away an afternoon browsing 30 shops, then contemplate dinner at one of several casual restaurants. ⊠ *Ho and Hum Rds.*

SPAS

Waldorf Astoria Spa. If you're seeking the serenity of the desert, this is the place. Influenced by Asian and Native American cultures, the soothing Southwestern spa is divided into two wings—east for relaxation and west for activity, which includes a movement studio for Pilates, tai chi, and yoga. Walk through the outdoor, Hopi-inspired tranquility labyrinth, or schedule a visit with the spa's resident astrologer. The services menu includes traditional treatments such as massages or facials, as well as signature Waldorf Astoria experiences such as chakra balancing, hypnotherapy, and detoxification. With a range of treatments like this, it's no wonder vacationers choose the Boulders specifically for its spa. ⊠ *The Boulders, a Waldorf Astoria Resort, 34631 N. Tom Darlington Dr.* 🖀 *480/595–3500* ⊕ *www.theboulders.com/waldorf-astoria-spa* ☞ *$145 50-minute massage, $145 50-minute facial; 4-hour spa day with complete massage, facial, wrap, and lunch from $39. Hair salon, sauna, soaking bath, pool (outdoor), steam room, whirlpool (outdoor). Gym with: cardiovascular machines, weight-training equipment. Services: acupuncture, aquatherapy, aromatherapy, facials, massage, reflexology, salon services, scrubs, Vichy shower, wraps. Classes and programs: guided hikes, guided walks, meditation, mountain biking, nature walk, personal training, Pilates, rock climbing, stretching, tai chi, water fitness, yoga.*

SPORTS AND THE OUTDOORS

GOLF

Boulders Resort Golf Club. There are two championship 18-hole courses at this club, which has one of the most unique settings in the Valley. The Jay Morrish–designed courses wind around the granite boulders for which the resort is named. ⊠ *The Boulders, 34631 N. Tom Darlington Dr., Carefree* 🖀 *480/488–9009, 888/579–2631* ⊕ *www.theboulders. com* 🖃 *$175* ⚑ *North Course: 18 holes, 6811 yards, par 72. South Course: 18 holes, 6726 yards, par 71.*

HORSEBACK RIDING

Spur Cross Stables. Well-cared-for horses will take you on one- to six-hour rides to the high Sonoran Desert of the Spur Cross Preserve and the Tonto National Forest. Some rides include visits to petroglyph sites and a saddlebag lunch. ⊠ *44029 Spur Cross Rd., Cave Creek* 🖀 *480/488–9117, 800/758–9530* ⊕ *www.horsebackarizona.com.*

WICKENBURG

70 miles northwest of Downtown Phoenix.

This town, land of guest ranches and tall tales, is named for Henry Wickenburg, whose nearby Vulture Mine was the richest gold strike in the Arizona Territory. In the late 1800s Wickenburg was a booming mining town on the banks of the Hassayampa River, with a seemingly endless supply of gold, copper, and silver. Nowadays Wickenburg's Old West history attracts visitors to its sleepy downtown and Western museum. There's a group of good antiques shops, most of which are on Tegner and Frontier streets.

GETTING HERE AND AROUND

Follow Interstate 17 north from Phoenix for about 15 miles to the Carefree Highway (AZ 74) junction. About 30 miles west on AZ 74, take U.S. 89/93 north and go another 10 miles to Wickenburg.

Maps for self-guided walking tours of the town's historic buildings are available at the Wickenburg Chamber of Commerce, in the town's old Santa Fe Depot.

ESSENTIALS

Visitor Information Wickenburg Chamber of Commerce ✉ *216 N. Frontier St.* ☎ *928/684–5479, 800/942–5242* 🌐 *www.wickenburgchamber.com.*

EXPLORING

FAMILY **Desert Caballeros Western Museum.** Boasting one of the best collections of Western art in the nation, this museum has paintings and sculpture by Frederic Remington, Albert Bierstadt, Joe Beeler (founder of the Cowboy Artists of America), and others. Kids enjoy the re-creation of a turn-of-the-20th-century Main Street that includes a general store, period clothing, and a large collection of cowboy gear. ✉ *21 N. Frontier St.* ☎ *928/684–2272* 🌐 *www.westernmuseum.org* 🎟 *$9* 🕒 *Mon.–Sat. 10–5, Sun. noon–4.*

Hassayampa River Preserve. Self-guided trails here wind through lush cottonwood-willow forests, mesquite trees, and around a 4-acre, spring-fed pond and marsh habitat. Waterfowl, herons, and Arizona's rarest raptors shelter here. ✉ *49614 U.S. 60, 3 miles southeast of Wickenburg* ☎ *928/684–2772* 🌐 *www.nature.org/hassayampa* 🎟 *$5* 🕒 *Mid-Sept.–mid-May, Wed.–Sun. 8–5. Summer hrs vary depending on fire danger and weather; call to confirm.*

Jail Tree. On the northeast corner of Wickenburg Way and Tegner Street, check out the Jail Tree, to which prisoners were chained, the desert heat sometimes finishing them off before their sentences were served.

WHERE TO EAT AND STAY

$ MEXICAN 🍴 **Anita's Cocina.** Reliable Tex-Mex fare is served at Anita's. The fresh tamales are tasty for lunch or dinner. Try a fruit burrito for dessert. [$] *Average main: $8* ✉ *57 N. Valentine St.* ☎ *928/684–5777* 🌐 *anitascocina.com.*

$$$$ RESORT FAMILY Fodor's Choice ★ 🏨 **Rancho de los Caballeros.** This 20,000-acre property combines the guest-ranch experience with first-class amenities. **Pros:** large rooms, casitas, and suites; abundant activity roster; a great place for family gatherings. **Cons:** remote location; long hikes to rooms. [$] *Rooms from: $485* ✉ *1551 S. Vulture Mine Rd.* ☎ *928/684–5484, 800/684–5030* 🌐 *www.sunc.com* 🛏 *79 casitas* 🕒 *Closed mid-May–early Oct.* 🍽 *All meals.*

NIGHTLIFE

Rancher Bar. Real live wranglers and cowboys meet up at this modern-day saloon to shoot some pool, and the breeze, after a hard day's work. ✉ *910 W. Wickenburg Way* ☎ *928/684–5957.*

ARCOSANTI

65 miles north of Downtown Phoenix.

Off the beaten path near Cordes Junction is the unusual community started by Italian architect Paolo Soleri, Arcosanti. Tourists visit partially to stretch their legs and see the grounds, but mostly to buy a sought-after wind chime.

GETTING HERE AND AROUND

From Phoenix, take Interstate 17 north 65 miles to Exit 262 (Cordes Junction). Follow the partly paved road 2½ miles northeast to the community.

EXPLORING

Arcosanti. The evolving complex and community of Arcosanti was masterminded by Italian architect Paolo Soleri to be a self-sustaining habitat in which architecture and ecology function in symbiosis. Building began in 1970, but Arcosanti hasn't quite achieved Soleri's original vision. It's still worth a stop to take a tour, have a bite at the café, and purchase one of the hand-cast bronze wind-bells made at the site. ⊠ *2 miles off I–17 Exit 262* ☎ *928/632–7135* ⊕ *www.arcosanti.org* ✄ *Tour $10* ☯ *Daily 9–5, tours hrly 10–4.*

CASA GRANDE RUINS NATIONAL MONUMENT

36 miles southeast of Downtown Phoenix.

Visitors have been fascinated by Casa Grande Ruins for more than 300 years, and it's no wonder. The buildings are a marvel of not just architecture, but also ancient astronomy.

GETTING HERE AND AROUND

Take U.S. 60 east (Superstition Freeway) to Florence Junction (U.S. 60 and AZ 89), and head south 16 miles on AZ 89 to Florence. Casa Grande is 9 miles west of Florence on AZ 287 or, from Interstate 10, 16 miles east on AZ 387 and AZ 87. Note: follow signs to ruins, not to town of Casa Grande. When leaving the ruins, take AZ 87 north 35 miles back to U.S. 60.

EXPLORING

Casa Grande Ruins National Monument. This site, whose original purpose still eludes archaeologists, was unknown to European explorers until Father Kino, a Jesuit missionary, first recorded the site's existence in 1694. The area was set aside as federal land in 1892 and named a national monument in 1918. Although only a few prehistoric sites can be viewed, more than 60 are in the monument area, including the 35-foot-tall—that's four stories—Casa Grande (Big House). The tallest known Hohokam building, Casa Grande was built in the early 14th century and is believed by some to have been an ancient astronomical observatory or a center of government, religion, trade, or education. Allow an hour to explore the site, longer if park rangers are giving a talk or leading a tour. On your way out, cross the parking lot by the covered picnic grounds and climb the platform for a view of a ball court and two platform mounds, said to date from the 1100s. ⊠ *1100 W. Ruins Dr., Coolidge* ☎ *520/723–3172* ⊕ *www.nps.gov/cagr* ⊠ *$5* ⊙ *Daily 9–5.*

THE APACHE TRAIL

Fodor's Choice President Theodore Roosevelt called this 150-mile drive "the most awe-
★ inspiring and most sublimely beautiful panorama nature ever created. "
A stretch of winding highway, the AZ 188 portion of the Apache Trail
closely follows the route forged through wilderness in 1906 to move
construction supplies for building the Roosevelt Dam, which lies at the
northernmost part of the loop.

PLANNING YOUR TIME
Although the drive itself can easily be completed in less than a day, you
could spend a night in Globe, continuing the loop back to Phoenix the
following day.

GETTING HERE AND AROUND
From the town of Apache Junction you can choose to drive the trail
in either direction; there are advantages to both. If you begin the loop
going clockwise—heading eastward on AZ 188 to the Superstition
Mountains, the Peralta Trail, Boyce Thompson Arboretum, Globe,
Tonto National Monument, Theodore Roosevelt Lake Reservoir &
Dam, and Tortilla Flat—your drive may be more relaxing; you'll be on
the farthest side of this narrow dirt road some refer to as the "white-
knuckle route," with its switchbacks and drop-offs straight down into
spectacular Fish Creek Canyon. ■TIP➔ This 42-mile section of the
drive isn't for anyone afraid of heights. But if you follow the route
counterclockwise—continuing on U.S. 60 past the town of Apache
Junction—you'll be able to appreciate each attraction better.

SUPERSTITION MOUNTAINS

30 miles east of Downtown Phoenix.

Folklore abounds in the Superstition Mountains, where visitors have
sought treasure from the Lost Dutchman Mine for generations.

GETTING HERE AND AROUND
From Phoenix, take Interstate 10 and then U.S. 60 (the Superstition
Freeway) east through the suburbs of Tempe, Mesa, and Apache
Junction.

EXPLORING
Superstition Mountains. As the Phoenix metro area gives way to cactus-
and creosote-dotted desert, the massive escarpment of the Superstition
Mountains heaves into view and slides by to the north. The Super-
stitions are supposedly where the legendary Lost Dutchman Mine is,
the location—not to mention the existence—of which has been hotly
debated since pioneer days. ⊠ *5470 N. Apache Trail, Apache Junction*
⊕ *www.azstateparks.com/parks/lodu.*

  Superstition Mountain Museum. The best place to learn about the
"Dutchman" Jacob Waltz and the Lost Dutchman Mine is at Superstition Mountain Museum. Exhibits include a collection of mining tools,

historical maps, and artifacts relating to the "gold" age of the Superstition Mountains. ⊠ *4087 N. Apache Trail (AZ 188) Apache Junction* ☎ *480/983–4888* ⊕ *www.superstitionmountainmuseum.org* ▧ *$5* ⊙ *Daily 9–4..*

Goldfield Ghost Town. Goldfield became an instant town of about 4,000 residents after a gold strike in 1892; it dried up five years later when the gold mine flooded. Today the Goldfield Ghost Town is an interesting place to grab a cool drink, pan for gold, go for a mine tour, or take a desert Jeep ride or horseback tour of the area. The ghost town's shops are open daily 10–5, the saloon daily 11–9, and gunfights are held hourly noon–4 on weekends. ⊠ *4650 N. Mammoth Mine Rd., 4 miles northeast of Apache Junction on AZ 188, Goldfield* ☎ *480/983–0333* ⊕ *www.goldfieldghosttown.com.*

PERALTA TRAIL

35 miles east of Downtown Phoenix, located in the Superstition Mountains.

This 4-mile hike offers a spectacular view of Weaver's Needle, which is one of Arizona's most famous sites in the folklore-rich Superstition Mountains. It takes a few hours to ascend the 1,400 feet. Bring water, food, and sunscreen.

GETTING HERE AND AROUND

About 11½ miles southeast of Apache Junction, off U.S. 60, take Peralta Trail Road, just past King's Ranch Road, an 8-mile, rough gravel road that leads to the start of the Peralta Trail.

SPORTS AND THE OUTDOORS

HIKING

Peralta Trail. The 4-mile round-trip Peralta Trail winds 1,400 feet up a small valley for a spectacular view of **Weaver's Needle,** a monolithic rock formation that is one of Arizona's more famous sights. Allow a few hours for this rugged and challenging hike, bring plenty of water, sunscreen, a hat, and a snack or lunch. Don't hike it in the middle of the day in summer. *Moderate.* ⊠ *Goldfield.*

BOYCE THOMPSON ARBORETUM

60 miles east of Downtown Phoenix, 30 miles southeast of the Peralta Trail.

If all that cacti get overwhelming, take a trip about an hour outside of Phoenix to the Boyce Thompson Arboretum, where you'll find a wonderland of exotic plants. Desert plants and tropical birds make this oasis worth the visit.

GETTING HERE AND AROUND

From Florence Junction, take U.S. 60 east for 12 miles.

EXPLORING

Boyce Thompson Arboretum. At the foot of Picketpost Mountain in Superior, the Boyce Thompson Arboretum is often called an oasis in the desert: the arid rocky expanse gives way to lush riparian glades home

DID YOU KNOW?

Road-weary travelers like to take a break from driving the Apache Trail and stretch their legs on the 4-mile round-trip Peralta Trail hike to see the iconic Weaver's Needle up close.

CLOSE UP

The Lost Dutchman Mine

Not much is known about Jacob "the Dutchman" Waltz, except that he was born around 1808 in Germany (he was "Deutsch," not "Dutch") and emigrated to the United States, where he spent several years at mining camps in the Southeast, in the West, and finally in Arizona. There's documentation that he did indeed have access to a large quantity of gold, though he never registered a claim for the mine that was attributed to him.

GOLDEN RUMORS

In 1868 Waltz appeared in the newly developing community of Pumpkinville, soon to become Phoenix. He kept to himself on his 160-acre homestead on the bank of the Salt River. From time to time he would disappear for a few weeks and return with enough high-quality ore to keep him in a wonderful fashion. Soon word was out that "Crazy Jake" had a vast gold mine in the Superstition Mountains, east of the city near the Apache Trail.

At the same time, stories about a wealthy gold mine discovered by the Peralta family of Mexico were circulating. Local Apaches raided the mine, which was near their sacred Thunder Mountain. In what became known as the Peralta Massacre, the Peraltas and more than 100 people working for them at the mine were killed. Rumors soon spread that Waltz had saved the life of a young Mexican who was part of Peralta's group—one of few who had escaped—and was shown the Peraltas' mine as a reward.

SEARCHING THE SUPERSTITIONS

As the legend of the Dutchman's mine grew, many opportunists attempted to follow Waltz into the Superstition Mountains. A crack marksman, Waltz quickly discouraged several who tried to track him. The flow of gold continued for several years.

In 1891 the Salt River flooded, badly damaging Waltz's home. When the floodwaters receded, neighbors found Waltz there in a weakened condition. He was taken to the nearby home and boardinghouse of Julia Thomas, who nursed the Dutchman for months. When his death was imminent, he reportedly gave Julia the directions to his mine.

Julia and another boarder searched for the mine fruitlessly. In her later years she sold maps to the treasure, based upon her recollections of Waltz's description. Thousands have searched for the lost mine, many losing their lives in the process—either to the brutality of fellow searchers or that of the rugged desert—and more than a century later gold seekers are still trying to connect the pieces of the puzzle.

THE LEGEND TODAY

There's no doubt that the Dutchman had a source of extremely rich gold ore. But was it in the Superstition Mountains, nearby Goldfield, or maybe even in the Four Peaks region? Wherever it was, it's still hidden. Perhaps the best-researched books on the subject are T. E. Glover's *The Lost Dutchman Mine of Jacob Waltz* and the companion book *The Holmes Manuscript*. Ron Feldman of OK Corral (☎ 480/982-4040 ⊕ *www.okcorrals. com*) in Apache Junction has become an expert on the subject during his 30-plus years in the region. He leads adventurers on pack trips into the mysterious mountains to relive the lore and legends.

to 3,200 different desert plants and more than 230 bird and 72 terrestrial species. The arboretum offers a living album of the world's desert and semiarid region plants, including exotic species such as Canary Islands date palms and Australian eucalyptus. Trails offer breathtaking scenery in the gardens and the exhibits, especially during the spring wildflower season. A variety of tours are offered year-round. Benches with built-in misters offer relief from the heat. Bring along a picnic and enjoy the beauty. ✉ *37615 U.S. 60, Milepost 223, Superior* ☎ *520/689–2811* ⊕ *azstateparks.com/Parks/ BOTH* 🎫 *$10* ☉ *Daily 8–5.*

> **WORD OF MOUTH**
>
> "I loved the Boyce Thompson Arboretum. It's a little bit of a drive from Phoenix, but you will see the desert in its unspoiled majesty. There are (easy) hiking trails and scenery to die for."
>
> –wliwl

EN ROUTE A few miles past the arboretum, **Superior** is the first of several modest mining towns and the launching point for a dramatic winding ascent through the Mescals to a 4,195-foot pass that affords panoramic views of this copper-rich range and its huge, dormant, open-pit mines. Collectors will want to watch for antiques shops, but be forewarned that quality varies considerably. A gradual descent will take you into **Miami** and **Claypool,** once-thriving boomtowns that have carried on quietly since major-corporation mining ground to a halt in the '70s. Working-class buildings are dwarfed by the mountainous piles of copper tailings. At a stoplight in Claypool, AZ 188 splits off northward to the Apache Trail, but continue on U.S. 60 another 3 miles to Globe.

GLOBE

Ninety miles east of Downtown Phoenix, 51 miles east of Apache Junction, 25 miles east of Superior, and 3 miles east of Claypool's AZ 188 turnoff, 30 miles east of Boyce Thompson.

In the southern reaches of Tonto National Forest, Globe is the most modern of the area's dilapidated mining towns. Initially, it was gold and silver that brought miners here—the city allegedly got its name from a large, circular boulder of silver, with lines like continents, found by prospectors—although the region is now known for North America's richest copper deposits. ■**TIP**➜ If you're driving the Apache Trail loop, stop in Globe to fill up the tank; it's the last chance to gas up until looping all the way back to U.S. 60 at Apache Junction.

GETTING HERE AND AROUND

Globe is at the intersection of U.S. 60 and AZ 188. At the Globe Chamber of Commerce, you can pick up brochures detailing the self-guided Historic Downtown Walking Tour.

ESSENTIALS

Visitor Information Globe Chamber of Commerce ✉ *1360 N. Broad St., 1¼ miles north of downtown on U.S. 60* ☎ *928/425–4495, 800/804–5623* ⊕ *www. globemiamichamber.com.*

Hikers in the Superstition Mountains—perhaps searching for the riches of the Lost Dutchman Mine

EXPLORING

FAMILY **Besh-Ba-Gowah Archaeological Park.** For a step 800 years back in time, tour the two acres of the excavated Salado Indian site at the Besh-Ba-Gowah Archaeological Park on the southeastern side of town. After a trip through the small museum and a video introduction, enter the area full of remnants of more than 200 rooms occupied here by the Salado during the 13th and 14th centuries. Public areas include the central plaza (also the principal burial ground), roasting pits, and open patios. Besh-Ba-Gowah is a name given by the Apaches, who, arriving in the 17th century, found the pueblo abandoned, and moved in. Loosely translated, the name means "metal camp," and remains left on the site point to it as part of an extensive commerce and trading network. ✉ *1324 S. Jesse Hayes Rd.* ☎ *928/425–0320* 🌐 *www.globeaz.gov/visitors/besh-ba-gowah* 🎟 *$5* 🕒 *Daily 9–4:30.*

WHERE TO EAT AND STAY

$ MEXICAN 🍴 **Chalo's.** This roadside spot offers top-notch Mexican and Tex-Mex food for a slightly different flavor than your average Mexican plate. Chalo's specialty is using green chiles. Fortunately, you can request mild or spicy versions of green-chile enchiladas, burros, and practically anything else on the menu. Be sure to ask for water. Try the savory stuffed sopapillas, filled with pork and beef, beans, and red or green chiles. It's a favorite among locals, so plan for an early lunch or dinner to avoid a wait. [$] *Average main: $9* ✉ *902 E. Ash St.* ☎ *928/425–0515* 🌐 *www.chalosglobe.com.*

$ B&B/INN 🏨 **Noftsger Hill Inn.** Built in 1907, this B&B was originally the North Globe Schoolhouse; now classrooms serve as guest rooms, filled with mining-era antiques and affording fantastic views of the Pinal Mountains and historic Old Dominion Mine. **Pros:** giant windows offer pleasant natural light; many rooms have original classroom chalkboards devoted to guest comments. **Cons:** city slickers might miss modern bath fixtures and amenities. [$] *Rooms from: $135* ✉ *425 North St.* ☎ *928/425–2260, 877/780–2479* 🌐 *www.noftsgerhillinn.com* 🛏 *6 rooms* 🍴 *Breakfast.*

TONTO NATIONAL MONUMENT

30 miles northwest of Globe.

One of the best preserved examples of Salado cliff dwellings, Tonto National Monument offers visitors a peek at 13th-century life.

GETTING HERE AND AROUND

Tonto National Monument is located off AZ 188, approximately 25 miles north of U.S. 60. It's about a two-hour drive from the Phoenix area. If you feel like a real journey, take AZ 88, otherwise known as the Apache Trail, to Tonto National Monument. Almost half of the 47-mile trail is gravel, so be prepared for a very long and bumpy ride.

EXPLORING

Tonto National Monument. You can visit a well-preserved complex of 13th-century Salado cliff dwellings at this site. There's a self-guided walking tour of the Lower Cliff Dwellings, but if you can, take a ranger-led tour of the 40-room Upper Cliff Dwellings, offered on selected mornings from November to April. Tour reservations are required and should be made as far as a month in advance. ✉ *26260 N. AZ 188, Roosevelt* ☎ *928/467–2241* 🌐 *www.nps.gov/tont* 🎟 *$3* 🕒 *Daily 8–5.*

THEODORE ROOSEVELT LAKE RESERVOIR AND DAM

5 miles northwest of Tonto National Monument on AZ 188, 125 miles north of Phoenix.

Water is a rarity in the desert, which is why Theodore Roosevelt Lake is one of the most popular recreation destinations in the area. Boaters, fishermen, and water-skiers flock here throughout the year.

GETTING HERE AND AROUND

Theodore Roosevelt Lake Reservoir and Dam is located off AZ 188, approximately 30 miles north of U.S. 60. It's on the same road as Tonto National Monument; the drive takes about two hours from Phoenix.

EXPLORING

Theodore Roosevelt Lake Reservoir & Dam. Flanked by the desolate Mazatzal and Sierra Anchas mountain ranges, Theodore Roosevelt Lake Reservoir & Dam is an aquatic recreational area—a favorite with bass anglers, water-skiers, and boaters. This is the largest masonry dam on the planet, and the massive bridge is the longest two-lane, single-span, steel-arch bridge in the nation. ✉ *Tonto Basin Ranger Station, Roosevelt* ☎ *928/467–3200.*

Past the reservoir, AZ 188 turns west and becomes a meandering dirt road, eventually winding its way back to Apache Junction via the magnificent, bronze-hued volcanic cliff walls of **Fish Creek Canyon**, with views of the sparkling lakes, towering saguaros, and, in the springtime, vast fields of wildflowers.

TORTILLA FLAT

18 miles southwest of Roosevelt Dam, 18 miles northeast of Apache Junction, 60 miles northeast of Phoenix.

Tortilla Flat might just be the closest thing to the end of the world you'll find. A sort of cowboy rest-stop, it's a favorite for travelers who want to stretch their legs after a bumpy, desolate ride in the desert.

GETTING HERE AND AROUND

Tortilla Flat is located off AZ 88, the bumpy and historic Apache Trail. It's about 60 miles from Downtown Phoenix, but leave at least two hours for the journey. Take U.S. 60 east of Phoenix through Apache Junction, then take the Idaho exit and head north toward AZ 88 and drive for approximately 18 miles. Be prepared for a bumpy and gravely ride on parts of AZ 88. It's historic for a reason.

EXPLORING

Tortilla Flat. Close to the end of the Apache Trail, this old-time restaurant and country store are what is left of an authentic stagecoach stop at Tortilla Flat. This is a fun place to stop for a well-earned rest and refreshment—miner- and cowboy-style grub, of course—before heading back the last 18 miles to civilization. Enjoy a hearty bowl of killer chili and some prickly-pear-cactus ice cream while sitting at the counter on a saddle barstool. ☎ *480/984–1776* ⊕ *www.tortillaflataz.com.*

GRAND CANYON
NATIONAL PARK

WELCOME TO GRAND CANYON NATIONAL PARK

TOP REASONS TO GO

★ **Its status:** This is one of those places where you really want to say, "Been there, done that!"

★ **Awesome vistas:** Painted Desert, sandstone canyon walls, pine and fir forests, mesas, plateaus, volcanic features, the Colorado River, streams, and waterfalls make for some jaw-dropping moments.

★ **Year-round adventure:** Outdoor junkies can bike, boat, camp, fish, hike, ride mules, whitewater raft, watch birds and wildlife, cross-country ski, and snowshoe.

★ **Continuing education:** Adults and kids can have fun learning, thanks to free park-sponsored nature walks and interpretive programs.

★ **Sky-high and river-low experiences:** Experience the canyon via plane, train, and automobile, as well as by helicopter, row- or motorboat, bike, mule, or foot.

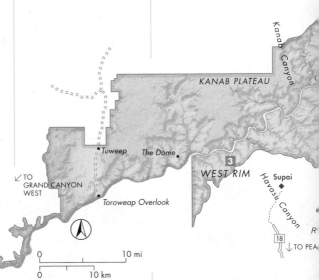

1 South Rim. The South Rim is where the action is: Grand Canyon Village's lodging, camping, eateries, stores, and museums, plus plenty of trailheads into the canyon. Visitor services and facilities are open and available daily, including holidays. Four free shuttle routes cover more than 35 stops, and visitors who'd rather relax than rough it can treat themselves to comfy hotel rooms and elegant restaurant meals (lodging and camping reservations are essential).

2 North Rim. Of the nearly 5 million people who visit the park annually, 90% enter at the South Rim, but many consider the North Rim even more gorgeous—and worth the extra effort. Open only from mid-May to the end of October (or the first good snowfall), the North Rim has legitimate bragging rights: at more than 8,000 feet above sea level (1,000 feet higher than the South Rim), it has precious solitude and seven developed viewpoints. Rather than staring into the canyon's depths, you get a true sense of its expanse.

3 West Rim and Havasu Canyon. Though not in Grand Canyon National Park, the far-off-the-beaten-path western end of the canyon,

3

KAIBAB
PLATEAU

MARBLE CANYON

67 ↑ TO
JACOB LAKE
AND SOUTH RIM

Colorado River

Great Thumb
Mesa

North Rim
Entrance Station

NORTH RIM
2

Colorado River

Point Imperial

Visitor Center

INNER GORGE

Vista Encantada

Roosevelt Point

Point
Sublime

Grand Canyon Lodge ◆ ● Bright Angel Point

HAVASUPAI
INDIAN
RESERVATION

Havasupai
Point

Roaring Springs

Bright Angel Creek

O PEACH SPRINGS

Bright Angel Trail

Walhalla Overlook

Cape Royal

Yavapai Point

Phantom Ranch

South Kaibab Trail

Pima Point

Hermit Rd.

Hermits Rest

Hopi
Point

Mather Point

Yaki Point

GRANITE GORGE

Navajo Point

Visitor Center

Lipan
Point

Desert
View

Grand Canyon
Village

Grandview
Point

South Entrance

Moran
Point

East
Entrance

Tusayan

64

SOUTH RIM

64

Grand Canyon
Airport

180 ↓ TO FLAGSTAFF,
WILLIAMS

TO CAMERON
AND NORTH RIM

often called the West Rim, has some spectacular scenery. In Havasu Canyon, on the Havasupai Reservation, you can view some of the most gorgeous waterfalls in the United States. On the Hualapai Reservation, the Skywalk has become a major draw. This U-shape glass-floored deck juts out 3,600 feet above the Colorado River and isn't for the faint of heart.

Desert view watchtower was designed by Mary Colter in 1932.

GETTING ORIENTED

Grand Canyon National Park is a superstar—biologically, historically, and recreationally. One of the world's best examples of arid-land erosion, the canyon provides a record of three of the four eras of geological time. Almost 2 billion years' worth of Earth's history is written in the colored layers of

rock stacked from the river bottom to the top of the plateau. In addition to its diverse fossil record, the park reveals long-ago traces of human adaptation to an unforgiving environment. It's also home to several major ecosystems, five of the world's seven life zones, three of North America's four desert types, and all kinds of rare, endemic, and protected plant and animal species.

Updated by
Mara Levin

When it comes to the Grand Canyon, there are statistics, and there are sensations. While the former are impressive—the canyon measures in at an average width of 10 miles, length of 277 river miles, and depth of 1 mile—they don't truly prepare you for that first impression. Seeing the canyon for the first time is an astounding experience—one that's hard to wrap your head around. In fact, it's more than an experience, it's an emotion, one that's only just beginning to be captured with the word "Grand." Hike or ride a trusty mule down into the canyon, bike or ramble along its rim, fly over, or raft through on the Colorado River—there are manifold ways to soak up the canyon's magnificence.

Roughly 5 million visitors come to the park each year. You can access the canyon via two main points—the South Rim and the North Rim—but the South Rim is much easier to get to and therefore much more visited. The width from the North Rim to the South Rim varies from 600 feet to 18 miles, but traveling between rims by road requires a 215-mile drive. Hiking arduous trails from rim to rim is a steep and strenuous trek of at least 21 miles, but it's well worth the effort. You'll travel through five of North America's seven life zones. (To do this any other way, you'd have to journey from the Mexican desert to the Canadian woods.) West of Grand Canyon National Park, the tribal lands of the Hualapai and the Havasupai lie along the so-called West Rim of the canyon, where you'll find the impressive glass Skywalk.

GRAND CANYON PLANNER

WHEN TO GO

There's no bad time to visit the canyon, though the busiest times of year are summer and spring break. Visiting during these peak seasons, as well as holidays, requires patience and a tolerance for crowds. Note that weather changes on a whim in this exposed high-desert region. The North Rim shuts down mid-October through mid-May due to weather conditions and related road closures.

FESTIVALS AND EVENTS

AUGUST **Grand Canyon Music Festival.** For three weekends in late August–early September, this festival brings mostly chamber music to the Shrine of Ages amphitheater at Grand Canyon Village. In the early 1980s, music aficionados Robert Bonfiglio and Clare Hoffman hiked through the Grand Canyon and decided the stunning spectacle should be accompanied by the strains of a symphony. One of the park rangers agreed, and the wandering musicians performed an impromptu concert. Encouraged by the experience, Bonfiglio and Hoffman started the festival. ☎ 928/638–9215, 800/997–8285 ⊕ www.grandcanyonmusicfest.org.

DECEMBER **Mountain Village Holiday.** Williams hails the winter holidays with a parade of lights, holiday decorations downtown, and live entertainment early December–early January. ☎ 928/635–4061 ⊕ www.experiencewilliams.com.

PLANNING YOUR TIME

Plan ahead: Mule rides require at least a six-month advance reservation, and longer for the busy season (most can be reserved up to 13 months in advance). Multiday rafting trips should be reserved at least a year in advance.

Once you arrive, pick up the free detailed map and the *Guide,* a newspaper with a schedule of free programs.

The park is most crowded on the South Rim, especially near the south entrance and in Grand Canyon Village, as well as on the scenic drives, particularly the 23-mile Desert View Drive.

GRAND CANYON IN 1 DAY

Start early, pack a picnic lunch, and drive to the South Rim's **Grand Canyon Visitor Center** just north of the south entrance, to pick up info and see your first incredible view at **Mather Point.** Continue east along **Desert View Drive** for about 2 miles to **Yaki Point.** Next, continue driving 7 miles east to **Grandview Point** for a good view of the buttes Krishna Shrine and Vishnu Temple. Go 4 miles east and catch the view at **Moran Point,** then 3 miles to the **Tusayan Ruin and Museum,** where a small display is devoted to the history of the Ancestral Puebloans. Continue another mile east to **Lipan Point** to view the Colorado River. In less than a mile, you'll arrive at **Navajo Point,** the highest elevation on the South Rim. **Desert View and Watchtower** is the final attraction along Desert View Drive.

On your return drive, stop off at any of the picnic areas for lunch. Once back at Grand Canyon Village, walk the paved **Rim Trail** to **Maricopa Point.** Along the way, pick up souvenirs in the village and stop at historic **El Tovar Hotel** for dinner (be sure to make reservations well in advance). If you have time, take the shuttle on **Hermit Road** to **Hermits Rest,** 7 miles away. Along that route, Hopi Point and Powell Point are excellent spots to watch the sunset.

GRAND CANYON IN 3 DAYS

On Day 1, follow the one-day itinerary for the morning, but spend more time exploring Desert View Drive and enjoy a leisurely picnic lunch. Later, drive 30 miles beyond Desert View to Cameron Trading Post, which has a good restaurant and is an interesting side trip. Travel Hermit Road on your second morning, and drive to Grand Canyon Airport for a late-morning small plane or helicopter tour. Have lunch in **Tusayan** and cool off at the IMAX film *Grand Canyon: The Hidden Secrets.* Back in the village, take a free ranger-led program. On your third day, hike partway down the canyon on **Bright Angel Trail.** It takes twice as long to hike back up, so plan accordingly. Get trail maps at **Grand Canyon Visitor Center,** and bring plenty of water.

Alternatively, spend Days 2 and 3 exploring the remote **West Rim,** 150 miles toward Nevada or California and far away from major highways. Fill the first day with a horseback ride along the rim, a helicopter ride into the canyon, or a pontoon boat ride on the Colorado River. The next day, raft the Class V-VII rapids. Another option is to get a tribal permit and spend Days 2 and 3 in **Havasu Canyon,** a truly spiritual backcountry experience. You can opt to hike, ride horseback, or take a helicopter 8 miles down to the small village of Supai and the Havasupai Lodge.

GETTING HERE AND AROUND
SOUTH RIM

AIR TRAVEL　North Las Vegas Airport in Las Vegas is the primary air hub for charter flights to the **Grand Canyon National Parks Airport** in Tusayan (*GCN* ☏ *928/638–2446*).

CAR TRAVEL　The best route into the park from the east or south is from Flagstaff. Take U.S. 180 northwest to the park's southern entrance and Grand Canyon Village. From the west on Interstate 40, the most direct route to the South Rim is taking Highway 64 from Williams to U.S. 180.

PARK SHUTTLE TRAVEL　The South Rim is open to car traffic year-round, though access to Hermits Rest is limited to shuttle buses part of the year. There are four free shuttle routes: The **Hermits Rest Route** operates March through November, between Grand Canyon Village and Hermits Rest. The **Village Route** operates year-round in the village area, stopping at lodgings, the general store, and the Grand Canyon Visitor Center. The **Kaibab Rim Route** goes from the visitor center to five viewpoints, including Yaki Point and a stop at the South Kaibab Trailhead. ■**TIP→** In summer, South Rim roads are congested, and it's easier, and sometimes required, to park your car and take the free shuttle. Running from one hour before sunrise until one hour after sunset, shuttles arrive every 15 to 30 minutes at 30 clearly marked stops.

TAXI AND SHUTTLE TRAVEL　Although there's no public transportation into the Grand Canyon, you can hire a taxi to take you to or from the Grand Canyon Airport or any of the Tusayan hotels. Arizona Shuttle is another option.

Taxi and Shuttle Contacts Arizona Shuttle. This shuttle has service between Phoenix, Sedona, Flagstaff, Williams, Tusayan, and Grand Canyon Village (at

Maswik Lodge). ☎ *928/226–8060, 877/226–8060* ⊕ *www.arizonashuttle.com.*
Xanterra. Xanterra offers 24-hour taxi service in Tusayan and the South Rim.
☎ *928/638–2822.*

TRAIN TRAVEL **Grand Canyon Railway.** There is no need to deal with all of the other drivers racing to the South Rim. Sit back and relax in the comfy train cars of the Grand Canyon Railway. Live music and storytelling enliven the trip as you journey past the landscape through prairie, ranch, and national park land to the log-cabin train station in Grand Canyon Village. You won't see the Grand Canyon from the train, but you can walk (¼ mile) or catch the shuttle at the restored, historic Grand Canyon Railway Station. The vintage train departs from the Williams Depot every morning, and makes the 65-mile journey in 2¼ hours. You can do the round trip in a single day; however, it's a more relaxing and enjoyable strategy to stay for a night or two at the South Rim before returning to Williams. ☎ *800/843–8724* ⊕ *www.thetrain.com* ◳ *$70–$178 round-trip.*

NORTH RIM

AIR TRAVEL The nearest airport to the North Rim is **St. George Municipal Airport** (☎ *435/627–4080* ⊕ *www.flysgu.com*) in Utah, 164 miles north, with regular service provided by both Delta and United Airlines.

CAR TRAVEL To reach the North Rim by car, take U.S. 89 north from Flagstaff past Cameron, turning left onto U.S. 89A at Bitter Springs. At Jacob Lake, take Highway 67 directly to the Grand Canyon North Rim. You can drive yourself to the scenic viewpoints and trailheads; the only transportation offered in the Park is a shuttle twice each morning that brings eager hikers from Grand Canyon Lodge to the North Kaibab Trailhead (a 2-mile trip). Note that services on the North Rim shut down in mid-October, and the road closes after the first major snowfall (usually the end of October); Highway 67 south of Jacob Lake is closed.

SHUTTLE TRAVEL From mid-May to mid-October, the **Trans Canyon Shuttle** (☎ *928/638–2820* ⊕ *www.trans-canyonshuttle.com*) travels daily between the South and North rims—the ride takes 4½ hours each way. One-way fare is $85, round-trip $160. Reservations are required.

PARK ESSENTIALS
PARK FEES AND PERMITS
A fee of $25 per vehicle or $12 per person for pedestrians and cyclists is good for one week's access at both rims.

The $50 Grand Canyon Pass gives unlimited access to the park for 12 months. The annual America the Beautiful **National Parks and Recreational Land Pass** (☎ *888/275–8747* ⊕ *store.usgs.gov/pass* ◳ *$80*) provides unlimited access to all national parks and federal recreation areas for 12 months.

No permits are needed for day hikers; but **backcountry permits** (☎ *928/638–7875* ⊕ *www.nps.gov/grca* ◳ *$10, plus $5 per person per night*) are necessary for overnight hikers camping below the rim. Permits are limited, so make your reservation as far in advance as possible—they're taken by fax (☎ *928/638–2125*), by mail (✉ *1824 S. Thompson St., Ste. 201, Flagstaff, AZ 86001*), or in person at the Backcountry Information Center in the village up to four months ahead of arrival. **Camping** in the park is restricted to designated campgrounds (☎ *877/444–6777* ⊕ *www.recreation.gov*).

PARK HOURS

The South Rim is open continuously every day of the year (weather permitting), while the North Rim is open mid-May through October. The park is in the Mountain Standard Time zone year-round. Daylight Saving Time isn't observed.

CELL PHONE RECEPTION

Cell phone coverage can be spotty at both the South Rim and North Rim—though Verizon customers report better reception at the South Rim. Don't expect a strong signal anywhere in the park.

RESTAURANTS

Within the park on the South Rim, you can find everything from cafeteria food to casual café fare to creatively prepared, Western- and Southwestern-inspired American cuisine. There's even a coffeehouse with organic joe. Reservations are accepted (and recommended) only for dinner at El Tovar Dining Room; they can be made up to six months in advance with El Tovar room reservations, 30 days in advance without. You should also make dinner reservations at the Grand Canyon Lodge Dining Room on the North Rim—as the only "upscale" dining option, the restaurant fills up quickly at dinner throughout the season (the two other choices on the North Rim are a cafeteria and a chuck wagon–style Grand Cookout experience). The dress code is casual across the board, but El Tovar is your best option if you're looking to dress up a bit and thumb through an extensive wine list. Drinking water and restrooms aren't available at most picnic spots.

Eateries outside the park generally range from mediocre to terrible—you didn't come all the way to the Grand Canyon for the food, did you? Our selections highlight your best options. Of towns near the park, Williams definitely has the leg up on culinary variety and quality, with Tusayan (near the South Rim) and Jacob Lake (the closest town to the North Rim) offering mostly either fast food or merely adequate sit-down restaurants. Near the park, even the priciest places welcome casual dress. On the Hualapai and Havasupai reservations in Havasu Canyon and on the West Rim, dining is limited and basic.

HOTELS

The park's accommodations include three "historic-rustic" facilities and four motel-style lodges, all of which have undergone significant upgrades over the past decade. Of the 922 rooms, cabins, and suites, only 203 are at the North Rim, all at the Grand Canyon Lodge. Outside El Tovar Hotel, the canyon's architectural highlight, accommodations are relatively basic but comfortable, and the most sought-after rooms have canyon views. Rates vary widely, but most rooms fall in the $100 to $180 range, though the most basic units at the South Rim go for just $83.

Reservations are a must, especially during the busy summer season. ■TIP→ If you want to get your first choice (especially Bright Angel Lodge or El Tovar), make reservations as far in advance as possible; they're taken up to 13 months ahead. You might find a last-minute cancellation, but you shouldn't count on it. Although lodging at the South

Rim will keep you close to the action, the frenetic activity and crowded facilities are off-putting to some. With short notice, the best time to find a room on the South Rim is in winter. And though the North Rim is less crowded than the South Rim, the only lodging available is at Grand Canyon Lodge.

Just south of the South Rim park boundary, Tusayan's hotels are in a convenient location but without bargains, while Williams (about an hour's drive) can provide price breaks on food and lodging, as well as a respite from the crowds. Extra amenities (e.g., swimming pools and gyms) are also more abundant. Reservations are always a good idea. At Grand Canyon West, lodging options are extremely limited; you can purchase a "package," which includes lodging and a visitation permit, through Hualapai Tourism. *Hotel reviews have been shortened. For full information, visit Fodors.com.*

Lodging Contacts Xanterra Parks & Resorts. Xanterra operates all lodging and dining services at the South Rim as well as Phantom Ranch, deep inside the canyon. ☏ *888/297–2757* ⊕ *www.grandcanyonlodges.com.*

WHAT IT COSTS				
	$	**$$**	**$$$**	**$$$$**
Restaurant	under $12	$12–$20	$21–$30	over $30
Hotel	under $120	$120–$175	$176–$250	over $250

Restaurant prices are the average cost of a main course at dinner or, if dinner is not served, at lunch. Hotel prices are the lowest cost of a standard double in high season, excluding taxes and service charges.

TOURS

Grand Canyon Field Institute. Instructors lead guided educational tours, hikes around the canyon, and weekend programs at the South Rim. With more than 200 classes a year, tour topics include everything from archaeology and backcountry medicine to photography and natural history. Contact GCFI for a schedule and price list. Private hikes can be arranged. Discounted classes are available for members; annual dues are $35. ⊠ *GCA Waehouse, 2-B Albright Ave., Grand Canyon Village* ☏ *928/638–2841, 866/471–4435* ⊕ *www.grandcanyon.org/ fieldinstitute* 🖃 *From $235.*

Xanterra Motorcoach Tours. Narrated by knowledgeable guides, tours include the Hermits Rest Tour, which travels along the old wagon road built by the Santa Fe Railway; the Desert View Tour, which glimpses the Colorado River's rapids and stops at Lipan Point; Sunrise and Sunset Tours; and combination tours. Children 16 and younger are free when accompanied by a paying adult. ☏ *303/297–2757, 888/297–2757* ⊕ *www.grandcanyonlodges.com* 🖃 *From $22.*

VISITOR INFORMATION

PARK CONTACT INFORMATION

Grand Canyon National Park. Before you go into the park, get the complimentary *Trip Planner,* updated regularly, from the Grand Canyon National Park. ☏ *928/638–7888* ⊕ *www.nps.gov/grca.*

VISITOR CENTERS

SOUTH RIM **Desert View Information Center.** Near the watchtower, at Desert View Point, the nonprofit Grand Canyon Association store and information center has a nice selection of books, park pamphlets, gifts, and educational materials. All sales from the Association stores go to support the park programs. ⊠ *East entrance* ☎ *800/858–2808, 928/638–7888* ⊙ *Daily 9–5; hrs vary in winter.*

Grand Canyon Verkamp's Visitor Center. This small visitor center is named for the Verkamp family, who operated a curios shop on the South Rim for over a hundred years. The building serves as an official visitor center, ranger station (get your Junior Ranger badges here), bookstore, and museum, with compelling exhibits on the Verkamps and other pioneers in this region. ⊠ *Desert View Dr. across from El Tovar Hotel, Grand Canyon Village* ☎ *928/638–7146* ⊙ *Daily 8–7, ranger station daily 8–5.*

Grand Canyon Visitor Center. The park's main orientation center, known formerly as Canyon View Information Plaza, provides pamphlets and resources to help plan your visit. It also holds engaging interpretive exhibits on the park. Rangers are on hand to answer questions and aid in planning canyon excursions. A daily schedule of ranger-led hikes and evening lectures is posted on a bulletin board inside, and a 20-minute film about the history, geology, and wildlife of the canyon plays every 30 minutes in the theater. The bicycle rental office, a small café, and a huge gift store are also in this complex. There's ample parking by the information center; from here, it's a short walk out to Mather Point, or a short ride on the shuttle bus, which can take you into Grand Canyon Village, too. The visitor center is also accessible via a leisurely 1-mile walk on the Greenway Trail—a paved pathway that meanders through the forest. ⊠ *East side of Grand Canyon Village, 450 Arizona 64, Grand Canyon* ☎ *928/638–7888* ⊕ *www.explorethecanyon.com* ⊙ *Daily 8–5, outdoor exhibits may be viewed anytime.*

Yavapai Geology Museum. Learn about the geology of the canyon at this museum and bookstore run by the Grand Canyon Association. You can also catch the park shuttle bus or pick up information for the Rim Trail here. The views of the canyon and Phantom Ranch from inside this historic building are stupendous. ⊠ *1 mile east of Market Plaza, Grand Canyon Village* ☎ *928/638–7888* ⊙ *Daily 8–8; hrs vary in winter.*

NORTH RIM **North Rim Visitor Center.** View exhibits, peruse the bookstore, and pick up useful maps and brochures at this visitor center. Interpretive programs are often scheduled in summer. If you're craving coffee, it's a short walk from here to the Roughrider Saloon at the Grand Canyon Lodge. ⊠ *Near the parking lot on Bright Angel Peninsula* ☎ *928/638–7864* ⊕ *www.nps.gov/grca* ⊙ *Mid-May–mid-Oct., daily 8–6.*

GRAND CANYON SOUTH RIM

Visitors to the canyon converge mostly on the South Rim, and mostly in summer. Grand Canyon Village is here, with most of the park's lodging and camping, trailheads, restaurants, stores, and museums, along with a nearby airport and railroad depot. Believe it or not, the average stay in the park is a mere half day or so; this is not advised! You need to spend several days to truly appreciate this marvelous place, but at the very least, give it a full day. Hike down into the canyon, or along the rim, to get away from the crowds and experience nature at its finest.

EXPLORING

SCENIC DRIVES

Desert View Drive. This heavily traveled 23-mile stretch of road follows the rim from the East entrance to Grand Canyon Village. Starting from the less-congested entry near Desert View, road warriors can get their first glimpse of the canyon from the 70-foot-tall watchtower, the top of which provides the highest viewpoint on the South Rim. Eight overlooks, the remains of an Ancestral Puebloan dwelling at the Tusayan Ruin and Museum, and the secluded and lovely Buggeln picnic area make for great stops along the South Rim. The Kaibab Trail Route shuttle bus travels a short section of Desert View Drive and takes 50 minutes to ride round-trip without getting off at any of the stops: Grand Canyon Visitor Center, South Kaibab Trailhead, Yaki Point, and Pipe Creek Vista, Mather Point, and Yavapai Geology Museum. ⊠ *Grand Canyon.*

> **WORD OF MOUTH**
>
> "Take Highway 64 toward Grand Canyon Village, which will take you along the East Rim and Desert View Drive. There are over a half-dozen viewpoints on this scenic road, each with its own features and perspective on the Grand Canyon." –K_Bot

Hermit Road. The Santa Fe Company built Hermit Road, formerly known as West Rim Drive, in 1912 as a scenic tour route. Nine overlooks dot this 7-mile stretch, each worth a visit. The road is filled with hairpin turns, so make sure you adhere to posted speed limits. A 1.5-mile Greenway trail offers easy access to cyclists looking to enjoy the original 1912 Hermit Rim Road. March through November, Hermit Road is closed to private auto traffic because of congestion; during this period, a free shuttle bus carries visitors to all the overlooks. Riding the bus round-trip without getting off at any of the viewpoints takes 75 minutes; the return trip stops only at Pima, Mohave, and Powell points. ⊠ *Hermit Rd.*

HISTORIC SITES

Kolb Studio. Built over several years beginning in 1904 by the Kolb brothers as a photographic workshop and residence, this building provides a view of Indian Garden, where, in the days before a pipeline was installed, Emery Kolb descended 3,000 feet each day to get the water he needed to develop his prints. Kolb was doing something right; he operated the studio until he died in 1976 at age 95. The gallery here has changing exhibitions of paintings, photography, and crafts. There's also a small Grand Canyon Association store here. During the winter months, a ranger-led tour of the studio illustrates the role the Kolb brothers had on the development of the Grand Canyon. Call ahead to sign up for the tour. ⊠ *Grand Canyon Village near Bright Angel Lodge* ☎ *928/638–2771* ⊕ *www.grandcanyon.org/kolb* 🎟 *Free* ☉ *Apr.–mid-Oct., daily 8–7; mid-Oct.–Apr., daily 8–6.*

Lookout Studio. Built in 1914 to compete with the Kolbs' photographic studio, the building was designed by architect Mary Jane Colter. The combination lookout point and gift shop has a collection of fossils and geologic samples from around the world. An upstairs loft provides another excellent overlook into the gorge below. ⊠ *About ¼ mile west of Hermit Rd. Junction on Hermit Rd.* 🎫 *Free* ☉ *Daily 9–5.*

Powell Memorial. A granite platform honors the memory of John Wesley Powell, who measured, charted, and named many of the canyons and creeks of the Colorado River. It was here that the dedication ceremony for Grand Canyon National Park took place on April 3, 1920. ⊠ *About 3 miles west of Hermit Rd. Junction on Hermit Rd.*

● **Tusayan Ruin and Museum.** Completed in 1932, this museum offers a quick orientation to the lifestyles of the prehistoric and modern Indian populations associated with the Grand Canyon and the Colorado Plateau. Adjacent, an excavation of an 800-year-old dwelling gives a glimpse of the lives of some of the area's earliest residents. Of special interest are split-twig figurines dating back 2,000 to 4,000 years ago, a replica of a 10,000-year-old spear point, and other artifacts left behind by ancient cultures. Twice daily, a ranger leads an interpretive tour of the Ancestral Puebloan village along a 0.1-mile, paved loop trail. ⊠ *About 20 miles east of Grand Canyon Village on E. Rim Dr.* 📞 *928/638–7888* 🎫 *Free* ☉ *Daily 9–5.*

SCENIC STOPS

◑ **The Abyss.** At an elevation of 6,720 feet, the Abyss is one of the most awesome stops on Hermit Road, revealing a sheer drop of 3,000 feet to the Tonto Platform, a wide terrace of Tapeats sandstone about two-thirds of the way down the canyon. From the Abyss you'll also see several isolated sandstone columns, the largest of which is called the Monument. ⊠ *About 5 miles west of Hermit Rd. Junction on Hermit Rd.*

Desert View and Watchtower. From the top of the 70-foot stone-and-mortar watchtower, even the muted hues of the distant Painted Desert to the east and the Vermilion Cliffs rising from a high plateau near the Utah border are visible. In the chasm below, angling to the north toward Marble Canyon, an imposing stretch of the Colorado River reveals itself. Up several flights of stairs, the watchtower houses a glass-enclosed observatory with powerful telescopes. ⊠ *About 23 miles east of Grand Canyon Village on Desert View Dr.* 📞 *928/638–2736* ☉ *Daily 8–8; hrs vary in winter.*

Grandview Point. At an elevation of 7,399 feet, the view from here is one of the finest in the canyon. To the northeast is a group of dominant buttes, including Krishna Shrine, Vishnu Temple, Rama Shrine, and Sheba Temple. A short stretch of the Colorado River is also visible. Directly below the point, and accessible by the steep and rugged Grandview Trail, is Horseshoe Mesa, where you can see remnants of Last Chance Copper Mine. ⊠ *About 12 miles east of Grand Canyon Village on Desert View Dr.*

Hermits Rest. This westernmost viewpoint and Hermit Trail, which descends from it, were named for "hermit" Louis Boucher, a 19th-century French-Canadian prospector who had a number of mining claims and a

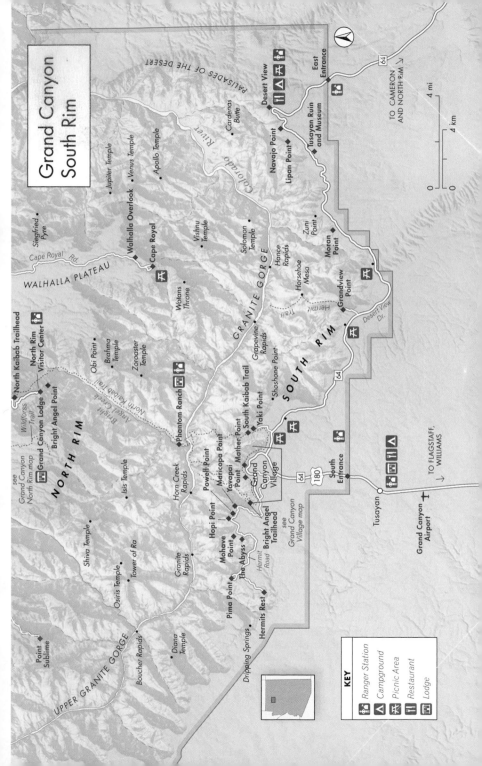

BEST GRAND CANYON VIEWS

The best time of day to see the canyon is before 10 am and after 4 pm, when the angle of the sun brings out the colors of the rock, and clouds and shadows add dimension. Colors deepen dramatically among the contrasting layers of the canyon walls just before and during sunrise and sunset.

Hopi Point is the top spot on the South Rim to watch the sun set; **Yaki** and **Pima** points also offer vivid views. For a grand sunrise, try **Mather** or **Yaki** points.

■ TIP→ Arrive at least 30 minutes early for sunrise views and as much as 90 minutes for sunset views at these points. For another point of view, take a leisurely stroll along the Rim Trail and watch the color change along with the views. Timetables are listed in the *Guide* and are posted at park visitor centers.

roughly built home down in the canyon. The trail served as the original mule ride down to Hermit Camp beginning in 1914. Views from here include Hermit Rapids and the towering cliffs of the Supai and Redwall formations. In the stone building at Hermits Rest you can buy curios and snacks. ⊠ *About 8 miles west of Hermit Rd. Junction on Hermit Rd.*

Fodor'sChoice
★
Hopi Point. From this elevation of 6,800 feet, you can see a large section of the Colorado River; although it appears as a thin line, the river is nearly 350 feet wide below this overlook. The overlook extends farther into the canyon than any other point on Hermit Road. The unobstructed views make this a popular place to watch the sunset.

Across the canyon to the north is Shiva Temple, which remained an unexplored section of the Kaibab Plateau until 1937. That year, Harold Anthony of the American Museum of Natural History led an expedition to the rock formation in the belief that it supported life that had been cut off from the rest of the canyon. Imagine the expedition members' surprise when they found an empty Kodak film box on top of the temple—it had been left behind by Emery Kolb, who felt slighted for not having been invited to partake of Anthony's tour.

Directly below Hopi Point lies Dana Butte, named for a prominent 19th-century geologist. In 1919, an entrepreneur proposed connecting Hopi Point, Dana Butte, and the Tower of Set across the river with an aerial tramway, a technically feasible plan that fortunately has not been realized. ⊠ *About 4 miles west of Hermit Rd. Junction on Hermit Rd.*

Lipan Point. Here, at the canyon's widest point, you can get an astonishing visual profile of the gorge's geologic history, with a view of every eroded layer of the canyon—you can also observe one of the longest stretches of visible Colorado River. The spacious panorama stretches to the Vermilion Cliffs on the northeastern horizon and features a multitude of imaginatively named spires, buttes, and temples—intriguing rock formations named after their resemblance to ancient pyramids. You can also see Unkar Delta, where a creek joins the Colorado to form powerful rapids and a broad beach. Ancestral Puebloan farmers worked the Unkar

Delta for hundreds of years, growing corn, beans, and melons. ⊠ *About 25 miles east of Grand Canyon Village on Desert View Dr.*

Maricopa Point. This site merits a stop not only for the arresting scenery, which includes the Colorado River below, but also for its view of a defunct mine operation. On your left, as you face the canyon, are the Orphan Mine, a mine shaft, and cable lines leading up to the rim. The mine, which started operations in 1893, was worked first for copper and then for uranium until the venture came to a halt in 1969. Little remains of the mine infrastructure today, but some displays along the Rim Trail discuss its history. The Battleship, the red butte directly ahead of you in the canyon, was named during the Spanish-American War, when warships were in the news. ⊠ *About 2 miles west of Hermit Rd. Junction on Hermit Rd.*

Mather Point. You'll likely get your first glimpse of the canyon from this viewpoint, one of the most impressive and accessible (next to the main Visitor Center Plaza) on the South Rim. Named for the National Park Service's first director, Stephen Mather, this spot yields extraordinary views of the Grand Canyon, including deep into the inner gorge and numerous buttes: Wotans Throne, Brahma Temple, and Zoroaster Temple, among others. The Grand Canyon Lodge, on the North Rim, is almost directly north from Mather Point and only 10 miles away—yet you have to drive 215 miles to get from one spot to the other. ⊠ *Near Grand Canyon Visitor Center* ☏ *928/638–7888* ⊕ *www.nps.gov/grca.*

Mohave Point. Some of the canyon's most magnificent stone spires and buttes visible from this lesser-known overlook include the Tower of Set; the Tower of Ra; and Isis, Osiris, and Horus temples. From here you can view the 5,401-foot Cheops Pyramid, a grayish rock formation behind Dana Butte, plus some of the strongest rapids on the Colorado River. ⊠ *About 5 miles west of Hermit Rd. Junction on Hermit Rd.*

Moran Point. This point was named for American landscape artist Thomas Moran, who was especially fond of the play of light and shadows from this location. He first visited the canyon with John Wesley Powell in 1873. "Thomas Moran's name, more than any other, with the possible exception of Major Powell's, is to be associated with the Grand Canyon," wrote noted canyon photographer Ellsworth Kolb. It's fitting that Moran Point is a favorite spot of photographers and painters. ⊠ *About 17 miles east of Grand Canyon Village on Desert View Dr.*

Navajo Point. A possible site of the first Spanish view into the canyon in 1540, this overlook is also at the highest natural elevation (7,461 feet) on the South Rim. ⊠ *About 21 miles east of Grand Canyon Village on Desert View Dr.*

Pima Point. Enjoy a bird's-eye view of Tonto Platform and Tonto Trail, which winds its way through the canyon for more than 70 miles. Also to the west, two dark, cone-shape mountains—Mount Trumbull and Mount Logan—are visible on the North Rim on clear days. They rise in stark contrast to the surrounding flat-top mesas and buttes. ⊠ *About 7 miles west of Hermit Rd. Junction on Hermit Rd.*

Trailview Overlook. Look down on a dramatic view of the Bright Angel and Plateau Point trails as they zigzag down the canyon. In the deep

DID YOU KNOW?

From the Grand Canyon's edge, the Colorado River is up to 1 mile deep. Almost 40 exposed bands of rock represent different geological periods—the oldest sections date back some 2 billion years.

Tips for Avoiding Grand Canyon Crowds

It's hard to commune with nature while you're searching for a parking place, dodging video cameras, and stepping away from strollers. However, this scenario is likely only during the peak summer months. One option is to bypass Grand Canyon National Park altogether and head to the West Rim of the canyon, tribal land of the Hualapai and Havasupai. If only the park itself will do, the following tips will help you to keep your distance and your cool.

TAKE ANOTHER ROUTE

Avoid road rage by choosing a different route to the South Rim, forgoing the traditional Highway 64 and U.S. 180 from Flagstaff. Take U.S. 89 north from Flagstaff instead, passing near Sunset Crater and Wupatki national monuments. When you reach the junction with Highway 64, take a break at Cameron Trading Post (1 mile north of the junction)—or stay overnight. This is a good place to shop for Native American artifacts, souvenirs, and the usual postcards, dream-catchers, recordings, and T-shirts. There are also high-quality Navajo rugs, jewelry, and other authentic handicrafts, and you can sample Navajo tacos. U.S. 64 to the west takes you directly to the park's east entrance; the scenery along the Little Colorado River gorge en route is eye-popping. It's 23 miles from the east entrance to the Grand Canyon Visitor Center in the village.

SKIP THE SOUTH RIM

Although the North Rim is just 10 miles across from the South Rim, the trip to get there by car is a five-hour drive of 215 miles. At first it might not sound like the trip would be worth it, but the payoff is huge. Along the way, you'll travel through some of the prettiest parts of the state and be granted even more stunning views than those on the more easily accessible South Rim. Those who make the North Rim trip often insist it has the canyon's most beautiful views and best hiking. To get to the North Rim from Flagstaff, take U.S. 89 north past Cameron, turning left onto U.S. 89A at Bitter Springs. En route you'll pass the area known as Vermilion Cliffs. At Jacob Lake, take Highway 67 directly to the Grand Canyon North Rim. North Rim services are closed from mid-October through mid-May because of heavy snow, but in summer months and early fall, it's a wonderful way to beat the crowds at the South Rim.

gorge to the north flows Bright Angel Creek, one of the region's few permanent tributary streams of the Colorado River. Toward the south is an unobstructed view of the distant San Francisco Peaks, as well as Bill Williams Mountain (on the horizon) and Red Butte (about 15 miles south of the canyon rim). ⊠ *About 2 miles west of Hermit Rd. Junction on Hermit Rd.*

Yaki Point. Stop here for an exceptional view of Wotan's Throne, a flat-top butte named by François Matthes, a U.S. Geological Survey scientist who developed the first topographical map of the Grand Canyon. The overlook juts out over the canyon, providing unobstructed views of inner-canyon rock formations, South Rim cliffs, and Clear Creek canyon. About a mile south of Yaki Point, you'll come to the trailhead for the South Kaibab Trail. The point is one of the best places on the South Rim to watch the sunset. ⊠ *2 miles east of Grand Canyon Village on Desert View Dr.*

Fodor'sChoice   **Yavapai Point.** This is also one of the best locations on the South Rim
★   to watch the sunset. Dominated by the Yavapai Geology Museum and Observation Station, this point displays panoramic views of the mighty gorge through a wall of windows. Exhibits at the museum include videos of the canyon floor and the Colorado River, a scaled diorama of the canyon with national park boundaries, fossils and rock fragments used to re-create the complex layers of the canyon walls, and a display on the natural forces used to carve the chasm. Rangers dig even deeper into Grand Canyon geology with free ranger programs daily. Check ahead for special events, guided walks, and program schedules. There's also a bookstore. ⊠ *Adjacent to Grand Canyon Village* 💲 *Free* ☉ *Daily 8–8; hrs vary in winter.*

EDUCATIONAL OFFERINGS
RANGER PROGRAMS
Interpretive Ranger Programs. The National Park Service sponsors all sorts of orientation activities, such as daily guided hikes and talks, which change with the seasons. The focus may be on any aspect of the canyon—from geology and flora and fauna to history and early inhabitants. For schedules on the South Rim, go to any of the Grand Canyon Visitor Centers, pick up a free copy of the *Guide,* or check online. ☎ *928/638–7888* ⊕ *www.nps.gov/grca* 💲 *Free.*

FAMILY   **Junior Ranger Program for Families.** The Junior Ranger Program provides a free, fun way to look at the cultural and natural history of this sublime destination. These hands-on educational activities for children ages 4 and up, available at the visitor centers, include guided adventure hikes, ranger-led "discovery" talks, and book readings. ☎ *928/638–7888* ⊕ *www.nps.gov/grca/forkids/beajuniorranger.htm* 💲 *Free.*

SPORTS AND THE OUTDOORS

AIR TOURS
Flights by plane and helicopter over the canyon are offered by a number of companies, departing from the Grand Canyon Airport at the south end of Tusayan. Though the noise and disruption of so many aircraft buzzing the canyon is controversial, flightseeing remains a popular, if expensive, option. You'll have more visibility from a helicopter, but they're louder and more expensive than the fixed-wing planes. Prices and lengths of tours vary, but you can expect to pay about $149 per adult for short plane trips and approximately $179–$250 for brief helicopter tours (and about $450 for tours leaving from Vegas). These companies often have significant discounts in winter—check the company websites to find the best deals.

TOURS
Grand Canyon Airlines. This company flies a fixed-wing on a 50-minute tour of the eastern edge of the Grand Canyon, the North Rim, and the Kaibab Plateau. All-day combination tours combine flightseeing with four-wheel-drive tours and float trips on the Colorado River. Grand Canyon Airlines

also schedules combination tours that leave from Las Vegas (plane flight from Las Vegas to Grand Canyon Airport, then helicopter flight into the canyon). ⊠ *Grand Canyon Airport, Tusayan* ☎ *928/638–2359, 866/235–9422* ⊕ *www.grandcanyonairlines.com* ✉ *From $159.*

Maverick Helicopters. Maverick Helicopters has 25- and 45-minute tours of the South Rim, North Rim, and Dragon Corridor of the Grand Canyon. Airplane tours are also provided. A landing tour option for those leaving from Las Vegas sets you down in the canyon for a short snack below the rim. ⊠ *Grand Canyon Airport, Grand Canyon* ☎ *928/638–2622, 800/962–3869* ⊕ *www.flymaverick.com* ✉ *From $165.*

Papillon Grand Canyon Helicopters. Leaving both from Grand Canyon Airport and Las Vegas, Papillon Grand Canyon Helicopters offers a variety of fixed-wing and helicopter tours of the canyon. Combination tour options include off-road jeep tours and smooth-water rafting trips. ⊠ *Grand Canyon Airport, Tusayan* ☎ *928/638–2764, 888/635–7272* ⊕ *www.papillon.com* ✉ *From $124.*

BICYCLING

The South Rim's limited opportunities for off-road biking, narrow shoulders on park roads, and heavy traffic may disappoint hard-core cyclists. Bicycles are permitted on all park roads and on the multiuse Greenway System, as well as Bridle Trail (⇨ *see North Rim*). Bikes are prohibited on all other trails, including the Rim Trail. Some find Hermit Road a good biking option, especially from March through November when it's closed to cars. You can ride west 8 miles and then put your bike on the free shuttle bus back into the village (or vice versa). Mountain bikers visiting the South Rim may be better off meandering through the ponderosa pine forest on the Tusayan Bike Trail. Rentals and guided bicycling tours are available April to October at the South Rim from Bright Angel Bicycles at the visitor center complex. Bicycle camping sites are available at Mather Campground for $6 per person.

HIKING

Although permits are not required for day hikes, you must have a backcountry permit for longer trips (⇨ *see Park Fees and Permits at the start of this chapter*). Some of the more popular trails are listed here; more detailed information and maps can be obtained from the Backcountry Information Centers. Also, rangers can help design a trip to suit your abilities.

Remember that the canyon has significant elevation changes and, in summer, extreme temperature ranges, which can pose problems for people who aren't in good shape or who have heart or respiratory problems. ■ **TIP→ Carry plenty of water and energy foods.** The majority of each year's 400 search-and-rescue incidents result from hikers underestimating the size of the canyon, hiking beyond their abilities, or not packing sufficient food and water.

⚠ **Under no circumstances should you attempt a day hike from the rim to the river and back.** Remember that when it's 80°F on the South Rim, it's 110°F on the canyon floor. Allow two to four days if you want to hike rim to rim (it's easier to descend from the North Rim, as it's more than 1,000 feet higher than the South Rim). Hiking steep trails from

Switchbacks on the canyon's trails make the steep grade level enough for hikers (and mules).

rim to rim is a strenuous trek of at least 21 miles and should only be attempted by experienced canyon hikers.

EASY

Fodor's Choice ★

Rim Trail. The South Rim's most popular walking path is the 12-mile (one-way) Rim Trail, which runs along the edge of the canyon from Pipe Creek Vista (the first overlook on Desert View Drive) to Hermits Rest. This walk, which is paved to Maricopa Point and for the last 1.5 miles to Hermits Rest, visits several of the South Rim's historic landmarks. Allow anywhere from 15 minutes to a full day, depending on how much of the trail you want to cover; the Rim Trail is an ideal day hike, as it varies only a few hundred feet in elevation from Mather Point (7,120 feet) to the trailhead at Hermits Rest (6,650 feet). The trail also can be accessed from several spots in Grand Canyon Village and from the major viewpoints along Hermit Road, which are serviced by shuttle buses during the busy summer months. ■TIP➔ On the Rim Trail, water is only available in the Grand Canyon Village area and at Hermits Rest. *Easy.*

MODERATE

Bright Angel Trail. This well-maintained trail is one of the most scenic hiking paths from the South Rim to the bottom of the canyon (9.6 miles each way). Rest houses are equipped with water at the 1.5- and 3-mile points from May through September and at Indian Garden (4 miles) year-round. Water is also available at Bright Angel Campground, 9.25 miles below the trailhead. Plateau Point, on a spur trail about 1.5 miles below Indian Garden, is as far as you should attempt to go on a day hike; the round trip will take six to nine hours.

Bright Angel Trail is the easiest of all the footpaths into the canyon, but because the climb out from the bottom is an ascent of 5,510 feet, the trip should be attempted only by those in good physical condition and should be avoided in midsummer due to extreme heat. The top of the trail can be icy in winter. Originally a bighorn sheep path and later used by the Havasupai, the trail was widened late in the 19th century for prospectors and is now used for both mule and foot traffic.

> **WORD OF MOUTH**
>
> "If you have pack space for 4 quarts of water and are feeling chipper then go for the gold standard, Kaibab. It's a much more scenic trail, with much fewer people and few mules compared to Bright Angel, and it's shorter, so you'll typically finish 30–60 minutes earlier." –Bill_H

Also note that mule trains have the right-of-way—and sometimes leave unpleasant surprises in your path. *Moderate.* ⊠ *Trailhead: Kolb Studio, Hermits Rd.*

DIFFICULT

Grandview Trail. Accessible from the parking area at Grandview Point, the trailhead is at 7,400 feet. The path heads steeply down into the canyon for 3 miles to the junction and campsite at East Horseshoe Mesa Trail. Classified as a wilderness trail, the route is aggressive and not as heavily traveled as some of the more well-known trails, such as Bright Angel and Hermit. There is no water available along the trail, which follows a steep descent to 4,800 feet at Horseshoe Mesa, where Hopi Indians once collected mineral paints. Hike 0.7 mile farther to Page Spring, a reliable water source year-round. Parts of this trail are icy in winter, and traction crampons are mandatory. *Difficult.* ⊠ *Trailhead: Grandview Point, Desert View Dr.*

Hermit Trail. Beginning on the South Rim just west of Hermits Rest (and 7 miles west of Grand Canyon Village), this steep, unmaintained, 9.7-mile (one-way) trail drops more than 5,000 feet to Hermit Creek, which usually flows year-round. It's a strenuous hike back up and is recommended for experienced long-distance hikers only; plan for six to nine hours. There's an abundance of lush growth and wildlife, including desert bighorn sheep, along this trail. The trail descends from the trailhead at 6,640 feet to the Colorado River at 2,300 feet. Day hikers should not go past Santa Maria Spring at 5,000 feet.

For much of the year, no water is available along the way; ask a park ranger about the availability of water at Santa Maria Spring and Hermit Creek before you set out. All water from these sources should be treated before drinking. The route leads down to the Colorado River and has inspiring views of Hermit Gorge and the Redwall and Supai formations. Six miles from the trailhead are the ruins of Hermit Camp, which the Santa Fe Railroad ran as a tourist camp from 1911 until 1930. *Difficult.* ⊠ *Trailhead: Hermits Rest, Hermits Rd.*

South Kaibab Trail. This trail starts near Yaki Point, 4 miles east of Grand Canyon Village, and is accessible via the free shuttle bus. Because the route is so steep (and sometimes icy in winter)—descending from the trailhead at 7,260 feet down to 2,480 feet at the Colorado River—and

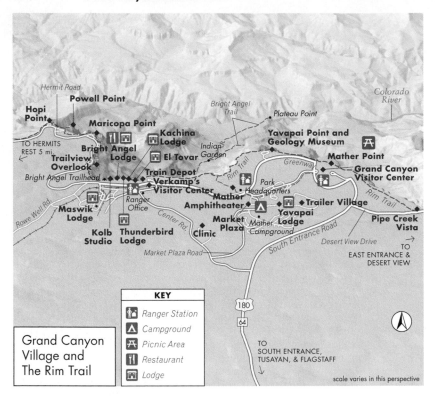

KEY

🚹	Ranger Station
⛺	Campground
⛲	Picnic Area
🍴	Restaurant
🏨	Lodge

Grand Canyon Village and The Rim Trail

Map labels: Hermit Road, Powell Point, Hopi Point, Maricopa Point, TO HERMITS REST 5 mi., Bright Angel Lodge, Trailview Overlook, Bright Angel Trailhead, Rowe Well Rd., Maswik Lodge, Kolb Studio, Thunderbird Lodge, Ranger Office, Center Rd., Verkamp's Visitor Center, Train Depot, Kachina Lodge, El Tovar, Indian Garden, Bright Angel Trail, Plateau Point, Yavapai Point and Geology Museum, Mather Point, Grand Canyon Visitor Center, Colorado River, Greenway, Rim Trail, Park Headquarters, Mather Amphitheater, Market Plaza, Clinic, Mather Campground, Yavapai Lodge, Trailer Village, Pipe Creek Vista, Market Plaza Road, South Entrance Road, Desert View Drive, TO EAST ENTRANCE & DESERT VIEW, 180, 64, TO SOUTH ENTRANCE, TUSAYAN, & FLAGSTAFF, scale varies in this perspective

has no water, many hikers take this trail down, then ascend via the less-demanding Bright Angel Trail. Allow four to six hours to reach the Colorado River on this 6.4-mile trek. At the river, the trail crosses a suspension bridge and runs on to Phantom Ranch. Along the trail there is no water and little shade. There are no campgrounds, though there are portable toilets at Cedar Ridge (6,320 feet), 1.5 miles from the trailhead. An emergency phone is available at the Tipoff, 4.6 miles down the trail (3 miles past Cedar Ridge). The trail corkscrews down through some spectacular geology. Look for (but don't remove) fossils in the limestone when taking water breaks. ■ TIP→ **Even though an immense network of trails winds through the Grand Canyon, the popular corridor trails (Bright Angel and South Kaibab) are recommended for hikers new to the region.** *Difficult.* ⊠ *Trailhead: Yaki Point, Desert View Dr.*

JEEP TOURS

Jeep rides can be rough; if you have had back injuries, check with your doctor before taking a 4X4 tour. It's a good idea to book a week or two ahead, and even further if you're visiting in summer or on busy weekends.

TOURS AND OUTFITTERS

Grand Canyon Jeep Tours & Safaris. If you'd like to get off the pavement and see parts of the park that are accessible only by dirt road, a jeep tour can be just the ticket. From March to November, this tour operator leads daily, 1½- to 4½-hour, off-road tours within the park, as well as in Kaibab National Forest. Sunset tours and combo tours adding helicopter or airplane rides are also available. ☎ *928/638–5337* ⊕ *www.grandcanyonjeeptours.com* ⊠ *From $67.*

Grand Canyon Store. This tour company offers off-road adventures year-round in comfortable cruisers (small luxury vans with heating and air-conditioning) rather than jeeps. Full-day tours go either to the South Rim, or to the bottom of the canyon on the Hualapai Indian Reservation. Helicopter tours or whitewater raft tours through the canyon are included in some of these trips. ⊠ *212 W. Rte. 66, Williams* ☎ *928/638–2000, 800/716–9389* ⊕ *www.discovergrandcanyon.com* ⊠ *From $249.*

Marvelous Marv's Grand Canyon Tours. For a personalized experience, take this private tour of the Grand Canyon and surrounding sights any time of year. Tours include round-trip transportation from your hotel or campground in Williams, Tusayan, or Grand Canyon; admission to the park; scenic viewpoint stops; a short hike; and personal narration of the geology and history of the area. Note that credit cards are not accepted. ⊠ *200 W. Bill Williams Ave., Williams* ☎ *928/707–0291* ⊕ *www.marvelousmarv.com* ⊠ *From $100.*

MULE RIDES

Fodor's Choice
★

Mule rides provide an intimate glimpse into the canyon for those who have the time, but not the stamina, to see the canyon on foot. ■TIP→ Reservations are essential and are accepted up to 13 months in advance.

These trips have been conducted since the early 1900s. A comforting fact as you ride the narrow trail: no one's ever been killed while riding a mule that fell off a cliff. (Nevertheless, the treks are not for the faint of heart or people in questionable health.)

OUTFITTERS

Fodor's Choice
★

Xanterra Parks & Resorts Mule Rides. These trips delve into the canyon from the South Rim to Phantom Ranch, or east along the canyon's edge (the Plateau Point rides were discontinued in 2009). Riders must be at least 55 inches tall, weigh less than 200 pounds (for the Phantom Ranch ride), and understand English. Children under 15 must be accompanied by an adult. Riders must be in fairly good physical condition, and pregnant women are advised not to take these trips.

The three-hour ride along the rim costs $114. An overnight with a stay at Phantom Ranch at the bottom of the canyon is $518 ($916 for two riders). Two nights at Phantom Ranch, an option available November through March, will set you back $731 ($1,218 for two). Meals are included. Reservations (by phone), especially during the busy summer months, are a must, but you can check at the Bright Angel Transportation Desk to see if there's last-minute availability. ☎ *888/297–2757* ⊕ *www.*

grandcanyonlodges.com ⚓ *Reservations essential* ⊘ *Phantom Ranch rides daily. Rim rides mid-Mar.– Oct., twice daily; Nov.–mid-Mar., once daily.*

SKIING

Tusayan Ranger District. Although you can't schuss down into the Grand Canyon, you can cross-country ski in the woods near the rim when there's enough snow, usually mid-December though early March. The ungroomed trails, suitable for beginner and intermediate skiers, begin at the Grandview Lookout and travel through the Kaibab National Forest. For details, contact the Tusayan Ranger District. ⊠ *176 Lincoln Log Loop, Grand Canyon* ☎ *928/638–2443* ⊕ *www.fs.usda.gov/kaibab.*

ARRANGING TOURS

Transportation-services desks are maintained at Bright Angel, Maswik Lodge, and Yavapai Lodge (closed in winter) in Grand Canyon Village. The desks provide information and handle bookings for sightseeing tours, taxi and bus services, and mule rides (but don't count on last-minute availability). There's also a concierge at El Tovar that can arrange most tours, with the exception of mule rides. On the North Rim, Grand Canyon Lodge has general information about local services.

SHOPPING

Nearly every lodging facility and retail store at the South Rim stocks Native American arts and crafts and Grand Canyon books and souvenirs. Prices are comparable to other souvenir outlets, though you may find some better deals in Williams. However, a portion of the proceeds from items purchased at Kolb Studio, Tusayan Museum, and all the park visitor centers go to the nonprofit Grand Canyon Association.

Desert View Trading Post. A mix of traditional Southwestern souvenirs and authentic Native American arts and crafts are for sale at Desert View Trading Post. ⊠ *Desert View Dr. near the watchtower at Desert View* ☎ *928/638–3150.*

Hopi House. This two-level shop has the widest selection of Native American art and handicrafts in the vicinity. ⊠ *Across from El Tovar Hotel, 4 El Tovar Rd., Grand Canyon Village* ☎ *928/638–2631.*

GRAND CANYON NORTH RIM

The North Rim stands 1,000 feet higher than the South Rim and has a more alpine climate, with twice as much annual precipitation. Here, in the deep forests of the Kaibab Plateau, the crowds are thinner, the facilities fewer, and the views even more spectacular. Due to snow, the North Rim is off-limits in winter. The buildings and concessions are closed mid-October through mid-May. The road and entrance gate close when the snow makes them impassable—usually by the end of November.

Lodgings are limited in this more remote park, with only one historic lodge (with cabins and hotel-type rooms as well as a restaurant) and a single campground. Dining options have opened up a little with the

GRAND CANYON NATIONAL PARK: TOP PICKS HIKING TRAILS

	Grade	Miles (One Way)	Beginning Elevation	Ending Elevation	Mules	Campground	Open Info*	Water	Shuttle Access	Ranger Station	Toilet/Restroom	Emergency Telephone	Hiking Level	Trail Conditions
SOUTH RIM														
Bright Angel Trail South	Steep	9.6 mi	6,785 ft	2,480 ft (Colorado River)	Y	Y	Y/R	(Seasonal)	Y	Y	Y	Y	Moderate-Difficult	Maintained
Grandview Trail	Very Steep	3.2 mi	7,400 ft	4,900 ft (Horseshoe Mesa)		Y	Y/R	Y		Y			Difficult	Unmaintained
Hermit Trail	Steep	9.7 mi	6,640 ft	2,300 ft (Colorado River)			Y/R	(Untreated)	Y		Y**	Y**	Difficult	Unmaintained
New Hance Trail	Steep	8 mi	6,982 ft	2,600 ft (Colorado River)			Y/R						Difficult	Unmaintained
Rim Trail	Level	9 mi	6,820 ft	7,120 ft (Mather Point)			Y/R	Y**	Y		Y	Y	Easy	Maintained
South Kaibab Trail	Steep	6.4 mi	7,200 ft	2,400 ft (Colorado River)		Y/R	Y**	Y	Y	Y	Y		Difficult	Maintained
NORTH RIM														
Cape Final Trail	Level/Incline	2.0 mi	7,840 ft	7,916 ft (Cape Final)			mid-May–mid-Oct.						Easy	Maintained
Ken Patrick Trail	Level/Incline	10 mi	8,250 ft	8,803 ft (Point Imperial)			mid-May–mid-Oct.						Difficult	Unmaintained
North Kaibab Trail	Steep	7.1 mi	8,241 ft	2,400 ft (Colorado River)	Y	Y	mid-May–mid-Oct.	Y	Y	Y	Y	Y	Difficult	Maintained
Transept Trail	Level	1.5 mi	8,255 ft	8,200 ft (Campground)			mid-May–mid-Oct.				Y	Y	Easy	Maintained
Uncle Jim Trail	Level	2.5 mi	8,300 ft	8,244 ft (Uncle Jim Point)	Y		mid-May–mid-Oct.						Moderate	Maintained
Widforss Trail	Level/Incline	4.9 mi	8,080 ft	7,900 ft (Widforss Point)			mid-May–mid-Oct.						Moderate	Unmaintained

*(South Rim trails occasionally close due to weather or trail conditions) **(Trailhead) Y/R = year-round

CLOSE UP

Freebies at the Grand Canyon

While you're here, be sure to take advantage of the many complimentary services offered at Grand Canyon National Park.

■ The most useful is undoubtedly the system of free shuttle buses at the South Rim; it caters to the road-weary, with four routes winding through or just outside the park—Hermits Rest Route, Village Route, Kaibab Rim Route, and Tusayan Route. Of the bus routes, the Hermits Rest Route runs only March through November and the Tusayan Route only in summer; the other two run year-round, and the Kaibab Trail Route provides the only access to Yaki Point. Hikers coming or going from the Kaibab Trailhead can catch the Hikers Express, which departs three times each morning from the Bright Angel Lodge, makes a quick stop at the Backcountry Information Center, and then heads out to the South Kaibab Trailhead.

■ Ranger-led programs are always free and offered year-round, though more are scheduled during the busy spring and summer seasons. These programs might include activities such as stargazing and topics such as geology and the cultural history of prehistoric peoples. Some of the more in-depth programs may include a fossil walk or a condor talk. Check with the visitor center for seasonal programs including wildflower walks and fire ecology.

■ Kids ages four and older can get involved with the park's Junior Ranger program, with ever-changing activities including hikes and hands-on experiments.

■ Despite all of these options, rangers will tell you that the best free activity in the canyon is watching the magnificent splashes of color on the canyon walls during sunrise and sunset.

addition of the Grand Cookout, offered nightly with live entertainment under the stars. Your best bet may be to pack your camping gear and hiking boots and take several days to explore the lush Kaibab Forest. The canyon's highest, most dramatic rim views also can be enjoyed on two wheels (via primitive dirt access roads) and on four legs (courtesy of a trusty mule).

EXPLORING

SCENIC DRIVE

Fodor's Choice
★

Highway 67. Open mid-May to roughly mid-November (or the first big snowfall), the two-lane paved road climbs 1,400 feet in elevation as it passes through the Kaibab National Forest. Also called the "North Rim Parkway," this scenic route crosses the limestone-capped Kaibab Plateau—passing broad meadows, sun-dappled forests, and small lakes and springs—before abruptly falling away at the abyss of the Grand Canyon. Wildlife abounds in the thick ponderosa pine forests and lush mountain meadows. It's common to see deer, turkeys, and coyotes as you drive through this remote region. Point Imperial and Cape Royal branch off this scenic drive, which runs from Jacob Lake to Bright Angel Point.

HISTORIC SITE

Grand Canyon Lodge. Built in 1937 by the Union Pacific Railroad (replacing the original 1928 building, which burned in a fire), the massive stone structure is listed on the National Register of Historic Places. Its huge sunroom has hardwood floors, high-beam ceilings, and a marvelous view of the canyon through plate-glass windows. On warm days, visitors sit in the sun and drink in the surrounding beauty on an outdoor viewing deck, where National Park Service employees deliver free lectures on geology and history. The dining room serves breakfast, lunch, and dinner; the Roughrider Saloon is a bar by night and a coffeeshop in the morning. ⊠ *10 Albright St., off Hwy. 67 near Bright Angel Point* ☎ *928/638–2631* ⊕ *www.grandcanyonlodges.com.*

SCENIC STOPS

Fodor's Choice
★

Bright Angel Point. This trail, which leads to one of the most awe-inspiring overlooks on either rim, starts on the grounds of the Grand Canyon Lodge and runs along the crest of a point of rocks that juts into the canyon for several hundred yards. The walk is only 0.5 mile round-trip, but it's an exciting trek accented by sheer drops on each side of the trail. In a few spots where the route is extremely narrow, metal railings ensure visitors' safety. The temptation to clamber out to precarious perches to have your picture taken should be resisted at all costs. ⊠ *North Rim Dr.*

Cape Royal. A popular sunset destination, Cape Royal showcases the canyon's jagged landscape; you'll also get a glimpse of the Colorado River, framed by a natural stone arch called Angels Window. In autumn, the aspens turn a beautiful gold, adding even more color to an already magnificent scene of the forested surroundings. The easy and rewarding 1-mile round-trip hike along **Cliff Springs Trail** starts here; it takes you through a forested ravine and terminates at Cliff Springs, where the forest opens to another impressive view of the canyon walls. ⊠ *Cape Royal Scenic Dr., 23 miles southeast of Grand Canyon Lodge.*

Point Imperial. At 8,803 feet, Point Imperial has the highest vista point at either rim; it offers magnificent views of both the canyon and the distant country: the Vermilion Cliffs to the north, the 10,000-foot Navajo Mountain to the northeast in Utah, the Painted Desert to the east, and the Little Colorado River canyon to the southeast. Other prominent points of interest include views of Mount Hayden, Saddle Mountain, and Marble Canyon. ⊠ *2.7 miles left off Cape Royal Rd. on Point Imperial Rd., 11 miles northeast of Grand Canyon Lodge.*

Fodor's Choice
★

Point Sublime. You can camp within feet of the canyon's edge at this awe-inspiring site. Sunrises and sunsets are spectacular. The winding road, through gorgeous high country, is only 17 miles, but it will take you at least two hours, one way. The road is intended only for vehicles with high-road clearance (pickups and four-wheel-drive vehicles). It is also necessary to be properly equipped for wilderness road travel. Check with a park ranger or at the information desk at Grand Canyon Lodge before taking this journey. You may camp here only with a permit from the Backcountry Information Center. ⊠ *North Rim Dr., about 20 miles west of North Rim Visitor Center.*

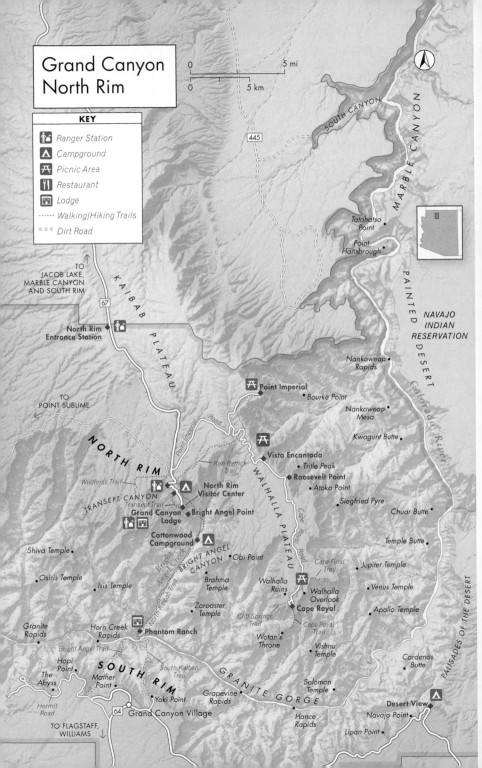

Grand Canyon
North Rim

KEY
- Ranger Station
- Campground
- Picnic Area
- Restaurant
- Lodge
- --- Walking/Hiking Trails
- === Dirt Road

0 ____ 5 mi
0 ____ 5 km

SOUTH CANYON

MARBLE CANYON

445

Tatahatso Point

Point Hansbrough

PAINTED DESERT

NAVAJO INDIAN RESERVATION

TO JACOB LAKE, MARBLE CANYON AND SOUTH RIM

67

KAIBAB PLATEAU

North Rim Entrance Station

Nankoweap Rapids

TO POINT SUBLIME

Point Imperial

Bourke Point

Nankoweap Mesa

Kwagunt Butte

Colorado River

NORTH RIM

Point Imperial Road

Ken Patrick Trail

Vista Encantada

Tritle Peak

Roosevelt Point

Atoko Point

Siegfried Pyre

Chuar Butte

Wildforss Trail

TRANSEPT CANYON

Transept Trail

North Rim Visitor Center

WALHALLA PLATEAU

Grand Canyon Lodge

Bright Angel Point

Cape Royal Road

Temple Butte

Cottonwood Campground

Shiva Temple

BRIGHT ANGEL CANYON

Obi Point

Cape Final Trail

Jupiter Temple

Osiris Temple

Isis Temple

Brahma Temple

Zoroaster Temple

Walhalla Ruins

Walhalla Overlook

Venus Temple

Apollo Temple

Cliff Springs Trail

Cape Royal

North Kaibab Trail

Cape Royal Trail

Granite Rapids

Horn Creek Rapids

Phantom Ranch

Wotan's Throne

Vishnu Temple

Cardenas Butte

Bright Angel Trail

Hopi Point

The Abyss

SOUTH RIM

Mather Point

Yaki Point

South Kaibab Trail

GRANITE GORGE

Grapevine Rapids

Solomon Temple

PALISADES OF THE DESERT

Hermit Road

TO FLAGSTAFF, WILLIAMS

64

Grand Canyon Village

Hance Rapids

Desert View

Navajo Point

Lipan Point

TO POINT SUBLIME

Roosevelt Point. Named after the president who gave the Grand Canyon its national monument status in 1908 (it was upgraded to national park status in 1919), Roosevelt Point is the best place to see the confluence of the Little Colorado River and the Grand Canyon. The cliffs above the Colorado River south of the junction are known as the Palisades of the Desert. A short woodland loop trail leads to this eastern viewpoint. ⊠ *Cape Royal Rd., 18 miles east of Grand Canyon Lodge.*

Vista Encantada. This point on the Walhalla Plateau offers views of the upper drainage of Nankoweap Creek, a rock pinnacle known as Brady Peak, and the Painted Desert to the east. This is an enchanting place for a picnic lunch. ⊠ *Cape Royal Rd., 16 miles southeast of Grand Canyon Lodge.*

Walhalla Overlook. One of the lowest elevations on the North Rim, this overlook has views of the Unkar Delta, a fertile region used by Ancestral Puebloans as farmland. These ancient people also gathered food and hunted game on the North Rim. A flat path leads to the remains of the Walhalla Glades Pueblo, which was inhabited from 1050 to 1150. ⊠ *Cape Royal Rd., 22.5 miles southeast of Grand Canyon Lodge.*

EDUCATIONAL OFFERINGS
RANGER PROGRAMS
FAMILY **Discovery Pack Junior Ranger Program.** In summer, children ages four and up can take part in hands-on educational programs and earn a Junior Ranger certificate and badge. Sign up at the North Rim Visitor Center for these independent and ranger-led activities. ☎ *928/638–7967* ⊕ *www.nps.gov/grca* ⊠ *Free.*

Interpretive Ranger Programs. Daily guided hikes and talks may focus on any aspect of the canyon—from geology and flora and fauna to history and the canyon's early inhabitants. For schedules, go to the Grand Canyon Lodge or download a free copy of the *Guide* to the North Rim from the park website. ☎ *928/638–7967* ⊕ *www.nps.gov/grca* ⊠ *Free.*

SPORTS AND THE OUTDOORS

BICYCLING
Mountain bikers can test the many dirt access roads found in this remote area. The 17-mile trek to Point Sublime is, well, sublime—though you'll share this road with high-clearance vehicles, it's rare to spot other people on most of these primitive pathways.

Bicycles and leashed pets are allowed on the well-maintained 1.2-mile (one way) **Bridle Trail,** which follows the road from Grand Canyon Lodge to the North Kaibab Trailhead. Bikes are prohibited on all other national park trails.

Flora and Fauna of the Grand Canyon

Eighty-nine mammal species inhabit Grand Canyon National Park, as well as 355 species of birds, 56 kinds of reptiles and amphibians, and 17 kinds of fish. The rare Kaibab squirrel is found only on the North Rim—you can recognize them by their all-white tails and black undersides. The pink Grand Canyon rattlesnake lives at lower elevations within the canyon. Hawks and ravens are visible year-round. The endangered California condor has been reintroduced to the canyon region. Park rangers give daily talks on the magnificent birds, whose wingspan measures 9 feet. In spring, summer, and fall, mule deer, recognizable by their large ears, are abundant at the South Rim. Don't be fooled by gentle appearances; these guys can be aggressive. It's illegal to feed them, as it'll disrupt their natural habitats, and increase your risk of getting bitten or kicked.

The best times to see wildlife are early in the morning and late in the afternoon. Look for out-of-place shapes and motions, keeping in mind that animals occupy all layers in a natural habitat and not just at your eye level. Use binoculars for close-up views. While out and about try to fade into the woodwork by keeping your movements limited and noise at a minimum.

More than 1,700 species of plants color the park. The South Rim's Coconino Plateau is fairly flat, at an elevation of about 7,000 feet, and covered with stands of piñon and ponderosa pines, junipers, and Gambel's oak trees. On the Kaibab Plateau on the North Rim, Douglas fir, spruce, quaking aspen, and more ponderosas prevail. In spring you're likely to see asters, sunflowers, and lupine in bloom at both rims.

HIKING
EASY
Cape Final Trail. This 4-mile (round-trip) gravel path follows an old jeep trail through a ponderosa pine forest to the canyon overlook at Cape Final with panoramic views of the northern canyon, the Palisades of the Desert, and the impressive spectacle of Juno Temple. *Easy.* ⊠ *Trailhead: dirt parking lot 5 miles south of Roosevelt Point on Cape Royal Rd.*

FAMILY **Roosevelt Point Trail.** This easy 0.2-mile round-trip trail loops through the forest to the scenic viewpoint. Allow 20 minutes for this relaxed, secluded hike. *Easy.* ⊠ *Trailhead: Cape Royal Rd.* ⊕ *www.nps.gov/grca.*

FAMILY **Transept Trail.** This 3-mile (round-trip), 1½-hour trail begins near the Grand Canyon Lodge at 8,255 feet. Well maintained and well marked, it has little elevation change, sticking near the rim before reaching a dramatic view of a large stream through Bright Angel Canyon. The route leads to a side canyon called Transept Canyon, which geologist Clarence Dutton named in 1882, declaring it "far grander than Yosemite." Check the posted schedule to find a ranger talk along this trail; it's also a great place to view fall foliage. Flash floods can occur any time of the year, especially June through September when thunderstorms develop rapidly. *Easy.* ⊠ *Trailhead: near the Grand Canyon Lodge's east patio.*

MODERATE

Uncle Jim Trail. This 5-mile, three-hour loop trail starts at 8,300 feet and winds south through the forest, past Roaring Springs and Bright Angel canyons. The highlight of this rim hike is Uncle Jim Point, which, at 8,244 feet, overlooks the upper sections of the North Kaibab Trail. *Moderate.* ⊠ *Trailhead: North Kaibab Trail parking lot.*

Fodor's Choice **Widforss Trail.** Round-trip, Widforss Trail is 9.8 miles, with an elevation ★ change of only 200 feet. Allow five to six hours for the hike, which starts at 8,080 feet and passes through shady forests of pine, spruce, fir, and aspen on its way to Widforss Point, at 7,900 feet. Here you'll have good views of five temples: Zoroaster, Brahma, and Deva to the southeast, and Buddha and Manu to the southwest. You are likely to see wildflowers in summer, and this is a good trail for viewing fall foliage. It's named in honor of artist Gunnar M. Widforss, renowned for his paintings of national park landscapes. *Moderate.* ⊠ *Trailhead: Point Sublime Rd.*

DIFFICULT

Ken Patrick Trail. This primitive trail, one of the longest on the North Rim, travels 10 miles one way (allow six hours each way) from the trailhead at 8,250 feet to Point Imperial at 8,803 feet. It crosses drainages and occasionally detours around fallen trees. The end of the road, at Point Imperial, brings the highest views from either rim. Note that there is no water along this trail. *Difficult.* ⊠ *Trailhead: east side of North Kaibab trailhead parking lot.*

North Kaibab Trail. At 8,241 feet, this trail leads into the canyon and down to Phantom Ranch. It is recommended for experienced hikers only, who should allow four days for the round-trip hike. The long, steep path drops 5,840 feet over a distance of 14.5 miles to Phantom Ranch and the Colorado River, so the National Park Service suggests that day hikers not go farther than Roaring Springs (5,020 feet) before turning to hike back up out of the canyon. After about 7 miles, Cottonwood Campground (4,080 feet) has drinking water in summer, restrooms, shade trees, and a ranger. *Difficult.* ■TIP➜ A free shuttle takes hikers to the North Kaibab trailhead twice daily from Grand Canyon Lodge; reserve a spot the day before. ⊠ *Trailhead: 2 miles north of the Grand Canyon Lodge.*

MULE RIDES

FAMILY **Canyon Trail Rides.** This company leads mule rides on the easier trails of the North Rim. A one-hour ride (minimum age seven) runs $40. Half-day trips on the rim or into the canyon (minimum age 10) cost $80. Weight limits are 200 pounds for canyon rides and 220 pounds for the rim rides. Available daily from May 15 to October 15, these excursions are popular, so make reservations in advance. ☎ *435/679–8665* ⊕ *www. canyonrides.com.*

THE WEST RIM AND HAVASU CANYON

Known as "The People" of the Grand Canyon, the Pai Indians—the Hualapai and Havasupai—have lived along the Colorado River and the vast Colorado Plateau for more than 1,000 years. Both tribes traditionally moved seasonally between the plateau and the canyon, alternately hunting game and planting crops. Today, they rely on their tourism offerings outside the national park as an economic base.

GRAND CANYON WEST

186 miles northwest of Williams, 70 miles north of Kingman.

The plateau-dwelling Hualapai ("people of the tall pines") acquired a larger chunk of traditional Pai lands with the creation of their reservation in 1883. Hualapai tribal lands include diverse habitats ranging from rolling grasslands to rugged canyons, and travel from elevations of 1,500 feet at the Colorado River to more than 7,300 feet at Aubrey Cliffs. In recent years, the Hualapai have been attempting to foster tourism on the West Rim—most notably with the spectacular Skywalk, a glass walkway suspended 70 feet over the edge of the canyon rim. Not hampered by the regulations in place at Grand Canyon National Park, Grand Canyon West offers helicopter flights down into the bottom of the canyon, horseback rides to rim viewpoints, and boat trips on the Colorado River.

The Hualapai Reservation encompasses a million acres in the Grand Canyon, along 108 miles of the Colorado River. Peach Springs, a two-hour drive from the West Rim on historic Route 66, is the tribal capital and the launch site for raft trips on this stretch of the river. Lodging is available both on the rim, at Hualapai Ranch, and in Peach Springs, at the Hualapai Lodge. Although increasingly popular, the West Rim is still relatively remote and visited by far fewer people than the South Rim—keep in mind that it's more than 120 miles away from the nearest interstate highways.

GETTING HERE AND AROUND

The West Rim is a five-hour drive from the South Rim of Grand Canyon National Park or a 2½-hour drive from Las Vegas. From Kingman, drive north 30 miles on U.S. 93, and then turn right onto Pierce Ferry Road and follow it for 28 miles. (A more scenic alternative is to drive 42 miles north on Stockton Hill Road, turning right onto Pierce Ferry Road for 7 miles, but this takes a bit longer because Stockton Hill Road has a lower speed limit than the wide, divided U.S. 93 highway.) Turn right (east) on to Diamond Bar Road and follow for 21 miles to Grand Canyon West entrance.

Visitors aren't allowed to travel in their own vehicles to the viewpoints once they reach the West Rim, and must purchase a tour package—which can range from day use to horseback or helicopter rides to lodging and meals—from Hualapai Tourism.

TOURS

In addition to the exploring options provided by the Hualapai tribe, more than 30 tour and transportation companies service Grand Canyon West from Las Vegas, Phoenix, and Sedona by airplane, helicopter, coach, SUV, and Hummer. Perhaps the easiest way to visit the West Rim from Vegas is with a tour.

Bighorn Wild West Tours. This full-day tour takes you to Grand Canyon West in the comfort of a hummer. Admission fees and lunch are included,

DID YOU KNOW?

Sure-footed mules take riders along the rim for half-day trips and down into the canyon for longer excursions. Two-day trips include an overnight stay at Phantom Ranch on the canyon floor.

as is a stop for photos at Hoover Dam. ☎ *702/385–4676* ⊕ *www.bighorntours.com* ✉ *From $249.*

VISITOR INFORMATION
Contacts Grand Canyon West
☎ *888/868–9378, 928/769–2636*
⊕ *www.hualapaitourism.com.*

EXPLORING
Hualapai Tourism. At the Welcome Center, Hualapai Tourism, run by the Hualapai tribe, offers the basic Hualapai Legacy tour package ($44 per person, including taxes and fees), which includes a Hualapai visitation permit and "hop-on, hop-off" shuttle transportation to three sites. The shuttle will take you to Eagle Point, where the Indian Village walking tour visits authentic

EXPLORING INDIAN COUNTRY

When visiting Native American reservations, respect tribal laws and customs. Remember you're a guest in a sovereign nation. Don't wander into residential areas or take photographs of residents without first asking permission. Possessing or consuming alcohol is illegal on tribal lands. In general, the Hualapai and Havasupai are quiet, private people. Offer respect and don't pursue conversations or personal interactions unless invited to do so.

dwellings. Educational displays there uncover the culture of five different Native American tribes (Havasupai, Plains, Hopi, Hualapai, and Navajo), and intertribal, powwow-style dance performances entertain visitors at the nearby amphitheater. The shuttle also goes to Hualapai Ranch, site of Western performances, cookouts, horseback and wagon rides, and the only lodging on the West Rim; and Guano Point, where the "High Point Hike" offers panoramic views of the Colorado River. At all three areas, local Hualapai guides and roaming "ambassadors" add a Native American perspective to a canyon trip that you won't find on North and South Rim tours.

For extra fees, you can add meals (there are cafés at each of the three stops), overnight lodging at Hualapai Ranch, a helicopter trip into the canyon, a pontoon boat trip on the Colorado, a horseback ride along the canyon rim, or a walk on the Skywalk. ⊠ *Grand Canyon West* ☎ *928/769–2636, 888/868–9378* ⊕ *www.hualapaitourism.com* ✉ *$44* ☉ *Daily.*

Grand Canyon Skywalk. This cantilevered glass terrace is suspended nearly 4,000 feet above the Colorado River and extends 70 feet from the edge of the Grand Canyon. Approximately 10 feet wide, the bridge's deck, made of tempered glass several inches thick, has 5-foot glass railings on each side creating an unobstructed open-air platform. Admission to the skywalk is a separate add-on to the basic Grand Canyon West admission. Visitors must store personal items, including cameras, cell phones, and video cameras, in lockers before entering. A professional photographer takes photographs of visitors, which can be purchased from the gift shop. ⊕ *www.hualapaitourism.com* ✉ *$32.*

SPORTS AND THE OUTDOORS
ADVENTURE TOURS

Hualapai River Runners. One-day combination river trips are offered by the Hualapai Tribe through the Hualapai River Runners mid-March through October. The trips leave from Peach Springs (a 2-hour drive from the West Rim) and include rafting, a hike, helicopter ride, and transport. Lunch, snacks, and beverages are provided. Children must be eight or older to take the trip, which runs several rapids with the most difficult rated as Class VII, depending on the river flow. ✉ *5001 Buck N Doe Rd., Peach Springs* ☎ *928/769–2636, 888/868–9378* ⊕ *www. hualapaitourism.com* ✈ *From $381.*

HAVASU CANYON

141 miles northwest from Williams to the head of Hualapai Hilltop.

With the establishment of Grand Canyon National Park in 1919, the Havasupai ("people of the blue green water") were confined to their summer village of Supai and the surrounding 518 acres in the 5-mile-wide and 12-mile-long Havasu Canyon. In 1975, the reservation was substantially enlarged, but is still completely surrounded by national park lands on all but its southern border. Each year, about 25,000 tourists fly, hike, or ride into Havasu Canyon to visit the Havasupai. Despite their economic reliance on tourism, the Havasupai take their guardianship of the Grand Canyon seriously, and severely limit visitation in order to protect the fragile canyon habitats. Dubbed the "Shangri-la of the Grand Canyon," the waterfalls have drawn visitors to this remote Native American reservation.

Major flooding in 2008 altered Havasu Canyon's famous landscape and it was closed to visitors for almost 10 months. Supai reopened in June 2009 but water and mud damage have changed some of the beautiful waterfalls, their streams and pools, and the amount of blue-green travertine. ■ TIP→ Be sure to call the Havasupai Tourist Enterprise (☎ 928/448–2121) to make reservations before visiting.

GETTING HERE AND AROUND

Hualapai Hilltop is reached via Indian Route 18, which you follow about 65 miles north from historic Route 66 (34 miles west of Seligman and 50 miles east of Kingman). The total driving distance from the South Rim of the Grand Canyon is about 200 miles and takes about four hours.

The Havasupai restrict the number of visitors to the canyon; you must call ahead and make reservations. The 8-mile Hualapai Trail begins at Hualapai Hilltop. You can park your car here (the parking lot is patrolled), but there is no gas, lodging, or water available. From an elevation of 5,200 feet, the trail travels down a moderate grade to Supai village at 3,200 feet. Bring plenty of water and avoid hiking during the middle of the day, when canyon temperatures can reach into the 100s. If you'd rather ride, you can rent a horse for the trip down for $187 round-trip, or $94 one-way. Riders must be able to mount and dismount by themselves; be at least 4 feet, 7 inches; and weigh less than 250 pounds. Reservations must be made at least six weeks in advance with Havasupai Tourist Enterprise, which requires a 50%

deposit. You'll need to spend the night if you're hiking or riding—you can camp at the campground 2 miles farther in ($17 per person) or stay at the Havasupai Lodge in the village.

Another option is a helicopter ride into the canyon with Air West Helicopters. Flights leave from Hualapai Hilltop and cost $85 per person each way. Reservations aren't accepted and visitors are transported on a first-come, first-served basis. Tribal members are boarded prior to tourists. All visitors who are camping or staying at the lodge must pay a $35 entrance fee and a $5 environmental fee.

ESSENTIALS

Transportation Contacts Air West Helicopters ☎ 623/516–2790 ⊗ Mid-Mar.–mid-Oct., Thurs., Fri., Sun., and Mon. 10–1; mid-Oct.–mid-Mar., Fri. and Sun. 10–1.

Visitor Information Havasupai Tourist Enterprise ☎ 928/448–2121 ⊕ www.havasupaitribe.com.

EXPLORING

Havasu Canyon. South of the middle part of Grand Canyon National Park's South Rim and away from the crowds, Havasu Canyon is the home of the Havasupai, a tribe that has lived in this isolated area for centuries. You'll discover why they are known as the "people of the blue green waters" when you see the canyon's waterfalls. Accumulated travertine formations in some of the most popular pools were washed out in massive flooding decades ago and again in 2008 and 2010, but it's still a magical place.

The village of Supai, which currently has about 600 tribal members living there, is accessed by the 8-mile-long **Hualapai Trail,** which drops 2,000 feet from the canyon rim to the tiny town.

To reach Havasu's waterfalls, you must hike downstream from the village of Supai. Both **Havasu Falls** and **Mooney Falls** are still flowing and as beautiful as ever, but the flooding in 2008 washed out well-known Navajo Falls completely. Pack adequate food and supplies. Prices for food and sundries in Supai are more than double what they would be outside the reservation. The tribe does not allow alcohol, drugs, pets, or weapons. Reservations are necessary for camping or staying at the Havasupai Lodge. ⊠ *Havasupai Tourist Enterprise, Supai* ☎ *928/448–2121 for camping and general info, 928/448–2201 for lodging reservations* ⊕ *www.havasupaitribe.com* ⊠ *$35 plus $5 impact fee.*

WHAT'S NEAR THE GRAND CANYON

The northwest section of Arizona is geographically fascinating. In addition to the Grand Canyon, it's home to national forests, national monuments, and national recreation areas. Towns, however, are small and scattered. Many of them cater to visiting adventurers, and Native American reservations dot the map.

NEARBY TOWNS

Towns near the canyon's South Rim include the tiny town of Tusayan, 1 mile south of the entrance station, and Williams, the "Gateway to the Grand Canyon," 58 miles south.

Tusayan (⇨ see Chapter 4) has lower-priced lodging than within the Park, basic amenities and an airport that serves as a starting point for airplane and helicopter tours of the canyon.

The cozy mountain town of **Williams** (⇨ see Chapter 4), founded in 1882 when the railroad passed through, was once a rough-and-tumble joint, replete with saloons and bordellos. Today it reflects a much milder side of the Wild West, with 3,300 residents and more than 25 motels and hotels. Wander along the main street—part of historic Route 66, but locally named, like the town, after trapper Bill Williams—and indulge in Route 66 nostalgia inside antiques shops or souvenir and T-shirt stores.

The communities closest to the North Rim—all of them tiny and with limited services—include Fredonia, 76 miles north; Marble Canyon, 80 miles northeast; Lees Ferry, 85 miles east; and Jacob Lake, 45 miles north.

Fredonia, a small community of about 1,050, approximately an hour's drive north of the Grand Canyon, is often referred to as the gateway to the North Rim; it's also relatively close to Zion and Bryce Canyon national parks in Utah. **Marble Canyon** marks the geographical beginning of the Grand Canyon at its northeastern tip. It's a good stopping point if you're driving U.S. 89 to the North Rim. En route from the South Rim to the North Rim is **Lees Ferry,** where most of the area's river rafts start their journey. The tiny town of **Jacob Lake,** nestled high in pine country at an elevation of 7,925 feet, was named after Mormon explorer Jacob Hamblin, also known as the "Buckskin Missionary." It has a hotel, café, campground, and lush mountain countryside.

VISITOR INFORMATION

Contacts **Kaibab National Forest, North District** ✉ 430 S. Main St., Fredonia ☎ 928/643–7395 ⊕ www.fs.usda.gov/kaibab. **Kaibab National Forest, Tusayan Ranger District** ✉ 176 Lincoln Log Loop ☎ 928/638–2443 ⊕ www.fs.usda. gov/kaibab. **Kaibab Plateau Visitor Center** ✉ U.S. 89A at AZ 67, Jacob Lake ☎ 928/643–7298 ⊕ www.fs.usda.gov/kaibab ⊙ Closed Nov.–mid-May.

MAIL BY MULE

Arguably the most remote mail route in the United States follows a steep 8-mile trail to the tiny town of Supai in Havasu Canyon. Havasupai tribal members living deep within the confines of the Grand Canyon rely on this route for the delivery of everything from food to furniture. During a typical week, more than a ton of mail is sent into the canyon by mule, with each animal carrying a cargo of about 130 pounds.

3

NEARBY ATTRACTIONS

Vermilion Cliffs National Monument. West of the town of Marble Canyon are these spectacular cliffs, more than 3,000 feet high in many places. Keep an eye out for condors; the giant endangered birds were reintroduced into

Lava Falls is the largest and best known of the rapids in the Grand Canyon.

the area in 1996. Reports suggest that the birds, once in captivity, are surviving well in the wilderness. ☎ *435/688–3200* ⊕ *www.blm.gov/az.*

SCENIC DRIVES

U.S. 89. The route north from Cameron Trading Post (Cameron, Arizona) on U.S. 89 offers a stunning view of the **Painted Desert** to the right. The desert, which covers thousands of square miles stretching to the south and east, is a vision of subtle, almost harsh beauty, with windswept plains and mesas, isolated buttes, and barren valleys in pastel patterns. About 30 miles north of Cameron Trading Post, the Painted Desert country gives way to sandstone cliffs that run for miles. Brilliantly hued and ranging in color from light pink to deep orange, the **Echo Cliffs** rise to more than 1,000 feet in many places. They are essentially devoid of vegetation, but in a few high places, thick patches of tall cottonwood and poplar trees, nurtured by springs and water seepage from the rock escarpment, manage to thrive. ⊠ *Grand Canyon.*

U.S. 89A. At Bitter Springs, 60 miles north of Cameron, U.S. 89A branches off from U.S. 89, running north and providing views of **Marble Canyon,** the geographical beginning of the Grand Canyon. Like the Grand Canyon, Marble Canyon was formed by the Colorado River. Traversing a gorge nearly 500 feet deep is **Navajo Bridge,** a narrow steel span built in 1929 and listed on the National Register of Historic Places. Formerly used for car traffic, it now functions only as a pedestrian overpass. ⊠ *Marble Canyon.*

AREA ACTIVITIES

SPORTS AND THE OUTDOORS

FISHING

The stretch of ice-cold, crystal clear water at Lees Ferry off the North Rim provides arguably the best trout fishing in the Southwest. Many rafters and anglers stay the night in a campground near the river or in nearby Marble Canyon before hitting the river at dawn.

Arizona Game and Fish Department. Fish for trout, crappie, catfish, and smallmouth bass at a number of lakes surrounding Williams. To fish on public land, anglers ages 14 and older are required to obtain a fishing license from the Arizona Game and Fish Department, either at their office or online. ⊠ *Flagstaff* ☎ *928/774–5045* ⊕ *www.azgfd.gov.*

Lees Ferry Anglers. There are guides, state fishing licenses, and gear for sale at Lees Ferry Anglers. ⊠ *Milepost 547, N. U.S. 89A, HC 67, Marble Canyon* ☎ *928/355–2261, 800/962–9755* ⊕ *www.leesferry.com.*

Marble Canyon Outfitters. This company sells Arizona fishing licenses and offers guided fishing trips. ⊠ *¼ mile west of Navajo Bridge on U.S. 89A, Marble Canyon* ☎ *928/645–2781, 800/533–7339* ⊕ *www. leesferryflyfishing.com.*

RAFTING

Fodor'sChoice ★ The National Park Service authorizes 16 concessionaires to run rafting trips through the canyon—you can view a full list at the park's website (⊕ *www.nps.gov/grca/planyourvisit/river-concessioners.htm*). Trips run from 3 to 16 days, depending on whether you opt for the upper canyon, lower canyon, or full canyon. You can also experience a one-day rafting trip, either running a few rapids in Grand Canyon West with the Hualapai tribe or floating through Glen Canyon near Page *(⇨ see Chapter 5, Northeast Arizona).* Here are a few of the best operators for multiday trips:

Arizona Raft Adventures. Arizona Raft Adventures organizes 6- to 16-day paddle and/or motor trips through the upper, lower, or "full" canyon, for all skill levels. Trips, which run $2,025 to $4,120 (all fees and taxes included), depart April through October. ⊠ *4050 E. Huntington Dr., Flagstaff* ☎ *928/526–8200, 800/786–7238* ⊕ *www.azraft.com.*

Canyoneers. With a reputation for high quality and a roster of 3- to 14-day trips, Canyoneers is popular with those who want to do some hiking as well. The five-day "Best of the Grand" trip includes a hike down to Phantom Ranch. The motorized and oar trips, available April through September, cost between $1,080 and $3,650. ⊠ *7195 N Hwy. 89, Flagstaff* ☎ *928/526–0924, 800/525–0924* ⊕ *www.canyoneers.com.*

Grand Canyon Expeditions. You can count on Grand Canyon Expeditions to take you down the Colorado River safely and in style: evening meals might include filet mignon, pork chops, or shrimp. The 8-day motorized and 14- or 16-day dory trips range from $2,650 to $4,199, and some trips focus on special interests like archaeology and photography. ☎ *435/644–2691, 800/544–2691* ⊕ *www.gcex.com.*

Wilderness River Adventures. One of the canyon's larger rafting outfitters, Wilderness River Adventures runs a wide variety of trips from 3 to 16

Continued on page 180

EXPLORING THE
COLORADO RIVER

By Carrie Frasure

High in Colorado's Rocky Mountains, the Colorado River begins as a catch-all for the snowmelt off the mountains west of the Continental Divide. By the time it reaches the Grand Canyon, the Colorado has been joined by multiple tributaries to become a raging river, red with silt as it sculpts spectacular landscapes. A network of dams can only partially tame this mighty river.

Snaking its way through five states, the Colorado River is an essential water source to the arid Southwest. Its natural course runs 1,450 miles from its origin in Colorado's La Poudre Pass Lake in Rocky Mountain National Park to its final destination in the Gulf of California, also called the Sea of Cortez. In northern Arizona, the Colorado River has been a powerful force in shaping the Grand Canyon, where it flows 4,000 to 6,000 feet below the rim. Beyond the canyon, the red river takes a lazy turn at the Arizona–Nevada border, where Hoover Dam creates the reservoir at Lake Mead. The Colorado continues at a relaxed pace along the Arizona–California border, providing energy and irrigation in Arizona, California, and Nevada before draining into northwestern Mexico.

A RIVER RUNS THROUGH IT

Stretching along 277 miles of the Colorado River is one of the seven natural wonders of the world: the Grand Canyon ranges in width from 4 to 18 miles, while the walls around it soar up to a mile high. Nearly 2 billion years of geologic history and majesty are revealed in exposed tiers of rock cut deep in the Colorado Plateau. What caused this incredible marvel of nature? Erosion by water coupled with driving wind are most likely the major culprits: under the sculpting power of wind and water, the shale layers eroded into slopes and the harder sandstone and limestone layers created terraced cliffs. Other forces that may have helped shape the canyon include ice, volcanic activity, continental drift, and earthquakes.

WHO LIVES HERE

Native tribes have lived in the canyon for thousands of years and continue to do so, looking to the river for subsistence. The plateau-dwelling Hualapai ("people of the tall pines") live on a million acres along 108 miles of the Colorado River in the West Rim. The Havasupai ("people of the blue green water") live deep within the walls of the 12-mile-long Havasu Canyon—a major side canyon connected to the Grand Canyon.

ENVIRONMENTAL CONCERNS

When the Grand Canyon achieved national park status in 1919, only 44,173 people made the grueling overland trip to see it—quite a contrast from today's nearly 5 million annual visitors. The tremendous increase in visitation has greatly impacted the fragile ecosystems, as has Lake Powell's Glen Canyon Dam, which was constructed in the 1950s and '60s. The dam has changed the composition of the Colorado River, replacing warm water rich in sediments (nature's way of nourishing the riverbed and banks) with mostly cool, much clearer water. This has introduced nonnative plants and animals that threaten the extinction of several native species. Air pollution has also affected visibility and the constant buzz of aerial tours has disturbed the natural solitude.

Above and right, views of Colorado River in the Grand Canyon from Toroweap.

DID YOU KNOW?

The North Rim's isolated Toroweap overlook (also called Tuweep) is perched 3,000 feet above the canyon floor: a height equal to stacking the Sears Tower and Empire State Building on top of each other.

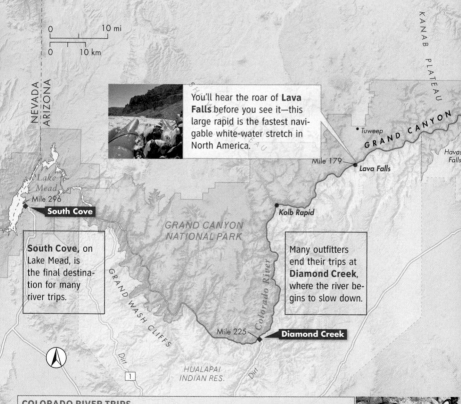

RIVER RAFTING THROUGH THE GRAND CANYON

Viewing the Colorado River from a canyon overlook is one thing, but looking up at the canyon from the middle of the river is quite another experience. If you're ready to tackle the churning white water of the Colorado River as it rumbles and hisses its way through the Grand Canyon, take a look at this map of what you might encounter along the way.

You'll hear the roar of **Lava Falls** before you see it—this large rapid is the fastest navigable white-water stretch in North America.

South Cove, on Lake Mead, is the final destination for many river trips.

Many outfitters end their trips at **Diamond Creek**, where the river begins to slow down.

Mile 296

South Cove

Mile 179

Lava Falls

Kolb Rapid

Mile 225

Diamond Creek

GRAND CANYON NATIONAL PARK

GRAND WASH CLIFFS

Colorado River

HUALAPAI INDIAN RES.

Tuweep

GRAND CANYON

Havasu Falls

KANAB PLATEAU

NEVADA / ARIZONA

Lake Mead

COLORADO RIVER TRIPS	
Time and Length	**Entry and Exit points**
1 day Float trip	Glen Canyon Dam to Lees Ferry (no rapids)
1 day Combo trip	Diamond Creek, then helicopter to West Rim
3–4 days	Lees Ferry to Phantom Ranch
6 days, 89 miles	Phantom Ranch to Diamond Creek
9–10 days, 136 miles	Lees Ferry to Diamond Creek
14–16 days, 225 miles	Lees Ferry to South Cove

*Trips either begin or end at Phantom Ranch/Bright Angel Beach at the bottom of the Grand Canyon, at river mile 87

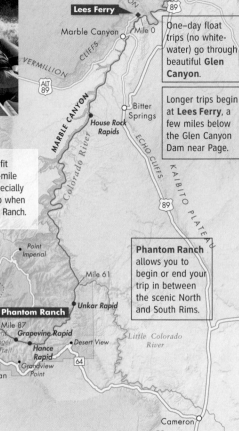

Kanab
89

Lake Powell

UTAH
ARIZONA

Glen Canyon Dam

Direction of Flow

Page
89

PARIA CANYON

Lees Ferry

Marble Canyon
Mile 0

VERMILLION CLIFFS

MARBLE CANYON

ALT 89

Bitter Springs

House Rock Rapids

ECHO CLIFFS

Colorado River

KAIBITO PLATEAU

89

One-day float trips (no white-water) go through beautiful **Glen Canyon**.

Longer trips begin at **Lees Ferry**, a few miles below the Glen Canyon Dam near Page.

⚠ You need to be very fit to hike the arduous 9.6-mile **Bright Angel Trail**, especially if you choose to hike up when departing from Phantom Ranch.

Deer Creek Falls

Great Thumb Mesa

Bedrock Rapid

NORTH RIM

67

Point Imperial

Fossil Rapid

Forester Rapid

Sapphire Rapid

Point Sublime

Bright Angel Point

Mile 61

Serpentine Rapid

Mile 98

HAVASU CANYON

HAVASUPAI INDIAN RES.

Crystal Rapid

Granite Rapid

Mather Pt

Bright Angel Trail

Phantom Ranch

Mile 87

Unkar Rapid

Grapevine Rapid

Hance Rapid

Desert View

Little Colorado River

Grand Canyon Village

Tusayan

Grandview Point

64

Phantom Ranch allows you to begin or end your trip in between the scenic North and South Rims.

If you begin at Phantom Ranch, you will soon plunge through the colossal waves of **Granite** and **Crystal Rapids**.

Cameron
TO FLAGSTAFF, 49 Miles

COCONINO PLATEAU

180
64

NOT JUST RAPIDS

Don't think that your experience will be nonstop white-water adrenaline. Most of the Colorado River features long, relaxing stretches of water, where you drift amid grandiose rock formations. You might even spot a mountain goat or two. Multiday trips include camping on the shore.

PLANNING YOUR RIVER RAFTING TRIP

OAR, MOTOR, OR HYBRID?

Base the type of trip you choose on the amount of effort you want to put in. Motor rafts, which are the roomiest of the choices, cover the most miles in less time and are the most comfortable. Guides do the rowing on oar boats and these smaller rafts offer a wilder ride. All-paddle trips are the most active and require the most involvement from guests. Hybrid trips are popular because they offer both the opportunity to paddle and to relax.

THE GEAR

Life jackets, beverages, tents, sheets, tarps, sleeping bags, dry bags, first aid, and food are provided—but you'll still need to plan ahead by packing clothing, hats, sunscreen, toiletries, and other sundries. Commercial outfitters allow each river runner two waterproof bags to store items during the day—just keep in mind that one of these will be filled up with the provided sleeping bag and tarp. ■TIP➜ Bring a rain suit: summer thunderstorms are frequent and chilly.

WHEN TO GO

Lots of people book trips for summer's peak period: June through August. If you're flexible, take advantage of the Arizona weather and go from May to early June or in September. ■TIP➜ Seats fill up quickly; make reservations for multi-day trips a year or two in advance.

TRIP LENGTH

Rafting options on the Colorado River range from one-day trips at either the east or west end of the Grand Canyon to leisurely, two-week paddle trips through the full length of Grand Canyon National Park. If you're short on time, take a one-day trip near Grand Canyon West, where you'll run several rapids and fly back to the West Rim by helicopter. Another action-packed choice is to raft the river for 3 or 4 days, disembark at Phantom Ranch, then hike up to the Grand Canyon South Rim. "Full Canyon" rafting trips can take 9 to 16 days.

Above, Getting wet—and loving it—on an oar boat.

DID YOU KNOW?

As you're hanging on for dear life, consider this: Civil War veteran John Wesley Powell chartered these treacherous rapids in 1869—not only were conditions more dangerous then, but he had only one arm.

days, oar or motorized, from April to October. Their most popular trip is the seven-day motor trip. ✉ *2040 E. Frontage Rd., Page* ☎ *928/645–3296, 800/992–8022* 🌐 *www.riveradventures.com.*

WHERE TO EAT

IN THE PARK

SOUTH RIM

$$$ STEAKHOUSE 🍴 **Arizona Room.** The canyon views from this casual Southwestern-style steakhouse are the best of any restaurant at the South Rim. The menu includes such delicacies as chile-crusted pan-seared wild salmon, chipotle barbecue baby back ribs, and half-pound buffalo burgers with Gorgonzola aioli. For dessert, try the cheesecake with prickly-pear syrup paired with one of the house's specialty coffee drinks. Seating is first-come, first-served, so arrive early to avoid the crowds. [$] *Average main: $22* ✉ *Bright Angel Lodge, Desert View Dr., Grand Canyon Village* ☎ *928/638–2631* 🌐 *www.grandcanyonlodges.com* ✍ *Reservations not accepted* ⏲ *Closed Jan. and Feb. No lunch Nov. and Dec.*

$ SOUTHWESTERN 🍴 **Bright Angel Restaurant.** No-surprises, affordable dishes here will fill your belly at breakfast, lunch, or dinner. Entrées include such basics as salads, steaks, lasagna, burgers, fajitas, and fish tacos (sandwiches are options at lunch). Or you can step it up a notch and order some of the same selections straight from the Arizona Room menu, including prime rib, baby back ribs, and wild salmon. For dessert try the warm apple grunt cake topped with vanilla ice cream. Be prepared to wait for a table: the dining room bustles all day long. The plain décor is broken up with large-pane windows and original artwork. [$] *Average main: $12* ✉ *Bright Angel Lodge, Desert View Dr., Grand Canyon Village* ☎ *928/638–2631* 🌐 *www.grandcanyonlodges.com* ✍ *Reservations not accepted.*

$ AMERICAN 🍴 **Canyon Café at Yavapai Lodge.** Open for breakfast, lunch, and dinner, this cafeteria in the Yavapai Lodge, across from Market Plaza, serves down-home staples like as chicken potpie, fried catfish, and fried chicken. Fast-food favorites include pastries, burgers, and pizza. There isn't a fancy bar, but you can order beer and wine with your meal. Resembling an old-fashioned diner, the large cafeteria has easy-to-read signs that point the way to your favorite foods. [$] *Average main: $7* ✉ *Yavapai Lodge, Desert View Dr., Grand Canyon Village* ☎ *928/638–2631* 🌐 *www.grandcanyonlodges.com/canyon-cafe-423.html* ✍ *Reservations not accepted* ⏲ *Closed Nov.–Feb. (except during Thanksgiving weekend and Christmas wk).*

$$$ SOUTHWESTERN Fodor's Choice ★ 🍴 **El Tovar Dining Room.** No doubt about it—this is the best restaurant for miles. Modeled after a European hunting lodge, this rustic 19th-century dining room built of hand-hewn logs is worth a visit. The cuisine is modern Southwestern with an exotic flair. Start with the smoked-salmon-and-goat-cheese crostini or the acclaimed black bean soup. The dinner menu includes such hearty yet creative dishes as cherry-merlot-glazed duck with roasted-poblano black-bean rice, grilled New York strip steak with cornmeal-battered onion rings, and a wild salmon tostada topped

TOP PICNIC SPOTS

Bring your picnic basket and enjoy dining alfresco surrounded by some of the most beautiful backdrops in the country. Be sure to bring water, as it's unavailable at many of these spots, as are restrooms.

■ **Buggeln,** 15 miles east of Grand Canyon Village on Desert View Drive, has some secluded, shady spots.

■ **Cape Royal,** 23 miles south of the North Rim Visitor Center, is the most popular designated picnic area on the North Rim due to its panoramic views.

■ **Grandview Point** has, as the name implies, grand vistas; it's 12 miles east of the village on Desert View Drive.

■ **Point Imperial,** 11 miles northeast of the North Rim Visitor Center, has shade and some privacy.

3

with organic greens and tequila vinaigrette. The dining room also has an extensive wine list. ■ **TIP→ Dinner reservations can be made up to six months in advance with room reservations and 30 days in advance for all other visitors.** If you can't get a dinner table, consider lunch or breakfast—the best in the region with dishes like polenta corncakes with prickly pear–pistachio butter, and blackened breakfast trout and eggs. $ *Average main: $27 ⊠ El Tovar Hotel, Desert View Dr., Grand Canyon Village ☎ 303/297–2757, 888/297–2757 reservations only ⊕ www. grandcanyonlodges.com/el-tovar-421.html ⌖ Reservations essential.*

$ ✕ **Maswik Cafeteria.** You can get a burger, hot sandwich, pasta, or Mexi-
AMERICAN can fare at this food court, as well as pizza by the slice and wine and beer in the adjacent Maswik Pizza Pub. This casual eatery is ¼ mile from the rim, and the Pizza Pub stays open until 11 pm (you can also order pizza to take out). Lines can be long during high-season lunch and dinner, but everything moves fairly quickly. $ *Average main: $7 ⊠ Maswik Lodge, Desert View Dr., Grand Canyon Village ⊕ www. grandcanyonlodges.com ⌖ Reservations not accepted.*

NORTH RIM

$ ✕ **Deli in the Pines.** Dining choices are limited on the North Rim, but
AMERICAN this is your best bet for a meal on a budget. Selections include pizza, salads, deli sandwiches, hot dogs, homemade breakfast pastries and burritos, and soft-serve ice cream. Best of all, there is an outdoor seating area for dining alfresco. It's open for lunch and dinner. $ *Average main: $6 ⊠ Grand Canyon Lodge, Bright Angel Point, North Rim ☎ 928/638–2611 ⊕ www.grandcanyonforever.com ⌖ Reservations not accepted ۞ Closed mid-Oct.–mid-May.*

$$ ✕ **Grand Canyon Lodge Dining Room.** The historic lodge has a huge, high-
AMERICAN ceilinged dining room with spectacular views and decent food, though
Fodor's Choice the draw here is definitely the setting. You might find pecan-glazed
★ pork chop, bison flank steak, and grilled ruby trout for dinner. The filling, simply prepared food here takes a flavorful turn with Southwestern spices and organic selections. It's also open for breakfast and lunch. A full-service bar and an impressive wine list add to the relaxed atmosphere of the only full-service, sit-down restaurant on the North

Rim. Dinner reservations are essential in summer and on spring and fall weekends. [$] *Average main: $20* ✉ *Grand Canyon Lodge, Bright Angel Point, North Rim* ☎ *928/638–2611* 🌐 *www.grandcanyonforever.com* 🕒 *Closed mid-Oct.–mid-May.*

$$$ AMERICAN FAMILY 🍴 **Grand Cookout.** Dine under the stars and enjoy live entertainment at this chuck-wagon-style dining experience—a popular family-friendly choice among the North Rim's limited dining options. Fill up on Western favorites at the all-you-can-eat buffet, including barbecue beef brisket, roasted chicken, baked beans, and cowboy biscuits. The food is basic and tasty, but the real draw is the nightly performance of Western music and tall tales. Transportation from the Grand Canyon Lodge to the cookout (1 mile away) is included in the price. Be sure to call before 4 pm for dinner reservations. Advance reservations are taken by phone (during winter months) or at the Grand Canyon Lodge registration desk. [$] *Average main: $30* ✉ *Grand Canyon Lodge, North Rim* ☎ *928/638–2611, 928/645–6865 (winter)* 🌐 *www.grandcanyonforever.com* ✍ *Reservations essential* 🕒 *Closed Oct.–May. No lunch.*

WHERE TO STAY

IN THE PARK

SOUTH RIM

$ HOTEL FAMILY 🏨 **Bright Angel Lodge.** Famed architect Mary Jane Colter designed this 1935 log-and-stone structure, which sits within a few yards of the canyon rim and blends superbly with the canyon walls. **Pros:** some rooms have canyon vistas; all are steps away from the rim; Internet kiosks and transportation desk for the mule-ride check-in are in the lobby; good value for the amazing location. **Cons:** the popular lobby is always packed; parking is a bit of a hike. [$] *Rooms from: $92* ✉ *Desert View Dr., Grand Canyon Village* ☎ *888/297–2757 for reservations only, 928/638–2631* 🌐 *www.grandcanyonlodges.com* 🛏 *37 rooms, 18 with bath; 50 cabins* 🍽 *No meals.*

$$$ HOTEL Fodor's Choice ★ 🏨 **El Tovar Hotel.** The hotel's proximity to all of the canyon's facilities, European hunting-lodge atmosphere, attractively updated rooms and tile baths, and renowned dining room make it the best place to stay on the South Rim. **Pros:** historic lodging just steps from the South Rim; fabulous lounge with outdoor seating and canyon views; best in-park dining on site. **Cons:** books up quickly. [$] *Rooms from: $183* ✉ *Desert View Dr., Grand Canyon Village* ☎ *888/297–2757 for reservations only, 928/638–2631* 🌐 *www.grandcanyonlodges.com* 🛏 *66 rooms, 12 suites* 🍽 *No meals.*

$$$ HOTEL 🏨 **Kachina Lodge.** The well-outfitted rooms at this motel-style lodge on the south rim are a good bet for families and are within easy walking distance of dining facilities at nearby lodges. **Pros:** partial canyon views in half the rooms; family-friendly; steps from the best restaurants in the park. **Cons:** check-in takes place at nearby El Tovar Hotel; limited parking; pleasant but bland furnishings. [$] *Rooms from: $178* ✉ *Desert View Dr., Grand Canyon Village* ☎ *888/297–2757 for reservations*

only, 928/638–2631 🌐 www.grandcanyonlodges.com 🛏 *49 rooms* 🍴 *No meals.*

$ HOTEL FAMILY 🏨 **Maswik Lodge.** Far from the noisy crowds, accommodations at this lodge are nestled in a shady ponderosa pine forest, with options ranging from rustic cabins to more modern motel-style rooms. **Pros:** larger rooms here than in older lodgings; good for families; affordable dining options. **Cons:** rooms lack historic charm; tucked away from the rim in the forest. [$] *Rooms from: $90* ✉ *Grand Canyon Village* ☎ *888/297–2757 for reservations only, 928/638–2631* 🌐 *www.grandcanyonlodges.com* 🛏 *278 rooms* 🍴 *No meals.*

DUFFEL SERVICE: LIGHTEN YOUR LOAD

Hikers staying at either Phantom Ranch or Bright Angel Campground can also take advantage of the ranch's duffel service: bags or packs weighing 30 pounds or less can be transported to the ranch by mule for a fee of $64.64 each way. As is true for many desirable things at the canyon, reservations are a must.

$ B&B/INN 🏨 **Phantom Ranch.** In a grove of cottonwood trees on the canyon floor, Phantom Ranch is accessible only to hikers and mule trekkers; there are 40 dormitory beds and 14 beds in cabins, all with shared baths. **Pros:** only inner-canyon lodging option; fabulous canyon views; remote access limits crowds. **Cons:** accessible only by foot or mule; few amenities or means of outside communication. [$] *Rooms from: $46* ✉ *On canyon floor, at intersection of Bright Angel and Kaibab trails* ☎ *303/297–2757, 888/297–2757* 🌐 *www.grandcanyonlodges.com* 🛏 *4 dormitories and 9 cabins (some cabins with outside showers reserved for mule riders)* 🍴 *Some meals.*

$$$ HOTEL 🏨 **Thunderbird Lodge.** This motel with comfortable, simple rooms has all the modern amenities you'd expect at a typical mid-price chain hotel. **Pros:** partial canyon views in some rooms; family-friendly. **Cons:** rooms lack personality; check-in takes place at nearby Bright Angel Lodge; limited parking nearby. [$] *Rooms from: $178* ✉ *Desert View Dr., Grand Canyon Village* ☎ *888/297–2757 for reservations only, 928/638–2631* 🌐 *www.grandcanyonlodges.com* 🛏 *55 rooms* 🍴 *No meals.*

$$ HOTEL 🏨 **Yavapai Lodge.** The largest motel-style lodge in the park is tucked in a piñon and juniper forest at the eastern end of Grand Canyon Village, across from Market Plaza. **Pros:** transportation-activities desk on site in the lobby; walk to Market Plaza in Grand Canyon Village; forested grounds. **Cons:** farthest in-park lodging from the rim (½ mile). [$] *Rooms from: $123* ✉ *10 Yavapai Lodge Rd., Grand Canyon Village* ☎ *888/297–2757 for reservations only, 928/638–2961* 🌐 *www.grandcanyonlodges.com* 🛏 *358 rooms* ⏲ *Closed Nov.–Feb., except during Thanksgiving weekend and Christmas wk* 🍴 *No meals.*

NORTH RIM

$$ HOTEL Fodor's Choice ★ 🏨 **Grand Canyon Lodge.** This historic property, constructed mainly in the 1920s and '30s, is the premier lodging facility in the North Rim area. **Pros:** steps away from gorgeous North Rim views; close to several easy hiking trails. **Cons:** as the only in-park North Rim lodging option, this lodge fills up fast; few amenities and limited Internet access. [$] *Rooms from: $124* ✉ *Grand Canyon National Park, Hwy. 67, North Rim*

Perched on the North Rim's edge—1,000 feet higher than the South Rim—is the Grand Canyon Lodge.

☎ 877/386–4383, 928/638–2611 May–Oct., 928/645–6865 Nov.–Apr. 🌐 www.grandcanyonforever.com 🛏 40 rooms, 178 cabins ⏲ Closed mid-Oct.–mid-May 🍴 No meals.

OUTSIDE THE PARK

JACOB LAKE

$ HOTEL 🏨 **Jacob Lake Inn.** The bustling lodge at Jacob Lake Inn is a popular stop for those heading to the North Rim, 45 miles south. **Pros:** grocery store, coffee shop, and restaurant; quiet rooms. **Cons:** worn furnishings and no TVs in cabins or motel rooms; old-fashioned key locks. *[$] Rooms from: $110 ✉ U.S. 89A at AZ 67, Jacob Lake ☎ 928/643–7232 🌐 www.jacoblake.com 🛏 32 rooms, 26 cabins 🍴 No meals.*

$ HOTEL 🏨 **Marble Canyon Lodge.** Popular with anglers and rafters, this Arizona Strip lodge offers two types of accommodations: standard rooms in the original lodge building and two-bedroom apartments in a newer building. **Pros:** convenience store, restaurant, and trading post; great fishing on the Colorado River. **Cons:** no-frills rustic lodging. *[$] Rooms from: $70 ✉ ¼ mile west of Navajo Bridge on U.S. 89A, Marble Canyon ☎ 928/355–2225, 800/726–1789 🌐 www.marblecanyoncompany.com 🛏 46 rooms, 8 apartments 🍴 No meals.*

WEST RIM

$$ HOTEL 🏨 **Havasupai Lodge.** These are fairly spartan accommodations, but you won't mind much when you see the natural beauty surrounding you. **Pros:** near the famous waterfalls; Native American perspective on the natural and cultural history of the Grand Canyon. **Cons:** accessible

CLOSE UP

Best Grand Canyon Campgrounds

Within the national park, camping is permitted only in designated campsites. Some campgrounds charge nightly camping fees in addition to entrance fees, and some accept reservations up to five months in advance through ⊕ www.recreation.gov. Others are first-come, first-served.

In-park camping outside of a developed rim campground requires a permit from the Backcountry Information Center, which also serves as your reservation. Permits can be requested by mail or fax only; applying well in advance is recommended. Call ☎ 928/638–7875 between 1 pm and 5 pm Monday through Friday for information.

Outside the park boundaries, there are campgrounds near the South and North rims, and in Havasu Canyon and the Kaibab National Forest. There's no camping on the West Rim, but you can pitch a tent on the beach near the Colorado River.

SOUTH RIM

Bright Angel Campground. This backcountry campground is near Phantom Ranch, at the bottom of the canyon. There are toilet facilities and running water, but no showers. ⊠ Intersection of South and North Kaibab trails, South Rim ☎ 928/638–7875.

Desert View Campground. Popular for spectacular views of the canyon from the nearby watchtower, this campground doesn't take reservations; show up before noon, as it fills up fast in summer. ⊠ Desert View Dr., 23 miles east of Grand Canyon Village off Hwy. 64, South Rim.

Indian Garden. Halfway down the canyon is this backcountry

campground, en route to Phantom Ranch on the Bright Angel Trail. Running water and toilet facilities are available, but not showers. ⊠ Bright Angel Trail, South Rim ☎ 928/638–7875.

NORTH RIM

North Rim Campground. The only designated campground at the North Rim of Grand Canyon National Park sits 3 miles north of the rim, near the general store, and has 84 RV and tent sites (no hookups). ⊠ Hwy. 67, North Rim ☎ 928/638–7888 ⊕ www. recreation.gov.

OUTSIDE THE PARK

Diamond Creek. You can camp on the banks of the Colorado River, but your peace might be interrupted since this beach is a launch point for river runners. The Hualapai permit camping on their tribal lands here, with an overnight camping permit of $32.10 per person per night, which can be purchased at the Hualapai Lodge. ☎ 928/769–2210, 888/255–9550 ⊕ www.hualapaitourism.com.

Havasu Canyon. You can stay in the primitive campgrounds in Havasu Canyon for $17 per person per night, in addition to the $35-per-person entry fee plus a $5 environmental-care fee. ☎ 928/448–2121, 928/448–2174, 928/448–2180, or 928/448–2141 ⊕ www.havasupaitribe.com.

Kaibab National Forest. Both developed and undeveloped campsites are available on a first-come, first-served basis May through September at this forest that surrounds Williams and extends to the Grand Canyon. ☎ 928/699–1239, 928/638–2443 ⊕ www.fs.usda.gov/kaibab.

3

only by foot, horseback, or helicopter; rooms are plain and worn; no phones, Internet, or TVs. $ Rooms from: $145 ⊠ 159 Supai, Supai Village Trail ☎ 928/448–2111, 928/448–2201 ⊕ www.havasupaitribe. com ⋧ 24 rooms ⦿ No meals.

$ ⊡ **The Hualapai Lodge.** In Peach Springs on the longest stretch of the
HOTEL original historic Route 66, the hotel has a comfortable lobby with a large fireplace that is welcoming on chilly nights. **Pros:** concierge desk arranges river trips with the Hualapai River Runners; good on-site restaurant with Native American dishes; Hualapai locals add a different perspective to the canyon experience. **Cons:** basic rooms lack historic charm; location is off the beaten path. $ Rooms from: $109 ⊠ 900 Rte. 66, Peach Springs ☎ 928/769–2230, 888/868–9378 ⊕ www. hualapaitourism.com ⋧ 60 rooms ⦿ Breakfast.

$$$$ ⊡ **Hualapai Ranch.** Accommodations at Hualapai Ranch, the only lodg-
B&B/INN ing on the West Rim, are available as a package through Hualapai Tourism, and hotel rates include continental breakfast, either lunch or dinner, a Hualapai visitation permit, and shuttle service to the rim overlooks at Guano Point and Eagle Point. **Pros:** front porches have nice desert views; rustlers tell tall tales while you roast s'mores at campfire programs; dining room serves meals all day long. **Cons:** no phones, Internet, or TVs. $ Rooms from: $308 ⊠ Grand Canyon West, Quartermaster Point Rd. ☎ 928/769–2636, 888/868–9378 ⊕ www. hualapaitourism.com ⋧ 26 cabins ⦿ Some meals.

NORTH-CENTRAL ARIZONA

WELCOME TO NORTH-CENTRAL ARIZONA

TOP REASONS TO GO

★ **Mother Nature:** Stunning red rocks, snow-capped mountains, and crisp country air rejuvenate the most cynical city dwellers. Nature lovers should visit either the Coconino or Prescott national forest.

★ **Father Time:** Ancient Native American sites, such as Walnut Canyon and Montezuma's Castle, show life before Columbus "discovered" America. You can learn their history in the excellent national monument visitor centers.

★ **Main Street charm:** Jerome and Prescott exude small-town hospitality with turn-of-the-20th-century architecture and charming bed-and-breakfasts.

★ **Cool escapes:** Beat the heat in the high desert; temperatures throughout north-central Arizona are typically 20°F cooler than in the Phoenix area.

★ **Free spirits:** The energy of Sedona is delightfully infectious; even skeptics might be tempted to get their aura read.

1 Williams and Tusayan. Take a historic train ride into the Grand Canyon from Williams, a cozy town along Route 66. Less than a mile from the Grand Canyon National Park entrance, tiny Tusayan has a half-dozen hotels and restaurants.

2 Flagstaff. College-town enthusiasm and high-country charm combine to make this one of Arizona's most outdoors-friendly towns. Hiking, biking, skiing, and climbing are local passions.

3 Sedona. Surrounded by the Coconino National Forest, Sedona's residents call their home a museum without walls. The town's red rocks lure visitors from around the world. You'll enjoy breathtaking views, fantastic cuisine, and a dash of New Age whimsy.

4 The Verde Valley, Jerome, and Prescott. Remote but still accessible, the towns of the Verde Valley embrace the life of yesteryear. You can take the Verde Canyon Railroad or visit Montezuma's Castle and see nature's untouched beauty and history. Whiskey Row in Prescott still exudes turn-of-the-20th-century charm, and Jerome is a hub for artisans and antiques dealers.

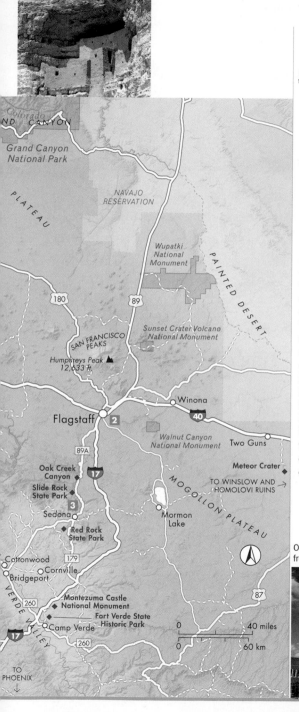

4

GETTING ORIENTED

Nestled between the Grand Canyon and Phoenix, north-central Arizona has enough natural beauty and sophisticated attractions to compete with its neighbors to the north and south. Most visitors flock to Sedona, world renowned for red rocks, pink jeeps, and New Age energy. The surrounding area of Verde Valley may not attract the same hordes, but this means some welcome peace and quiet. Flagstaff is surrounded by the Coconino National Forest and wrapped around the base of the San Francisco Peaks, the tallest mountains in the state. Phoenicians flee the summertime heat to cool off in the mountains and explore Prescott and Jerome.

Old Flagstaff sandstone courthouse from 1894.

Map labels

Colorado
ND CANYON
Grand Canyon National Park
PLATEAU
NAVAJO RESERVATION
Wupatki National Monument
PAINTED DESERT
180
89
SAN FRANCISCO PEAKS
Sunset Crater Volcano National Monument
Humphreys Peak 12,633 ft.
Winona
Flagstaff
40
2
89A
Walnut Canyon National Monument
Two Guns
Meteor Crater
17
TO WINSLOW AND HOMOLOVI RUINS
Oak Creek Canyon
Slide Rock State Park
3
MOGOLLON PLATEAU
Sedona
Mormon Lake
Red Rock State Park
Cottonwood
179
Cornville
Bridgeport
VERDE VALLEY
260
Montezuma Castle National Monument
Fort Verde State Historic Park
87
17
Camp Verde
260
0   40 miles
0   60 km
TO PHOENIX

Updated by
Mara Levin

Red-rock buttes ablaze in the slanting light of late afternoon, majestic mountains tipped white from a fresh snowfall, pine forests clad in dark green needles—north-central Arizona is rich in natural beauty, a landscape of vast plateaus punctuated by steep ridges and canyons. North-central Arizona is also rich in artifacts from its earliest inhabitants—well-preserved cliff dwellings and petroglyphs provide glimpses into Native American cultures dating back over a thousand years. Geological wonders, like huge craters formed by meteorites and volcanoes, add yet another layer to exploring in the region.

North of Flagstaff the San Francisco Peaks, a string of tall volcanic mountains, rise over 12,000 feet. To the south, ponderosa pines cover the Colorado Plateau before the terrain plunges dramatically into Oak Creek Canyon. The canyon then opens to reveal red buttes and mesas in the high-desert areas surrounding Sedona. The desert gradually descends to the Verde Valley, crossing the Verde River before reaching the 7,000-foot Black Range, over which lies the Prescott Valley.

Flagstaff, the hub of this part of Arizona, was historically a way station en route to Southern California via the railroads and then Route 66. Many of those who were "just passing through" stayed and built a community, revitalizing downtown with cafés, an activity-filled square, eclectic shops, and festivals. The town's large network of bike paths and parks abuts hundreds of miles of trails and forest roads, an irresistible lure for outdoors enthusiasts. Not surprisingly, the typical resident of Flagstaff is outdoorsy, young, and has a large, friendly dog in tow.

Down in Sedona, the average age and income rises considerably. This was once a hidden hamlet used by Western filmmakers, but New Age enthusiasts flocked to the region in the 1980s, believing it was the center of spiritual powers. Well-off executives and retirees followed soon after. Sophisticated restaurants, upscale shops, luxe accommodations, and New Age entrepreneurs cater to both these populations, and to the thriving tourist trade.

Pioneers and miners are now part of north-central Arizona's past, but the wild and woolly days of the Old West aren't forgotten. The preserved fort at Camp Verde recalls frontier life, and the decrepit facades of the funky former mining town of Jerome have an infectious charm. The jumble of saloons and Victorian houses in temperate Prescott attest to the attempt to bring "civilization" to Arizona's territorial capital.

■TIP→ It's wise, especially if you're an outdoors enthusiast, to start in the relatively lowland areas of Prescott and the Verde Valley, climbing gradually to Sedona and Flagstaff—it can take several days to grow accustomed to the high elevation in Flagstaff.

NORTH-CENTRAL ARIZONA PLANNER

WHEN TO GO

Autumn, when the wet season ends, the stifling desert temperatures moderate (it's 20°F cooler than Phoenix), and the mountain aspens reach their full golden splendor, is a great time to visit this part of Arizona. During the summer months many Phoenix residents travel north to escape the 100°F temperatures, meaning excessive traffic along Interstate 17 just north of Phoenix on Friday and Sunday evenings. Hotels are less expensive in winter, but mountain temperatures dip below zero, and snowstorms can occur weekly, especially near Flagstaff.

Sedona has springlike temperatures even in January, when it's snowing in Flagstaff, but summer temperatures above 90°F are common.

FESTIVALS AND EVENTS

JUNE **Northern Arizona Barbeque Festival.** Forty teams compete for prize money at this cook-off in downtown Williams in mid-June, where you'll find barbeque tasting, a beer garden, and live music. ✉ *200 Railroad Ave., Williams* ☎ *928/635–4061* ⊕ *www.experiencewilliams.com.*

SEPTEMBER **Festival of Science.** This 10-day series of exhibits, activities, and talks in Flagstaff is a fun and interactive way to learn about current research in astronomy, geology, and biology. ☎ *800/842–7293* ⊕ *www.scifest.org.*

Flagstaff Route 66 Days. Classic and muscle cars roar into Flagstaff in early September for this fun auto show with live music and a host of vendors. ☎ *928/451–1204* ⊕ *www.route66carclub.com.*

PLANNING YOUR TIME

Sedona will probably occupy most of your time, so plan to spend at least two days there, hiking or shopping. Oak Creek Canyon and Chapel of the Holy Cross are must-sees. Then, depending on your preferences, spend your time looking (window-shopping or stargazing) or doing (hiking, exploring). If you can, plan to be in Sedona midweek, when the weekend crowds aren't around.

Outdoors enthusiasts should head to Flagstaff for a day to enjoy the Mount Elden Trail System or hit the slopes at Arizona Snowbowl. The evening can be spent enjoying dinner at one of downtown Flagstaff's

HIKING HIGHLIGHTS

Ancient seas, colliding landmasses, spewing volcanoes, and other geological forces have cast and recast northern Arizona into a sprawling sculpture of contrasts. Hikes along canyon rims often look out among red-rock monoliths, and treks to the barren crests of the San Francisco Peaks overlook verdant forests stretching to the edge of the Grand Canyon to the north and the Mogollon Rim to the south. You can hike through thick woods in the Verde Valley and the Prescott National Forest (and even ascend a volcano), and amid rock formations around Sedona. Check out ⊕ *www. fs.usda.gov/coconino* for info on the Coconino, and ⊕ *www.fs.usda.gov/ prescott* for more info on Prescott.

many restaurants, followed by constellation viewing at the Lowell Observatory.

Prescott and Jerome can be combined for a day or less. You can check out the pulse of downtown Prescott's art and music scene on famous Whiskey Row, then spend a night in a historic hotel; Jerome has several quaint B&Bs, as well as a shopping district with more affordable treasures than Sedona.

GETTING HERE AND AROUND
Don't plan on flying into Flagstaff, Sedona, or Prescott: commercial flights are limited, and besides, getting here is half the fun. The scenery is gorgeous, you'll definitely want a car, and north-central Arizona is only a two-hour drive from Phoenix.

It makes sense to rent a car in this region, since trails and monuments stretch miles past city limits and many area towns can't be reached by the major bus companies. The major rental agencies have offices in Flagstaff, Prescott, and Sedona. Avoid interstates when possible; the back ways can be more direct and have the best views of the stunning landscape. Instead of Route 17, take AZ 89A through Verde Valley and Oak Creek Canyon. Weekend traffic around Sedona can be heavy, so leave early and allow extra time.

RESTAURANTS
You'll find lots of American comfort food in this part of the country: barbecue restaurants, steak houses, and burger joints predominate. If you're looking for something different, Sedona and Flagstaff have the majority of good, multiethnic restaurants in the area, and if you're craving Mexican, you're sure to find something authentic and delicious (note that burritos are often called "burros" around here). Sedona is the best place in the area for fine dining, although Flagstaff and Prescott now boast a few upscale eateries. Some area restaurants close in January and February—the slower months in the area—so call ahead. Reservations are suggested April through October.

HOTELS

Flagstaff and Prescott have the more affordable lodging options, with lots of comfortable motels and B&Bs, but no real luxury. The opposite is true in Sedona, which is filled with opulent resorts and hideaways, most offering solitude and spa services—just don't expect a bargain. Reservations are essential for Sedona and suggested for Flagstaff and Prescott. Little Jerome has a few B&Bs, but call ahead if you think you might want to spend the night. If you're in for a thrill, many of the historic hotels have haunted rooms. *Hotel reviews have been shortened. For full information, visit Fodors.com.*

WHAT IT COSTS				
	$	$$	$$$	$$$$
Restaurants	under $13	$13–$20	$21–$30	over $30
Hotels	under $121	$121–$175	$176–$250	over $250

Restaurant prices are the average cost of a main course at dinner or, if dinner is not served, at lunch. Hotel prices are the lowest cost of a standard double room in high season, excluding taxes and service charges.

WILLIAMS AND TUSAYAN

If you are heading to the Grand Canyon from points west, Williams makes sense as a base, especially if you want to take the Grand Canyon Railway. Tusayan is much closer to the canyon; instead of a one-hour drive or two-hour train ride, this tiny town with good accommodations and restaurants sits just outside the National Park entrance gate.

WILLIAMS

59 miles south of Grand Canyon National Park, 36 miles west of Flagstaff.

The mountain town of Williams encompasses a nicely preserved half-mile of Route 66 to accommodate adventurous cross-country motorists. Sure, there are kitschy 1950s diners and souvenir shops, along with cowboys who enact staged gun-fights on the streets. But you'll also find good restaurants, a microbrewery, and outdoor activities like hiking, biking, and fishing.

GETTING HERE AND AROUND

From Flagstaff, you can take Exit 165 to reach the historic downtown area. You'll end up on Railroad Avenue, the one-way westbound street. If you're coming from points west, take Exit 163, Grand Canyon Boulevard, into the heart of town. Most shops and restaurants are along Route 66 (also called Main Street) and Railroad Avenue, which runs parallel. The Williams Visitor Center is on the corner of Railroad Avenue and Grand Canyon Boulevard, and there's a free parking lot next to it. The Grand Canyon Railway Depot is across the tracks.

ESSENTIALS

Visitor Information Williams Visitor Center ✉ *200 W. Railroad Ave., at Grand Canyon Blvd.* ☎ *928/635–4061* 🌐 *www.experiencewilliams.com* 🕘 *Daily 8–5.*

EXPLORING

FAMILY **Planes of Fame Air Museum.** A good stop 30 miles north of Williams, at the junction of U.S. 180 and State Route 64 in Valle, is this satellite of the Air Museum Planes of Fame in Chino, California. The museum chronicles the history of aviation with an array of historic and modern aircraft. One of the featured pieces is a C-121A Constellation "Bataan," the personal aircraft General MacArthur used during the Korean War. Guided tours of this historic plane are offered for an extra $3 fee. Visitors are not allowed inside the cockpits. ✉ *755 Mustang Way, Valle* ☎ *928/635–1000* 🌐 *www.planesoffame.org* 🎫 *$6.95* 🕘 *Daily 9–5; extended summer hrs.*

WHERE TO EAT

$$ AMERICAN FAMILY 🍴 **Cruisers Café 66.** Patterned after a '50s-style, high-school hangout (but with cocktail service), this diner pleases kids and adults with a large menu of family-priced American classics—good burgers and fries, barbecue pork sandwiches, salads, and thick malts, plus a choice steak that'll set you back about $20. The Grand Canyon Brewery, accessed by a side entrance, adds to the casual fun—just saddle up to a hand-carved log barstool and order one of five microbrews on tap. A large mural of the town's heyday along the "Mother Road" and historic cars out front make this a Route 66 favorite. Kids enjoy the relaxed atmosphere and jukebox tunes. [$] *Average main: $15* ✉ *233 W. Rte. 66* ☎ *928/635–2445* 🌐 *www.cruisers66.com.*

$$ MEXICAN 🍴 **Pancho McGullicuddy's Southwestern Bar & Grill.** Established in 1893 as the Cabinet Saloon, this restaurant is on the National Register of Historic Places. Gone are the spittoons and pipes—the colorful dining area now has Mexican-inspired décor and serves such specialties as "armadillo eggs" (deep-fried jalapeños stuffed with cheese). Other favorites include fish tacos, buzzard wings—better known as "hot wings"—and *pollo verde* (chicken breasts smothered in a sauce of cheese, sour cream, and green chiles). The bar has TVs tuned to sporting events and pours more than 30 tequilas. There's live country music most evenings during the summer season. [$] *Average main: $14* ✉ *141 Railroad Ave.* ☎ *928/635–4150* 🌐 *www.vivapanchos.com.*

$$$ ECLECTIC Fodor's Choice ★ 🍴 **Red Raven Restaurant.** This dapper storefront bistro in the heart of downtown Williams features warm lighting and romantic booth seating. Creatively presented fare blends American, Italian, and Asian ingredients. Specialties include a starter of crisp tempura shrimp salad with a ginger-sesame dressing, and mains like charbroiled salmon with basil butter over cranberry–pine nut couscous, and pork tenderloin with cilantro pesto, served with mashed potatoes and sautéed local vegetables. The well-selected wine and beer list is one of the most extensive in the region. [$] *Average main: $21* ✉ *135 W. Rte. 66* ☎ *928/635–4980* 🌐 *www.redravenrestaurant.com.*

$ AMERICAN FAMILY 🍴 **Twisters.** Kick up some Route 66 nostalgia at this old-fashioned soda fountain, bar, and kitschy gift shop built in 1926. Dine on burgers and hot dogs, a famous Twisters sundae (topped with raspberry sauce, nuts, and hot fudge), Route 66 beer float, or cherry phosphate—all to the sounds of '50s tunes. The kids' menu features cartoon characters and a selection of corn dogs, hot dogs, hamburgers, chicken strips, and peanut-butter-and-jelly sandwiches. The gift shop is a blast from the past, with Route 66 tchotchkes, classic Coca-Cola memorabilia, and fanciful items celebrating the careers of Betty Boop, James Dean, Elvis, and Marilyn Monroe. If you're thirsty, the attached bar has 20 beers on tap. [$] *Average main: $7* ✉ *417 E. Rte. 66* ☎ *928/635–0266* 🌐 *www.route66place.com* 🕒 *Closed Sun., and Jan. and Feb.*

WHERE TO STAY

$ HOTEL FAMILY 🏨 **Canyon Motel and RV Park.** Railcars, cabooses, and cottages make up this 13-acre property on the outskirts of Williams. **Pros:** family-friendly property with hiking, horseshoes, playground, and indoor swimming pool; general store; friendly and helpful owners. **Cons:** short drive to restaurants and shops; RV park traffic. [$] *Rooms from: $76* ✉ *1900 E. Rodeo Rd., Rte. 66* ☎ *928/635–9371, 800/482–3955* 🌐 *www.thecanyonmotel.com* 🛏 *18 rooms, 5 railcar suites* 🍴 *No meals.*

$$ HOTEL 🏨 **Grand Canyon Railway Hotel.** Designed to resemble the train depot's original Fray Marcos lodge, this hotel features attractive Southwestern-style accommodations with large bathrooms and comfy beds with upscale linens. **Pros:** railway package options; game room and outdoor playground; short walk from historic downtown restaurants and bars. **Cons:** large-scale property. [$] *Rooms from: $169* ✉ *233 North Grand Canyon Blvd.* ☎ *928/635–4010, 800/843–8724* 🌐 *www.thetrain.com* 🛏 *287 rooms, 11 suites* 🍴 *No meals.*

$$ B&B/INN 🏨 **The Red Garter.** This restored saloon and bordello from 1897 now houses a small, antiques-filled B&B. **Pros:** on-site coffeehouse and bakery; decorated in antiques and period pieces; steps from several restaurants and bars. **Cons:** all rooms are only accessible by stairs; parking is across the street. [$] *Rooms from: $135* ✉ *137 Railroad Ave.* ☎ *928/635–1484, 800/328–1484* 🌐 *www.redgarter.com* 🛏 *4 rooms* 🍴 *Breakfast.*

$$ B&B/INN 🏨 **Sheridan House Inn.** Nestled among 2 acres of pine trees a half-mile uphill from Route 66, this upscale B&B has decks with good views and a flagstone patio with a hot tub. **Pros:** quiet location; scrumptious breakfasts. **Cons:** a long drive to the canyon and a short drive from downtown Williams; no children under 16. [$] *Rooms from: $170* ✉ *460 E. Sheridan Ave.* ☎ *928/635–8991* 🌐 *www.grandcanyonbedandbreakfast.com* 🛏 *6 rooms, 2 suites* 🍴 *Breakfast.*

SPORTS AND THE OUTDOORS

BICYCLING

Historic Route 66 Mountain Bike Tour. Cyclists can enjoy the scenery along abandoned sections of Route 66 on the Historic Route 66 Mountain Bike Tour. Maps of the tour, which include the 6-mile **Ash Fork Hill Trail** and the 5-mile **Devil Dog Trail,** are available at the Williams Visitor Center. 🌐 *www.experiencewilliams.com.*

FISHING

Arizona Game and Fish Department. Fish for trout, crappie, catfish, and smallmouth bass at a number of lakes surrounding Williams. To fish on public land, anglers ages 14 and older are required to obtain a fishing license from the Arizona Game and Fish Department, either at their office or online. ⊠ *Flagstaff* ☎ *928/774–5045* ⊕ *www.azgfd.gov.*

SKIING

FAMILY **Elk Ridge Ski and Outdoor Recreation.** This ski area is usually open mid-December through much of March, weather permitting. There are four groomed runs (including one for beginners), areas suitable for cross-country skiing, and a hill set aside for tubing. The lodge rents skis, snowboards, and inner tubes. From Williams, take South 4th Street/ Perkinsville Road for 2½ miles, and then turn right at Ski Run Road/ Forest Road 106 and go another 1½ miles. During heavy snows, four-wheel drive or chains may be necessary. ⊠ *Ski Run Rd.* ☎ *928/814– 5038* ⊕ *www.elkridgeski.com.*

TUSAYAN

57 miles north of Williams, 1 mile south of Grand Canyon National Park.

The small hamlet of Tusayan, incorporated as a town only in 2010, is little more than a place to sleep and eat when visiting the Grand Canyon's South Rim. The main attractions here are an IMAX theater, where you can see a film about the Canyon and purchase tickets for air and jeep tours, and the Grand Canyon Airport, the takeoff point for plane and helicopter tours.

GETTING HERE AND AROUND

Tusayan's quarter-mile strip of hotels, eateries, and services sits right on Highway 64, the road leading into Grand Canyon National Park. Parking lots are plentiful.

EXPLORING

National Geographic Visitor Center Grand Canyon. Here you can schedule and purchase tickets for air tours, and buy a national park pass, which enables you to access the park by special entry lanes. However, the biggest draw at the visitor center is the six-story IMAX screen that features the short movie, *Grand Canyon: The Hidden Secrets.* You can learn about the geologic and natural history of the canyon, soar above stunning rock formations, and ride the rapids through the rocky gorge. The film is shown every hour on the half-hour; the adjoining gift store is huge and well stocked. ⊠ *450 State Rte. 64, 2 miles south of the Grand Canyon's south entrance* ☎ *928/638–2468* ⊕ *www.explorethecanyon. com* 🖾 *$13.72 for IMAX movies* ⊙ *Mar.–Oct., daily 8 am–10 pm; Nov.–Feb., daily 10:30–6:30.*

WHERE TO EAT

$$ ✕ **Canyon Star Steakhouse and Saloon.** Relax in the rustic timber-and-
AMERICAN stone dining room at the Grand Hotel for reliable if uninspired Ameri-
FAMILY can food, with an emphasis at dinner on steaks and barbecue. Other popular options include barbecue chicken and ribs, and Mexican fare.

Most nights there's live guitar or banjo music. There's a kids' menu, and the Canyon Star also serves breakfast and lunch daily. In summer, be sure to reserve a table at dinner. There's also a coffee bar in the hotel lobby. [$] *Average main: $18* ✉ *149 Hwy. 64* ☎ *928/638–3333* 🌐 *www.grandcanyongrandhotel.com* 🕒 *No lunch during winter.*

$$$ AMERICAN 🍴 **The Coronado Room.** Inside the Best Western Grand Canyon Squire Inn is the most sophisticated cuisine in Tusayan in an upscale dining room with attentive service. The menu includes well-prepared, hearty American food, with an emphasis on game (elk, venison, buffalo), plus grilled seafood, escargot, and oversize desserts. There's a good-size wine list, too. Although classier than most eateries in these parts, dress is still casual and the vibe relaxed. Reservations are a good idea, particularly in the busy season. [$] *Average main: $22* ✉ *100 Hwy. 64* ☎ *928/638–2681* 🌐 *www.grandcanyonsquire.com* 🕒 *No lunch.*

4

WHERE TO STAY

$$$ HOTEL FAMILY 🏨 **Best Western Grand Canyon Squire Inn.** About 1 mile from the park's south entrance, this motel lacks the historic charm of the older lodges at the canyon rim, but has more amenities, including a small cowboy museum in the lobby, an upscale gift shop, and one of the better restaurants in the region. **Pros:** a cool pool in summer and a hot tub for cold winter nights; children's activities at the Family Fun Center; close to South Rim. **Cons:** hall noise can be an issue with all of the in-hotel activities. [$] *Rooms from: $239* ✉ *100 Hwy. 64, Grand Canyon* ☎ *928/638–2681, 800/622–6966* 🌐 *www.grandcanyonsquire.com* 🛏 *250 rooms, 4 suites* 🍽 *Breakfast.*

$$$ HOTEL 🏨 **The Grand Hotel.** At the south end of Tusayan, this popular hotel has bright, clean rooms decorated in Southwestern colors, a cozy stone-and-timber lobby, and free Wi-Fi. **Pros:** coffee stand for a quick morning pick-me-up; gift shop stocked with outdoor gear and regional books. **Cons:** somewhat generic property. [$] *Rooms from: $249* ✉ *149 State Hwy. 64, Grand Canyon* ☎ *928/638–3333, 888/634–7263* 🌐 *www.grandcanyongrandhotel.com* 🛏 *121 rooms* 🍽 *No meals.*

$$ HOTEL 🏨 **Red Feather Lodge.** About 2 miles from the canyon, this motel and adjacent hotel are a good value. **Pros:** good price for being so close to park. **Cons:** motel rooms are small, with shower only. [$] *Rooms from: $140* ✉ *300 Hwy. 64* ☎ *928/638–2414, 800/538–2345* 🌐 *www.redfeatherlodge.com* 🛏 *215 rooms, 1 suite* 🍽 *No meals.*

SPORTS AND THE OUTDOORS

BICYCLING

Arizona Bike Trail. Pedal the depths of the Kaibab National Forest on the Arizona Bike Trail–Tusayan Bike Trails System. Following linked loop trails at an elevation of 6,750 feet, you can bike as few as 3 miles or as many as 38 miles round-trip along old logging roads (parts of it paved) through ponderosa pine forest. Keep an eye out for elk, mule deer, hawks, eagles, pronghorn antelope, turkeys, coyote, and porcupines. Open for biking year-round (but most feasible March through October), the trail is accessed on the west side of Highway 64, a half mile north of Tusayan. ✉ *Tusayan Ranger District, Hwy. 64, Box 3088* ☎ *928/638–2443* 🌐 *www.fs.usda.gov/kaibab.*

HORSEBACK RIDING

Apache Stables. There's nothing like a horseback ride to immerse you in the Western experience. From stables near Tusayan, these folks offer gentle horses and a ride through the forest. Choose from one- and two-hour trail rides or the popular campfire rides and horse-drawn wagon excursions. ⊠ *Forest Service Rd. 328, 1 mile north of Tusayan* ☎ *928/638–2891* ⊕ *www.apachestables.com* ✉ *From $44* ☉ *Apr.– Nov., daily (weather permitting).*

FLAGSTAFF

146 miles northwest of Phoenix, 27 miles north of Sedona via Oak Creek Canyon.

Few travelers slow down long enough to explore Flagstaff, a town of 66,000 known locally as "Flag"; most stop only to spend the night at one of the town's many motels before making the last leg of the trip to the Grand Canyon, 80 miles north. Flag makes a good base for day trips to ancient Native American sites and the Navajo and Hopi reservations, as well as to Petrified Forest National Park and the Painted Desert, but the city is a worthwhile destination in its own right. Set against a lovely backdrop of pine forests and the snowcapped San Francisco Peaks, downtown Flagstaff retains a frontier flavor.

In summer, Phoenix residents head here seeking relief from the desert heat, because at any time of the year temperatures in Flagstaff are about 20°F cooler than in Phoenix. They also come to Flagstaff in winter to ski at the small Arizona Snowbowl, about 15 miles northeast of town among the San Francisco Peaks.

GETTING HERE AND AROUND

Flagstaff lies at the intersection of Interstate 40 (east–west) and Interstate 17 (running south from Flagstaff), 146 miles north of Phoenix via Interstate 17. If you're driving from Sedona to Flagstaff or the Grand Canyon, head north on AZ 89A through the wooded Oak Creek Canyon: it's the most scenic route.

Flagstaff Pulliam Airport is 3 miles south of town off Interstate 17 at Exit 337. US Airways flies from Phoenix to Flagstaff. A taxi from Flagstaff Pulliam Airport to downtown should cost about $15. Cabs aren't regulated; some, but not all, have meters, so it's wise to agree on a rate before you leave for your destination.

Amtrak comes into the downtown Flagstaff station twice daily. There's no rail service into Prescott or Sedona, but Arizona Shuttle provides transportation via shuttle van or private car between Phoenix, Sedona, Flagstaff, Williams, and the Grand Canyon. Sun Taxi will take you around Flagstaff or to any place in northern Arizona.

A walking-tour map of the area is available at the visitor center in the Tudor Revival–style train depot, an excellent place to begin sightseeing.

PLANNING YOUR TIME

You can see most of Flagstaff's attractions in a day—especially if you visit the Lowell Observatory or the Northern Arizona University Observatory in the evening, which is also when the Museum Club is best experienced.

Consult the schedule of tour times if you want to visit the Riordan State Historic Park. Devote at least an hour to the excellent Museum of Northern Arizona. The Historic Downtown District is a good place for lunch or dinner and shopping. If you're a skier, spend part of a winter's day at the Arizona Snowbowl; in summer you can spend a couple of hours on the skyride and scenic trails at the top. Take your time enjoying the trails on Mount Elden, and remember to pace yourself in the higher elevations; allow a full day for hiking. The Lava River Cave is an easy—if dark—hike that can be done comfortably in an hour; Walnut Canyon, where you can walk through ancient cliff dwellings, is only 20 minutes east of town.

ESSENTIALS

Transportation Contacts A Friendly Cab ☎ *928/774–4444* ⊕ *www. afriendlycab.com.* **Arizona Shuttle** ☎ *800/888–2749* ⊕ *www.arizonashuttle.com.* **Sun Taxi and Tours** ☎ *928/779–1111* ⊕ *www.suntaxiandtours.com.*

Visitor Information Flagstaff Visitor Center ✉ *Santa Fe Depot, 1 E. Rte. 66, Downtown* ☎ *928/774–9541, 800/842–7293* ⊕ *www.flagstaffarizona.org.*

EXPLORING

TOP ATTRACTIONS

Arizona Snowbowl. Although the Arizona Snowbowl is still one of Flagstaff's biggest attractions, snowy slopes can be a luxury in times of drought. Fortunately, visitors can enjoy the beauty of the area year-round, with or without the fluffy white stuff. The Agassiz ski lift climbs to a height of 11,500 feet in 25 minutes, and doubles as a skyride through the Coconino National Forest in summer. From this vantage point you can see up to 70 miles; views may even include the North Rim of the Grand Canyon. There's a lodge at the base with a restaurant, bar, and ski school. To reach the ski area, take U.S. 180 north from Flagstaff; it's 7 miles from the Snowbowl exit to the skyride entrance. ✉ *Snowbowl Rd., North Flagstaff* ☎ *928/779–1951* ⊕ *www.arizonasnowbowl. com* ☞ *Skyride $15* ⊙ *Skyride: Memorial Day–early Sept., daily 10–4; early Sept.–mid-Oct., Fri.–Sun. 10–4 (weather permitting).*

Historic Downtown District. Storied Route 66 runs right through the heart of downtown Flagstaff. The late-Victorian, Tudor Revival, and early art deco architecture in this district recalls the town's heyday as a logging and railroad center. ✉ *Downtown Historic District, Rte. 66 north to Birch Ave., and Beaver St. east to Agassiz St., Downtown.*

Santa Fe Depot. The Santa Fe Depot now houses the visitor center for the Historic District. ✉ *1 E. Rte. 66, Downtown.*

Hotel Monte Vista. Highlights of the historic district include the 1927 Hotel Monte Vista, built after a community drive raised $200,000 in 60 days. The construction was promoted as a way to bolster the burgeoning

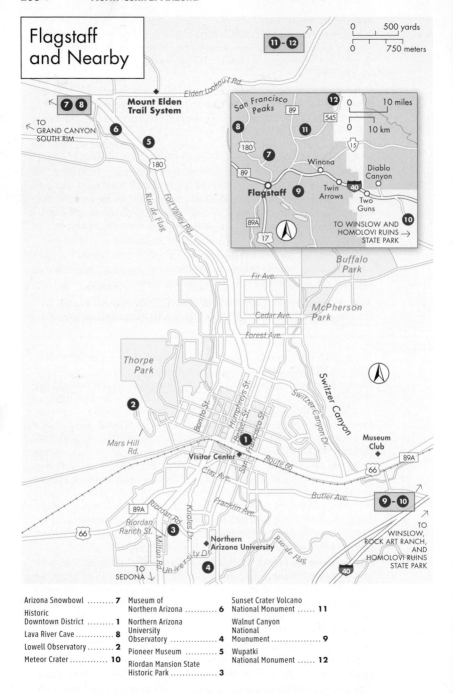

Flagstaff and Nearby

tourism industry in the region. The hotel was held publicly until the early 1960s. Rendezvous, a coffee house/martini bar with a wraparound window, is a great place for people-watching, and the subterranean Cocktail Lounge hosts live music on weekends. ⊠ *100 N. San Francisco St., Downtown* ☎ *928/779–6971* ⊕ *www.hotelmontevista.com.*

Babbitt Brothers Building. The 1888 Babbitt Brothers Building was constructed as a building-supply store and then turned into a department store by David Babbitt, the mastermind of the Babbitt empire. The Babbitts are one of Flagstaff's wealthiest founding families. Bruce Babbitt, the most recent member of the family to wield power and influence, was the governor of Arizona from 1978 through 1987 and Secretary of the Interior under President Clinton (1993–2001). ⊠ *12 E. Aspen Ave., Downtown.*

Vail Building. Most of the area's first businesses were saloons catering to railroad construction workers, which was the case with the 1888 Vail Building, a brick art deco–influenced structure covered with stucco in 1939. Crystal Magic, a New Age shop, is the building's current tenant. ⊠ *5 N. San Francisco St., Downtown.*

QUICK
BITES

Macy's European Coffee House and Bakery. Students, skiers, new and aging hippies, and just about everyone else who likes good coffee (and delicious vegetarian fare) jam into Macy's European Coffee House and Bakery for the best cup in town. ⊠ *14 S. Beaver St., Downtown* ☎ *928/774–2243* ⊕ *www.macyscoffee.net.*

Mix on the Square. You can create your own salads, or enjoy breakfast (try the carrot cake pancakes), homemade soups (gluten-free), and sandwiches through dinnertime at Mix. ⊠ *Heritage Square, 120 N. Leroux St., Downtown* ☎ *928/774–8200* ⊕ *www.mixflagstaff.com.*

FAMILY
Fodor's Choice
★

Lowell Observatory. In 1894 Boston businessman, author, and scientist Percival Lowell founded this observatory from which he studied Mars. His theories of the existence of a ninth planet sowed the seeds for the discovery of Pluto at Lowell in 1930 by Clyde Tombaugh. The 6,500-square-foot Steele Visitor Center hosts exhibits and lectures and has a gift shop. Several interactive exhibits—among them Pluto Walk, a scale model of the solar system—appeal to children. Visitors are invited, on some evenings, to peer through the 24-inch Clark telescope and the McAllister, a 16-inch reflector telescope. Day and evening viewings are offered year-round, but call ahead for a schedule. ■TIP→ The Clark observatory dome is open and unheated, so dress for the outdoors. To reach the observatory, less than 2 miles from downtown, drive west on Route 66, which resumes its former name, Santa Fe Avenue, before it merges into Mars Hill Road. ⊠ *1400 W. Mars Hill Rd., West Flagstaff* ☎ *928/233–3212, 928/233–3211 for recorded info* ⊕ *www.lowell.edu* ☞ *$12* ⊗ *Hrs vary by season; call ahead.*

FAMILY
Museum of Northern Arizona. This institution, founded in 1928, is respected worldwide for its research and its collections centering on the natural and cultural history of the Colorado Plateau. Among the

permanent exhibitions are an extensive collection of Navajo rugs and a Hopi *kiva* (men's ceremonial chamber).

A gallery devoted to area geology is usually a hit with children: it includes a life-size model dilophosaurus, a carnivorous dinosaur that once roamed northern Arizona. Outdoors, a life-zone exhibit shows the changing vegetation from the bottom of the Grand Canyon to the highest peak in Flagstaff. A nature trail, open only in summer, heads down across a small stream into a canyon and up into an aspen grove. Also in summer, the museum hosts exhibits and the works of Native American artists, whose wares are sold in the museum gift shop. ⊠ *3101 N. Fort Valley Rd., North Flagstaff* ☎ *928/774–5213* ⊕ *www.musnaz. org* 🖾 *$10* ⊙ *Daily 9–5.*

WORTH NOTING

● **Lava River Cave.** Subterranean lava flow formed this mile-long cave roughly 700,000 years ago. Once you descend into its boulder-strewn maw, the cave is spacious, with 40-foot ceilings, but claustrophobes take heed: about halfway through, the cave tapers to a 4-foot-high squeeze that can be a bit unnerving. A 40°F chill pervades the cave throughout the year so take warm clothing.

To reach the turnoff for the cave, go approximately 9 miles north of Flagstaff on U.S. 180, then turn west onto FR 245. Turn left at the intersection of FR 171 and look for the sign to the cave. The trip is approximately 45 minutes from Flagstaff. Although the cave is on Coconino National Forest Service property, the only thing here is an interpretive sign, so it's definitely something you tackle at your own risk. ■ TIP➜ Pack a flashlight (or two). ⊠ *FR 171B.*

● **Northern Arizona University Observatory.** This observatory was built in 1952 by Dr. Arthur Adel, a scientist at Lowell Observatory whose study of infrared astronomy pioneered research into molecules that absorb light passing through Earth's atmosphere. Today's studies of Earth's shrinking ozone layer rely on some of Dr. Adel's early work. Visitors to the observatory—which houses one of the largest research-grade telescopes that the public is allowed to move and manipulate—are usually hosted by friendly students and faculty members of the university's Department of Physics and Astronomy. Dr. Adel's 24-inch telescope—the first infrared scope—is also on display. ⊠ *Bldg. 47, Northern Arizona Campus Observatory, Dept. of Physics and Astronomy, S. San Francisco St. just north of Walkup Skydome, University* ☎ *928/523–7170* ⊕ *www.physics.nau.edu* 🖾 *Free* ⊙ *Viewings Fri. 7:30–10 pm, weather permitting.*

Pioneer Museum. The Arizona Historical Society operates this museum in a volcanic-rock building constructed in 1908. The structure was Coconino County's first hospital for the poor, and the current displays include one of the depressingly small nurses' rooms, an old iron lung, and a reconstructed doctor's office. Most of the exhibits, however, touch on more cheerful aspects of Flagstaff history—like road signs and pioneer children's games.

The museum holds folk-crafts festivals in the summer, with blacksmiths, weavers, spinners, quilters, and candle makers. Their crafts, and those of other local artisans, are sold in the museum's gift shop. In a wooded residential section at the northwest end of town, the museum is part of the Fort Valley Park complex. ✉ *2340 N. Fort Valley Rd., North Flagstaff* ☎ *928/774–6272* 🌐 *www.arizonahistoricalsociety.org* 🎟 *$6* 🕒 *Mon.–Sat. 9–5.*

Riordan Mansion State Historic Park. This artifact of Flagstaff's logging heyday is near Northern Arizona University. The centerpiece is a mansion built in 1904 for Michael and Timothy Riordan, lumber-baron brothers who married two sisters. The 13,300-square-foot, 40-room log-and-stone structure—designed by Charles Whittlesley, who was also responsible for El Tovar Hotel at the Grand Canyon—contains furniture by Gustav Stickley, father of the American Arts and Crafts design movement. One room holds "Paul Bunyan's shoes," a 2-foot-long pair of boots made by Timothy in his workshop. Everything on display is original to the house. The inside of the mansion may be explored only by guided tour (hourly on the hour); reservations are suggested. ✉ *409 W. Riordan Rd., University* ☎ *928/779–4395* 🌐 *www.arizonahistoricalsociety.org* 🎟 *$10* 🕒 *June–Aug., daily 10:30–5; Sept.–May, Thurs.–Mon. 10:30–5.*

4

WHERE TO EAT

● $ AMERICAN 🍴 **Beaver Street Brewery.** This restaurant and microbrewery is a casual and family-friendly place. Popular wood-fired pizzas include the Enchanted Forest—with Brie, portobello mushrooms, roasted red peppers, spinach, and artichoke pesto. Expect serious amounts of garlic with whichever pie you choose. Sandwiches, such as the Margarita chicken (marinated in tequila and lime), come with a hefty portion of tasty fries. You won't regret ordering one of the down-home desserts, like the super-gooey chocolate bread pudding. Among the excellent microbrews on tap, the Bramble Berry ale is a local favorite. [$] *Average main: $12* ✉ *11 S. Beaver St., Downtown* ☎ *928/779–0079* 🌐 *www.beaverstreetbrewery.com* ✍ *Reservations not accepted.*

$$$ AMERICAN 🍴 **Black Bart's Steakhouse Saloon.** The Wild West décor at this rollicking, brightly lit barn of a restaurant is a bit cornball, but the steaks and barbecued chicken are tender and flavorful; just don't expect to see vegetables on your plate unless they're deep-fried. A big attraction here is the Northern Arizona University music students that entertain while waiting tables, so don't be surprised if your server suddenly jumps onstage to belt out some show tunes. [$] *Average main: $25* ✉ *2760 E. Butler Ave., Downtown* ☎ *928/779–3142* 🌐 *www.blackbartssteakhouse.com* 🕒 *No lunch.*

$$$ AMERICAN 🍴 **Brix Restaurant & Wine Bar.** A redbrick carriage house, built around 1910 as a garage for one the first automobiles in Flagstaff, is home to one of the city's most sophisticated restaurants. With a seasonally updated menu, the chef pairs locally raised pork and roasted duck entrées with wines from a list of almost 200 bottles ("brix" refers to the sugar content of grapes at harvest). The cheese plate, served with poached natural apricots, is a great accompaniment to a glass of wine at the counter bar. The servers are friendly, the vibe is casually upscale, and

the food is outstanding. [$] *Average main: $25* ✉ *413 N. San Francisco St., Downtown* ☎ *928/213–1021* 🌐 *www.brixflagstaff.com* 🕒 *Closed Mon. No lunch.*

$$$ EUROPEAN 🍴 **Cottage Place.** Regarded by locals as one of the best special-occasion dining venues in the area, this restaurant in a cottage built in 1909 has intimate dining rooms and an extensive wine list. The menu strays slightly from Continental to include some classic American dishes, such as charbroiled lamb chops. The grilled herb salmon and the chateaubriand for two are recommended. Small plates of items such as stuffed mushrooms and grilled shrimp are less pricey and perfect for a lighter meal. [$] *Average main: $30* ✉ *126 W. Cottage Ave., Downtown* ☎ *928/774–8431* 🌐 *www.cottageplace.com* 🕒 *Closed Mon. and Tues. No lunch.*

$ ITALIAN 🍴 **Pizzicletta.** When you take your first bite of any one of the five expertly crafted pizzas on the menu—like the simple tomato, basil, and mozzarella, or the mascarpone, pecorino, arugula, and prosciutto—you'll understand why this small eatery has quickly developed a fierce following. Plates of paper-thin cured meats and olives and salads with chevre and pine nuts are equally delicious. And don't skip out on the homemade gelato. [$] *Average main: $12* ✉ *203 W. Phoenix Ave., Downtown* ☎ *928/774–3242* 🌐 *www.pizzicletta.com* 🕒 *Closed Mon. No lunch.*

$ MEXICAN 🍴 **Salsa Brava.** This cheerful Mexican restaurant, with light-wood booths and colorful designs, eschews heavy Sonoran-style fare in favor of the grilled dishes found in Guadalajara. It's considered the best Mexican food in town. The fish tacos are particularly good, and you can substitute grilled vegetables for the rice and beans if you prefer a lower-carb meal. [$] *Average main: $11* ✉ *2220 E. Rte. 66, East Flagstaff* ☎ *928/779–5293* 🌐 *www.salsabravaflagstaff.com.*

$$$ MODERN AMERICAN Fodor's Choice ★ 🍴 **Tinderbox Kitchen.** This trendy spot downtown serves modern comfort food to local professionals as well as foodies from out of town. Try the slow-roasted pork belly or a board of house-cured meats and cheeses for starters. Signature entrées include juniper-cured venison with blue cheese grits and a grownup, Southwestern take on mac 'n' cheese, with spicy jalapeno and duck-leg confit. For cocktails and lighter fare (or if the wait for restaurant seating is lengthy), check out the sister bar next door, The Annex—it's just as hip and delicious. [$] *Average main: $25* ✉ *34 S. San Francisco St., Downtown* ☎ *928/226–8400* 🌐 *www.tinderboxkitchen.com* 🕒 *No lunch.*

WHERE TO STAY

Trains pass through the downtown area along Route 66 about every 15 minutes throughout the day and night. Light sleepers may prefer to stay in the south or east sections of town to avoid hearing trains rumbling through; at least the whistles are no longer blown within the downtown district.

$$ B&B/INN 🏨 **Abineau Lodge.** This contemporary mountain inn with a rustic feel is on 4 acres bordering the immense Coconino National Forest. **Pros:** pleasant common areas; pretty setting; sauna. **Cons:** 7 miles south of town. [$] *Rooms from: $144* ✉ *1080 Mountainaire Rd., South Flagstaff*

☎ *928/525–6212, 888/715–6386* 🌐 *www.abineaulodge.com* 🛏 *8 rooms, 1 suite* 🍴 *Breakfast.*

$$$ HOTEL 🏨 **Drury Inn & Suites.** So clean it sparkles, the Drury Inn sits at the edge of Northern Arizona University's campus and packs in the amenities, like a free hot breakfast and happy hour drinks, an indoor pool, and comfy lounge areas with mountain views. **Pros:** plenty of extras; great location (walk to campus and historic district). **Cons:** large-scale property. [$] *Rooms from: $180* ✉ *300 S. Milton Rd., Downtown* ☎ *928/773–4900* 🌐 *www.druryhotels.com* 🛏 *160 rooms* 🍴 *Breakfast.*

$$ B&B/INN 🏨 **The Inn at 410.** This downtown B&B in a beautifully restored 1907 residence is an inviting alternative to Flagstaff's chain motels. **Pros:** convenient downtown location; romantic; complimentary cookies and cocktails every afternoon. **Cons:** some train noise. [$] *Rooms from: $165* ✉ *410 N. Leroux St., Downtown* ☎ *928/774–0088, 800/774–2008* 🌐 *www.inn410.com* 🛏 *8 suites* 🍴 *Breakfast.*

$$ HOTEL 🏨 **Little America Hotel Flagstaff.** This deservedly popular hotel is a little distance from the roar of the trains, the grounds are surrounded by evergreen forests, and it's one of the few places in Flagstaff with room service. **Pros:** large, clean rooms; many amenities including walking trails. **Cons:** large-scale property; a few miles east of the shopping and dining district. [$] *Rooms from: $139* ✉ *2515 E. Butler Ave., Downtown* ☎ *928/779–7900, 800/865–1401* 🌐 *flagstaff.littleamerica.com* 🛏 *247 rooms* 🍴 *No meals.*

$$ B&B/INN 🏨 **Starlight Pines Bed and Breakfast.** If you prefer the clean lines of 1920s design to Victorian froufrou, consider staying at this stylish B&B on the city's east side. **Pros:** pretty, immaculate rooms; hospitable hosts. **Cons:** a 10-minute drive from downtown. [$] *Rooms from: $159* ✉ *3380 E. Lockett Rd., East Flagstaff* ☎ *928/527–1912, 800/752–1912* 🌐 *www.starlightpinesbb.com* 🛏 *4 rooms* 🍴 *Breakfast.*

4

NIGHTLIFE AND THE ARTS

NIGHTLIFE

Flagstaff's large college contingent has plenty of places to gather after dark; most are in historic downtown and charge little or no cover. It's easy to walk from one rowdy spot to the next. Use the Ale Trail Map (🌐 *www.flagstaffaletrail.com*) to guide you to six breweries within a 1-mile radius. During the summer months, catch free, family-friendly performances (music, theater, and dance) and movies Thursday to Saturday evening outdoors at Heritage Square. For information on what's going on, pick up the free *Flagstaff Live.*

The Green Room. An environmentally conscious bar, typically filled with college students, The Green Room rolls out an eclectic mix of live music and hardy stout nightly until 2 am. ✉ *15 N. Agassiz St., Downtown* ☎ *928/226–8669* 🌐 *www.flagstaffgreenroom.com.*

Hotel Weatherford. You'll find a double bill here: Charly's Pub hosts late-night jazz and blues bands, while the Exchange Bar tends to attract folksy ensembles. ✉ *23 N. Leroux St., Downtown* ☎ *928/779–1919* 🌐 *www.weatherfordhotel.com.*

Monte Vista Lounge. This lounge in the historic Hotel Monte Vista packs 'em in with nightly live blues, jazz, classic rock, and punk. ⊠ *Hotel Monte Vista, 100 N. San Francisco St., Downtown* ☎ *928/779–6971* ⊕ *www.hotelmontevista.com.*

Museum Club Roadhouse and Danceclub. Fondly known as the Zoo, this building housed an extensive taxidermy collection in the 1930s and is now a popular country-and-western club (a few owls still perch above the dance floor). A gigantic log cabin constructed around five trees, with a huge, wishbone-shape pine as the entryway, the venue offers a taste of Route 66 color along with live music and other events. ⊠ *3404 E. Rte. 66, Downtown* ☎ *928/526–9434* ⊕ *www.themuseumclub.com.*

THE ARTS

There's no shortage of cultural entertainment in Flagstaff, including several summer festivals.

A Celebration of Native American Art. During the summer months, art festivals highlighting the Zuni (May), Hopi (July), and Navajo (August) cultures take place at the Museum of Northern Arizona. ⊠ *3101 N. Fort Valley Rd., North Flagstaff* ☎ *928/774–5213* ⊕ *www.musnaz.org.*

Flagstaff Arts Council/Coconino Center for the Arts. Many excellent art exhibitions, theatrical productions, and music performances take place at Coconino Center for the Arts, under the direction of the Flagstaff Arts Council. ⊠ *2300 N. Fort Valley Rd., North Flagstaff* ☎ *928/779–2300* ⊕ *www.flagartscouncil.org.*

Flagstaff Symphony Orchestra. Year-round concerts, mostly held in Ardrey Auditorium on the NAU campus, are given by the Flagstaff Symphony Orchestra. ☎ *928/774–5107, 888/520–7214 for NAU ticket office* ⊕ *www.flagstaffsymphony.org.*

Orpheum Theater. The 1917 Orpheum Theater, in the heart of the historic district, features music acts, films, lectures, and plays. ⊠ *15 W. Aspen St., Downtown* ☎ *928/556–1580* ⊕ *www.orpheumpresents.com.*

Theatrikos Theatre Company. This highly regarded performance-art group produces five mainstage productions annually using a diverse base of local talent. ⊠ *11 W. Cherry Ave., Downtown* ☎ *928/774–1662* ⊕ *www.theatrikos.com.*

SHOPPING

The Artists Gallery. For fine arts and crafts—everything from ceramics and stained glass to weaving and painting—visit the Artists Gallery, a local artists' cooperative. ⊠ *17 N. San Francisco St., Downtown* ☎ *928/773–0958* ⊕ *www.flagstaffartistsgallery.com.*

Babbitt's Backcountry Outfitters. Just about all your sporting-goods needs can be met at Babbitt's Backcountry Outfitters. ⊠ *12 E. Aspen Ave., Downtown* ☎ *928/774–4775* ⊕ *www.babbittsbackcountry.com.*

Black Hound Gallerie. This downtown gallery specializes in posters, prints, and funky kitsch of all kinds. ⊠ *120 N. Leroux St., Downtown* ☎ *928/774–2323* ⊕ *www.blackhoundgallerie.com.*

A visit to Meteor Crater complements Arizona's many observatories for a different look at the impact of the heavens.

Bookmans. Packed solid with used books, music, and movies, Bookmans is also a cybercafe and a place to see live folk music. ✉ *1520 S. Riordan Ranch St., University* ☎ *928/774–0005* ⊕ *www.bookmans.com.*

Carriage House Antique & Gift Mall. Vendors sell vintage clothing and jewelry, furniture, fine china, Mexican folk art, and other collectibles at Carriage House Antique & Gift Mall. ✉ *413 N. San Francisco St., Downtown* ☎ *928/774–1337.*

Flagstaff Soap Company. Organic bath and body products, including beautiful bar soaps, bubble baths, and lip balms, are handmade on-site at the earthy Flagstaff Soap Company. ✉ *21 N. San Francisco St., Downtown* ☎ *928/774–9178* ⊕ *www.flagstaffsoap.com.*

Museum of Northern Arizona Gift Shop. High-quality Native American art, jewelry, and crafts can be found at the Museum of Northern Arizona Gift Shop. ✉ *3101 N. Fort Valley Rd., North Flagstaff* ☎ *928/774–5213* ⊕ *www.musnaz.org.*

Winter Sun Trading Company. This company sells medicinal herbs, unique fragrances, and Native American jewelry and crafts. ✉ *107 N. San Francisco St., Ste. 1, Downtown* ☎ *928/774–2884* ⊕ *www.wintersun.com.*

Zani Cards and Gifts. Hip jewelry and gifts, handmade paper, and greeting cards are stocked at Zani. ✉ *107 W. Phoenix Ave., Downtown* ☎ *928/774–9409* ⊕ *www.zanigifts.com.*

SPORTS AND THE OUTDOORS

HIKING

You can explore Arizona's alpine tundra in the San Francisco Peaks, part of the Coconino National Forest, where more than 80 species of plants grow on the upper elevations. The habitat is fragile, so hikers are asked to stay on established trails (there are lots of them). ■ TIP→ Flat-landers should give themselves a day or two to adjust to the altitude before lengthy or strenuous hiking. The altitude here will make even the hardiest hikers breathe a little harder, so anyone with cardiac or respiratory problems should be cautious about overexertion. Note that most of the forest trails aren't accessible during winter due to snow.

Coconino National Forest–Flagstaff Ranger District. The rangers of the Coconino National Forest maintain many of the region's trails, and can provide you with details on hiking in the area; both the forest's main office in North Flagstaff and the ranger station in East Flagstaff (✉ *5075 N. U.S 89*) are open weekdays 8–4. ✉ *1824 S. Thompson St., North Flagstaff* ☎ *928/527–3600 for North Flagstaff (main office), 928/526–0866 for East Flagstaff* ⊕ *www.coconinoforest.us.*

Mount Elden Trail System. Most trails in the Coconino National Forest's 35-mile-long Mount Elden Trail System lead to stunning views from the dormant volcanic field, across the vast ponderosa pine forest, all the way to Sedona. Keep in mind that most of the forest trails are not accessible for hiking December through March due to snow. ⊕ *www. cocnino.us.*

Elden Lookout Trail. The most challenging trail in the Mount Elden system, which happens to be the route with the most rewarding views, is along the steep switchbacks of the Elden Lookout Trail. If you traverse the full 3 miles to the top, keep your focus on the landscape rather than the tangle of antennae and satellite dishes that greets you at the end. *Difficult.* ✉ *Trailhead: Off U.S. 89, 3 miles east of downtown Flagstaff.*

Humphreys Peak Trail. This trail is 9 miles round-trip, with a vertical climb of 3,843 feet to the 12,643-foot summit of Arizona's highest mountain. *Difficult.* ✉ *Trailhead: Snowbowl Rd., 7 miles north of U.S. 180.*

Kachina Trail. Those who don't want a long hike can do just the first mile of the 5-mile-long Kachina Trail; gently rolling, this route is surrounded by huge stands of aspen and offers fantastic vistas. In fall, changing leaves paint the landscape shades of yellow, russet, and amber. *Moderate.* ✉ *Trailhead: Snowbowl Rd., 7 miles north of U.S. 180.*

Sunset Trail. The 4-mile-long Sunset Trail proceeds with a gradual pitch through the pine forest, emerging onto a narrow ridge nicknamed the Catwalk. By all means take pictures of the stunning valley views, but make sure your feet are well placed. The access road to this trail is closed in winter. *Moderate.* ✉ *Trailhead: Off U.S. 180, 3 miles north of downtown Flagstaff, then 6 miles east on FR 420/Schultz Pass Rd.*

MOUNTAIN BIKING

With 50 miles of urban bike trails and more than 30 miles of challenging forest and mountain trails a short ride from town, it was inevitable that one of Flagstaff's best-kept secrets would leak out. The mountain biking on Mount Elden is on par with that of more celebrated trails in Colorado and Utah. While there isn't a concise loop trail such as those in Moab, Utah, experienced bikers can create one by connecting Schultz Creek Trail, Sunset Trail, and Elden Lookout Road. Beginners (as well as those looking for rewarding scenery with less of an incline) may want to start with Lower Fort Valley and Campbell Mesa. Local bike shop staff can help with advice and planning.

Coconino National Forest. Some of the best mountain biking trails in the region are in the Coconino National Forest. ☎ 928/527–3600 for North Flagstaff (main office), 928/526–0866 for East Flagstaff ⊕ www. coconino.us.

Lower Oldham Trail. Originating on the north end of Buffalo Park in Flagstaff, the Lower Oldham Trail is steep in some sections, but rewarding. The terrain rolls, climbing about 800 feet in 3 miles, and the trail is difficult in spots but easy enough to test your tolerance of the elevation. Many fun trails spur off this one; it's best to stop in at the local bike shop to get trail maps and discuss rides with staff who know the area. ⊠ Trailhead: Cedar St.

Schultz Creek Trail. The popular Schultz Creek Trail is fun and suitable for strong beginners, although seasoned experts will be thrilled as well. Most opt to start at the top of the 600-foot-high hill and swoop down the smooth, twisting path through groves of wildflowers and stands of ponderosa pines and aspens, ending at the trailhead 4 giddy miles later. ⊠ Trailhead: Schultz Pass Rd., near intersection with U.S. 180.

Sunset Trail. Near the summit of Mount Elden, Sunset Trail has amazing views off the ridge rendered barren by a 1977 fire. The trail narrows into the aptly nicknamed Catwalk, with precipitous drops a few feet on either side. Fear, either from the 9,000-foot elevation or the sheer exposure, is not an option. You need to be at least a moderately experienced mountain biker to attempt this trail. When combined with Elden Lookout Road and Schultz Creek Trail, the usual loop, the trail totals 15 miles and climbs almost 2,000 feet. You can avoid the slog up Mount Elden by parking one vehicle at the top of Elden Lookout Road, at the trailhead, and a friend's vehicle at the bottom. ⊠ Trailhead: Elden Lookout Rd., 7 miles from intersection with Schultz Pass Rd.

Flagstaff Nordic Center. From mid-June to mid-October, the Flagstaff Nordic Center opens its cross-country trails—good for families and beginners, because they're scenic and not technically challenging. ⊠ U.S. 180, 16 miles north of Flagstaff, North Flagstaff ☎ 928/220–0550 ⊕ www. flagstaffnordiccenter.com.

Flagstaff Urban Trails System (FUTS). A map of the Urban Trails System, available at the Flagstaff Visitor Center, details low- and no-traffic bike routes around town. ⊠ Flagstaff Visitor Center, 1 E. Rte. 66, Downtown ☎ 928/774–9541, 800/842–7293 ⊕ www.flagstaffarizona.org.

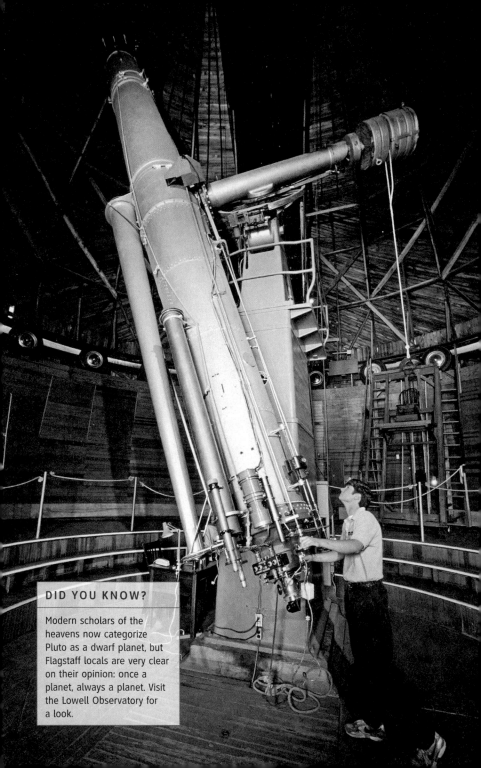

DID YOU KNOW?

Modern scholars of the heavens now categorize Pluto as a dwarf planet, but Flagstaff locals are very clear on their opinion: once a planet, always a planet. Visit the Lowell Observatory for a look.

EQUIPMENT AND RENTALS

Absolute Bikes. You can rent mountain bikes, get good advice and gear, and purchase trail maps at Absolute Bikes. ⊠ *202 E. Route 66, Downtown* ☎ *928/779–5969* ⊕ *www.absolutebikes.net.*

ROCK CLIMBING

Flagstaff Climbing Center. The tallest indoor climbing walls in the Southwest can be found at this rock-climbing gym. Flagstaff Climbing also offers guided climbing excursions around the Flagstaff area. ⊠ *205 S. San Francisco St., Downtown* ☎ *928/556–9909* ⊕ *www. flagstaffclimbing.com.*

SKIING AND SNOWBOARDING

The ski season usually starts in mid-December and ends in mid-April.

Arizona Snowbowl. Seven miles north of Flagstaff off U.S. 180, the Arizona Snowbowl has 32 downhill runs (37% beginner, 42% intermediate, and 21% advanced), four chairlifts, and a vertical drop of 2,300 feet. There are a couple of good bump runs, but it's better for beginners or those with moderate skill; serious area skiers take a road trip to Telluride. Still, it's a fun place to ski or snowboard. The Hart Prairie Lodge has an equipment-rental shop and a SKIwee center for ages four to seven.

All-day adult lift tickets are $59. Half-day discounts are available, and group-lesson packages for skiing or snowboarding (including two hours of instruction, an all-day lift ticket, and equipment rental) are a good buy at $90. A children's program, which includes lunch and supervision from 9 to 3, runs $89 (reservations are required). Some Flagstaff motels have ski packages that include transportation to Snowbowl. ⊠ *Snowbowl Rd., North Flagstaff* ☎ *928/779–1951, 928/779–4577 for snow report* ⊕ *www.arizonasnowbowl.com.*

Flagstaff Nordic Center. Nine miles north of Snowbowl Road, the Flagstaff Nordic Center has 25 miles of well-groomed cross-country trails here that are open 9–4 daily (when there's enough snow). Coffee, hot chocolate, and snacks are served at the lodge. A day pass for skiing costs $15 on weekdays and $18 on weekends. An instruction package costs $30, including equipment, day pass, and a 90-minute group lesson. Renting equipment by itself is $16. ⊠ *U.S. 180, 16 miles north of Flagstaff, North Flagstaff* ☎ *928/220–0550* ⊕ *www.flagstaffnordiccenter.com.*

SIDE TRIPS NEAR FLAGSTAFF

Travelers heading straight through town bound for the Grand Canyon often neglect the area north and east of Flagstaff, but a detour has its rewards. If you don't have time to do everything, take a quick drive to Walnut Canyon—it's only about 15 minutes out of town.

EAST OF FLAGSTAFF

Within an hour's drive of east Flagstaff you'll find plenty of natural and cultural attractions, from craters and volcanoes to Native American art and architecture. After exploring sites like Walnut Canyon and

Homolovi Ruins, you can take a break by "standing on a corner in Winslow, Arizona," and then tour the beautifully restored La Posada Hotel.

GETTING HERE AND AROUND
From Flagstaff, follow Interstate 40 a few miles east to Exit 204 for Walnut Canyon National Monument. Continue east along the highway for Meteor Crater off Exit 233, a 45-minute drive. Continue east on Interstate 40, to the town of Winslow, about 50 miles from Flagstaff; head 4 miles northeast to see the Hopi pueblos at Homolovi Ruins State Park.

EXPLORING
Homolovi Ruins State Park. *Homolovi* is a Hopi word meaning "place of the little hills." The pueblo sites here at Homolovi Ruins State Park are thought to have been occupied between AD 1200 and 1425, and include 40 ceremonial kivas and two pueblos containing more than 1,000 rooms each. The Hopi believe their immediate ancestors inhabited this place, and they consider the site sacred. Many rooms have been excavated and recovered for protection; rangers conduct guided tours. The Homolovi Visitor Center has a small museum with Hopi pottery and Ancestral Puebloan artifacts; it also hosts workshops on native art, ethnobotany, and traditional foods. Campsites, with or without hookups, are $25 and can be reserved in advance. ☒ *AZ 87, 3.5 miles northeast of Winslow* ☎ *928/289–4106* ⊕ *www.azstateparks.com* ☒ *$7* ☉ *Visitor center daily 8–5.*

FAMILY **Meteor Crater.** A natural phenomenon in a privately owned park 43 miles east of Flagstaff, Meteor Crater is impressive if for no other reason than its sheer size. A hole in the ground 600 feet deep, nearly 1 mile across, and more than 3 miles in circumference, Meteor Crater is large enough to accommodate the Washington Monument or 20 football fields. It was created by a meteorite crash 49,000 years ago. The area looks so much like the surface of the moon that NASA made it one of the official training sites for the Project Apollo astronauts.

You can't descend into the crater because of the efforts of its owners to maintain its condition—scientists consider this to be the best-preserved crater on Earth—but guided rim tours give useful background information, and telescopes along the rim offer you a closer look. There's a sandwich shop on site, and the Rock Shop sells specimens from the area and jewelry made from native stones. Take Interstate 40 east of Flagstaff to Exit 233, then drive 6 miles south on Meteor Crater Road. ☒ *I–40, Exit 233, Winslow* ☎ *928/289–5898, 800/289–5898* ⊕ *www.meteorcrater.com* ☒ *$16* ☉ *June–Aug., daily 7–7; Sept.–May, daily 8–5.*

Rock Art Ranch. The Ancestral Puebloan petroglyphs of this working cattle ranch in Chevelon Canyon are startlingly vivid after more than 1,000 years. Ranch owner Brantly Baird will guide you along the ¼-mile trail, explaining Western and archaeological history. It's mostly easy walking, except for the climb in and out of Chevelon Canyon, where there are handrails. Baird houses his Native American artifacts and pioneer farming implements in his own private museum. It's out of the way and on a dirt road, but you'll see some of the best rock art in northern Arizona. Reservations are required. ☒ *Off AZ 87, 13 miles southeast of*

Winslow ☎ *928/386–5047* ✉ *$35 per person for 1 or 2 people; less per person for larger groups* ⊘ *By appointment only.*

Fodor'sChoice ★ **Walnut Canyon National Monument.** The group of cliff dwellings that make up Walnut Canyon National Monument were constructed by the Sinagua people, who lived and farmed in and around the canyon starting around AD 700. The more than 300 dwellings here were built between 1080 and 1250, and abandoned, like those at so many other settlements in Arizona and New Mexico, around 1300. The Sinagua traded far and wide with other Native Americans, including people at Wupatki. Even macaw feathers, which would have come from tribes in what is now Mexico, have been excavated in the canyon.

> **THE SINAGUA PEOPLE**
>
> The achievements of the Sinagua people, who lived in north-central Arizona from the 8th through the 15th century, reached their height in the 12th and 13th centuries, when related groups occupied most of the San Francisco Volcanic Field and a large portion of the upper and middle Verde Valley. The Sinagua sites around modern-day Camp Verde, Clarkdale, and Flagstaff provide a window onto this remarkable culture. Some of the best examples of surviving Sinagua architecture can be found at Walnut Canyon and Wupatki National Monument, northeast of Flagstaff.

4

Early Flagstaff settlers looted the site for pots and "treasure"; Woodrow Wilson declared this a national monument in 1915, which began a 30-year process of stabilizing the site.

Part of the fascination of Walnut Canyon is the opportunity to enter the dwellings, stepping back in time to an ancient way of life. Some of the Sinagua homes are in near-perfect condition in spite of all the looting, because of the dry, hot climate and the protection of overhanging cliffs. You can reach them by descending 185 feet on the 1-mile, 240-stair, stepped **Island Trail,** which starts at the visitor center. As you follow the trail, look across the canyon for other dwellings not accessible on the path. Island Trail takes about an hour to complete at a normal pace. Those with health concerns should opt for the easier 0.5-mile **Rim Trail,** which has overlooks from which dwellings, as well as an excavated, reconstructed pit house, can be viewed. Picnic areas dot the grounds and line the roads leading to the park. Do not rely on a GPS to get here; stick to I–40. ✉ *Walnut Canyon Rd., 3 miles south of I–40, Exit 204, Winona* ☎ *928/526–3367* ⊕ *www.nps.gov/waca* ✉ *$5* ⊘ *Nov.–Apr., daily 9–5; May–Oct., daily 8–5.*

Winslow. Frequent flooding on the Little Colorado River frustrated the attempts of Mormon pioneers to settle here, but with the coming of the railroad the town roared into life. Later, Route 66 sustained the community until Interstate 40 passed north of town. New motels and restaurants sprouted near the interstate exits, and the downtown was all but abandoned. Still, visitors wishing to find themselves "standing on a corner in Winslow, Arizona" abound thanks to a song by the Eagles; and the historic masterpiece, La Posada, remains one of the best places to sleep and dine in the state. The town is 58 miles east of Flagstaff on Interstate 40.

WHERE TO STAY

$ 🔲 **La Posada Hotel.** One of the great railroad hotels, La Posada ("rest-
HOTEL   ing place") exudes the charm of an 18th-century Spanish hacienda and
Fodor's Choice   its restoration has been a labor of love. **Pros:** historic charm; unique
★   architecture; impressive restaurant. **Cons:** mazes of staircases aren't
wheelchair-friendly. $ *Rooms from: $129* ✉ *303 E. 2nd St., Winslow*
☎ *928/289–4366* ⊕ *www.laposada.org* ↩ *53 rooms* ⦿ *No meals.*

SAN FRANCISCO VOLCANIC FIELD

The San Francisco Volcanic Field north of Flagstaff encompasses 2,000 square miles of fascinating geological phenomena, including ancient volcanoes, cinder cones, valleys carved by water and ice, and the San Francisco Peaks themselves, some of which soar to almost 13,000 feet. There are also some of the most extensive Native American dwellings in the Southwest: don't miss Sunset Crater and Wupatki. These national monuments can be explored in relative solitude during much of the year. ■**TIP**➜ The area is short on services, so fill up on gas and consider taking a picnic.

> **MARY JANE COLTER**
>
> Pick a historic hotel or site of significance built in the late 19th or early 20th century in northern or eastern Arizona, and there's a good chance architect Mary Jane Colter was part of it. A student of Frank Lloyd Wright, Colter designed La Posada in Winslow, the Painted Desert Inn, and several structures at the Grand Canyon, including the Hopi House. She also decorated the canyon's El Tovar Hotel.

GETTING HERE AND AROUND

To get to both Sunset Crater and Wupatki national monuments, take U.S. 89 north out of Flagstaff. After 12 miles, turn right for Sunset Crater. Wupatki National Monument is another 19 miles north on this road.

EXPLORING

Sunset Crater Volcano National Monument. Sunset Crater, a cinder cone that rises 1,000 feet, was an active volcano 900 years ago. Its final eruption contained iron and sulfur, which give the rim of the crater its glow and thus its name. You can walk around the base, but you can't descend into the huge, fragile cone. The **Lava Flow Trail,** a half-hour, mile-long, self-guided walk, provides a good view of the evidence of the volcano's fiery power: lava formations and holes in the rock where volcanic gases vented to the surface.

If you're interested in hiking a volcano, head to **Lenox Crater,** about 1 mile east of the visitor center, and climb the 280 feet to the top of the cinder cone. The cinder is soft and crumbly, so wear closed, sturdy shoes. From **O'Leary Peak,** a 5-mile hike from the visitor center on Forest Route 545A, enjoy great views of the San Francisco Peaks, the Painted Desert, and beyond. The trail is an unpaved, rutted road (closed during winter), with a steep 2.5-mile hike to the top. Bonito Campground, just outside the monument, is open May–October ($18) and has toilets but no hook-ups. To get to the area from Flagstaff, take

Santa Fe Avenue east to U.S. 89, and head north for 12 miles; turn right onto the road marked Sunset Crater and go another 2 miles to the visitor center. ✉ *6082 Sunset Crater Rd., 14 miles northeast of Flagstaff* ☎ *928/526–0502* ⊕ *www.nps.gov/sucr* 🖱 *$5, includes Wupatki National Monument and Doney Mountain* ⊙ *Nov.–Apr., daily 9–5; May–Oct., daily 8–5.*

Wupatki National Monument. Families from the Sinagua and other Ancestral Puebloans are believed to have lived together in harmony on the site that is now Wupatki National Monument, farming and trading with one another and with those who passed through. The eruption of Sunset Crater may have influenced migration to this area a century after the event, as freshly laid volcanic cinders held in moisture needed for crops. Although there's evidence of earlier habitation, most of the settlers moved here around 1100 and left the pueblo by about 1250. The 2,700 identified sites contain archaeological evidence of a Native American settlement.

The national monument was named for the Wupatki ("tall house" in Hopi) site, which was originally three stories high, built above an unexplored system of underground fissures. The structure had almost 100 rooms and an open ball court—evidence of Southwestern trade with Mesoamerican tribes for whom ball games were a central ritual. Next to the ball court is a blowhole, a geologic phenomenon in which air is forced upward by underground pressure.

Other sites to visit are Wukoki, Lomaki, and the Citadel, a pueblo on a knoll above a limestone sink. Although the largest remnants of Native American settlements at Wupatki National Monument are open to the public, other sites are off-limits. If you're interested in an in-depth tour, consider a ranger-led overnight hike to the **Crack-in-Rock Ruin.** The 14-mile (round-trip) trek covers areas marked by ancient petroglyphs and dotted with well-preserved sites. The trips are only conducted in April and October; call by February or August if you'd like to take part in the lottery for one of the 100 available places on these $50 hikes. Between the Wupatki and Citadel ruins, **Doney Mountain** affords 360-degree views of the Painted Desert and the San Francisco Volcanic Field. It's a perfect spot for a sunset picnic. In summer, rangers give lectures. ✉ *Sunset Crater–Wupatki Loop Rd., 19 miles north of Sunset Crater visitor center* ☎ *928/679–2365* ⊕ *www.nps.gov/wupa* 🖱 *$5, includes Sunset Crater National Monument and Doney Mountain* ⊙ *Daily 9–5.*

SEDONA AND OAK CREEK CANYON

27 miles south of Flagstaff on AZ 89A, 114 miles north of Phoenix, Interstate 17 to AZ 179 to AZ 89A, 60 miles northeast of Prescott, U.S. 89 to AZ 89A.

It's easy to see what draws so many people to Sedona. Red-rock buttes—Cathedral Rock, Bear Mountain, Courthouse Rock, and Bell Rock, among others—reach up into an almost always blue sky, and both colors are intensified by dark-green pine forests. Surrealist Max

Sedona Vortex Tour

What is a vortex? The word "vortex" comes from the Latin *vertere*, which means "to turn or whirl." In Sedona, a vortex is a funnel created by the motion of spiraling energy. Sedona has long been believed to be a center for spiritual power because of the vortexes of subtle energy in the area. This energy isn't described as electricity or magnetism, though it's said to leave a slight residual magnetism in the places where it's strongest.

New Agers believe there are four major vortexes in Sedona: Airport, Cathedral Rock, Boynton Canyon, and Bell Rock. Each manifests a different kind of energy, and this energy interacts with the individual in its presence. People come from all over the world to experience these energy forms, hoping for guidance in spiritual matters, health, and relationships.

Juniper trees, which are all over the Sedona area, are said to respond to vortex energy in a way that reveals where this energy is strongest. The stronger the energy, the more axial twist the junipers bear in their branches.

Airport Vortex is said to strengthen one's "masculine" side, aiding in self-confidence and focus. **Cathedral Rock Vortex** nurtures one's "feminine" aspects, such as patience and kindness. You'll be directed to **Boynton Canyon Vortex** if you're seeking balance between the masculine and feminine. And finally **Bell ✪ Rock Vortex**, the most powerful of all, strengthens all three aspects: masculine, feminine, and balance.

These energy centers are easily accessed, and vortex maps are available at crystal shops all over Sedona.

Ernst, writer Zane Grey, and many filmmakers drew inspiration from these vistas—more than 80 Westerns were shot in the area in the 1940s and '50s alone.

These days, Sedona lures enterprising restaurateurs and gallery owners from the East and West coasts. New Age followers, who believe that the area contains some of Earth's more important vortexes (energy centers), also come in great numbers, seeking a "vibe" here that confers a sense of balance and well-being, and enhances creativity.

Expansion since the early 1980s has been rapid, and lack of planning has taken its toll in the form of unattractive developments and increased traffic.

The city of Sedona is young, and there are few historic sites; as many visitors conclude, you don't come to Sedona to tour the town itself. The main downtown activity is shopping, mostly for Southwestern-style paintings, clothing, rugs, jewelry, and Native American artifacts. Just beyond the shops and restaurants, however, canyons, creeks, ancient dwellings, and the red rocks beckon. The area is relatively easy to hike or bike, or you can take a jeep tour into the hills.

GETTING HERE AND AROUND

Sedona stretches along AZ 89A, its main thoroughfare, which runs roughly east–west through town. Uptown, the section with most of the shops and restaurants, is at the east end. Free parking is plentiful

Sedona and
Oak Creek Canyon

throughout Sedona, but especially in Uptown: the visitor center, a half block off 89A on Forest Road, has an adjacent parking lot; parking spaces along the streets are free for three hours; or park all day in the large municipal lot a few blocks farther east, off Jordan Road.

The most scenic route into town from Phoenix is taking Interstate 17 to AZ 260 toward Cottonwood, then going northeast on AZ 89A. To reach Sedona more directly from Phoenix, take Interstate 17 north for 107 miles until you come to AZ 179; it's another winding 7½ miles on that road, past the Village of Oak Creek, into town. The trip should take about 2 hours. The 27-mile drive north from Sedona to Flagstaff on AZ 89A, which winds its way through Oak Creek Canyon, is breathtaking.

Sedona Airport, in West Sedona, is a base for several air tours but has no regularly scheduled flights.

The Arizona Shuttle makes eight trips daily between Sedona and Phoenix; the fare is $47 one-way. You can also get on or off at Camp Verde, Cottonwood, or the Village of Oak Creek (7 miles outside Sedona on AZ 179). Reservations are required.

Weekend traffic near Sedona, especially during summer months, can approach gridlock on the narrow highways. Leave for your destination at first light to bypass the day-trippers, late risers, and midday heat.

Sedona is roughly divided into three neighborhoods: Uptown, which is a walkable shopping district that encompasses the areas just north and south of the "Y" (where AZ 179 and AZ 89A intersect); West Sedona, which is a 4-mile-long commercial strip; and the Village of Oak Creek, which lies a few miles south of the "Y" along AZ 179. The Verde Lynx provides bus transportation (and has wheelchair lifts) east and west along AZ 89A until 7 pm for $1 each way. Sedona Taxi is handy for getting to and from restaurants or trailheads.

FLAGSTAFF AND SEDONA

There might only be 27 miles separating Flagstaff and Sedona, but they're very different places. Flagstaff's natural terrain and earthiness lend a "granola-y" feel to the city, and the Northern Arizona University students here enhance it. Meanwhile, Sedona's beauty is no secret, and residents (full- and part-time) pay a premium to enjoy it.

Sedona Trolley offers two types of daily orientation tours, both departing from the main bus stop in Uptown and lasting less than an hour. One goes along AZ 179 to the Chapel of the Holy Cross; the other passes through West Sedona to Boynton Canyon (Enchantment Resort). Rates are $15 for one or $25 for both.

If you want to explore the red rocks of Sedona on your own, you can rent a four-wheel-drive vehicle from an agency such as Barlow Jeep Rentals; most visitors opt for a jeep tour.

PLANNING YOUR TIME

In warmer months visit air-conditioned shops at midday and do hiking and jeep tours in the early morning or late afternoon, when the light is softer and the heat less oppressive. Many of the most memorable spots in Sedona are considered energy centers; pick up a vortex map of the area at the visitor center.

The vistas of Sedona from Airport Mesa at sunset can't be beat. The Upper Red Rock Loop has great photo opportunities.

ESSENTIALS

Transportation Contacts Barlow Jeep Rentals ☎ 928/282-8700 ⊕ www.barlowjeeprentals.com. **Arizona Shuttle** ☎ 800/448-7988 in Arizona ⊕ www.arizonashuttle.com. **Sedona Taxi** ☎ 928/204-9111. **Sedona Trolley** ☎ 928/282-4211 ⊕ www.sedonatrolley.com. **Verde Lynx** ☎ 928/634-5526 ⊕ www.verdelynx.az.gov.

Visitor Information Sedona Visitor Center ✉ 331 Forest Rd., just off AZ 89A ☎ 928/282-7722, 800/288-7336 ⊕ www.visitsedona.com.

EXPLORING

TOP ATTRACTIONS

Bell Rock. With its distinctive shape right out of your favorite Western film and its proximity to the main drag, this popular butte ensures a steady flow of admirers, so you may want to arrive early in the day. The parking lot next to the Bell Rock Pathway often fills by mid-morning, even midweek. The views from here are good, but an easy and fairly accessible path follows mostly gentle terrain for 1 mile to the base of the butte. Mountain bikers, parents with all-terrain baby strollers, and not-so-avid hikers should have little problem getting there. No official paths climb the rock itself, but many forge their own routes (at their own risk). ⊠ *AZ 179, several hundred yards north of Bell Rock Blvd., Village of Oak Creek.*

Cathedral Rock. It's almost impossible not to be drawn to this butte's towering, variegated spires. The approximately 1,200-foot-high Cathedral Rock looms dramatically over town. When you emerge from the narrow gorge of Oak Creek Canyon, this is the first recognizable formation you'll spot. ■ TIP➔ The butte is best seen toward dusk from a distance. Hikers may want to drive to the Airport Mesa and then hike the rugged but generally flat path that loops around the airfield. The trail is 0.5 mile up Airport Road off AZ 89A in West Sedona; the reward is a panoramic view of Cathedral Rock without the crowds. Those not hiking should drive through the Village of Oak Creek and 5 miles west on Verde Valley School Road to its end, where you can view the butte from a beautiful streamside vantage point and take a dip in Oak Creek if you wish. ⊠ *5 miles to end of Verde Valley School Rd., west off AZ 179, Village of Oak Creek.*

Cathedral Rock Trail. A vigorous but nontechnical 1.5-mile scramble up the slickrock (smooth, rather than slippery, sandstone), this path leads to a nearly 360-degree view of red-rock country. Follow the cairns (rock piles marking the trail) and look for the footholds in the rock. Carry plenty of water: though short, the trail offers little shade and the pitch is steep. You can see the Verde Valley and Mingus Mountain in the distance. Look for the barely discernible "J" etched on the hillside marking the former ghost town of Jerome 30 miles away. ⊠ *Trailhead: about ½ mile down Back O' Beyond Rd. off AZ 179, 3 miles south of Sedona.*

🕙 **Chapel of the Holy Cross.** You needn't be religious to be inspired by the setting and the architecture here. Built in 1956 by Marguerite Brunwige Staude, a student of Frank Lloyd Wright, this modern landmark, with a huge cross on the facade, rises between two red-rock peaks. Vistas of the town and the surrounding area are spectacular. Though there is only one regular service—a beautiful Taizé service of prayer and song on Monday at 5 pm—all are welcome for quiet meditation.

A small gift shop sells religious artifacts and books. A trail east of the chapel leads you—after a 20-minute walk over occasional loose-rock surfaces—to a seat surrounded by voluptuous red-limestone walls, worlds away from the bustle and commerce around the chapel. ⊠ *Chapel Rd. off AZ 179, Village of Oak Creek* ☎ *928/282–4069* ⊕ *www. chapeloftheholycross.com* ⊠ *Free* ⊗ *Daily 9–5.*

🕙 **Oak Creek Canyon.** Whether you want to swim, hike, picnic, or enjoy beautiful scenery framed through a car window, head north through the wooded Oak Creek Canyon. It's the most scenic route to Flagstaff and the Grand Canyon, and worth a drive-through even if you're not heading north. The road winds through a steep-walled canyon, where you crane your neck for views of the dramatic rock formations above. Although the forest is primarily evergreen, the fall foliage is glorious. Oak Creek, which runs along the bottom, is lined with tent campgrounds, fishing camps, cabins, motels, and restaurants. ✉ *AZ 89A, beginning 1 mile north of Sedona, Oak Creek Canyon.*

FAMILY **Slide Rock State Park.** A good place for a picnic, Slide Rock is 7 miles north of Sedona. On a hot day you can plunge down a natural rock slide into a swimming hole (bring an extra pair of jeans or a sturdy bathing suit and river shoes to wear on the slide). The site started as an early-20th-century apple orchard, and the natural beauty attracted Hollywood—a number of John Wayne and Jimmy Stewart movies were filmed here.

A few easy hikes run along the rim of the gorge. One downside is the traffic, particularly on summer weekends; you might have to wait to get into the park after mid-morning. Unfortunately, the popularity of the stream has led to the occasional midsummer closing due to E. coli contamination; the water is tested daily and there is a water-quality hotline at ☎ 602/542–0202. ✉ *6871 N. Hwy. 89A, Oak Creek Canyon* ☎ *928/282–3034* ⊕ *www.azstateparks.com* 💲 *$10 per vehicle for up to 4 persons; $20 per vehicle in summer* ☉ *Oct.–Apr., daily 8–5; May–Sept., daily 8–6 (last admission is 1 hr before closing).*

FAMILY **Snoopy Rock.** Kids love this butte that looks uncannily like the famed *Peanuts* beagle lying atop red rock instead of his doghouse. You can distinguish the formation from several places around town, including the mall in Uptown Sedona, but to get a clear view, venture up Schnebly Hill Road. Park by the trailhead on the left immediately before the paved road deteriorates to dirt. Marg's Draw, one of several trails originating here, is worthwhile, gently meandering 100 feet down-canyon, through the tortured desert flora to Morgan Road. Backtrack to the parking lot for close to a 3-mile hike. ✉ *Schnebly Hill Rd. off AZ 179, Central.*

WORTH NOTING

Courthouse Butte. Toward sunset, when this monolith is free of shadow, the red sandstone seems to catch on fire. From the highway, Courthouse Butte sits in back of Bell Rock and can be viewed without any additional hiking or driving. ✉ *AZ 179, Village of Oak Creek.*

Red Rock State Park. Two miles west of Sedona via AZ 89A is the turn-off for this 286-acre state park, a less crowded alternative to Slide Rock State Park, though without the possibility of swimming. The 5 miles of interconnected trails are well marked, and provide beautiful red rock vistas. There is a daily naturalist-led nature walk at 10 am, a featured program at 2 pm, and bird-watching excursions on Wednesday and Saturday at 9 am. ✉ *4050 Red Rock Loop Rd., West Sedona* ☎ *928/282–6907* ⊕ *www.azstateparks.com* 💲 *$5* ☉ *Daily 8–5.*

CLOSE UP

Red-Rock Geology

It's hard to imagine that the landlocked desert surrounding Sedona was, for much of prehistoric time, an area of dunes and swamps on the shore of an ancient sea. The ebb and flow of this sea shaped the land. When the sea rose, it planed the dunes before dropping more sediment on top. The process continued for a few hundred million years. Eventually the sediment hardened into gray layers of limestone on top of the red sandstone. When North America collided with another continental plate, the land buckled and lifted, forming the Rocky Mountains and raising northern Arizona thousands of feet. Volcanoes erupted in the area, capping some of the rock with erosion-resistant basalt.

Oak Creek started flowing at this time, eroding through the layers of sandstone and limestone. Along with other forces of erosion, the creek carved out the canyons and shaped the buttes. Sedona's buttes stayed intact because a resilient layer of lava had hardened on top and slowed the erosion process considerably. As iron minerals in the sandstone were gradually exposed to the elements, they turned red in a process similar to rusting. The iron minerals, in turn, stained the surrounding colorless quartz and grains of sand—it only takes 2% red-iron material to give the sandstone its red color.

Like the rings of a tree, the striations in the rock document the passage of time and the events: limestone marking the rise of the sea, sandstone indicating when the region was coastline.

WHERE TO EAT

Some Sedona restaurants close in January and February, so call before you go; if you're planning a visit in high season (April to October), make reservations.

$ AMERICAN 🍴 **Coffee Pot Restaurant.** Locals and tourists alike swarm to this spacious diner for scrumptious breakfast and brunch food served by a friendly waitstaff. One hundred and one omelet options are the stars of the show, and include such concoctions as the quirky peanut butter and jelly or the basic ham and cheese. Warm homemade biscuits always hit the spot. An extensive lunch menu that includes everything from Mexican dishes to a Greek salad rounds out the offerings. [$] *Average main: $9* ✉ *2050 W. AZ 89A,* ☎ *928/282–6626* 🌐 *www.coffeepotsedona.com* 🕑 *No dinner.*

$$$ STEAKHOUSE 🍴 **Cowboy Club.** At this restaurant catering to carnivores, you can hang out in the casual Cowboy Club or dine in the more formal Silver Saddle Room, where suede booths are surrounded by cowboy art and a pair of large cattle horns. High-quality cuts of beef are the specialty, but the burgers, grilled trout, and vegetable pot pies are delicious, too. [$] *Average main: $25* ✉ *241 N. AZ 89A, Uptown* ☎ *928/282–4200* 🌐 *www.cowboyclub.com.*

$$$ ITALIAN 🍴 **Dahl & Di Luca Ristorante Italiano.** At this popular Italian restaurant, expect to find delicious homemade soups like white bean with ham

and hearty minestrone. Specialties here include potato gnocchi with a vodka sauce and *pollo piccata* (chicken in a lemon, capers, and chardonnay sauce). Any pasta dish can be made gluten-free with a corn fusilli. Renaissance reproductions and café seating give the impression of a Roman piazza. Make reservations or you can sit at the bar—good food but far less romantic. [$] *Average main: $25* ✉ *2321 W. AZ 89A,* ☎ *928/282–5219* 🌐 *www.dahlanddiluca.com* ⏲ *No lunch.*

$$ MEXICAN Fodor's Choice ★ 🍴 **Elote Café.** Traditional Mexican recipes get a creative and tasty update at this popular restaurant. Start with the namesake *elote,* roasted corn on a stick; this favorite street food in Mexico is transformed into an addictive dip of grilled corn kernels, *cotija* cheese, lime, and chiles. Small plates like chicken tacos with mole sauce are delicious and affordable, and larger dishes like braised lamb shank in ancho chile sauce or chiles rellenos are equally satisfying. Enjoy the colorful interior or sit on the open-air deck for fabulous Sedona views. Just come prepared for a wait, because the word is out and they don't take reservations. [$] *Average main: $19* ✉ *771 AZ 179, Kings Ransom Sedona Hotel, Central* ☎ *928/203–0105* 🌐 *www.elotecafe.com* ✍ *Reservations not accepted* ⏲ *Closed Sun. and Mon. No lunch.*

$$$ EUROPEAN Fodor's Choice ★ 🍴 **Heartline Café.** Fresh flowers and innovative cuisine that even the staff struggles to characterize are this attractive café's hallmarks. Local ingredients pepper the menu, giving a Sedona twist to Continental fare; favorites include pecan-crusted, Sedona-raised trout with Dijon sauce and chicken breast with pesto cream sauce. Appealing vegetarian plates are also available, and breakfast specialties (served until 3 pm) include lemon creme–stuffed French toast and crab Benedict. Lunch sandwiches and wraps can be ordered to go for a gourmet picnic in the red rocks. Desserts include a phenomenal crème brûlée and a marzipan-filled poached pear with caramel sauce. [$] *Average main: $26* ✉ *1610 W. AZ 89A,* ☎ *928/282–0785* 🌐 *www.heartlinecafe.com.*

$$$$ FRENCH 🍴 **L'Auberge.** The most formal dining room in Sedona, on the L'Auberge de Sedona resort property, promises a quiet, civilized evening of indulgence. The menu, a fusion of American cuisine with French influences, is offered as a two-, three-, or four-course meal, and can be paired with selections from the resort's 1,200-bottle wine cellar. Among the house favorites are the filet mignon and the Scottish salmon. The lavish Sunday brunch is well worth the splurge; or have cocktails and lighter fare creekside at the Veranda Bar. [$] *Average main: $54* ✉ *L'Auberge de Sedona, 301 L'Auberge La., Uptown* ☎ *928/282–1661* 🌐 *www.lauberge.com.*

$ CAFÉ 🍴 **New Frontiers Natural Marketplace.** The healthful fare at this mostly organic grocery and deli runs the gamut from grab-and-go sandwiches and the well-stocked salad bar to hot items like honey-glazed salmon, cheese or chicken enchiladas, and turkey meat loaf. Get supplies for your red-rock picnic or relax at the indoor-outdoor dining area. [$] *Average main: $7* ✉ *1420 W. AZ 89A,* ☎ *928/282–6311* 🌐 *www.newfrontiersmarket.com/sedona.*

$$ MEXICAN 🍴 **Oaxaca Restaurant.** Tasty standards complement some of the best Uptown canyon vistas at this modern Mexican restaurant with a lovely balcony. The smoky kick of the salsa, along with the sun-kissed scenery,

Jeep tours get you close to Sedona's red rocks while someone else does the driving.

may transport you south of the border, but dishes are prepared under the auspices of owner Carla Butler, a dietitian who shuns the traditional use of lard and cholesterol-containing oils in favor of healthier options—with delicious results. A south-of-the-border breakfast is served on weekends. $ *Average main: $16* ✉ *321 N. AZ 89A, Uptown* ☎ *928/282–4179* ⊕ *www.oaxacarestaurant.com.*

$$$$
EUROPEAN

× **René at Tlaquepaque.** Ease into the plush banquettes at this quiet, lace-curtained restaurant for classic French and Continental dishes. Recommended starters include French onion soup and the spinach-and-wild-mushroom salad in a hazelnut vinaigrette. Rack of lamb is the house specialty, and the Dover sole is a real find, far from the white cliffs. Crêpes suzette for two, prepared tableside, is an impressive dessert. There's a well-selected wine list, too. Service is formal, but resort-casual attire is acceptable. $ *Average main: $31* ✉ *Tlaquepaque Arts & Crafts Village, Unit B–117, AZ 179, Central* ☎ *928/282–9225* ⊕ *www. rene-sedona.com.*

$
SOUTHERN

× **Sally's B.B.Q.** Although it offers limited indoor seating, this Uptown hideaway behind a long row of tourist shops is worth a visit. It's super-casual, with just an ordering window where you can select pulled-pork sandwiches and homemade comfort food such as beans or coleslaw. The barbecue sauce has a bit of a kick, and the french fries (also made from scratch) are fabulous. Hours vary with the season (during winter they close at 7), so call ahead. $ *Average main: $8* ✉ *250 Jordan Rd., No. 9, Uptown* ☎ *928/282–6533* ⊕ *www.sallysbbq.com.*

$$$$ AMERICAN Fodor's Choice ★ 🍴 **Shugrues Hillside.** Almost everything is good here—including the red-rock views from every seat, which have made this one of the most popular restaurants in Sedona—but the salads and meats are particularly noteworthy. The Caesar salad is refreshingly traditional, and the inventive ginger-walnut chicken salad is large enough to share. Rack of lamb and filet mignon are prepared and presented simply, and there's a small, well-priced wine list. Full entrées include soup or salad; smaller à la carte selections are lower priced. Service is friendly rather than formal, and dining views don't get much better than the upstairs deck. [$] *Average main: $31* ✉ *671 AZ 179, Central* ☎ *928/282–5300* 🌐 *www.shugrueshillside.com.*

WHERE TO STAY

$$$ B&B/INN 🏨 **Adobe Village Graham Inn.** All of the rooms at this inn south of Sedona have either wood-burning or gas fireplaces, and some of them also have Jacuzzi tubs and balconies that look out onto the red rocks. **Pros:** above-average hospitality; variety of accommodations; close to hiking and biking trails. **Cons:** the villas and suites are pricey. [$] *Rooms from: $179* ✉ *150 Canyon Circle Dr., Village of Oak Creek* ☎ *928/284–1425, 800/228–1425* 🌐 *www.adobevillagegrahaminn.com* 🛏 *6 rooms, 5 suites, 4 private villas* 🍽 *Breakfast.*

$$$ B&B/INN 🏨 **Alma de Sedona Bed and Breakfast Inn.** This enchanting bed-and-breakfast has spectacular views and ultracomfortable beds. **Pros:** spacious and private rooms; excellent views. **Cons:** décor could use updating; some rooms require climbing stairs. [$] *Rooms from: $209* ✉ *50 Hozoni Dr.,* ☎ *928/282–2737, 800/923–2282* 🌐 *www.almadesedona.com* 🛏 *12 rooms* 🍽 *Breakfast.*

$$$ RESORT 🏨 **Amara Resort Hotel & Spa.** You might not expect to find a boutique hotel in small, outdoorsy Sedona, but at the Amara, next to gurgling Oak Creek, sleek rooms deviate from the usual Sedona look, with low-slung beds and work desks with ergonomic seating. **Pros:** good spa and restaurant; walk to Uptown. **Cons:** city-chic feels somewhat incongruous with natural setting. [$] *Rooms from: $229* ✉ *100 Amara La., Uptown* ☎ *928/282–4828, 800/815–6152* 🌐 *www.amararesort.com* 🛏 *92 rooms, 8 suites* 🍽 *No meals.*

$$$ B&B/INN 🏨 **Boots & Saddles.** At this quiet inn tucked behind the main street in West Sedona, the romantic rooms are decorated in an upscale Western motif, complete with genuine cowboy artifacts, and most have decks with hot tubs and telescopes for stargazing. **Pros:** hosts go the extra mile to pamper and advise; private decks. **Cons:** first-floor rooms can get noise from upstairs guests. [$] *Rooms from: $190* ✉ *2900 Hopi Dr.,* ☎ *928/282–1944, 800/201–1944* 🌐 *www.oldwestbb.com* 🛏 *6 rooms* 🍽 *Breakfast.*

$$$ B&B/INN 🏨 **Briar Patch Inn.** This B&B in verdant Oak Creek canyon exudes rustic elegance in its Southwestern-themed rooms in charming wooden cabins, many with decks overlooking the creek. **Pros:** private and quiet; tranquil creekside setting with beautiful gardens. **Cons:** pricey; some cabins can be dark. [$] *Rooms from: $225* ✉ *3190 N. AZ 89A, Oak Creek Canyon* ☎ *928/282–2342, 888/809–3030* 🌐 *www.briarpatchinn.com* 🛏 *19 cottages* 🍽 *Breakfast.*

$$
B&B/INN

▦ **The Canyon Wren.** The best value in the Oak Creek canyon area, this small and serene B&B across the road from the creek has freestanding cabins with views of the canyon walls. **Pros:** romantic yet homey; wonderful hosts and breakfast. **Cons:** some cabins are close to road; 6 miles to town. $ *Rooms from: $165* ✉ *6425 N. AZ 89A, Oak Creek Canyon* ☎ *928/282–6900, 800/437–9736* ⊕ *www.canyonwrencabins.com* ☞ *4 cabins* ⦙◎⦙ *Breakfast.*

$
HOTEL

▦ **Desert Quail Inn.** Close to a lion's share of the trailheads, this is a good base for outdoor adventures, and the front desk has plenty of maps and advice on offer. **Pros:** large, clean rooms. **Cons:** older, two-story roadside motel. $ *Rooms from: $95* ✉ *6626 AZ 179, Village of Oak Creek* ☎ *928/284–1433, 800/385–0927* ⊕ *www.desertquailinn.com* ☞ *40 rooms* ⦙◎⦙ *No meals.*

$$$
B&B/INN
Fodor'sChoice
★

▦ **El Portal Sedona Hotel.** This stunning hacienda is one of the most beautifully designed boutique hotels in the Southwest. **Pros:** attractive rooms; next to Tlaquepaque shops and restaurants; pet-friendly rooms have private outdoor yard space. **Cons:** breakfast is expensive; location not as secluded as some. $ *Rooms from: $229* ✉ *95 Portal La., Central* ☎ *928/203–9405, 800/313–0017* ⊕ *www.elportalsedona.com* ☞ *12 rooms* ⦙◎⦙ *No meals.*

$$$$
RESORT
Fodor'sChoice
★

▦ **Enchantment Resort.** A few miles outside of town, serene Boynton Canyon is the setting for this luxurious resort and its world-class destination spa, Mii Amo. **Pros:** gorgeous setting, next to great hiking trails; state-of-the-art spa; numerous on-site activities. **Cons:** 20-minute drive into town. $ *Rooms from: $355* ✉ *525 Boynton Canyon Rd.,* ☎ *928/282–2900, 800/826–4180* ⊕ *www.enchantmentresort.com* ☞ *107 rooms, 115 suites* ⦙◎⦙ *No meals.*

$$$
RESORT

▦ **Junipine Resort.** These one- and two-bedroom cabins nestled in a juniper and pine forest (hence the name) are spacious and airy, with vaulted ceilings, wood-burning fireplaces, and large decks overlooking either the creek or the canyon. **Pros:** huge, well-equipped cabins (some with hot tubs); trailheads on site. **Cons:** individually owned condo units have been individually decorated; creek views and hot tubs push up the cost; the group appeal can mean some partying neighbors. $ *Rooms from: $179* ✉ *8351 N. AZ 89A, Oak Creek Canyon* ☎ *928/282–3375, 800/742–7463* ⊕ *www.junipine.com* ☞ *50 suites* ⦙◎⦙ *No meals.*

$$$$
RESORT
Fodor'sChoice
★

▦ **L'Auberge de Sedona.** This elegant resort consists of private hillside units with spectacular views and cozy cottages in the woods along Oak Creek. **Pros:** luxurious rooms and cabins; secluded setting yet close to town. **Cons:** in-house restaurant very pricey. $ *Rooms from: $255* ✉ *301 L'Auberge La., Uptown* ☎ *928/282–1661, 800/905–5745* ⊕ *www.lauberge.com* ☞ *25 lodge rooms, 15 cottage suites, 4 junior suites, 62 cottages* ⦙◎⦙ *No meals.*

$$$
B&B/INN

▦ **Lodge at Sedona.** Rooms in this rambling wood-and-stone Craftsman house have a refined rustic style; most have fireplaces, and some have jetted tubs, redwood decks, or hot tubs. **Pros:** tranquil setting yet short walk from West Sedona; friendly staff. **Cons:** limited views. $ *Rooms from: $219* ✉ *125 Kallof Pl.,* ☎ *928/204–1942, 800/619–4467* ⊕ *www.lodgeatsedona.com* ☞ *5 rooms, 9 suites* ⦙◎⦙ *Breakfast.*

Local arts and crafts often represent the Native American heritage in Arizona.

$ **Sky Ranch Lodge.** There may be no better vantage point in town from
HOTEL which to view Sedona's red-rock canyons and sunsets than the private
patios and balconies at Sky Ranch Lodge, near the top of Airport Mesa.
Pros: good value; great views. **Cons:** older rooms are somewhat worn;
driving up and down the hill into town. *$ Rooms from: $85* ⊠ *Top
of Airport Rd., 1105 Airport Rd.,* ☎ *928/282–6400, 800/708–6400*
⊕ *www.skyranchlodge.com* ⤵ *92 rooms, 2 cottages* ⦿⧀ *No meals.*

$ **Sugar Loaf Lodge.** Though it may be hard to believe, there are still
HOTEL bargains in Sedona, and this one-story, family-run motel delivers.
Pros: cheap and clean. **Cons:** older, basic furnishings. *$ Rooms from:
$60* ⊠ *1870 W. AZ 89A,* ☎ *928/282–9451, 877/282–0632* ⊕ *www.
sedonasugarloaf.com* ⤵ *15 rooms* ⦿⧀ *Breakfast.*

NIGHTLIFE AND THE ARTS

Nightlife in Sedona tends to be sedate, although on high-season weekends there's usually live music at the Enchantment Resort. Shugrue's
Hillside also regularly presents local musicians. Options vary from jazz
to rock and pop; in all cases, call ahead.

NIGHTLIFE

Relics Restaurant & Lounge at Rainbow's End. The closest thing to a rollick-
ing cowboy bar in Sedona is Relics Restaurant & Lounge at Rainbow's
End, a steakhouse with a wooden dance floor and live rock or country-
and-Western music most nights. ⊠ *3235 W. AZ 89A,* ☎ *928/282–1593*
⊕ *www.relicsrestaurant.com.*

Sound Bites Grill. This casual restaurant and bar offers live music, mostly jazz, Tuesday through Sunday night. It also has reasonably priced appetizers and cocktails, and excellent views of the sun setting over the red rocks if you're lucky enough to grab a table on the outside deck. ⊠ *101 N. AZ 89A, Uptown* ☎ *928/282–2713* ⊕ *www.soundbitesgrill.com.*

THE ARTS

Chamber Music Sedona. October through May, Chamber Music Sedona hosts a concert series. They also host the "Met Live in HD" opera performances, a JazzFest in March, and a bluegrass festival in early summer. ☎ *928/204–2415* ⊕ *www.chambermusicsedona.org.*

Sedona Arts Center. In addition to offering classes in all mediums, this center hosts First Fridays, when you can ride the free trolley to any member galleries in town, meet the artists, and view their work. It takes place from 5 to 8 pm the first Friday of each month. ⊠ *15 Art Barn Rd., Uptown* ☎ *928/282–3809* ⊕ *www.sedonaartscenter.com.*

Sedona International Film Festival. The nine-day Sedona International Film Festival takes place in late February, and features independent films from all over the world. ⊠ *2030 W. AZ 89A,* ☎ *928/282–1177* ⊕ *www. sedonafilmfestival.org.*

SHOPPING

With a few exceptions, most of the stores in Uptown Sedona north of the "Y" (running along AZ 89A to the east of its intersection with AZ 179) cater to the tour-bus trade with Native American jewelry and New Age souvenirs. If this isn't your style, the largest concentration of stores and galleries is along AZ 179, just south of the "Y," with plenty of offerings for serious shoppers.

ARTS AND CRAFTS

Esteban's. Native American crafts and ceramics are the focus at Esteban's. ⊠ *Tlaquepaque, 336 AZ 179, No. 103, Bldg. B, Uptown* ☎ *928/ 282–4686* ⊕ *www.estebanssedona.com.*

Garland's Navajo Rugs. There's a collection of new and antique rugs at Garland's Navajo Rugs, as well as Native American kachina dolls, pottery, and baskets. ⊠ *411 AZ 179, Uptown* ☎ *928/282–4070* ⊕ *www. garlandsrugs.com.*

James Ratliff Gallery. There are fun and functional pieces by up-and-coming artists at the James Ratliff Gallery. ⊠ *Hillside Sedona, 671 AZ 179, A1 and A2, Uptown* ☎ *928/282–1404* ⊕ *www.jamesratliffgallery.com.*

Kuivato Glass Gallery. There's gorgeous glass lining the shelves at the Kuivato Glass Gallery . ⊠ *Tlaquepaque, 336 AZ 179, No. 125, Bldg. B, Uptown* ☎ *928/282–1212* ⊕ *www.kuivato.com.*

Lanning Gallery. Mostly Southwestern art and jewelry is for sale at the Lanning Gallery. ⊠ *Hozho Center, 431 AZ 179, Uptown* ☎ *928/282–6865* ⊕ *www.lanninggallery.com.*

Sedona Pottery. There's an eclectic mix of pieces available at Sedona Pottery, including flower-arranging bowls, egg separators, and life-size ceramic statues. ✉ *Garland Building, 411 AZ 179, Uptown* ☎ *928/282–1192* ⊕ *www.sedonapottery.net.*

CLOTHING

Looking West. The spiffiest cowgirl-style getups in town fill the racks at Looking West. ✉ *242 N. AZ 89A, Uptown* ☎ *928/282–4877* ⊕ *www.sedonaclothing.com.*

JEWELRY

🟢 `**Crystal Magic.** This shop dabbles in the metaphysical, with crystals, jewelry, and books for the New Age. ✉ *2978 W. AZ 89A,* ☎ *928/282–1622.*

SHOPPING CENTERS

There are three main art-gallery complexes in Sedona—Hozho, Tlaquepaque, and Hillside, all located just south of the "Y." Each has smaller galleries within the larger complex.

4

Hillside Sedona. Half a dozen galleries and three restaurants, including Shugrues Hillside, are housed in the Hillside Sedona complex. ✉ *671 AZ 179, Uptown* ☎ *928/282–4500* ⊕ *www.hillsidesedona.net.*

Hozho Center. A minute or two north of Hillside Sedona shopping complex on AZ 179, the Hozho Center is a small, upscale complex in a beige Santa Fe–style building, with galleries and fine-art souvenirs. ✉ *431 AZ 179, Uptown.*

Fodor's Choice ★ **Tlaquepaque Arts & Crafts Village.** Home to more than 100 shops and galleries and several restaurants, Tlaquepaque Arts & Crafts Village remains one of the best places for travelers to find mementos from their trip to Sedona. The complex of clay-tile-roofed buildings arranged around a series of courtyards shares its name and architectural style with a crafts village just outside Guadalajara. It's a lovely place to browse, but beware: prices tend to be high, and locals joke that it's pronounced "to-lock-your-pocket." ✉ *AZ 179 just south of "Y," Uptown* ☎ *928/282–4838* ⊕ *www.tlaq.com.*

SPORTING GOODS

Canyon Outfitters. This shop in West Sedona is good for gearing up with maps, clothing, and camping equipment before your outdoor adventures. ✉ *2701 W. AZ 89A,* ☎ *928/282–5294* ⊕ *www.canyonoutfitterssedona.com.*

The Hike House. A unique shopping experience, The Hike House can not only outfit you from head to toe, they can also match you with a suitable and satisfying hiking itinerary through their interactive Trail Finder service. If you'd rather go on a guided hike, staff can arrange that as well. Grab some trail mix, scones, and strong coffee in the adjoining cafe. ✉ *Hozho Center, 431 AZ 179, Uptown* ☎ *928/282–5820* ⊕ *www.thehikehouse.com.*

SPAS

While some prefer to harness Sedona's rejuvenating energy at a vortex site, others seek renewal at one of the many spas in town. From all-inclusive spa retreats nestled in red-rock canyons to inexpensive bodywork performed by healing arts students, Sedona has relaxing options for every budget and preference.

With its history of Native American traditions, Sedona is thought of as one of the most sacred healing spots on Earth. Spas incorporate indigenous materials, like red-rock clay, into their spa services—and choosing your treatments is part of the pleasure. Some of Sedona's spas are destinations in themselves, offering experiences tailored to individual needs and desires.

Fodor's Choice
★

Mii Amo Spa. Set in spectacular Boynton Canyon, Mii Amo is a state-of-the-art facility with indoor and outdoor pools and treatment rooms. Meditate in the sand-floor crystal grotto before your Watsu water therapy or deep-tissue massage. Take a guided hike or try a tai chi, dance, or photography class. Afterward, dine in the spa's healthful and tasty café (no egg yolks in these omelets), wearing only your spa robe if you like. All-inclusive spa packages are definitely the prime selection for a rejuvenating getaway—stay in one of the beautifully appointed spa casitas steps away from resort activities (three meals and two spa treatments each day are included). Otherwise, regular guests at the Enchantment Resort are welcome to partake in spa services, classes, and dining before and after their jeep tours. ⊠ *Enchantment Resort, 525 Boynton Canyon Rd.,* ☏ *928/203–8500, 888/749–2137* ⊕ *www. miiamo.com* ↺ *$160 60-minute massage, $235 90-minute massage; from $2,265–$5,560 for 3- to 7-night all-inclusive packages. Hot tubs, pools, sauna, steam room. Gym with: cardiovascular machines, free weights, weight-training equipment. Services: bodywork, facials, massage, scrubs, nutritional counseling. Classes and programs: dance, flexibility training, guided hikes, meditation, Pilates, tai chi, tennis, yoga.*

NAMTI. Students and faculty at the Northern Arizona Massage Therapy Institute (NAMTI) offer quality one-hour and 90-minute massage, craniosacral, reflexology, and facial treatments at much lower prices than you'll pay at resort spas in the area. A particularly invigorating treatment is the specialized Thai Massage, a two-hour combination of deep-pressure massage and stretching movements (while on the floor, clothed) that improves flexibility and relieves tension. Discounts are given for multiple treatments, such as a facial and a massage, and for adding on shorter treatments like the fine line–reducing Opal Sonic facial massage. ⊠ *2120 W. AZ 89A,* ☏ *928/282-7737* ⊕ *www.namti.com* ↺ *$59 60-min massage or facial, $79 90-min massage or facial, $109 for massage and facial. Services: aromatherapy, facials massage, waxing.*

Sedona New Day Spa. The popular Sedona New Day Spa uses local ingredients for clay masks, body wraps, and crystal therapy. Their signature treatment, Body and Soul Reviver—which begins with a dry-brush skin exfoliation, transitions to a scented, candle-lit bath, and finishes with a hot stone massage—may just be the ultimate pampering experience. Or choose a "Soul Journey," for a psychic reading of your chakras along with a massage. For couples, they have several luxurious packages. ⊠ *1449 W. AZ 89A,* ☏ *928/282-7502* ⊕ *www.sedonanewdayspa.com* ↺ *$125 60-min massage, $165 90-min massage; $140 60-min facial. Services: baths, body wraps, facials, massage, nail treatment, waxing.*

The Spa at L'Auberge. As one of Sedona's upscale resorts, L'Auberge offers an array of spa amenities for both resort guests and those lodging elsewhere. Here you can indulge in an outdoor massage on the bank of gurgling Oak Creek, or restore balance to your being with an Energy Healing Therapy such as Reiki. Their signature service is the 90-minute Sedona Dreams, which incorporates a ginger-lime exfoliating scrub, aromatherapy, and a hot-stone massage. The spa is intimate, with a rustic yet elegant vibe. ⊠ *301 L'Auberge La, Uptown* ☎ *800/905–5745, 928/282–1661* ⊕ *www.lauberge.com* ☞ *$135 60-min massage, $195 90-min massage, facial, or energy work; additional $30 for creekside treatments. Outdoor hot tub, steam rooms. Gym with: cardiovascular machines, free weights. Services: body wraps, facials, massage. Classes: yoga (resort guests only).*

Fodor's Choice ★ **The Spa at Sedona Rouge.** This spa is like an understated healing environment. Deepak Chopra chooses this simple and tranquil setting for his weeklong "SynchroDestiny" workshop each year. Skilled spa therapists meet with clients first to discuss individual goals before embarking on treatments like the Seven Sacred Pools Massage, which brings balance to the body's seven energy centers, or chakras. Mind-body coaching services, ayurvedic treatments, and tarot readings are also popular. The gardens and interior lounges contribute to the overall nourishing experience. Yoga classes ($10) meet daily at 8 am. ⊠ *Sedona Rouge Hotel and Spa, 2250 W. AZ 89A,* ☎ *866/312–4111, 928/203–4111* ⊕ *www.sedonarouge.com* ☞ *$120 60-min massage, $180 90-min massage, $215 90-min coaching/stress management session. Hot tub, pool, steam room. Gym with: cardiovascular machines, free weights, weight-training equipment. Services: massage, facials, scrubs, wraps, waxing, and tinting. Classes and programs: clairvoyant coaching, harmonious healing mind/body/spirit integration, yoga.*

SPORTS AND THE OUTDOORS

The Brins Fire consumed 4,500 acres in Sedona in 2006. Although no people or structures were harmed, the human-ignited fire threatened the Oak Creek Canyon area and serves as a reminder about fire safety. Take precautions and use common sense. Extinguish all fires with water. Never toss a cigarette butt. And don't hesitate to ask questions of local park rangers.

■ **TIP➜ A Red Rock Pass is required to park in the Coconino National Forest from Oak Creek Canyon through Sedona and the Village of Oak Creek.** Passes cost $5 for the day, $15 for the week, or $20 for an entire year, and can be purchased online and at the **Coconino Forest Service Red Rock Ranger Station** (⊠ *8375 AZ 179, just south of Village of Oak Creek* ☎ *928/203–7500* ⊕ *www.redrockcountry.org*), which is open daily and has copious information on regional outdoor activities. Passes are also available from vending machines at popular trailheads—including Boynton Canyon and Bell Rock—and at the Sedona Chamber of Commerce, Circle K stores, and many Sedona hotels. Locals widely resent the pass, feeling that free access to national forests is a right. The Forest Service counters that it doesn't receive enough federal funds to maintain the land surrounding Sedona, trampled by 5 million visitors each year, and that a parking fee is the best way to raise revenue.

BALLOONING

Northern Light Balloon Expeditions. One of only two companies with permits to fly over Sedona, Northern Light Balloon Expeditions offers sunrise flights that include a post-flight breakfast picnic. ☎ 928/282–2274, 800/230–6222 ⊕ www. northernlightballoon.com.

Red Rock Balloon Adventures. Fly over the red rocks for one to two hours with a Red Rock Balloon Adventures tour; you'll be served a picnic upon landing, along with a souvenir DVD of the flight. ☎ 800/258–3754 ⊕ www.redrockballoons.com.

FISHING

Rainbow Trout Farm. North-central Arizona may not be the most obvious fishing destination, but this stocked farm is a fun way to spend a few hours if you're so inclined. Anglers young and old almost always enjoy a sure catch, and you can rent a cane pole here with a hook and bait for $1. There's no charge if your catch is under 8 inches; above that it's $8 to $12, depending on the length. The real bargain is that the staff will clean and pack your fish for $0.50 each. ✉ 3500 N. AZ 89A, 3 miles north of Sedona, Oak Creek Canyon ☎ 928/282–5799 ⊕ www.sedonarainbowtroutfarm.com ▨ $1 (includes fishing pole and bait) ⊙ Daily 9–5.

GOLF

Oak Creek Country Club. This semiprivate 18-hole, par-72 course was designed by the father-son team of Robert Trent Jones Sr. and Robert Trent Jones Jr. It is a traditional (rather than desert) course with long, tree-lined fairways and slightly elevated greens amid lovely red-rock views. Providing challenges for beginner through advanced golfers, this course is described as "player-friendly." It's budget-friendly, too, in the afternoons—tee off after 2:30 pm and the greens fee is only $49. ✉ 690 Bell Rock Blvd., Village of Oak Creek ☎ 928/284–1660 ⊕ www. oakcreekcountryclub.com ▨ $99, $79 after 1 pm, $49 after 2:30 pm ⚑ 18 holes, 6824 yards, par 72.

Fodor's Choice **Sedona Golf Resort.** A gorgeous course, Sedona Golf Resort was designed
★ by Gary Panks to take advantage of the many changes in elevation and scenery. Golf courses are a dime a dozen in Arizona, but this one is regarded as one of the best in the state. Don't let the stunning views around every bend distract your focus from the undulating greens and fairways. The restaurant—with panoramic red-rock vistas—serves breakfast and lunch daily. ✉ 35 Ridge Trail Dr., Village of Oak Creek ☎ 928/284–9355, 877/733–6630 ⊕ www.sedonagolfresort.com ▨ $99 ⚑ 18 holes, 6646 yards, par 71.

HIKING AND BACKPACKING

Coconino National Forest-Red Rock Ranger District. For free detailed maps, hiking advice, and information on campgrounds, contact the rangers of the Coconino National Forest. Ask here or at your hotel for directions to trailheads for Doe's Mountain (an easy ascent, with many switchbacks), Loy Canyon, Devil's Kitchen, and Long Canyon. ⊠ *8375 AZ 179, Village of Oak Creek* ☎ *928/203–7500* ⊕ *www.redrockcountry. org* ⊙ *Daily 9–4:30.*

West Fork Trail. Among the paths in Coconino National Forest, the popular West Fork Trail traverses Oak Creek Canyon for a 3-mile hike. A walk through the woods between sheer red-rock walls and a dip in the stream make a great summer combo. The trailhead is about 3 miles north of Slide Rock State Park. ⊠ *Trailhead: AZ 89A, 9.5 miles north of Sedona.*

Any backpacking trip in the **Red Rock–Secret Mountain Wilderness** near Sedona guarantees stunning vistas, otherworldly rock formations, and Zen-like serenity, but little water, so pack a good supply. ∎**TIP→** Plan your trip for spring or fall: summer brings 100°F heat and sudden thunderstorms that flood canyons without warning. Most individual trails in the wilderness are too short for anything longer than an overnighter, but several trails can be linked up to form a memorable multiday trip. Contact Coconino National Forest's Red Rock Ranger District in Sedona for full details.

HORSEBACK RIDING

M Diamond Ranch. Ride on horseback through varied terrain for views of red rocks and the Verde Valley with wranglers at the M Diamond Ranch. One- and two-hour trail rides, as well as cowboy cookouts, are offered, starting at $75 ($55 for children). ⊠ *3255 FR 618, Verde* ☎ *928/300–6466* ⊕ *www.sedonahorsebackrides.com.*

Trail Horse Adventures. Among the tour options at Trail Horse Adventures are a midday ride with picnic and a ride along the Verde River to Native American cliff dwellings. Rides range from $65 for an hour to $125 for a three-hour ride with lunch. ⊠ *675 Dead Horse Ranch Rd., Cottonwood* ☎ *928/634–5276, 866/958–7245* ⊕ *www.trailhorseadventures.com.*

JEEP TOURS

Several jeep-tour operators headquartered along Sedona's main Uptown drag conduct excursions, some focusing on geology, some on astronomy, some on vortexes, some on all three. You can even find a combination jeep tour and horseback ride. Prices start at about $60 per person for two hours and go upward of $100 per person for four hours. Although all the excursions are safe, many aren't for those who dislike heights or bumps.

A Day in the West. With this tour operator, you can go to all the prime spots and combine a jeep tour with a horseback ride or local wine tasting. ☎ *928/282–4320, 800/973–3662* ⊕ *www.adayinthewest.com.*

Pink Jeep Tours. The ubiquitous Pink Jeep Tours are a popular choice for driving through the red rocks. ⊠ *204 N. AZ 89A, Uptown* ☎ *800/873– 3662* ⊕ *www.pinkjeeptours.com.*

Red Rock Western Jeep Tours. This reliable operator spins some good cowboy tales on its jeep tours. ⌧ *301 N. AZ 89A, Uptown* ☎ *928/ 282–6667, 8/848–7728* ⊕ *www. redrockjeep.com.*

MOUNTAIN BIKING

Given the red-rock splendor, challenging terrain, miles of single track, and mild weather, you might think Sedona would be a mountain-biking destination on the order of Moab or Durango. Inexplicably, you won't find the Lycra-clad throngs patronizing pasta bars or throwing back microbrews on the Uptown mall, but all the better for you: the mountain-biking culture remains fervent but low-key. A few excellent, strategically located bike shops can outfit you and give advice.

> **BOYNTON CANYON**
>
> You might want to drive out to Boynton Canyon, sacred to the Yavapai Apache, who believe it was their ancient birthplace. This is also the site of Enchantment Resort, where all are welcome to hike the canyon and stop in for lunch or a late-afternoon drink on the terrace.

As a general rule, mountain bikes are allowed on all trails and jeep paths unless designated as wilderness or private property. The rolling terrain, which switches between serpentine trails of buff red clay and mounds of slickrock, has few sustained climbs, but be careful of blind drop-offs that often step down several feet in unexpected places. The thorny trailside flora makes carrying extra inner tubes a must, and an inner-tube sealant is a good idea, too. If you plan to ride for several hours, pack a gallon of water and start early in the morning on hot days. Shade is rare, and with the exception of (nonpotable) Oak Creek, water is nonexistent.

Bell Rock Pathway. For the casual rider, Bell Rock Pathway is a scenic and easy ride traveling 3 miles through some of the most breathtaking scenery in red-rock country. Several single-track trails spur off this one, making it a good starting point for many other rides in Sedona. ⌧ *Trailhead: 5 miles south of Sedona on AZ 179.*

Fodor's Choice ★ **Broken Arrow-Submarine Rock Trail.** There's good reason why the Broken Arrow-Submarine Rock Trail is perhaps the most popular single-track loop in the area. The 10-mile trail is a heady mixture of prime terrain and scenery following slickrock and twisty trails up to Chicken Point, a sandstone terrace overlooking colorful buttes. The trail continues as a bumpy romp through washes, almost all downhill. Be wary of blind drop-offs in this section. It wouldn't be overly cautious to scout any parts of the trail that look sketchy. ⌧ *Trailhead: 2 miles south of Sedona, off AZ 179; take Morgan Rd. to Broken Arrow Trail parking lot.*

TOURS AND OUTFITTERS

Absolute Bikes. Close to several biking trails, Absolute Bikes is a good source for rentals, equipment, and advice on trails and conditions. ⌧ *6101 AZ 179, Village of Oak Creek* ☎ *928/284–1242* ⊕ *www. absolutebikes.net.*

Sedona Bike and Bean. About a block south of Bell Rock Pathway, the friendly folks at Bike and Bean offer rentals, equipment, trail maps, and their own blend of coffee. ✉ *75 Bell Rock Plaza, at AZ 179, Village of Oak Creek* ☎ *928/284–0210* ⊕ *www.bike-bean.com.*

THE VERDE VALLEY, JEROME, AND PRESCOTT

About 90 miles north of Phoenix, as you round a curve approaching Exit 285 off Interstate 17, the valley of the Verde River suddenly unfolds in a panorama of grayish-white cliffs, tinted red in the distance and dotted with desert scrub, cottonwood, and pine. For hundreds of years many Native American communities, especially those of the southern Sinagua people, lined the Verde River. Rumors of great mineral deposits brought Europeans to the Verde Valley as early as 1583, when Hopi Indians guided Antonio de Espejo here, but it wasn't until the second half of the 19th century that this wealth was commercially exploited. The discovery of silver and gold in the Black Hills, which border the valley on the southwest, gave rise to boomtowns like Jerome—and to military installations such as Fort Verde, set up to protect the white settlers and wealth seekers from the Native American tribes they displaced. Mineral wealth was also the impetus behind the establishment of Prescott as a territorial capital by President Lincoln and other Unionists who wanted to keep the riches out of Confederate hands.

VERDE VALLEY

18 miles southwest of Sedona on U.S. 89A, 94 miles north of Phoenix on Interstate 17.

Often overlooked by travelers on trips to Sedona or Flagstaff, the Verde Valley offers several enjoyable diversions, including wine tasting in Cornville and the historical wonders at Montezuma Castle and Tuzigoot. And if you're tired of the car, the Verde Canyon Railroad in Clarkdale is a great way to get off-road without doing the driving.

GETTING HERE AND AROUND

From Phoenix, it's a leisurely and picturesque route through Verde Valley. Follow Interstate 17 north 25 miles past Cordes Junction until you see the turnoff for AZ 260, which will take you to Cottonwood in 12 miles. Here you can pick up AZ 89A, which leads southwest to Prescott (41 miles) or northeast to Sedona (19 miles).

EXPLORING
TOP ATTRACTIONS

Montezuma Castle National Monument. The five-story, 20-room cliff dwelling at Montezuma Castle National Monument was named by explorers who believed it had been erected by the Aztecs. Southern Sinagua Native Americans actually built the roughly 600-year-old structure, which is one of the best-preserved prehistoric dwellings in North America—and one of the most accessible. An easy paved trail (0.3 mile round-trip) leads to the dwelling and to the adjacent Castle A, a badly deteriorated six-story living space with about 45 rooms. No one is permitted to enter the site, but the viewing area is close by. From Interstate 17, take Exit 289 and follow signs to Montezuma Castle Road. ✉ *Montezuma Castle*

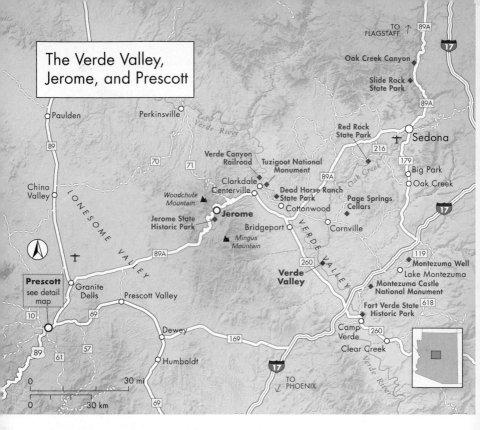

The Verde Valley,
Jerome, and Prescott

Rd., 7 miles northeast of Camp Verde ☎ 928/567–3322 ⊕ www.nps.
gov/moca ☑ $5 for Montezuma Castle ⊘ Daily 8–5

Montezuma Well. Somewhat less accessible than Montezuma Castle—but equally striking—is Montezuma Well, a unit of the national park. Although there are some Sinagua and Hohokam sites here, the limestone sinkhole with a limpid blue-green pool lying in the middle of the desert is the main attraction. This cavity—55 feet deep and 365 feet across—is all that's left of an ancient subterranean cavern; the water remains at a constant 76°F year-round. It's a short hike, but the peace, quiet, and views of the Verde Valley reward the effort. To reach Montezuma Well from Montezuma Castle, return to Interstate 17 and go north to Exit 293; signs direct you to the well, which is 4 miles east of the freeway (11 miles from Montezuma Castle National Monument). ☎ 928/567–4521 ☑ Free ⊘ Daily 8–5.

Fodor'sChoice
★
Verde Canyon Railroad. Train buffs come to the Verde Valley to catch the 22-mile Verde Canyon Railroad, which follows a dramatic route through the Verde Canyon, the remains of a copper smelter, and much unspoiled desert that is inaccessible by car. The destination—the city of Clarkdale—might not be that impressive, but the ride is undeniably scenic. Knowledgeable announcers regale riders with the area's

colorful history and point out natural attractions along the way—in winter you're likely to see bald eagles.

This 4-hour trip is especially popular in fall-foliage season and in spring, when the desert wildflowers bloom; book well in advance. Round-trip rides cost $54.95. For $79.95 you can ride the more comfortable, living-room-like first-class cars, where hors d'oeuvres and a champagne toast are included in the price (a cash bar is also available). ■TIP→ Reservations are essential. ✉ *Arizona Central Railroad, 300 N. Broadway, Clarkdale* ☏ *800/320–0718* ⊕ *www.verdecanyonrr.com* ✉ *$54.95.*

> ### DID SOMEONE SAY DEAD HORSES?
>
> In the late 1940s, when Calvin "Cap" Ireys asked his family to help him choose between the ranches he was thinking about buying in the Verde Valley, his son immediately picked "the one with the dead horse on it." Ireys sold the land to the state in 1973 at one-third of its value, with the stipulation that the park into which it was to be converted retain the ranch's colorful name.

WORTH NOTING

Dead Horse Ranch State Park. The 423-acre spread of Dead Horse Ranch State Park, which combines high-desert and wetlands habitats, is a pleasant place to while away the day. You can fish in the Verde River or the well-stocked Park Lagoon, or hike on some 6 miles of trails that begin in a shaded picnic area and wind along the river; adjoining forest service pathways are available for hikers and mountain bikers who enjoy longer journeys. Birders can check off more than 100 species from the Arizona Audubon Society lists provided by the rangers. Bald eagles perch along the Verde River in winter, and the common black hawks—a misnomer for these threatened birds—nest here in summer. Campsites and cabins are also available (reserve by phone or online). The park is 1 mile north of Cottonwood, off Main Street. ✉ *675 Dead Horse Ranch Rd., Cottonwood* ☏ *928/634–5283* ⊕ *www.azstateparks.com/Parks/deho* ✉ *$7 per car (up to 4 persons)* ◷ *Daily 8–4:30.*

Fort Verde State Historic Park. The military post for which Fort Verde State Historic Park is named was built between 1871 and 1873 as the third of three fortifications in this part of the Arizona Territory. To protect the Verde Valley's farmers and miners from Tonto Apache and Yavapai raids, the fort's administrators oversaw the movement of nearly 1,500 Native Americans to the San Carlos and Fort Apache reservations. A museum details the history of the area's military installations, and three furnished officers' quarters show the day-to-day living conditions of the top brass—it's a good break from the interstate if you've been driving for too long. Signs from any of Interstate 17's three Camp Verde exits will direct you to the 10-acre park. ✉ *125 E. Hollamon St.* ☏ *928/567–3275* ⊕ *www.azstateparks.com/Parks/fove* ✉ *$5* ◷ *Thurs.–Mon. 9–5.*

Tuzigoot National Monument. Impressive in scope, Tuzigoot National Monument is a complex of the Sinagua people, who lived on this land overlooking the Verde Valley from about AD 1000 to 1400. The pueblo, constructed of limestone and sandstone blocks, once rose three stories and incorporated 110 rooms. Inhabitants were skilled dry farmers and traded with peoples hundreds of miles away. Implements used for food preparation, as well as jewelry, weapons, and farming tools excavated from the site, are displayed in the visitor center. Within the site, you can step into a reconstructed room. ✉ *25 W. Tuzigoot Rd., 3 miles north of Cottonwood between Cottonwood's Old Town and Clarkdale* ☎ *928/634–5564* 🌐 *www.nps.gov/tuzi* 🎟 *$5* 🕒 *Daily 8–5.*

WINERIES

The high-desert soil of the Verde Valley seems to be working for growing grapes, and several vineyards have sprouted on the hillsides above Lower Oak Creek. Three notable vineyards are nestled together along Page Springs Road in Cornville—recently dubbed Winery Row—and offer wine tastings daily.

Javelina Leap Vineyard & Winery. Predominantly red wines with bold, dry flavors are produced by Javelina Leap Vineyard. Taste a few here and you'll be welcomed by the owners as if you were family. ✉ *1565 N. Page Springs Rd., Cornville* ☎ *928/649–2681* 🌐 *www.javelinaleapwinery.com* 🕒 *Daily 11–5.*

Oak Creek Vineyards & Winery. This winery offers syrah, merlot, chardonnay, and dessert wines. You can also pick up fixings for a picnic here—salami, cheeses, crackers, and chocolates. ✉ *1555 N. Page Springs Rd., Cornville* ☎ *928/649–0290* 🌐 *www.oakcreekvineyards.net* 🕒 *Daily 10–6.*

Fodor's Choice ★ **Page Springs Cellars.** The award-winning wines at Page Springs Cellars focus on grapes popular in the Rhône wine region of France. Sit outside on the deck overlooking Oak Creek and enjoy the wines, as well as antipasti plates and flatbread pizzas. There's live music Thursday through Sunday evenings, and you can take a tour on Friday and Sunday. ✉ *1500 N. Page Springs Rd., Cornville* ☎ *928/639–3004* 🌐 *www.pagespringscellars.com* 🕒 *Mon.–Wed. 11–7, Thurs.–Sun. 11–9.*

WHERE TO EAT

$$$ EUROPEAN 🍴 **Manzanita Restaurant.** You might not expect to find sophisticated cooking in Cornville, 6 miles east of Cottonwood, but a European-born chef prepares Continental and German fare here, using organic produce and locally raised meat whenever possible. Specialties include wild game such as alligator and buffalo. Shrimp scampi and lamb shank in burgundy sauce are beautifully presented; and the sauerbraten and wiener schnitzel don't disappoint. A lower-priced light menu is also available. [$] *Average main: $22* ✉ *11425 E. Cornville Rd., Cornville* ☎ *928/634–8851* 🌐 *www.themanzanitarestaurant.com* 🕒 *Closed Mon.*

SPORTS AND THE OUTDOORS

Black Canyon Trail. This trail is a bit of a slog, rising more than 2,200 feet in 6 miles, but the reward is grand views from the gray cliffs of Verde Valley to the red buttes of Sedona to the blue range of the San Francisco Peaks. ✉ *AZ 260, 4 miles south of Cottonwood, east on FR 359 4.5 miles.*

Prescott National Forest-Verde Ranger District. The Verde Ranger District office of the Prescott National Forest is a good resource for places to

Getting there is the fun with a classic train ride on the Verde Canyon Railroad.

hike, fish, and boat along the Verde River. ⊠ *300 E. AZ 260* ☎ *928/567–4121* ⊕ *www.fs.usda.gov/prescott.*

JEROME

20 miles northwest of Camp Verde, 3½ miles southwest of Clarkdale, 33 miles northeast of Prescott, 25 miles southwest of Sedona on AZ 89A.

Fodor'sChoice ★ Jerome was once known as the Billion Dollar Copper Camp, but after the last mines closed in 1953 the booming population of 15,000 dwindled to 50 determined souls. Although its population has risen back to almost 500, Jerome still holds on to its "ghost town" designation, and several B&Bs and eateries regularly report spirit sightings. It's hard to imagine that this town was once the location of Arizona's largest JCPenney store and one of the state's first Safeway supermarkets. Jerome saw its first revival during the mid-1960s, when hippies arrived and turned it into an arts colony of sorts, and it has since become a tourist attraction. In addition to its shops and historic sites, Jerome is worth visiting for its scenery: it's built into the side of Cleopatra Hill, and from here you can see Sedona's red rocks, Flagstaff's San Francisco Peaks, and even eastern Arizona's Mogollon Rim country.

Jerome is about a mile above sea level, but structures within town sit at elevations that vary by as much as 1,500 feet, depending on whether they're on Cleopatra Hill or at its foot. Blasting at the United Verde (later Phelps Dodge) mine regularly shook buildings off their foundations—the town's jail slid across a road and down a hillside, where it

Cliff dwellings of the Sinagua people have been preserved for about 600 years at Montezuma Castle.

sits today. And that's not all that was unsteady about Jerome. In 1903 a reporter from a New York newspaper called Jerome "the wickedest town in America," due to its abundance of drinking and gambling establishments; town records from 1880 list 24 saloons. Whether by divine retribution or drunken accidents, the town burned down several times.

GETTING HERE AND AROUND

You can get a map of the town's shops and its attractions at the visitor-information trailer on AZ 89A (which becomes Hull Street). The three streets in the main shopping area—Hull, Main, and Hill—run parallel to each other on the hillside. Street parking is easy to come by, but be prepared for some steep climbing up and down Cleopatra Hill when you're exploring by foot.

PLANNING YOUR TIME

The town can easily be explored in an afternoon with a stop for lunch, but the historic charm and shopping opportunities entice some visitors to stay overnight. Jerome currently has around 50 retail establishments (that's more than one for every 10 residents). Attractions and businesses don't always stay open as long as their stated hours if things are slow.

ESSENTIALS

Visitor Information Jerome Chamber of Commerce & Visitor Center ⊠ *310 Hull St.* ☏ *928/634–2900* ⊕ *www.jeromechamber.com.*

EXPLORING

Jerome State Historic Park. Of the three mining museums in town, the most inclusive is part of Jerome State Historic Park. At the edge of town, signs on AZ 89A will direct you to the turnoff for the park, reached by a short, precipitous road. The museum occupies the 1917 mansion of Jerome's mining king, Dr. James "Rawhide Jimmy" Douglas Jr., who purchased Little Daisy Mine in 1912. You can see tools and heavy equipment used to grind ore, and some minerals are on display, but accounts of the town's wilder elements—such as the House of Joy brothel—are not so prominently featured. Just outside the mansion/park gates is Audrey Head Frame Park, where you can peer 1,900 feet down into the Daisy Mineshaft. ✉ *100 Douglas Rd.* ☎ *928/634–5381* 🌐 *www.azstateparks.com* 🎟 *$5* 🕒 *Daily 8:30–5.*

4

Mine Museum. Run by the Jerome Historical Society, the Mine Museum in downtown Jerome focuses on the social history of miners in the area. The museum's collection of mining stock certificates alone is worth the (small) price of admission—the amount of money that changed hands in this town 100 years ago boggles the mind. ✉ *200 Main St.* ☎ *928/634–5477* 🌐 *www.jeromehistoricalsociety.com* 🎟 *$2* 🕒 *Daily 9:30–4:30.*

WHERE TO EAT

$$$ AMERICAN Fodor's Choice ★ 🍴 **The Asylum Restaurant.** Don't be put off by the name, a tribute to its past identity—this charming restaurant inside the Jerome Grand Hotel is the standout choice in town for fine dining, good wines, and wonderful vistas. Burgundy interior walls hung with local artists' work create a warm and romantic setting. Signature dishes include achiote-rubbed pork tenderloin and sea bass with a poblano chile–chardonnay lemon sauce. The roasted butternut squash soup, with just the right blend of sweetness and spice, is divine. [$] *Average main: $26* ✉ *200 Hill St.* ☎ *928/639–3197* 🌐 *www.asylumrestaurant.com.*

$ AMERICAN 🍴 **Flatiron Cafe.** Ask where to have lunch or a late-afternoon snack, and nearly every Main Street shop owner will direct you to a tiny eatery at the fork in the road. The menu includes healthful sandwiches, such as black-bean hummus with feta cheese, and many coffee drinks. Breakfast is also served. [$] *Average main: $10* ✉ *416 Main St.* ☎ *928/634–2733* 🕒 *Closed Tues. No dinner.*

$ AMERICAN 🍴 **Haunted Hamburger/Jerome Palace.** After the climb up the stairs from Main Street to this former boardinghouse, you'll be ready for the hearty burgers, chili, cheese steaks, and ribs that dominate the menu. Lighter fare, including such meatless selections as the guacamole quesadilla, is also available. Eat on the outside deck overlooking Verde Valley or in the upstairs dining room, where "Claire," the resident ghost, purportedly hangs out. [$] *Average main: $10* ✉ *410 Clark St.* ☎ *928/634–0554* 🌐 *www.thehauntedhamburger.com.*

WHERE TO STAY

$ B&B/INN 🏨 **Ghost City Inn.** The outdoor veranda at this 1898 B&B affords sweeping views of the Verde Valley and Sedona. **Pros:** authentic historic charm; fabulous views. **Cons:** some rooms are small. [$] *Rooms from: $105* ✉ *541 N. Main St.* ☎ *928/634–4678, 888/634–4678* 🌐 *www.ghostcityinn.com* 🛏 *6 rooms* 🍽 *Breakfast.*

$ HOTEL

Jerome Grand Hotel. This full-service hotel at the highest point in town is housed in the Jerome's former hospital, built in 1927. **Pros:** great restaurant; historic property; great ghost-hunting. **Cons:** creaky. [$] *Rooms from: $130* ✉ *200 Hill St.* ☎ *928/634–8200, 888/817–6788* 🌐 *www.jeromegrandhotel.com* *25 rooms* 🍴 *Breakfast.*

$$ B&B/INN Fodor's Choice ★

The Surgeon's House. Plants, knickknacks, bright colors, and plenty of sunlight make this Mediterranean-style home a welcoming place to stay. **Pros:** friendly host; knockout vistas; unique gardens. **Cons:** rigid breakfast time; climbing some stairs is required. [$] *Rooms from: $145* ✉ *101 Hill St.* ☎ *928/639–1452, 800/639–1452* 🌐 *www.surgeonshouse.com* *2 rooms, 2 suites* 🍴 *Breakfast.*

NIGHTLIFE

Jerome's a ghost town, so don't expect a hopping nightlife—although there are some places to have fun.

Paul & Jerry's Saloon. The two pool tables and old wooden bar at Paul & Jerry's Saloon attract a regular crowd (relatively speaking). ✉ *206 Main St.* ☎ *928/634–2603.*

Spirit Room. On weekends there's live music and a lively scene at the Spirit Room. The mural over the bar harks back to the days when it was a dining spot for the prostitutes of the red-light district. ✉ *166 Main St.* ☎ *928/634–8809* 🌐 *www.spiritroombar.com.*

SHOPPING

Jerome has its share of art galleries (some perched precariously on Cleopatra Hill), along with boutiques, and they're funkier than those in Sedona. Main Street and, just around the bend, Hull Avenue are Jerome's two primary shopping streets. Your eyes may begin to glaze over after browsing through one boutique after another, most offering tasteful Southwestern paraphernalia.

Aurum. About 30 artists are represented at Aurum, which focuses on contemporary art jewelry in silver and gold. ✉ *369 Main St.* ☎ *928/634–3330* 🌐 *www.aurumjewelry.com.*

Designs on You. This boutique carries attractively styled women's clothing and accessories. ✉ *367 Main St.* ☎ *928/634–7879* 🌐 *www.designsonyoujeromeaz.com.*

Jerome Artists Cooperative Gallery. The focus at this gallery is on jewelry, sculpture, painting, and pottery by local artists. ✉ *502 Main St.* ☎ *928/639–4276* 🌐 *www.jeromecoop.com.*

Nellie Bly Kaleidoscopes and Art Glass. This shop specializes in art glass and outstanding kaleidoscopes—in fact, they claim to have the world's largest collection of them. ✉ *136 Main St.* ☎ *928/634–0255* 🌐 *www.nbscopes.com.*

Raku Gallery. You'll find wrought-iron furniture, free-blown glass, and fountains at Raku Gallery, which stocks the work of about 300 artists. ✉ *250 Hull Ave.* ☎ *928/639–0239* 🌐 *www.rakugallery.com.*

Sky Fire. There are two floors of clothing and furniture at Sky Fire, from Southwestern-pattern dishes to handcrafted Mission-style hutches. ✉ *140 Main St.* ☎ *928/634–8081* 🌐 *www.skyfirejerome.com.*

EN
ROUTE

Prescott National Forest. The drive down a mountainous section of AZ 89A from Jerome to Prescott is gorgeous (if somewhat harrowing in bad weather), filled with twists and turns through Prescott National Forest. A scenic turnoff near Jerome provides one last vista and a place to apply chains during surprise snowstorms. There's camping, picnicking, and hiking at the crest of Mingus Mountain. If you're coming to Prescott from Phoenix, the route that crosses the Mogollon Rim, overlooking the Verde Valley, has nice views of rolling hills and is less precipitous. ⊕ *www.fs.usda.gov/prescott.*

PRESCOTT

33 miles southwest of Jerome on AZ 89A to U.S. 89, 100 miles northwest of Phoenix via Interstate 17 to AZ 69.

In a forested bowl 5,300 feet above sea level, Prescott is a prime summer refuge for Phoenix-area dwellers. It was proclaimed the first capital of the Arizona Territory in 1864 and settled by Yankees to ensure that gold-rich northern Arizona would remain a Union resource. (Tucson and southern Arizona were strongly pro-Confederacy.) Although early territorial settlers thought that the area's original inhabitants were of Aztec origin, today it's believed that they were ancestors of the Yavapai, whose reservation is on the outskirts of town. The Aztec theory—inspired by *The History and Conquest of Mexico,* a popular book by historian William Hickling Prescott, for whom the town was named—has left its mark on such street names as Montezuma, Cortez, and Alarcon.

Despite a devastating downtown fire in 1900, Prescott remains the "West's most Eastern town," with a rich trove of late-19th-century New England–style architecture. With two institutions of higher education, Yavapai College and Prescott College, Prescott could be called a college town, but it doesn't really feel like one, perhaps because so many retirees also reside here, drawn by the temperate climate and low cost of living.

The 1916 Yavapai County Courthouse stands in the heart of Prescott, bounded by Gurley, Goodwin, Cortez, and Montezuma streets, and guarded by an equestrian bronze of turn-of-the-20th-century journalist and lawmaker Bucky O'Neill, who died while charging San Juan Hill in Cuba with Teddy Roosevelt during the Spanish-American War. Those interested in architecture will enjoy the Victorian neighborhoods. Many Queen Annes have been beautifully restored, and a number are now B&Bs.

GETTING HERE AND AROUND

The most direct route to Prescott from Phoenix is to take Interstate 17 north for 60 miles to Cordes Junction and then drive northwest on AZ 69 for 36 miles into town. Interstate 17, a four-lane divided highway, has several steep inclines and descents (complete with a number of runaway-truck ramps), but it's generally an easy and scenic thoroughfare.

Prescott Municipal Airport is 8 miles north of town on U.S. 89. United Airlines affiliate Great Lakes Airlines (⊕ *www.flygreatlakes.com*) offers service to Prescott Municipal Airport from Los Angeles and Denver.

4

The city's main drag is Gurley Street, which AZ 69 turns into from the east. You can usually find street parking along Gurley or on the side streets as you approach town; or use the free public garage on Granite Street, between Gurley and Goodwin. Most of the town's Victorian neighborhoods, shops, and restaurants, best explored on foot, are within walking distance of the Courthouse Plaza, sitting just off Gurley Street on Montezuma. Art galleries and saloons line Cortez and Montezuma streets to the north and west of the courthouse. The Chamber of Commerce and Visitor Center is on Goodwin Street, across from the courthouse and next to the post office.

PLANNING YOUR TIME

Tourism in Prescott can be bustling on weekends but is rarely overwhelming. Any day will do to tour the Victorian homes and antiques shops, but if you enjoy museums, note that museum hours are limited on Sunday, and you won't want to rush through the extensive grounds of the Sharlot Hall Museum. Devoting a full day to tour Prescott is ample, and an overnight allows for hearing plenty of live music on Whiskey Row.

ESSENTIALS

Transportation Contact Prescott Municipal Airport ☎ *928/777–1114* ⊕ *www.prescott-az.gov.*

Visitor Information Prescott Chamber of Commerce & Visitor Center ✉ *117 W. Goodwin St., across from Courthouse* ☎ *928/445–2000, 800/266–7534* ⊕ *www.prescott.org* ⊗ *Weekdays 9–5, weekends 10–2.*

EXPLORING

Phippen Museum. The paintings and bronze sculptures of George Phippen, along with works by other artists of the West, form the permanent collection of this museum about 5 miles north of Downtown. Phippen met with a group of prominent cowboy artists in 1965 to form the Cowboy Artists of America, a group dedicated to preserving the Old West as they saw it. He became the president but died the next year. A memorial foundation set up in his name opened the doors of this museum in 1984. ✉ *4701 U.S. 89N* ☎ *928/778–1385* ⊕ *www.phippenartmuseum. org* 🎟 *$7* ⊗ *Tues.–Sat. 10–4, Sun. 1–4.*

FAMILY **Sharlot Hall Museum.** Local history is documented at this remarkable museum. Along with the original ponderosa pine log cabin, which housed the territorial governor, and the museum, named for historian and poet Sharlot Hall, the parklike setting contains three fully restored period homes and a transportation museum. Territorial times are the focus, but natural history and artifacts of the area's prehistoric peoples are also on display. Kids under 13 get in free. ✉ *415 W. Gurley St., 2 blocks west of Courthouse Plaza, Downtown* ☎ *928/445–3122* ⊕ *www. sharlot.org* 🎟 *$7* ⊗ *Mon.–Sat. 10–4, Sun. noon–4.*

The Smoki Museum. The 1935 stone-and-log building, which resembles an Indian pueblo, is almost as interesting as the Native American artifacts inside. Baskets, kachinas, pottery, rugs, and beadwork make up the collection, which represents Native American culture from the pre-Columbian period to the present. ✉ *147 N. Arizona Ave., Downtown*

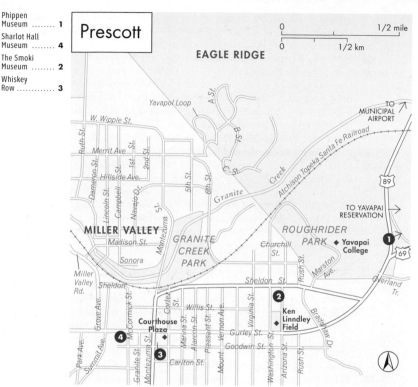

928/445–1230 ⊕ *www.smokimuseum.org* $7 ⊗ *Mon.–Sat. 10–4, Sun. 1–4; closed 1st 2 wks in Jan.*

Whiskey Row. Twenty saloons and houses of pleasure once lined this stretch of Montezuma Street, along the west side of Courthouse Plaza. Social activity is more subdued these days, although live music pulses every evening, and the buildings have been beautifully restored. The historic bars provide an escape from the street's many boutiques. ⊠ *Montezuma St., Downtown.*

WHERE TO EAT

$ ✕ **Bistro St. Michael.** This is a great place to enjoy a coffee, eggs Benedict,
AMERICAN or a bowl of black-bean chili while watching the people on Whiskey Row. The café-bar, which serves breakfast and lunch (and is open until 4 pm on weekends), has been restored to its original 1901 style. The service at the counter is brisk, and will leave you plenty of time for antiquing or museum-browsing for the remainder of the day. $ *Average main: $9* ⊠ *205 W. Gurley St., Downtown* 928/776–1999 ⊕ *www.stmichaelhotel.com* ⊗ *No dinner.*

$$ ✕ **Genovese's.** Reasonably priced, classic southern Italian fare makes this
ITALIAN restaurant near Courthouse Plaza a local favorite. The décor is right out of 1975, but the family recipes, like chicken marsala, are fresh and flavorful and the service is extra friendly. Try the cannelloni stuffed with

shrimp, crab, ricotta cheese, and spinach. Save room for spumoni ice cream or a cannoli. Ⓢ *Average main: $15* ⊠ *217 W. Gurley St., Downtown* ☎ *928/541–9089* ⊕ *www.genovesesrestaurant.com.*

$$$
AMERICAN
✕ **Murphy's.** Mesquite-grilled meats and beer brewed exclusively for the restaurant are the specialties at this classy bar and grill, a sort of local institution set in a restored, polished-up 1890 mercantile building. The baby back ribs, fresh steamed clams, and fresh fried catfish are standouts. Businessfolk do their moving and shaking at lunchtime here, and the spirited bar stays open until 10 pm. Ⓢ *Average main: $24* ⊠ *201 N. Cortez St., Downtown* ☎ *928/445–4044* ⊕ *www.rgtaz.com.*

$$
AMERICAN
✕ **The Palace Restaurant and Saloon.** Legend has it that the patrons who saved the Palace's ornately carved 1880s Brunswick bar from a Whiskey Row fire in 1900 continued drinking at it while the row burned across the street. Whatever the case, the bar remains the centerpiece of the beautifully restored turn-of-the-20th-century structure, with a high, pressed-tin ceiling. Steaks and chops are the stars here, but the grilled fish and hearty corn chowder are fine, too. Ⓢ *Average main: $20* ⊠ *120 S. Montezuma St., Downtown* ☎ *928/541–1996* ⊕ *www.historicpalace. com* ⊘ *No lunch weekends.*

$
AMERICAN
✕ **Prescott Brewing Company.** Good beer, good food, good service, and good prices—for a casual meal, it's hard to beat this cheerful restaurant on the town square. In addition to burgers, chili, fish-and-chips, and British-style bangers-and-mash, vegetarian pot-pies and salads are on the menu. Ponderosa IPA and Lodgepole Light are two popular microbrews; fresh-baked beer bread comes with many entrées. Ⓢ *Average main: $12* ⊠ *130 W. Gurley St., Downtown* ☎ *928/771–2795* ⊕ *www. prescottbrewingcompany.com.*

$$$
AMERICAN
✕ **The Rose Restaurant.** In a well-maintained Victorian home, the Rose serves inspired dishes that straddle nouvelle and Continental fare. Choose from entrées like chateaubriand, duck breast with sweetpotato cake and blackberry-bourbon sauce, or almond-crusted halibut as Sinatra music plays softly in the background. Desserts, especially the apple-caramel tart, are equally stellar. Ⓢ *Average main: $28* ⊠ *234 S. Cortez St., Downtown* ☎ *928/777–8308* ⊕ *www.theroserestaurant. com* ⊘ *Closed Mon. and Tues. No lunch.*

WHERE TO STAY

$$
HOTEL
▦ **Hassayampa Inn.** Built in 1927 for early automobile travelers, the Hassayampa Inn oozes character; the ceiling in the lobby is hand-painted, and some rooms still have the original furnishings. **Pros:** central location; historic charm. **Cons:** thin walls; small bathrooms. Ⓢ *Rooms from: $159* ⊠ *122 E. Gurley St., Downtown* ☎ *928/778–9434, 800/322–1927* ⊕ *www.hassayampainn.com* ↝ *58 rooms, 10 suites* ⦿ *No meals.*

$
B&B/INN
▦ **Hotel Vendome.** This World War I–era hostelry has seen miners, health seekers, and celebrities walk through its doors. **Pros:** central location; historical; good value. **Cons:** creaky floors raise noise factor. Ⓢ *Rooms from: $99* ⊠ *230 S. Cortez St., Downtown* ☎ *928/776–0900* ⊕ *www. vendomehotel.com* ↝ *16 rooms, 4 suites* ⦿ *Breakfast.*

$
HOTEL
▦ **The Motor Lodge.** Impeccably renovated to reflect its heyday as a circa-1960 motor hotel, this boutique property delivers great value as well as a fun blast from the past. **Pros:** inexpensive; comfortable beds; cheery

sixties décor. **Cons:** a long-ish walk to downtown. [$] *Rooms from: $79* ✉ *503 S. Montezuma St.* ☎ *928/717–0157* 🌐 *www.themotorlodge.com* 🛏 *12 rooms* 🍴 *No meals.*

$ RESORT 🏨 **Prescott Resort and Conference Center.** On a hill on the outskirts of town, this upscale property run by the Yavapai tribe has views of the mountain ranges surrounding Prescott and the valley, although many guests hardly notice, so riveted are they by the poker machines and slots in Prescott's only hotel casino. **Pros:** comfortable, nicely updated rooms; great views on the higher floors. **Cons:** large-scale property may feel impersonal; drive to town center. [$] *Rooms from: $119* ✉ *1500 AZ 69* ☎ *928/776–1666, 888/957–4637* 🌐 *www.prescottresort.com* 🛏 *160 rooms* 🍴 *No meals.*

4

NIGHTLIFE AND THE ARTS

NIGHTLIFE

Montezuma Street's Whiskey Row, off Courthouse Plaza, is nowhere near as wild as it was in its historic heyday, but most bars have live music—with no cover charge—on weekends.

Hassayampa Inn. This upscale, art nouveau piano bar is a quieter venue for conversation than the Whiskey Row bars across the square. ✉ *122 E. Gurley St., Downtown* ☎ *928/778–9434* 🌐 *www.hassayampainn.com.*

Jersey Lilly Saloon. Located above the Palace, the Jersey Lilly Saloon is a former brothel with live entertainment, a great patio, and a large dance floor. ✉ *116 S. Montezuma St., Downtown* ☎ *928/541–7854* 🌐 *www.jerseylillysaloon.com.*

Lyzzard's Lounge. The classic Brunswick bar at Lyzzard's Lounge was shipped from England via the Colorado River. ✉ *120 N. Cortez St., Downtown* ☎ *928/778–2244* 🌐 *www.lyzzards.com.*

Matt's Saloon. For live country-and-western music and two-stepping on the dance floor, mosey on over to Matt's Saloon. ✉ *112 S. Montezuma St., Downtown* ☎ *928/776–2974* 🌐 *www.mattssaloon.com.*

Raven Cafe. A contemporary and attractive coffeehouse and bar, Raven Cafe serves excellent organically grown food and doubles as a live-music venue on weekends. ✉ *142 N. Cortez St., Downtown* ☎ *928/717–0009* 🌐 *www.ravencafe.com.*

THE ARTS

Cowboy Poets Gathering. In August the Cowboy Poets Gathering at Yavapai Community College brings together campfire bards from around the country. 🌐 *www.azcowboypoets.org.*

Frontier Days. The town had its first organized cowboy competition in 1888, and lays claim to having the world's oldest rodeo: the annual Frontier Days roundup, held on July 4th weekend at the Prescott Rodeo Grounds. 🌐 *www.worldsoldestrodeo.com.*

Prescott Bluegrass Festival. Prescott's popular Bluegrass Festival takes place downtown at Courthouse Plaza in June. ☎ *928/445–2000* 🌐 *www.prescottbluegrassfestival.com.*

Prescott Center for the Arts. Musicals and dramas, plays for children, and a concert series are put on by the Prescott Center for the Arts. The association's gallery also presents rotating exhibits by local, regional, and national artists. ✉ *208 N. Marina St., Downtown* ☎ *928/445–3286* ⊕ *www.pfaa.net.*

Yavapai Symphony Association. Performances by the Phoenix and Flagstaff symphonies are hosted by the Yavapai Symphony Association and held at Yavapai City College; call ahead for schedules and venues. ✉ *228 N. Alarcon St., Ste. B, Downtown* ☎ *928/776–4255* ⊕ *www. yavapaisymphony.org.*

SHOPPING

Shops selling antiques and collectibles line Cortez Street, just north of Courthouse Plaza. You'll find fun stuff—especially Western kitsch—as well as some good buys on valuable pieces. Courthouse Plaza, especially along Montezuma Street, is lined with artist cooperatives, specialty stores, and gift shops. Many match those in Sedona for quality.

Arts Prescott Gallery. Be sure to check out Arts Prescott, a cooperative gallery of talented local artisans. ✉ *134 S. Montezuma St., Downtown* ☎ *928/776–7717* ⊕ *www.artsprescott.com.*

Bella Home Furnishings. Vintage home furnishings and artwork are sold at this colorful store. ✉ *115 W. Willis St., Downtown* ☎ *928/445–0208* ⊕ *www.bellahomefurnishings.com.*

Jenny Longhorn. There's upscale Western wear for women and men at Jenny Longhorn, as well as jewelry, artwork, and home furnishings. ✉ *152 S. Montezuma St., Downtown* ☎ *928/778–1204* ⊕ *www. jennylonghorn.com.*

The Merchandise Mart Antique Mall. At 14,000 square feet, the Merchandise Mart Antique Mall houses the largest array of antiques dealers in town. ✉ *205 N. Cortez St., Downtown* ☎ *928/776–1728.*

Van Gogh's Ear. Exquisite work by local and national artists is beautifully displayed at Van Gogh's Ear. ✉ *156 S. Montezuma St., Downtown* ☎ *928/776–1080* ⊕ *www.vgegallery.com.*

SPORTS AND THE OUTDOORS

HIKING

Prescott National Forest–Bradshaw Ranger District. Contact the Bradshaw Ranger District for information about hiking trails and campgrounds in the Prescott National Forest south of town down to Horse Thief Basin. Campgrounds near Prescott are generally not crowded. ✉ *344 S. Cortez St.* ☎ *928/443–8000* ⊕ *www.fs.usda.gov/prescott.*

Thumb Butte Loop Trail. A 2-mile trek on a paved yet steep loop, the Thumb Butte Loop Trail takes you 600 feet up near the crest of its namesake. The vistas are large, but you won't be alone on this popular trail. *Easy–Moderate.* ✉ *Trailhead: Thumb Butte Rd., 3 miles west of Prescott following Gurley St., which turns into Thumb Butte.*

HORSEBACK RIDING

Granite Mountain Stables. This company offers guided 1-, 2-, and 4-hour trail rides, as well as Western riding lessons. ✉ *2400 Shane Dr., 7 miles northeast of Prescott* ☎ *928/771–9551* ⊕ *www.granitemountainstables. com* 🖃 *From $35.*

NORTHEAST ARIZONA

WELCOME TO NORTHEAST ARIZONA

TOP REASONS TO GO

★ **Drive the rim roads at Canyon de Chelly:** Visit one of the most spectacular natural wonders in the Southwest—it rivals the Grand Canyon for jaw-dropping views, albeit on a much smaller scale. It's a must for photography buffs.

★ **Go boating at Glen Canyon:** Get to know this stunning, mammoth reservoir by taking a boat out amid Lake Powell's towering cliffs.

★ **Explore Hubbell Trading Post:** Take the self-guided tour to experience the relationship between early traders and the Navajo.

★ **Shop for handmade crafts on the Hopi Mesas:** Pick up crafts by some of Arizona's leading Hopi artisans, who sustain their culture through continuous occupation of the ancient villages on these mesas.

★ **Take a jeep tour through Monument Valley:** See firsthand the landscape depicted in such iconic Western films as *Stagecoach* and *The Searchers*.

1 Navajo Nation East. Vastly underrated Canyon de Chelly National Monument offers some of the most spectacular panoramas in the Southwest, and Window Rock is the governmental and cultural hub of the Navajo people.

2 The Hopi Mesas. An artistically rich and dramatically situated tribal land entirely surrounded by the Navajo Nation, the minimally developed Hopi Mesas rise above the high-desert floor, rife with trading posts and art studios selling fine weavings, jewelry, and crafts. Expect very few services, even relative to the rest of northeastern Arizona.

3 Navajo Nation West. Just 80 miles east of the Grand Canyon's South Rim, the bustling community of Tuba City anchors the western portions of the Navajo Nation and Hopi tribal lands—it's an excellent base for checking out

the region's painted-desert landscapes and Navajo trading posts, and for booking a tour of Hopi Mesa art studios.

4 Monument Valley. You've probably seen images of this Ancestral Puebloan stomping ground in everything from classic Western movies to Ansel Adams photos; you can explore this sweeping valley

GETTING ORIENTED

Relatively few visitors experience the vast, sweeping northeast quadrant of Arizona, which comprises the Navajo and Hopi reservations, but efforts to spend a few days here are rewarded with stunning scenery and the chance to learn about some of the world's most vibrant indigenous communities. This is part of the West's great Four Corners Region, home to the underrated and spectacular Canyon de Chelly National Monument as well as the dramatic buttes and canyons of Monument Valley. The one portion of the area outside tribal lands is Page, the base for exploration of crystalline Lake Powell's nearly 2,000 miles of shoreline.

5

on a variety of Navajo-led tours. The region spans the Arizona and Utah borders, extending northeast from Kayenta, Arizona, nearly to Bluff, Utah.

5 Glen Canyon Dam and Lake Powell. The one section of northeastern Arizona not set on tribal lands is dominated by the nation's second-largest man-made body of water, Lake Powell, and 710-foot-tall Glen Canyon Dam. It's a boating paradise, and the town of Page has the region's greatest number of hotels, restaurants, and bars.

NATIVE AMERICAN EXPERIENCE

With roots tracing back thousands of years, Native Americans have lived in Arizona for hundreds of generations. Today, more than 250,000 people reside in sovereign nations within Arizona's state borders. Alongside ancient cliff dwellings and stunning natural monuments, the reality of the 21 tribes' cultures is best experienced on the reservations.

Above: Colorful beadwork is a popular adornment for clothing. Top right: Apache warrior Geronimo Bottom right: Each Navajo community is known for specific rug colors and designs.

Arizona's tribes live on reservations that comprise more than a quarter of the state's lands. Though some tribes are similar to one another in certain aspects, most are culturally and spiritually distinct. Many tribes live on lands that enable them to derive income from natural resources, such as coal, but most rely to some extent on tourism for revenue. Some tribes, such as the Navajo, open up much of their culture to visitors. Native American artisans are famed for handmade items popular with tourists, but casinos are increasingly vital to tribal economies. These often include dining, lodging, and entertainment as well.

RESERVATION REALITIES

For all the richness in culture, reservations are places where poverty is often prevalent. Some liken the tourist experience to that of visiting a developing country. Some panhandlers cluster at shopping centers and viewpoints. Visitors should respond to panhandlers with a polite but firm "no." If you wish to help, make a donation to a legitimate organization.

NAVAJO NATION AND HOPI RESERVATION RULES

Each reservation has its own government that dictates and enforces visitation rules.

Alcohol and drugs: The possession and consumption of alcoholic beverages or illicit drugs is illegal on Hopi and Navajo land.

Camping: No open fires are allowed in reservation campgrounds; you must use grills or fireplaces. You may not gather firewood on the reservation—bring your own. Camping areas have quiet hours from 11 pm to 6 am. Pets must be kept on a leash or confined.

Hopi shrines: Hopi spirituality is intertwined with daily life, and objects that seem ordinary to you may have deeper significance. If you see a collection of objects at or near the Hopi Mesas do not disturb them.

Permits and permissions: No off-trail hiking, rock climbing, or other off-road travel is allowed unless you're accompanied by a local guide. A tribal permit is required for fishing. Violations of fish and game laws are punishable by heavy fines, imprisonment, or both.

Photography: Always ask permission before taking photos of locals. Even if no money is requested, consider offering a dollar or two to the person whose photo you've taken. The Navajo are very open about photographs; the Hopi don't allow photographs at all, including videos and tape recordings.

Religious ceremonies: Should you see a ceremony in progress, look for posted signs indicating who is welcome or check with local shops or the village community. Unless you're specifically invited, stay out of *kivas* (ceremonial rooms) and stay on the periphery of dances or processions.

Respect for the land: Do not wander through residential areas or disturb property. Do not disturb or remove animals, plants, rocks, petrified wood, or artifacts.

TRIBAL TIMELINE

950 The first settlements are built at Keet Seel.

1120–1210 Ancestral Puebloans occupy Wupatki Pueblo.

1150 The Hopi build the village of Old Orabi.

1250 Ancestral Puebloans are living at Keet Seel.

1276–1300 Tribes abandon northern Arizona during the "big drought."

1540–1542 Francisco Vásquez de Coronado leads an expedition in search of gold.

1863 Congress creates the Arizona Territory.

1864 Navajos forced to march 300 miles to Fort Sumner during the "Long Walk."

1868 The Navajo and the United States sign a treaty.

1886 Geronimo surrenders after evading U.S. troops for over a year.

1907 Arizona outlaws gambling.

1912 Arizona becomes 48th state.

1993 16 Arizona tribes sign gambling compacts with state.

5

SHOPPING TIPS

For big-ticket items, buy directly from the craftspeople themselves or a reputable dealer. Most products sold on the Hopi and Navajo reservations are authentic, but fakes are not unheard of.

If you're traveling in Navajo land, the Cameron Trading Post north of Flagstaff and the Hubbell Trading Post at Ganado are two spots where you can find exemplary items.

In Phoenix, the Heard Museum offers some of the finest Native American handicrafts at reasonable prices.

Trading posts are reliable, as are most roadside stands, which can offer some outstanding values, but be wary of solo vendors around parking lots.

If you're planning on shopping on the Hopi Reservation or elsewhere outside the Navajo trading posts, it's a good idea to carry cash, as not all vendors accept credit cards.

Proud craftspeople have individual logos or personal marks that are put into each piece. Authentic pieces will also indicate that the silver is sterling.

CULTURE

Heritage flavors: Native American food staples are well adapted to living in Arizona's arid lands. Corn is a universal ingredient—ground into flour to make tortillas, included in stew, or simply steamed and left on the cob. The fruits of the saguaro, prickly pear, and other cacti are commonly harvested by tribes as well as tepary beans grown from seeds handed down over generations. Fry bread—pillow-shape fried dough—is the basis of the popular Navajo taco, usually topped with beans, ground beef, and shredded cheese.

Song and dance: Ceremonies involving music and dance are central to Native American culture. Not every ceremony is accessible to visitors. Cultural centers and museums, such as the Heard in Phoenix, frequently hold powwows and other festivals that often celebrate more than one tribe.

Sacred spaces: The Hopi kivas are square- or circular-walled, mostly underground structures that are used exclusively for religious ceremonies, and often accessed by a ladder from above. Most kivas, including ruins, are off-limits to tourists. The hogan is the traditional dwelling of the Navajo and the door always faces east to welcome the rising sun. Though used as homes, hogans play an important part in Navajo spirituality and represent the universe and all things in it.

Arts and crafts: Many of the craftspeople on the reservations sell their wares, with specialties that include pottery, turquoise and sterling-silver jewelry, handwoven baskets, and Navajo wool rugs. As the Spanish ventured northward from Mexico in the late 1500s and early 1600s, they taught the Native Americans their silver-crafting skills, while tribes specializing in pottery and weaving carry on a tradition that began hundreds of years ago. Native beadwork traces its origins to trade beads from early explorers.

THE NAVAJO AND THE HOPI PEOPLE

Both the Navajo and Hopi base their cultures on the land, but they're very different from one another. The Navajo refer to themselves as the Diné (pronounced din-*eh*)—"the people"—and live on 17 million acres in Arizona, New Mexico, Utah, and Colorado, the largest Native American reservation in the country. The Hopi trace their roots to the original settlers of the area, whom they call the Hisatsinom, or "people of long ago"—they are also known as Anasazi, meaning both "ancient ones" and "ancient enemies." Hopi culture is more structured than that of the Navajo, and their religion has remained stronger and purer. For both tribes, unemployment is high on the reservation and poverty an ongoing concern.

The **Navajo** use few words and have a subtle sense of humor that can pass you by if you're not a good listener. They're taught not to talk too much, be loud, or show off. Eye contact is considered impolite; if you're conversing with Navajos, some may look down or away even though they're paying attention to you. Likewise, touching is seen differently; handshaking may be the only physical contact that you see. When shaking hands, a light touch is preferred to a firm grip, which is considered overbearing. Some of these traits are changing with younger generations, especially as technology and travel lead to less insular communities.

Although most Navajos speak English, listen closely to the language of the Diné. Stemming from the Athabascan family of languages, it's difficult for outsiders to learn because of subtle accentuation. The famous Marine Corps Navajo "code talkers" of World War II saved thousands of lives in the South Pacific by creating a code within their native Navajo language. A few code talkers still living today reside around Tuba City.

The **Hopi** Reservation is surrounded by the far larger Navajo Reservation and has begun to open up a bit more to visitors, who can now book guided tours of artists' studios. Over the years the proximity of the two tribes has been the cause of contention, often involving the assistance of the United States Government in settling land claims, yet the spirituality of the Hopi—"the peaceful ones"—is decidedly antiwar. In fact, Hopi mythology holds that a white-skinned people will save the tribe from its difficult life. Long ago, however, in the face of brutal treatment by whites, most Hopi became convinced that salvation would originate elsewhere.

ON THE GROUND

Visiting the Navajo: The Navajo are generally more relaxed than the Hopi with recording, but always ask for permission before taking someone's picture. If you aren't asked for a gratuity, consider giving one. Canyon De Chelly, Chaco Canyon, Monument Valley Navajo Tribal Park, and Navajo National Monument offer glimpses into the past and present of Native American life and culture, including ruins of ancient dwellings and visitor centers with informative dioramas.

Visiting the Hopi: Recordings, including photographs, are prohibited in the Hopi Reservation, except in limited cases by permit. Central to the reservation are Hopi Mesas that contain two of the oldest continually inhabited villages in North America. Though Hopi villages offer visitors limited access, visitors can buy handicrafts from Hopi artisans at many shops or book a studio tour through the Moenkopi Legacy Inn in Tuba City.

(Above: A traditional Navajo hogan dwelling)

Updated
by Andrew
Collins

Northeast Arizona is a vast and magnificent land of lofty buttes, towering cliffs, and turquoise skies. Most of the land in the area belongs to the Navajo and Hopi, who adhere to ancient traditions based on spiritual values, kinship, and an affinity for nature. Spend time at some of the region's most spectacular sites, such as Canyon de Chelly, Lake Powell, and surrounding Glen Canyon, and Monument Valley, and you'll quickly come to appreciate why indigenous locals so revere the landscape.

Life here has changed little during the last two centuries, and visiting this land can feel like traveling to a foreign country or going back in time, although a handful of distinctive, inviting hotels have opened in the region in recent years, helping to entice overnight visitors aiming to venture off the beaten path without necessarily foregoing creature comforts.

In such towns as Tuba City and Window Rock it's not uncommon to hear the gliding vowels and soft consonants of the Navajo language, a tongue as different from Hopi as English is from Chinese. As you drive in the vicinity, tune your radio to 660 AM KTNN (⊕ *www.ktnnonline. com*), the Voice of the Navajo Nation since 1985. You'll quickly understand why the U.S. Marine Navajo "code talkers" communicating in their native tongue were able to devise a code within their language that was never broken by the Japanese.

In the Navajo Nation's approximate center sits the nearly 2,350-square-mile Hopi Reservation, a series of adobe villages built on high mesas overlooking the cultivated land. On Arizona's borders, where the Navajo Nation continues into Utah and New Mexico, the Navajo and Canyon de Chelly national monuments contain haunting cliff dwellings of ancient people who lived in the area some 1,500 years ago. Glen Canyon Dam, which abuts the northwestern corner of the reservation, holds back 185 miles of emerald waters known as Lake Powell.

Most of northeast Arizona is high desert, but it's far from monochromatic: eerie and spectacular rock formations as colorful as desert sunsets highlight immense mesas, canyons, and cliffs; towering stands of ponderosa pine cover the Chuska Mountains to the north and east of Canyon de Chelly. Navajo Mountain to the north and west in Utah soars more than 10,000 feet, and the San Francisco Peaks climb to similar heights to the south and west by Flagstaff. According to the Navajo creation myth, these are two of the four mountainous boundaries of the sacred land where the Navajo first emerged from Earth's interior.

NORTHEAST ARIZONA PLANNER

WHEN TO GO

FESTIVALS AND EVENTS

SEPTEMBER **Navajo Nation Annual Tribal Fair.** The world's largest Native American fair includes a rodeo, traditional Navajo music and dances, food booths and fry bread competitions, a Miss Navajo Nation Pageant, and an intertribal powwow during the first week of September, at Window Rock. ☎ *928/871–6478* ⊕ *www.navajonationfair.com.*

Suminangwa Harvest Festival. This celebration, which features Harvest and Butterfly social dances, is typically held the third weekend of September in the village of Sichomovi, between First Mesa and Second Mesa. ☎ *928/737–2754* ⊕ *www.sipaulovihopiinformationcenter.org/ events.html.*

DECEMBER **Monument Valley Balloon Event.** This well-attended, mid-December, three-day weekend of hot-air ballooning at Monument Valley Navajo Tribal Park includes concerts, a family fun walk, a balloon "night glow" over the small airport at Goulding's Lodge, and a launch of more than 20 colorful balloons each morning. ☎ *435/727–5870* ⊕ *www. navajonationparks.org.*

PLANNING YOUR TIME

Northeastern Arizona encompasses an enormous area but relatively few key attractions, so it's best to use one or two primary communities (Page or Tuba City on the west side, Kayenta on the north, and Chinle or Window Rock on the east) as bases for day trips to outlying attractions.

If your time is limited, put Canyon de Chelly and Monument Valley at the top of your list—if you're ambitious, you could explore these two sites on consecutive days, spending the night in Chinle, Kayenta, or in Monument Valley itself. Focus on the South Rim Drive at Canyon de Chelly, and in Monument Valley book a jeep tour with the highly respected Sacred Monument Tours. On travel days from one base community to another, plan a scenic drive, such as AZ 264 from Tuba City to Window Rock (don't miss the great crafts shopping at Second Mesa) or AZ 98 to U.S. 160 to U.S. 191 from Page to Chinle. Give yourself at least two days to get to know any one part of the region, and as much as a week to fully explore all of it.

■ TIP➔ Unlike the rest of Arizona (including the Hopi Reservation), the Navajo Reservation observes Daylight Saving Time. Thus for half the year—mid-March to early November—it's an hour later on the Navajo

Reservation than everywhere else in the state.

GETTING HERE AND AROUND

CAR TRAVEL

It's virtually impossible to see much of northeastern Arizona without a car—this is your best bet not only for getting here, but also for visiting attractions and communities throughout the region.

Many visitors see northeastern Arizona as part of a road-tripping adventure through the Four Corners Region, perhaps combining their visit with trips to the national parks of southern Utah and southwestern Colorado. This "en route" road-tripping strategy makes the most sense, especially given the region's stunningly scenic drives. The Navajo Nation has a terrific website (⊕ *www. navajoscenicroads.com*) geared toward road-tripping.

HIKING IN NORTHEAST ARIZONA

Some of the best hikes in this region are in Canyon de Chelly, up the streambed between the soaring vermilion, orange, and white sandstone cliffs, with the remains of the ancient Ancestral Puebloan communities frequently in view. The Navajo National Monument offers impressive hikes to Betatakin, a settlement dating back to AD 1250, and Keet Seel, which dates back as far as AD 950. Both are in alcoves at the base of gigantic overhanging cliffs. Remember, you can't hike or camp on private property or tribal land without a backcountry permit.

ROAD CONDITIONS AND SERVICES Most of the 27,400 square miles of the Navajo Reservation and other areas of northeastern Arizona are off the beaten track. It's prudent to stay on the well-maintained paved thoroughfares. If you don't have the equipment for wilderness travel—including a four-wheel-drive vehicle and provisions—and lack backcountry experience, stay off dirt roads unless they're signed and graded and the skies are clear. Be on the lookout for ominous rain clouds in summer or signs of snow in winter. Never drive into dips or low-lying areas during a heavy rainstorm, and be vigilant for both wildlife and livestock (the Navajo Nation is open range, meaning cattle roam freely). If you heed these simple precautions, car travel through the region is as safe as anywhere else in the Southwest. ■TIP→ While driving around the Navajo Nation, tune in to 660 AM (KTNN) for local news and weather.

A tour of Navajo-Hopi country can involve driving significant distances between widely scattered communities, so a detailed, up-to-date road map is essential (relying on smartphone GPS isn't a great idea, as cell coverage is spotty). Gas stations are in all major towns, but distances between them can be considerable—it's best to service your vehicle before venturing into the Navajo and Hopi reservations, and to carry emergency equipment and supplies.

RESTAURANTS

Northeastern Arizona is a vast area with small hamlets and towns scattered miles apart, and there are few stores or restaurants. With the exception of Page, which has slightly more culinary variety, the region's restaurants mostly serve basic but tasty Native American, Southwestern, and frontier-inspired American (steaks, burgers) cuisine. Navajo and Hopi favorites include mutton stew, Hopi *piki* (paper-thin, blue-corn bread), and Navajo fry bread.

HOTELS

Page has the area's greatest concentration of lodgings, most of them fairly standard chain motels and hotels, but this base camp for exploring Lake Powell also has a few B&Bs as well as houseboat rentals, and just over the border in Utah is the ultraluxurious Amangiri resort. You'll find a handful of well-maintained chains in the Navajo Nation, in Kayenta, Chinle, Tuba City, and Window Rock. Additionally, the Navajo's View Hotel in Monument Valley, and the Hopi's Moenkopi Legacy Inn in Tuba City are beautifully designed, contemporary hotels. This is a popular area for both tent and RV camping—you can obtain a list of campgrounds from the Page/Lake Powell Tourism Bureau and the Navajo Nation Tourism Office. *Hotel reviews have been shortened. For full information, visit Fodors.com.*

WHAT IT COSTS				
	$	$$	$$$	$$$$
Restaurants	under $12	$12–$20	$21–$30	over $30
Hotels	under $121	$121–$175	$176–$250	over $250

Restaurant prices are the average cost of a main course at dinner or, if dinner is not served, at lunch. Hotel prices are the lowest cost of a standard double in high season, excluding taxes and service charges.

NAVAJO NATION EAST

Land has always been central to the history of the Navajo people: it's embedded in their very name. The Tewa were the first to call them *Navahu*, which means "large area of cultivated land." But according to the Navajo creation myth, they were given the name *ni'hookaa diyan diné* ("holy earth people") by their creators. Today tribal members call themselves the Diné (pronounced din-*eh*)—"the people." The eastern portion of the Arizona Navajo Nation (in Navajo, *diné bikéyah*) is a dry but often surprisingly green land, especially in the vicinity of the aptly named Beautiful Valley, south of Canyon de Chelly along U.S. 191. A landscape of rolling hills, wide arroyos, and small canyons, the area is dotted with traditional Navajo hogans, sheepfolds, cattle tanks, and wood racks. The region's easternmost portion is marked by tall mountains and towering sandstone cliffs cut by primitive roads that are generally accessible only on horseback or with four-wheel-drive vehicles.

ESSENTIALS

Visitor Information Navajo Nation Tourism Office ☎ *928/871–6436* ⊕ *www. discovernavajo.com.*

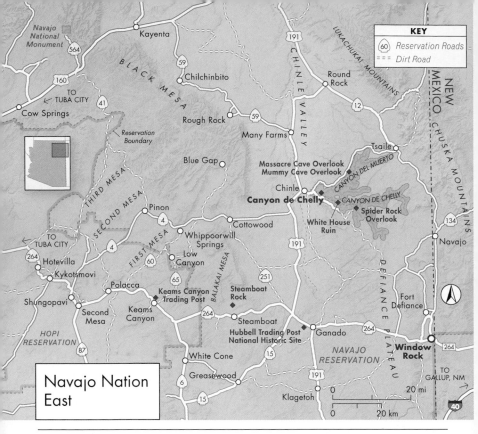

KEY

🔵 60 *Reservation Roads*
=== *Dirt Road*

Navajo National Monument

564

Kayenta

BLACK MESA

59

Chilchinbito

160

TO TUBA CITY

41

Cow Springs

Rough Rock

59

Many Farms

Reservation Boundary

THIRD MESA

SECOND MESA

Blue Gap

Chinle

Canyon de Chelly

Massacre Cave Overlook
Mummy Cave Overlook

CANYON DEL MUERTO

CANYON DE CHELLY

Spider Rock Overlook

White House Ruin

134

Navajo

Pinon

4

Cottowood

191

TO TUBA CITY

4

Hotevilla

264

Whippoorwill Springs

Low Canyon

60

Kykotsmovi

FIRST MESA

65

251

Polacca

BALAKAI MESA

Keams Canyon Trading Post

Steamboat Rock

DEFIANCE PLATEAU

Fort Defiance

Shungopavi

Second Mesa

Keams Canyon

264

Steamboat

Ganado

264

Window Rock

264

HOPI RESERVATION

87

Hubbell Trading Post National Historic Site

NAVAJO RESERVATION

TO GALLUP, NM

White Cone

15

Greasewood

6

191

Klagetoh

0   20 mi

0   20 km

40

191

CHINLE VALLEY

LUKACHUKAI MOUNTAINS

Round Rock

12

Tsaile

NEW MEXICO

CHUSKA MOUNTAINS

15

Navajo Nation East

WINDOW ROCK

192 miles from Flagstaff, 26 miles from Gallup, New Mexico.

Named for the immense arch-shape "window" in a massive sandstone ridge above the city, Window Rock is the capital of the Navajo Nation and the center of its tribal government. With a population of around 2,710, this community serves as the business and social center for Navajo families throughout the reservation. Window Rock is a good place to stop for food, supplies, and gas.

GETTING HERE AND AROUND

From Flagstaff follow Interstate 40 east for 160 miles, then Highway 12 north. From Gallup, New Mexico, follow U.S. 491 north and then NM 264 west (which becomes AZ 264). Window Rock lies on the border between the two states, with most businesses on the Arizona side.

EXPLORING

Navajo Nation Council Chambers. The murals on the walls of this handsome structure, built to resemble a large ceremonial hogan, depict scenes from the history of the tribe, and the bell beside the entrance was a gift to the tribe by the Santa Fe Railroad to commemorate the thousands of Navajos who built the railroad. Visitors can observe sessions of the council, where 88 delegates representing 110 reservation chapters meet on the third Monday of January, April, July, and October. Turn east off Indian Highway 12, about ½ mile north of AZ 264, to reach the Council Chambers. Nearby **Window Rock Navajo Tribal Park & Veteran's Memorial** is a memorial park honoring Navajo veterans, including the famous World War II code talkers. ✉ *AZ 264* ☎ *928/871–6417* 🌐 *www.navajonationcouncil.org* 🕒 *Weekdays 8–5; call for weekend hrs.*

FAMILY **Navajo Nation Fair.** Many all-Indian rodeos are held near the center of downtown at the fairgrounds. The community hosts the annual multi-day Fourth of July celebration with a major rodeo, ceremonial dances, and a parade. The Navajo Nation Tribal Fair, much like a traditional state fair, is held in early September. It offers standard county-fair rides, midway booths, contests, powwow competitions, and an all-Indian rodeo. ✉ *AZ 264* ☎ *928/871–7941* 🌐 *www.navajonationfair.com* 🎟 *$5.*

FAMILY **Navajo Nation Museum.** Located on the grounds of the former Tse Bonito Park off AZ 264, this museum is devoted to the art, culture, and history of the Navajo people and has an excellent library on the Navajo Nation. Each season brings new exhibitions by native artists each season; call for a list of shows. There are also permanent exhibits on the Long Walk, during which the Navajo were tragically and temporarily relocated to Fort Sumner, New Mexico, and on culture and philosophies of the Navajo people. In the same building is the Navajo Nation Visitor Center, a great resource for all sorts of information on reservation activities. ✉ *AZ 264 and Loop Rd., next to Quality Inn Navajo Nation* ☎ *928/871–7941* 🌐 *www.navajonationmuseum.org* 🎟 *Free* 🕒 *Mon.–Sat. 8–5.*

FAMILY **The Navajo Nation Zoological & Botanical Park.** Amid the sandstone monoliths on the border between Arizona and New Mexico, the Navajo Nation Zoological & Botanical Park displays about 50 species of domestic and wild animals, birds, and amphibians that figure in Navajo legends, as well as examples of plants used by traditional people. Most of the animals here were brought in as orphans or after sustaining injuries—they include black bears, mountain lions, Mexican gray wolves, bobcats, cougars, golden eagles, Gila monsters, and prairie rattlesnakes. It's the nation's only Native American–owned zoo. ✉ *AZ 264, just east of Quality Inn; shares parking lot with Navajo Nation Museum* ☎ *928/871–6574* 🌐 *www.navajozoo.org* 🎟 *Free* 🕒 *Mon.–Sat. 10–4:30.*

WHERE TO EAT AND STAY

$ AMERICAN 🍴 **Blake's Lotaburger.** The westernmost branch of a beloved New Mexico chain of old-school burger joints is technically in the Land of Enchantment (i.e. New Mexico) but just a few hundred feet over the Arizona state line, and within walking distance of the Quality Inn and Window Rock museums. Blake's began in 1952 in Albuquerque and enjoys a cult following for its Angus-beef green-chile cheeseburgers, seasoned fries, breakfast burritos, and cherry milkshakes. [$] *Average main: $5* ✉ *NM 264, at Alma Dr., Gallup, New Mexico* ☎ *505/371–5400* 🌐 *www.lotaburger.com.*

$ HOTEL 🏨 **Quality Inn Navajo Nation Capital.** Rooms in this two-story beam-and-stucco hotel near the Navajo Museum are decorated with an earthy Navajo-inspired palette that complements the rustic pine furniture.

Pros: within walking distance of Navajo Museum; decent on-site restaurant; rooms are bright and attractively furnished. **Cons:** on busy road with dull setting. *$ Rooms from: $89 ✉ 48 W. AZ 264, at Hwy. 12 ☎ 928/871–4108 🌐 www.qualityinnwindowrock.com 56 rooms 🍽 Breakfast.*

SHOPPING

Fodor's Choice ★ **Navajo Arts and Crafts Enterprises.** This outlet of the Navajo Arts and Crafts Enterprises stocks tribal art purchased from craftspeople across Navajo Nation, including stunning silverwork and traditional Navajo dolls, pottery, and rugs. Local artisans are occasionally at work here. There are six other outlets; four are in northeastern Arizona (Cameron, Chinle, Kayenta, Navajo National Monument), and one is in northwestern New Mexico (Shiprock). Major credit cards are accepted. *✉ AZ 264 at Hwy. 12, next to Quality Inn Navajo Nation Capital ☎ 928/871–4090, 888/831–7384 🌐 www.gonavajo.com.*

CANYON DE CHELLY

30 miles west of Window Rock on AZ 264, then 25 miles north on U.S. 191.

Comprising two long canyons, each one more than 1,000 feet deep, Canyon de Chelly is one of the sites in the Four Corners region. It's somewhat overshadowed by the Grand Canyon and some of southern Utah's national parks, and you can only venture into the canyons with an authorized guide, but visitors with just a little time can experience Canyon de Chelly's dramatic viewing areas along two park roads (there's no admission fee) that snake along the canyon rims.

GETTING HERE AND AROUND

U.S. 191 runs north–south through Chinle, the closest town to the Canyon de Chelly entrance.

Guided tours allow visits directly into the canyons, not just the park drives high above them; jeep tours even have the option of camping overnight. Each kind of tour has its pros and cons: you'll cover the most ground in a jeep; horseback trips get you close to one of the park's most notable geological formations, Spider Rock; and guided walks provide the most leisurely pace and an excellent opportunity to interact with your guide and ask questions. You can also plan custom treks lasting several days.

PLANNING YOUR TIME

To get even a basic sense of the park's scope and history, spend at least a full day here. If time is short, the best strategy is to visit the visitor center, where you can watch an informative 23-minute video about the canyons, and then drive the most magnificent of the two park roads, South Rim Drive. You could, if you're ambitious, drive both park roads in one day, but it's better to set aside a second day for North Rim Drive, or take the North Rim Drive as an alternative route to Kayenta, by way of Tsaile. From the different overlooks along the park roads you'll be treated to amazing photo ops of the valley floors below, and you can

CLOSE UP

Who Were the Cliff Dwellers?

The first inhabitants of the canyons arrived more than 2,000 years ago—anthropologists call them the basket makers, because baskets were the predominant artifacts they left behind. By AD 750, however, the basket makers had disappeared—their reason for leaving the region is unknown, but some speculate they were forced to leave because of encroaching cultures or climatic changes—and they were replaced by Pueblo tribes who constructed stone cliff dwellings. The departure of the Pueblo people around AD 1300 is widely believed to have resulted from changing climatic conditions, soil erosion, dwindling local resources, disease, and internal conflict. Present-day Hopi see these people as their ancestors. Beginning around AD 780, Hopi farmers settled here, followed by the Navajo around 1300. Evidence indicates that the Navajo migrated from far northern Canada, although the timing of their initial voyage south isn't clear. Despite evidence to the contrary, most Navajos hold that their people have always lived here and that the Diné passed through three previous underworlds before emerging into this, the fourth or Glittering World.

also access certain dwellings. For a more in-depth experience, book one of the guided hiking, jeep, or horseback tours into the canyon.

Both Canyon de Chelly and Canyon del Muerto have a paved rim drive with turnoffs and parking areas. Each drive takes a minimum of two hours—allow more if you plan to hike to White House Ruin, picnic, or spend time photographing the sites. Overlooks along the rim drives provide incredible views of the canyon; be sure to stay on trails and away from the canyon edge, and to control children and pets at all times.

The visitor center has exhibits on the history of the cliff dwellers and provides information on scheduled hikes, tours, and National Park Service programs offered throughout the summer months.

ESSENTIALS

Visitor Information Canyon de Chelly Visitor Center ✉ *Indian Hwy. 7, 3 miles east of U.S. 191, Chinle* 🕾 *928/674–5500* ⊕ *www.nps.gov/cach.*

EXPLORING

Fodor'sChoice **Canyon de Chelly.** Home to Ancestral Puebloans from AD 350 to 1300, ★ the nearly 84,000-acre Canyon de Chelly (pronounced d'*shay*) is one of the most spectacular natural wonders in the Southwest. On a smaller scale, it rivals the Grand Canyon for beauty. Its main gorges—the 26-mile-long Canyon de Chelly ("canyon in the rock") and the adjoining 35-mile-long Canyon del Muerto ("canyon of the dead")—comprise sheer, heavily eroded sandstone walls that rise to 1,100 feet over dramatic valleys. Ancient pictographs and petroglyphs decorate some of the cliffs, and within the canyon complex there are more than 7,000 archaeological sites. Stone walls rise hundreds of feet above streams, hogans, tilled fields, and sheep-grazing lands.

You can view prehistoric sites near the base of cliffs and perched on high, sheltering ledges, some of which you can access from the park's two main drives along the canyon rims. The dwellings and cultivated fields of the present-day Navajo lie in the flatlands between the cliffs, and those who inhabit the canyon today farm much the way their ancestors did. Most residents leave the canyon in winter but return in early spring to farm.

Canyon de Chelly's South Rim Drive (36 miles round-trip with seven overlooks) starts at the visitor center and ends at **Spider Rock Overlook,** where cliffs plunge nearly 1,000 feet to the canyon floor. The view here is of two pinnacles, Speaking Rock and Spider Rock. Other highlights on the South Rim Drive are Junction Overlook, where Canyon del Muerto joins Canyon de Chelly; White House Overlook, from which a 2.5-mile round-trip trail leads to the **White House Ruin,** with remains of nearly 60 rooms and several kivas; and Sliding House Overlook, where you can see dwellings on a narrow, sloped ledge across the canyon. The carved and sometimes narrow trail down the canyon side to White House Ruin is the only access into Canyon de Chelly without a guide—but if you have a fear of heights, this may not be the hike for you.

The only slightly less breathtaking **North Rim Drive** (34 miles round-trip with four overlooks) of Canyon del Muerto also begins at the visitor center and continues northeast on Indian Highway 64 toward the town of Tsaile. Major stops include Antelope House Overlook, a large site named for the animals painted on an adjacent cliff; **Mummy Cave Overlook,** where two mummies were found inside a remarkably unspoiled pueblo dwelling; and **Massacre Cave Overlook,** which marks the spot where an estimated 115 Navajo were killed by the Spanish in 1805. (The rock walls of the cave are still pockmarked by the Spaniards' ricocheting bullets.) ✉ *Indian Hwy. 7, 3 miles east of U.S. 191, Chinle* ☎ *928/674–5500 for visitor center* 🌐 *www.nps.gov/cach* 🎫 *Free* 🕒 *Daily 8–5.*

Chuska Mountains. To the north of Tsaile are the impressive Chuska Mountains, covered with sprawling stands of ponderosa pine. There are no established hiking trails in the mountains, but up-to-date hiking information and backcountry-use permits (rarely granted if a Navajo guide does not accompany the trip) can be obtained through the Navajo Nation. ✉ *Navajo Nation Parks and Recreation Department, Bldg. 36A, E. AZ 264, Window Rock* ☎ *928/871–6647* 🌐 *www.navajonationparks.org.*

WHERE TO EAT

Chinle is the closest town to Canyon de Chelly. There are lodgings with basic restaurants, as well as a supermarket and a campground. Be aware that you may be approached by panhandlers in the grocery store parking lot.

$$ AMERICAN 🍴 **Garcia's Restaurant.** The lobby restaurant at Chinle's Holiday Inn is low-key, a bit lacking in natural light, and rather ordinary, but people come here because it is one of the area's only non-fast-food dining options. It's a reliable—if unspectacular—choice for dinner. You can count on well-prepared Navajo and American fare, such as mutton stew with fry bread and honey. It also sells a box lunch. [$] *Average main:*

$13 ✉ *Indian Hwy. 7, Chinle* ☎ *928/674–5000* 🌐 *www.holidayinn.com* 🕓 *Limited hrs mid-Nov.–Mar.; call ahead.*

$ AMERICAN 🍴 **The Junction.** Across the parking lot from the Best Western Canyon de Chelly Inn, this sun-filled, airy dining room with cream-color walls, large windows, a long granite counter, and a mix of attractive booths and tables has a cheerier feel than any other restaurant in town. The kitchen turns out pretty tasty American, Southwestern, and Chinese food, too. Specialties include *posole* stew (a Mexican dish made with pork), chicken-fried steak, and sheepherder's sandwiches (consisting of a tortilla or fry bread stuffed with steak, Swiss cheese, grilled onions, chiles, and tomatoes). A small kiosk by the front door sells gifts and jewelry. [$] *Average main: $10* ✉ *100 Main St., Chinle* ☎ *928/674–5875* 🌐 *www.bestwestern.com.*

WHERE TO STAY

$ HOTEL 🏨 **Best Western Canyon de Chelly Inn.** This two-story motel about 3 miles from Canyon de Chelly but close to the junction with U.S. 191 has cheerful rooms with modern, no-frills oak furnishings. **Pros:** affordable; fun retro-motel exterior; indoor pool with hot tub and sauna is open until 9 pm. **Cons:** not within walking distance of the park; ordinary rooms. [$] *Rooms from: $119* ✉ *100 Main St., Chinle* ☎ *928/674–5874, 800/327–0354* 🌐 *www.bestwestern.com* 🛏 *104 rooms* 🍽 *No meals.*

$ HOTEL 🏨 **Holiday Inn Canyon de Chelly.** Once Garcia's Trading Post, this well-kept hotel near Canyon de Chelly is less generic than you might expect: the exterior is territorial fort in style, although the rooms are predictably pastel and contemporary. **Pros:** attractive adobe-style building; nice pool and gym; a short drive from park entrance. **Cons:** room décor not especially memorable; dull roadside setting; slightly pricier than other options in town. [$] *Rooms from: $110* ✉ *Indian Hwy. 7, Chinle* ☎ *928/674–5000, 888/465–4329* 🌐 *www.holidayinn.com* 🛏 *108 rooms* 🍽 *No meals.*

$ HOTEL FAMILY 🏨 **Sacred Canyon Lodge.** Purchased in 2013 by the team behind the View Hotel in Monument Valley, this pleasant if basic establishment has an ideal location within the national monument's borders—the stone-and-adobe units that match the site's original 1896 trading post. **Pros:** only hotel inside the actual park borders; atmospheric architecture and décor is steeped in history; tours offered right from hotel. **Cons:** rustic décor; area cell phone service is spotty. [$] *Rooms from: $99* ✉ *Indian Hwy. 7, Chinle* ☎ *928/674–5841, 800/679–2473* 🌐 *www.tbirdlodge.com* 🛏 *70 rooms* 🍽 *No meals.*

SHOPPING

Navajo Arts and Crafts Enterprises. This branch of the respected Navajo gallery carries an excellent selection of locally made crafts and works of art. ✉ *AZ 64 at U.S. 191, Chinle* ☎ *928/328–8116* 🌐 *www.gonavajo.com.*

SPORTS AND THE OUTDOORS

HIKING

From about late May through early September, free three-hour ranger hikes depart most mornings from the Canyon de Chelly Visitor Center—call ahead for times and to reserve a spot. Year-round, you can book a Navajo guide–led day hike or overnight camping trip through

5

CLOSE UP

Best Northeast Arizona Campgrounds

Cottonwood Campground. This sometimes cramped and noisy campground has RV and tent sites right in Canyon de Chelly. ⊠ *Indian Hwy. 7 near Canyon de Chelly Visitor Center, Chinle* ☎ *928/674–2106* ⊕ *www.nps.gov/cach.*

Goulding's Good Sam Campground. Views of Monument Valley are the draw at this clean, modern campground. ⊠ *Monument Valley Rd., off U.S. 163 just north of UT/AZ border, 24 miles north of Kayenta, Monument Valley Navajo Tribal Park* ☎ *435/727–3231* ⊕ *www.gouldings.com.*

Mitten View Campground. Sites are crowded together, but most offer spectacular views of Monument Valley. ⊠ *Monument Valley Navajo Tribal Park, near visitor center, Monument Valley Rd., off U.S. 163 just north of UT/AZ border, 24 miles north of Kayenta* ☎ *435/727–5870* ⊕ *www.navajonationparks.org.*

Navajo National Monument Campground. Beautiful and serene with no fee, this campground has no hookups, and open fires aren't allowed (you must use camp stoves). ⊠ *AZ 564, Shonto* ☎ *928/672–2700* ⊕ *www.nps.gov/nava.*

Spider Rock Campground. Cordial Navajo owner Howard Smith makes everyone feel comfortable at this informal campground nestled in low piñons within a few hundred yards of the canyon. ⊠ *Indian Hwy. 7, 10 miles east of Canyon de Chelly Visitor Center* ☎ *928/674–8261* ⊕ *www.spiderrockcampground.com.*

Wahweap/Lake Powell RV & Campground. This campground in the Wahweap Marina complex, which is run by the National Park Service concessionaire, has views of the lake and serves both RVers and tent campers. ⊠ *U.S. 89, 5 miles north of Page near shore of Lake Powell, Wahweap* ☎ *888/896–3829* ⊕ *www.lakepowell.com.*

Ancient Canyon Tours. Some trails are strenuous and steep; others are easy or moderate. Those with health concerns or a fear of heights should proceed with caution.

Only one hike within Canyon de Chelly National Monument—the **White House Ruin Trail** on the South Rim Drive—can be undertaken without an authorized guide. The trail starts near White House Overlook and runs along sheer walls that drop about 550 feet. If you have concerns about heights, be aware that the path gets narrow and requires careful footing. The hike is 2½ miles round-trip, and hikers should carry their own drinking water.

Ancient Canyon Tours. This Navajo-owned tour company offers both day-hiking and overnight-camping excursions into the park's two canyons, de Chelly and del Muerto. The moderately difficult day hikes venture into some of the park's most spectacular backcountry and can last from three to four hours, if covering the lower parts of the canyons; and to as long as nine hours for excursions into the higher terrain. The cost is $40 per hour (three-hour minimum) for up to 15 hikers; there are additional $30-per-guide and $50-per-night land-use fees for overnight trips. ⊠ *Chinle* ☎ *928/380–1563* ⊕ *www.ancientcanyontours. com* ✉ *From $40/hr.*

HORSEBACK RIDING

Fodor'sChoice **Totsonii Ranch.** Thirteen miles from the visitor center at the end of the
★ paved portion of South Rim Drive (follow the signs from there), this
ranch offers several types of horseback tours into different parts of
Canyon de Chelly: Canyon Rim (two hours), Three Turkey Ruins (four
hours), Spider Rock (four hours), White House Ruins (six hours), Canyon de Chelly overview (eight hours), and one- and two-night treks.
Some of these trips are geared only toward skilled adult riders, such as
the Canyon Rim trips, which encounter steep terrain and offer amazing
views. Spider Rock is a great choice for virtually any skill level, and can
be done in a half day—the ride leads right to the base of this 800-foot
iconic pillar. Per person rates range from $65 to $250 for day trips,
and $360 (one night) to $525 (two nights) for overnight adventures.
⊠ *South Rim Dr., Chinle* ☎ *928/551–0109* ⊕ *www.totsoniiranch.com*
✉ *From $65/person.*

JEEP TOURS

Canyon de Chelly Tours. Book a private jeep tour into Canyon de Chelly
or choose from group tours, overnight camping in the canyon, late-
afternoon and evening tours, and bus tours along South Rim Drive.
Entertainment such as storytellers, music, and Navajo legends can be
arranged with an advance reservation. Rates begin at $82 per person
for three-hour tours, or $55 per hour per vehicle if you use your own
SUV. (There's roughly a 10% discount if you pay in cash.) ⊠ *Canyon
de Chelly Visitor Center parking lot, Chinle* ☎ *928/349–1600* ⊕ *www.
canyondechellytours.com* ✉ *From $82/person.*

WALKING TOURS

Footpath Journeys. Hoof it into Canyon de Chelly on a scheduled or
custom four- to seven-day trek. ⊠ *Chinle* ☎ *928/724–3366* ⊕ *www.
footpathjourneys.com* ✉ *From $800/person, not including food.*

HUBBELL TRADING POST NATIONAL HISTORIC SITE

*40 miles south of Canyon de Chelly, off AZ 264, 30 miles west of
Window Rock.*

Administered by the national park service, this well-preserved Navajo
trading post provides a glimpse into the region's legacy as a trading
hub of fine weavings. High-quality, handmade rugs are still sold in the
park store.

GETTING HERE AND AROUND

The site is just off AZ 264, well marked from the road, and easily
explored on foot once you arrive. The National Park Service Visitor
Center exhibits illustrate the post's history, and you can take a self-
guided tour of the grounds and Hubbell home, and visit the Hubbell
Trading Post, which contains a fine display of Native American artistry.
The visitor center has a fairly comprehensive bookstore specializing in
Navajo history, art, and culture; local weavers often demonstrate their
craft on site.

EXPLORING

Fodor's Choice
★ **Hubbell Trading Post National Historic Site.** John Lorenzo Hubbell, a merchant and friend of the Navajo, established this trading post in 1876. Hubbell taught, translated letters, settled family quarrels, and explained government policy to the Navajo, and during an 1886 smallpox epidemic he turned his home into a hospital and ministered to the sick and dying. He died in 1930 and is buried near the trading post. Visitors today can tour the historic home and explore the grounds and outbuildings.

The Hubbell Trading Post National Historic Site is famous for "Ganado red" Navajo rugs, which are sold at the store here. Rugs can cost anywhere from $100 to more than $30,000, but considering the quality and time that goes into weaving each one, the prices are quite reasonable. It's hard to resist the beautiful designs and colors, and it's a pleasure just to browse around this rustic spot, where Navajo artists frequently show their work. Documents of authenticity are provided for all works. Note: When photographing weavers, ask permission first. They expect a few dollars in return. ⊠ *AZ 264, 1 mile west of U.S. 191, Ganado* ☎ *928/755–3475* ⊕ *www.nps.gov/hutr* ⊠ *Free, $2 to tour Hubbell home* ⊙ *May–Sept., daily 8–6; Oct.–Apr., daily 8–5.*

■ EN
ROUTE
Steamboat Rock. This immense, jutting peninsula of stone resembles an early steamboat, complete with a geologically formed waterline. At Steamboat Rock you are only 5 miles from the eastern boundary of the Hopi Reservation. ⊠ *AZ 264, about 20 miles west of Hubbell Trading Post, Steamboat.*

THE HOPI MESAS

The Hopi occupy 12 villages in regions referred to as First Mesa, Second Mesa, and Third Mesa. Although these areas have similar languages and traditions, each has its own individual features. Generations of Hopitu, "the peaceful people," much like their Puebloan ancestors, have lived in these largely agrarian settlements of stone-and-adobe houses, which blend in with the earth so well that they appear to be natural formations. Television antennae, satellite dishes, and automobiles notwithstanding, these Hopi villages still exude the air of another time.

Descendants of the ancient Hisatsinom, the number of Hopi living among the villages today is about 7,000. Their culture can be traced back more than 2,000 years, making them one of the oldest known tribes in North America. They successfully developed "dry farming," and grow many kinds of vegetables and corn (called maize) as their basic food—in fact the Hopi are often called the "corn people." They incorporate nature's cycles into most of their religious rituals. In the celebrated Snake Dance ceremony, dancers carry venomous snakes in their mouths to appease the gods and to bring rain. In addition to farming the land, the Hopi create fine pottery and basketwork and excel at carving wooden kachina dolls.

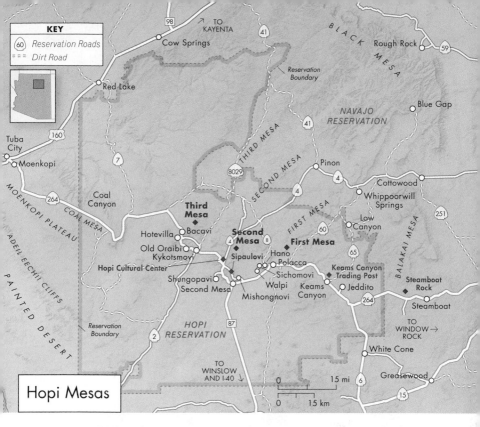

Hopi Mesas

VISITOR INFORMATION

Hopi Tribe. Staff at the Hopi Tribe offices can answer basic questions and provide guidance for visiting the Hopi Mesas. ☎ 928/734–3202 ⊕ www.hopi-nsn.gov.

Moenkopi Legacy Inn. Although the Hopi Tribe offices can provide basic information to travelers, the staff at the Moenkopi Legacy Inn in Tuba City has become the tribe's de facto visitor information center and best overall tourism resource. The staff here can also arrange tours led by Hopi-certified guides. ☎ 928/283–4500 ⊕ www.experiencehopi.com.

KEAMS CANYON TRADING POST

43 miles west of Hubbell Trading Post on AZ 264.

The trading post established by Thomas Keam in 1875 to do business with local tribes is now the area's main tourist attraction, offering a primitive campground, restaurant, service station, and shopping center, all set in a dramatic rocky canyon. An administrative center for the Bureau of Indian Affairs, Keams Canyon also has a number of government buildings. A road, accessible by passenger car, winds northeast 3 miles into the 8-mile wooded canyon. At **Inscription Rock,** about

2 miles down the road, frontiersman Kit Carson engraved his name in stone. There are several picnic spots in the canyon.

GETTING HERE AND AROUND

Keams Canyon is along AZ 264, the main route between Window Rock and Tuba City.

WHERE TO EAT

$ ✕ **Keams Canyon Restaurant.** This typical no-frills roadside diner with
AMERICAN Formica tabletops offers both American and Native American dishes, including Navajo tacos heaped with ground beef, chili, beans, lettuce, and grated cheese. Daily specials, offered at $1 to $2 off the regular price, may include anything from barbecued ribs to lamb chops to crab legs. There's an ice-cream stand in the same building. Come early because both the diner and ice cream counter close around 8 pm. $ *Average main: $8* ✉ *Keams Canyon Shopping Center, AZ 264, Keams Canyon* ☎ *928/738–2296* ⊘ *Closed Sun. No dinner Sat.*

SHOPPING

McGee's Indian Art. Head upstairs from the Keams Canyon Restaurant to peruse first-rate, high-quality Hopi crafts such as handcrafted jewelry, pottery, beautiful carvings, basketry, and artwork. ✉ *AZ 264, Keams Canyon* ☎ *928/738–2295* ⊕ *www.hopiart.com.*

FIRST MESA

11 miles west of Keams Canyon, on AZ 264.

The easternmost of the three main Hopi mesas, First Mesa comprises several centuries-old communities acclaimed for polychrome pottery and kachina-doll carving. Hano, Sichomovi, and Walpi—with its dramatic setting beneath sheer cliffs—are the key communities at First Mesa.

GETTING HERE AND AROUND

The first village that you approach is Polacca; the older and more impressive villages of Hano, Sichomovi, and Walpi are at the top of the sweeping mesa. From Polacca a paved road (off AZ 264) angles up to a parking lot near the village of Sichomovi, and to the Punsi Hall Visitor Center. ■ TIP→ You must get permission to take the guided walking tour of Hano, Sichomovi, and Walpi. Tour times vary; call ahead to the Moenkopi Legacy Inn in Tuba City for more information.

EXPLORING

Fodor's Choice **First Mesa.** First Mesa villages are renowned for their polychrome pottery
★ and kachina-doll carvings. The older Hopi villages have structures built of rock and adobe mortar in simple architectural style. **Hano** actually belongs to the Tewa, a New Mexico Pueblo tribe. In 1696 the Tewa Indians sought refuge with the Hopi on First Mesa after an unsuccessful rebellion against the Spanish in the Rio Grande Valley. Today the Tewa live close to the Hopi but maintain their own language and ceremonies.

Sichomovi is built so close to Hano that only the residents can tell where one ends and the other begins. Constructed in the mid-1600s, this village is believed to have been built to ease overcrowding at Walpi, the highest point on the mesa. **Walpi,** built on solid rock and surrounded by steep cliffs, frequently hosts ceremonial dances. It's the most pristine of

5

the Hopi villages, with cliffside houses and vast scenic vistas. Inhabited for more than 1,100 years (dating back to 900 AD), Walpi's cliffside houses seem to grow out of the terrain. Today only about 10 residents occupy this settlement, which has neither electricity nor running water; one-hour guided tours of the village are available daily, except when certain ceremonies are taking place (call for hours). Note that Walpi's steep terrain makes it a less than ideal destination for acrophobes. ⊠ *Punsi Hall Visitor Center, AZ 264, at milepost 392, First Mesa* ☎ *928/737–2670* ⊕ *www.experiencehopi.com/walpi.html* 🖃 *Guided tours $20.*

SECOND MESA

8 miles southwest of First Mesa, on AZ 264.

Dubbed the "Center of the Universe" of Hopi culture, Second Mesa contains the communities of Shungopavi and Mishongnovi; in the former, you'll find the Hopi Cultural Center, which contains a museum, trading post, and no-frills hotel and restaurant.

GETTING HERE AND AROUND

The Second Mesa communities are reached via the main highway (AZ 264) through the Hopi Reservation.

TOURS

Fodor'sChoice
★

Hopi Arts Trail and Tours. This Hopi-authorized tour company, run out of Tuba City's Moenkopi Legacy Inn, specializes in studio tours of the Hopi Villages, including not just Second Mesa's artists but those in nearby villages, such as Walpi and Sipaulovi. The tours are led by knowledgeable guides and are a great way to undertake an arts-shopping adventure, especially given that many of the individual galleries keep irregular hours and can be hard to find. At the hotel you can alternatively pick up a copy of the Hopi Arts Trail brochure and passport, which lists several galleries and more than a dozen artists in the Hopi Villages with studios open to the public; present the brochure when visiting these establishments for discounts. Visit the Hopi Art Trails website for full descriptions of all participating galleries and artists. In terms of cost, some short (one to two hours) tours to certain villages are as little as $15, while a full-day tour including a few villages could be as much as $140 per person. ⊠ *AZ 164 at U.S. 160, Tuba City* ☎ *928/283–4500* ⊕ *www.hopiartstrail.com.*

EXPLORING

Second Mesa. The Mesas are the Hopi universe, and Second Mesa is the "Center of the Universe." **Shungopavi,** the largest and oldest village on Second Mesa, which was founded by the Bear Clan, is reached by a paved road angling south off AZ 264, between the junction of AZ 87 and the Hopi Cultural Center. The villagers here make silver overlay jewelry and coil plaques. Coil plaques are woven from galleta grass and yucca and are adorned with designs of kachinas, animals, and corn. The art of making the plaques has been passed from mother to daughter for generations, and fine coil plaques have become highly sought-after collector's items. The famous Hopi snake dances (closed to the public) are held here in August during even-numbered years.

Two smaller villages are off a paved road that runs north from AZ 264, about 2 miles east of the Hopi Cultural Center. **Mishongnovi**, the easternmost settlement, was established in the late 1600s.

Sipaulovi Hopi Information Center. Set on a high mesa with views for more than 100 miles in every direction, Sipaulovi was originally at the base of the mesa before moving to its present site in 1680. You can learn more about the community and its centuries-old traditions by watching a video at the small visitor center and taking one of the guided walking tours through the community. On these tours you have the chance to stop by local studios and talk with artists. ✉ *Second Mesa* ☎ *928/ 737–5426* ⊕ *www.experiencehopi.com/sipaulovi.html* ⚐ *Guided tours $15* ⊙ *Tours weekdays 9–4.*

Hopi Cultural Center. Here you can stop for the night, learn about the people and their communities, and eat authentic Hopi cuisine. The center's museum is dedicated to preserving Hopi traditions and to presenting those traditions to non-Hopi visitors. A gift shop sells works by local Hopi artisans at reasonable prices, and a modest picnic area on the west side of the building is a pleasant spot for lunch with a view of the San Francisco Peaks. ✉ *AZ 264, Second Mesa* ☎ *928/734–2401* ⊕ *www. hopiculturalcenter.com* ⚐ *Museum $3* ⊙ *Mid-Mar.–Oct., weekdays 8–5, weekends 9–3; Nov.–mid-Mar., weekdays 8–5.*

WHERE TO EAT AND STAY

$ ✕ **Hopi Cultural Center Restaurant.** The restaurant at the Hopi Cultural
SOUTHWESTERN Center is an attractive, light-filled room where you can sample traditional tribal fare. Authentic dishes include Indian tacos, Hopi blue-corn pancakes, *piki* (paper-thin, blue-corn bread), fry bread (delicious with honey or salsa), and *nok qui vi* (a tasty stew made with tender bits of lamb, hominy, and mild green chiles). Breakfast is served starting at 7. $ *Average main: $9* ✉ *AZ 264, 5 miles west of AZ 87, Second Mesa* ☎ *928/734–2401* ⊕ *www.hopiculturalcenter.com.*

$ ⬚ **Hopi Cultural Center Inn.** This small Hopi-run motel, the only place to
HOTEL eat or sleep in the immediate area, occupies an attractive adobe building with a tan-and-reddish-brown exterior and clean, quiet, moderately priced rooms with coffeemakers. **Pros:** adjacent to cultural center; only place to stay for miles in either direction; peaceful setting. **Cons:** remote unless you are here to explore Hopi culture; basic, dated rooms; Wi-Fi in rooms can be slow and unreliable. $ *Rooms from: $105* ✉ *AZ 264, 5 miles west of AZ 87, Second Mesa* ☎ *928/734–2401* ⊕ *www. hopiculturalcenter.com* ⇆ *33 rooms, 1 suite* ⦿ *No meals.*

SHOPPING

Hopi Arts and Crafts Silvercraft Cooperative Guild. This venerable guild, just west of the Hopi Cultural Center and in existence since the 1940s, hosts craftspeople selling their wares; you might even see silversmiths at work here. You can stop by on your own or arrange a tour through the operators of the Hopi Arts Trail, based out of the Moenkopi Legacy Inn in Tuba City. ✉ *383 AZ 264, Second Mesa* ☎ *928/283–4500* ⊕ *www. hopiartstrail.com/hopi-artists/silversmiths.html.*

Hopi Cultural Center. This collection of shops carries the works, including pottery, baskets, and dolls, of local artists and artisans. ✉ *AZ 264, Second Mesa* ☎ *928/734–2401* ⊕ *www.hopiculturalcenter.com.*

Tsa-Kursh-Ovi. At this small shop, 1½ miles east of the Hopi Cultural Center, Hopi come to buy bundles of sweetgrass and sage, deer hooves with which to make rattles, and ceremonial belts adorned with seashells. Proprietors Joseph and Janice Day (she is a renowned Hopi basket maker) are a font of information on local artwork, and the shop has one of the largest collections of Hopi baskets in the Southwest. ✉ *AZ 264, Second Mesa* ☎ *928/734–2478.*

THIRD MESA

12 miles northwest of Second Mesa, on AZ 264.

Home to a number of studios in which artisans create weavings, wicker baskets, and jewelry, the Hopi tribe's Third Mesa has four main communities: Kykotsmovi, Old Oraibi, Hotevilla, and Bacavi.

GETTING HERE AND AROUND

The Third Mesa communities are the closest to Tuba City, about 50 miles away along AZ 264.

TOURS

Ancient Pathways Tours. A knowledgeable guide and member of a Hopi clan from Old Oraibi, Bertram "Tsaava" Tsavadawa leads three-hour tours of the Third Mesa area, including trips to see the Taawa Petroglyphs, which are marked with symbols of the people who resided here for more than 1,000 years. ☎ *928/797–8145* ⊕ *www.ancientpathwaystours.com.*

EXPLORING

Third Mesa. Third Mesa villages are known for their agricultural accomplishments, textile weaving, wicker baskets, silver overlay, and plaques. You'll find crafts shops and art galleries, as well as occasional roadside vendors, along AZ 264. ■TIP➜ Visit the Hopi Tribal Headquarters in Kykotsmovi first for necessary permissions to visit the villages of Third Mesa.

At the eastern base of Third Mesa, **Kykotsmovi,** literally "ruins on the hills," is named for the sites on the valley floor and in the surrounding hills. Present-day Kykotsmovi was established by Hopi people from Oraibi—a few miles west—who either converted to Christianity or who wished to attend school and be educated. Kykotsmovi is the seat of the Hopi Tribal Government.

Old Oraibi, a few miles west and on top of Third Mesa at about 7,200 feet in elevation, is believed to be the oldest continuously inhabited community in the United States, dating from around AD 1150. It was also the site of a rare, bloodless conflict between two groups of the Hopi people; in 1906, a dispute, settled uniquely by a "push of war" (a pushing contest), sent the losers off to establish the town of Hotevilla. Oraibi is a dusty spot and, as a courtesy, tourists are asked to park their cars outside and approach the village on foot.

Hotevilla and **Bacavi** are about 4 miles west of Oraibi, and their inhabitants are descended from the former residents of that village. The men of Hotevilla continue to plant crops and beautiful gardens along the mesa slopes. ⊠ *Cultural Preservation Office, AZ 264, Kykotsmovi* ☎ *928/734–3613* ⊕ *www.nau.edu/~hcpo-p* ⊙ *Weekdays 8:30–5.*

EN ROUTE **Coal Canyon.** Beyond Hotevilla, AZ 264 descends from Third Mesa, exits the Hopi Reservation, and crosses into Navajo territory, past Coal Canyon, where Native Americans have long mined coal from the dark seam just below the rim. The colorful mudstone, dark lines of coal, and bleached white rock have an eerie appearance, especially by the light of the moon. Twenty miles west of the canyon, at the junction of AZ 264 and U.S. 160, is the town of Moenkopi, the last Hopi outpost. Established as a farming community, it was settled by the descendants of former Oraibi residents.

NAVAJO NATION WEST

5

The Hopi Reservation is like a doughnut hole surrounded by the Navajo Nation. If you approach the Grand Canyon from U.S. 89, via Flagstaff, north of the Wupatki National Monument, you'll find two significant sites in the western portions of the Navajo Reservation, the Cameron Trading Post and Tuba City (which also partly occupies Hopi land). Situated 45 miles west of the Hopi town of Hotevilla, Tuba City is a good stopover if you're traveling east to the Hopi Mesas or northeast to Page.

At Cameron, a turnoff point for the South Rim of the Grand Canyon, the Cameron Trading Post was built in 1916 and commemorates Ralph Cameron, a pre-statehood territorial-legislative delegate. The sheer walls of the Little Colorado River canyon about 10 miles west of U.S. 89 along AZ 64 are quite impressive, and also worth a stop.

TUBA CITY

52 miles northwest of Third Mesa on AZ 264.

Tuba City, believed to be named after a Hopi chief "Tsuve," has about 8,600 permanent residents and is the administrative center for the western portion of the Navajo Nation. Most of the population is Navajo, but there's also a small Hopi community—this is where you'll find the Moenkopi Legacy Inn, which acts as something of a general information center and tour desk for the Hopi tribe. In addition to two hotels and a few restaurants, this small town has a hospital, a bank, a trading post, and a movie theater. In mid- to late October Tuba City hosts the Western Navajo Fair, a celebration combining traditional Navajo song and dance with a parade, pageant, and countless arts-and-crafts exhibits.

GETTING HERE AND AROUND

Tuba City is one of the main base communities in the Navajo and Hopi region as well as a potential base for exploring either rim of the Grand Canyon from the east. The town lies about midway between Flagstaff and Page (80 miles from each) via U.S. 89 and U.S. 160, and 60 miles

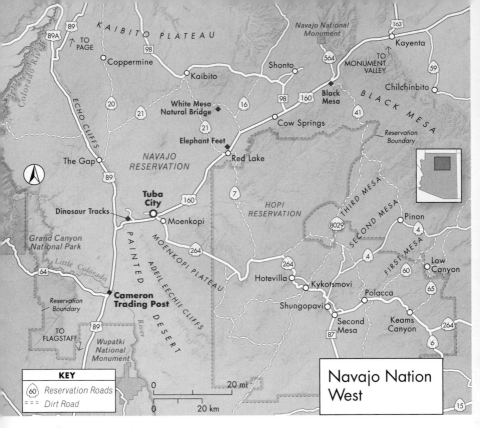

from the eastern entrance to the South Rim of the Grand Canyon via AZ 64, U.S. 89, and U.S. 160.

EXPLORING

FAMILY **Dinosaur Tracks.** About 5½ miles west of Tuba City, between mileposts 316 and 317 on U.S. 160, is a small sign for the Dinosaur Tracks. It's free to see these tracks that a dilophosaurus—a carnivorous bipedal reptile over 10 feet tall—left in mud that turned to sandstone. Ask the locals about guiding you to the nearby petroglyphs and freshwater springs.

Fodor's Choice **Explore Navajo Interactive Museum.** The tribe operates this enlightening ★ 7,000-square-foot museum, which is set inside a geodesic dome-shape structure that is meant to recall a traditional Navajo hogan. Inside the dome is a vast trove of artifacts, photos, artwork, and memorabilia. One of the more poignant exhibits tells of the infamous "Long Walk" of 1864, when the U.S. military forced the Navajo to leave their native lands and march to an encampment at Fort Sumner, New Mexico, where they were confined for more than four years. Admission also includes entry to the small **Navajo Code Talkers Memorial Museum** in the back of the Tuba City Trading Post next door. Both facilities are adjacent to the Quality Inn Navajo Nation. ⊠ *10 N. Main*

St., at Moenave St. ☎ *928/640–0684* 🌐 *www.explorenavajo.com* 🎟 *$9* 🕒 *Mon.–Sat. 8–6, Sun. noon–6.*

Painted Desert. The junction of U.S. 160 with U.S. 89, 4 miles west of the Dinosaur Tracks, is one of the most colorful regions of the Painted Desert, with amphitheaters of maroon, orange, and red rocks facing west; it's especially glorious at sunset.

Tuba City Trading Post. The octagonal store, founded in the early 1870s, sells groceries and authentic, reasonably priced Navajo rugs, pottery, baskets, and jewelry—it's adjacent to the Quality Inn Navajo Nation and Explore Navajo Museum. ✉ *Main St. at Moenave Rd.* ☎ *928/283–5441.*

WHERE TO EAT

$$ SOUTHWESTERN

🍴 **Hogan's Restaurant.** The fare at this spot adjacent to the Quality Inn Navajo Nation is mostly Southwestern and American, but the kitchen also serves a few basic Mexican and Navajo dishes. Highlights include tasty barbecue ribs, honey-glazed ham, and herb-roasted chicken. The chicken enchiladas and beef tamales are also quite good. Breakfast is served, too. [$] *Average main: $13* ✉ *10 Main St.* ☎ *928/283–5260* 🌐 *www.qualityinntubacity.com.*

$ AMERICAN

🍴 **Tuuvi Café.** This casual spot inside the largest truck stop and travel center in the region serves simple but well-prepared Southwestern and American food, from Native fry bread tacos to charbroiled burgers. There's always a stew of the day—perhaps corn-squash-and-mutton, or green-chile-and-chicken—and homemade peach pie is a dessert specialty. Noteworthy, too, are the hearty breakfasts, such as chicken-fried steak with eggs, and the Hopi Special of eggs, bacon or Spam, and homemade biscuits and gravy. [$] *Average main: $7* ✉ *U.S. 160 (Navajo Trail), at AZ 264* ☎ *928/283–4374* 🌐 *www.experiencehopi.com/tuuvicafe.html.*

WHERE TO STAY

$$ HOTEL FAMILY Fodor's Choice ★

🏨 **Moenkopi Legacy Inn & Suites.** Operated by the Hopi tribe and situated across from the Tuuvi Travel Center, this striking, contemporary hotel contains light-filled, boldly colored rooms with flat-screen TVs, work desks, and coffeemakers. **Pros:** high-quality furnishings and linens; pool is perfect spot to end a day of hiking; hotel offers guided tours to nearby Hopi villages. **Cons:** no restaurant on site (although the Hopi-run Tuuvi Café across the street and there's a Denny's next door); at a busy intersection. [$] *Rooms from: $139* ✉ *U.S. 160 at AZ 264* ☎ *928/283–4500* 🌐 *www.experiencehopi.com* 🛏 *84 rooms, 16 suites* 🍽 *Breakfast.*

$ HOTEL

🏨 **Quality Inn Navajo Nation.** Tuba City's longest-running hotel has upgraded its rooms in an effort to better compete with the snazzy Moenkopi Legacy Inn down the street, but it's still a pretty run-of-the-mill property. **Pros:** rooms have attractive Navajo-style prints and art; Navajo museum and trading post are across parking lot; dining on site. **Cons:** rates are a little high for what you get; an older property. [$] *Rooms from: $112* ✉ *10 N. Main St., at Moenave Rd.* ☎ *928/283–4545, 800/644–8383* 🌐 *www.qualityinn.com* 🛏 *78 rooms, 2 suites* 🍽 *Breakfast.*

SHOPPING

Native American swap meet. Bargain hunters can find great deals on jewelry, jewelry-making supplies, semiprecious stones, rugs, pottery, and other arts and crafts behind the To'Nanees'Dizi (formerly called Tuba City) Chapter House, near the town's transfer station, every Friday from 8 am. There are also food concessions and booths selling herbs. ⊠ *Edgewater Dr. and Peshlaki Ave., beside To'Nanees'Dizi Chapter House.*

CAMERON TRADING POST

25 miles southwest of Tuba City on U.S. 89.

Cameron Trading Post and Motel, established in 1916 overlooking a spectacular gorge and vintage suspension bridge, is one of the few remaining authentic trading posts in the Southwest. A convenient stop if you're driving from the Hopi Mesas to the Grand Canyon, it has reasonably priced dining, lodging, camping, and shopping.

GETTING HERE AND AROUND

The trading post is along the main highway (U.S. 89) between Flagstaff and Page and just 30 miles from the eastern entrance to the South Rim of the Grand Canyon.

WHERE TO STAY

$ 🖾 **Cameron Trading Post.** At the turnoff for the western entrance to the
HOTEL   Grand Canyon's South Rim, this trading post dates back to 1916 and contains handsome Southwestern-style rooms with carved-oak furniture, tile baths, and balconies overlooking the Colorado River. **Pros:** impressive collection of Southwestern art in the trading post gallery and gift shop; restaurant serves Native American specialties and American favorites; historic lodging with campground next door. **Cons:** high traffic volume; occasional highway noise; somewhat remote. $ *Rooms from: $99* ⊠ *466 U.S. 89* 🕾 *928/679–2231, 800/338–7385* ⊕ *www. camerontradingpost.com* ➳ *62 rooms, 4 suites* ⦿⏐*No meals.*

SHOPPING

Navajo Arts and Crafts Enterprises. Fine authentic Navajo products are sold at this outlet of the Navajo Arts and Crafts Enterprises, open since 1941. ⊠ *U.S. 89 at AZ 64* 🕾 *928/679–2244* ⊕ *www.gonavajo.com.*

**▌EN
ROUTE**

As you proceed toward Kayenta, 22 miles northeast of Tuba City on U.S. 160, you'll come to the tiny community of Red Lake. Off to the left of the highway is a geologic phenomenon known as **Elephant Feet.** These massive eroded-sandstone buttes offer a great family photo opportunity: pose under the enormous columns. Northwest of here at the end of a graded dirt road in Navajo backcountry is **White Mesa Natural Bridge,** a massive arch of white sandstone that extends from the edge of White Mesa. The long **Black Mesa** plateau runs for about 15 miles along U.S. 160. Above the prominent escarpments of this land formation, mining operations—a major source of revenue for the Navajo Nation—delve into the more than 20 billion tons of coal deposited there.

MONUMENT VALLEY

The magnificent Monument Valley stretches to the northeast of Kayenta into Utah. At a base altitude of about 5,500 feet, the sprawling, arid expanse was once populated by Ancestral Puebloan people (more popularly known by the Navajo word *Anasazi*, which means both "ancient ones" and "ancient enemies") and in the last few centuries has been home to generations of Navajo farmers. The soaring red buttes, eroded mesas, deep canyons, and naturally sculpted rock formations of Monument Valley are easy to enjoy on a leisurely drive.

> **WORD OF MOUTH**
>
> "If you can get to Monument Valley on the afternoon before spending a night in Kayenta, you could do a tour that would include sunset and then have plenty of time the next day to get to Page, perhaps with a stop at Antelope canyon on the way. Check what time sunset is when you go and be aware that Page does not do daylight savings time as it is on Arizona time, but the Navajo parks do." –emalloy

At U.S. 163 and the Monument Valley entrance is a street of disheveled buildings called Vendor Village. Here you can purchase trinkets and souvenirs; bartering is perfectly acceptable and expected.

KAYENTA

75 miles northeast of Tuba City, on U.S. 160, 22 miles south of Monument Valley.

Kayenta, a small and rather dusty town with a couple of convenience stores, three hotels, and a hospital, is a good base for exploring nearby Monument Valley Navajo Tribal Park and the Navajo National Monument. The Burger King in town has an excellent "Navajo Code Talker" exhibit, with lots of memorabilia relating to this heroic World War II marine group.

GETTING HERE AND AROUND

Kayenta is the first sizable Arizona community you reach if driving to the Navajo Nation via the Four Corners on U.S. 160 or U.S. 163.

EXPLORING

FAMILY **Navajo Cultural Center of Kayenta.** Take a self-guided walking tour through the Navajo Cultural Center of Kayenta, which includes the small Shadehouse Museum and a 2-acre outdoor cultural park. The museum is designed to resemble an authentic shade house (these wood-frame, rather crude, structures are used to shelter sheepherders in the region's often unforgiving high desert). Inside, visitors will find an extensive collection of Navajo Code Talkers memorabilia and local artwork, as well as exhibits on the beliefs and traditions that have shaped North America's largest Native American tribe. As you walk through the grounds of the cultural park, note the different types of traditional hogans and sweat lodges. ⊠ *U.S. 160 between Hampton Inn and Burger King* ☎ *928/697–3170* ⊒ *Free* ⊘ *Daily 7 am–sunset.*

WHERE TO EAT

$ ✕ **Amigo Cafe.** The tables are packed with locals who frequent this small
SOUTHWESTERN establishment, where everything is made from scratch. The delicious
fry bread is the real draw. If you've never had a Navajo taco or Navajo
hamburger, this is a good place to be initiated. The café also serves
excellent Mexican fare and traditional American dishes. Dine on the
adobe-walled patio in warm weather. $ *Average main: $9* ⊠ *U.S. 163,
just north of U.S. 160* ☎ *928/697–8448* ☉ *Closed Sun.*

$$ ✕ **Reuben Heflin Restaurant.** Hampton Inn hotels aren't known for their
AMERICAN restaurants, but this attractive spot just off the lobby serves the best food
in town. Upholstered Navajo-print chairs with rustic lodgepole frames,
hammered-tin sconces, a wood-beam ceiling, and a mammoth adobe
fireplace set an inviting mood for the American fare with a regional
bent. The Mazalon club sandwich (ham, turkey, bacon, lettuce, and
tomato in a Navajo taco) is a local favorite, but also consider rosemary-
citrus chicken, New York steak with grilled shrimp, fajitas, and black-
bean and mesquite-chicken pizzas. $ *Average main: $17* ⊠ *Hampton
Inn, U.S. 160* ☎ *928/697–3170* ☉ *No lunch mid-Oct.–mid-Mar.*

WHERE TO STAY

$$ ☷ **Hampton Inn of Kayenta.** This warm and inviting hotel is the best
HOTEL accommodation in Kayenta, although it's much like any other hotel in
FAMILY the chain except for its unusually good restaurant and Navajo-inspired
Fodor'sChoice design. **Pros:** clean and updated rooms; welcoming staff; excellent res-
★ taurant. **Cons:** books up many weeks in advance in summer; pricey
for a Hampton Inn; on busy, unattractive stretch of road. $ *Rooms
from: $169* ⊠ *U.S. 160* ☎ *928/697–3170* ⊕ *www.hamptoninn.hilton.
com* ⤳ *73 rooms* ❑ *Breakfast.*

$$ ☷ **Wetherill Inn.** This clean but very basic two-story, red-tile-roofed
HOTEL motel, located in an area with few lodging options, has Southwestern
décor and plain but new furnishings. **Pros:** a little closer to Monu-
ment Valley than other properties in Kayenta; well-kept guest rooms.
Cons: bland setting; rates a little high for such basic accommodations.
$ *Rooms from: $140* ⊠ *1000 U.S. 163* ☎ *928/697–3231* ⊕ *www.
wetherill-inn.com* ⤳ *54 rooms* ❑ *Breakfast.*

MONUMENT VALLEY NAVAJO TRIBAL PARK

24 miles northeast of Kayenta, off U.S. 163.

Even first-time visitors to Monument Valley typically recognize the
otherworldly landscape of red-rock towers and buttes—the landscape
has appeared in countless Hollywood feature films. Straddling the Ari-
zona/Utah border, the Monument Valley Navajo Tribal Park contains a
17-mile drive through this dramatic scenery as well as one of the most
beautifully situated hotels in Arizona.

GETTING HERE AND AROUND

It's impossible not to drive slowly on this park's bumpy roads, which
are best conquered with an SUV or all-wheel-drive vehicle (especially
during rainy times of year), but if you take your time and exercise cau-
tion, you can make the entire drive in a conventional car. If in doubt,

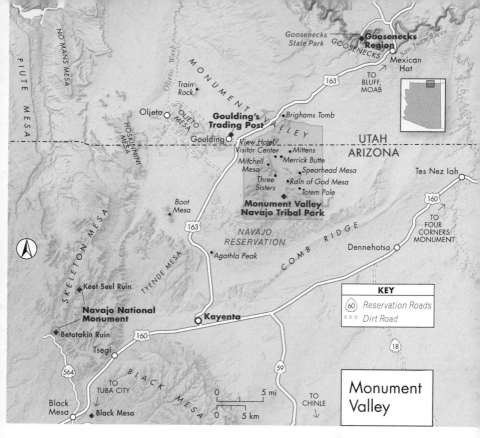

Monument Valley

inquire at the drive's entrance gate. Call ahead for road conditions in winter. The park is just off U.S. 163 north of the Arizona/Utah border and very well marked.

EXPLORING

Monument Valley Navajo Tribal Park. For generations, the Navajo have grown crops and herded sheep in Monument Valley, considered to be one of the most scenic and mesmerizing destinations in the Navajo Nation. Within Monument Valley lies the 30,000-acre Monument Valley Navajo Tribal Park, home as well to the View Hotel, where eons of wind and rain have carved the mammoth red-sandstone monoliths into memorable formations. The monoliths, which jut hundreds of feet above the desert floor, stand on the horizon like sentinels, frozen in time and unencumbered by electric wires, telephone poles, or fences—a scene virtually unchanged for centuries. These are the very same nostalgic images so familiar to movie buffs who recall the early Western films of John Wayne. A 17-mile self-guided driving tour on an extremely rough dirt road (there's only one road, so you can't get lost) passes the memorable **Mittens** and **Totem Pole** formations, among others. Also be sure to walk (15 minutes round-trip) from North Window around the end of Cly Butte for the views. ⊠ *Monument Valley Rd., off U.S. 163, just north of AZ/UT border, Monument Valley, Utah* ☎ *435/727–5874* ⊕ *www.navajonationparks.org.*

DID YOU KNOW?

If Monument Valley looks familiar, it probably should. Scenes from many movies, including *How the West Was Won, Forrest Gump, Stagecoach, 2001: A Space Odyssey,* and *Wind Talkers,* have been filmed here.

org/htm/monumentvalley.htm ▨ *$5* ⊙ *May–Sept., daily 6 am–8 pm; Oct.–Apr., daily 8–5.*

Monument Valley Visitor Center. The handsome center contains an extensive crafts shop and exhibits devoted to ancient and modern Native American history, including a display on the World War II Navajo Code Talkers. Most of the independent guided group tours, which leave from the center, use enclosed vans and charge about $75 per person for 2½ to 3 hours; private tours are also often available, starting around $150 for up to two people. You can generally

find Navajo guides—who will escort you to places that you are not allowed to visit on your own—in the center or at the booths in the parking lot. It adjoins the stunning View Hotel (and restaurant), which sits on a gradual rise overlooking the valley and its magnificent red-rock monoliths, with big-sky views in every direction. ⊠ *Monument Valley Rd., off U.S. 163, just north of AZ/UT border, 24 miles north of Kayenta, Monument Valley Tribal Park, Utah* ☎ *435/727–5874* ⊕ *www. navajonationparks.org* ▨ *$5 (tours extra)* ⊙ *May–Sept., daily 6 am– 8 pm; Oct.–Apr., daily 8–5.*

WHERE TO EAT AND STAY

$$
SOUTHWESTERN
Fodor's Choice
★

✕ **View Restaurant.** Connected to the View Hotel through a second-floor breezeway, this airy space comprises a few high-ceilinged rooms with massive plate-glass windows framing mesmerizing views of the valley—in warm weather you can dine outside on a terrace, awed by the same panorama. Navajo rugs and local art hang on the walls above the light-wood tables and chairs, and the tribal visitor center's extensive curio shop is attached. The food has continued to improve over the years as more-experienced chefs have come aboard, adding fresh, local ingredients, Navajo influences, and an artful flourish to typically Southwestern fare. Consider red chile–posole stew, the Navajo taco sampler plate (comprising four minitacos), thick steaks, and the like. There's also a smaller self-serve section, where you can grab sandwiches and light snacks. $ *Average main: $18* ⊠ *Monument Valley Rd., off U.S. 163 jusrt north of AZ/UT border, 24 miles north of Kayenta* ☎ *435/727– 5555* ⊕ *www.monumentvalleyview.com.*

$$$
HOTEL
Fodor's Choice
★

▥ **View Hotel.** The Navajo tribe operates this sleek red-stucco hotel, the only lodging inside Monument Valley Navajo Tribal Park and one of the most spectacularly situated hotels in the Southwest, with astounding vistas that help the hotel live up to its name. **Pros:** only hotel in the park; design reflects the surroundings and Navajo culture; unbelievable panoramas from every room; eco-conscious bath products, appliances, and buildings standards; rates are similar to or less than run-of-the-mill hotels nearby. **Cons:** books up weeks in advance in summer; Wi-Fi

5

doesn't reach all rooms. [$] *Rooms from: $219* ✉ *Monument Valley Rd., off U.S. 163 just north of AZ/UT border, 24 miles north of Kayenta* ☎ *435/727–5555* 🌐 *www.monumentvalleyview.com* 🛏 *96 rooms* 🍴 *No meals.*

SPORTS AND THE OUTDOORS

TOURS

Black's Monument Valley Tours. A wide variety of tour options—from jeep and horseback adventures to hiking—are available with this respected tour operator. You can also book an overnight stay in a Navajo hogan. ✉ *Monument Valley, Utah* ☎ *928/429–1959* 🌐 *www.blacksmonumentvalleytours.com* 🎟 *From $75/person.*

Monument Valley Tours. Some of the jeep tours on offer include entertainment and outdoor barbecues, and custom hikes into the valley as well. The all-day, 60-mile Monument Valley and Mystery Valley tour, which includes lunch, is especially popular. ☎ *435/727–3313* 🌐 *www.monumentvalleytours.net* 🎟 *From $75/person.*

Sacred Monument Tours. Native guides lead hiking, jeep, photography, and horseback-riding tours into Monument Valley. ✉ *Monument Valley, Utah* ☎ *435/727–3218, 435/459–2501* 🌐 *www.monumentvalley.net* 🎟 *From $68/person.*

Simpson's Trailhandler Tours. This operator offers four-wheel-drive jeep trips, photography tours, and guided hikes, plus the chance to stay overnight in a traditional Navajo hogan. If you don't have time or interest for one of the several-hour hiking tours, Simpson's can also customize a fairly easy one-hour guided hike, tailored to your interest and skill level. ✉ *Monument Valley, Utah* ☎ *435/727–3362, 888/723–6236* 🌐 *www.trailhandlertours.com* 🎟 *From $35/person.*

OFF THE BEATEN PATH

Four Corners Monument. An inlaid brass plaque marks the only point in the United States where four states meet: Arizona, New Mexico, Colorado, and Utah. Despite the Indian wares and booths selling greasy food, there's not much else to do here but pay a fee and stay long enough to snap a photo; you'll see many a twisted tourist trying to get an arm or a leg in each state. The monument is a 75-mile drive from Kayenta and is administered by the Navajo Nation Parks and Recreation Department. ✉ *4 Corners Rd., 7 miles northwest of the U.S. 160 and U.S. 64 junction, Teec Nos Pos* ☎ *928/871–6647 for Navajo Parks and Recreation Dept.* 🌐 *www.navajonationparks.org/htm/fourcorners.htm* 🎟 *$3* ⏲ *Oct.–Apr., daily 8–5; May–Sept., daily 8–7.*

GOOSENECKS REGION, UTAH

Fodor's Choice ★

33 miles north of Monument Valley Navajo Tribal Park, on U.S. 163.

Monument Valley's scenic route, U.S. 163, continues from Arizona into Utah, where the land is crossed, east to west, by a stretch of the San Juan River known as the Goosenecks—named for its myriad twists and curves. This barren, erosion-blasted gorge has a stark beauty, and is a well-known take-out point for white-water runners on the San Juan, a river that vacationing sleuths will recognize as the setting of many of Tony Hillerman's Jim Chee mystery novels. The small village of Bluff (population 260), which lies at the northeastern end of the region, has an excellent hotel and restaurant, and is a good base for exploring Goosenecks and the northern reaches of Monument Valley.

GETTING HERE AND AROUND

The scenic overlook for the Goosenecks is reached by turning west from U.S. 163 onto UT 261, 4 miles north of the tiny community of **Mexican Hat,** then proceeding on UT 261 for 1 mile to a directional sign at the road's junction with UT 316. Turn left onto UT 316 and proceed 4 miles to the vista-point parking lot. To take in spectacular scenery, drive northeast on U.S. 163 Kayenta through Monument Valley all the way past Mexican Hat to Bluff, then turn south on U.S. 191 back into Arizona, and then turn west onto U.S. 160 back to Kayenta; the 140-mile loop takes three hours without stops, but allow a full day for breaks and lunch in Bluff.

WHERE TO EAT AND STAY

$$ ECLECTIC Fodor's Choice ★ 🍴 **Twin Rocks Cafe.** It's hard to miss this low-slung, timber-frame roadhouse-style restaurant in Bluffs—it's tucked beneath a sandstone ridge crowned by two rock pillars that look as though they might topple in a bad storm. Here you'll find the most varied menu and consistently delicious food in the Monument Valley region. It's well worth the 40-mile drive from Monument Valley Tribal Park for surprisingly excellent barbecue ribs and brisket for this part of the world, plus pizzas (using Navajo fry bread), country-fried steaks, and French toast breakfasts. An extensively stocked trading post lies at one end of the dining room, and there's seating on the patio during the warmer months. [$] *Average main: $13* ✉ *913 E. Navajo Twins Dr., off U.S. 191, Bluff* ☎ *435/672–2341* 🌐 *www.twinrockscafe.com.*

$$ HOTEL Fodor's Choice ★ 🏨 **Desert Rose Inn and Cabins.** This nicely maintained motel with a handsome timber-frame facade and panoramic views of the surrounding red rocks is in Bluffs, 25 miles northeast of Mexican Hat; it's an excellent base for exploring Goosenecks State Park, the northern end of Monument Valley, and even Canyonlands National Park, to the north. **Pros:** family-owned and run by a great staff; scenic setting; good base if you're coming from points north or east. **Cons:** a 40-minute drive to Monument Valley Tribal Park (though a beautiful drive). [$] *Rooms from: $140* ✉ *701 W. U.S. 191, Bluff* ☎ *435/672–2303, 888/475–7673* 🌐 *www.desertroseinn.com* 🛏 *30 rooms, 6 suites* 🍽 *No meals.*

$ HOTEL 🏨 **San Juan Inn & Trading Post.** This quirky motel's well-maintained, Southwestern-style, rustic rooms overlook the San Juan River in Mexican Hat, Utah, and the setting, against the red rocks, is quite inspiring, even if accommodations have few frills. **Pros:** magnificent setting; affordable rooms; parking is right outside your room. **Cons:** basic room décor—it's all about the setting. [$] *Rooms from: $94* ✉ *U.S. 163, at the San Juan River, Mexican Hat* ☎ *800/447–2022, 435/683–2220* 🌐 *www.sanjuaninn.net* 🛏 *36 rooms* 🍽 *No meals.*

5

GOULDING'S TRADING POST

2 miles west of entrance road to Monument Valley Navajo Tribal Park, off U.S. 163 on Indian Hwy. 42.

Established in 1924 by Harry Goulding and his wife "Mike," this trading post provided a place where Navajos could exchange livestock and handmade goods for necessities. Goulding's is probably best known, though, for being used as a headquarters by director John Ford when he filmed the Western classic *Stagecoach*. Today the compound has a lodge, restaurant, museum, gift shop, grocery store, and campground. The Goulding Museum displays Native American artifacts and Goulding family memorabilia, as well as an excellent multimedia show about Monument Valley.

WHERE TO STAY

$$$ HOTEL Fodor's Choice ★ **Goulding's Lodge.** Nestled beneath a massive red-rock monolith, this two-level property affords spectacular views of Monument Valley from each room's private balcony. **Pros:** right in heart of Monument Valley; incredibly peaceful; indoor pool open all year. **Cons:** remote location; not cheap; books up weeks in advance in summer. [$] *Rooms from: $222* ✉ *Monument Valley Rd. (U.S. 163 just north of state border), 24 miles north of Kayenta, Monument Valley, Utah* ☎ *435/727–3231, 800/727–3231* 🌐 *www.gouldings.com* 🛏 *62 rooms, 8 suites* 🍴 *No meals.*

NAVAJO NATIONAL MONUMENT

53 miles southwest of Goulding's Trading Post, 21 miles west of Kayenta.

It takes a little effort to reach this remote national monument designated on the site of two prominent, 13th-century pueblos, each with well over 100 rooms. You can sign up for a guided ranger-led hike to both ruins or set out on a handful of shorter treks on your own.

GETTING HERE AND AROUND

From Kayenta, take U.S. 160 southwest to AZ 564 and follow signs 9 miles north to monument.

AZ 564 turns north off U.S. 160 at the Black Mesa gas station and convenience store, and leads to the visitor center. No food, gasoline, or hotel lodging is available at the monument, but Kayenta is about a 40-minute drive.

The visitor center houses a small museum, exhibits of prehistoric pottery, and a good crafts shop. Free campground and picnic areas are nearby, and rangers sometimes present campfire programs in summer.

EXPLORING

Fodor's Choice ★ **Navajo National Monument.** Two unoccupied 13th-century cliff pueblos, Betatakin and Keet Seel, stand under the overhanging cliffs of Tsegi Canyon. The largest ancient dwellings in Arizona, these stone-and-mortar complexes were built by Ancestral Puebloans, obviously for permanent occupancy, but abandoned after less than half a century.

The well-preserved, 135-room **Betatakin** (Navajo for "ledge house") is a cluster of cliff dwellings from AD 1250 that seem to hang in midair before a sheer sandstone wall. When discovered in 1907 by a passing American rancher, the apartments were full of baskets, pottery, and preserved grains and ears of corn—as if the occupants had been chased away in the middle of a meal. For an impressive view of Betatakin, walk to the rim overlook about ½ mile from the visitor center. Ranger-led tours (a 5-mile, four-hour, strenuous round-trip hike including a 700-foot descent into the canyon) leave once or twice a day from late May to early September, and on weekends (weather-permitting) the rest of the year. No reservations are accepted; groups of no more than 25 form on a first-come, first-served basis.

Keet Seel (Navajo for "broken pottery") is also in good condition in a serene location, with 160 rooms and five kivas dating from AD 950. Explorations of Keet Seel, which lies at an elevation of 7,000 feet and is 8½ miles from the visitor center on foot, are restricted: only 20 people are allowed to visit per day, and only between late May and early September, when a ranger is present at the site. A permit—which also allows campers to stay overnight nearby—is required. ■TIP→ Trips to Keet Seel are very popular, so reservations are taken up to two months in advance. Anyone who suffers from vertigo might want to avoid this trip: the trail leads down a 1,100-foot, near-vertical rock face. ⊠ *AZ 564, 10 miles north of junction with U.S. 160, Shonto* ☎ *928/672–2700* ⊕ *www.nps.gov/nava* ⊠ *Free* ☉ *Late May–mid-Sept., daily 8–5:30; mid-Sept.–late May, daily 9–5.*

SPORTS AND THE OUTDOORS
HIKING
Navajo National Monument Hiking Trails. Hiking is the best way for adventurous souls to see the Navajo National Monument. It's a fairly strenuous 5-mile hike to the Betatakin sites, permissible only with a guide from the visitor center, but if you're fit, it's well worth it to visit one of the best-preserved ancient dwellings in the Southwest. It's free, but the trail is open daily only during the summer months (May through September), and on weekends the rest of the year, when weather permits; there are two Betatakin hikes each morning. Call ahead to make a reservation—it's a good idea to reserve at least four weeks in advance. There are also three shorter self-guided hikes, open year-round, leaving from the visitor center. All are between a half mile and a full mile round-trip. The Sandal Trail leads to a viewpoint overlooking the Betatakin/Talastima cliff dwellings, and the Canyon Trail ends at a historic ranger station and takes in expansive views of Tsegi Canyon. ⊠ *Shonto* ☎ *928/672–2700* ⊕ *www.nps.gov/nava.*

GLEN CANYON DAM AND LAKE POWELL

Lake Powell is the heart of the huge Glen Canyon National Recreation Area, which at 1.25 million acres is about the size of Grand Canyon National Park. Created by the barrier of Glen Canyon Dam in the Colorado River, Lake Powell is ringed by red cliffs that twist off into 96 major canyons and countless inlets (most accessible only by boat) with huge, red-sandstone buttes randomly jutting from the sapphire waters. It extends through terrain so rugged it was the last major area of the United States to be mapped. You could spend 30 years exploring the lake and still not experience everything there is to see. In the 1990s, the Sierra Club and Glen Canyon Institute started a movement to drain the lake to restore water-filled Glen Canyon, which some believe was more spectacular than the Grand Canyon, but these efforts failed to gain significant momentum, and the lake is likely to be around for years to come.

South of Lake Powell the landscape gives way to **Echo Cliffs,** orange-sandstone formations rising 1,000 feet and more above the highway in places. At **Bitter Springs** the road ascends the cliffs and provides a spectacular view of the 9,000-square-mile Arizona Strip to the west and the 3,000-foot Vermilion Cliffs to the northwest.

PAGE

90 miles west of the Navajo National Monument, 136 miles north of Flagstaff on U.S. 89.

Built in 1957 as a Glen Canyon Dam construction camp, Page is now a tourist spot and a popular base for day trips to Lake Powell; it's also become a major point of entry to the Navajo Nation. The nearby Vermilion Cliffs are where the California condor, an endangered species, has been successfully reintroduced into the wild. The town's human population of about 7,310 makes it the largest community in far-northern Arizona, and each year more than 3 million people come to play at Lake Powell.

GETTING HERE AND AROUND

Most of the motels, restaurants, and shopping centers are concentrated along **Lake Powell Boulevard,** the name given to U.S. 89 as it loops through the business district.

The only airline that offers service directly to northeastern Arizona is Great Lakes Airlines, which flies into Page Municipal Airport (PGA) from Phoenix and Prescott, as well as from Las Vegas, Denver, and Farmington, New Mexico.

ESSENTIALS

Transportation Contacts Great Lakes Airlines ☏ *800/554–5111* ⊕ *www. greatlakesav.com.* **Page Municipal Airport** ⊠ *238 10th Ave.* ☏ *928/645–4232* ⊕ *www.cityofpage.org/airport.*

Visitor Information Page/Lake Powell Tourism Bureau. There's a visitor information center inside the Powell Museum, at 6 North Lake Powell Boulevard. ☏ *888/261–7243, 928/645–9496* ⊕ *www.visitpagelakepowell.com.*

EXPLORING

John Wesley Powell Memorial Museum. At the corner of North Navajo Drive and Lake Powell Boulevard is the John Wesley Powell Memorial Museum, whose namesake led the first known expeditions down the Green River and the rapids-choked Colorado through the Grand Canyon between 1869 and 1872. Powell mapped and kept detailed records of his trips, naming the Grand Canyon and many other geographic points of interest in northern Arizona. Artifacts from his expeditions are

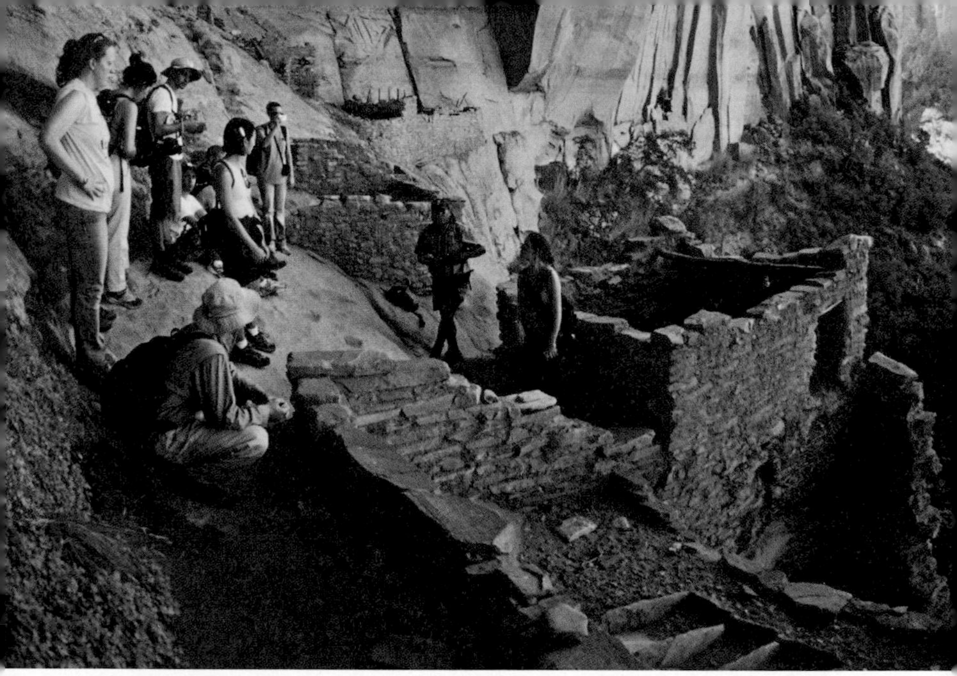

Ancestral Puebloans' construction methods and their mysterious fate are worth pondering during a visit to Navajo National Monument.

displayed in the museum. The museum also doubles as the town's visitor information center. A travel desk dispenses information and allows you to book boating tours, raft trips, scenic flights, accommodations in Page, or Antelope Canyon tours. When you sign up for tours here, concessionaires give a donation to the nonprofit museum with no extra charge to you. ✉ *6 N. Lake Powell Blvd.* ☎ *928/645–9496* 🌐 *www.powellmuseum.org* 🎟 *$5* 🕑 *Apr.–Oct., Mon.–Sat. 9–5; Nov.–Mar., weekdays 9–5.*

WHERE TO EAT

$$ AMERICAN 🍴 **Dam Bar and Grille.** The vaguely industrial-looking décor is quite urbane for this part of the world, and the kitchen turns out filling, well-prepared food. Consider the 8-ounce cowboy steak topped with sautéed mushrooms and Swiss cheese, the smoked baby back ribs, the Southwest Cobb salad, or the burger topped with bacon, cheddar, and barbecue sauce. The Dam also operates two adjacent establishments: the very good Blue Buddha Sushi Lounge and Blue, a coffeehouse and bakery by day and a wine and tapas bar in the evenings. These are all popular nightlife options as well. [$] *Average main: $17* ✉ *644 N. Navajo Dr.* ☎ *928/645–2161* 🌐 *www.damplaza.com.*

$$ MEXICAN 🍴 **El Tapatio.** This small, casual cantina inside a modest-looking former fast-food restaurant is part of an affordable and consistently good chain. Take a seat in the simple but colorfully decorated dining room and peruse the astoundingly long menu, which reveals a mix of Americanized and authentic Mexican dishes, including a "cocktail" of shrimp, abalone, and octopus ceviche; charcoal-grilled *carne asada* (skirt steak); and *borrego ranchero* (grilled lamb with pico de gallo and guacamole).

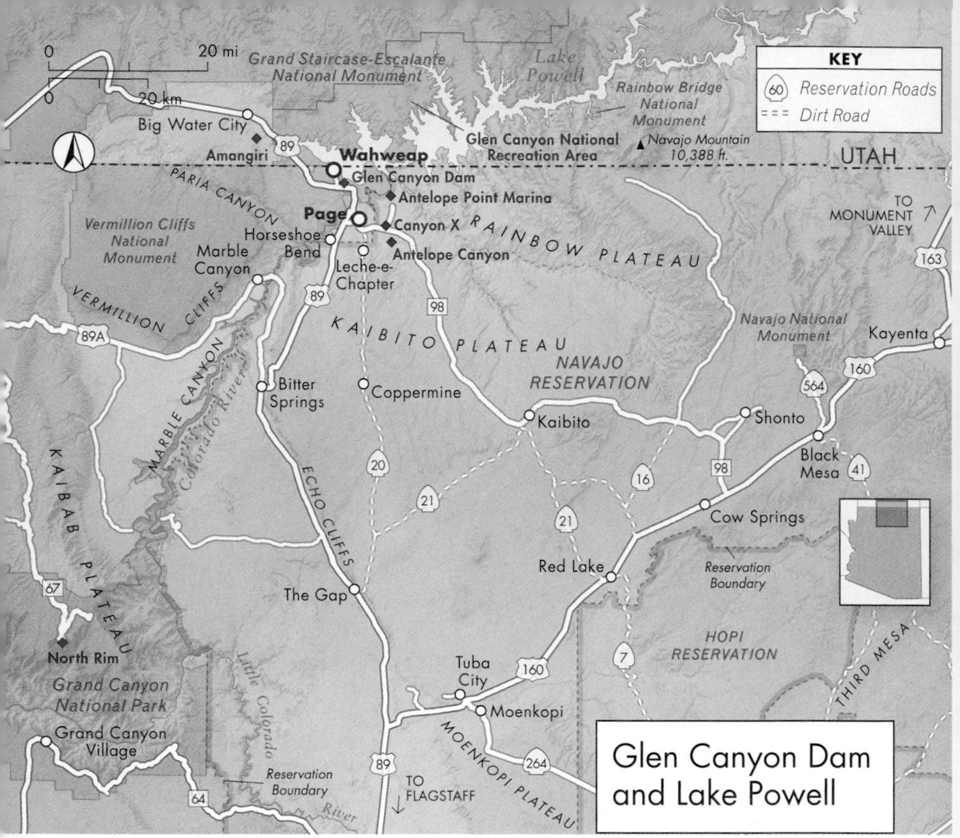

Glen Canyon Dam and Lake Powell

Mojitos, margaritas, and other colorful cocktails are served, too. $ *Average main: $12* ✉ *25 Lake Powell Blvd.* ☎ *928/645–4055.*

WHERE TO STAY

$$$ HOTEL 🏨 **Best Western Plus at Lake Powell.** This modern, three-story motel on a high bluff overlooking Glen Canyon Dam features dazzling views of the Vermilion Cliffs. **Pros:** excellent views; close to downtown shopping and dining; rates drop significantly late fall through late spring. **Cons:** run-of-the-mill décor and amenities don't merit the soaring summer high-season rates. $ *Rooms from: $229* ✉ *208 N. Lake Powell Blvd.* ☎ *928/645–5988, 888/794–2888* 🌐 *www.bestwestern.com* 🛏 *106 rooms, 26 suites* 🍴 *Breakfast.*

$$ B&B/INN 🏨 **Canyon Colors Bed and Breakfast.** Run by personable New England transplants Bev and Rich Jones, this desert-country B&B occupies a simple, modern house in a quiet residential neighborhood near downtown. **Pros:** personal attention; peaceful setting; central location. **Cons:** very small; need to book well ahead in summer. $ *Rooms from: $130* ✉ *225 S. Navajo Dr.* ☎ *928/645–5979* 🌐 *www.canyoncolors.com* 🛏 *3 rooms* 🍴 *Breakfast.*

$$$$ HOTEL 🏨 **Courtyard Page at Lake Powell.** Situated just below the stunning grounds of Lake Powell National Golf Course, Page's most upscale hotel boasts airy rooms with plush bedding, large TVs, and bathrooms

with marble accents. **Pros:** lovely setting by golf course; good restaurant; the best and most modern room amenities in town. **Cons:** uphill walk to downtown restaurants and shopping; restaurant closed for dinner during slower months; steep rates in July and August. [$] *Rooms from: $269* ✉ *600 Clubhouse Dr.* ☎ *928/645–5000, 877/905–4495* 🌐 *www.marriott.com* 🛏 *153 rooms* 🍴 *No meals.*

$$ HOTEL 🏨 **Lake Powell Days Inn & Suites.** It may be part of an uneven budget chain, but this particular Days Inn—an attractive Southwest-style building atop a plateau with expansive views—is the best among value-oriented accommodations in the region. **Pros:** many rooms have balconies; super-friendly staff; panoramic views. **Cons:** need a car to get to downtown shopping and restaurants; on a busy road at the edge of town; better rates than competitors but can still be pricey in summer. [$] *Rooms from: $154* ✉ *961 U.S. 89* ☎ *928/645–2800, 877/525–3769* 🌐 *www.daysinn.net* 🛏 *82 rooms* 🍴 *Breakfast.*

SHOPPING

There are numerous gift shops and clothing stores in the downtown area along Lake Powell Boulevard. There's a lot of junk, but you can find authentic Native American arts and crafts, too.

Big Lake Trading Post. At this post there is a gas station, convenience store, car wash, and coin laundry. ✉ *1505 Coppermine Rd., at AZ 98* ☎ *928/645–2404* 🌐 *www.biglaketradingpost.com.*

Fodor's Choice ★ **Blair's Dinnebito Trading Post.** Authentic Native American arts and crafts are only a small part of what this store, which has been around for more than half a century, sells. Need tack equipment, rodeo ropes, rugs, saddlery, or pottery? It's all here and reasonably priced. Wander upstairs and visit the Elijah & Claudia Blair collection and memorabilia rooms. ✉ *626 N. Navajo Dr.* ☎ *928/645–3008* 🌐 *www.blairstradingpost.com.*

SPORTS AND THE OUTDOORS

For water sports on Lake Powell, see Wahweap.

Glen Canyon Recreation Area. Check out the park website to help plan your Glen Canyon trip. ☎ *928/608–6200* 🌐 *www.nps.gov/glca.*

AIR TOURS

FAMILY Fodor's Choice ★ **Colorado River Discovery.** This respected outfitter offers waterborne tours, including a 5½-hour guided rafting excursion down a calm portion of the Colorado River on comfortable, motorized pontoon boats ($85). The scenery—multicolor-sandstone cliffs adorned with Native American petroglyphs—is spectacular. The trips are offered twice daily May through September, and once a day in March, April, October, and November. The company also offers full-day rowing trips along the river, using smaller boats maneuvered by well-trained guides ($161). These trips—offered Sunday, Monday, and Wednesday—are quieter and more low-key, and provide a more intimate brush with this magnificent body of water. The above prices exclude a $6-per-person river-use fee. And there's also a combination tour that includes rafting on the Colorado in the morning and kayaking on Lake Powell in the afternoon ($194), and a rafting tour through a slot canyon ($193). ✉ *130 6th Ave.* ☎ *888/522–6644* 🌐 *www.raftthecanyon.com* 🎫 *From $85/person.*

5

GOLF

Lake Powell National Golf Course. Wide fairways, tiered greens with some of the steepest holes in the Southwest, and a generous lack of hazards make for a pleasant golfing experience. From the fairways you can enjoy spectacular vistas of Glen Canyon Dam and Lake Powell. ⊠ *400 Clubhouse Dr., off U.S. 89* ☎ *928/645–2023* ⊕ *www. lakepowellgolfing.com* ⊠ *$52* ⟟ *18 holes, 7064 yds, par 72.*

HIKING

Glen Canyon Hike. This hike, a short walk from the parking lot down a flight of uneven rock steps, takes you to a viewpoint on the canyon rim high above the Colorado River, and provides fantastic views of the Colorado as it flows through Glen Canyon. ⊠ *Off U.S. 89* ✛ *To reach the parking lot, turn west on Scenic View Drive, 1½ miles south of Carl Hayden Visitor Center.*

Horse Shoe Bend Trail. The views along this hike are well worth the steep up-and-down paths and the bit of deep sand to maneuver. The trail leads up to a bird's-eye view of Glen Canyon and the Colorado River downstream from Glen Canyon Dam. There are some sheer drop-offs here, so watch children. To reach the trail, drive 4 miles south of Page on U.S. 89 and turn west (right) onto a blacktop road just south of mile marker 545. It's a ¾-mile hike from the parking area to the top of the canyon, and the entire hike can easily be done in an hour round-trip. *Difficult.* ⊠ *Off U.S. 89* ⊕ *www.lakepowell.com/media/225945/ HorseshoeBendTrailGuide.pdf.*

> ### LAKE POWELL FAST FACTS
>
> ■ Lake Powell is 185 miles long with nearly 2,000 miles of shoreline—longer than America's Pacific Coast.
>
> ■ This is the second-largest man-made lake in the nation and it took 17 years to fill.
>
> ■ The Glen Canyon Dam is a 710-foot-tall wall of concrete.

ANTELOPE CANYON

4 miles east of Page on the Navajo Reservation, on AZ 98.

It's saying a lot that in the blessedly beautiful swath of northeastern Arizona, Antelope Canyon is arguably the favorite destination of both professional and amateur photographers. Accessible only if accompanied by a licensed Navajo guide, Antelope Canyon is a narrow, red-sandstone slot canyon famous for the mesmerizing way sunlight filters through it.

GETTING HERE AND AROUND

Access to Antelope Canyon is restricted by the Navajo tribe to licensed tour operators. The tribe charges a $6-per-person fee, included in the price of tours offered by the licensed concessionaires in Page. The easiest way to book a tour is in town at the John Wesley Powell Memorial Museum Visitor Center; you pay nothing extra for the museum's service. If you'd like to go directly to the tour operators, you can do that, too; visit ⊕ *www.navajonationparks.org/htm/antelopecanyon.htm* for a list of approved companies. Most companies offer 1- to 1½-hour sightseeing tours for about $35 to $45, or longer photography tours

Houseboats are a unique lodging option; they're also great for exploring Lake Powell's almost 2,000 miles of shoreline.

for around $80. ■TIP→ The best time to see the canyon is between 8 am and 2 pm.

TOURS

Antelope Canyon Navajo Tours. One-hour sightseeing tours ($40) and two-hour photography tours ($80) are available at Antelope Canyon. The canyon's $6 admission fee is covered within the cost of the tour. ☎ 928/698–3384 ⊕ *www.navajotours.com* ✉ *From $40/person.*

Antelope Canyon Tours. For sightseers and photographers, there are several tours daily, from 8 am to 4:30 pm. Sightseeing tours run 90 minutes and cost $35 to $46; photo tours last two-and-a-half-hours, cost $80, and give both serious and amateur photographers the opportunity to wait for the right light to photograph the canyon and get basic information on equipment setup. ☎ 928/645–9102, 435/675–9109 ⊕ *www.antelopecanyon.com* ✉ *From $35/person.*

John Wesley Powell Memorial Museum. The visitor center in the museum offers 1½-hour tours and 2½-hour photography tours, which leave at different times throughout the morning and early afternoon. You can book online or by stopping at the museum. ☎ 928/645–9496 ⊕ *www.powellmuseum.org/tours.php* ✉ *From $35/person.*

Overland Canyon Tours. Navajo guide Charly Moore, through his company, Overland Canyon Tours, offers the only access to the isolated slot canyon known as Canyon X, on private property. Only one tour, which will include coverage of the canyon's history and geology, is given per day (departure times vary), and tours are offered by advance reservation only. Because the area is rugged, children aren't allowed and participants should have good physical mobility to climb crevasses and some rough terrain. The company also operates popular tours to Antelope Canyon, both during the day and at night, as well as several other photo-intensive excursions in the region. ☎ *928/608–4072* 🌐 *www.overlandcanyontours.com* 🎟 *From $37/person.*

EXPLORING

Fodor's Choice ★ **Antelope Canyon.** You've probably seen dozens of photographs of Antelope Canyon, a narrow, red-sandstone slot canyon with convoluted corkscrew formations, dramatically illuminated by light streaming down from above. And you're likely to see assorted shutterbugs waiting patiently for just the right shot of these colorful, photogenic rocks, which are actually petrified sand dunes. The best photos are taken at high noon, when light filters through the slot in the canyon surface. **■TIP→ Be prepared to protect your camera equipment against blowing dust.** ✉ *AZ 98, 3 miles east of Page* ☎ *928/698–2808* 🌐 *www.navajonationparks.org/htm/antelopecanyon.htm* 🎟 *$6* 🕒 *Mid-Mar.–Oct., daily 8–5; Nov.–mid-Mar., daily 9–3.*

WHERE TO EAT

$$ AMERICAN 🍴 **Ja'di' To'oh at Antelope Point Marina.** The floating, sandstone restaurant and lounge at the Navajo-operated Antelope Point Marina serves reliably well-prepared American food with contemporary accents—wood-fire pizzas, fish tacos, buffalo burgers, and filet mignon with garlic-herb butter—and has one of the region's better wine lists. As good as the food is, the dramatic dining room with soaring windows overlooking a red-rock-wall section of Lake Powell is what really makes this place special. It's a long walk from the parking area to the front door, but staff whisk visitors to and fro in golf carts. The restaurant's name is Navajo for "Antelope Springs." **■TIP→ Hours can vary a bit in the slower winter season—call ahead to make sure it's open before driving all the way from Page.** [$] *Average main: $17* ✉ *537 Marina Pkwy., end of Indian Hwy. 22B, off AZ 98, 9 miles northeast of Page* ☎ *928/645–5900* 🌐 *www.antelopepointlakepowell.com* 🕒 *Closed Mon.–Wed. in winter.*

SPORTS AND THE OUTDOORS

BOATING

Antelope Point Marina. About 5 miles north of AZ 98, opposite the turnoff for Antelope Canyon, the Navajo Nation built Antelope Point Marina in the early 2000s on a scenic canyon of Lake Powell. This impressive 27,000-square-foot floating village has 300 wet slips for houseboats and watercraft, a variety of boat and houseboat rentals, the very good Ja'di' To'oh restaurant and lounge, a seasonal ice-cream stand, a fishing dock, and a market. From here, boaters can access the other points along the lake, including the development at Wahweap. Eventually the Navajo plan to add luxury casitas and a Navajo Cultural Center to this dramatic compound. ✉ *End of Indian Rte. N22B, off AZ 98, 9 miles northeast of Page* ☎ *928/645–5900* 🌐 *www.antelopepointlakepowell.com.*

GLEN CANYON NATIONAL RECREATION AREA

1 mile north of Page on U.S. 89.
Roughly the same size as Grand Canyon National Park, this stunning recreation area takes in the easily accessible shores of Lake Powell close to Glen Canyon Dam as well as many square miles of rugged, remote lakefront and rock formations best visited by tour boat or houseboat.

GETTING HERE AND AROUND
Just off the highway at the north end of the bridge is the **Carl Hayden Visitor Center,** where you can learn about the controversial creation of Glen Canyon Dam and Lake Powell, enjoy panoramic views of both, and take guided tours of the dam ($5). To enter the visitor center you must go through a metal detector. Absolutely no bags or food are allowed inside, but cameras, wallets, and clear water bottles are welcome.

SLOT CANYONS

Slot canyons are unique to the Southwest. Carved through sandstone by wind and water, they're narrow at the top—some are only a foot wide on the surface—and wider at the bottom, which can be more than 100 feet below ground level. The play of light as it filters down through the slot onto the sandstone walls makes them remarkable subjects for photographs, but they're dangerous, particularly during the summer rainy season when flash floods can rush through them and sweep away an unwary hiker. Before hiking into a slot canyon, consult with locals and pay attention to weather forecasts.

EXPLORING

Fodor's Choice ★ **Glen Canyon Dam National Recreation Area.** Once you leave the Page business district heading northwest, the Glen Canyon Dam National Recreation Area and Lake Powell behind it immediately become visible. This concrete-arch dam—all 5 million cubic feet of it—was completed in September 1963, its power plant an engineering feat that rivaled the Hoover Dam. The dam's crest is 1,560 feet across and rises 710 feet from bedrock and 583 feet above the waters of the Colorado River. When Lake Powell is full, it's 560 feet deep at the dam. The plant generates some 1.3 million kilowatts of electricity when each generator's 40-ton shaft is producing nearly 200,000 horsepower. Power from the dam serves a five-state grid consisting of Colorado, Arizona, Utah, California, and New Mexico, and provides energy for more than 1.5 million users.

With only 8 inches of annual rainfall, the Lake Powell area enjoys blue skies nearly year-round. Summer temperatures range from the 60s to the 90s. Fall and spring are usually balmy, with daytime temperatures often in the 70s and 80s, but chilly weather can set in. Nights are cool even in summer, and in winter the risk of a cold spell increases, but all-weather houseboats and tour boats make for year-round cruising.

Boaters and campers should note that regulations require the use of portable toilets on the lake and lakeshore to prevent water pollution. ✉ *U.S. 89, 2 miles northwest of Page* ☎ *928/608–6200* ⊕ *www.nps.gov/*

glca 🎫 *$15/vehicle or $7/person (entering on foot or by bicycle), good for up to 7 days; $16/wk boating fee* 🕒 *Carl Hayden Visitor Center: June–Aug., daily 8–6; Sept.–Oct. and Mar.–May, daily 8–5; Nov.–Feb., daily 8:30–4:30.*

WAHWEAP

5 miles north of Glen Canyon Dam on U.S. 89.

Most waterborne-recreational activity on the Arizona side of the lake is centered on this vacation village, where everything needed for a lakeside holiday is available: tour boats, fishing, boat rentals, dinner cruises, and more. The Lake Powell Resorts have excellent views of the lake area, and you can take a boat tour from the Wahweap Marina.

GETTING HERE AND AROUND

Wahweap has two well-marked entrance roads off U.S. 89, one just north of Glen Canyon Dam, and the other about 3½ miles north and more direct if arriving from Utah. Keep in mind that you must pay the Glen Canyon National Recreation Area entry fee on entering Wahweap—this is true even if you're just passing through or having a meal at Lake Powell Resorts (although the fee collection stations are often closed in winter, meaning you can pass through freely).

EXPLORING

Rainbow Bridge National Monument. The 290-foot red-sandstone arch is the world's largest natural bridge, and can be reached by boat or strenuous hike *(⇨ see Hiking)* and can also be viewed by air. A boat tour to the monument is a great way to see not only the monument but also the enormity of the lake and its incredible, rugged beauty. However, the lake level is down due to the prolonged drought throughout the region, so expect a 1½-mile hike from the boat dock to the monument. To the Navajos this is a sacred area with deep religious and spiritual significance, so outsiders are asked not to hike underneath the arch itself. ☎ *928/608–6200, 800/528–6154 for boat tour info* 🌐 *www.nps.gov/rabr.*

WHERE TO EAT AND STAY

$$$ AMERICAN Fodor's Choice ★

🍴 **Rainbow Room.** The bilevel signature restaurant at the Lake Powell Resort occupies a cavernous round room affording 270-degree views of the lake, surrounding vermilion cliffs, and massive Navajo Mountain in the distance. Serving the best food in the region, the kitchen focuses on organic, healthful ingredients in producing such toothsome dishes as a maple-peppercorn pork chop with smoked bacon, wild-mushroom-and-goat-cheese bread pudding, wilted greens, and smoked-chile aioli; and pecan-crusted salmon with creamy green-chile rice, heirloom tomato–corn salad, and a smoky cumin–lime vinaigrette. There's an expansive breakfast buffet in the mornings, but you can also order à la carte. When Rainbow Room is closed in the winter, you can dine at the resort's casual Driftwood Lounge restaurant. [$] *Average main: $23* ✉ *100 Lake Shore Dr., off U.S. 89, 7 miles north of Page* ☎ *928/645–2433* 🌐 *www.lakepowell.com/dining/wahweap-dining.aspx* 🕒 *Closed Nov.–Feb.*

$$$$ RESORT Fodor'sChoice ★ **Amangiri.** One of just two U.S. properties operated by the famously luxurious Aman resort company, this ultraplush 34-suite compound lies just a few miles north of Lake Powell on a 600-acre plot of rugged high desert, soaring red-rock cliffs, and jagged mesas. **Pros:** stunning accommodations inside and out; exceedingly gracious and professional staff; world-class restaurant and spa. **Cons:** it's many times more expensive than most accommodations in the area; extremely remote. [$] *Rooms from: $1200* ✉ *1 Kayenta Rd., 15 miles northwest of Page off U.S. 89, Canyon Point, Utah* ☎ *435/675–3999, 877/695–3999* 🌐 *www.amanresorts.com* ⇒ *34 suites* 🍴 *No meals.*

$$ B&B/INN **Dreamkatchers' B&B.** This sleek, contemporary Southwestern-style home in Utah sits on a bluff a few miles northwest of Lake Powell and 15 miles from Page, its grounds affording dramatic views of the lake, mountains, and sweeping high-desert mesas. **Pros:** peaceful and secluded location that's perfect for stargazing at night; delicious breakfasts; laid-back, friendly hosts. **Cons:** often booked more than a couple of months in advance; two-night minimum stay. [$] *Rooms from: $135* ✉ *1055 S. American Way, Big Water, Utah* ☎ *435/675–5828* 🌐 *www.dreamkatcherslakepowell.com* ⇒ *3 rooms* ⏲ *Closed mid-Nov.–early Apr.* 🍴 *Breakfast.*

$$$ RESORT FAMILY **Lake Powell Resorts & Marinas.** This sprawling property consisting of several one- and two-story buildings, run by Aramark, sits on a promontory above Lake Powell and serves as the center for recreational activities in the area—guests can relax beside two seasonal swimming pools. **Pros:** stunning lake setting; couldn't be closer to the water; all rooms have patios or balconies. **Cons:** it can be a long way from your room to the restaurant and lobby. [$] *Rooms from: $189* ✉ *100 Lake Shore Dr., off U.S. 89, 7 miles north of Page* ☎ *888/896–3829* 🌐 *www.lakepowell.com* ⇒ *350 rooms* 🍴 *No meals.*

HOUSEBOATS

Without a doubt, the most popular and fun way to vacation on Lake Powell is to rent a houseboat. Houseboats, ranging in size from 46 to 75 feet and sleeping 6 to 22 people, come complete with marine radios, fully equipped kitchens, and bathrooms with hot showers; you need only bring sheets and towels. The larger, luxury boats are a good choice in hot summer months, since they have air-conditioning.

Lake Powell Resorts & Marinas. Houseboat rentals at this marina—the only concessionaire that rents boats on Lake Powell—range widely in size, amenities, and price, depending on season. A smaller, more basic houseboat that sleeps up to 12 runs from $3,300 for a week in winter to about $4,500 for a week during the summer peak. At the other end of the spectrum, 75-foot luxury houseboats, some of which can sleep up to 22, cost as much as $145,000 in high season for seven nights. You receive hands-on instruction before you leave the marina. You may want to rent a powerboat or personal watercraft along with a houseboat to explore the many narrow canyons and waterways on the lake. A 19-foot powerboat for seven passengers runs approximately $400 and up per day. Kayaks rent for $45 per day, and wakeboards, water skis, stand-up paddleboards, and jet skis are also available. There are

Midday light on Antelope Canyon's sandstone walls is a favorite shot for many photographers.

many vacation packages available. ☎ *928/645–2433, 888/896–3829* ⊕ *www.lakepowell.com.*

SHOPPING

Lake Powell Resort. The gift shop at Lake Powell Resort carries authentic Native American rugs, pottery, jewelry, and baskets, as well as tourist T-shirts and postcards. ⊠ *100 Lake Shore Dr.* ☎ *888/896–3829* ⊕ *www. lakepowell.com.*

SPORTS AND THE OUTDOORS

BOATING

One of the most scenic lakes of the American West, Lake Powell has 185 miles of clear sapphire waters edged with vast canyons of red and orange rock. Ninety-six major side canyons intricately twist and turn into the main channel of Lake Powell, into what was once the main artery of the Colorado River through Glen Canyon. In some places the lake is 500 feet deep, and by June the lake's waters begin to warm and stay that way well into October.

Wahweap Marina. The largest and most impressive of the five full-service Lake Powell marinas run by Aramark's Lake Powell Resorts & Marinas has more than 900 slips and the most facilities, including a decent diner, public launch ramp, camping, extensive docks, fishing guide and private tour services, and a marina store, where you can buy fishing licenses and other necessities. It's the only full-service marina on the Arizona side of the lake (the other four—Dangling Rope, Hite, Bullfrog, and Halls Crossing—are in Utah). ⊠ *100 Lake Shore Dr.* ☎ *888/896–3829* ⊕ *www.lakepowell.com/executive-marina.aspx.*

TOURS **Lake Powell Resort.** Excursions on double-decker scenic cruisers piloted by experienced guides leave from the dock of Lake Powell Resort. The most popular tour is the full-day trip to Rainbow Bridge National Monument for $125 (a box lunch is included); a half-day version is available, too. There's also a two-hour sunset dinner cruise ($75) featuring a prime-rib dinner (vegetarian option available in advance). It's served on the fully enclosed decks of the sleek and modern *Canyon Princess* ship. Two-hour Antelope Canyon cruises are another favorite, costing about $45, and there's also a longer and more extensive Canyon Adventure tour that visits both Antelope Canyon and Navajo Canyon for $70. Tours generally run spring through early fall. ⊠ *100 Lake Shore Dr.* ☎ *928/645–2433, 888/896–3829* ⊕ *www.lakepowell. com/tours/scenic-boat-tours.aspx* 🖾 *From $45/person.*

CAMPING
Beautiful campsites are abundant on Lake Powell, from large beaches to secluded coves, with the most desirable areas accessible only by boat. You're allowed to camp anywhere along the shores of the lake unless it's restricted by the National Park Service; however, camping within ¼ mile of the shoreline requires a portable toilet or bathroom facilities on your boat. Campfires are allowed on the shoreline, but since there's little firewood available around the lake you'll need to bring your own.

FISHING
Marina Store at Wahweap Marina. Anglers delight in the world-class bass fishing on Lake Powell. You'll hear over and over how the big fish are "biting in the canyons," so you'll need a small vessel if you plan on fishing for the big one. Landing a 20-pound striper isn't unusual (the locals' secret is to use anchovies for bait). Fishing licenses for both Arizona and Utah are available at the Marina Store at Wahweap Marina. ⊠ *100 Lake Shore Dr.* ☎ *888/896–3829* ⊕ *www.lakepowell.com/executive-marina.aspx.*

Stix Bait & Tackle. Come here for supplies and fishing guide recommendations. ⊠ *5 S. Lake Powell Blvd., Page* ☎ *928/645–2891.*

HIKING
Bring plenty of water when hiking and drink often. It's important to remember when hiking at Lake Powell to watch the sky for storms: it may not be raining where you are, but flooding can occur in downstream canyons—particularly slot canyons—from a storm miles away.

Lake Powell Navajo Tribal Park Office. Here at this office 3 miles south of downtown Page, you can purchase backcountry permits ($12 per person, per 24-hour period), which are required before hiking to Rainbow Bridge or elsewhere on wilderness lands in the Navajo Nation. The office is open weekdays 8 to 5. ⊠ *Coppermine Rd., 2 miles south of junction with AZ 98, Lechee* ☎ *928/698–2808* ⊕ *www.navajonationparks.org/permits.htm.*

Rainbow Bridge. Only seasoned hikers in good physical condition will want to try either of the trails leading to Rainbow Bridge; both are about 26 to 28 miles round-trip through challenging and rugged terrain. This site is considered sacred by the Navajo, and it's requested that visitors show respect by not walking under the bridge. Take Indian Highway 16 north toward the Utah state border. At the fork in the road, take either direction for about 5 miles to the trailhead leading to Rainbow Bridge. Excursion boats pull in at the dock near the arch, but no supplies are sold there. *Difficult.*

EASTERN
ARIZONA

WELCOME TO EASTERN ARIZONA

TOP REASONS TO GO

★ **Get outside:** No place for couch potatoes, Eastern Arizona is home to some of the state's best recreation areas for skiing, fishing, camping, and exploring. If you love the outdoor life, you might fall in love with this place.

★ **Be petrified:** Marvel at huge fossilized logs and the dazzling colors of nature at Petrified Forest National Park.

★ **View nature's handiwork at Salt River Canyon:** Watch the desert cacti disappear as the country's pines delight your senses. U.S. 60 dramatically switchbacks down—and back up—2,000 feet of eroded canyon.

★ **Hit the road:** Whether you're traveling the Coronado Trail National Scenic Byway or getting your kicks on Route 66, these roads were made for travelers.

★ **Discover native traditions:** The rich culture and heritage of Native American tribes permeates this area.

1 The White Mountains. In a state known for its extreme temperatures, residents of the White Mountains are proud of their home's relatively staid climate. The comfortable conditions and panoramic mountain views draw thousands here in summer, making the region a playground for golfers, hikers, and fishermen.

2 The Round Valley and Coronado Trail. Considered one of the most scenic drives in the country this 123-mile stretch of highway takes you through terrifying switchbacks and majestic pine forests. Fill up your gas tank in Springerville, head south toward Clifton, and enjoy the ride.

3 The Petrified Forest and Around. Forget about indoor natural history exhibits—the Petrified Forest actually takes you back in time, with fossils that help you see the plant and animal life of a former ecosystem. One of Arizona's most unusual sites, the park has yielded animal fossils, some even as large as nearly 200 feet! The forest itself is like exploring an outdoor museum, and it's worth the trip just to see the park's beautiful Painted Desert.

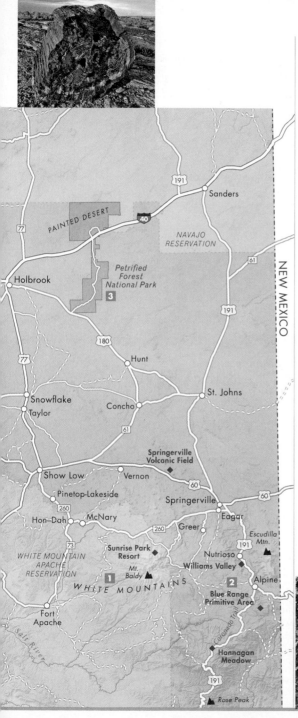

GETTING ORIENTED

Eastern Arizona is a large, somewhat loosely defined series of small towns and historic sites along the Mogollon Rim. Pronounced "*muh*-gee-on," the rim is a 200-mile-long area of volcanic and sedimentary rock that marks a distinct change in the topography of the state. Say goodbye to cacti and desert, and hello to forests of towering trees. Visitors searching for an escape from the desert heat head for the White Mountains and their majestic vistas of ponderosa pines. Others seek history and head northeast to the 221,000-acre Petrified Forest National Park and the Painted Desert. Throughout the region you can experience the area's local flavor, whether it's through perusing Native American crafts or driving through a town whose name was derived from a winning hand of cards (Show Low).

6

Updated by
Elise Riley

As a state of dramatic natural wonders, Eastern Arizona is often overlooked. This is unfortunate, as it's one of Arizona's great outdoor playgrounds. In the White Mountains, northeast of Phoenix, you can hike, fish, swim, and at night gaze upward at millions of twinkling stars. The region's winter sports are just as varied: you can ski downhill or cross-country, snowboard, snowshoe, and snowmobile. Any time of year, you can glimpse age-old fossils and brilliant colors on a drive through the Petrified Forest, where the Painted Desert showcases hues of red and orange you never thought existed in nature.

The White Mountains are unspoiled high country at its best. In vast tracts of preserved primitive wilderness, the air is punctuated with piercing cries of hawks and eagles, and majestic herds of elk graze in verdant, wildflower-laden meadows. Past volcanic activity has left the land strewn with cinder cones, and the whole region is bounded by the Mogollon Rim—a 200-mile geologic upthrust that splits the state—made famous as the "Tonto Rim" in the books of the best-selling Western author Zane Grey. Much of the plant life is unique to this region; this is one of the few places in the country where such desert plants as juniper and manzanita grow intermixed with mountain pines and aspen.

Volcanic activity also gave us the Petrified Forest and the Painted Desert. Once a great steamy swampland, the area experienced seismic activity that forced the swamp's decaying plant matter underground, where it eventually turned to stone. The Painted Desert, which cuts through Petrified Forest National Park, is famous for its multihued sedimentary layers.

The human aspects of the landscape are equally appealing. Historic Western towns are outposts of down-home hospitality, and the prehistoric sites are reminders of the native cultures that once flourished here and are still a vital presence. The Fort Apache Indian Reservation, home to the White Mountain Apache tribe, is to the north of the Salt River, and the San Carlos Apache Indian Reservation is to the south. Visitors are welcome to explore most reservation lands with a permit, which can be obtained from tribal offices. In the more recent past, historic Route 66 made its imprint on the region.

EASTERN ARIZONA PLANNER

WHEN TO GO

If you're not a winter-sports enthusiast, it's best to plan your trip to Eastern Arizona for the high season (May through October). You'll be joined by residents of Phoenix and Tucson, who flock here in summer to escape the unbearably hot temperatures in their hometowns, but you can find some solitude if you rent a cabin or choose a small, remote resort or bed-and-breakfast.

If you're a skier, winter is the time to tour the White Mountains. Sunrise Park Resort has 10 lifts and 65 trails, and a private snowboarders' park. ■TIP→ Eastern Arizona is enjoyable year-round, but many lodging facilities, restaurants, and tourist attractions are closed in autumn and winter. It's wise to call ahead November through April, as the opening and closing dates of many seasonal properties are dependent on when the snow starts (and when it melts). Snowstorms can close the highways that lead into the area, so if you plan on making the trip from Phoenix or even Flagstaff, make sure you have an alternative plan.

PLANNING YOUR TIME

The Petrified Forest is the main attraction for most of Eastern Arizona's visitors; it's easy to see the fossils and petroglyphs in just a few hours. Plan to reserve a day for the park and the surrounding Painted Desert, with one or two additional days for exploring the nearby towns and areas. Depending on your preferences, you can add day trips and excursions. Fans of the great outdoors have their choice of activities in the White Mountains. Those who like a little less sweat in their vacations can hit the open road and explore historic Route 66 or the Coronado Trail.

Pinetop-Lakeside, with its wide range of lodging facilities and amenities, might be the best base for your trip. Neighboring area towns, such as Snowflake-Taylor, have memorable motels and B&Bs. If solitude is your goal, consider staying at a lodge surrounded by private forest.

GETTING HERE AND AROUND
CAR TRAVEL

There isn't much choice: you'll be driving to and around Eastern Arizona. Amtrak runs limited service, but it isn't that helpful for travelers. Part of the experience in Eastern Arizona is the drive. Rent a car in Phoenix or Tucson, or even Flagstaff, and enjoy the open road.

If you're arriving from points west via Flagstaff, Interstate 40 leads directly to Holbrook, where drivers can take AZ 77 south into Show Low or U.S. 180 southeast to Springerville-Eagar. From Phoenix, take the scenic drive northeast on U.S. 60, or the slightly faster (and less curvy) AZ 87 north to AZ 260 east, both of which lead to Show Low. From Tucson, AZ 77 north connects with U.S. 60 at Globe, and continues through Show Low up to Holbrook. For those who want to drive the Coronado Trail south-to-north, U.S. 70 and AZ 78 link up with U.S. 191 from Globe to the west and New Mexico to the east, respectively.

WINTER ROAD CONDITIONS Weather conditions change rapidly in Eastern Arizona. Before heading out on a daylong excursion—particularly in winter—be sure to call the Arizona Department of Transportation's Traveler Information Service (☎ 511).

RESTAURANTS

Luxury travel this is not. Fine dining is difficult to find; home-style cooking, steakhouses, and the occasional authentic Mexican joint pepper most towns. Casual is the norm. A pair of jeans will gain you entrance to just about any eatery in the area—anything dressier and you might be overdone. Reservations are helpful during the busy summer months, and remember that some places are closed from November to April.

HOTELS

Most places supply clean rooms without many frills. These aren't the world-class resorts and spas of Phoenix, but that isn't necessarily a bad thing. "Resort" in this area means you'll probably have a room with a kitchenette and occasional (but not daily) maid service in a picturesque, woodsy setting. Plan on bringing your own toiletries and the like (there's a reason some of these prices are so affordable). *Hotel reviews have been shortened. For full information, visit Fodors.com.*

WHAT IT COSTS			
$	**$$**	**$$$**	**$$$$**
Restaurants under $12	$12–$20	$21–$30	over $30
Hotels under $121	$121–$175	$176–$250	over $250

Restaurant prices are the average cost of a main course at dinner or, if lunch is not served, at lunch. Hotel prices are of the lowest cost of a standard double room in high season, excluding taxes and service charges.

THE WHITE MOUNTAINS

With elevations climbing to more than 11,000 feet, the White Mountains area of east-central Arizona is a winter wonderland and a summer haven from the desert heat. In the 1870s, the U.S. soldier John Gregory Bourke wrote in his diary that the White Mountains region was "a strange upheaval, a freak of nature, a mountain canted up on one side; one rides along the edge and looks down two or three thousand feet . . . into a weird scene of grandeur and rugged beauty." The area, although much less remote than in Bourke's time, is still grand and rugged, carved by deep river canyons and tall cliffs covered with ponderosa pine.

TOP OUTDOOR ACTIVITIES IN EASTERN ARIZONA

Hiking: Hikers and mountain bikers of all abilities enjoy the White Mountains' 225 miles of interconnecting loop trails, open to visitors on foot or on nonmotorized wheels. Ranger stations have maps. Allow an hour for every 2 miles of trail, plus an additional hour for every 1,000 feet gained in altitude. Carry water, wear sunscreen, and watch out for poison ivy.

Fishing: Anglers flock to the more than 65 lakes, streams, and reservoirs in the White Mountains. Artificial lures and flies are permitted in winter only. An Arizona fishing license is required; on tribal land you'll also need a White Mountain Apache fishing license. Want an easier catch? Some lodges have private lakes stocked with trout.

Golfing: The high country's links draw golfers from all over, and these mountain fairways angle through lush forests and past lakes and springs.

Skiing: The 11,000-foot White Mountains have hilly, wooded landscapes that invite downhill and cross-country skiing adventurers. Greer's nearby Pole Knoll Trail System and surrounding Forest Service roads make for 33 miles of cross-country trails. No matter where you stay in the White Mountains, Sunrise Park Resort is never more than an hour's drive away.

6

SALT RIVER CANYON

40 miles north of Globe on U.S. 60.

Carved from years of erosion, the multicolor spires, buttes, mesas, and walls of the Salt River Canyon—which dramatically drop 2,000 feet—have inspired this marvel's nickname, the Mini-Grand Canyon. But you don't need mules (or your feet) to get to the canyon floor. From Phoenix, U.S. 60 climbs through rolling hills as it approaches the Salt River Canyon, and the terrain changes from high desert with cactus and mesquite trees to forests of ponderosa pine. After entering the San Carlos Indian Reservation, the highway descends sharply into the canyon, making a series of hairpin turns to reach the Salt River. **Hieroglyphic Point** is just one of the viewpoints along the scenic drive. Stop to stretch your legs at the viewing and interpretive display area before crossing the bridge. Wander along the banks below and enjoy the rock-strewn rapids. On hot days slip your shoes off and dip your feet into the chilly water. ■TIP→ The river and canyon are open to hiking, fishing, and white-water rafting, but you need a permit, as this is tribal land. For information and recreational permits, contact the individual tribes.

The Apache people migrated to the Southwest around the 10th century. Divided into individual bands instead of functioning as a unified tribe, they were a hunting and gathering culture, moving with the seasons to gather food, and their crafts—baskets, beadwork, and cradleboards (traditional baby-carriers)—were compatible with their mobile lifestyle. The U.S. government didn't understand that different Apache bands

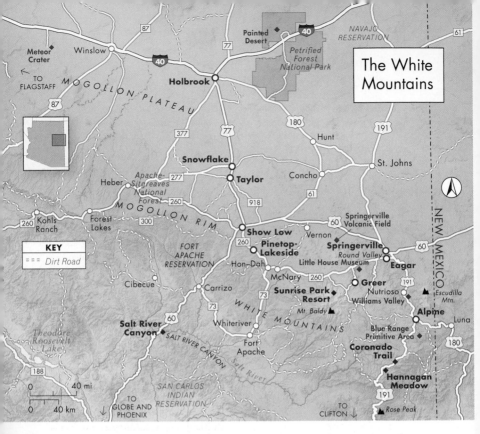

The White Mountains

might be hostile to each other, and tried to gather separate tribes on one reservation, compounding relocation problems. Eventually, the government established the San Carlos Apache Indian Reservation in 1871 and the Fort Apache Indian Reservation in 1897. Both tribes hold on fiercely to their cultures. The native language is still spoken and taught in schools, and tribal ceremonies continue to be held. Both tribes have highly acclaimed "hot-shot" crews that immediately respond to forest fires throughout the West. The Salt River forms the boundary between these two large Apache reservations in Eastern Arizona.

WHEN TO GO
As with most of Eastern Arizona, it's best to visit Salt River Canyon in summer, when there are no worries about winter storms.

GETTING HERE AND AROUND
From the Phoenix area, take U.S. 60 east through Globe, and then continue north for 40 miles. From rim to rim, the road into the canyon is only 9 miles, but allow plenty of time for slowing down for the tight turns—and for enjoying the views. It's a three-hour drive from Phoenix through Globe.

CLOSE UP

Camping Resources

Apache-Sitgreaves National Forests has a listing of all public camping facilities in the region, most of which operate from April to November. ☎ *928/333–4301* ⊕ *www.fs.usda.gov/asnf.*

To reserve a site at a fee campground, use the National Recreation Reservation Service, which charges a reservation fee of $10 per transaction. ☎ *877/444–6777* ⊕ *www.recreation.gov.*

Book your campground site well in advance with the Game and Fish Department of the White Mountain Apache Tribe. ☎ *928/338–4385* ⊕ *www.wmatoutdoors.org.*

ESSENTIALS

Recreational Permits and Information San Carlos Apache Tribe ☎ *928/475–2343* ⊕ *www.sancarlosapache.com.* White Mountain Apache Tribe ☎ *928/338–4346* ⊕ *www.wmat.nsn.us.*

EXPLORING

Apache Cultural Museum. The entrance price buys access to three great places to visit on the Fort Apache Indian Reservation. The museum explains the history, culture, and artistic traditions of the Apaches, and sells local crafts and books. The **Fort Apache Historical Park** harks back to cavalry days with horse barns, parade grounds, log cabins, and officers' homes. **Kinishba Ruins,** 5 miles west of Fort Apache (get directions and a map at the Cultural Center), is a partly restored sandstone pueblo, and the only Native American ruin on the reservation open to visitors. ⊠ *½ mile east of junction of AZ 73 and Indian Rte. 46, 5 miles south of Whiteriver* ☎ *928/338–4625* ⊕ *www.wmat.nsn.us/fortapachepark.htm* ⊠ *$5* ⊙ *Weekdays 8–5.*

Cultural Center. Exhibits on Apache history and culture are displayed at the San Carlos Apache Cultural Center, along with explanations of cultural traditions, such as the Changing Women Ceremony, a girls' puberty rite. Crafts are sold here as well. ⊠ *U.S. 70, milepost 272, Peridot* ☎ *928/475–2894* ⊠ *$4* ⊙ *Weekdays 9–5.*

Fort Apache Indian Reservation. The elevation of the tribal lands ranges from 3,000 feet at the bottom of Salt River to 11,000 feet in the White Mountains, and the area provides some of the best outdoor recreation in the state. The 2,500-square-mile reservation is the ancestral home of the White Mountain Apache Tribe; most of the more than 15,000 tribal members live in nine towns, and the largest of these towns, Whiteriver (population 5,200), serves as tribal headquarters. Tribal enterprises include Sunrise Ski Resort, Hon-Dah Resort Casino, cattle ranching, and lumber. ⊠ *Whiteriver* ☎ *928/338–4346* ⊕ *www.wmat.nsn.us.*

San Carlos Apache Indian Reservation. Established in 1871 for various Apache tribes, the San Carlos Apache Indian Reservation covers 1.8

U.S. 60 descends 2,000 feet into the Salt River Canyon on a series of tight switchbacks with great views.

million acres southeast of Salt River Canyon. One-third of the reservation is covered with forest, and the rest is desert. The San Carlos Apaches number about 12,500 and are noted for their beadwork and basketry. Peridot, a beautiful yellow-green stone resembling the emerald, is mined near the town of the same name and made into jewelry. You need a permit to stop and visit the reservation's attractions; pick one up at the office 1½ miles east of the AZ 170 junction for San Carlos (closed on Sunday). ⊠ *Off Hwy. 170, San Carlos* ☎ *928/475–2361 for tribal offices* ⊕ *www.sancarlosapache.com.*

▌EN ROUTE The road out of the Salt River Canyon climbs along the canyon's northern cliffs, providing views of this truly spectacular chasm, unfairly overlooked in a state full of world-famous gorges. The highway continues some 50 miles northward to the **Mogollon Rim**—a huge geologic ledge that bisects much of Arizona—and its cool upland pinewoods.

SHOW LOW

60 miles north of the Salt River Canyon on U.S. 60.

Show Low has little of the charm of its neighboring White Mountains communities, but it's the main commercial center for the high country. The city is also a crossing point for east–west traffic along the Mogollon Rim and traffic headed for Holbrook and points north. If you're heading up to the Painted Desert and Petrified Forest from Phoenix, you might want to spend the night here.

WHEN TO GO

You'll have to pass through the Salt River Canyon to reach Show Low (or take highways 87 and 260 through Payson). Either way, it means you'll be driving through mountains; be prepared in winter for storms and cold weather.

GETTING HERE AND AROUND

Show Low is a fairly good central location from which to explore Eastern Arizona by car. You can take AZ 260 south to reach Pinetop-Lakeside, or travel north on AZ 77 to Snowflake-Taylor and, eventually, Petrified Forest National Park.

WHERE TO EAT

$$
MEXICAN

✕**Licano's Mexican Food and Steakhouse.** Along with what locals claim are the best enchiladas on the mountain, Licano's serves shrimp tacos, prime rib, and lobster tail, making for a fairly broad menu. The spacious lounge, with a weekday happy hour from 4:30 to 6:30, stays open to 9 nightly. The convenient downtown location places Licano's within walking distance from most Show Low hotels. $ *Average main: $11* ✉ *573 W. Deuce of Clubs* ☎ *928/537–8220* ⊕ *www.licanos.net.*

$
AMERICAN

✕**Native New Yorker.** With 30 TVs in the dining room and the adjacent sports bar, this regional chain restaurant is a good place to keep up with the team. As you might expect, it's famous for its wings and bar food, but its chili will warm you up, too. If you're looking for a late-night scene, this is your best bet for the area: the bar stays open on weekends until 2 am. $ *Average main: $9* ✉ *391 W. Deuce of Clubs* ☎ *928/532–5100* ⊕ *www.nativenewyorker.com.*

WHERE TO STAY

$
HOTEL

🏨 **Best Western Paint Pony Lodge.** Spacious rooms have wood accents and picture windows overlooking the pine-studded high country. **Pros:** affordable, large rooms; free hot breakfast; modern conveniences. **Cons:** no frills. $ *Rooms from: $95* ✉ *581 W. Deuce of Clubs* ☎ *928/537–5773* ⊕ *www.bestwestern.com* 🛏 *48 rooms, 2 suites* ⊙❙ *Breakfast.*

$
HOTEL

🏨 **Holiday Inn Express.** Larger rooms and more conveniences than much of its competition make for a comfortable night's rest. **Pros:** the closest thing to a "big city" hotel in Show Low; everything you expect from a brand-name property. **Cons:** limited sightseeing opportunities nearby mean this is better for a pit stop than a vacation base. $ *Rooms from: $118* ✉ *151 W. Deuce of Clubs* ☎ *928/537–5115* ⊕ *www.hiexpress.com* 🛏 *71 rooms* ⊙❙ *Breakfast.*

$
HOTEL

🏨 **KC Motel.** Victorian decorating and large rooms help this not-so-typical two-story motel stand out. **Pros:** good value; Continental breakfast included. **Cons:** as expected for a motel, there are few frills; style not for everyone. $ *Rooms from: $72* ✉ *60 W. Deuce of Clubs* ☎ *928/537–4433, 800/531–7152* ⊕ *www.kcmotelshowlow.com* 🛏 *35 rooms* ⊙❙ *Breakfast.*

SPORTS AND THE OUTDOORS

FISHING

Fool Hollow Lake Recreational Area. In addition to fishing, this year-round park is popular for boating, camping, and wildlife-viewing. Set amid a piney 800 acres, the lake is stocked with rainbow trout, walleye, and bass. There are five fishing platforms available, plus two fish-cleaning stations at the park. ⊠ *1500 N. Fool Hollow Lake Rd., 2 miles north of U.S. 60 off AZ 260, Show Low* ☎ *928/537–3680* ⊕ *www.azstateparks. com/parks/FOHO/index.html.*

FAMILY **Show Low Lake.** South of town and 1 mile off AZ 260, Show Low Lake holds the state record for the largest walleye catch. The water is well stocked with largemouth bass, bluegill, and catfish. Some anglers have pulled out 9-pound rainbow trout. Facilities include a bait shop, a marina with boat rentals, and campsites with bathrooms and showers. ⊠ *Show Low Lake Rd.* ☎ *928/537–4126.*

GOLF

Bison Golf. Designed by Billy Mayfair, Bison Golf has a back nine in the pines and a front nine in a more open meadow. The course is open year-round, but expect to encounter course closings throughout the winter. The club also has a fitness center. ⊠ *860 N. 36th Dr., at AZ 260* ☎ *928/537–4564* ⊕ *www.bisongolf.net* ⊠ *$52 weekends, $48 weekdays* ⅄ *18 holes, 5969 yards, par 71.*

Silver Creek Golf Club. This championship course opened to rave reviews in the 1980s, and was voted by the PGA as one of the top 10 golf courses in Arizona—no small feat in a state that lives and breathes golf. It's also one of the more affordable courses in the area. Given its lower elevation, this course is usually a few degrees warmer than Show Low and stays open year-round. Sandbaggers Bar & Grill has breakfast and lunch (dinner on weekends). The golf club is 5 miles east of town on U.S. 60, then 7½ miles north on Bourdon Ranch Road. ⊠ *2051 Silver Lake Blvd.* ☎ *928/537–2744, 888/537–3673* ⊕ *www. silvercreekgolfclub.com* ⊠ *$60 weekends, $56 weekdays* ⅄ *18 holes, 6,813 yards, par 71.*

PINETOP-LAKESIDE

15 miles southeast of Show Low on AZ 260.

At 7,200 feet, the community of Pinetop-Lakeside borders the world's largest stand of ponderosa pine. Two towns, Pinetop and Lakeside, were incorporated in 1984 to form this municipality—although they still retain separate post offices. The year-round population is just 4,200, but in summer months it can jump to as high as 30,000. Once popular only with retirees and those with summerhouses, the city now lures thousands of "flatlanders" up from the Valley of the Sun with gorgeous scenery, excellent multiuse trails, premier golf courses, and temperatures that rarely exceed 85°F.

WHEN TO GO

Desert dwellers flock to Pinetop-Lakeside in summer to escape the heat. In winter, it's a wonderland of snow and mountains, but be prepared, as U.S. 60 and Interstate 40 are routinely closed and impassable during snowstorms.

GETTING HERE AND AROUND

A 15-minute drive from Show Low, Pinetop-Lakeside is ideal for exploring by car. The main drag is known as both AZ 260 and White Mountain Boulevard.

WHERE TO EAT

$$$ STEAKHOUSE 🍴 **Charlie Clark's Steak House.** Attracting golfers relishing a successful day on the links as well as locals in search of good food, Charlie Clark's has been the meeting place of the White Mountains since it opened in 1938. Furnished with lots of wood, the building has been added on to in the decades since. Prime rib is the house specialty, and make sure to try a cup of the French onion soup. Minnesota walleye adds a Midwestern spin to the menu. [$] *Average main: $23* ✉ *1701 E. White Mountain Blvd., Pinetop* ☎ *928/367–4900, 888/333–0259* 🌐 *www.charlieclarks.com.*

$ MEXICAN 🍴 **Los Corrales.** Bright yellows and oranges make this a cheerful family-style eatery. Locals come for Mexican seafood dishes such as *camarones a la crema* (shrimp and mushrooms in cream sauce) and lunch specials. Dessert specialties include fried ice cream and apple *chimichanga.* [$] *Average main: $8* ✉ *845 E. White Mountain Blvd., Lakeside* ☎ *928/367–5585.*

6

WHERE TO STAY

$$ HOTEL 🏨 **Hon-Dah Resort Casino and Conference Center.** Stuffed high-country animals atop a mountain of boulders welcome you to Hon-Dah, which is operated by the White Mountain Apache Tribe (the name means "welcome to my home" in Apache), where the main draw is the casino, with hundreds of slot machines, live poker and blackjack, and live entertainment on weekends. **Pros:** best destination for travelers who aren't interested in roughing it; big draw for the casino crowd. **Cons:** can get noisy in the evening, and the term "resort" can be misleading. [$] *Rooms from: $124* ✉ *777 AZ 260, Pinetop* ☎ *928/369–0299, 800/929–8744* 🌐 *www.hon-dah.com* 🛏 *126 rooms, 2 suites* 🍽 *No meals.*

$ RESORT 🏨 **Lake of the Woods Resort.** Whether you're looking for a modern cabin with most of the creature comforts or something a little more cozy and rustic, this resort can satisfy both cravings. **Pros:** on Lakeside's main street, with a rural, but not removed, atmosphere; stocked private lake. **Cons:** only phone for guests is a pay phone in the main building; Internet in lobby only. [$] *Rooms from: $99* ✉ *2244 W. White Mountain Blvd., Lakeside* ☎ *928/368–5353* 🌐 *www.lakeofthewoodsaz.com* 🛏 *26 cabins, 7 houses* 🍽 *No meals.*

$ RESORT FAMILY 🏨 **Northwoods Resort.** Each of the 14 fully furnished cottages at this mountain retreat has its own covered porch and a grill, and inside, the fully electric kitchens have refrigerators, ovens, microwaves, and adjacent dinette sets. **Pros:** no highway noise; ideal for a family vacation in solitude; Wi-Fi available. **Cons:** cabins are close together, so there isn't a lot of privacy. [$] *Rooms from: $99* ✉ *AZ 260, milepost 352* ☎ *928/367–2966, 800/813–2966* 🌐 *www.northwoodsaz.com* 🛏 *14 cabins* 🍽 *No meals.*

$ RESORT 🏨 **Whispering Pines Resort.** On 12 acres bordering the Apache-Sitgreaves National Forest, these well-maintained cabins are in walking distance of Woodland Lake and Walnut Creek. **Pros:** great accommodations for large parties; extremely private. **Cons:** older furnishings in rooms; icy roads in the resort can be difficult to navigate in winter; no daily housekeeping. [$] *Rooms from: $99* ✉ *237 E. White Mountain Blvd. (AZ 260), just beyond milepost 352* ☎ *928/367–4386, 800/840–3867* 🌐 *www.whisperingpinesaz.com* 🛏 *38 cabins* 🍴 *No meals.*

SHOPPING

Shops that specialize in antiques, collectibles, Western wares, and gifts are located on White Mountain Boulevard, the main thoroughfare in town. Many shops are only open a couple of months during the year, so call ahead before embarking on any retail-therapy expedition. A few to antiques shops worth checking out if they're open are **Antique Mercantile Company** (☎ *928/368–9090*), **Harvest Moon Antiques** (☎ *928/367–6973*), and **Lilly Bear Antiques** (☎ *928/367–5979*).

SPORTS AND THE OUTDOORS

BICYCLING AND HIKING

Listed in the American Hiking Society's "Trail Town Hall of Fame," Pinetop-Lakeside is the primary trailhead for the White Mountains Trails System, which includes roughly 200 miles of interconnecting multiuse loop trails that span the White Mountains. All these trails are open to mountain bikers, horseback riders, and hikers.

Apache-Sitgreaves National Forests. You can get trail brochures or other information from the Apache-Sitgreaves National Forests, including a $2 booklet on the White Mountains Trail System. ✉ *Lakeside Ranger Station, 2022 W. White Mountain Blvd., Lakeside* ☎ *928/368–2100* 🌐 *www.fs.usda.gov/asnf.*

Big Springs Environmental Study Area. Half a mile off AZ 260 on Woodland Road, Big Springs Environmental Study Area is a 0.5-mile loop trail that wanders by riparian meadows, two streams, and a spring-fed pond. A series of educational signs is devoted to the surrounding flora and fauna. *Easy.* ✉ *Woodland Rd. and AZ 260, Lakeside* ☎ *928/368–6700* 🌐 *ci.pinetop-lakeside.az.us/bigsprings.htm.*

Country Club Trail. The trailhead for Country Club Trail is at the junction of Forest Service roads 182 and 185 (but it's more helpful to ask for directions at the ranger station). These 3.5 miles of moderately difficult mountain-biking and hiking trails can be spiced up by following the spur-trail to the top of Pat Mullen Mountain and back. *Moderate.*

Mogollon Rim Interpretive Trail. The well-traveled and easy Mogollon Rim Interpretive Trail follows a small part of the 19th-century **Crook Trail** along the Mogollon Rim; the ¼-mile path, with a trailhead just west of the Pinetop-Lakeside city limits, is well marked with placards describing local wildlife and geography. *Easy.* ✉ *3 miles west of Lakeside Ranger Station on AZ 260, follow signs for trail.*

Panorama Trail. The 8-mile Panorama Trail, rated moderate, comes with astonishing views from the top of extinct double volcanoes known as the Twin Knolls and passes through a designated wildlife habitat area; the trailhead is 6 miles east on Porter Mountain Road, off AZ 260. *Moderate.*

FISHING

Hawley Lake. East of Pinetop-Lakeside and 9 miles south of AZ 260, 260-acre Hawley Lake sits on Apache territory and yields mostly rainbow trout; rental boats are available in the marina. Tribal permits are required for all recreational activities: contact **White Mountain Apache Game & Fish Department** (☎ 928/338–4385 ⊕ *www.wmatoutdoors. org*) for details. ⊠ *AZ 473, Hawley Lake.*

Paradise Creek Anglers. Sharing business space with Skiers Edge, Paradise Creek Anglers offers fishing advice, lessons, and equipment rentals. ⊠ *560 W. White Mountain Blvd., Lakeside* ☎ *928/367–6200, 800/231– 3831* ⊕ *www.paradisecreekanglers.com.*

GOLF

Pinetop Lakes Golf & Country Club. Open April to October, Pinetop Lakes Golf & Country Club has fewer trees than other area courses, but it includes several water hazards to compensate. The shorter course is wonderful for public play. The club also has tennis courts. ⊠ *4643 Buck Springs Rd., Pinetop* ☎ *928/369–4531* ⊕ *www.pinetoplakesgolf. com* ⊑ *$63* ⅃. *18 holes, 4558 yards, par 63.*

SKIING AND SNOW SPORTS

The Skier's Edge. Rent cross-country and downhill skis as well as snowboards and boots. The Skier's Edge shares space with Paradise Creek Anglers, so you can get service and advice here year-round. ⊠ *560 W. White Mountain Blvd., Pinetop* ☎ *928/367–6200, 800/231–3831* ⊕ *www.skiersedgepinetop.com.*

Snowriders Board & Ski Rentals. December through mid-March, Snowriders Board & Ski Rentals sells and rents skis, snowboards, and gear, weather permitting. ⊠ *857 E. White Mountain Blvd., Pinetop* ☎ *928/367–5638* ⊕ *www.azsnowriders.com.*

SNOWFLAKE-TAYLOR

30 miles north of Pinetop-Lakeside on Route 260 and AZ 77.

Snowflake and Taylor is a good jumping-off point for exploring Eastern Arizona, especially if you want to get away from the crowds during summer trips into the nearby White Mountains. Most Phoenix weekenders head for the higher towns of Pinetop and Lakeside, so Snowflake and Taylor don't get the crush of summer visitors that results in higher prices at hotels and restaurants. Yet, because they're sandwiched between the White Mountains and the Colorado Plateau, the communities enjoy year-round pleasant weather, with summer highs in the 90s. Yes, as the name suggests, it snows in Snowflake, but it seldom lasts more than a day. It's also an easy day trip to the Petrified Forest.

Snowflake and Taylor were settled by Mormons in the 1870s and named for Mormon church leaders. Snowflake's unusual name is a combination of Erastus Snow, an apostle in the early Mormon church of Salt Lake City, and William Flake, one of the town founders. One of Arizona's two Mormon temples sits on Temple Hill (to the west of Snowflake), and the towns still have a large Mormon contingent in their combined population of 9,000. You can take a walking tour of Snowflake's historical district, which has pioneer homes and antiques stores.

WHEN TO GO

Since Snowflake-Taylor isn't as far into the White Mountains as other communities it's somewhat easier to reach in winter. Still, most visitors explore this area in summer.

GETTING HERE AND AROUND

From Show Low off AZ 77, Snowflake-Taylor is about one-third of the way to Interstate 40.

EXPLORING

Stinson Museum. James Stinson, the first rancher in the valley, was the original resident of this small adobe home that once served as a schoolhouse. William J. Flake bought out Stinson's holdings and founded the town of Snowflake. Flake added on to the structure, which today is a museum containing pioneer memorabilia, quilts, Native American artifacts, and a small gift shop. ✉ *102 N. 1st St. East, Snowflake* ☎ *928/536–4331 for Snowflake-Taylor Chamber of Commerce* 🎟 *Donations accepted* 🕒 *April–Sept., Mon.–Sat. 10–2; Oct.–May, by appointment only.*

Taylor Museum. A small local museum with pioneer and Native American exhibits, the Taylor Museum celebrates July 4th by "firing the anvil" to begin the day. At 4 am revelers place an anvil on the ground, a newspaper and gunpowder on top, then another anvil. When the gunpowder is lighted, the anvil flies a few feet into the air with a deafening bang. The rest of the year, the anvil resides at the museum along with the Jennings drum, which was brought to town by early Mormon settlers. ✉ *2 North Main St., Taylor* ☎ *928/536–4331 Snowflake-Taylor Chamber of Commerce* 🎟 *Donations accepted* 🕒 *Mon.,Tues., and Thurs.–Sat. 10–2. By appointment only Oct.–May.*

WHERE TO EAT

$$ ITALIAN 🍴 **Enzo's Ristorante Italiano.** At the only Italian restaurant in town, sauces and breads are made from scratch by Enzo himself, and although they may take a while, the minestrone soup, baked pastas, and shrimp alfredo are worth the wait. Bring your own bottle of wine; Enzo provides the glasses. [$] *Average main: $15* ✉ *423 W. 3rd St. N, Snowflake* ☎ *928/243–0450* ✍ *Reservations not accepted* 💳 *No credit cards* 🕒 *Closed Sun.–Tues. No lunch.*

$ MEXICAN 🍴 **La Cocina de Eva.** Any trip to Arizona should become a tour of different styles of Mexican food, and if you like trying different interpretations of Sonoran cuisine, stop here. The green-corn tamales and enchiladas are delicious, and locals go for the bean burrito smothered in green-chile sauce. Portions are large, and the service is friendly at this popular spot, which is decorated in a homey combination of south-of-the-border knickknacks and Western paintings. [$] *Average main: $8* ✉ *201 N. Main St., Snowflake* ☎ *928/536–7683* 🕒 *Closed Sun.*

$ AMERICAN 🍴 **Trapper's Cafe.** Opened in 1973 by "Trapper" Hatch, this family-owned diner is decorated with Hatch's old trapping equipment and animal paintings by local artists. Chicken-fried steak and homemade barbecue sauce draw a loyal crowd, as do the steaks. People drive out of their way just for a piece of pie, especially the banana cream. Have a slice at the counter with a cup of coffee. [$] *Average main: $8* ✉ *9 S. Main St., Taylor* ☎ *928/536–7758* 🕒 *Closed Sun.*

WHERE TO STAY

$ B&B/INN Fodor's Choice ★ 🏨 **Heritage Inn Bed & Breakfast.** Elegantly furnished with Victorian antiques and decorated pioneer style, this popular redbrick bed-and-breakfast has charm to spare. **Pros:** quiet B&B setting with modern conveniences, including Internet access and DVD players; exceptional service and great breakfast. **Cons:** some rooms only have a Jacuzzi tub with no shower. [$] *Rooms from: $105* ✉ *161 N. Main St., Snowflake* ☎ *928/536–3322, 866/486–5947* 🌐 *www.heritage-inn.net* 🛏 *10 rooms, 1 cottage* 🍴 *Breakfast.*

$ B&B/INN 🏨 **Rodeway Inn Silver Creek Inn.** Simply furnished, clean, and handy to fast-food restaurants, Rodeway Inn Silver Creek Inn attracts regulars who travel through the area often. **Pros:** convenient town location; inexpensive; free Wi-Fi. **Cons:** intended for travelers just passing through; no on-site restaurant. [$] *Rooms from: $59* ✉ *825 N. Main St., Taylor* ☎ *928/536–2600* 🌐 *www.rodewayinn.com* 🛏 *42 rooms* 🍴 *Breakfast.*

SPORTS AND THE OUTDOORS

GOLF

Snowflake Municipal Golf Course. One of the least expensive golf courses in the White Mountains, the Snowflake Municipal Golf Course is open year-round, with fees that are lower October through April. With scenic red rocks and waterfalls, the course also includes a water hazard. The restaurant is open May through October. ✉ *90 N. Country Club Dr.* ☎ *928/536–7233* 🌐 *www.snowflakegolfcourse.com* 🎫 *$33* ⛳ *18 holes, 6,172 yards, par 72.*

HIKING

Petroglyph Hike. At the junction of Silver Creek Canyon and Five-Mile Canyon, 5 miles north of Snowflake, ancient peoples left petroglyphs made by carving through dark varnish, revealing the light sandstone of the canyon walls. Petroglyph Hike, the trail from the canyon top down to the petroglyphs, is short but steep. Trail access is regulated by the city of Snowflake. To check in and get directions, contact the **Snowflake-Taylor Chamber of Commerce** (☎ *928/536–4331* 🌐 *www.snowflaketaylorchamber.org*). *Moderate.* ✉ *Silver Creek Canyon.*

SUNRISE PARK RESORT

27 miles southeast of Pinetop-Lakeside on AZ 260 and AZ 273.

One of the Arizona's favorite locations for snowplay, Sunrise Park Resort is a prime destination for desert-dwellers looking to ski or snowboard—or build a snowman. In summer, it's a great place to ride horses or just take in the beauty of the ponderosa pines.

6

WHEN TO GO

Sunrise is one of Arizona's top two destinations for skiing and winter recreation. However, you can also visit in summer, when activities include horseback riding, mountain biking, and chairlift rides—all with great views of the White Mountains.

GETTING HERE AND AROUND

The resort is 7 miles south of the intersection of AZ 260 and AZ 273.

WHERE TO STAY

$$ HOTEL **Sunrise Park Resort.** Catering to those who want to be as close as possible to the lifts, this hotel has comfortable rooms with ski racks and runs a shuttle to the slopes every half hour. **Pros:** convenient location and proximity to slopes; free Wi-Fi. **Cons:** this is not a resort like many travelers are accustomed to—accommodations are no-frills. [$] *Rooms from: $129* ✉ *AZ 273, 7 miles south of AZ 260* ☎ *928/735–7669* 🌐 *www.sunriseskipark.com* 🛏 *100 rooms, 1 suite* 🕑 *Closed Apr.–Memorial Day and mid-Oct.–mid-Nov.* 🍴 *No meals.*

SPORTS AND THE OUTDOORS

SKIING

FAMILY **Sunrise Park Resort.** In winter and early spring, skiers and other snow lovers flock to Sunrise Park Resort. There's plenty more than downhill and cross-country skiing here, including snowboarding, snowmobiling, snowshoeing, ice fishing, and sleigh rides. The resort has 10 lifts and 65 trails on three mountains rising to 11,000 feet. Eighty percent of the downhill runs are for beginning or intermediate skiers, and many less-intense trails begin at the top, so skiers of varying skill levels can ride the chairlifts together. There's a "ski-wee" hill for youngsters. The Sunrise Express high-speed chairlift anchors the 10 lifts. One-day lift tickets are $63. Sunrise's Snowboard Park has jumps of all difficulty levels and its own sound system, and is exclusively for snowboarders—so there's no tension on the hill between boarders and skiers. Cross-country skiers enjoy 13½ miles of interconnecting trails. You can rent equipment at the ski shop. In summer a marina is open for boat rentals on Sunrise Lake. ✉ *AZ 273, 7 miles south of AZ 260, 12 miles west of Greer* ☎ *928/735–7669* 🌐 *www.sunriseskipark.com.*

GREER

12 miles east of Sunrise Park Resort, 35 miles southeast of Pinetop-Lakeside, 15 miles southwest of Springerville-Eagar on AZ 260.

The charming community of Greer sits among pine, spruce, willow, and aspen on the banks of the Little Colorado River. At an elevation of 8,500 feet, this portion of gently sloping National Forest land is covered with meadows and reservoirs and is dominated by 11,590-foot Baldy Peak. Much of the surrounding area remains under the control of the White Mountain Apache Tribe, which has its own laws regulating camping and hiking.

Eastern Arizona attracts outdoors lovers for horseback riding, hiking, fishing, golfing, and skiing.

WHEN TO GO
When compared to other areas of Eastern Arizona, Greer is relatively temperate. As in most towns in the area, summers are great here for getting away from the heat; winters are snowy but not frigid.

GETTING HERE AND AROUND
Take AZ 373 south from AZ 260. AZ 373 is also Greer's main street, and after it crosses the Little Colorado River it eventually comes to a dead end. It's affectionately called the Road to Nowhere.

EXPLORING
Butterfly Lodge Museum. Listed on the National Register of Historic Places, the Butterfly Lodge Museum was built as a hunting lodge in 1914 for author James Willard Schultz and his artist son, Lone Wolf, a prolific painter of Indian and Western scenes. There's a small gift shop, where you can buy prints of his work as well as other art and books on pioneer life and Arizona history. Take time to watch the surrounding meadow come to life with the lodge's fluttering butterflies. (The lodge was built by John Butler, the husband of "Aunt Molly," of Molly Butler Lodge fame.) ⊠ *AZ 373 at CR 1126* 🕾 *928/735-7514* ⊕ *www.butterflylodgemuseum.org* 🖃 *$2* ☉ *June–Aug., Thurs.–Sun. 10–5.*

WHERE TO EAT AND STAY
$ ✕**Greer Mountain Resort Country Cafe.** Decorated with hanging plants,
AMERICAN this diner-café has a straightforward, unremarkable interior and exterior. Grab a seat by the fireplace and sample the homemade ranch beans, a grilled-cheese sandwich with tomato and green chiles—because every dish in Arizona tastes better with green chiles—or fresh-baked cobbler. When it's cold outside, the homemade soups will take away

the chill. The cafe is open daily 7 am to 3 pm. [$] *Average main: $7* ✉ *38742 AZ 373, 1½ miles south of AZ 260* ☎ *928/735–7560* 🌐 *www.greermountainresort.com* 🕘 *No dinner.*

$ AMERICAN 🍴 **Rendezvous Diner.** This popular local diner has earned a reputation for serving some of Greer's tastiest dishes, not to mention the area's best hot spiced cider, a perfect choice during the chilly winter months. Of particular note are the pineapple teriyaki, green-chile burgers, and generous portions of homemade cobblers; the rhubarb is a specialty. The place is open year-round for breakfast and lunch. [$] *Average main: $7* ✉ *117 Main St.* ☎ *928/735–7483* 🕘 *Closed Tues. No dinner.*

$ RENTAL 🏨 **Greer Mountain Resort.** Budget travelers and families appreciate these cabin-style accommodations. **Pros:** on-site restaurant and in-room kitchens; good value. **Cons:** small resort with few other amenities. [$] *Rooms from: $95* ✉ *AZ 373, 1½ miles south of AZ 260* ☎ *928/735–7560* 🌐 *www.greermountainresort.com* 🛏 *9 units* 🍽 *No meals.*

$$ RENTAL 🏨 **Molly Butler Lodge & Cabins.** Colorful quilts and wood furnishings fill the history-theme rooms at Arizona's oldest lodge, which also includes dozens of cabins in the Greer area for larger parties and extended stays. **Pros:** historic charm; range of accommodations (some cabins sleep up to 8). **Cons:** minimal services; you're on your own (which could be a good thing). [$] *Rooms from: $125* ✉ *109 Main St.* ☎ *928/735–7617* 🌐 *www.mollybutlerlodge.com* 🛏 *7 rooms, 51 cabins* 🍽 *No meals.*

$$ RESORT 🏨 **Greer Lodge Resort & Cabins.** This resort runs through the main thoroughfare of Greer, and its accommodations range from basic motel rooms to spacious cabins. **Pros:** great place for city slickers to escape but still feel spoiled; range of accommodations. **Cons:** quaint setting can feel isolated after a few days. [$] *Rooms from: $125* ✉ *44 Main St.* ☎ *928/735–7216* 🌐 *www.greerlodgeaz.com* 🛏 *10 rooms, 10 cabins* 🍽 *No meals.*

NIGHTLIFE

Molly Butler Lodge. Tiny Greer's nightlife is limited to the bar and lounge of the Molly Butler Lodge, where you can listen to vintage tunes on the jukebox, sink into a cozy seat near the fireplace, play an arcade game, or challenge a local to a game of pool or darts. The bar usually closes by 11 in winter and just past midnight during the busier summer months. ✉ *109 Main St.* ☎ *928/735–7226* 🌐 *www.mollybutlerlodge.com.*

SPORTS AND THE OUTDOORS

Lazy Trout Trading Post. Fishing licenses, groceries, sleds in winter, tackle in the summer, and other supplies are for sale here, which is helpful considering the nearest large grocery store is more than a half hour away. You can grab a cup of joe, buy supplies for an afternoon picnic, and feel free to use the Wi-Fi for a quick email check. ✉ *38940 AZ 373* ☎ *928/735–7540* 🌐 *www.lazytrout.com.*

FISHING

Greer Lakes. The three Greer Lakes are actually the Bunch, River, and Tunnel reservoirs. Bait and fly-fishing options are scenic and plentiful, and there are several places to launch a boat. Winding through Greer, the Little Colorado River's West Fork is well stocked with brook and rainbow trout, and has 23 miles of fishable waters.

HIKING

Mount Baldy Trail. The difficult but accessible Mount Baldy Trail begins at **Sheeps Crossing,** southwest of Greer on AZ 273. In just under 8 miles (one-way) the trail climbs the northern flank of 11,590-foot Mount Baldy, the second-highest peak in Arizona. Note that the summit of Baldy is on the White Mountain Apache Reservation. Considered sacred land, this final ¼ mile is off-limits to non-Apaches. Please respect this boundary, no matter how much you wish to continue to the peak. *Moderate.* ☎ *928/333–6200 for Springerville Ranger District.*

SKIING

Apache-Sitgreaves National Forests. Trail maps for winter sports, including cross-country skiing, are available from the Apache-Sitgreaves National Forests outpost. ✉ *Springerville Ranger District, 165 S. Mountain Ave., Springerville* ☎ *928/333–6200* ⊕ *www.fs.usda.gov/asnf.*

Pole Knoll Trail System. Cross-country skiers find Greer an ideally situated hub for some of the mountain's best trails. About 2½ miles west of AZ 373 on AZ 260, a trailhead marks the starting point for the Pole Knoll Trail System, nearly 30 miles of well-marked, groomed cross-country trails interlacing through the Apache-Sitgreaves National Forests and color-coded by experience level. ✉ *Springerville Ranger District, 165 S. Mountain Ave., Springerville* ☎ *928/333–6200* ⊕ *www.fs.usda.gov/asnf.*

6

THE ROUND VALLEY AND CORONADO TRAIL

Named by Basque settlers in the late 1800s, the "Valle Redondo," or Round Valley, is a circular, high-mountain basin on the back side of the massive 10,912-foot Escudilla Mountain. This area once served as a unique Old West haven for the lawless—it was a great place to conceal stolen cattle and hide out for a while. Butch Cassidy, the Clantons, and the Smith Gang all spent time here. Home to sister cities Springerville and Eagar, the Round Valley is the ideal start to any journey on the Coronado Trail, a historic 123-mile switchback highway that starts in pine forests and ends with the cacti of the Sonoran Desert in Clifton. Along the way, you'll find quaint towns, charming inns, and plenty of reasons to marvel at what Mother Nature created.

CORONADO TRAIL

The 123-mile stretch of U.S. 191 from Springerville to Clifton.

One of the most picturesque drives in Arizona—and one of the curviest, too—the Coronado Trail is a 123-mile stretch of off-the-beaten-path road, where you'll find quaint inns, wandering meadows, steep cliffs, and a feast for the eyes. Start the journey with a full tank of gas, and don't be shy about turning around if the curves become too much.

WHEN TO GO

It's best to drive in summer. The majority of the road is anything but straight—it was once called the Devil's Highway for a reason. Don't drive on it in snow or ice.

GETTING HERE AND AROUND

Take U.S. 191 for 123 miles from Springerville to Clifton, and be prepared for an eye-opening ride. Allow a good four hours to make the steep, winding drive, more if you plan on making stops and having a leisurely trip.

EXPLORING

Coronado Trail. Surely one of the world's curviest roads, the twisting Coronado Trail portion of U.S. 191 was referred to as the Devil's Highway in its prior incarnation as U.S. 666. The route parallels the one allegedly followed more than 450 years ago by Spanish explorer Francisco Vásquez de Coronado on his search for the legendary Seven Cities of Cibola, where he'd heard that the streets were paved with gold and jewels.

This 123-mile stretch of highway is renowned for the transitions of its spectacular scenery over a dramatic 5,000-foot elevation change—from rolling meadows to spruce- and ponderosa pine–covered mountains, down into the Sonoran Desert's piñon pine, grassland savannas, juniper stands, and cacti. A trip down the Coronado Trail crosses through the Apache-Sitgreaves National Forests, as well as the Fort Apache and San Carlos Apache Indian reservations.

Pause at **Blue Vista,** perched on the edge of the Mogollon Rim, about 30 miles outside Alpine, to take in views of the Blue Range Mountains to the east and the succession of tiered valleys dropping some 4,000 feet back down into the Sonoran Desert. Still above the rim, this is one of your last opportunities to enjoy the blue spruce, ponderosa pine, and high-country mountain meadows.

About 17 miles south of Blue Vista, the Coronado Trail continues to twist and turn, eventually crossing under 8,786-foot **Rose Peak.** Named for the wild roses growing on its mountainside, Rose Peak is also home to a fire lookout tower from which peaks more than 100 miles away can be seen on a clear day. This is a great picnic-lunch stop.

After Rose Peak, enjoy the remaining scenery some 70 more miles until you reach the less scenic towns of Clifton and Morenci, homes to a massive copper mine. U.S. 191 then swings back west, links up with U.S. 70, and provides a fairly straight shot to Globe. ⊠ *From Springerville to Globe.*

SPRINGERVILLE-EAGAR

17 miles northeast of Greer, 45 miles east of Pinetop-Lakeside on AZ 260, 67 miles southeast of Petrified Forest National Park on U.S. 180.

Sister cities Springerville and Eagar are the self-proclaimed "Gateway to the White Mountains." Insulated by the unique geography of the Round Valley where they sit, Springerville and Eagar occupy a different climate belt from nearby Greer and Sunrise Park Resort, which means less-severe winter temperatures and lighter snowfall than in neighboring mountain towns.

WHEN TO GO

■ TIP➔ The Round Valley is the favorite of skiers in the know, who appreciate the location as they commute to the lifts at Sunrise with the sun always at their back—important when you consider the glare off those blanketed snowscapes between the resort and Pinetop-Lakeside. There's also a lot less traffic on this less-icy stretch of AZ 260.

On the other hand, although Springerville-Eagar doesn't get as much snow as other parts of the region, it remains a very remote area. It can be hard to reach—and leave—in winter.

GETTING HERE AND AROUND

It's about an hour drive from Pinetop-Lakeside to this isolated area.

**EN
ROUTE**

Springerville Volcanic Field. The junction of U.S. 180/191 and U.S. 60, just north of Springerville, is the perfect jumping-off spot for a driving tour of the Springerville Volcanic Field, which covers an area larger than the state of Rhode Island. On the southern edge of the Colorado Plateau, it's spread across a high-elevation plain similar to the Tibetan Plateau. Six miles north of Springerville on U.S. 180/191 are sweeping westward views of the double volcanoes **Twin Knolls.** As you travel west on U.S. 60, Green's Peak Road and various south-winding Forest Service roads make for a leisurely, hour-long drive past **St. Peter's Dome** and a stop for impressive views from **Green's Peak,** the topographic high point of the Springerville Field. A free, detailed driving-tour brochure of the Springerville Volcanic Field is available from the **Springerville-Eagar Regional Chamber of Commerce** (✉ *318 Main St., Springerville* ☎ *928/333-2123* ⊕ *www.sechamber.com*).

6

EXPLORING

Casa Malpais Archaeological Park. Built in the 13th century, the 14½-acre Casa Malpais Archaeological Park pueblo complex has a series of narrow terraces lining eroded edges of basalt (hardened lava flow) cliff, as well as an extensive system of subterranean rooms nestled within Earth's fissures underneath. Strategically designed gateways in the walls of the "House of the Badlands," as Spanish settlers called it, allow streams of sunlight to illuminate significant petroglyphs prior to the setting equinox or solstice sun. Casa Malpais's Great Kiva (any kiva over 30 feet is considered great) is square-cornered instead of round, consistent with Ancestral Puebloan practice. Some archaeologists believe the pueblo served as a regional ceremonial center for the Mogollon people. Both the Hopi and Zuni tribes trace their history to Casa Malpais. Start your visit at the Springerville Heritage Center, home of the Casa Malpais Museum. Two-hour tours leave at 9, 11, and 2. ✉ *418 E. Main St.* ☎ *928/333-5375* ⊕ *www.casamalpais.org* ☞ *$10* ☉ *Museum Mon.–Sat. 8–4, weather permitting; call ahead to confirm. Tours Mar.–Nov., Mon.–Sat. at 9, 11, and 2.*

Little House Museum. About 10 minutes' drive from Greer, the Little House Museum has a collection of local pioneer and ranching memorabilia, but it's the mesmerizing tones from a rare collection of automatic musical instruments that you remember—as well as the museum's colorful curator, Wink Crigler, with her tales of this region's lively past. Tours to archaeological digs and petroglyphs are available by appointment.

To reach the ranch, go 10 miles southwest of Eagar on AZ 260, turn south onto South Fork Road, and go 3 miles. ✉ *X Diamond Ranch, S. Fork Rd., 10 miles southwest of Eagar* ☎ *928/333–2286* 🌐 *www.xdiamondranch.com/museum.html* 🎫 *$12* 🕒 *By reservation only.*

Renée Cushman Art Collection Museum. One of the highlights of the Springerville Heritage Center is the Renée Cushman Art Collection Museum, which holds an extensive collection of objets d'art—some acquired on Ms. Cushman's travels, some collected with the accumulated resources of three wealthy husbands, and some willed to her by her artistic father. The items here include a Rembrandt engraving, pen-and-inks by Tiepolo, and some impressive European antiques, some dating back to the 15th century. ✉ *Springerville Heritage Center, 418 E. Main St.* ☎ *928/333–2123* 🎫 *Donations only* 🕒 *Mon.–Sat. 8–4.*

WHERE TO EAT

$ MEXICAN 🍴 **Booga Reds.** The delicious comfort food here, such as fish-and-chips and a roast-beef dinner, is worth a stop. Should your palate demand something spicier, try one of the many Mexican dishes—the enchiladas are wonderful. Save room for the daily fruit or cream pie. Booga Reds closes at 8 pm, so make your dinner an early one. If you're feeling like a libation or two, visit the on-site bar, Tequila Reds. [$] *Average main: $8* ✉ *521 E. Main St.* ☎ *928/333–2640.*

$ AMERICAN 🍴 **Java Blues.** With a coffeehouse vibe (overstuffed couches and stained-glass windows), this isn't your typical mountain eatery. Salads, soups, sandwiches, and a Greek Board—a variety of meats and cheeses served with toasted baguette—are on the lunch menu. A separate dinner menu and a full bar make it a favorite evening spot, too—don't miss the chicken-fried steak. The restaurant opens early and serves dinner every day but Sunday. [$] *Average main: $7* ✉ *341 E. Main St.* ☎ *928/333–2233* 🕒 *No dinner Sun.*

WHERE TO STAY

$ HOTEL 🏨 **Reed's Lodge.** This is an older motel but a town favorite, thanks to the helpful staff and a handful of perks. **Pros:** well-priced; fantastic service; gift shop on site. **Cons:** modest accommodations; few frills; some rooms in need of updating. [$] *Rooms from: $58* ✉ *514 E. Main St.* ☎ *928/333–4323, 800/814–6451* 🌐 *www.k5reeds.com* 🛏 *45 rooms, 5 suites* 🍽 *No meals.*

$ B&B/INN 🏨 **Rode Inn.** Two cardboard figures of John Wayne in full cowboy regalia are perched on a walkway above the lobby, and his photos decorate the walls, but there's more to this place than "The Duke" motif—the rooms and service here are excellent. **Pros:** comfortable; free Wi-Fi. **Cons:** take away the kitschy accessories and it's just an old Ramada Inn. [$] *Rooms from: $80* ✉ *242 E. Main St.* ☎ *928/333–4365* 🌐 *www.rodeinnmotels.com* 🛏 *60 rooms, 3 suites* 🍽 *Breakfast.*

$ RESORT 🏨 **X Diamond Ranch.** This magnificent ranch has log cabins complete with porches, fireplaces, and full kitchens, and a slew of activities—fly-fishing, horseback riding, and tours of Little Bear archaeological site among them. **Pros:** one of the best-known and most picturesque spots in the area. **Cons:** no on-site restaurant, so plan on making your own meals. [$] *Rooms from: $110* ✉ *S. Fork Rd., 10 miles southwest*

The White Mountains' elevation makes the area a great place to stay cool in summer.

of Eagar off AZ 260 ☎ *928/333–2286* ⊕ *www.xdiamondranch.com* ⇨ *7 cabins* ⦿ *No meals.*

SHOPPING

Reed's Lodge / K5 Adventures & Gallery. Here you can buy wares created by White Mountains artists and local craftspeople, including those from nearby reservations. The gallery teems with Western-themed paintings, books on local history, wildlife, cowboy poetry, and even John Wayne paper dolls. ✉ *Reed's Lodge, 514 E. Main St.* ☎ *928/333–4323* ⊕ *www. k5reeds.com.*

SPORTS AND THE OUTDOORS

Sweat Shop. For your mountain-sports needs, the Sweat Shop rents skis, snowboards, and mountain bikes. ✉ *42 N. Main St., Eagar* ☎ *928/333–2950.*

FISHING

Becker Lake. Trout fishing is the specialty at Becker Lake; call for seasonal bait requirements. ✉ *U.S. 60, 2 miles northwest of Springerville* ☎ *928/367–4281* ⊕ *www.azgfd.gov.*

Big Lake. Known to many as the "queen of all trout lakes," Big Lake is stocked each spring and fall with rainbow, brook, and cutthroat trout. ✉ *Springerville Ranger District, AZ 273, 24 miles south of AZ 260* ☎ *928/333–6200.*

Nelson Reservoir. Between Springerville-Eagar and Alpine, Nelson Reservoir is well stocked with rainbow, brown, and brook trout. ✉ *U.S. 191, Nutrioso* ☎ *928/333–4301.*

TOURS AND OUTFITTERS

Western United Drug. Open 365 days a year, Western United Drug has a well-stocked sporting-goods and outdoor-equipment section. ✉ *105 E. Main St.* ☎ *928/333–4321.*

ALPINE

27 miles south of Springerville-Eagar on U.S. 191.

Known as the Alps of Arizona, the tiny, scenic village of Alpine promotes its winter recreation opportunities most heavily, but outdoors enthusiasts find that the town, sitting on the lush plains of the San Francisco River, is also an ideal base for hiking, fishing, and mountain-biking excursions during the warmer months. There are summer cabins tucked in the pines, campgrounds, 11 lakes, and 200 miles of trout streams within a 30-mile radius.

WHEN TO GO

This area of the Apache-Sitgreaves National Forests is as remote as it gets, and the name Alpine should indicate the climate. If you're here in winter, expect road closures or delays if there's a storm. In summer, this is a great place to transition from green forests to, eventually, brown desert and cacti.

GETTING HERE AND AROUND

Take U.S. 191 south from Springerville for 27 miles. This is a good stop along the Coronado Trail.

EXPLORING

Blue Range Primitive Area. Directly east of Hannagan Meadow, these unspoiled 170,000 acres, lovingly referred to by locals as "the Blue," are the last designated primitive area in the United States. The diverse terrain surrounds the Blue River and is crossed by the Mogollon Rim from east to west. No motorized or mechanized equipment is allowed, and that includes mountain bikes; passage is restricted to foot or horseback. Many trails interlace the Blue: prehistoric paths of the ancient native peoples, cowboy trails to move livestock between pastures and water sources, access routes to lookout towers and fire trails. Avid backpackers and campers may want to spend a few days exploring the dozens of hiking trails. Even though trail access is fairly good, hikers need to remember that this is primitive, rough country, and it's essential to carry adequate water and other supplies. Access it off Highway 191; get directions and instructions from the Alpine Ranger District. ✉ *Alpine Ranger District* ☎ *928/339–5000.*

WHERE TO STAY

$ RENTAL

🏨 **Downs' Ranch Hide-Away.** If you're looking for a vacation that is really back-of-beyond, do as the locals do and go "down on the Blue." **Pros:** a truly one-of-a-kind way to commune with Mother Nature; open year-round. **Cons:** zero amenities; no credit cards. [$] *Rooms from: $75* ✉ *738 Downs Ranch Rd., on Forest Service Rd. 281, 35 miles south of Alpine* ☎ *928/339–4952* 🌐 *www.dcoutfitters.com/downsRanch.php* 🛏 *4 cabins* 💳 *No credit cards* 🍴 *No meals.*

$ B&B/INN

🏨 **Tal-Wi-Wi Lodge.** This lodge draws many repeat visitors—particularly driving and motorcycle enthusiasts—to its lush meadows, a favorite for bird-watchers. **Pros:** best place to stay in Alpine; in-room Wi-Fi. **Cons:** only a few rooms have king-size beds; no phones in room (cell phones may not work well in this remote area); only open nine months a year. [$] *Rooms from: $90* ✉ *U.S. 191* ☎ *928/339–4319* 🌐 *www.talwiwilodge.com* 🛏 *20 rooms* 🕒 *Closed Jan.–Mar.* 🍴 *No meals.*

SPORTS AND THE OUTDOORS

BICYCLING

Luna Lake Trail. The 8-mile Luna Lake Trail, 5 miles east of U.S. 191, is a good two-hour ride for beginner and intermediate cyclists. The trailhead is on the north side of the lake, before the campground entrance. ✉ *Apline Ranger District, U.S. 180* ☎ *928/339–5000.*

FISHING

Luna Lake. A divergence of the San Francisco River's headwaters, 80-acre Luna Lake, 5 miles east of U.S. 191, is well stocked with rainbow trout. ✉ *Alpine Ranger District, U.S. 180* ☎ *928/339–5000.*

Tackle Shop. At the junction of U.S. 180 and 191, Tackle Shop carries trout and fly-fishing supplies. ✉ *Junction U.S. 180 E and 191 S* ☎ *928/339–4338* 🌐 *www.thetackleshopaz.com.*

HIKING

Escudilla National Recreation Trail. A 3-mile trail that is more idyllic than arduous, the Escudilla National Recreation Trail winds through the Escudilla Wilderness to the summit of towering, 10,912-foot **Escudilla Mountain,** Arizona's third-tallest peak. The trail climbs 1,300 feet to a fire tower ¼ mile from the summit. From Alpine, take U.S. 191 north and follow the signs to Hulsey Lake (about 5 miles). *Moderate.* ✉ *Alpine Ranger District, U.S. 191, Hulsey Lake* ☎ *928/339–5000.*

SNOW SPORTS

Williams Valley Winter Sports Area. This winter recreation area, 2.5 miles west of town, has 12.5 miles of cross-country and snowshoe trails of varying difficulty. Toboggan Hill is a favorite with families who sled, toboggan, and tube. Shelters, picnic facilities, and toilets are available. Pick up an Apache-Sitgreaves National Forests map and "Winter Sports" brochure from the Alpine Ranger District, and call for conditions prior to heading out. ✉ *Alpine Ranger District, Forest Service Rd. 249* ☎ *928/339–5000.*

6

HANNAGAN MEADOW

23 miles south of Alpine, 50 miles south of Springerville-Eagar.

Remote even for Eastern Arizona standards, Hannagan Meadow is located along the picturesque Coronado Trail. Stop and have a bite to eat at the lodge, fill up your gas tank (bring cash), or linger a bit and rest your head for the night. This is solitude at its finest.

WHEN TO GO

Just like other towns in Eastern Arizona, Hannagan Meadow is warm (not hot!) in summer and cold and snowy in winter. It's a good place to stop for the night and enjoy some time away from it all.

GETTING HERE AND AROUND

The Coronado Trail stretch of U.S. 191 passes through this remote part of the state.

EXPLORING

Hannagan Meadow. This lush, isolated, and mesmerizing spot at a 9,5000-foot elevation is home to elk, deer, and range cattle, as well as blue grouse, wild turkeys, and the occasional eagle. Adjacent to the meadow is the Blue Range Primitive Area, which provides access to miles of untouched wilderness and some stunning rugged terrain. It's a designated recovery area for the endangered Mexican gray wolf. Francisco Vásquez de Coronado and his party may have come through the meadow on their famed expedition in 1540 to find the Seven Cities of Cibola. ⊠ *Alpine Ranger District, Hannagan Meadow* ☎ *928/339–5000.*

WHERE TO STAY

$

RESORT

⛄ **Hannagan Meadow Lodge.** Antiques and floral prints impart a genteel, Victorian quality to this lodge, while log cabins are more rustic. **Pros:** gorgeous surroundings and fantastic service. **Cons:** you should not rely on daily room cleaning; much more lodge than hotel. [$] *Rooms from: $85* ⊠ *Hannagan Meadow, U.S. 191, 22 miles south of Alpine, HC 61, P.O. Box 335* ☎ *928/339–4370* ⊕ *www.hannaganmeadow.com* ⌨ *7 rooms, 8 cabins* ⎮⊙⎮ *No meals.*

SPORTS AND THE OUTDOORS

Want to get away from it all? The **Apache Ranger District** of the Apache-Sitgreaves National Forests has secluded spaces for outdoor adventures year-round. Hikers and anglers can check out the 11,000-acre **Bear Wallow Wilderness Area** (west of U.S. 191 and bordered by Forest Service roads 25 and 54), which has cool, flowing streams stocked with native Apache trout. The **Rose Spring Trail** is a pleasant 5½-mile hike with a moderate gradient and magnificent views from the Mogollon Rim's edge; the trailhead is at the end of Forest Service Road 54. **Reno Trail** and **Gobbler Trail** both drop into the main canyon from well-marked trailheads off Forest Service Road 25. Reno Trail meanders 2 miles through conifer forest and aspen, while Gobbler Trail is 2½ miles long, with views overlooking the Black River and Fort Apache Indian Reservation. This designated wilderness (and some of its trails) borders the San Carlos Apache Indian Reservation, where an advance permit is required for entry.

Hannagan Meadow Winter Recreation Area. In winter, try the 8.5 miles of groomed cross-country trails of the Hannagan Meadow Winter Recreation Area, which also is part of the Apache-Sitgreaves National Forest. The 4.5-mile **Clell Lee Loop** is an easy route; the more advanced, ungroomed **KP Rim Loop** traverses upper elevations of the Blue Range Primitive Area and provides some of the most varied (and tranquil) remote skiing in the state. The area just northeast of U.S. 191 is a snowmobiling playground. Trailheads are at U.S. 191 and Forest Service Road 576. There are no rental shops nearby, so bring your own equipment.

CLOSE UP

Petroglyphs: The Writing on the Wall

The rock art of early Native Americans is carved or painted on basalt boulders, on canyon walls, and on the underside of overhangs throughout the area. No one knows the exact meaning of these signs, and interpretations vary; they've been seen as elements in shamanistic or hunting rituals, as clan signs, maps, or even indications of visits by extraterrestrials.

WHERE TO FIND IT

Susceptible to (and often already damaged by) vandalism, many rock-art sites aren't open to the public. Two good petroglyphs to check out at **Petrified Forest National Park** are Newspaper Rock, an overlook near mile marker 12, and Puerco Pueblo, near mile marker 11. Other sites in Arizona include **Hieroglyphic Point** in Salt River Canyon, and **Five-Mile Canyon** in Snowflake.

DETERMINING ITS AGE

It's just as difficult to date a "glyph" as it is to understand it. Archaeologists try to determine a general time frame by judging the style, the date of the ruins and pottery in the vicinity, the amount of patination (formation of minerals) on the design, or the superimposition of newer images on top of older ones. Most of Eastern Arizona's rock art is estimated to be at least 1,000 years old, and many of the glyphs were created even earlier.

VARIED IMAGES

Some glyphs depict animals like bighorn sheep, deer, bear, and mountain lions; others are geometric patterns. The most unusual are the anthropomorphs, strange humanlike figures with elaborate headdresses. Concentric circles are a common design. A few of these circles served as solstice signs, indicating the summer and winter solstice and other important dates. At the solstice, when the angle of the sun is just right, a shaft of light shines through a crack in a nearby rock, illuminating the center of the circle. Archaeologists believe that these solar calendars helped determine the time for ceremonies and planting.

Many solstice signs are in remote regions, but you can visit Petrified Forest National Park around June 20 to see a concentric circle illuminated during the summer solstice. The glyph, reached by a paved trail just a few hundred yards from the parking area, is visible year-round, but light shines directly in the center during the week of the solstice. The phenomenon occurs at 9 am.

■TIP➜ Do not touch petroglyphs or pictographs—the oil from your hands can damage the images.

6

Contact **Apache-Sitgreaves National Forests'** Alpine Ranger District (☎ *928/339–5000* ⊕ *www.fs.usda.gov/asnf*) for trail maps and information. ✉ *Alpine Ranger District, U.S. 191, Hannagan Meadow.*

THE PETRIFIED FOREST AND AROUND

Only about 1½ hours from Show Low and the lush, verdant forests of the White Mountains, Arizona's diverse and dramatic landscape changes from pine-crested mountains to sunbaked terrain. Inside the lunar landscape of the Painted Desert is the fossil-filled Petrified Forest.

PETRIFIED FOREST NATIONAL PARK

Northern Entrance: 160 miles north of Hannagan Meadow on AZ 191 and Interstate 40, 27 miles east of Holbrook on Interstate 40. Southern Entrance: 18 miles east of Holbrook on U.S. 180.

There are few places where the span of geologic and human history is as wide or apparent as it is at Petrified Forest National Park. Fossilized trees and countless other fossils date back to the Triassic Period, while a stretch of the famed Route 66 of more modern lore is protected within park boundaries. Ancestors of the Hopi, Zuni, and Navajo left petroglyphs, pottery, and even structures built of petrified wood. Nine park sites are on the National Register of Historic Places; one, the Painted Desert Inn, is one of only 3% of such sites that are also listed as National Historic Landmarks.

The good thing is that most of Petrified Forest's treasures can easily be viewed without a great amount of athletic conditioning. Much can be seen by driving along the main road, from which historic sites are readily accessible. By combining a drive along the park road with a short hike here and there and a visit to one of the park's landmarks, you can see most of the sights in as little as half a day.

WHEN TO GO

The park is rarely crowded. Weatherwise, the best time to visit is autumn, when nights are chilly but daytime temperatures hover near 70°F. Half of all yearly rain falls between June and August, so it's a good time to spot blooming wildflowers. The park is least crowded in winter, because of cold winds and occasional snow, though daytime temperatures are in the 50s and 60s.

PLANNING YOUR TIME

● PETRIFIED
FOREST IN
ONE DAY

A nonstop drive through the park (28 miles) takes only 45 minutes, but you can spend a half day or more exploring if you stop along the way. From almost any vantage point you can see the multicolor rocks and hills, where small Triassic dinosaurs are believed to have once roamed (a few of their fossils have been unearthed here).

Entering from the north, stop at **Painted Desert Visitor Center** for a 20-minute introductory film. Two miles in, the **Painted Desert Inn National Historic Landmark** provides guided ranger tours. Drive south 8 miles to reach **Puerco Pueblo,** a 100-room pueblo built before 1400. Continuing south, you'll encounter **Newspaper Rock,** marked with Puebloan petroglyphs, and, just beyond, **the Tepees,** cone-shape rock formations.

Blue Mesa is roughly the midpoint of the drive, and the start of a 1-mile, moderately steep loop hike that leads you around badland hills made of bentonite clay. Drive on for 5 miles until you come to **Jasper Forest,**

just past **Agate Bridge,** with views of the landscape strewn with petrified logs. **Crystal Forest,** about 20 miles south of the north entrance, is named for the smoky quartz, amethyst, and citrine along the 0.8-mile loop trail. **Rainbow Forest Museum,** at the park's south entrance, has restrooms, a bookstore, and exhibits. Just behind Rainbow Forest Museum is **Giant Logs,** a 0.4-mile loop that takes you to "Old Faithful," the largest log in the park, estimated to weigh 44 tons.

> ### LOOK AND TOUCH— BUT DON'T TAKE
>
> One of the most commonly asked questions about the Petrified Forest is, "Can I touch the wood?" Yes! Feel comfortable to touch anything, pick it up, inspect it . . . just make sure you put it back where you found it. It's illegal to remove even a small sliver of fossilized wood from the park.

GETTING HERE AND AROUND

Holbrook, the nearest large town with services such as gas or food, is on U.S. 40, roughly 30 miles from either of the park's two entrances.

Parking is free, and there's ample space at all trailheads, as well as at the visitor center and the museum. The main park road extends 28 miles from the Painted Desert Visitor Center (north entrance) to the Rainbow Forest Museum (south entrance). For park road conditions, call ☎ 928/524–6228.

PARK ESSENTIALS

ACCESSIBILITY   The visitor center, museum, and overlooks on the scenic drive are wheelchair accessible. All trails are paved, and all are accessible except Blue Mesa, which is very steep.

PARK FEES
AND PERMITS   Entrance fees are $10 per car for seven consecutive days or $5 per person on foot, bicycle, motorcycle, or bus. Backcountry hiking and camping permits are free (limit of 15 days) at the Painted Desert Visitor Center or the Rainbow Forest Museum before 4 pm.

PARK HOURS   It's a good idea to call ahead or check the website, because the park's hours vary so much; as a rule of thumb, the park is open daily from sunrise to sunset. Hours are approximately: 8 am to 5 pm from November to February, daily 7–6:30 in March, daily 7–7 in April, daily 7 am–7:30 pm in May, daily 7 am–8 pm in June and July, daily 7 am–7:30 pm in August, and daily 7–6 in September and October. Keep in mind that the area does not observe daylight saving time.

VISITOR INFORMATION

Park Contact Information Petrified Forest National Park ⊠ *1 Park Rd., Petrified Forest* ☎ *928/524–6228* ⊕ *www.nps.gov/pefo.*

VISITOR
CENTERS   **Painted Desert Inn National Historic Landmark.** This third visitor center at the park isn't as large as the others, but here you can get information as well as view cultural history exhibits. ⊠ *2 miles north of Painted Desert Visitor Center.*

Painted Desert Visitor Center. This is the place to go for general park information and an informative 20-minute film. Proceeds from books purchased here will fund continued research and interpretive activities

Walking Petrified Forest's short trails can be a nice break from driving along Interstate 40, which crosses the park.

for the park. ⊠ *North entrance, off I–40, 27 miles east of Holbrook* ☎ *928/524–6228.*

Rainbow Forest Museum and Visitor Center. Be sure to see Gurtie, a skeleton of a phytosaur (a crocodilelike carnivore) among the artifacts of early reptiles, dinosaurs, and petrified wood housed here. ⊠ *South entrance, off U.S. 180, 18 miles southeast of Holbrook* ☎ *928/524–6228.*

EXPLORING
HISTORIC SITES

Agate House. This eight-room pueblo is thought to have been built entirely of petrified wood 700 years ago. Researchers believe it might have been used as a temporary dwelling by seasonal farmers or traders from one of the area tribes. ⊠ *Rainbow Forest Museum parking area.*

Newspaper Rock. See huge boulders covered with petroglyphs believed to have been carved by the Pueblo Indians more than 500 years ago. ■TIP→ Look through the binoculars that are provided here—you'll be surprised at what the naked eye misses. ⊠ *6 miles south of Painted Desert Visitor Center on the main park road.*

Painted Desert Inn National Historic Landmark. A nice place to stop and rest in the shade, this site offers vast views of the Painted Desert from several lookouts. Inside, cultural-history exhibits, murals, and Native American crafts are on display. ⊠ *2 miles north of Painted Desert Visitor Center on the main park road.*

Puerco Pueblo. This is a 100-room pueblo, built before 1400 and said to have housed Ancestral Puebloan people. Many visitors come to see

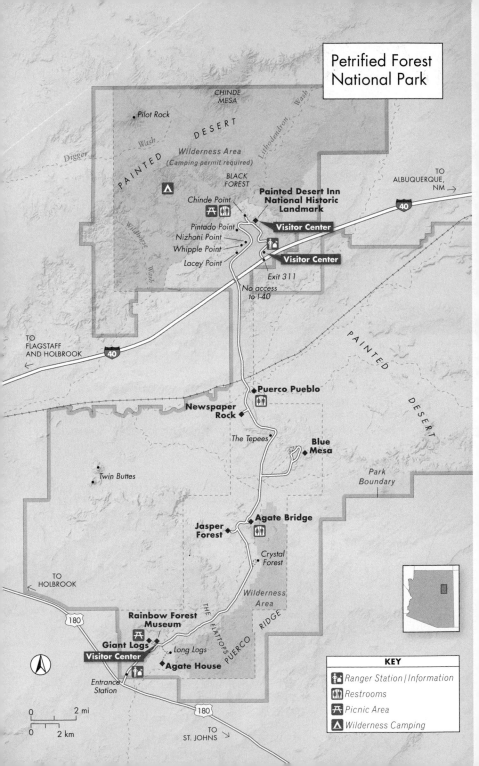

Petrified Forest National Park

CHINDE MESA

• Pilot Rock

PAINTED   DESERT

Digger   Wash

Wash

Lithodendron   Wash

TO ALBUQUERQUE, NM →

*Wilderness Area
(Camping permit required)*

BLACK FOREST

Wilderness   Wash

△

Chinde Point •
⛰ 🚻

Painted Desert Inn National Historic Landmark

◆ **Visitor Center**

Pintado Point •
Nizhoni Point •
Whipple Point •
Lacey Point •

🚹 ◆ **Visitor Center**

Exit 311

No access to I-40

40

TO FLAGSTAFF AND HOLBROOK ←
40

P A I N T E D

🚻 ◆ **Puerco Pueblo**

Newspaper Rock ◆

The Tepees

◆ **Blue Mesa**

D E S E R T

• Twin Buttes

Park Boundary

Jasper Forest ◆

◆ 🚻 **Agate Bridge**

Crystal Forest

TO HOLBROOK ←

180

THE FLATTOPS

PUERCO RIDGE

Wilderness Area

Rainbow Forest Museum ⛰

Giant Logs ◆
◆ *Long Logs*

◆ **Visitor Center**
🚹

◆ **Agate House**

Entrance Station

180

TO ST. JOHNS ↗

| 0 | 2 mi |
| 0 | 2 km |

KEY

🚹🚹 *Ranger Station / Information*
🚻 *Restrooms*
⛰ *Picnic Area*
△ *Wilderness Camping*

Petrified Forest Flora and Fauna

Engelmann's asters and sunflowers are among the blooms in the park each summer. Juniper trees, cottonwoods, and willows grow along Puerco River wash, providing shelter for all manner of wildlife. You might spot mule deer, coyotes, prairie dogs, and foxes, while other inhabitants, like porcupines and bobcats, tend to hide. Bird-watchers should keep an eye out for mockingbirds, red-tailed and Swainson's hawks, roadrunners, swallows, and hummingbirds. Look for all three kinds of lizards—collared, side-blotched, and southern prairie—in rocks.

Beware of rattlesnakes. They're common but can generally be easily avoided: Watch where you step, and don't step anywhere you can't see. If you do come across a rattler, give it plenty of space, and let it go its way before you continue on yours. Other reptiles are just as common but not as dangerous. The gopher snake looks similar to a rattlesnake, but is nonpoisonous. The collared lizard, with its yellow head, can be seen scurrying out of your way in bursts measured at up to 15 mph. They aren't poisonous, but they will bite in the rare instance of being caught.

petroglyphs, as well as a solar calendar. ⊠ *10 miles south of the Painted Desert Visitor Center on the main park road.*

SCENIC DRIVE

Painted Desert Scenic Drive. A 28-mile scenic drive takes you through the park from one entrance to the other. If you begin at the north end, the first 5 miles of the drive take you along the edge of a high mesa, with spectacular views of the Painted Desert. Beyond lies the desolate Painted Desert Wilderness Area. After the 5-mile point, the road crosses Interstate 40, then swings south toward the Puerco River across a landscape covered with sagebrush, saltbrush, sunflowers, and Apache plume. Past the river, the road climbs onto a narrow mesa leading to Newspaper Rock, a panel of Pueblo Indian rock art. Then the road bends southeast, enters a barren stretch, and passes teepee-shape buttes in the distance. Next you come to Blue Mesa, roughly the park's midpoint and a good place to stop for views of petrified logs. The next stop on the drive is Agate Bridge, really a 100-foot log over a wide wash. The remaining overlooks are Jasper Forest and Crystal Forest, where you can get a further glimpse of the accumulated petrified wood. On your way out of the park, stop at the Rainbow Forest Museum for a rest and to shop for a memento. ⊠ *Begins at Painted Desert Visitor Center.*

SCENIC STOPS

Agate Bridge. Here you'll see a 100-foot log spanning a 40-foot-wide wash. ⊠ *19 miles south of Painted Desert Visitor Center on the main park road.*

Crystal Forest. The fragments of petrified wood strewn here once held clear quartz and amethyst crystals. ⊠ *20 miles south of Painted Desert Visitor Center on the main park road.*

Different minerals in different concentrations cause the rich colors in petrified wood and in the Painted Desert.

Giant Logs Interpretive Loop Trail. A short walk leads you past the park's largest log, known as Old Faithful. It's considered the largest because of its diameter (9 feet, 9 inches), as well as how tall it once was. ⊠ *28 miles south of Painted Desert Visitor Center on the main park road, 1 Park Rd.*

Jasper Forest. More of an overlook than a forest, this spot has a large concentration of petrified trees in jasper or red. ⊠ *17 miles south of Painted Desert Visitor Center on the main park road.*

The Tepees. Witness the effects of time on these cone-shaped rock formations colored by iron, manganese, and other minerals. ⊠ *8 miles south of Painted Desert Visitor Center on the main park road.*

WHERE TO EAT AND STAY

There's no lodging or campgrounds within the Petrified Forest. Backcountry camping is allowed if you obtain a free permit at the visitor center or museum; the only camping allowed is minimal-impact camping in a designated zone in the wilderness area. Group size is limited to eight. RVs aren't allowed. There are no fire pits, nor is any shade available. Also note that if it rains, that pretty Painted Desert rock formation turns to sticky clay.

Dining in the park is limited to a cafeteria in the Painted Desert Visitor Center and snacks in the Rainbow Forest Museum. You may want to pack a lunch and eat at one of the park's picnic areas.

SPORTS AND THE OUTDOORS

Because the park goes to great pains to maintain the integrity of the fossil- and artifact-strewn landscape, sports and outdoors options in the park are limited to on-trail hiking.

HIKING

All trails begin off the main road, with restrooms at or near the trailheads. Most maintained trails are relatively short, paved, clearly marked, and, with a few exceptions, easy to moderate in difficulty. Hikers with greater stamina can make their own trails in the wilderness area, located just north of the Painted Desert Visitor Center. Watch your step for rattlesnakes, which are common in the park—if left alone and given a wide berth, they're passed easily enough.

EASY **Crystal Forest Trail.** This easy ¾-mile loop leads you past petrified wood that once held quartz crystals and amethyst chips. *Easy.* ⊠ *Trailhead: 20 miles south of the Painted Desert Visitor Center.*

Giant Logs Trail. At 0.4 miles, Giant Logs is the park's shortest trail. The loop leads you to Old Faithful, the park's largest petrified log—9 feet, 9 inches at its base, weighing an estimated 44 tons. *Easy.* ⊠ *Trailhead: directly behind Rainbow Forest Museum, 28 miles south of Painted Desert Visitor Center.*

Long Logs Trail. Although barren, this easy 1.6-mile loop passes the largest concentration of wood in the park. *Easy.* ⊠ *Trailhead: 26 miles south of Painted Desert Visitor Center.*

FAMILY **Puerco Pueblo Trail.** A relatively flat and interesting 0.3-mile trail takes you past remains of a home of the Ancestral Puebloan people, built before 1400. The trail is paved and wheelchair accessible. *Easy.* ⊠ *Trailhead: 10 miles south of Painted Desert Visitor Center.*

MODERATE
Fodor's Choice
★
Agate House. A fairly flat 1-mile trip takes you to an eight-room pueblo sitting high on a knoll. *Moderate.* ⊠ *Trailhead: 26 miles south of Painted Desert Visitor Center.*

Blue Mesa. Although it's only 1 mile long and significantly steeper than the rest, this trail at the park's midway point is one of the most popular and worth the effort. *Moderate.* ⊠ *Trailhead: 14 miles south of Painted Desert Visitor Center.*

Painted Desert Rim. The 1-mile trail is at its best in early morning or late afternoon, when the sun accentuates the brilliant red, blue, purple, and other hues of the desert and petrified forest landscape. *Moderate.* ⊠ *Trail runs between Tawa Point and Kachina Point, 1 mile north of Painted Desert Visitor Center; drive to either point from Visitor Center.*

DIFFICULT **Kachina Point.** This is the trailhead for wilderness hiking at Petrified Forest National Park. A 1-mile trail leads to the Wilderness Area, but from there you're on your own. There are no developed trails, so hiking here is cross-country style. Expect to see strange formations, beautifully colored landscapes, and maybe, just maybe, a pronghorn antelope. *Difficult.* ⊠ *Trailhead: on the northwest side of the Painted Desert Inn National Historic Landmark.*

6

HOLBROOK

27 miles west of Petrified Forest National Park via Interstate 40.

Downtown Holbrook is a monument to Route 66 kitsch. The famous "Mother Road" traveled through the center of Holbrook before Interstate 40 replaced it as the area's major east–west artery, and remnants of the "good ol' days" can be found all over town. It's probably not worth staying overnight in Holbrook, although the town's iconic Wigwam Motel is a quirky and iconic option if you do find yourself here.

GETTING HERE AND AROUND

Holbrook is on Interstate 40, approximately 90 miles east of Flagstaff, and 30 miles west of Petrified Forest National Park. You can access AZ 77, en route to Snowflake, Taylor, and other Eastern Arizona recreation towns, directly from Interstate 40 in Holbrook.

WHERE TO STAY

$ HOTEL **Wigwam Motel.** On the National Register of Historic Places, the Wigwam consists of 15 bright-white concrete tepees. **Pros:** impeccably kitschy; one of the signature spots along Route 66. **Cons:** very sparse accommodations that can fit no more than two. [$] *Rooms from: $62* ✉ *811 West Hopi Dr., Holbrook* ☎ *928/524–3048* 🌐 *www.galerie-kokopelli.com/wigwam* 🛏 *15 rooms* 🍴 *No meals.*

TUCSON

WELCOME TO TUCSON

TOP REASONS TO GO

★ **Get close to the cacti:** Unique to this region, the saguaro is the quintessential symbol of the Southwest. See them at Sabino Canyon and Saguaro National Park.

★ **Enjoy Mexican food:** Tucson boasts that it's the "Mexican Food Capital," and you won't be disappointed at any of the authentic restaurants.

★ **Explore the Arizona–Sonora Desert Museum:** Anyone who thinks that museums are boring hasn't been here, where you can learn about the region's animals, plants, and geology up close in a gorgeous, mostly outdoor setting.

★ **Tour Mission San Xavier del Bac:** The "White Dove of the Desert" is the oldest building in Tucson. Ornate carvings and frescoes inside add to the mystical quality of this active parish on the Tohono O'odham Reservation.

★ **Stroll the U of A campus:** Stop in at one of the five museums, then walk University Boulevard and 4th Avenue for a taste of Tucson's hipper element.

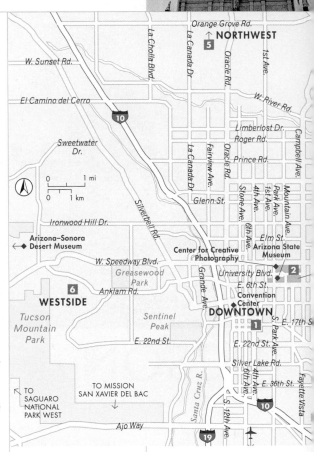

1 Downtown. Three historic districts—Barrio Historico, El Presidio, and Armory Park—encompass the Downtown area, and Congress Street is the hub of Tucson nightlife.

2 The University of Arizona. The 353-acre campus, classified as an arboretum, has several top-rated museums. At the west entrance, University Boulevard is lined with boutiques, cafés, and bookstores.

3 Central and Eastside. This mostly residential area is home to Tucson's zoo, its largest indoor shopping mall (Park Place), and its best municipal golf course (Randolph Park).

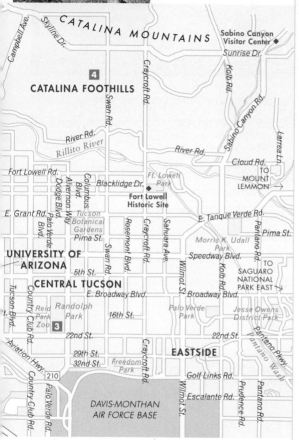

CATALINA MOUNTAINS

Sabino Canyon
Visitor Center ◆

Sunrise Dr.

[4]
CATALINA FOOTHILLS

Campbell Ave.
Skyline Dr.
Craycroft Rd.
Kolb Rd.
Swan Rd.
Sabino Canyon Rd.
Larrea Ln.

River Rd.
Rillito River
River Rd.
Cloud Rd.

Fort Lowell Rd.
Columbus Blvd.
Alvernon Way
Dodge Blvd.
Blacklidge Dr.
Ft. Lowell Park
TO MOUNT LEMMON →
Fort Lowell Historic Site

E. Grant Rd.
Palo Verde Blvd.
Tucson Botanical Gardens
Pima St.
Rosemont Blvd.
Craycroft Rd.
Sahuara Ave.
E. Tanque Verde Rd.
Pantano Rd.
Pima St.

UNIVERSITY OF ARIZONA
Swan Rd.
Morris K. Udall Park
Speedway Blvd.
Wilmot St.
Kolb Rd.
TO SAGUARO NATIONAL PARK EAST ↘

Tucson Blvd.
5th St.
CENTRAL TUCSON
E. Broadway Blvd.
Broadway Blvd.
Palo Verde Park
Jesse Owens District Park

Country Club Rd.
Reid Park Zoo
Randolph Park
16th St.
[3]
22nd St.
29th St.
32nd St.
Freedom Park
Craycroft Rd.
22nd St.
EASTSIDE
Pantano Pkwy
Pantano Wash

Aviation Hwy.
210
Palo Verde Rd.
Country Club Rd.
DAVIS-MONTHAN AIR FORCE BASE
Golf Links Rd.
Wilmot St.
Escalante Rd.
Prudence Rd.
Pantano Rd.

GETTING ORIENTED

The metropolitan Tucson area covers more than 500 square miles in a valley ringed by mountains—the Santa Catalinas to the north, the Santa Ritas to the south, the Rincons to the east, and the Tucson Mountains to the west. Saguaro National Park bookends Tucson, with one section on the far east side and the other out west near the Arizona–Sonora Desert Museum. The central portion of the city has most of the shops, restaurants, and businesses, but not many tourist sites. Downtown's historic district and the neighboring university area are much smaller and easily navigated on foot. Up north in the Catalina Foothills are first-class resorts, restaurants, and hiking trails, most with spectacular views of the entire valley.

7

[4] Catalina Foothills.
North of River Road the land becomes hilly and streets wind up to beautiful homes and resorts. At the east end, Sabino Canyon is a must for hikers.

[5] Northwest. Suburban sprawl at its finest, this part of town just keeps growing. A dude ranch and a few

riding stables are holdouts from a quieter era.

[6] Westside. The untamed Tucson Mountain region embraces miles of saguaro forests, the Arizona–Sonora Desert Museum, and Mission San Xavier del Bac on the Tohono O'odham Reservation.

Updated by
Mara Levin

The Old Pueblo, as Tucson is affectionately known, is built upon a deep Native American, Spanish, Mexican, and Old West foundation, and you can find elements of these influences in the city's architecture, restaurants, and friendly, relaxed vibe. Arizona's second-largest city is both a bustling center of business and development and a laid-back university and resort town, with abundant hiking trails and nature preserves. Tucson is particularly popular among golfers and spa-goers. Saguaro National Park, along with the four mountain ranges surrounding the city, provides a variety of outdoor activities.

Metropolitan Tucson has more than 850,000 residents, including thousands of snowbirds, who flee colder climes to enjoy the sun that shines on the city more than 340 days out of 365. The city's tricultural population (Hispanic, Anglo, Native American) offers visitors the chance to see how these cultures interact and to sample their flavorful cuisine.

The city also has a youthful energy, largely due to the population of students attending the University of Arizona. Although high-tech industries have moved into the area, the economy still relies heavily on the university and tourism. Come summer, though, you'd never guess; when the snowbirds and students depart, Tucson can be a sleepy place.

TUCSON PLANNER

WHEN TO GO

Summer lodging rates (late May to September) are hugely discounted, even at many of the resorts, but there's a good reason: summer in Tucson is hot! Swimming and indoor activities like visiting museums (and spa treatments) are doable; but only the hardiest hikers and golfers stay out past noon in summer.

Tucson averages only 12 inches of rain a year. Winter temperatures hover around 65°F during the day and 38°F at night. Summers are unquestionably hot—July averages 104°F during the day and 75°F at night—but, as Tucsonans are fond of saying, "It's a dry heat."

The International Gem and Mineral Show descends on Tucson the first two weeks in February; book your hotel in advance or you'll be hard-pressed to find a room.

FESTIVALS AND EVENTS

FEBRUARY **Tubac Festival of the Arts.** This rural artisan extravaganza in February brings artists from around the country to exhibit their eclectic, fine, and tourist-oriented art in the charming village of Tubac. ⊠ *Tubac Plaza, Tubac* ☎ *520/398–2704* ⊕ *www.tubacaz.com/festival.*

Tucson Gem and Mineral Show. This huge two-week trade show in February, with multiple venues in and around downtown, is the largest of its kind in the world. Most vendors sell to the public as well as to wholesalers. The Tucson Convention & Visitors Bureau website (⊕ *www. visittucson.org/events/gem-show*) has a lot of information about the event. ☎ *520/322–5773* ⊕ *www.tgms.org.*

La Fiesta de los Vaqueros. America's largest outdoor midwinter rodeo is at the Tucson Rodeo Grounds the third weekend in February. ☎ *520/294– 8896* ⊕ *www.tucsonrodeo.com.*

MAY **4th Avenue Street Fair.** Feeling casual and eclectic? Hit Tucson's 4th Avenue Street Fair, usually held in May and December, where you can buy local hand-crafted wares while munching on every kind of festival food imaginable. ☎ *520/624–5004* ⊕ *www.fourthavenue.org.*

JUNE/JULY **Saguaro Harvest.** The majestic saguaro's fruit is harvested at Colossal Cave Mountain Park around late June. ☎ *520/647–7121* ⊕ *www. colossalcave.com.*

OCTOBER **Tucson Originals World Margarita Championship.** In October, Tucson Originals, a group of independent local restaurants, hosts the World Margarita Championship. Sample foods, wines, and killer margaritas—then cast your votes—prepared by more than 40 local indie chefs. ☎ *520/343–9985* ⊕ *www.tucsonoriginals.com.*

PLANNING YOUR TIME

Even if you have only one day, you can experience both the wild and developed parts of Tucson. You can visit the Arizona–Sonora Desert Museum in the morning and combine it with a stop at Mission San Xavier del Bac or Old Tucson Studios. On the way back to town, stop in Downtown's Barrio Historico and El Presidio neighborhoods to meander through the adobe-lined streets, then have dinner at one of the outstanding Mexican restaurants in Downtown or South Tucson.

Another option is spending a half day in Saguaro National Park. ■TIP→ Set out for a desert visit in the early morning when it's cooler and the liveliest time for wildlife. If you're based in the Foothills, you can choose Sabino Canyon instead; the saguaros are almost as plentiful and the vistas are equally rewarding. Nature in the morning can be

7

combined with an afternoon in the university area: visit any of the five campus museums, then stroll University Boulevard and 4th Avenue for ethnic eats and vintage boutiques.

If you have another day for exploring and like to shop, head south toward the Mexican border. If you haven't seen Mission San Xavier yet, it's directly en route to Tubac, an artists' colony with historic sights as well as galleries. You can then head back toward Tucson, stopping at the Titan Missile Museum or at one of the casinos.

GETTING HERE AND AROUND

You can fly to Tucson International Airport (TUS), which is 8½ miles south of Downtown, off the Valencia exit of Interstate 10, but cheaper, nonstop flights into Phoenix—a two-hour drive away on Interstate 10—are often easier to find. Once in town, a car is essential to get to the outlying tourist sights.

AIR TRAVEL

Air Contacts Tucson International Airport (TUS) ☎ *520/573–8100* ⊕ *www.flytucson.com.*

GROUND TRANSPOR-TATION Many hotels have a courtesy airport shuttle; inquire when making reservations. The Arizona Stagecoach shuttle, which has a service counter at the airport, will carry you between the airport and all parts of Tucson and Green Valley for $5 to $45, depending on the location.

Ground Transportation Contact Arizona Stagecoach ☎ *520/889–1000* ⊕ *www.azstagecoach.com.*

BUS TRAVEL

Within the city limits, public transportation, which is geared primarily to commuters, is available through Sun Tran, Tucson's bus system.

Bus Contact Sun Tran ☎ *520/792–9222* ⊕ *www.suntran.com.*

CAR TRAVEL

You'll need a car to get around Tucson and the surrounding area, and it makes sense to rent at the airport; all the major car-rental agencies are represented. To save a little on cost, Carefree Rent-a-Car, a local company, rents reliable used cars at good rates.

Driving time from the airport to the center of town varies, but it's usually less than a half hour; add 15 minutes to any destination during rush hours (7:30 to 9 am and 4:30 to 6 pm). Parking isn't a problem in most parts of town, except near the university, where there are several pay lots.

Car Rental Contact Carefree Rent-a-Car ✉ *6941 E. 22nd St., Eastside* ☎ *520/790–2655.*

TAXI TRAVEL

Taxi rates vary widely because they're unregulated, but the taxi companies listed here charge around $2 per mile plus an initial pickup fee of $15 from the airport. It's always wise to inquire about the cost before getting into a cab. It should be about $30 from the airport to central Tucson. AAA Sedan transports travelers in a little more comfort (in Lincoln Town Cars or SUVs) for a little more money (the rate into central

Tucson is $40). VIP Taxi and Yellow Cab dispatchers and drivers speak English and Spanish.

Taxi Contacts AAA Sedan ☎ *520/594-9444* ⊕ *www.azlimousines. com.* **VIP Taxi** ☎ *520/798-1111* ⊕ *www.taximagic.com.* **Yellow Cab** ☎ *520/624-6611, 520/300-0000* ⊕ *www.aaayellowaz.com.*

TRAIN TRAVEL

Amtrak serves the city with westbound trains (to Los Angeles, CA) and eastbound trains daily.

Train Contact Amtrak ✉ *400 E. Toole Ave., Downtown* ☎ *800/872-7245* ⊕ *www.amtrak.com.*

VISITOR INFORMATION

Contacts Metropolitan Tucson Convention and Visitors Bureau. The visitor center in La Placita Village is open 9–5 weekdays and 9–4 weekends. ✉ *100 S. Church Ave., Ste. 7199, Downtown* ☎ *520/624-1817, 800/638-8350* ⊕ *www.visittucson.org.*

NATIVE CULTURES

Mexican-Americans make up about 30% of Tucson's population, and play a major role in all aspects of daily life. The city's south-of-the-border soul is visible in its tile-roof architecture, mariachi festivals, and abundance of Mexican restaurants. Native Americans have a strong presence as well, especially the Tohono O'odham and the Pascua Yaqui. Mission San Xavier del Bac, a thriving reservation parish, is a good spot to experience religious festivals and to sample fry bread, a favorite Indian snack.

EXPLORING

Central Tucson—which has most of the shops, restaurants, and businesses—is roughly bounded by Craycroft Road to the east, Oracle Road to the west, River Road to the north, and 22nd Street to the south. The older Downtown section, east of Interstate 10 off the Broadway-Congress exit, is smaller and easy to navigate on foot. Downtown streets don't run on any sort of grid, however, and many are one way, so it's best to get a good, detailed map. The city's Westside area is the vast region west of Interstates 10 and 19, which includes the western section of Saguaro National Park and the San Xavier Indian Reservation.

DOWNTOWN TUCSON

The area bordered by Franklin Street on the north, Cushing Street on the south, Church Avenue on the east, and Main Avenue on the west contains more than two centuries of Tucson's history, dating from the original walled fortress, El Presidio de Tucson, built by the Spanish in 1776, when Arizona was still part of New Spain. A good deal of the city's history was destroyed in the 1960s, when large sections of Downtown's barrio were bulldozed to make way for the Tucson Convention Center, high-rises, and parking lots.

However, within the area's three small historic districts it's still possible to explore Tucson's cultural and architectural past. Adobe—brick made of mud and straw, cured in the hot sun—was used widely as a building

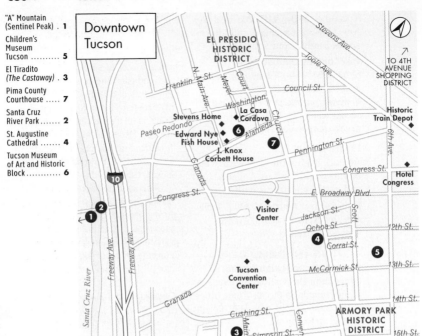

material in early Tucson because it provides natural insulation from the heat and cold and because it's durable in Tucson's dry climate. When these buildings are properly made and maintained, they can last for centuries. Driving around Downtown Tucson, you'll see adobe houses painted in vibrant hues such as bright pink and canary yellow.

Revitalization is in full swing Downtown, especially along Congress Street, where multiple restaurants and bars are now thriving, and a new streetcar line—scheduled for completion in mid-2014—will shuttle riders between Downtown and the 4th Avenue–University areas.

GETTING HERE AND AROUND
Downtown only approaches "bustling" on weekdays at lunchtime and for the evening rush hour (5 to 6 pm). It's possible to find metered street parking (free after 6 pm); otherwise, there is ample parking in several parking garages all within a few blocks of Congress Street.

TOP ATTRACTIONS
"A" Mountain. The original name of this mountain, Sentinel Peak, west of Downtown, came from its function as a lookout point for the Spanish, though the Pima village and cultivated fields that once lay at the base of the peak are long gone. In 1915 fans of the University of Arizona football team whitewashed a large "A" on its side to celebrate a victory, and the tradition has been kept up ever since—the permanent "A" is

now red, white, and blue. During the day the peak's a great place to get an overview of the town's layout; at night the city lights below form a dazzling carpet, but the teenage hangout/make-out scene may make some uncomfortable. ⊠ *Congress St. off Sentinel Peak Rd., Downtown.*

FAMILY **Children's Museum Tucson.** Youngsters are encouraged to touch and explore the science, language, and history exhibits here. They can examine a patient in the Medical Center and shop for healthy food in the Wellness Town Grocery Store. Investigation Station has air-pressure tubes where balls and scarves whiz around, and there's an Enchanted Forest for all ages to climb, build, and burn off steam. ⊠ *200 S. 6th Ave., Downtown* ☎ *520/792–9985* ⊕ *www.childrensmuseumtucson. org* ☎ *$8* ☉ *Tues.–Fri. 9–5, weekends 10–5.*

Downtown Historic Districts. North of the Convention Center and the government buildings that dominate Downtown, **El Presidio Historic District** is an architectural thumbnail of the city's former self. The north–south streets Court, Meyer, and Main are sprinkled with traditional Mexican adobe houses sitting cheek by jowl with territorial-style houses with wide attics and porches. Paseo Redondo, once called Snob Hollow, is the wide road along which wealthy merchants built their homes.

The area most closely resembling 19th-century Tucson is the **Barrio Historico,** also known as Barrio Viejo. The narrow streets of this neighborhood, including Convent Avenue, have a good sampling of thick-walled adobe houses. The colorfully painted houses are close to the street, hiding the yards and gardens within.

To the east of the Barrio Historico, across Stone Avenue, is the **Armory Park** neighborhood, mostly constructed by and for the railroad workers who settled here after the 1880s. The brick or wood territorial-style homes here were the Victorian era's adaptation to the desert climate.

El Tiradito (*The Castaway*). No one seems to know the details of the story behind this little shrine, but everyone agrees a tragic love triangle was involved. A bronze plaque indicates only that it's dedicated to a sinner who is buried here on unconsecrated ground. The candles that line the cactus-shrouded spot attest to its continuing importance in local Catholic lore. People light candles and leave *milagros* ("miracles," or little icons used in prayers for healing) for loved ones. A modern-day miracle: the shrine's inclusion on the National Register of Historic Places helped prevent a freeway from plowing through this section of the Barrio Historico. ⊠ *Main Ave., south of Cushing St., Downtown.*

Pima County Courthouse. This pink Spanish colonial–style building with a mosaic-tile dome is among Tucson's most beautiful historic structures. Still in use, it was built in 1927 on the site of the original single-story adobe court of 1869; a portion of the old presidio wall can be seen in the south wing of the courthouse's second floor. At the side of the building, the county assessor's office has a diorama depicting the area's early days. ⊠ *115 N. Church Ave., between Alameda and Pennington sts., Downtown* ⊕ *www.sc.pima.gov* ☎ *Free* ☉ *Weekdays 8–4:30, Sat. 8–noon.*

Tucson Museum of Art and Historic Block. The five historic buildings on this block are listed in the National Register of Historic Places. You can

7

tour La Casa Cordova, the Stevens Home, the J. Knox Corbett House, and the Edward Nye Fish House, but the Romero House, believed to incorporate a section of the presidio wall, is now used for the museum's ceramics education program. You can also visit the main museum of art itself. The museum building houses a permanent collection of modern, contemporary, and Asian art and hosts traveling shows. A gift shop featuring local artisans' work is also here. In the center of the museum complex, connecting the main museum to the surrounding historic houses, is the Plaza of the Pioneers, honoring Tucson's early citizens.

La Casa Cordova, one of the oldest buildings in Tucson, is also one of the best local examples of a Sonoran row house. This simple but elegant design is a Spanish style adapted to adobe construction. The oldest section of La Casa Cordova, constructed around 1848, has been restored to its original appearance, and is the Mexican Heritage Museum. El Nacimiento, a permanent installation of nativity scenes and depictions of Mexican family life, is on display here from November through March.

The **Stevens Home** was where the wealthy politician and cattle rancher Hiram Stevens and his Mexican wife, Petra Santa Cruz, entertained many of Tucson's leaders during the 1800s. A drought brought the Stevens's cattle ranching to a halt in 1893, and Stevens killed himself in despair after unsuccessfully attempting to shoot his wife (the bullet was deflected by the comb she wore in her hair). The 1865 house was restored in 1980, and now houses the Tucson Museum of Art's permanent collections of pre-Columbian, Spanish-colonial, and Latin American folk art.

The **J. Knox Corbett House** was built in 1906–07 and occupied by members of the Corbett family until 1963. The original occupants were J. Knox Corbett, a successful businessman, postmaster, and mayor of Tucson, and his wife, Elizabeth Hughes Corbett, an accomplished musician and daughter of Tucson pioneer Sam Hughes. Tucson's Hi Corbett field (now the baseball field for the U of A Wildcats) is named for their grandnephew, Hiram. The two-story, Mission Revival–style residence has been furnished with Arts and Crafts pieces: Stickley, Roycroft, Tiffany, and Morris are among the more famous manufacturers represented.

Permanent and changing exhibitions of Western art fill the **Edward Nye Fish House,** an 1868 adobe that belonged to an early merchant, entrepreneur, and politician, and his wife. The building is notable for its 15-foot beamed ceilings and saguaro cactus–rib supports.

Admission to the museum and all four homes is free on the first Sunday of every month. There are free docent tours of the museum, and you can pick up a self-guided tour map of El Presidio district. ■ TIP→ There's free parking in a lot behind the museum at Washington and Meyer streets. ⊠ 140 N. Main Ave., Downtown ☎ 520/624–2333 ⊕ www. tucsonmuseumofart.org ⬛ $10 ☉ Tues., Wed., Fri., and Sat. 10–5, Thurs. 10–8, Sun. noon–5. Free guided tours Oct.–Apr., Wed.–Sat. at 11 and 2, Sun. at 11.

QUICK BITES

Cafe A La C'Art. On the patio of the Stevens Home, part of the Tucson Museum of Art and Historic Block, this gem of a café serves breakfast frittatas, burritos, and pancakes as well as delightful salads, soups, and sandwiches daily from 8 to 3, and is open for happy hour and dinner Thursday through Saturday until 9. ⊠ *150 N. Main Ave., Downtown* ☎ *520/628–8533* ⊕ *www.cafealacarttucson.com.*

WORTH NOTING

Santa Cruz River & River Park. When Europeans arrived in what is now Arizona, the Santa Cruz River had wide banks suitable for irrigation; over time its banks have been narrowed and contained and are now lined by River Park. These days it's a dry wash, or *arroyo*, most of the year, but sudden summer thunderstorms and rainwater from upper elevations can turn it into a raging river in a matter of hours. It's a favorite spot for walkers, joggers, and bicyclists. The park has a bike path, restrooms, drinking fountains, and sculptures created by local artists. ⊠ *W. Congress St. at Bonita Ave., Downtown* ⊕ *www.pima. gov/nrpr/parks.*

St. Augustine Cathedral. Although the imposing white-and-beige, late-19th-century, Spanish-style building was modeled after the Cathedral of Queretaro in Mexico, a number of its details reflect the desert setting. For instance, above the entryway, next to a bronze statue of St. Augustine, are carvings of local desert scenes with saguaro cacti, yucca, and prickly pears—look closely and you'll find the horned toad. Compared with the magnificent facade, the modernized interior is a bit disappointing. Call for the schedule of English and Spanish masses. ■TIP→ For a distinctly Southwestern experience, attend the mariachi mass celebrated Sunday at 8 am. ⊠ *192 S. Stone Ave., Downtown* ☎ *520/623–6351* ⊕ *www.staugustinecathedral.org* ⊠ *Free* ☺ *Daily 7–6.*

THE UNIVERSITY OF ARIZONA

The U of A (as opposed to rival ASU, in Tempe) is a major economic influence in Tucson, with a student population of more than 34,000. The land for the university was "donated" by a couple of gamblers and a saloon owner in 1891—their benevolence reputedly inspired by a bad hand of cards—and $25,000 of territorial (Arizona was still a territory back then) money was used to build Old Main, the original building, and hire six faculty members. Money ran out before Old Main's roof was placed, but a few enlightened citizens pitched in funds to finish it. Most of the city's populace was less than enthusiastic about the institution: They were disgruntled when the 13th Territorial Legislature granted the University of Arizona to Tucson and awarded Phoenix what was considered the real prize—an insane asylum and a prison.

The university's flora is impressive—it represents a collection of plants from arid and semiarid regions around the world. An extremely rare mutated, or "crested," saguaro grows at the northeast corner of the Old Main building. The long, grassy mall in the heart of campus—itself once a vast cactus garden—sits atop a huge underground student activity center, and makes for a pleasant stroll on a balmy evening.

7

GETTING HERE AND AROUND

If you drive, leave your car in a university garage or lot; those on 2nd Street at Mountain Avenue, on Speedway Boulevard at Park Avenue, on Tyndall Avenue south of University Boulevard, and on 2nd Street at Euclid Avenue are the most convenient. Parking is free in these garages on weekends and holidays. Both the campus and the shopping/dining district just west along University Boulevard are best explored on foot. The new streetcar route, scheduled to be completed in early 2014, runs west along University Boulevard, down 4th Avenue and into Downtown.

PLANNING YOUR TIME

Call ahead to verify hours for the university's museums, or visit the University of Arizona website (⊕ *www.arizona.edu*) for parking maps and the latest visitor information.

TOP ATTRACTIONS

4th Avenue. Students and counterculturists favor this ½-mile strip of 4th Avenue, between University Boulevard and 8th Street, where vintage-clothing stores rub shoulders with ethnic eateries from Guatemalan to Greek. After dark, 4th Avenue bars pulse with live and recorded music. ⊠ *University* ⊕ *www.fourthavenue.org.*

FAMILY   **Arizona History Museum.** The museum houses the headquarters of the state Historical Society and has exhibits exploring the history of southern Arizona, starting with the Hohokam Indians and Spanish explorers. The harrowing "Life on the Edge: A History of Medicine in Arizona" exhibit promotes a new appreciation of modern drugstores in present-day Tucson. Children enjoy the exhibit on copper mining (with an atmospheric replica of a mine shaft and camp) and the stagecoaches in the transportation area.

Flanking the entrance to the museum are statues of two men: Father Kino, the Jesuit who established San Xavier del Bac and a string of other missions, and John Greenaway, indelibly linked to Phelps Dodge, the copper-mining company that helped Arizona earn statehood in 1912.

The library has an extensive collection of historic Arizona photographs and sells inexpensive reprints. Park in the garage at the corner of 2nd and Euclid streets and get a free parking pass in the museum. ⊠ *949 E. 2nd St., University* ☎ *520/628–5774* ⊕ *www.arizonahistoricalsociety. org/museums* ☑ *$5* ⊙ *Mon.–Sat. 10–4, library weekdays 9–4.*

FAMILY   **Arizona State Museum.** Inside the main gate of the university is Arizona's oldest museum, dating from territorial days (1893) and recognized as one of the world's most important resources for the study of Southwestern cultures. Exhibits include the largest collections of Southwest Indian pottery and basketry, as well as "Paths of Life: American Indians of the Southwest"—a permanent exhibit that explores the cultural traditions, origins, and contemporary lives of 10 native tribes of Arizona and Sonora, Mexico. Admission is free for children under 18. ⊠ *1013 E. University Blvd., at Park Ave., University* ☎ *520/621–6302* ⊕ *www. statemuseum.arizona.edu* ☑ *$5* ⊙ *Mon.–Sat. 10–5.*

Center for Creative Photography. Ansel Adams conceived the idea of a photographer's archive and donated the majority of his negatives to

CLOSE UP

U of A Campus Walking Tour

This tour takes in the highlights of the university area: Start at the northwest corner of campus, at Euclid and 2nd streets, at the public parking garage, then walk a half block east on 2nd Street to the **Arizona History Museum** to see how far the Old Pueblo has come in 100 years. A block south on Park Avenue, just inside the main gate of the university, is the **Arizona State Museum**, the place to explore Native American culture. Heading east on University Boulevard and deeper into the campus, you'll pass Old Main and the crested saguaro. As the road curves to the left, University Boulevard turns into the campus mall. The Student Union, which houses a huge food court, and University Bookstore are on your left; the sculpture in front of the complex depicts Arizona–Mexico border struggles. Cross over to the south side of the mall (watch out for Frisbees) and take a peek inside the old gymnasium, then continue east, passing the steps leading down to the underground activity center, and you'll come to the **Flandrau Science Center and Planetarium.** Check telescope-viewing schedules, see a light show, or stock up on science-oriented gifts here.

Walk north on Cherry, then turn left onto 2nd Street, passing several fraternity and sorority houses. Turn right on Olive Road to find the **Center for Creative Photography,** home to most of photographer Ansel Adams's negatives and a slew of other exhibits in this medium. Across from the center is the **University of Arizona Museum of Art.** From here it's a short walk west on Speedway Boulevard to Park Avenue, where you can go south to 2nd Street and return to the Arizona Historical Society's Museum and the parking lot.

For more college culture, continue down Park to University Boulevard and turn right. This area is the hub of off-campus activity, with restaurants, cafés, and trendy boutiques. You can walk or take the new streetcar along University to **4th Avenue,** Tucson's last bastion of bohemia, for shopping and people-watching.

If you drive, leave your car in a university garage; those on 2nd Street at Mountain Avenue, on Speedway Boulevard at Park Avenue, on Tyndall Avenue south of University Boulevard, and on 2nd Street at Euclid Avenue are the most convenient. Parking is free in these garages on weekends and holidays.

7

this museum. In addition to its superb collection of his work, the center has works by other major photographers, including Paul Strand, W. Eugene Smith, Edward Weston, and Louise Dahl-Wolfe. Changing exhibits in the main gallery display selected pieces from the collection. On the first Friday of every month, a themed display of photos from the archives is set up, unframed, in the print study room for up-close viewing and discussion with docents. ✉ *1030 N. Olive Rd., north of 2nd St., University* ☎ *520/621–7968* ⊕ *www.creativephotography.org* ✆ *Free* ☉ *Weekdays 9–5, weekends 1–4.*

FAMILY **Flandrau Science Center and Planetarium.** Attractions at the university's science museum include a 16-inch public telescope for evening

The University of Arizona

stargazing, hands-on science exhibits, planetarium shows, and the Mineral Museum, which displays more than 2,000 rocks and gems, some quite rare. ⊠ *1601 E. University Blvd., at Cherry Ave., University* ☎ *520/621–4515, 520/621–7827 for recorded message* ⊕ *www.flandrau.org* ⊙ *$7 for museum, $5 for planetarium/laser show, observatory free* ⊙ *Museum Mon.–Wed. 10–3, Thurs.–Fri. 10–3 and 6–9, Sat. 10–9, Sun. 1–4. Planetarium and laser shows Thurs.–Sun.; call for schedule. Observatory hrs vary; call for schedule.*

QUICK BITES

Just outside the west campus gate, University Boulevard is lined with student-oriented eateries.

Gentle Ben's Brewing Company. Beer lovers should head to Gentle Ben's, a friendly, laid-back burger-and-brew pub that also makes a scrumptious veggie burger. The deck upstairs offers a good view of the sunset. ⊠ *865 E. University Blvd., University* ☎ *520/624–4177* ⊕ *www.gentlebens.com.*

Kababeque. From curry to kebab, the tasty and plentiful dishes at Kababeque satisfy for a quick bite Indian-style. ⊠ *845 E. University Blvd., University* ☎ *520/388–4500* ⊕ *www.tucsonindianrestaurant.com.*

Sinbad's. Nestled in the verdant Geronimo Plaza, Sinbad's serves falafel and other Middle Eastern fare, and has a great patio. ⊠ *810 E. University Blvd., University* ☎ *520/623–4010.*

WORTH NOTING

University of Arizona Museum of Art. This small campus museum houses a collection of more than 6,000 artworks, mainly European and American paintings from the Renaissance through modern day, including works by Georgia O'Keeffe and Jackson Pollock. A highlight is the Kress Collection's *retablo* from Ciudad Rodrigo: 26 panels of an altarpiece made in the 1490s by Fernando Gallego. ⊠ *Fine Arts Complex, 1031 N. Olive Rd., north of 2nd St., University* ☎ *520/621–7567* ⊕ *www.artmuseum. arizona.edu* ☜ *$5* ۞ *Tues.–Fri. 9–5, weekends noon–4.*

CENTRAL TUCSON

Tucson expanded north and east from the university during the 1950s and '60s, and currently continues to spread southeast. The east–west thoroughfares of Broadway, Speedway, and Grant are lined with small and large businesses and eateries, mostly in unattractive strip malls. Sights worth seeing in this area include the Reid Park Zoo, the Tucson Botanical Gardens, and a couple of eccentric museums.

PLANNING YOUR TIME

If it's warm, visit outdoor attractions such as the zoo or Tucson Botanical Gardens in the morning; the museums and shopping malls are cooler options for the afternoon.

7

TOP ATTRACTIONS

FAMILY **Fort Lowell Park and Museum.** Fertile soil and proximity to the Rillito River once enticed the Hohokam to construct a village on this site. Centuries later, a fort (in operation from 1873 to 1891) was built here to protect the fledgling city of Tucson against the Apaches. The former commanding officer's quarters at this quirky fort museum has artifacts from military life in territorial days. The park has a playground, ball fields, tennis courts, and a duck pond. Admission to the museum is two-for-one on the first Saturday of every month. ⊠ *2900 N. Craycroft Rd., Central* ☎ *520/885–3832* ⊕ *www.arizonahistoricalsociety. org* ☜ *Museum $3* ۞ *Fri. and Sat. 10–4.*

The Mini Time Machine. When Pat Arnell began collecting miniatures in the late 1970s, she probably didn't imagine that her hobby would eventually outgrow her house and become an offbeat but effective vehicle for people of all ages to explore history and culture. The modern museum displays more than 275 doll houses and room boxes, antique through contemporary, from the U.S., Europe, and Asia. There are also plenty of wee folk—like fairies, wizards, and Kewpie dolls—and even tiny appliance "samples" that were carried door-to-door by traveling salesmen. Take a free, docent-led tour Tuesday through Friday and Sunday at 1 and Saturday at 11:30 and 2. ⊠ *4455 E. Camp Lowell Dr., Central* ☎ *520/881–9307* ⊕ *www.theminitimemachine.org* ☜ *$9* ۞ *Closed Mon.*

Colorful adobe buildings come in many shades beyond the natural clay color.

FAMILY **Reid Park Zoo.** This small but well-designed zoo won't tax the children's—or your—patience. There are plenty of shady places to sit, a well-stocked gift shop, and a snack bar to rev you up when your energy flags. You can feed carrots to the zoo's friendly giraffes each morning at about 9:30 ($2). The African elephants habitat and the South American section with rain forest exhibits and exotic birds are also popular. If you're visiting in summer, go early in the day when the animals are active. The park surrounding the zoo has a number of imaginative playground structures and a lake where you can feed ducks and rent paddleboats. ⊠ *Reid Park, 1100 S. Randolph Way, off 22nd St., Central* ☎ *520/791–4022* ✉ *$9* ☉ *Sept.–May daily 9–4; June–Aug. daily 8–3.*

WORTH NOTING

Tucson Botanical Gardens. The five acres are home to a variety of experiences: a tropical greenhouse; a sensory garden, where you can touch and smell the plants and listen to the abundant birdlife; historical gardens that display the Mediterranean landscaping the property's original owners planted in the 1930s; a garden designed to attract birds; and a cactus garden. Other gardens showcase wildflowers, Australian plants, and Native American crops and herbs. From October to April, interact with butterflies from all over the world in their own greenhouse. A delightful café is open for breakfast and lunch daily October through May. All paths are wheelchair accessible. ⊠ *2150 N. Alvernon Way, Central* ☎ *520/326–9686* ⊕ *www.tucsonbotanical.org* ✉ *$13 Oct.–Apr., $8 May–Sept.* ☉ *Daily 8:30–4:30.*

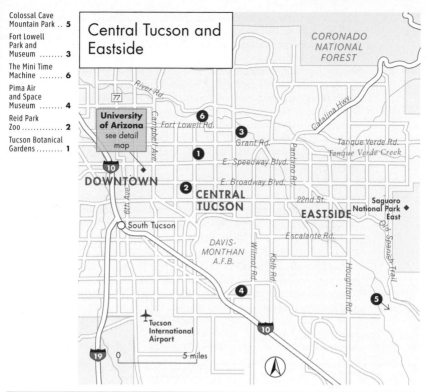

Central Tucson and Eastside

7

EASTSIDE

The sprawling east side of Tucson is mostly residential, but there are a few gems on the southeastern outskirts that are well worth the journey: the Pima Air and Space Museum, Colossal Cave, and Saguaro National Park's east district.

PLANNING YOUR TIME

Because of copious traffic lights, it's a 30- to 45-minute drive across town to the far eastside. Because this area is not particularly scenic, you can take I–10 instead (if you're starting from downtown or the west/ northwest). During the summer months, plan the outdoor sights for the morning. Note that Colossal Cave stays at a constant cool temperature, which makes it a good option on a warm afternoon.

TOP ATTRACTIONS

Pima Air and Space Museum. This huge facility ranks among the largest private collections of aircraft in the world. More than 300 airplanes are on display in hangars and outside, including a presidential plane used by both John F. Kennedy and Lyndon B. Johnson; a full-scale replica of the Wright brothers' 1903 Wright Flyer; the SR-71 reconnaissance jet; and a mock-up of the X-15, the world's fastest aircraft. World War II planes are particularly well represented.

Meander on your own (even leashed pets are allowed) or take a free walking tour led by volunteer docents. The open-air tram tour (an additional $6 fee) narrates all outside aircraft. Hour-long van tours of Aerospace Maintenance and Regeneration Group (AMARG)—affectionately called "The Boneyard"—at nearby Davis-Monthan Air Force Base provide an eerie glimpse of hundreds of mothballed aircraft lined up in rows on a vast tract of desert. This $7 AMARG tour, available only on weekdays on a first-come, first-served basis, is a photographer's delight. An on-site restaurant, The Flight Grill, is open daily from 9:30 to 4:30. ⊠ *6000 E. Valencia Rd., I–10 Exit 267, Eastside* ☎ *520/574– 0462* ⊕ *www.pimaair.org* ⊠ *$15.50* ☉ *Daily 9–5, last admission at 4.*

WORTH NOTING

FAMILY **Colossal Cave Mountain Park.** This limestone grotto 20 miles east of Tucson is the largest dry cavern in the world. Guides discuss the fascinating crystal formations and relate the many romantic tales surrounding the cave, including the legend that an enormous sum of money stolen in a stagecoach robbery is hidden here.

Forty-five-minute cave tours begin every 30 minutes and require a ½-mile walk and a climb of 363 steps. The park includes a ranch area with trail rides ($30 per hour), a gemstone-sluicing area, a small museum, a desert tortoise habitat, nature trails, a butterfly garden and a gift shop. Parking is $5 per vehicle. Take Broadway Boulevard or 22nd Street east to Old Spanish Trail. ⊠ *16721 E. Old Spanish Trail, Eastside* ☎ *520/647–7275* ⊕ *www.colossalcave.com* ⊠ *Cave tour $13* ☉ *Oct.–mid-Mar., daily 9–5; mid-Mar.–Sept., daily 8–5.*

CATALINA FOOTHILLS

Considered by some to be the "Beverly Hills of Tucson," the Catalina Foothills area is home to posh resorts and upscale shopping. Because the neighborhood abuts the beautiful Santa Catalina Mountains, it also has an abundance of hiking trails.

PLANNING YOUR TIME

It may be hard to choose from the shopping, hiking, golf, and spa options along the Skyline Drive/Sunrise Drive corridor, but you can plan to spend at least a few hours strolling, hiking, or taking the tram through Sabino Canyon. Shopping and dining at La Encantada or the smaller complexes across the road can easily fill the other half of a day. If you want to venture farther into the mountains, head northeast up to Mount Lemmon. It's time-consuming (a one-hour drive each way), but the higher elevation and cooler temperatures make it an excellent destination in summer.

TOP ATTRACTIONS

Mount Lemmon. Part of the Santa Catalina range, Mount Lemmon— named for Sara Lemmon, the first woman to reach the peak of this mountain, in 1881—is the southernmost ski slope in the continental United States. But you don't have to be a skier to enjoy the area: in summer, it's a popular place for picnicking, and there are 150 miles of marked and well-maintained trails for hiking. The mountain's

CLOSE UP

Tucson History: City in the Foothills

Native Americans have lived along the waterways in this valley for thousands of years. During the 1500s, Spanish explorers arrived to find Pima Indians growing crops in the area. Father Eusebio Francisco Kino, a Jesuit missionary whose influence is still strongly felt throughout the region, first visited the area in 1687, and returned a few years later to build missions.

NATIVE AMERICANS AND THE PRESIDIO

The name "Tucson" came from the Native American word *stjukshon* (pronounced *stook*-shahn), meaning "spring at the foot of a black mountain." The springs at the foot of Sentinel Peak, made of black volcanic rock, are now dry. The name was pronounced *tuk*-son by the Spanish explorers who built a wall around the city in 1776 to keep Native Americans from reclaiming it. At the time, this *presidio* (fortified city), called San Augustín del Tucson, was the northernmost Spanish settlement in the area, and present-day Main Avenue is a quiet reminder of the former Camino Real ("royal road") that stretched from this tiny walled fort all the way to Mexico City.

CHANGING ALLEGIANCES

Four flags have flown over Tucson— Spanish, Mexican, Confederate, and, finally, the Stars and Stripes. Tucson's allegiance changed in 1820 when Mexico declared independence from Spain, and again in 1853 when the Gadsden purchase made it part of the United States, though Arizona didn't become a state until 1912. In the 1850s the Butterfield stage line was extended to Tucson, bringing adventurers, a few settlers, and more than a handful of outlaws. The arrival of the railroad in 1880 marked another spurt of growth, as did the opening of the University of Arizona in 1891.

MODERN TIMES

Tucson's 20th-century growth occurred after World War I, when veterans with damaged lungs sought the dry air and healing power of the sun, and again during World War II with the opening of Davis-Monthan Air Force Base and the rise of local aeronautical industries. The advent of air-conditioning in the 1960s made the desert climate hospitable year-round.

7

9,157-foot elevation brings relief from summer heat (temperatures are typically 25 degrees lower than in Tucson).

Mount Lemmon Highway twists for 28 miles up the mountainside; driving time from mid-town is about an hour. Every 1,000-foot climb in elevation is equivalent, in terms of climate, to traveling 300 miles north. You'll move from typical Sonoran Desert plants in the foothills to vegetation similar to that found in southern Canada at the top. Rock formations along the way look as though they were carefully balanced against each other by sculptors from another planet.

Even if you don't make it to the top of the mountain, you'll find stunning views of Tucson at Windy Point, about halfway up. Look for a road on your left between the Windy Point and San Pedro lookouts; it leads to Rose Canyon lake, a lovely reservoir.

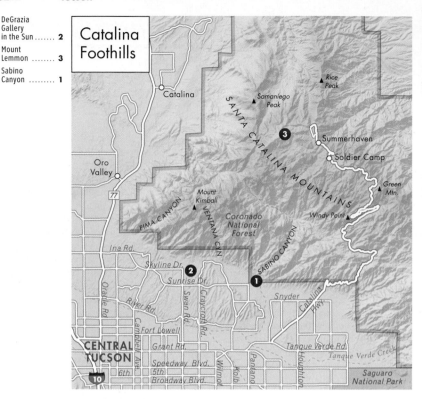

Just before you reach the ski area, you'll pass through the tiny alpine-style village of **Summerhaven,** which has some casual restaurants, gift shops, and pleasant lodges.

■**TIP**➔ There are no gas stations on Mount Lemmon Highway, so gas up before you leave town and check the road conditions in winter. To reach the highway, take Tanque Verde Road to Catalina Highway, which becomes Mount Lemmon Highway as you head north. ⊠ *Mount Lemmon Hwy., Northeast* ☎ *520/576–1400 for recorded snow report, 520/547–7510 for winter road conditions* 🖭 *Free* ⊙ *Daily, depending on snow in winter.*

Mt. Lemmon Ski Valley. Follow Mount Lemmon Highway to its end and you're at Mount Lemmon Ski Valley. Skiing and snowboarding here depend on natural conditions; there's no artificial snow, so call ahead. There are 21 runs, ranging from beginner to advanced. Lift tickets cost $40 for an all-day pass and $35 for a half-day pass starting at 12:30 pm. Equipment rentals and instruction are available.

Off-season you can take a ride on the chairlift ($10), which whisks you to the top of the slope—some 9,100 feet above sea level. Many ride the lift, then hike on one of several trails that crisscross the summit. There are some concessions right at the ski lift; the Iron Door Restaurant, across the road, serves sandwiches, soups, and homemade pies, which you can enjoy with gorgeous views. ✉ *10300 Ski Run Rd., Mount Lemmon* ☎ *520/576–1321* ⊕ *www.skithelemmon.com* ⊙ *Closed Tues.–Wed.*

FAMILY **Mt. Lemmon Sky Center.** At the University of Arizona's research observatory on Mount Lemmon, visitors can plumb the night sky on the highest mountain in the area using the largest public-viewing telescope in the Southwest. A five-hour stargazing program is offered nightly (weather permitting), and includes astronomy lessons, telescope viewing, and a light dinner. The cost is half price for kids. ✉ *Ski Run Rd., Mt. Lemmon* ☎ *520/626–8122* ⊕ *www.skycenter.arizona.edu* ✉ *$60.*

Fodor'sChoice **Sabino Canyon.** Year-round, but especially in summer, locals flock to ★ Coronado National Forest to hike, picnic, and enjoy the waterfalls, streams, swimming holes, saguaros, and shade trees. No cars are allowed, but a narrated tram ride (about 45 minutes round-trip) takes you up a WPA-built road to the top of the canyon; you can hop off and on at any of the nine stops or hike any of the numerous trails.

There's also a shorter tram ride (or you can walk) to adjacent Bear Canyon, where a rigorous but rewarding hike leads to the popular Seven Falls. (It'll take about 1½ to 2 hours each way from the drop-off point, so carry plenty of water). If you're in Tucson near a full moon between April and November, take the special night tram and watch the desert come alive with nocturnal critters. ✉ *Sabino Canyon Rd. at Sunrise Dr., Foothills* ☎ *520/749–2861 for recorded tram info, 520/749–8700 for visitor center* ⊕ *www.fs.fed.us/r3/coronado* ✉ *$5 per vehicle, tram $3–$8* ⊙ *Visitor center daily 8–4:30; call for tram schedules.*

WORTH NOTING

DeGrazia Gallery in the Sun. Arizonan artist Ted DeGrazia, who depicted Southwest Native American and Mexican life in a manner some find kitschy and others adore, built this sprawling, spacious, single-story museum with the assistance of Native American friends, using only natural material from the surrounding desert.

You can visit DeGrazia's workshop, former home, tranquil chapel, and grave. Although the original works are not for sale, the museum's gift shop has a wide selection of prints, ceramics, and books by and about the colorful artist. ✉ *6300 N. Swan Rd., Foothills* ☎ *520/299–9191* ⊕ *www.degrazia.org* ✉ *Free* ⊙ *Daily 10–4.*

NORTHWEST TUCSON AND WESTSIDE

Once a vast, open space dotted with horse ranches, Northwest Tucson is now a rapidly growing residential area encompassing the townships of Oro Valley and Marana. Families and retirees are moving here in droves, and the traffic congestion proves the point, but you'll also find first-rate golf resorts and restaurants here, as well as the oases of Tohono Chul Park and Catalina State Park, which calm the senses.

The Westside is far less developed, and beautiful vistas of saguaro-studded hills are around every bend. Saguaro National Park West, the Desert Museum, Old Tucson Studios, and the San Xavier mission are all in this section of town. If you're interested in the flora and fauna of the Sonoran Desert—as well as some of its appearances in the cinema—heed the same advice given the pioneers: go west.

PLANNING YOUR TIME

A good idea is to start the morning at Saguaro National Park and then head over to the Arizona–Sonora Desert Museum, where you can lunch at Ironwood Terrace or the more upscale Ocotillo Café. How long you spend at Saguaro National Park depends on whether you choose a short walk to see petroglyphs at Signal Hill on the Loop Drive (an hour should suffice) or hike a longer mountain trail, but leave yourself at least two hours for your visit at the Desert Museum. The hottest part of an afternoon can be spent ducking in and out of attractions at Old Tucson Studios or enjoying the indoor sanctuary of San Xavier mission, although the mission is also a good stop if you're heading out of town to Tubac or Tumacácori.

TOP ATTRACTIONS

FAMILY
Fodor's Choice
★
Arizona–Sonora Desert Museum. The name "museum" is a bit misleading, since this delightful site is actually a zoo, aquarium, and botanical garden featuring the animals, plants and, even fish of the Sonoran Desert. Hummingbirds, coatis, rattlesnakes, scorpions, bighorn sheep, bobcats, and Mexican wolves all busy themselves in ingeniously designed habitats.

An Earth Sciences Center has an artificial limestone cave to climb through and an excellent mineral display. The coyote and *javelina* (wild, piglike mammals with oddly oversize heads) exhibits have "invisible" fencing that separates humans from animals, and at the Raptor Free Flight show (October through April daily at 10 and 2), you can see the powerful birds soar and dive, untethered, inches above your head.

The restaurants are above average, and the gift shop, which carries books, jewelry, and crafts, is outstanding. ■TIP➜ June through August, the museum stays open until 10 pm every Saturday, which provides a great opportunity to see nocturnal critters. ⌂ *2021 N. Kinney Rd., Westside* ☎ *520/883–2702* ⊕ *www.desertmuseum.org* ✉ *$19.50* ⓧ *Mar.–Sept., daily 7:30–5; Oct.–Feb., daily 8:30–5.*

Fodor's Choice
★
Mission San Xavier del Bac. The oldest Catholic church in the United States still serving the community for which it was built, San Xavier was founded in 1692 by Father Eusebio Francisco Kino, who established 22 missions in northern Mexico and southern Arizona. The current structure was made out of native materials by Franciscan missionaries between 1777 and 1797, and is owned by the Tohono O'odham tribe.

The beauty of the mission, with elements of Spanish, baroque, and Moorish architectural styles, is highlighted by the stark landscape against which it is set, inspiring an early-20th-century poet to dub it "the White Dove of the Desert."

Inside, there's a wealth of painted statues, carvings, and frescoes. Paul Schwartzbaum, who helped restore Michelangelo's masterwork in

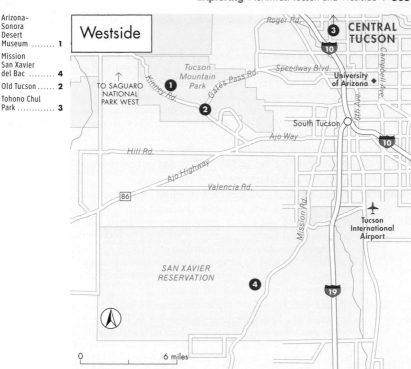

Rome, supervised Tohono O'odham artisans in the restoration of the mission's artwork, completed in 1997. Schwartzbaum has called the mission the Sistine Chapel of the United States. Mass is celebrated at 8:30 am Tuesday through Friday in the church, Saturday afternoon at 5:30, and three times on Sunday morning. Call ahead for information about special celebrations.

Across the parking lot from the mission, San Xavier Plaza has a number of crafts shops selling the handiwork of the Tohono O'odham tribe, including jewelry, pottery, friendship bowls, and woven baskets with man-in-the-maze designs. ⊠ *1950 W. San Xavier Rd., 9 miles southwest of Tucson on I–19, Westside* ☎ *520/294–2624* ⊕ *www.sanxaviermission.org* ⊠ *Free* ☺ *Church daily 7–5, museum and gift shop daily 8–5.*

QUICK BITES

Wa:k Snack Shop. For wonderful Indian fry bread—large, round pieces of dough taken fresh from the hot oil and served with sweet or savory toppings like honey, powdered sugar, beans, meats, or green chiles—stop in the Wa:k Snack Shop at the back of San Xavier Plaza. You can also have breakfast or a lunch of Mexican food here, and if you're lucky, local dancers will be performing for one of the many tour groups that stop here. ⊠ *San*

Xavier Plaza, 1950 W. San Xavier Rd., 9 miles southwest of Tucson on I-19, Westside.

Tohono Chul Park. A 48-acre desert garden retreat designed to promote the conservation of arid regions, Tohono Chul—"desert corner" in the language of the Tohono O'odham—uses demonstration gardens, a greenhouse, and a geology wall to explain this unique desert area. Nature trails, a small art gallery, gift shops (including a great selection of desert plants), and a bistro can all be found at this peaceful spot. You can visit the restaurant and gift shops without paying admission. ⊠ *7366 N. Paseo del Norte, Northwest* ☎ *520/742–6455* ⊕ *www. tohonochulpark.org* ⌨ *$10* ☉ *Park and restaurant daily 8–5.*

WORTH NOTING

OFF THE
BEATEN
PATH

Biosphere 2. In the town of Oracle, about 30 minutes northwest of Tucson, this unique, self-contained cluster of ecosystems opened in 1991 as a facility to test nature technology and human interaction with it. Now managed by the University of Arizona, the biomes include tropical rain forest, savanna, desert, thorn scrub, marsh, and ocean areas. The newest biome, the Landscape Evolutionary Observatory, tracks rainfall in simulated desert environments to study the effects of climate change on water sources and plant life in this region.

Guided walking tours, which last about an hour, take you inside the biomes, and a brief film gives an overview of Biosphere projects, from the original "human missions"—where scientists literally ate, slept, and breathed their work in a closed system—to current research. A snack bar overlooks the Santa Catalina Mountains. ⊠ *32540 S. Biosphere Rd., AZ 77, Milepost 96.5, Oracle* ☎ *520/838–6200* ⊕ *www.b2science. org* ⌨ *$20* ☉ *Daily 9–4.*

FAMILY **Old Tucson.** This film studio–theme park, originally built for the 1940 motion picture *Arizona*, has been used to shoot countless movies, such as *Rio Bravo* (1959) and *The Quick and the Dead* (1994), and the TV shows *Gunsmoke, Bonanza,* and *Highway to Heaven.* Actors in Western garb perform and roam the streets talking to visitors.

Youngsters enjoy the simulated gunfights, rides, stunt shows, and petting farm, while adults might appreciate the screenings of old Westerns, studio tour, and the little-bit-bawdy Grand Palace Hotel's Dance Hall Revue. There are plenty of places to eat and to buy souvenirs. Horseback riding and stagecoach rides are available at an additional charge. ⊠ *Tucson Mountain Park, 201 S. Kinney Rd., Westside* ☎ *520/883–0100* ⊕ *www.oldtucson.com* ⌨ *$16.95* ☉ *Jan.–Apr., daily 10–5; May and Oct.–Dec., Fri.–Sun. 10–5.*

WHERE TO EAT

Tucson boldly proclaims itself to be the "Mexican Food Capital of the United States," and most of the Mexican food in town is Sonoran-style. This means prolific use of cheese, mild peppers, corn tortillas, pinto beans, and beef or chicken. It's the birthplace of the *chimichanga*

(Spanish for "whatchamacallit"), a flour tortilla filled with meat or cheese, rolled, and deep-fried.

The best Mexican restaurants are concentrated in South Tucson and Downtown, although some favorites have additional locations around town. If Mexican's not your thing, there are plenty of other options: you won't have any trouble finding excellent sushi, Thai, Italian, and Ethiopian food at reasonable prices.

For sampling regional flavors, there are several notable Southwestern restaurants in town. In the Foothills, upscale Southwestern cuisine flourishes at Acacia and the Grill at Hacienda del Sol. A recent trend in Tucson dining is combining hip restaurants with chic shopping locations. Choose from sushi, steak, Italian, or Mexican at La Encantada in the Foothills. Casas Adobes Plaza, in the Northwest, is home to upscale shops alongside Wildflower Grill, Bluefin Seafood Bistro, and trendy, thin-crust pizza at Sauce—and the gelato shop, Frost, is handy for dessert. Downtown has recently exploded with first-rate dining and drinking establishments, from modern comfort food and homemade ice cream to gourmet pizzas, craft beers, and contemporary Mexico City cuisine.

Tasty fare as varied as Indian, Guatemalan, and Middle Eastern can be enjoyed on the west side of U of A's campus, along University Boulevard and 4th Avenue—another great area for people-watching and barhopping as well as quelling hunger pangs.

On Friday and Saturday nights and during the Gem Show (first two weeks of February), reservations are usually a good idea at upscale and popular restaurants. Dress ranges from casual to casual-dressy here; jackets for men aren't required at any restaurant, even at resorts.

WHAT IT COSTS				
	$	$$	$$$	$$$$
At Dinner	under $13	$13–$20	$21–30	over $30

Restaurant prices are the average cost of a main course at dinner or, if dinner is not served, at lunch.

Use the coordinate (✛ B2) at the end of each listing to locate a site on the corresponding map.

DOWNTOWN TUCSON

$$ ✕ **47 Scott.** Hip in an understated way, this relatively new restaurant and bar is already at the top of local "best of Tucson" lists, and its cocktails have garnered national attention. The minimalist setting—walnut banquets, exposed pipes, and bare-bulb lighting—contrasts with the great care taken in preparing entrées like phyllo-wrapped chicken stuffed with spinach and goat cheese, or steamed mussels with andouille sausage and pommes frites. Try a bold, herb-infused cocktail such as the Brick House Old Fashioned, with bacon-washed rye. Brunch specialties like veggie scrambles and sourdough french toast attract crowds on the weekends.

MODERN
AMERICAN

BEST BETS FOR TUCSON DINING

Fodor's offers a listing of quality dining experiences at every price range, from the city's best cheap eateries to its most upscale restaurants. Here, we've compiled our top picks by price and experience. The best properties—in other words, those that provide a remarkable experience in their price range—are designated in the listings with the Fodor's Choice logo.

Fodor's Choice ★

Beyond Bread, $,
p. 371
Café Poca Cosa, $$,
p. 369
Elvira's, $$, p. 413
Maynards, $$$, p. 370

Best by Price

$

Beyond Bread, p. 371
El Minuto Café, p. 369
Sauce, p. 378
Tucson Tamale
Company, p. 374
Zinburger, p. 377

$$

47 Scott, p. 367
Bangkok Cafe, p. 371
Café Poca Cosa,
p. 369
Downtown Kitchen &
Cocktails, p. 369
Feast, p. 371

$$$–$$$$

Acacia, p. 375
The Grill at Hacienda
del Sol, p. 375
Maynards, p. 370

Best by Cuisine

AMERICAN

47 Scott, $$, p. 367
Feast, $$, p. 371
Kingfisher Bar and
Grill, $$$, p. 371
Wildflower Grill, $$,
p. 378

ITALIAN

Tavolino, $$, p. 377
Vivace, $$$, p. 377

MEXICAN

Café Poca Cosa, $$,
p. 369
El Charro Café, $$,
p. 369
El Minuto Café, $,
p. 369
Micha's, $, p. 378
Mi Nidito, $, p. 378

SOUTHWESTERN

Acacia, $$$, p. 375
The Grill at Hacienda
del Sol, $$$$, p. 375

Best by Experience

BEST BREAKFAST

The B Line, $, p. 370
Cup Café, $$, p. 369

BEST PATIO DINING

Cup Café, $$, p. 369
Maynards, $$$, p. 370
Vivace, $$$, p. 377

GOOD FOR GROUPS

Bluefin Seafood
Bistro, $$$, p. 377
Feast, $$, p. 371
Tavolino, $$, p. 377

HOT SPOTS

47 Scott, $$, p. 367
Café Poca Cosa, $$,
p. 369
Cup Café, $$, p. 369

LATE-NIGHT DINING

Cup Café, $$, p. 369
Kingfisher Bar and
Grill, $$$, p. 371
Zinburger, $, p. 377

MOST KID-FRIENDLY

Beyond Bread, $,
p. 371
Pinnacle Peak Steak-
house, $$, p. 375
Sauce, $, p. 378

SPECIAL OCCASION

Acacia, $$$, p. 375
The Grill at Hacienda
del Sol, $$$$, p. 375
Maynards, $$$, p. 370

$ *Average main: $17* ✉ *47 N. Scott Ave., Downtown* ☎ *520/624–4747* ⊕ *www.47scott.com* ۞ *No lunch weekdays* ✛ *B5.*

$$
MEXICAN
Fodor's Choice
★

✕ **Café Poca Cosa.** At what is arguably Tucson's most creative Mexican restaurant, the chef prepares recipes inspired by different regions of her native country. The menu, which changes daily, might include chicken mole or pork *pibil* (made with a tangy Yucatecan barbecue seasoning). Servings are plentiful, and each table gets a stack of warm corn tortillas and a bowl of beans to share. Order the daily Plato Poca Cosa, and the chef will select one beef, one chicken, and one vegetarian entrée for you to sample. The bold-color walls of the contemporary interior are hung with Latin American art. $ *Average main: $16* ✉ *110 E. Pennington St., Downtown* ☎ *520/622–6400* ⊕ *www.cafepocacosatucson.com* ⌂ *Reservations essential* ۞ *Closed Sun. and Mon.* ✛ *B5.*

$$
AMERICAN

✕ **Cup Café.** This charming spot off the lobby of Hotel Congress is at the epicenter of Tucson's hippest Downtown scene, but it's also a down-home, friendly place. Try the eggs, potatoes, chorizo, and cheese for breakfast or an ahi tuna salad for lunch. The "Heartbreaker" appetizer—Brie melted over artichoke hearts and apple slices on a baguette—complements such entrées as chicken cordon bleu, house-smoked beef brisket, or potato-wrapped salmon. It's open late—until 10 pm weeknights and midnight on weekends—and becomes crowded in the evening with patrons from Club Congress, the hotel's nightclub. $ *Average main: $13* ✉ *Hotel Congress, 311 E. Congress St., Downtown* ☎ *520/798–1618* ⊕ *www.hotelcongress.com* ✛ *B5.*

$$
MODERN
AMERICAN

✕ **Downtown Kitchen & Cocktails.** Ever-evolving maverick and master chef Janos Wilder returned to the Downtown dining scene a few years ago, delighting city planners striving to energize this district. The menu draws inspiration from warm-weather regions around the world. Dishes like calamari with mango, roasted peanuts, and green-chile vinaigrette, and honey-soy-ginger duck breast fused beautifully with Janos's French technique and Southwestern flavors. The interior, decorated in soft blues and greens and exposed brick walls, affords relaxation and quiet conversation. Janos's emphasis on locally grown, organic foods informs the seasonally changing menu, but you can always get his signature J Dawg, a Sonoran hot dog with black beans, bacon, and smoked–poblano chile crema. $ *Average main: $20* ✉ *135 S. 6th Ave., Downtown* ☎ *520/623–7700* ⊕ *www.downtownkitchen.com* ۞ *No lunch* ✛ *B5.*

$$
MEXICAN

✕ **El Charro Café.** Started by Monica Flin in 1922, the oldest Mexican restaurant in town still serves splendid versions of the Mexican-American staples Flin claims to have originated, most notably chimichangas and cheese crisps. The tortilla soup and *carne seca* chimichanga, made with beef that is air-dried on the premises—on the roof, actually—are delicious. Located in an old stone house in El Presidio Historic District, the colorful restaurant and bar exude festive if slightly touristy vibes. $ *Average main: $14* ✉ *311 N. Court Ave., Downtown* ☎ *520/622–1922* ⊕ *www.elcharrocafe.com* ✛ *B5.*

$
MEXICAN

✕ **El Minuto Café.** Popular with local families and the business crowd at lunch, this bustling restaurant is in Tucson's Barrio Historico neighborhood and stays open until 11 pm Friday and Saturday and 10 pm the rest of the week. For more than 50 years El Minuto has served *topopo*

7

salads (a crispy tortilla shell heaped with beans, guacamole, and many other ingredients), huge burritos, and green-corn tamales (in season) made just right. The spicy *menudo* (tripe soup) is reputed to be a great hangover remedy. $ *Average main: $11* ⊠ *354 S. Main Ave., Downtown* ☎ *520/882–4145* ⊕ *www.elminutocafe.com* ✛ *B5.*

$$$
FRENCH
Fodor's Choice
★

✕ **Maynards.** An anchor in the downtown district, this French-inspired bistro, bar, and gourmet market–café takes up part of Tucson's historic train depot. Clever thematic touches—a dining room fashioned long and narrow like a train car, with wheel-like divider walls and lamps made from rail spikes—and the attentive yet relaxed service evoke the romance of a largely bygone era. Choose a table by the window and watch the trains go by. Or if you prefer, sit outside on the vast patio overlooking the tracks. Menu choices range from starters like fresh oysters and steak tartare to bouillabaisse, coq au vin, and burgers served with pommes frites. The market, open from 7 am to 8 pm daily, sells pastries, sandwiches, and lighter fare to take out or dine in, as well as locally made wines, tamales, and ice cream. $ *Average main: $25* ⊠ *400 N. Toole Ave., Downtown* ☎ *520/545–0577* ⊕ *www.maynardsmarket. com* ☾ *No lunch Mon.–Sat.* ✛ *B5.*

UNIVERSITY OF ARIZONA

$$$$
EUROPEAN

✕ **Arizona Inn Restaurant.** At one of Tucson's oldest and most elegant restaurants, dine on the patio overlooking the lush grounds or enjoy the view from the dining room, which has Southwestern details from the 1930s. The culinary range here is broad, from roasted duck in a tart cherry demi-glace to a vegetarian tomato and mushroom cannelloni. Locals mostly come for weekday power breakfasts, business or special occasion lunches, and Sunday brunch. $ *Average main: $34* ⊠ *Arizona Inn, 2200 E. Elm St., University* ☎ *520/325–1541* ⊕ *www. arizonainn.com* ✛ *C4.*

$$
GREEK

✕ **Athens on 4th Avenue.** The tranquil dining room in this Greek spot off 4th Avenue is furnished with lace curtains, white stucco walls, and potted plants. Enjoy classics like *kotopoulo stin pita* (grilled chicken breast with a yogurt-cucumber sauce on fresh pita), moussaka, or the *pastitsio* (a casserole made with pasta, meat, and béchamel). The house favorite is braised lamb shoulder in a light tomato sauce over pasta or potatoes—call to reserve your order of the lamb ahead of time. The housemade lemon cheesecake will melt in your mouth. $ *Average main: $18* ⊠ *500 N. 4th Ave., at 6th St., University* ☎ *520/624–6886* ⊕ *athenson4thave.com* ☾ *Closed Sun.* ✛ *B5.*

$
AMERICAN

✕ **The B Line.** In the heart of 4th Avenue's amalgam of antique clothing stores, pubs, and natural-food grocers, this casual café in a converted 1920s bungalow attracts a mix of students, professors, downtown professionals, and artists with its simple but refined meals and desserts. Homemade biscuit sandwiches and excellent coffee start the day; the lunch–dinner menu features soups, salads, pastas, burritos, and 13 brews on tap. People-watching as a secondary pleasure doesn't get any better than sitting against the wraparound window looking out on 4th Avenue. $ *Average main: $10* ⊠ *621 N. 4th Ave., University* ☎ *520/882–7575* ⊕ *www.blinerestaurant.com* ✛ *B4.*

CENTRAL TUCSON

$$ THAI 🍴 **Bangkok Cafe.** This is not only the best Thai food in town, it is top-notch for Thai-food fans. The bright, spacious café serves favorite Thai dishes, along with exceptionally pleasant service; the Thoong Tong appetizer of fried veggie-filled pouches is blissfully good. The spice-heat level of any dish can be adjusted at your request, from 1 through 5 (just keep in mind that a 5 might cause steam to blow out the top of your head). There are plenty of options for vegetarians, and tofu can be added to any dish. Try to avoid the dinner rush (6:30–8:30) on weekends, or you might wait a while to be seated. [$] *Average main: $14* ✉ *2511 E. Speedway Blvd., Central* ☎ *520/323–6555* 🌐 *www.bangkokcafe.net* ✍ *Reservations not accepted* 🕒 *Closed Sun.* ✥ *C4.*

$ CAFÉ Fodor's Choice ★ 🍴 **Beyond Bread.** Twenty-seven varieties of bread are made at this bustling bakery with Central, Eastside, and Northwest locations, and highlights from the menu of generously-sized sandwiches include Annie's Addiction (hummus, tomato, sprouts, red onion, and cucumber) and Brad's Beef (roast beef, provolone, onion, green chiles, and Russian dressing); soups, salads, and breakfast items are equally scrumptious. Eat inside or on the patio, or order takeout, but either way, splurge on one of the incredible desserts. The other locations—larger and just as busy—are at 6260 East Speedway Boulevard and 421 West Ina Road. [$] *Average main: $8* ✉ *3026 N. Campbell Ave., Central* ☎ *520/322–9965* 🌐 *www.beyondbread.com* 🕒 *No dinner Sun.* ✥ *C3, F4.*

$$ ECLECTIC 🍴 **Feast.** One of Tucson's most popular upscale bistros, Feast has a contemporary setting that is bright, cheerful, and conducive to conversation. The eclectic menu, which changes monthly, is filled with interesting combinations of flavors such as rosemary–goat cheese risotto with artichoke hearts and tomatoes, and orange-glazed chicken breast with roasted beets on sesame-cream noodles. Many of the herbs and veggies are grown in the restaurant's garden. A similarly eclectic array of wines is available for both dining and retail. Though the cuisine may be hard to categorize, it is always yummy—including the homemade desserts. [$] *Average main: $20* ✉ *3719 E. Speedway, Central* ☎ *520/326–9363* 🌐 *www.eatatfeast.com* 🕒 *Closed Mon.* ✥ *D4.*

$$$ AMERICAN 🍴 **Kingfisher Bar and Grill.** A standout for classic American cuisine, Kingfisher has an emphasis on fresh seafood, especially oysters and mussels, but the kitchen does baby back ribs and steak with equal success. Try the delicately battered fish-and-chips or the clam chowder on the late-night menu, served from 10 pm to midnight daily. Bright panels of turquoise and terra-cotta, black banquettes, and neon lighting make for a chic space in the main dining room, or sit in the cozy bar area with locals who appreciate a good meal with their cocktails. [$] *Average main: $21* ✉ *2564 E. Grant Rd., Central* ☎ *520/323–7739* 🌐 *www.kingfishertucson.com* 🕒 *No lunch Sat.–Sun.* ✥ *C4.*

$ MEXICAN 🍴 **Molina's Midway.** Tucked into a side street just north of Speedway, this charming, unassuming Mexican restaurant holds its own against any in South Tucson. Specialties include "Sinchiladas" (chicken or beef with chiles, cheese, and a cream sauce) and *carne asada* (chunks of mildly spiced steak) wrapped in soft corn or flour tortillas. Seating is plentiful and the service is friendly; several smaller rooms keep the noise level

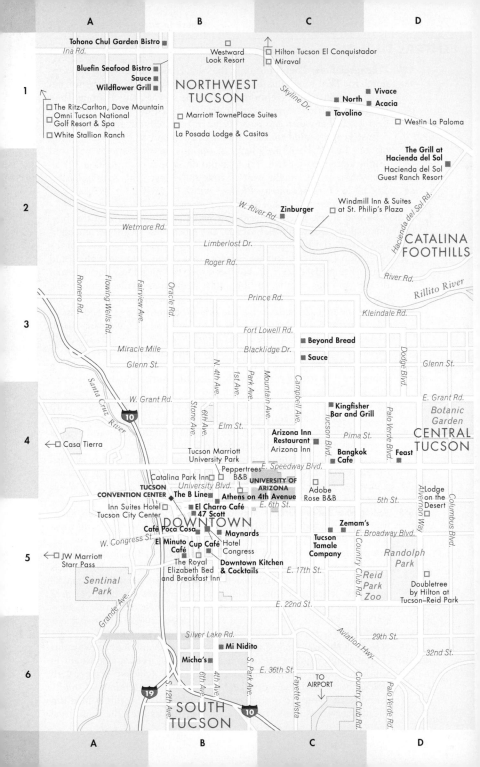

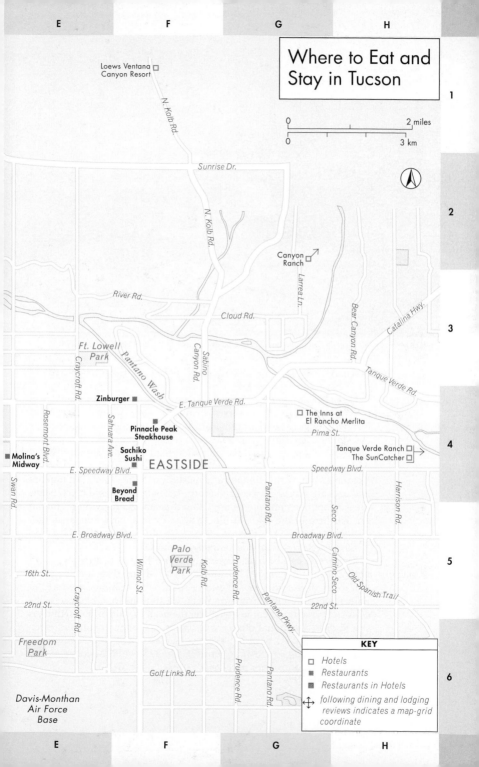

Work up your appetite hiking through the desert before enjoying some of the best Mexican food north of the border.

down. $ *Average main: $9* ✉ *1138 N. Belvedere, Central* ☎ *520/325–9957* ⊘ *Closed Mon.* ✛ *E4.*

MEXICAN $ ✕ **Tucson Tamale Company.** A good homemade tamale is special and a restaurant that prepares and serves them fresh every day with all sorts of creative fillings is a find indeed. Carnivores can indulge in beef, pork, or chicken tamales while vegetarians can opt for traditional, cheese-filled green-corn tamales, or "Blue" tamales, made of blue corn and filled with squash, onion, tomato, and cheese; there are also vegan choices like the Austin, with a spinach and mushroom filling. Breakfast tamales and eggs are served on weekend mornings. Salad, rice, and black beans are side options; most items are gluten-free and made without animal fat. Eat here in the no-frills dining area, or take your tamales to go. $ *Average main: $8* ✉ *2545 E. Broadway Blvd., Central* ☎ *520/305–4760* ⊕ *www.tucsontamalecompany.com* ✛ *C5.*

ETHIOPIAN $ ✕ **Zemam's.** It can be hard to get a table in this small, friendly eatery with a loyal following. The sampler plate of any three items allows you to try dishes like *yesimir wat* (a spicy lentil dish) and *lega tibs* (a milder beef dish with a tomato sauce). Most of the food has a stewlike consistency, so don't come if you feel the need to crunch. Everything is served on a communal platter with *injera*, a spongy bread, and eaten with the hands. Alcohol is "bring your own." $ *Average main: $12* ✉ *2731 E. Broadway Blvd., Central* ☎ *520/323–9928* ⊕ *www.zemams. com* ⬥ *Reservations not accepted* ⊘ *Closed Mon.* ✛ *C5.*

EASTSIDE

$$ STEAKHOUSE FAMILY 🍴 **Pinnacle Peak Steakhouse.** Anybody caught eating newfangled foods like fish tacos here would probably be hanged from the rafters—along with the ties snipped from city slickers who overdressed. This cowboy steakhouse serves basic, not stellar, fare: mesquite-broiled steak, ribs, chicken, and grilled fish with salad and pinto beans. The restaurant is part of the somewhat kitschy, family-friendly Trail Dust Town, a re-creation of a turn-of-the-20th-century town, complete with a working antique carousel, a narrow-gauge train, and Western stunt shows staged outside nightly at 7 and 8. Expect a long wait on weekends. [$] *Average main: $16* ✉ *6541 E. Tanque Verde Rd., Eastside* ☎ *520/296–0911* 🌐 *www.traildusttown.com* ✍ *Reservations not accepted* 🕒 *No lunch* ✣ *F4.*

$$ JAPANESE 🍴 **Sachiko Sushi.** Don't let the bland interior or the strip-mall setting dissuade you: many locals consider this the best Japanese restaurant in Tucson. Inside, perfectly prepared sushi and sashimi and generous combinations of tempura and teriyaki await, along with friendly service. The owner's wife is Korean, so the menu also has quite a few Korean classics, like beef and pork *bulgogi* (barbecued with vegetables) and tofu kimchi. Try a bowl of udon noodles, served in broth with assorted meat, seafood, or vegetables; it's a satisfying meal in itself. [$] *Average main: $13* ✉ *1101 N. Wilmot Rd., Eastside* ☎ *520/886–7000* 🌐 *www.sachikosushitucson.com* ✣ *F4.*

7

CATALINA FOOTHILLS

$$$ SOUTHWESTERN 🍴 **Acacia.** One of Tucson's premier chefs, Albert Hall, relocated his fine-dining restaurant to high in the Catalina Foothills, so now patrons can enjoy stunning city views from both the restaurant and the expansive, more casual bar. Roasted plum tomato and basil soup, a recipe from Hall's mom, is a favorite starter. Creative dishes like wild salmon with a pecan honey-mustard glaze and wood-roasted quail filled with pancetta, mozzarella, roasted tomatoes, and Oaxacan risotto are among the many tempting, organically grown (or raised) entrées. Vegetarians have choices here, too, including a sweet-corn and green-chile custard with roasted vegetables, fettuccine, and wild mushrooms, and an Asian noodle salad. [$] *Average main: $26* ✉ *3001 E. Skyline Dr., Gallery Row, Foothills* ☎ *520/232–0101* 🌐 *www.acaciatucson.com* ✣ *D1.*

$$$$ SOUTHWESTERN 🍴 **The Grill at Hacienda del Sol.** Tucked into the foothills and surrounded by spectacular flowers and cactus gardens, this special-occasion restaurant, a favorite among locals hosting out-of-town visitors, provides an alternative to the chile-laden dishes of most Southwestern nouvelle cuisine. Wild-mushroom bisque, grilled buffalo in dark chocolate mole, and pan-seared sea bass are among the menu choices at this luxurious guest ranch resort. Lower-priced tapas such as tequila-steamed mussels and carne asada tacos can be enjoyed on the more casual outdoor patio, accompanied by live flamenco guitar music on weekends. The lavish Sunday brunch buffet is worth a splurge. [$] *Average main: $38* ✉ *Hacienda del Sol Guest Ranch Resort, 5501 N. Hacienda Del Sol*

CLOSE UP

Tucson Food: North of the Border

Although Tucson ensures that authentic south-of-the-border culinary and cultural influences aren't lost in translation, it also cooks up plenty of cross-border sway. The growing University metropolis boasts eats from around the world and mixes these tastes with more local flavors.

Emerging from an era of meat and potatoes and carne and frijoles—all of which it still does exceptionally well—Tucson has become a foodie tour de force. You can indulge in authentic chicken *mole* (rich sauce including chiles and chocolate) and *carne seca* (dried beef); fill up on some local/world fusion food; or get good and greasy with a Sonoran hot dog.

Start with some classic Mexican dishes such as *tamales* (filled masa dough wrapped in a corn husk) or *enchiladas* (corn tortillas filled with meat or cheese). But today even Mexican-American foods are evolving into a new generation of creations. Do you prefer the chimichangas that purportedly originated at El Charro Café or the mango-filled ones at Mi Nidito for dessert? Taste and decide for yourself.

SAY CHEESE

Many identify Mexican food by bright, glistening layers of cheddar that render the entrée below it unrecognizable. Not that there's anything wrong with that, but true Mexico-style meals are untouched by orange cheese. Authentic dishes are served with much smaller rations of white cheese, usually *queso blanco* or *panela*—mild cheeses that become soft and creamy when heated, but don't melt—and *cotija*, a Mexican-style Parmesan. These cheeses now appear on non-Hispanic menus, too.

PICK A PEPPER

Another key to authentic Mexican food is its heat source: fresh peppers. These heat-tolerant plants were once a south-of-the-border specialty; increased demand has led to their being raised in the southern United States, where they've had a growing impact on regional cuisine. There are endless varieties of the spicy fruit, but here are some more commonly seen on local menus.

Green and Red: Often roasted and peeled for stews and broths, sauces, rubs, marinades, confectionery, chili, and chiles rellenos. Green chiles are unripe, with mild to medium-high heat. Red chiles are ripe, with maximum heat.

Jalapeño: These flavorful green peppers can range from mild to hot and are served pickled, canned, deep-fried for "poppers," or as a garnish for everything from salads to nachos.

Chipotle: When select jalapeños mature from green to a deep red, they're prime for the wood-smoking process that creates *chipotle* (chee-pote-lay) peppers. Their distinct flavor is popular in sauces, marinades, and salsas.

Habañero: This thumb-shape pepper is one of the hottest. A little goes a long way in cooking. It's most often found in chili recipes and hot sauces.

Poblano: This green pepper, aka *pasilla*, is usually mild, but can sometimes pack a punch. Dried, it's an *ancho* chile. The poblano is used for moles.

Rd., Foothills ☎ *520/529–3500* 🌐 *www.haciendadelsol.com/dining/the-grill.htm* ✥ *D2.*

$$ ITALIAN 🍴 **North.** This trendy eatery in upscale La Encantada Shopping Center melds an urban-loft look with rustic Italian touches, including bright red chairs and metal tables. North draws crowds who come for the excellent thin-crust pizzas, pasta, fish, and steak, all prepared in the open kitchen. Alfresco dining on the wraparound patio affords views of the city and quieter conversation; on most evenings the expansive bar area inside buzzes with Tucson's young professionals. [$] *Average main: $18* ✉ *La Encantada Shopping Center, 2995 E. Skyline Dr., Foothills* ☎ *520/299–1600* 🌐 *www.foxrc.com* ✥ *C1.*

$$ ITALIAN 🍴 **Tavolino.** Italian classics like lasagna del forno, ravioli del zucca, and osso buco have never tasted better than at Chef Mossimo's Tavolino, tucked into a small complex of art galleries across from La Encantada Mall. All the pastas are house-made, and even the bread—a pizza dough recipe—is scrumptious. Wood-fired pizzas and the slow-roasted pork loin are deservedly popular. The mostly Italian wine list includes some excellent selections from Pietro Rinaldi (Mossimo's brother's vineyards), just to keep it all in the family. [$] *Average main: $19* ✉ *2890 E. Skyline Dr., Foothills* ☎ *520/531–1913* 🌐 *www.tavolinoristorante.com* ✥ *C1.*

$$$ ITALIAN 🍴 **Vivace.** A nouvelle Italian bistro in a lovely Foothills setting, Vivace has long been a favorite with Tucsonans. Wild mushrooms and goat cheese in puff pastry is hard to resist as a starter. The fettuccine with grilled salmon is a nice, lighter alternative to such entrées as a rich osso buco. For dessert, the molten chocolate cake with spumoni is worth the 20 minutes it takes to create. Patio seating, with either city or mountain views, is especially inviting on warm evenings. [$] *Average main: $26* ✉ *6440 N. Campbell Ave., Foothills* ☎ *520/795–7221* 🌐 *www.vivacetucson.com* 🕒 *Closed Sun.* ✥ *C1.*

$ AMERICAN 🍴 **Zinburger.** Have a glass of wine or a cocktail with your gourmet burger and fries at this high-energy, somewhat noisy, and unquestionably hip burger joint. Zinburger delivers tempting burgers—try the Kobe beef with cheddar and wild mushrooms—and decadent milkshakes made of exotic combinations like dates and honey or melted chocolate with praline flakes. A few creative salads, including one with ahi tuna, round out the menu. The restaurant also has a second location on the northeast side of town. [$] *Average main: $10* ✉ *1865 E. River Rd., Foothills* ☎ *520/299–7799* 🌐 *www.foxrc.com* ✥ *C2, F4.*

7

NORTHWEST TUCSON

$$$ SEAFOOD 🍴 **Bluefin Seafood Bistro.** What's a nice little fish restaurant doing in the middle of the desert? Consistently turning out fresh, well-prepared seafood like cashew-crusted mahimahi, Scottish salmon, and a mixed grill of lobster, shrimp, and scallops in a classy setting, that's what. Tucked into the Casas Adobes Plaza, the two-story bistro has three comfortable seating areas: in the brick-walled bar (where Mussel Madness is a daily happy-hour lure), upstairs in the mellow dining room, and outside on the patio. The bar menu, which includes New England and Manhattan

clam chowder, is served until 10 pm on Friday and Saturday, providing a less expensive, lighter option in this part of town. $ *Average main: $22* ⊠ *Casas Adobes Plaza, 7053 N. Oracle Rd., Northwest* ☎ *520/531–8500* ⊕ *www.bluefintucson.com* ✛ *B1.*

$ ✕ **Sauce.** Modern Italian fuses with fast food here at North Restaurant's casual little sister in Casas Adobes Plaza. Delicious thin-crust

ITALIAN pizzas, chopped salads, pastas, and panini are ordered at the counter in this lively, family-friendly spot decorated in a contemporary twist on the colors of Italy's flag—green, white, and tomato-red. The food is fast, fresh, and affordable, without sacrificing sophisticated taste. Two additional locations, on East Broadway in Eastside and North Campbell in Central, are identical in both décor and menu. $ *Average main: $9* ⊠ *Casas Adobes Plaza, 7117 N. Oracle Rd., Northwest* ☎ *520/297–8575* ⊕ *www.foxrc.com* ✛ *B1, C3.*

$$ ✕ **Tohono Chul Garden Bistro.** The food at Tohono Chul Garden Bistro is

SOUTHWESTERN fine, but what many come for is the location inside a wildlife sanctuary, surrounded by flowering desert gardens. The Southwestern interior has Mexican tile, light wood, and a cobblestone courtyard. Dine on the back patio to watch hummingbirds and butterflies. House favorites include prickly pear and pistachio chicken on croissant, "vegan quiche" (a tofu-and-garbanzo custard with veggies), burgers, and assorted salads. Open daily 8 to 4:30, the bistro also serves breakfast, a popular choice on weekends. $ *Average main: $15* ⊠ *Tohono Chul Park, 7366 N. Paseo del Norte, Northwest* ☎ *520/742–6455* ⊕ *www. tohonochulpark.org* ⊘ *No dinner* ✛ *B1.*

$$ ✕ **Wildflower Grill.** A glass wall separates the bar from the dining area,

AMERICAN where an open kitchen, high ceiling with painted flowers, and blue-green banquettes complete the light and airy effect. Wildflower Grill is well known for its creative American fare and stunning presentation, and the menu has compelling choices like a salmon and seafood bouillabaisse; bow-tie pasta with grilled chicken, tomatoes, spinach, and pine nuts; and red wine-braised shortribs. The decadently huge desserts are equally top-notch. Request a banquette or seating on the patio in the evening if you want quiet conversation, as the room can be noisy. $ *Average main: $20* ⊠ *Casa Adobes Plaza, 7037 N. Oracle Rd., Northwest* ☎ *520/219–4230* ⊕ *www.foxrc.com/restaurants/wildflower-american-cuisine* ✛ *B1.*

SOUTH TUCSON

$ ✕ **Micha's.** Family owned for 39 years, this local institution in the heart

MEXICAN of South Tucson is a nondescript Mexican diner serving some of the best Sonoran classics this side of the border. House specialties include *machaca* (shredded beef) enchiladas and chimichangas, and *cocido*, a hearty vegetable-beef soup. Homemade chorizo spices up breakfast, which is served daily. $ *Average main: $10* ⊠ *2908 S. 4th Ave., South* ☎ *520/623–5307* ⊕ *www.michascatering.com* ⊘ *No dinner Mon.* ✛ *B6.*

$ ✕ **Mi Nidito.** A perennial favorite among locals (the wait is worth it), Mi

MEXICAN Nidito—"my little nest"—has also hosted its share of visiting celebrities. Following President Clinton's lunch here, the rather hefty Presidential Plate (bean tostada, taco with barbecued meat, chiles rellenos, chicken enchilada, and beef tamale with rice and beans) was added to the menu. Top that off with the mango chimichangas for dessert, and you're talkin' executive privilege. [$] *Average main: $10* ✉ *1813 S. 4th Ave., South* ☎ *520/622–5081* 🌐 *www.miniditо.net* 🕒 *Closed Mon. and Tues.* ✥ *B6.*

WHERE TO STAY

When it comes to places to spend the night, the options in Tucson run the gamut: there are luxurious desert resorts, dude ranches, bed-and-breakfasts in modest homes or historic estates, and small-scale to medium-size hotels and motels.

If you like being able to walk to sights, shops, and restaurants, plan on staying in either the Downtown or University neighborhood. Downtown's Hotel Congress is a hot scene, with nightly music pulsing at Club Congress or the Rialto Theatre across the street. For a quieter but equally convenient base, opt for one of the charming B&Bs near the U of A campus.

The posh resorts, primarily situated in the Catalina Foothills and Northwest areas, although farther away from town, have many activities on site, as well as some of Tucson's top-rated restaurants, golf courses, and spas; resort staff can arrange transportation to shopping and sights. Tucson's JW Marriott Starr Pass is the only one southwest of town; seemingly isolated, it's actually closer to Downtown and the Westside sights.

For a unique experience, you can check into one of several Southwestern-style dude ranches—among them a former cattle ranch from the 1800s—on the outskirts of town (unless otherwise indicated, price categories for guest ranches include all meals and most activities).

If you're seeking accommodations that can change your life, book a stay at one of Tucson's world-class health spas, Canyon Ranch or Miraval. Both provide pampering, serenity, and guidance for attaining an improved sense of well-being.

Summer rates (late May through September) are up to 60% lower than those in winter. Note that unless you book months in advance, you'll be hard-pressed to find a Tucson hotel room at any price the week before and during the huge gem and mineral show, which is held the first two weeks in February *(⇨ see "Festivals and Events" in Tucson Planner)*. Also, resorts typically charge an additional daily fee for "use of facilities," such as pools, tennis courts, and exercise classes and equipment, so be sure to ask what's included when you book a room.

WHAT IT COSTS

	$	$$	$$$	$$$$
For two people	under $151	$151–$225	$226–$350	over $350

Hotel prices are the lowest cost of a standard double room in high season.

7

Hotel reviews have been shortened. For full information, visit Fodors.com. Use the coordinate (✢ B2) at the end of each listing to locate a site on the corresponding map.

DOWNTOWN TUCSON

$ HOTEL Fodor's Choice ★ 🏨 **Hotel Congress.** This hotel, built in 1919, has been artfully restored to its original Western version of art deco; it's now the center of Tucson's hippest scene and a great place for younger and adventurous travelers to stay. **Pros:** prime location; good restaurant; funky and fun. **Cons:** no elevator to guest rooms; no TVs in rooms; noise from nightclub. [$] *Rooms from: $109* ✉ *311 E. Congress St., Downtown* ☎ *520/622–8848, 800/722–8848* 🌐 *www.hotelcongress.com* 🛏 *40 rooms* 🍴 *No meals* ✢ *B5.*

$ HOTEL 🏨 **Inn Suites Hotel Tucson City Center.** Just north of the Presidio district of Downtown, this circa 1980 hotel is next to Interstate 10 but quiet nevertheless. **Pros:** free breakfast and two cocktails; affordable. **Cons:** little character; long walk to Downtown attractions (but there is a free shuttle service). [$] *Rooms from: $79* ✉ *475 N. Granada Ave., Downtown* ☎ *520/622–3000, 877/446–6589* 🌐 *www.innsuites.com* 🛏 *265 rooms, 35 suites* 🍴 *Breakfast* ✢ *B5.*

$$ B&B/INN 🏨 **The Royal Elizabeth Bed and Breakfast Inn.** Fans of Victoriana adore this B&B in the Armory Park historic district. **Pros:** large and well-appointed rooms; beautiful common areas; a sense of privacy as well as B&B camaraderie. **Cons:** a bit pricey for Downtown; neighbors aren't very lively (next door to a funeral home). [$] *Rooms from: $185* ✉ *204 S. Scott Ave., Downtown* ☎ *520/670–9022* 🌐 *www.royalelizabeth.com* 🛏 *6 rooms* 🍴 *Breakfast* ✢ *B5.*

UNIVERSITY OF ARIZONA

$ B&B/INN 🏨 **Adobe Rose Bed and Breakfast.** In the historic Sam Hughes neighborhood, the well-maintained inn just east of the university is within easy walking distance of shops and restaurants. **Pros:** sumptuous breakfasts that can be prepared gluten-free; homelike yet private. **Cons:** some rooms are small; about a mile walk to University Boulevard and 4th Avenue sights. [$] *Rooms from: $135* ✉ *940 N. Olsen Ave., University* ☎ *520/318–4644, 800/328–4122* 🌐 *www.aroseinn.com* 🛏 *6 rooms* 🍴 *Breakfast* ✢ *C4.*

$$$ HOTEL Fodor's Choice ★ 🏨 **Arizona Inn.** Although near the university and many sights, the beautifully landscaped lawns and gardens of this 1930 inn seem far from the hustle and bustle. **Pros:** unique historical property; emphasis on service. **Cons:** rooms may not be modern enough for some; close to University Medical Center but long walk (1½ miles) from the main campus. [$] *Rooms from: $299* ✉ *2200 E. Elm St., University* ☎ *520/325–1541, 800/933–1093* 🌐 *www.arizonainn.com* 🛏 *72 rooms, 20 suites, 3 casitas* 🍴 *No meals* ✢ *C4.*

$ B&B/INN 🏨 **Catalina Park Inn Bed & Breakfast.** Classical music plays softly in the living room of this beautifully restored 1927 neoclassical house in the University of Arizona vicinity. **Pros:** rooms are large and quiet with up-to-date technology (DVDs, flat-screen TVs, and iPod docks);

BEST BETS FOR TUCSON LODGING

Fodor's offers a selective listing of quality lodging experiences at every price range, from the city's best budget motel to its most sophisticated luxury hotel. Here, we've compiled our top recommendations by price and experience. The very best properties—in other words, those that provide a particularly remarkable experience in their price range—are designated in the listings with the Fodor's Choice logo.

Fodor'sChoice ★

Arizona Inn, $$$, p. 380

Canyon Ranch, $$$$, p. 383

Casa Tierra, $$, p. 385

Hacienda del Sol Guest Ranch Resort, $$, p. 383

Hotel Congress, $, p. 380

Loews Ventana Canyon Resort, $$$, p. 383

White Stallion Ranch, $$$$, p. 385

Best by Price

$

Adobe Rose Bed and Breakfast, p. 380

Catalina Park Inn Bed & Breakfast, p. 380

Hotel Congress, p. 380

Inn Suites Hotel Tucson City Center, p. 380

La Posada Lodge and Casitas, p. 384

Peppertrees Bed & Breakfast, p. 382

$$

Casa Tierra, p. 385

Hacienda del Sol Guest Ranch Resort, p. 383

The Inns at El Rancho Merlita, p. 382

Lodge on the Desert, p. 382

Westward Look Resort, p. 384

$$$–$$$$

Arizona Inn, p. 380

JW Marriott Starr Pass, p. 385

Loews Ventana Canyon Resort, p. 383

The Ritz-Carlton, Dove Mountain, p. 384

Westin La Paloma, p. 383

White Stallion Ranch, p. 385

Best By Experience

BEST B&BS

Casa Tierra, $$, p. 385

Catalina Park Inn Bed & Breakfast, $, p. 380

Peppertrees Bed & Breakfast, $, p. 382

Royal Elizabeth Bed and Breakfast Inn, $$, p. 380

BEST RESORTS

JW Marriott Starr Pass, $$$, p. 385

Loews Ventana Canyon Resort, $$$, p. 383

The Ritz-Carlton, Dove Mountain, $$$$, p. 384

Westin La Paloma, $$$, p. 383

BEST SPAS

Canyon Ranch, $$$$, p. 383

JW Marriott Starr Pass, $$$, p. 385

Miraval, $$$$, p. 384

The Ritz-Carlton, Dove Mountain, $$$$, p. 384

Westin La Paloma, $$$, p. 383

GREAT VIEWS

Casa Tierra, $$, p. 385

JW Marriott Starr Pass, $$$, p. 385

Loews Ventana Canyon Resort, $$$, p. 383

Tanque Verde Ranch, $$$, p. 383

Westward Look Resort, $$, p. 384

MOST KID-FRIENDLY

Hilton Tucson El Conquistador, $$, p. 384

Tanque Verde Ranch, $$$, p. 383

Westin La Paloma, $$$, p. 383

White Stallion Ranch, $$$$, p. 385

MOST ROMANTIC

Arizona Inn, $$$, p. 380

Hacienda del Sol Guest Ranch Resort, $$, p. 383

JW Marriott Starr Pass, $$$, p. 385

The Ritz-Carlton, Dove Mountain, $$$$, p. 384

7

comfortable beds; charming hosts. **Cons:** west University location is not quite as bucolic as east of campus; closed late summer. [$] *Rooms from: $145* ✉ *309 E. 1st St., University* ☎ *520/792–4541, 800/792–4885* 🌐 *www.catalinaparkinn.com* 🛏 *5 rooms* 🕓 *Closed July–Aug.* 🍴 *Breakfast* ✥ *B4.*

$ B&B/INN 🏨 **Peppertrees Bed & Breakfast.** This restored 1905 Victorian, filled with antiques and just west of the U of A campus, has both rooms and self-contained apartment units. **Pros:** comfortably furnished and meticulously clean; very convenient. **Cons:** often booked far in advance. [$] *Rooms from: $145* ✉ *724 E. University Blvd., University* ☎ *520/622–7167* 🌐 *www.peppertreesinn.com* 🛏 *2 rooms, 1 suite, 2 guesthouses* 🍴 *Breakfast* ✥ *B4.*

$$ HOTEL 🏨 **Tucson Marriott University Park.** With the University of Arizona less than a block from the front door, this clean, contemporary hotel is an ideal place to stay when visiting the campus. **Pros:** excellent location; clean. **Cons:** generic rooms; uninspired restaurant. [$] *Rooms from: $169* ✉ *880 E. 2nd St., University* ☎ *520/792–4100, 888/236–2427* 🌐 *www.marriott.com* 🛏 *234 rooms, 16 suites* 🍴 *No meals* ✥ *B4.*

CENTRAL TUCSON

$ HOTEL 🏨 **Doubletree by Hilton at Tucson–Reid Park.** A sprawling, 1970s-era hotel and conference center, the Doubletree sits directly across the street from Randolph Park, Tucson's best municipal golf course, and Reid Park, which houses the city zoo, a lake with paddleboats, and numerous play areas. **Pros:** attractive gardens; close to recreation and restaurants. **Cons:** large, older property; smallish rooms. [$] *Rooms from: $129* ✉ *445 S. Alvernon Way, Central* ☎ *520/881–4200, 800/222–8733* 🌐 *doubletree3.hilton.com* 🛏 *295 rooms* 🍴 *No meals* ✥ *D5.*

$$ HOTEL 🏨 **Lodge on the Desert.** A charming hacienda-style hotel originally built in the 1930s has gotten a long-awaited face-lift and now offers modern comfort in an old-world setting. **Pros:** quiet, garden setting; central location. **Cons:** no gym or spa (though in-room massages and gym passes are available, for a fee). [$] *Rooms from: $169* ✉ *306 N. Alvernon Way, Central* ☎ *520/320–2000, 877/498–6776* 🌐 *www.lodgeonthedesert.com* 🛏 *83 rooms, 20 suites* 🍴 *No meals* ✥ *D5.*

EASTSIDE

$$ B&B/INN 🏨 **The Inns at El Rancho Merlita.** Few bed-and-breakfasts deliver the historic charm, elegance, and pampering of this midcentury Southwestern estate, the former retreat of cosmetics mogul Merle Norman. **Pros:** historic, charming home and grounds; excellent breakfast. **Cons:** a little far from town for some. [$] *Rooms from: $179* ✉ *1924 N. Corte El Rancho Merlita, Eastside* ☎ *520/495–0071, 888/218–8418* 🌐 *www.ranchomerlita.com* 🛏 *8 rooms* 🍴 *Breakfast* ✥ *G4.*

$$ B&B/INN 🏨 **The SunCatcher.** The three rooms in this serene B&B near the national park are decorated in honor of three groups who settled the Old West: Cowboys, Native Americans, and Spaniards. **Pros:** quiet escape from civilization; all rooms have separate entrances; scrumptious European breakfasts. **Cons:** on the far east side of town. [$] *Rooms from: $180*

✉ *105 N. Avenida Javelina, Eastside* ☎ *520/885–0883, 877/775–8355* ⊕ *www.suncatchertucson.com* ➳ *3 rooms* ⭐ *Breakfast* ✛ *H4.*

$$$ 🏨 **Tanque Verde Ranch.** The most upscale of Tucson's guest ranches and
ALL-INCLUSIVE one of the oldest in the country, the Tanque Verde sits on 640 beautiful
FAMILY acres in the Rincon Mountains next to Saguaro National Park East.
Pros: authentic Western experience; loads of all-inclusive activities;
great riding. **Cons:** at the eastern edge of town; all-inclusive package
excludes alcohol. $ *Rooms from: $350* ✉ *14301 E. Speedway Blvd.,
Eastside* ☎ *520/296–6275, 800/234–3833* ⊕ *www.tanqueverderanch.
com* ➳ *49 rooms, 25 suites* ⭐ *All-inclusive* ✛ *H4.*

CATALINA FOOTHILLS

$$$$ 🏨 **Canyon Ranch.** This award-winning resort draws an international
ALL-INCLUSIVE crowd of well-to-do health seekers to its superb spa facilities on 70
Fodor's Choice acres in the desert foothills. **Pros:** a stay here can be a life-changing
★ experience; gorgeous setting. **Cons:** very pricey; not family-friendly.
$ *Rooms from: $900* ✉ *8600 E. Rockcliff Rd., Foothills* ☎ *520/749–
9000, 800/742–9000* ⊕ *www.canyonranch.com* ➳ *240 rooms* ⭐ *All-
inclusive* ✛ *G2.*

$$ 🏨 **Hacienda del Sol Guest Ranch Resort.** This 32-acre hideaway in the
RESORT Santa Catalina Foothills is a charming and more intimate alternative
Fodor's Choice to the larger resorts, and is partly a guest ranch, with riding stables
★ down the road. **Pros:** outstanding restaurant and bar; buildings and
landscaping are stunningly beautiful. **Cons:** not enough resort amenities
for some (no golf or spa, just a few massage rooms). $ *Rooms from:
$189* ✉ *5501 N. Hacienda Del Sol Rd., Foothills* ☎ *520/299–1501,
800/728–6514* ⊕ *www.haciendadelsol.com* ➳ *22 rooms, 8 suites* ⭐ *No
meals* ✛ *D2.*

$$$ 🏨 **Loews Ventana Canyon Resort.** This is one of the most luxurious and
RESORT prettiest of the big resorts, with dramatic stone architecture and an
FAMILY 80-foot waterfall cascading down the mountains. **Pros:** this place has
Fodor's Choice everything: great golf, full spa, hiking, and even a kids' playground.
★ **Cons:** some rooms overlook the parking lot. $ *Rooms from: $239*
✉ *7000 N. Resort Dr., Foothills* ☎ *520/299–2020, 800/234–5117*
⊕ *www.loewshotels.com/Ventana-Canyon-Resort* ➳ *384 rooms, 14
suites* ⭐ *No meals* ✛ *F1.*

$$$ 🏨 **Westin La Paloma.** Popular with business travelers and families, this
RESORT sprawling resort has grand views of the Santa Catalina Mountains
FAMILY above and the city below. **Pros:** top-notch golf, tennis, and spa. **Cons:**
so big it can feel crowded at pool areas and mazelike going to and from
guest rooms. $ *Rooms from: $239* ✉ *3800 E. Sunrise Dr., Foothills*
☎ *520/742–6000, 800/937–8461* ⊕ *www.westinlapalomaresort.com*
➳ *455 rooms, 32 suites* ⭐ *No meals* ✛ *D1.*

$ 🏨 **Windmill Inn & Suites at St. Philip's Plaza.** Set in a chic shopping plaza
HOTEL filled with boutiques, galleries, good restaurants, and a weekend farmers' market, this all-suites hotel provides a range of amenities, including
complimentary coffee, muffins, juice, and a newspaper delivered to your
door. **Pros:** many shops and restaurants to walk to; free Wi-Fi; bicycles
are available for treks along the adjacent Rillito River Path. **Cons:** it's
a suite, but both rooms are on the small side. $ *Rooms from: $149*

7

✉ *4250 N. Campbell Ave., Foothills* ☎ *520/577–0007, 800/547–4747* 🌐 *www.windmillinns.com* 🛏 *122 suites* 🍴 *Breakfast* ✥ *C2.*

NORTHWEST TUCSON

$$ RESORT FAMILY 🏨 **Hilton Tucson El Conquistador.** A huge copper mural of cowboys and cacti, and a wide view of the Santa Catalina Mountains grace the lobby of this golf and tennis resort. **Pros:** great variety of on-site activities; low-key. **Cons:** huge place; location is farther northwest than most resorts, which means longer driving time to restaurants and in-town sights. [$] *Rooms from: $189* ✉ *10000 N. Oracle Rd., Northwest* ☎ *520/544–5000, 800/325–7832* 🌐 *www.hiltonelconquistador.com* 🛏 *328 rooms, 57 suites, 43 casitas* 🍴 *No meals* ✥ *C1.*

$ HOTEL 🏨 **La Posada Lodge and Casitas.** This 1960s motor lodge has been reborn as a Santa Fe–style boutique hotel with a Latin theme. **Pros:** good location; good value; attractive grounds. **Cons:** hotel is on a busy road, so front-facing rooms are not as tranquil; rooms are not large. [$] *Rooms from: $99* ✉ *5900 N. Oracle Rd., Northwest* ☎ *520/887–4800, 800/810–2808* 🌐 *laposada.org* 🛏 *72 rooms* 🍴 *Breakfast* ✥ *B1.*

$ HOTEL 🏨 **Marriott TownePlace Suites.** With full kitchens in all of its studio, one-bedroom, and two-bedroom suites, this property is suitable for short or extended stays. **Pros:** convenient location; well-equipped units. **Cons:** no on-site restaurant; kind of sterile-looking. [$] *Rooms from: $129* ✉ *405 W. Rudasill Rd., Northwest* ☎ *520/292–9697* 🌐 *www.marriott.com/towneplace* 🛏 *76 suites* 🍴 *Breakfast* ✥ *B1.*

$$$$ RESORT 🏨 **Miraval.** This New Age health spa 30 miles north of Tucson, popular with celebrities, has a secluded desert setting and beautiful Southwestern rooms. **Pros:** very high-end getaway in the middle of nowhere; tranquil. **Cons:** very posh attitude makes some uncomfortable; expensive. [$] *Rooms from: $1000* ✉ *5000 E. Via Estancia Miraval, Catalina* ☎ *520/825–4000, 800/232–3969* 🌐 *www.miravalresorts.com* 🛏 *102 rooms* 🍴 *All meals* ✥ *C1.*

$$ RESORT 🏨 **Omni Tucson National Golf Resort & Spa.** Perfect for couples with differing ideas on how to spend a vacation, the friendly Omni Tucson National is both a premier golf resort and a full-service European-style spa, where you can be coiffed, waxed, and wrapped to your heart's content. **Pros:** outstanding golf; relaxed yet luxurious; convenient to shopping and restaurants in thriving Northwest area. **Cons:** a little farther from central Tucson than others, as it's tucked away in Northwest Tucson; too sedate for some. [$] *Rooms from: $179* ✉ *2727 W. Club Dr., Northwest* ☎ *520/297–2271, 800/843–6664* 🌐 *www.omnihotels.com* 🛏 *143 rooms, 24 suites* 🍴 *No meals* ✥ *A1.*

$$$$ RESORT 🏨 **The Ritz-Carlton, Dove Mountain.** The most elegant and exclusive of Tucson's golf and tennis resorts is the ever-posh Ritz-Carlton, set in the rolling hills of Marana, about 20 miles northwest of central Tucson. **Pros:** great golf; top-notch service. **Cons:** somewhat isolated location in the far Northwest. [$] *Rooms from: $399* ✉ *15000 N. Secret Springs Dr., Marana* ☎ *520/572–3000, 800/241–3333* 🌐 *www.ritzcarlton.com/dovemountain* 🛏 *250 rooms* 🍴 *No meals* ✥ *A1.*

$$ RESORT 🏨 **Westward Look Resort.** Originally the 1912 homestead of William and Mary Watson, this laid-back lodging with gorgeous city views and

Downtown Tucson is close to the Tucson Mountains, which fill with blooms in springtime.

desert gardens has Southwestern character and all the amenities you expect at a major resort. **Pros:** horseback riding; excellent spa and tennis; pleasant nature trails; you can actually park near your room. **Cons:** no golf (privileges at private club 4 miles away); pool areas are rather plain. $ *Rooms from: $199* ⊠ *245 E. Ina Rd., Northwest* ☎ *520/297–1151, 800/722–2500* ⊕ *www.westwardlook.com* ⊅ *244 rooms* ⦿ *No meals* ✛ *B1.*

$$$$
ALL-INCLUSIVE
Fodor'sChoice
★
🖬 **White Stallion Ranch.** A 3,000-acre working cattle ranch run by the hospitable True family since 1965, this place is the real deal, satisfying for families as well as singles or couples. **Pros:** solid dude-ranch experience; very charming hosts; airport shuttle. **Cons:** no TV in rooms; alcohol not included in the rate—pay extra or bring your own. $ *Rooms from: $400* ⊠ *9251 W. Twin Peaks Rd., Northwest* ☎ *520/297–0252, 888/977–2624* ⊕ *www.wsranch.com* ⊅ *24 rooms, 17 suites* ⦿ *All-inclusive* ✛ *A1.*

WESTSIDE

$$
B&B/INN
Fodor'sChoice
★
🖬 **Casa Tierra.** For a real desert experience, head to this B&B on five acres near the Desert Museum and Saguaro National Park West. **Pros:** peaceful; great Southwest character. **Cons:** far from town (30-minute drive); two-night minimum stay; closed in summer. $ *Rooms from: $165* ⊠ *11155 W. Calle Pima, Westside* ☎ *520/578–3058, 866/254–0006* ⊕ *www.casatierratucson.com* ⊅ *3 rooms, 1 suite* ⊙ *Closed mid-June–mid-Aug.* ⦿ *Breakfast* ✛ *A4.*

$$$
RESORT
🖬 **JW Marriott Starr Pass.** Set amid saguaro forests and mesquite groves in the Tucson Mountains (yet only 15 minutes from Downtown), this is the

city's largest resort. **Pros:** posh and beautiful; excellent spa; great walking-hiking paths. **Cons:** expensive; parking structure is quite far from lobby areas and guest rooms. [$] *Rooms from: $299* ✉ *3800 W. Starr Pass Blvd., Westside* ☎ *520/792–3500* 🌐 *www.jwmarriottstarrpass.com* 🛏 *538 rooms, 37 suites* 🍴 *No meals* ✣ *A5.*

NIGHTLIFE AND THE ARTS

NIGHTLIFE

The majority of Tucson's bars and clubs, many with live music or a DJ, are clustered along Congress Street Downtown and on 4th Avenue. A proliferation of craft breweries and gastro-pubs are now pouring local brews in this district. In addition, most of the major resorts have late spots for drinks or dancing. The Westward Look Resort's Lookout Bar, with its expansive view and classic rock band on Friday and Saturday nights, is popular for dancing. The bars at Westin La Paloma, Hacienda del Sol, and Loews Ventana have live acoustic music on weekends.

DOWNTOWN TUCSON

BARS AND CLUBS

Club Congress. The city's main venue for cutting-edge bands and singer-songwriters, Club Congress has a mixed-bag crowd of alternative rockers, international travelers, young professionals, and college kids. There is live indie rock and folk/roots during the week, while Friday and Saturday nights bring more rock and dance parties. ✉ *Hotel Congress, 311 E. Congress St., Downtown* ☎ *520/622–8848* 🌐 *www.hotelcongress.com.*

La Cocina. Hear some of the best local talent play folk-rock, blues, and jazz Wednesday to Saturday nights at this restaurant and bar in the courtyard of Old Town Artisans. Sit under the stars and order from the late-night menu until 2 am. Closed Sunday and Monday nights. ✉ *Old Town Artisans, 201 N. Court Ave., Downtown* ☎ *520/622–0351* 🌐 *www.lacocinatucson.com.*

Playground. Three distinct spaces at this bar offer something for everyone—everyone who likes a modern, urban vibe, that is. The spacious rooftop deck has a DJ and dancing most nights, plus a good view of town. Downstairs, the sleek, minimalist bar, with large-screen TVs and happy-hour specials, has occasional live music. Check out the intimate covered patio for quieter conversation with your cocktails. ✉ *278 E. Congress St., Downtown* ☎ *520/396–3691* 🌐 *www.playgroundtucson.com.*

UNIVERSITY OF ARIZONA

BARS AND CLUBS

GAY AND LESBIAN **IBT's (It's 'Bout Time).** Tucson's most popular gay men's bar, IBT's (It's 'Bout Time) has rock and disco DJ music and drag shows Wednesday and Saturday nights. Expect long lines on weekends. ✉ *616 N. 4th Ave., University* ☎ *520/882–3053* 🌐 *www.ibtstucson.com.*

ROCK **Plush.** Alternative-rock bands like Camp Courageous and Greyhound Soul are hosted at the intimate Plush, as well as local performers with a loyal following. ✉ *340 E. 6th St., at 4th Ave., University* ☎ *520/798–1298* ⊕ *www.plushtucson.com.*

CENTRAL TUCSON AND EASTSIDE
BARS AND CLUBS

BLUES AND JAZZ **Boondocks.** The unofficial home of the Blues Heritage Foundation, Boondocks hosts local and touring jazz and classic rock singer-songwriters five or six nights a week. ✉ *3306 N. 1st Ave., Central* ☎ *520/690–0991* ⊕ *www.boondockslounge.com.*

Old Pueblo Grille. This Southwestern restaurant and bar has live jazz on Sunday nights. ✉ *60 N. Alvernon Way, Central* ☎ *520/326–6000* ⊕ *www.oldpueblogrille.com.*

COUNTRY AND WESTERN **The Maverick Live Country Club.** An excellent house band gets the crowd two-stepping Tuesday through Saturday night. ✉ *6622 E. Tanque Verde Rd., Eastside* ☎ *520/298–0430* ⊕ *www.tucsonmaverick.com.*

ROCK **The Shelter.** Sip a martini and go totally retro at the Shelter, a former bomb shelter decked out in plastic 1960s kitsch, lava lamps, and JFK memorabilia. Watch Elvis videos and listen to music of Burt Bacharach, as well as current alternative rock. ✉ *4155 E. Grant Rd., Central* ☎ *520/326–1345* ⊕ *www.thesheltercocktaillounge.com.*

SOUTH TUCSON
BARS AND CLUBS

Nimbus Brewing Company. This is the place for acoustic blues, folk, and bluegrass, not to mention good, cheap food and microbrew beer. ✉ *3850 E. 44th St., Southeast* ☎ *520/745–9175* ⊕ *www.nimbusbeer.com.*

CASINOS

Two Native American tribes operate casinos on their Tucson-area reservations west of the airport. They're quite unlike their distant and much grander cousins in Las Vegas and Atlantic City. Don't expect much glamour, ersatz or otherwise: these casinos are more like glorified video arcades, though you can lose money much faster. You'll be greeted by a wall of cigarette smoke (the reservation is exempt from antismoking laws) and the wail of slot machines, video poker, blackjack, roulette, and craps machines. Casino del Sol has expanded into a resort, with comfortable hotel rooms, first-class dining, a spa, and an 18-hole golf course. The only "live" gaming is keno, bingo, blackjack, and certain types of poker. No one under age 21 is permitted.

Casino del Sol. A few miles west of the Casino of the Sun is the Pascua Yaqui tribe's newer, larger facility, Casino del Sol, with live poker and blackjack, bingo, and slots. A first-rate Asian-fusion restaurant, an excellent steakhouse, and several casual eateries provide multiple dining options. A 215-room hotel and conference center opened in 2012, followed by a golf course in 2013. An adjacent 4,600-seat outdoor amphitheater books entertainers like Counting Crows and James Taylor. ✉ *5655 W. Valencia Rd., Westside* ☎ *520/838–6506, 855/765–7829* ⊕ *www.casinodelsol.com.*

Casino of the Sun. The Pascua Yaqui tribe's original gaming venture has slot and video-gambling machines only, and one casual restaurant. ✉ *7406*

7

S. Camino de Oeste, off W. Valencia Rd. about 5 miles west of I–19, Southwest ☎ *520/838–6506, 855/765-7829* ⊕ *www.casinodelsol.com.*

Desert Diamond Casinos Tucson. The Tohono O'odham tribe operates the Desert Diamond Casinos, which has an indoor concert venue, a hotel and conference center, and plenty of one-armed bandits and video poker in addition to live blackjack and poker, keno, and bingo. ⊠ *7350 S. Old Nogales Hwy., 1 mile south of Valencia, just west of airport, South* ☎ *520/294–7777, 866/332–9467* ⊕ *www.desertdiamondcasino.com.*

THE ARTS

For a city of its size, Tucson is abuzz with cultural activity. It's one of only 14 cities in the United States with a symphony as well as opera, theater, and ballet companies. Wintertime, when Tucson's population swells with vacationers, is the high season, but the arts are alive and well year-round. The low cost of Tucson's cultural events comes as a pleasant surprise to those accustomed to paying East or West Coast prices: concert tickets are as little as $20 for some performances, and touring Broadway musicals can often be seen for $35. Parking is plentiful and frequently free.

The free *Tucson Weekly* (⊕ *www.tucsonweekly.com*) and the "Caliente" section of the *Arizona Daily Star* (⊕ *www.azstarnet.com*) both hit the stands on Thursday, and have listings of what's going on in town.

MAJOR VENUES

Centennial Hall. Dance, music, and other performances take place at the University of Arizona's Centennial Hall. The UA Presents series is held here during the academic year (September through May); a few performances by other entities are held here in summer. ⊠ *1020 E. University Blvd., University* ☎ *520/621–3341* ⊕ *www.uapresents.org.*

Fox Tucson Theatre. A refurbished old movie palace, the art deco Fox Theatre hosts film festivals and mostly folk-rock concerts. ⊠ *17 W. Congress St., Downtown* ☎ *520/547–3040* ⊕ *www.foxtucsontheatre.org.*

Rialto Theatre. One of Tucson's hottest venues, the Rialto Theatre, once a silent-movie theater, now reverberates with the sounds of hard rock, jazz, folk, and world-music concerts. You can experience great musicians up close for reasonable ticket prices. ⊠ *318 E. Congress St., Downtown* ☎ *520/740–1000* ⊕ *www.rialtotheatre.com.*

Tucson Convention Center. Much of the city's cultural activity, including opera, touring Broadway shows, and Tucson Symphony concerts, takes place at the Tucson Convention Center. Also part of this complex are the Music Hall and the smaller Leo Rich Theater. ⊠ *260 S. Church Ave., Downtown* ☎ *520/791–4101* ⊕ *www.tucsonaz.gov/tcc.*

TICKETS **Ticketmaster.** Each season brings visiting opera, theater, and dance companies to Tucson. Tickets to many events can be purchased through Ticketmaster, which has outlets at a few Fry's Marketplace stores around town. ☎ *800/745–3000* ⊕ *www.ticketmaster.com.*

MUSIC

Arizona Friends of Chamber Music. A Wednesday-night chamber-music series is hosted by the Arizona Friends of Chamber Music at the Leo Rich Theater in the Tucson Convention Center October through April. There's also a music festival the first week of March. ⊠ *260 S. Church St., Downtown* ☎ *520/577–3769* ⊕ *www.arizonachambermusic.org.*

Arizona Opera Company. This Phoenix-based company puts on five major productions each year at the Tucson Convention Center's Music Hall. ⊠ *260 S. Church St., Downtown* ☎ *520/293–4336* ⊕ *www.azopera.com.*

Arizona Symphonic Winds. In winter the Arizona Symphonic Winds performs a series of free indoor concerts and then goes outdoors with a spring–summer concert schedule at Udall Park in Northeast Tucson; performances in the park are usually at 7 pm, but you need to arrive at least an hour early for a good spot on the grass. ⊠ *László Veres Amphitheater, Udall Park, 7200 E. Tanque Verde Rd., Tucson* ⊕ *www.azsymwinds.org.*

Tucson Jazz Society. The small but vibrant jazz scene in Tucson encompasses everything from afternoon jam sessions in the park to Sunday jazz brunches at resorts in the Foothills. Call the Tucson Jazz Society for information. ☎ *520/903–1265* ⊕ *www.tucsonjazz.org.*

Tucson Pops Orchestra. In May, June, and September the Tucson Pops Orchestra gives free concerts on Sunday evenings at the DeMeester Outdoor Performance Center in Reid Park. Arrive about an hour before the music starts (usually at 7 pm) to stake your claim on a viewing spot. ☎ *520/722–5853* ⊕ *www.tucsonpops.org.*

Tucson Symphony Orchestra. Part of Tucson's cultural scene since 1929, this orchestra performs at the Tucson Convention Center and at sites in the Foothills and the Northwest October through May. ⊠ *Box Office, 2175 N. 6th Ave., Downtown* ☎ *520/882–8585 for box office* ⊕ *www.tucsonsymphony.org.*

POETRY

Tucson Poetry Festival. The first weekend in April brings the Tucson Poetry Festival and its four days of readings and related events, including workshops, panel discussions, and a poetry slam. Such internationally acclaimed poets as Jorie Graham and Sherman Alexie have participated. ⊠ *Hotel Congress, 311 E. Congress St.* ⊕ *www.tucsonpoetryfestival.org.*

THEATER

Arizona Repertory Theatre. Performances by students occur throughout the academic year on campus at this University of Arizona theater. ⊠ *1025 N. Olive St., University* ☎ *520/621–7008* ⊕ *www.tftv.arizona.edu.*

Arizona Theatre Company. September through May, Arizona's state theater performs classical pieces, contemporary drama, and musical comedy at the historic Temple of Music and Art. It's worth coming just to see the beautifully restored historic Spanish colonial–Moorish-style theater; dinner at the adjoining Temple Café is a tasty prelude. ⊠ *Temple of Music and Art, 330 S. Scott Ave., Downtown* ☎ *520/622–2823 for box office* ⊕ *www.arizonatheatre.org.*

Borderlands Theater. This company presents new plays about Southwest border issues—often multicultural and bilingual—at venues throughout Tucson, usually October through April. ⊠ 40 W. Broadway, Downtown ☎ 520/882–7406 ⊕ www.borderlandstheater.org.

FAMILY **Gaslight Theatre.** Children of all ages love the clever, original melodramas at the Gaslight Theatre, where hissing at the villain and cheering the hero are part of the audience's duty. ⊠ 7010 E. Broadway, Eastside ☎ 520/886–9428 ⊕ www.thegaslighttheatre.com.

Invisible Theatre. Contemporary plays and musicals are presented in an intimate 80-seat theater by this highly regarded nonprofit company. ⊠ 1400 N. 1st Ave., Central ☎ 520/882–9721 ⊕ www.invisibletheatre. com.

SHOPPING

Much of Tucson's retail activity is focused around malls, but shops with more character and some unique wares can be found in the city's open plazas: Old Town Artisans (Meyer Avenue and Washington Street), St. Philip's Plaza (River Road and Campbell Avenue), Casas Adobes Plaza (Oracle and Ina roads), and La Encantada (Skyline Drive and Campbell Avenue).

The 4th Avenue neighborhood near the University of Arizona—especially between 2nd and 9th streets—is fertile ground for unusual items in the artsy boutiques, galleries, and secondhand-clothing stores. For in-town deals, the outlet stores at the Foothills Mall in Northwest Tucson score high marks.

If you're seeking work by regional artists, there are excellent galleries Downtown and in the Catalina Foothills; or you might want to drive down to Tubac, a community 45 miles south of Tucson (⇨ see Side Trips Near Tucson).

San Xavier Plaza, across from San Xavier mission and also part of the Tohono O'odham Reservation, is a good place to find vendors and stores selling the work of this and other area tribes.

DOWNTOWN TUCSON

GALLERIES

Etherton Gallery. This gallery specializes in vintage, classic, and contemporary photography but also represents artists in other mediums. ⊠ 135 S. 6th Ave., Downtown ☎ 520/624–7370 ⊕ www.ethertongallery.com ☺ Closed Sun. and Mon.

Obsidian Gallery. This gallery in the historic train station sells exquisite glass, ceramic, and jewelry pieces, as well as sculpture and paintings. ⊠ Historic Depot, 410 N. Toole Ave., #130, Downtown ☎ 520/577–3598 ⊕ www.obsidian-gallery.com ☺ Closed Mon. and Tues.

Philabaum Glass Gallery and Studio. Magnificent handblown glass pieces by Tom Philabaum and others, including vases, artwork, table settings, and jewelry, are made and sold at this gallery. ⊠ 711 S. Sixth Ave., Downtown ☎ 520/884–7404 ⊕ www.philabaumglass.com ☺ Closed Sun. and Mon.

MALLS AND SHOPPING CENTERS

Old Town Artisans Complex. Across from the Tucson Museum of Art, the Old Town Artisans complex of adobe buildings dating back to the 1850s has a large selection of Southwestern wares, including Native American jewelry, baskets, Mexican handicrafts, pottery, and textiles, as well as La Cocina Restaurant and bar. ⊠ *201 N. Court Ave., Downtown* ☎ *520/622–0351* ⊕ *www.oldtownartisans.com.*

UNIVERSITY OF ARIZONA

ARTS AND CRAFTS

Del Sol. This shop specializes in Mexican folk art, jewelry, and Southwest-style clothing. ⊠ *435 N. 4th Ave., University* ☎ *520/628–8765* ⊕ *www.delsolstores.com.*

Native Seeds/SEARCH. Dedicated to preserving native crops and traditional farming methods, Native Seeds/SEARCH sells 350 kinds of seeds as well as Native American foods, baking mixes, and crafts. ⊠ *3061 N. Campbell Ave., University* ☎ *520/622–5561* ⊕ *www.nativeseeds. org* ☉ *Closed Sun.*

BOOKS

Antigone Books. This lovely independent bookstore on 4th Avenue specializes in books by and about women, and sells creative cards, gifts, and T-shirts as well as a broad range of books. ⊠ *411 N. 4th Ave., University* ☎ *520/792–3715* ⊕ *www.antigonebooks.com.*

Book Stop. This is a wonderful browsing place for used, rare, and out-of-print books. ⊠ *214 N. 4th Ave., University* ☎ *520/326–6661* ⊕ *www. bookstoptucson.com.*

CENTRAL TUCSON

BOOKS

Bookmans Entertainment Exchange. A Tucson institution, Bookmans carries an enormous and eclectic selection of used and new books, movies, music, magazines, games, and musical instruments in three spacious locations. ⊠ *1930 E. Grant Rd., Central* ☎ *520/325–5767* ⊕ *www. bookmans.com.*

CLOTHING

Arizona Hatters. For that Stetson you've always wanted, Arizona Hatters is your best bet. ⊠ *2790 N. Campbell Ave., Central* ☎ *520/292–1320* ⊕ *www.arizonahatters.com* ☉ *Closed Sun.*

MALLS AND SHOPPING CENTERS

Broadway Village. Tucson's first shopping center, Broadway Village, was built in 1939. Although small by today's standards, this outdoor complex and neighboring strip of shops houses several noteworthy stores: Zocalo for colonial Mexican furniture and art, Yikes! for fabulous off-the-wall toys, and Picante for a wonderful assortment of Mexican/Latin American clothing and crafts. ⊠ *2926 E. Broadway Blvd., at Country Club Rd., Central* ⊕ *www.broadwayvillagetucson.com.*

The Lost Barrio Tucson. Located in an old warehouse district, The Lost Barrio is a cluster of 10 shops with Southwestern and ethnic art, furniture, and funky gifts (both antique and modern). ⊠ *Park Ave. and 12th St., south of Broadway, Central.*

Local ceramics and other arts and crafts are popular in Tucson and the nearby town of Tubac.

EASTSIDE
ARTS AND CRAFTS
B&B Cactus Farm. You'll pass this cactus farm en route to Saguaro National Park East. There's a huge selection of cacti and succulents, and they'll ship anywhere in the country. ✉ *11550 E. Speedway Blvd., Eastside* ☎ *520/721–4687* ⊕ *www.bandbcactus.com* ☾ *Closed Sun. and Mon.*

JEWELRY
Abbott Taylor Jewelers. In business since the 1970s, Abbott Taylor specializes in creating custom designs in diamonds and other precious stones. ✉ *6383 E. Grant Rd., Eastside* ☎ *520/745–5080* ⊕ *www.atdiamonds. com* ☾ *Closed Sun. and Mon.*

MALLS AND SHOPPING CENTERS
Park Place. This busy enclosed mall has an extensive food court, a 20-screen cineplex, and more than 120 stores, including Macy's and Dillard's department stores. ✉ *5870 E. Broadway Blvd., Eastside* ☎ *520/747–7575* ⊕ *www.parkplacemall.com.*

CATALINA FOOTHILLS
ARTS AND CRAFTS
Bahti Indian Arts. This shop is owned and run by Mark Bahti, whose father, Tom, literally wrote the book on Native American art, including an early definitive work on kachinas. The store sells high-quality jewelry, pottery, rugs, art, and more. ✉ *St. Philip's Plaza, 4330 N. Campbell Ave., Foothills* ☎ *520/577–0290* ⊕ *www.bahti.com.*

Grey Dog Trading Company. There's an ample selection of Native American jewelry, katsinas, weaving, pottery, and Zuni fetishes at this store. ✉ *St. Philip's Plaza, 4320 N. Campbell Ave., Ste. 130, Foothills* ☎ *520/881–6888* ⊕ *www.greydogtrading.com.*

GALLERIES

Gallery Row at El Cortijo. Galleries that collectively represent regional and national artists working in all mediums, including Native American, Western, and contemporary painting, crafts, and jewelry make up this complex, across the street from La Encantada. The acclaimed Acacia restaurant is also here. ✉ *3001 E. Skyline Dr., at Campbell Ave., Foothills.*

Madaras Gallery. Bright watercolor prints of cacti, desert scenes, and animals by the popular local artist Diana Madaras can be found at this gallery, in the El Cortijo complex. ✉ *El Cortijo, 3001 E. Skyline Dr., #101, Foothills* ☎ *520/615–3001* ⊕ *www.madaras.com.*

JEWELRY

Beth Friedman. For unsurpassed designs in silver and semiprecious stones, visit Beth Friedman's. The store also carries an eclectic selection of ladies' apparel, fine art, and home furnishings. ✉ *Joesler Village, 1865 E. River Rd., Ste. 121, Foothills* ☎ *520/577–6858* ⊕ *www.bethfriedman.com.*

MALLS AND SHOPPING CENTERS

La Encantada. The newest outdoor mall in the area, La Encantada has close to 50 stores (and five restaurants) decidedly aimed at affluent consumers. North, a nouvelle Italian bistro, and Ra Sushi are the standout eateries. Trendy tenants include Crate & Barrel, Pottery Barn, Coach, Apple, and Tiffany & Co., plus AJs, a gourmet grocery that also serves casual meals. ✉ *Skyline Dr. and Campbell Ave., Foothills* ☎ *520/615–2561* ⊕ *www.laencantadashoppingcenter.com.*

St. Philip's Plaza. More than a dozen chic boutiques and galleries are arranged around Spanish-style outdoor courtyards at St. Philip's Plaza. The restaurant Union Public House, serving food and drink into the wee hours, is located here, and an excellent farmers' market is held on weekend mornings. ✉ *4280 N. Campbell Ave., at River Rd., Foothills* ⊕ *www.stphilipsplaza.com.*

Tucson Mall. This indoor mall has Dillard's, Macy's, H&M, and more than 200 specialty shops. For tasteful Southwestern-style T-shirts, belts, jewelry, and prickly pear candies, check out the shops on "Arizona Avenue," a section on the first floor that's devoted to regional items. The popular Cheesecake Factory is also here, on the mall's perimeter. ✉ *4500 N. Oracle Rd., at Wetmore Rd., Central* ☎ *520/293–7330* ⊕ *www.tucsonmall.com.*

NORTHWEST TUCSON AND WESTSIDE

ARTS AND CRAFTS

Antigua de Mexico. This place sells well-made furniture and crafts from Mexico that you are not likely to find elsewhere in town. ✉ *3235 W. Orange Grove Rd., Northwest* ☎ *520/742–7114* ⊕ *www.antiguademexico.us* ⊙ *Closed Sun.*

Tucson's Map and Flag Center. For topographical and colorful maps of just about anywhere, including specialty guides to Arizona, visit Tucson's

Map and Flag Center. ✉ *3239 N. 1st Ave., Northwest* ☎ *520/887–4234* ⊕ *www.mapsmithus.com.*

MALLS AND SHOPPING CENTERS

Casas Adobes Plaza. This outdoor, Mediterranean-style shopping center originally served the ranchers and orange-grove owners in this once remote part of town, now the city's fastest-growing area. There's a Whole Foods grocery store, the superb Wildflower and Bluefin restaurants, a gelato shop, upscale pizzas at Sauce, Starbucks, and diverse boutiques and gift shops. ✉ *7001–7153 N. Oracle Rd., Northwest* ⊕ *www.casasadobesplaza.com.*

Foothills Mall. This mall has a Barnes & Noble Superstore and many outlets, including Saks Fifth Avenue, Old Navy, Nike, and Adidas. A 16-screen cineplex (including Tucson's only IMAX theater), several casual restaurants, and the brewpub Thunder Canyon Brewery round out the place. ✉ *7401 N. La Cholla Blvd., at Ina Rd., Northwest* ☎ *520/219–0650* ⊕ *www.shopfoothillsmall.com.*

SOUTH TUCSON

CLOTHING

Stewart Custom Boots. This humble company has been making handmade leather boots since the 1940s. It is open Monday through Thursday, and by appointment Friday and Saturday. ✉ *30 W. 28th St., at S. Sixth Ave., South* ☎ *520/622–2706* ⊕ *www.stewartbootcompany.com.*

SPAS

From day spas to top-rated destination spas to a multitude of posh resorts, the array of wellness treatments in Tucson is wide. Many Tucson spas feature treatments that incorporate Native American traditions and desert plants. Most of the resorts and destination spas—including Canyon Ranch (⇨ *see Where to Stay)*—lie in the Foothills or Northwest, while popular day spas are located around town.

Gadabout. Pampering from head to toe is what awaits at this popular day spa with five locations around town. Hair stylists and "nail therapists" are friendly and skilled; massages, facials, waxing, and makeup lessons are also on the menu, at lower prices than you'll pay at a resort. Each 50-minute facial includes a soothing neck, shoulder, hand, and foot moisturizing massage. If you want your friends back home to envy your Arizona tan, even if you don't have hours to spend soaking up rays, try the "Sun Glow" massage, an exfoliating scrub, and UV-free tanning application all in one. ✉ *3207 E. Speedway, Central* ☎ *520/325–0000* ⊕ *www.gadabout.com* ☞ *$70 50-minute massage. Hair salon. Services: facials, massage, nail treatment, scrubs, waxing, and tinting.*

Hashani Spa at JW Marriott Starr Pass. The trilevel modern Hashani Spa, built on a hillside just east of the JW Marriott, connects to the main resort via a walkway above a wildlife area, but it feels a world away. The top level houses the salon and a shop selling activewear and high-end skin and beauty products. Sleek, Asian-inspired indoor/outdoor lounge areas, a gym, and a dance/yoga studio occupy the middle level;

the lower floor is for heavenly treatments like the hot desert-stone massage and the signature creosote body wrap. After your spa service, lie out or lunch poolside; then make your own aromatherapy sachet to take home. ✉ *3800 W. Starr Pass Blvd., Southwest* ☎ *520/791–6117* ⊕ *www. hashanispa.com* ☞ *$130 50-minute massage. Hair salon, hot tub, pool, steam room. Gym with: cardio machines, free weights, weight-training equipment. Services: aromatherapy, body wraps, facials, massage, nail treatment, scrubs, waxing, and tinting. Classes and programs: dance classes, fitness analysis, guided hikes, nutritional counseling, personal training, tone and cardio, yoga.*

Lakeside Spa at Loews Ventana Canyon Resort. Quiet and unassuming, the Lakeside Spa has an abundant array of fitness opportunities and beauty treatments. For example, take in the sweeping desert views along the trail on the daily 7-mile guided power walk or from the serene pool area during an aqua fitness class, and fortify your skin for the dry climate by choosing a signature spa treatment like the Sedona Sacred Ritual, which begins with an Arizona red-clay wrap, adds a face and scalp massage, and finishes with an ultra-hydrating body massage using jojoba lotion. On your way back to reality, indulge in a sundress, yoga pants, or locally made lotions from the well-stocked spa shop. ✉ *7000 N. Resort Dr., Foothills* ☎ *520/529–7830* ⊕ *www.loewshotels.com/en/ Ventana-Canyon-Resort/spa* ☞ *$115 50-minute massage, $190 80-minute Sacred Sedona Ritual. Hair salon, outdoor hot tub, pool, saunas, steam rooms. Gym with: cardio machines, free weights, weight-training equipment. Services: aromatherapy, body wraps, facials, massage, nail treatments, scrubs, waxing and tinting. Classes and programs: aerobics, aqua fitness, guided power walks, personal training, Pilates, yoga.*

The Red Door Spa at Westin La Paloma. Glamour and body bliss combine at this Elizabeth Arden spa connected to the Westin La Paloma Resort. Renowned for its state-of-the-art skin and makeup products—including the aptly named anti-aging line, Prevage for Face—the Red Door also delivers first-rate Swedish and hot-stone massages, which can be experienced in an outdoor cabana. Check yourself in for an Ultimate Arden facial or the 110-minute "Stress Melter Ritual" (exfoliating scrub, custom body wrap, and signature massage); either way, you'll leave feeling and looking *"mah-velous."* ✉ *3666 E. Sunrise Dr., Foothills* ☎ *520/742–7866* ⊕ *www.reddoorspas.com/locations/westin-la-paloma-0* ☞ *$140 50-minute massage or facial, $255 110-minute Stress Melter Ritual. Hair salon, outdoor hot tub, saunas, steam rooms. Services: aromatherapy, body wraps, facials, makeup application, massage, nail treatment, scrubs, waxing and tinting.*

The Ritz-Carlton Spa, Dove Mountain. Are you an earth element who needs a little more fire in your life? Perhaps your wood, water, and metal are out of balance. "Embracing Your Elements," the signature service at the 17,000-square-foot Dove Mountain Spa, may help you realign all five elements in a rejuvenating 90-minute massage, skin brush, aromatherapy, and face/scalp treatment based upon your birthdate. Before and after, relax indoors in the men's, ladies', or co-ed lounge areas, or by the secluded infinity pool with a tanning "island" in the center. As you might expect from Ritz-Carlton, spas don't come much more luxurious

than this. ⊠ *15000 N. Secret Springs Dr., Marana* ☎ *520/572–3030,
800/542–8680* ⊕ *www.ritzcarlton.com/dovemountain* ⤳ *$150 50-minute massage, $185 75-minute massage, $245 90-minute "Embracing
Your Elements" treatment. Hair salon, outdoor hot tub, pool, sauna.
Gym with cardio machines, free weights, weight-training equipment.
Services: aromatherapy, body wraps, facials, massage, nail treatment,
scrubs, Vichy shower, waxing. Classes and programs: Pilates, yoga,
Zumba.*

SPORTS AND THE OUTDOORS

Fall, winter, and spring in Tucson are mild with little rainfall, making
the Tucson area wonderful for outdoor sports. The city has miles of
bike paths (shared by joggers and walkers), plenty of open spaces with
memorable desert views, and some of the best golf courses in the country. Hikers enjoy the desert trails in Saguaro National Park, Sabino Canyon, and Catalina State Park—all within 20 minutes of central Tucson.
In summer there are cooler treks in nearby mountain ranges—Mount
Lemmon to the north and Madera Canyon to the south. Equestrians
can find scenic trails at one of the many area stables or dude ranches.

ADVENTURE TOURS

Baja's Frontier Tours. This operator explores the natural and cultural
history of Tucson and the greater Southwest by van and motorcoach.
Tours range from one-day trips exploring Mexican cultural traditions
in Southern Arizona, such as Day of the Dead and Barrio Christmas
($99), to a six-day tour of the Hopi Mesas ($1,895). ☎ *520/887–2340*
⊕ *www.bajasfrontiertours.com.*

Southwest Trekking. This outfitter arranges top-notch guided mountain
biking, hiking, and camping outings. Custom-designed tours, based on
the groups' interests and abilities, might consist of a 4-hour bike ride
($150, bicycles provided) or an all-day hike among the spectacular boulders of the Cochise Stronghold ($250, includes breakfast in Tombstone).
☎ *520/296–9661* ⊕ *www.swtrekking.com* ✉ *From $150.*

BALLOONING

Balloon America. Passengers can soar above Sabino Canyon and the Santa
Catalinas in a hot-air balloon. Two-hour tours ($349 includes in-flight
photos and a champagne toast) depart from the east side of Tucson,
October through May. ⊠ *1501 N. Houghton Rd.* ☎ *520/299–7744*
⊕ *www.balloonrideusa.com.*

Fleur de Tucson Balloon Tours. Operating out of Northwest Tucson October through April, this company flies over the Tucson Mountains and
Saguaro National Park West. Flights cost $275 and include photos from
your flight as well as a continental champagne brunch after you arrive
back on the ground. Meet your balloon guide at a parking lot near Ina
Road and Interstate 10. ☎ *520/403–8547* ⊕ *www.fleurdetucson.net.*

BICYCLING

Tucson is one of America's top bicycling cities and has well-maintained bikeways, routes, lanes, and paths all over the city. Scenic-loop roads in both sections of Saguaro National Park are rewarding rides for all levels of cyclists, though the West district's road is unpaved.

GABA (*Greater Arizona Bicycling Association*). Most bike stores in Tucson carry the monthly newsletter of the Tucson chapter of GABA, which lists rated group rides, local bike resources, and more. ⊕ *www. bikegaba.org.*

Pima Association of Governments. You can pick up a map of Tucson-area bike routes here. ⊠ *177 N. Church Ave., Ste. 405, Downtown* ☎ *520/792–1093* ⊕ *www.pagnet.org.*

EQUIPMENT AND RENTALS

Cycle Tucson. This company rents road, mountain, and hybrid bikes, and delivers them to your door. ⊠ *7049 E. Tanque Verde Rd., Ste. 126, Foothills* ☎ *520/245–6011* ⊕ *www.cycletucson.com.*

Fair Wheel Bikes. Mountain bikes and road bikes can be rented by the day or week here. The company also organizes group rides of varying difficulty. ⊠ *1110 E. 6th St., University* ☎ *520/884–9018* ⊕ *fairwheelbikes.com.*

BIRD-WATCHING

The naturalist and illustrator Roger Tory Peterson (1908–96) considered Tucson one of the country's top birding spots, and avid "life listers"—birders who keep a list of all the birds they've sighted and identified—soon see why. In the early morning and early evening Sabino Canyon is alive with cactus and canyon wrens, hawks, and quail. Spring and summer, when species of migrants come in from Mexico, are great hummingbird seasons. In the nearby Santa Rita Mountains and Madera Canyon you can see elegant trogons nesting in early spring. The area also supports species usually found only in higher elevations.

Tucson Audubon Society and Nature Shop. You can get the latest birding word on the local Audubon Society's 24-hour line; sightings of rare or interesting birds in the area are recorded regularly. The society's shop organizes free local outings for birders and carries field guides, bird feeders, binoculars, and natural-history books. ⊠ *300 E. University Blvd., Ste. 120, University* ☎ *520/629–0510* ⊕ *www.tucsonaudubon.org.*

Wild Bird Store. This shop is an excellent resource for birding information, feeders, books, and trail guides. Free bird walks are offered most Sundays. ⊠ *3160 E. Fort Lowell Rd., Central* ☎ *520/322–9466* ⊕ *www. wildbirdsonline.com.*

TOURS

Several companies operate birding tours in the Tucson area.

Borderland Tours. Bird-watching tours throughout the state and internationally are led by this company, whose owner, Richard Taylor, has written several photo field guides, including *Birds of Southeastern Arizona.* Seven-day tours of Southeastern Arizona cost $2,195, including all meals, accommodations, and transportation from Tucson. ⊠ *2550*

Don't let the name fool you—the Arizona–Sonora Desert Museum is also a zoo and botanical garden.

W. Calle Padilla, Northwest ☎ *520/882–7650* ⊕ *www.borderland-tours.com.*

Wings. This elite Tucson-based company leads ornithological expeditions worldwide and locally. Its Southern Arizona tours—sighting owls, hawks, warblers, hummingbirds, and more—have a maximum group size of seven and range from 8 days ($2,350) to 10 days ($3,100). ☎ *520/320–9868, 866/547–9868* ⊕ *www.wingsbirds.com.*

GOLF

Tee off after 1 pm at many of Tucson's courses, and you can shave off nearly half the greens fee. The city's public courses also have lower fees Monday through Thursday. All Tucson area courses dramatically reduce their greens fees in summer.

RESOURCES

Golf Stop Inc. This shop, owned and run by two LPGA pros, can fit you with pro shop brands and custom clubs, repair your old irons, or give you lessons. ⊠ *6155 E. Broadway, Eastside* ☎ *520/790–0941* ⊕ *www.golfstopinc.biz.*

Tucson Parks and Recreation Department. To reserve a tee time at one of the city's municipal courses, call the Tucson Parks and Recreation Department or reserve online up to six days in advance. ☎ *520/791–4653 for general golf info, 520/791–4336 for automated tee-time reservations* ⊕ *www.tucsoncitygolf.com.*

MUNICIPAL COURSES

One of Tucson's best-kept secrets is that the city's five low-priced municipal courses are maintained to standards usually found only at the best country clubs. All five have pro shops, driving ranges and putting greens, snack bars, and rental clubs.

Dell Urich Golf Course. Adjacent to Randolph Golf Course and formerly known as Randolph South, Dell Urich is a pretty 18-hole in-town course with tall trees and dramatic elevation changes. The mountain views are beautiful from every hole. ⊠ *600 S. Alvernon Way, Central* ☎ *520/791–4161* ⊕ *www.tucsoncitygolf.com/dell-urich-golf-course.html* ⊠ *$25 for 9 holes, $50 for 18 holes* ⅄. *18 holes, 6633 yards, par 70.*

El Rio Golf Course. This is a par-70 course with 18 holes of tight fairways, small greens, and two lakes on fairly flat terrain west of downtown. You'll have nice views of the nearby Tucson Mountains. ⊠ *1400 W. Speedway Blvd., Westside* ☎ *520/791–4229* ⊕ *www.tucsoncitygolf. com/el-rio-golf-course.html* ⊠ *$19 for 9 holes, $38 for 18 holes* ⅄. *18 holes, 6936 yards, par 70.*

Fred Enke Golf Course. This hilly, semi-arid (less grass and more native vegetation) 18-hole course is in the southeastern part of town. ⊠ *8251 E. Irvington Rd., Eastside* ☎ *520/791–2539* ⊕ *www.tucsoncitygolf. com/fred-enke-golf-course.html* ⊠ *$17 for 9 holes, $38 for 18 holes* ⅄. *18 holes, 6567 yards, par 72.*

Fodor's Choice ★ **Randolph Park Golf Course–North Course.** This scenic 18-hole course has hosted the LPGA Tour for many years and is the flagship of Tucson's municipal courses. It's also the longest of Tucson's municipal courses, with great mountain views and tall trees lining the fairways. ⊠ *600 S. Alvernon Way, Central* ☎ *520/791–4161* ⊕ *www.tucsoncitygolf.com/ randolph-north-golf-course.html* ⊠ *$25 for 9 holes, $50 for 18 holes* ⅄. *18 holes, 6863 yards, par 72.*

Silverbell Golf Course. With spacious fairways and ample greens, this course has an 18-hole layout along the Santa Cruz River northwest of town. Two large lakes create water hazards on five holes. Greens fee includes a cart here. ⊠ *3600 N. Silverbell Rd., Northwest* ☎ *520/791–5235* ⊕ *www.tucsoncitygolf.com/silverbell-golf-course.html* ⊠ *$21 for 9 holes, $42 for 18 holes* ⅄. *18 holes, 6936 yards, par 70.*

PUBLIC COURSES

Arizona National Golf Club. This is a gorgeous 18-hole, Robert Trent Jones Jr.–designed course at the base of the Santa Catalina Mountains on the northeastern edge of town. You won't need to go to Saguaro National Park after playing here—the saguaro-studded hillsides around the course are as magnificent and plentiful. ⊠ *9777 E. Sabino Greens Dr., Eastside* ☎ *520/749–4089* ⊕ *www.arizonanationalgolfclub.com* ⊠ *$105* ⅄. *18 holes, 6776 yards, par 71.*

Dorado Golf Course. With an 18-hole, par-62 executive course, Dorado Golf Course is good for those who want to play just a few short rounds. There's a putting green but no driving range or lessons. ⊠ *6601 E. Speedway Blvd., Eastside* ☎ *520/885–6751* ⊠ *$22 for 9 holes, $32 for 18 holes* ⅄. *18 holes, 3751 yards, par 62.*

Esplendor Resort & Country Club. South of Tucson, this reasonably priced Robert Trent Jones Sr.–designed course, with loads of shade trees and bent grass greens, is one of Arizona's lesser-known gems. The restaurant and country club facilities are comparable to many higher-priced resorts. At a higher elevation, it's also cooler than Tucson, making for a great golf getaway in summer. ⊠ *1069 Camino Carampi, Rio Rico* ☎ *800/288–4746, 520/281–8567* ⊕ *www.esplendor-resort.com* ⊠ *$48* ⟨. *18 holes, 6135 yards, par 72.*

San Ignacio Golf Club. Designed by renowned architect Arthur Hills, San Ignacio is a challenging 18-hole desert target course, which puts a premium on accuracy. Set in Green Valley, a 40-minute drive south of Tucson, it has nice mountain views and low greens fees. ⊠ *4201 S. Camino del Sol, Green Valley* ☎ *520/648–3469* ⊕ *www.sanignaciogolf. com* ⊠ *$25 for 9 holes, $59 for 18 holes* ⟨. *18 holes, 5865 yards, par 71.*

Tubac Golf Resort. A par-71 course 45 minutes south of Tucson, Tubac Golf Resort will look familiar to you if you've seen the movie *Tin Cup*. The rolling hills and pastoral land surrounding these 27 holes are a change from desert golf environs. This resort has an on-site pro shop, excellent restaurant, and a cantina. ⊠ *1 Ave. De Otero Rd., Tubac* ☎ *520/398–2211* ⊕ *www.tubacgolfresort.com* ⊠ *$45 for 9 holes, $99 for 18 holes* ⟨. *27 holes, 6375 yards, par 71.*

RESORT COURSES

Avid golfers check into one of Tucson's many tony resorts and head straight for the links. The resort courses listed here are open to the public, but resort guests pay slightly lower greens fees. All have complete country-club facilities. Those who don't mind getting up early to beat the heat will find some excellent golf packages at these places in summer.

Hilton Tucson El Conquistador. This resort has 45 holes of golf tucked into the Santa Catalina Foothills. All three courses—one par-72, one par-71, and the 9-hole Pusch Ridge course—have panoramic views of the city. You'll pay less to play here, without sacrificing any of the resort or clubhouse amenities. ⊠ *10555 N. La Canada Dr., Northwest* ☎ *520/544–1800* ⊕ *www.hiltonelconquistador.com* ⊠ *$29 for 9 holes, $89 for 18 holes* ⟨. *Cañada Course: 18 holes, 6713 yards, par 72; El Conquistador Course: 18 holes, 6801 yards, par 71; Pusch Ridge Course: 9 holes, 2788 yards, par 35.*

Fodor'sChoice ★ **Lodge at Ventana Canyon.** There are two beautiful 18-hole Tom Fazio–designed courses here. The signature hole, No. 3 on the mountain course, is a favorite of golf photographers for its panoramic views and majestic saguaros. Guests staying up the road at Loews Ventana Canyon Resort have privileges here. ⊠ *6200 N. Clubhouse La., Foothills* ☎ *520/577–1400, 800/828–5701* ⊕ *www.thelodgeatventanacanyon. com* ⊠ *$159* ⟨. *Canyon Course: 18 holes, 6819 yards, par 72; Mountain Course: 18 holes, 6898 yards, par 72.*

Omni Tucson National Golf Resort. Cohost of an annual PGA winter open, this resort offers 36 holes: the Catalina Course, designed by Robert Van Hagge and Bruce Devlin, a traditional par-73 course with eight lakes and gorgeous, long par 4s; and the Sonoran, a par-70 desert course. After a day on the links, the Legends restaurant is a great place to watch the sun set on the mountains. ⊠ *2727 W. Club Dr., Northwest* ☎ *520/297–2271* ⊕ *www.tucsonnational.com* ✉ *$190* ⚑. *Catalina Course: 18 holes, 6610 yards, par 7; Sonoran Course: 18 holes, 6065 yards, par 70.*

Starr Pass Golf Resort. With 27 magnificent holes in the Tucson Mountains, Starr Pass was developed as a Tournament Player's Course. Managed by Arnold Palmer, it's become a favorite of visiting pros; playing its No. 15 signature hole has been likened to threading a moving needle. Guests at the JW Marriott Starr Pass Resort have privileges (and pay lower greens fees) here. ⊠ *3645 W. Starr Pass Blvd., Westside* ☎ *520/670–0406* ⊕ *www.jwmarriottstarrpass.com* ✉ *$100 for 9 holes, $179 for 18 holes* ⚑. *27 holes, 6731 yards, par 71.*

HIKING

For hiking inside Tucson's city limits, you can test your skills climbing up "A" Mountain (Sentinel Peak), a moderately easy trail with excellent views, but there are also hundreds of other trails in the immediate Tucson area. The Santa Catalina Mountains, Sabino Canyon, and Saguaro National Park East and West beckon hikers with waterfalls, birds, critters, and huge saguaro cacti. ⇨ *For hiking trails in Saguaro, see Saguaro National Park in this chapter.*

FAMILY
Fodor'sChoice
★

Bear Canyon Trail. Also known as Seven Falls Trail, this route in Sabino Canyon is a three- to four-hour, 7.8-mile round trip that is moderately easy and fun, crossing the stream several times on the way up the canyon.

Be sure to bring plenty of water. Kids enjoy the boulder-hopping, and all hikers are rewarded with pools and waterfalls as well as views at the top. The trailhead can be reached from the parking area by either taking a five-minute Bear Canyon Tram ride or walking the 1.8-mile tram route. *Moderate.* ⊠ *Sabino Canyon Rd. at Sunrise Dr., Foothills* ☎ *520/749–2861* ⊕ *www.fs.usda.gov/coronado.*

Catalina State Park. This park is crisscrossed by hiking trails. One of them, the moderately easy, two-hour, 5.5-mile round-trip **Romero Canyon Trail** leads to Romero Pools, a series of natural *tinajas,* or stone "jars," filled with water much of the year. The trailhead is on the park's entrance road, past the restrooms on the right side. *Moderate.* ⊠ *11570 N. Oracle Rd., Northwest* ☎ *520/628–5798* ⊕ *www.pr.state. az.us/parks/cata/index.html.*

RESOURCES

Sierra Club. The Club's local chapter, The Rincon Group, welcomes out-of-towners on weekend hikes, ranging in level of difficulty. ⊠ *738 N. 5th Ave., University* ☎ *520/620–6401* ⊕ *www.arizona.sierraclub. org/rincon.*

Summit Hut. For hiking on your own, this store has an excellent collection of hiking reference materials, supplies, and a friendly staff who will help you plan your trip. Packs, tents, bags, and climbing shoes can be rented and purchased here. The other store branch is located in the northwest at 7745 North Oracle Road. ⊠ *5045 E. Speedway Blvd., Eastside* ☎ *520/325–1554* ⊕ *www.summithut.com.*

7

HORSEBACK RIDING

Bandit Outfitters. This friendly stable leads riders on one-hour, two-hour, sunset, and cowboy cookout rides near Saguaro National Park East and through Colossal Cave Park. ⊠ *16600 Colossal Cave Rd., Eastside* ☎ *520/647–3450* ⊕ *www. banditoutfitters.com.*

Cocoraque Ranch. Wranglers lead riders through their working cattle ranch and along trails into Saguaro National Park West. Cattle drives also can be arranged. ⊠ *6255 N. Diamond Hills La., Westside* ☎ *520/682–8594* ⊕ *www.cocoraque.com.*

WORD OF MOUTH

"In the American West, temperature is more a function of elevation rather than how far north or south you are. This is why you can be enjoying a swimming pool in Tucson but then drive to the top of Mt. Lemmon for snow (in February) and alpine conditions. This is also why Tucson will be cooler than Phoenix even though it is farther south." –peterboy

Pantano Riding Stables. This is a reliable operator of one-hour or longer rides on the far east side of town and into Saguaro National Park East. ⊠ *4450 S. Houghton Rd., Eastside* ☎ *520/298–8980* ⊕ *www. horsingaroundarizona.com.*

Pusch Ridge Stables. Adjacent to Catalina State Park, Pusch Ridge Stables takes riders along the beautiful western side of the Santa Catalina Mountains on one-hour, two-hour and sunset rides. You can also sign up for a cowboy-style breakfast, lunch, or dinner on the trail or at the ranch. ⊠ *13700 N. Oracle Rd., Northwest* ☎ *520/825–1664* ⊕ *www. puschridgestables.com.*

RODEO

FAMILY **Tucson Rodeo.** In late February, Tucson hosts **Fiesta de Los Vaqueros,** the largest annual winter rodeo in the United States, a nine-day extravaganza with more than 600 events and a crowd of more than 44,000 spectators a day at the Tucson Rodeo Grounds.

The rodeo kicks off with a 2-mile parade of Western and fancy-dress Mexican *charros*, wagons, stagecoaches, and horse-drawn floats; it's touted as the largest nonmotorized parade in the world. Local schoolkids especially love the celebration—they get a two-day holiday from school. Daily seats at the rodeo range from $12 to $26. ⊠ *4823 S. 6th Ave., South* ☎ *520/741–2233* ⊕ *www.tucsonrodeo.com.*

SAGUARO NATIONAL PARK

Saguaro National Park West: 14 miles west of central Tucson; Saguaro National Park East: 12 miles east of central Tucson.

Saguaro National Park's two distinct sections flank the city of Tucson. Perhaps the most familiar emblem of the Southwest, the towering saguaros are found only in the Sonoran Desert. Saguaro National Park preserves some of the densest stands of these massive cacti.

Known for their height (often 50 feet) and arms reaching out in weird configurations, these slow-growing giants can take 15 years to grow a foot high and up to 75 years to grow their first arm. The cacti can live up to 200 years and weigh up to 2 tons. In late spring (usually May), the succulent's top is covered with tiny white blooms—the Arizona state flower. The cacti are protected by state and federal laws, so don't disturb them.

ORIENTATION

Saguaro West. Also called the Tucson Mountain District, this is the park's smaller, more-visited section. At the visitor center is a Native American video about saguaros; also in the park's western part are hiking trails, an ancient Hohokam petroglyph site at Signal Hill, and a scenic drive through the park's densest desert growth. This section is near the Arizona–Sonora Desert Museum in Tucson's Westside, and many visitors combine these sights.

Saguaro East. Also called the Rincon Mountain District, this area encompasses 57,930 acres of designated wilderness area, an easily accessible scenic loop drive, several easy and intermediate trails through the cactus forest, and opportunities for adventure and backcountry camping at six rustic campgrounds.

WHEN TO GO

Saguaro never gets crowded; however, most people visit in milder weather, October through April. December through February can be cool and are likely to see gentle rain showers. The spring days of March through May are bright and sunny with wildflowers and cacti in bloom. Because of high temperatures, from June through September it's best to visit the park in the early morning or late afternoon. The intense summer heat puts off most hikers, at least at lower elevations, but lodging is much cheaper—rates at top resorts in Tucson drop by as much as 70%. Cooler temperatures return in October and November, providing perfect weather for hiking and camping throughout the park.

PLANNING YOUR TIME

SAGUARO IN ONE DAY

Before setting off, choose which section of the park to visit and pack a lunch (there's no food service in either park district). Also bring plenty of water—you're likely to get dehydrated in the dry climate—or purchase a reusable bottle at the visitor center (there are water stations in both districts of the park).

In the western section, start out by watching the 15-minute video at the **Red Hills Visitor Center,** then stroll along the ½-mile-long **Desert Discovery Trail.**

Drive north along Kinney Road, then turn right onto the graded dirt **Bajada Loop Drive.** Before long you'll soon see a turnoff for the **Hugh Norris Trail** on your right. If you're game for a steep 45-minute hike uphill, this trail leads to a perfect spot for a picnic. Hike back down and drive along the Bajada Loop Drive until you reach the turnoff for **Signal Hill.** From here it's a short walk to the **Hohokam petroglyphs.**

Alternatively, in the eastern section, pick up a free map of the hiking trails at the **Saguaro East Visitor Center.** Drive south along the paved **Cactus Forest Drive** to the Javelina picnic area, where you'll see signs for the **Freeman Homestead Trail,** an easy 1-mile loop that winds through a stand of mesquite as interpretive signs describe early inhabitants in the Tucson basin. If you're up for more difficult hiking, you might want to tackle part of the **Tanque Verde Ridge Trail,** which affords excellent views of saguaro-studded hillsides.

Along the northern loop of Cactus Forest Drive is **Cactus Forest Trail,** which branches off into several fairly level paths. You can easily spend the rest of the afternoon strolling among the saguaros.

GETTING HERE AND AROUND
Both districts are about a half-hour drive from Central Tucson. To reach Rincon Mountain District (east section) from Interstate 10, take Exit 275, then go north on Houghton Road for 10 miles. Turn right on Escalante and left onto Old Spanish Trail, and the park will be on the right side. If you're coming from town, go east on Speedway Boulevard to Houghton Road. Turn right on Houghton and left onto Old Spanish Trail.

To reach the Tucson Mountain District (west section) from Interstate 10, take Exit 242 or Exit 257, then go west on Speedway Boulevard (the name will change to Gates Pass Road), follow it to Kinney Road, and turn right.

As there's no public transportation to or within Saguaro, a car is a necessity. In the western section, Bajada Loop Drive takes you through the park and to various trailheads; Cactus Forest Drive does the same for the eastern section.

PARK ESSENTIALS
PARK FEES AND PERMITS
Admission to Saguaro is $10 per vehicle and $5 for individuals on foot or bicycle; it's good for seven days from purchase at both park districts. Annual passes cost $25. For camping at one of the primitive campsites in the east district (the closest campsite is 6 miles from the trailhead), obtain a required backcountry permit for $6 nightly from the Saguaro East Visitor Center up to two months in advance.

PARK HOURS
The park opens at sunrise and closes at sunset. It's in the mountain time zone.

VISITOR INFORMATION
PARK CONTACT INFORMATION
Saguaro National Park ⊠ *3693 S. Old Spanish Trail, Tucson* ☎ *520/733–5158 for Saguaro West, 520/733–5153 for Saguaro East* ⊕ *www.nps.gov/sagu.*

VISITOR CENTERS
Red Hills Visitor Center. Take in gorgeous views of nearby mountains and the surrounding desert from the center's large windows and shaded outdoor terrace. A spacious gallery is filled with educational exhibits, and a lifelike display simulates the flora and fauna of the region. A 15-minute slideshow, "Voices of the Desert," provides a poetic, Native American perspective of the saguaro. Park rangers and volunteers provide maps and suggest hikes to suit your interests. The gift shop sells books, trinkets, a few basic snacks like dried fruit and trail mix, and reusable water

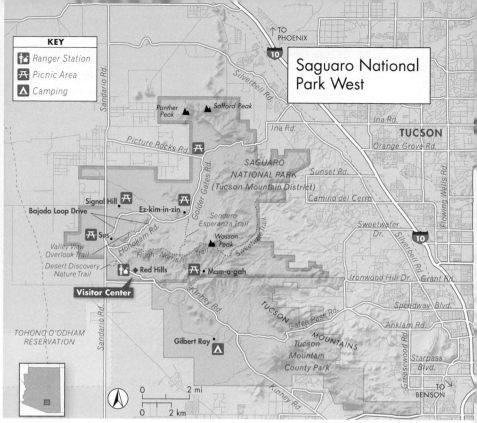

KEY

👫 Ranger Station
🏕 Picnic Area
⛰ Camping

Saguaro National Park West

TO PHOENIX

TUCSON

SAGUARO NATIONAL PARK (Tucson Mountain District)

Panther Peak
Safford Peak
Silverbell Rd.
Picture Rocks Rd.
Ina Rd.
Ina Rd.
Orange Grove Rd.
Sandario Rd.
Golder Gates Rd.
Sunset Rd.
Camino del Cerro
Signal Hill
Ez-kim-in-zin
Bajada Loop Drive
Sendero Esperanza Trail
Sweetwater Dr.
Flowing Wells Rd.
Valley View Overlook Trail
Sus
Wasson Peak
Hohokam Rd.
Hugh Norris Trail
Sweetwater Trail
Desert Discovery Nature Trail
Red Hills
Mam-a-gah
Ironwood Hill Dr.
Grant Rd.
Visitor Center
Kinney Rd.
TUCSON Gates Pass Rd.
Speedway Blvd.
Anklam Rd.
TOHONO O'ODHAM RESERVATION
Sandario Rd.
Gilbert Ray
Tucson Mountain County Park
MOUNTAINS
Greasewood Rd.
Starpass Blvd.
Kinney Rd.
TO BENSON
0 2 mi
0 2 km

bottles that you can fill at water stations outside. ✉ *2700 N. Kinney Rd., Saguaro West* ☎ *520/733–5158* ⊙ *Daily 9–5.*

Saguaro East Visitor Center. Stop here to pick up free maps and printed materials on various aspects of the park, including maps of hiking trails and backcountry camping permits (Red Hills Visitor Center, in Saguaro West, does not offer permits). Exhibits at the center are comprehensive, and a relief map of the park lays out the complexities of this protected landscape.

Two 20-minute slide shows explain the botanical and cultural history of the region, and there is a short self-guided nature walk along the paved Cactus Garden Trail. A small, select variety of books and other gift items, along with energy bars, beef jerky, and refillable water bottles, are sold here. ✉ *3693 S. Old Spanish Trail, Saguaro East* ☎ *520/733–5153* ⊙ *Daily 9–5.*

EXPLORING

SCENIC DRIVES

Unless you're ready to lace up your hiking boots for a long desert hike, the best way to see Saguaro National Park is from the comfort of your car.

Bajada Loop Drive. This 6-mile drive winds through thick stands of saguaros and past two picnic areas and trailheads to a few short hikes, including one to a petroglyph site. Although the road is unpaved and somewhat bumpy, it's a worthwhile trade-off for access to some of the park's densest desert growth. It's one way between Hugh Norris Trail and Golden Gate Road, so if you want to make the complete circuit, travel counterclockwise. The road is susceptible to flash floods during the monsoon season (July and August), so check road conditions at the visitor center before proceeding. This loop route is also popular among bicyclists. ⊠ *Saguaro West.*

Cactus Forest Drive. This paved 8-mile drive provides a great overview of all Saguaro East has to offer. The one-way road, which circles clockwise, has several turnouts with roadside displays that make it easy to pull over and admire the scenery; you can also stop at two picnic areas and three easy nature trails. This is a good bicycling route as well, but watch out for snakes and javelinas traversing the roads. This road is open daily from 7 am to sunset. ⊠ *Saguaro East.*

HISTORIC SITES

Manning Camp. The summer home of Levi Manning, onetime Tucson mayor, was a popular gathering spot for the city's elite in the early 1900s. The cabin can be reached only on foot or horseback via one of several challenging high-country trails: Douglas Spring Trail to Cow Head Saddle Trail (12 miles), Turkey Creek Trail (7.5 miles), or Tanque Verde Ridge Trail (15.4 miles). The cabin itself is not open for viewing. ⊠ *Douglas Spring Trail (6 miles) to Cow Head Saddle Trail (6 miles), Saguaro East.*

SCENIC STOPS

FAMILY **Signal Hill.** The most impressive petroglyphs, and the only ones with explanatory signs, are on the Bajada Loop Drive in Saguaro West. An easy five-minute stroll from the signposted parking area takes you to one of the largest concentrations of rock carvings in the Southwest. You'll have a close-up view of the designs left by the Hohokam people between AD 900 and 1200, including large spirals some believe are astronomical markers. ⊠ *Bajada Loop Dr., 4.5 miles north of visitor center, Saguaro West.*

EDUCATIONAL OFFERINGS

Junior Ranger Program. Usually offered during June in the East District, a day camp for kids ages 5 through 12 includes daily hikes and workshops on pottery and petroglyphs. In the **Junior Ranger Discovery program,** young visitors can pick up an activity pack any time of the year at either visitor center and complete it within an hour or two. ⊠ *Saguaro East and Red Hills visitor centers* ☎ *520/733–5153.*

Orientation Programs. Daily programs at both park districts introduce visitors to the desert. You might find presentations on bats, birds, or desert blooms, and naturalist-led hikes (including moonlight hikes). Check online or call for the current week's activities. ⊠ *Saguaro East and Red Hills visitor centers* ☎ *520/733–5153* ⬜ *Free* ☉ *Daily.*

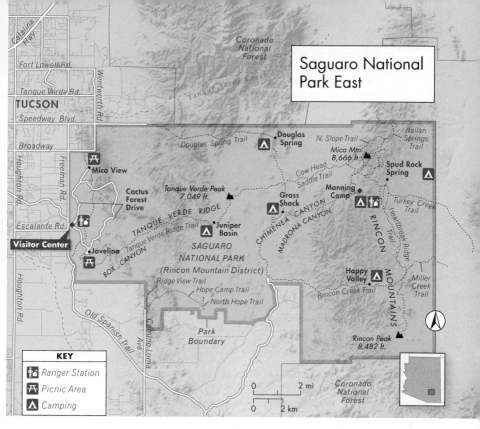

Saguaro National
Park East

KEY

👫	Ranger Station
🏕	Picnic Area
⚠	Camping

Ranger Talks. The assortment of talks by national park rangers are a great way to hear about wildlife, geology, and archaeology. ✉ *Saguaro East and Red Hills visitor centers* ☎ *520/733–5153* 🎟 *Free* ⏱ *Nov.–Apr.*

SPORTS AND THE OUTDOORS

BICYCLING

Scenic drives in the park—Bajada Loop in the west and Cactus Forest Drive in the east—are also popular among cyclists, though you'll have to share the roads with cars. Bajada Loop Drive is a gravel and dirt road, so it's quite bumpy and only suitable for mountain bikers. In the east section, Cactus Forest Trail is a great unpaved path for both beginning and experienced mountain bikers who don't mind sharing the trail with hikers and the occasional horse; Hope Camp Trail is also open to mountain bikes.

BIRD-WATCHING

To check out the more than 200 species of birds living in or migrating through the park, begin by focusing your binoculars on the limbs of the saguaros, where many birds make their home. In general, early morning and early evening are the best times for sightings. In winter and spring, volunteer-led birding hikes begin at the visitor centers.

The finest areas to flock to in Saguaro East (the Rincon Mountain District) are the Desert Ecology Trail, where you may find rufous-winged sparrows, verdins, and Cooper's hawks along the washes, and the Javelina picnic area, where you'll most likely spot canyon wrens and black-chinned sparrows. At Saguaro West (the Tucson Mountain District), sit down on one of the visitor center benches and look for ash-throated flycatchers, Say's phoebes, curve-billed thrashers, and Gila woodpeckers. During the cooler months, keep a lookout for wintering neotropical migrants such as hummingbirds, swallows, orioles, and warblers.

HIKING

The park has more than 100 miles of trails. The shorter hikes, such as the Desert Discovery and Desert Ecology trails, are perfect for those looking to learn about the desert ecosystem without expending too much energy.

■**TIP➔** Rattlesnakes are commonly seen on trails; so are coyotes, javelinas, roadrunners, Gambel's quail, and desert spiny lizards. Hikers should keep their distance from all wildlife.

EASY

Cactus Garden Trail. This 100-yard paved trail in front of the Saguaro East Visitor Center is wheelchair accessible and has resting benches and interpretive signs about common desert plants. *Easy.* ⊠ *Trailhead: next to Saguaro East Visitor Center, Saguaro East.*

FAMILY **Desert Discovery Trail.** Learn about plants and animals native to the region on this paved path in Saguaro West. The ½-mile loop is wheelchair accessible, and has resting benches and ramadas (wooden shelters that supply shade for your table). *Easy.* ⊠ *Trailhead: 1 mile north of Red Hills Visitor Center, Saguaro West* ☎ *520/733–5158.*

FAMILY **Desert Ecology Trail.** Exhibits on this ¼-mile loop near the Mica View picnic area explain how local plants and animals subsist on limited water. *Easy.* ⊠ *Trailhead: 2 miles north of Saguaro East Visitor Center.*

Freeman Homestead Trail. Learn a bit about the history of homesteading in the region on this 1-mile loop. Look for owls living in the cliffs above as you make your way through the lowland vegetation. *Easy.* ⊠ *Trailhead: next to Javelina picnic area, 2 miles south of Saguaro East Visitor Center.*

Signal Hill Trail. This ¼-mile trail in Saguaro West is a simple, rewarding ascent to ancient petroglyphs carved a millennium ago by the Hohokam people. *Easy.* ⊠ *Trailhead: 4½ miles north of Red Hills Visitor Center on Bajada Loop Dr., Saguaro West.*

MODERATE

Cactus Forest Trail. This 2.5-mile one-way loop in the east district is open to pedestrians, bicyclists, and equestrians. It is a moderately easy walk along a dirt path that passes historic lime kilns and a wide variety of Sonoran Desert vegetation. While walking this trail, keep in mind that it is one of the only off-road trails for bicyclists. *Moderate.* ⊠ *Trailhead: 2 miles south of Saguaro East Visitor Center, off Cactus Forest Dr., Saguaro East.*

CLOSE UP

Saguaro National Park Flora and Fauna

The saguaro may be the centerpiece of Saguaro National Park, but more than 1,200 plant species, including 50 types of cactus, thrive in the park. Among the most common cacti here are the prickly pear, barrel cactus, and teddy bear cholla—so named because it appears cuddly, but rangers advise packing a comb to pull its barbed hooks from unwary fingers.

For many of the desert fauna, the saguaro functions as a high-rise hotel. Each spring the Gila woodpecker and gilded flicker create holes in the cactus and then nest there. When they give up their temporary digs, elf owls, cactus wrens, sparrow hawks,

and other birds move in, as do dangerous Africanized honeybees.

You may not encounter any of the park's six species of rattlesnake or the Gila monster, a venomous lizard, but avoid sticking your hands or feet under rocks or into crevices. Look where you're walking; if you do get bitten, get to a clinic or hospital as soon as possible. Not all snakes pass on venom; 50% of the time the bite is "dry" (nonpoisonous).

Wildlife, from bobcats to jackrabbits, is most active in early morning and at dusk. In spring and summer, lizards and snakes are out and about but tend to keep a low profile during the midday heat.

7

Douglas Spring Trail. This challenging 6-mile trail, steep in some parts, leads almost due east into the Rincon Mountains. After a half mile through a dense concentration of saguaros you reach the open desert. About 3 miles in is Bridal Wreath Falls, worth a slight detour in spring when melting snow creates a larger cascade. Blackened tree trunks at the Douglas Spring Campground are one of the few traces of a huge fire that swept through the area in 1989. *Moderate.* ⊠ *Trailhead: eastern end of Speedway Blvd., Saguaro East.*

Fodor's Choice
★

Hope Camp Trail. Well worth the 5-mile round-trip trek, this Rincon Valley Area route rewards hikers with gorgeous views of the Tanque Verde Ridge and Rincon Peak. The trail is also open to mountain bicyclists. *Moderate.* ⊠ *Trailhead: from Camino Loma Alta trailhead to Hope Camp, Saguaro East.*

Sendero Esperanza Trail. Follow a sandy mine road for the first section of this 6-mile trail in Saguaro West, then ascend via a series of switchbacks to the top of a ridge and cross the Hugh Norris Trail. Descending on the other side, you'll meet up with the King Canyon Trail. The Esperanza ("Hope") Trail is often rocky and sometimes steep, but rewards include ruins of the Gould Mine, dating back to 1907. *Moderate.* ⊠ *Trailhead: 1½ miles east of the intersection of Bajada Loop Dr. and Golden Gate Rd., Saguaro West.*

Sweetwater Trail. Though technically within Saguaro West, this trail is on the eastern edge of the district, and affords access to Wasson Peak from the eastern side of the Tucson Mountains. After gradually climbing 3.4 miles it ends at King Canyon Trail (which would then take you on a fairly steep 1.2-mile climb to Wasson Peak). Long and meandering, this little-used trail allows more privacy to enjoy the natural surroundings than some of the more frequently used trails. *Moderate.* ✉ *Trailhead: western end of El Camino del Cerro Rd., Saguaro West.*

Valley View Overlook Trail. On clear days you can spot the distinctive slope of Picacho Peak from this 1.5-mile trail in Saguaro West. Even on an overcast day there are splendid vistas of Avra Valley. *Moderate.* ✉ *Trailhead: 3 miles north of Red Hills Visitor Center on Bajada Loop Dr., Saguaro West.*

DIFFICULT

Fodor'sChoice **Hugh Norris Trail.** This 10-mile trail through the Tucson Mountains is
★ one of the most impressive in the Southwest. It's full of switchbacks, and some sections are moderately steep, but the top of 4,687-foot Wasson Peak treats you to views of the saguaro forest spread across the *bajada* (the gently rolling hills at the base of taller mountains). *Difficult.* ✉ *Trailhead: 2½ miles north of Red Hills Visitor Center on Bajada Loop Dr., Saguaro West.*

King Canyon Trail. This 3.5-mile trail is the shortest, but steepest, route to the top of Wasson Peak in Saguaro West. It meets the Hugh Norris Trail less than half a mile from the summit. The trail, which begins across from the Arizona–Sonora Desert Museum, is named after the Copper King Mine. It leads past many scars from the search for mineral wealth. Look for petroglyphs in this area. *Difficult.* ✉ *Trailhead: 2 miles south of Red Hills Visitor Center, Saguaro West.*

Tanque Verde Ridge Trail. Be rewarded with spectacular scenery on this 18-mile round-trip trail that takes you through desert scrub, oak, alligator juniper, and piñon pine at the 6,000-foot peak, where views of the surrounding mountain ranges from both sides of the ridge delight. *Difficult.* ✉ *Trailhead: Javelina picnic area, 2 miles south of Saguaro East Visitor Center.*

SHOPPING

The visitor centers in both districts sell books, gifts, film, and single-use cameras, as well as a few necessities such as sunscreen, bug repellent, snacks, and reusable water bottles. For other items, you'll have to drive a few miles back toward town.

SIDE TRIPS NEAR TUCSON

Interstate 19 heads south from Tucson through Tubac to Nogales at the border of Mexico, carrying with it history buffs, bird-watchers, hikers, art enthusiasts, duffers, and shoppers. The road roughly follows the Camino Real (King's Road), which the conquistadors and missionaries traveled from Mexico up to what was once the northernmost portion of New Spain.

THE ASARCO MINERAL DISCOVERY CENTER

15 miles south of Tucson off Interstate 19.

The American Smelting and Refining Company (abbreviated as ASARCO) gives visitors a glimpse not only of a vast, open-pit mine but also of the complex processes involved in extracting minerals like copper from the earth.

GETTING HERE AND AROUND

From Interstate 19 south take Exit 80. Turn right (west) onto Pima Mine Road and the entrance will be almost immediately on your left.

EXPLORING

ASARCO Mineral Discovery Center. This mining operations center elucidates the importance of mining to everyday life. Exhibits include a walk-through model of an ore crusher, video stations that explain refining processes, and a film about how minerals are actually extracted. The big draw, though, is the yawning open pit of the Mission Mine, some 2 miles long and 1¾ miles wide because so much earth has to be torn up to extract the 1% that is copper. It's impressive, but doesn't bolster the case the center tries to make about how environmentally conscious mining has become. Tours of the pit take a little over an hour; the last one starts at 3:30. In summer, pit mine tours are only on Saturday. ⊠ *1421 W. Pima Mine Rd.* ☎ *520/625–8233* ⊕ *www.mineraldiscovery. com* ✉ *$9* ◷ *Tues.–Sat. 9–5.*

TITAN MISSILE MUSEUM

25 miles south of Tucson.

The Titan Missile Museum houses one of the 54 missile silos built around the country during the "cold war" of the 1960s, in case the United States needed to deploy nuclear bombs. A guided tour gives you a sense of the military mindset during this era.

GETTING HERE AND AROUND

From Interstate 19, take Exit 69 (Duval Mine Road) approximately 1 mile west to the museum.

EXPLORING

Titan Missile Museum. Now a National Historic Landmark, the Titan Missile Museum makes for a sobering visit. During the cold war Tucson was ringed by 18 of the 54 Titan II missiles maintained in the United States. After the SALT II treaty with the Soviet Union was signed in 1979, this was the only missile-launch site left intact.

Guided tours, running every hour on the hour, last about an hour and take you down 55 steps into the command post, where a ground crew of four lived and waited. Among the sights is the 103-foot, 165-ton, two-stage liquid-fuel rocket. Now empty, it originally held a nuclear warhead with 214 times the explosive power of the bomb that destroyed Hiroshima. ⊠ *1580 W. Duval Mine Rd., I–19, Exit 69, Green Valley* ☎ *520/625–7736* ⊕ *www.titanmissilemuseum.org* ✉ *$9.50* ◷ *Daily 9–5; last tour departs at 4.*

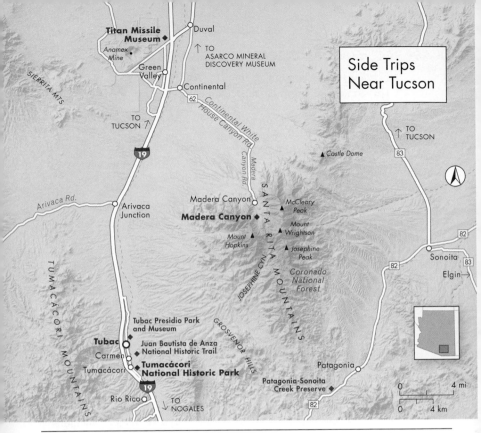

MADERA CANYON

61½ miles southeast of Tucson.

This prime hiking and birding area south of Tucson is where the Coronado National Forest meets the Santa Rita Mountains. Higher elevations and thick pine cover make it especially popular with Tucsonans looking to escape the summer heat.

GETTING HERE AND AROUND

From Interstate 19, take Exit 63 (Continental Road) east for about a mile, then turn right (southeast) on White House Canyon Road for 12½ miles (it turns into Madera Canyon Road).

EXPLORING

Madera Canyon. With approximately 200 miles of scenic trails, the recreation area of Madera Canyon—which includes Mount Wrightson, the highest peak in southern Arizona, at 9,453 feet—is a haven for hikers and birders. Trails vary from a steep trek up Mount Baldy to a paved, wheelchair-accessible path. Birders flock here year-round; about 400 avian species have been spotted in the area.

There are picnic tables and ramadas near the parking area, and camping is available for $10 per night on a first-come, first-served basis (the 13 campsites have drinking water and restrooms, but no showers or electric hook-ups). The Santa Rita Lodge, with charming cabins and a gift shop, is also here. ⊠ *Madera Canyon Rd., Madera Canyon* ☎ *520/281–2296 for Nogales Ranger District office* ⊕ *www.fs.usda. gov/coronado* ⊡ *$5* ⊙ *Daily.*

TUBAC

45 miles south of Tucson at Exit 40 off Interstate 19.

Established in 1726, Tubac is the site of the first European settlement in Arizona. A year after the Pima Indian uprising in 1751, a military garrison was established here to protect Spanish settlers, missionaries, and peaceful Native American converts of the nearby Tumacácori Mission. It was from here that Juan Bautista de Anza led 240 colonists across the desert—the expedition resulted in the founding of San Francisco in 1776. In 1860 Tubac was the largest town in Arizona. Today, the quiet little town is a popular art colony. More than 80 shops sell such crafts as carved wooden furniture, hand-thrown pottery, delicately painted tiles, and silkscreen fabrics (many shops are closed Monday). You can also find Mexican pottery and trinkets without having to cross the border. The annual **Tubac Festival of the Arts** has been held in February for more than 50 years *(⇨ see Tucson Planner)*.

<aside>
WORD OF MOUTH

"Titan Missile [Museum] on Duval Mine Road in Green Valley is often highly praised for being a worthwhile stop. It is especially good if you like (or remember) history from the '60s." –CollegeMom
</aside>

GETTING HERE AND AROUND
When you exit Interstate 19 at Tubac Road, signs will point you east into Tubac village. There's plenty of free parking, and you can pick up a free map of the village at Tubac Chamber of Commerce and at most of the shops.

ESSENTIALS
Visitor Information Tubac Chamber of Commerce ⊠ *12B Tubac Rd.* ☎ *520/398–2704* ⊕ *www.tubacaz.com.*

EXPLORING
Tubac Presidio Park and Museum. There's an archaeological display of portions of the original 1752 fort at this museum, run by volunteers of the Tubac Historical Society. In addition to the visitor center and the adjoining museum, which has detailed exhibits on the history of the early colony, the park includes Tubac's well-preserved 1885 schoolhouse. ⊠ *1 Burruel St.* ☎ *520/398–2252* ⊕ *www.tubacpresidiopark. com* ⊡ *$5* ⊙ *Daily 9–5.*

WHERE TO EAT AND STAY
$$
MEXICAN
Fodor's Choice
★

✕ Elvira's. This colorful and deservedly popular restaurant, a fixture in Nogales, Mexico, since 1927, moved across the border and now serves delicious Sonoran classics in Tubac village. Try one of the five Chicken moles (a sauce using chocolate as its base), ranging from sweet to nutty to spicy, and you'll know why Chef Ruben has such a devoted following. Chiles rellenos, enchiladas, and heartier steak and fish selections don't disappoint either. Save room for the divine flan dessert, a creamier version of traditional Mexican custard with caramel sauce. Live music on Friday and Saturday nights adds festivity to this gem of an eatery in a quiet little town. [$] *Average main: $18* ✉ *2221 E. Frontage Rd.* ☎ *520/398–9421* 🌐 *www.elvirasrestaurant.com* 🕒 *Closed Mon. No dinner Sun.*

$ AMERICAN 🍴 **Tubac Deli & Coffee Co.** Smack in the middle of Tubac village, this is a very convenient and friendly place to "set awhile" with the locals. From freshly roasted coffee and breakfast pastries to generous sandwiches, salads, and soups, this pleasant little eatery is open daily from 6:30 am until 5 pm. [$] *Average main: $8* ✉ *6 Plaza Rd.* ☎ *520/398–3330* 🌐 *www.tubacdeli.com.*

$ B&B/INN 🏨 **Amado Territory Inn.** Although this quiet, friendly B&B is directly off the highway frontage road, it feels worlds away. **Pros:** good breakfast; pleasant garden areas for strolling. **Cons:** only the 3-bedroom Hacienda has a TV; a short drive to Tubac village. [$] *Rooms from: $129* ✉ *3001 E. Frontage Rd., off Exit 48 of I–19, Amado* 🌐 *www.amadoterritoryinn.com* 🛏 *9 rooms, 1 3-bedroom house* 🍽 *Breakfast.*

$ B&B/INN 🏨 **Tubac Country Inn.** Down the lane from the shops and eateries of Tubac village is this charming two-story inn. **Pros:** rooms are spacious, comfortably furnished, and have separate entrances; in Tubac village. **Cons:** no B&B camaraderie here—it feels more like you're staying in someone's guest cottage. [$] *Rooms from: $130* ✉ *13 Burruel St.* ☎ *520/398–3178* 🌐 *www.tubaccountryinn.com* 🛏 *5 rooms* 🍽 *Breakfast.*

SPORTS AND THE OUTDOORS

HIKING

Juan Bautista de Anza National Historic Trail. You can tread the same road as the conquistadors: the first 4.5 miles of the Juan Bautista de Anza National Historic Trail from Tumacácori to Tubac were dedicated in 1992. You'll have to cross the Santa Cruz River—which is usually low—three times to complete the hike, and the path is rather sandy, but it's a pleasant journey along the tree-shaded banks of the river. *Moderate.* ☎ *415/623–2344* 🌐 *www.nps.gov/juba.*

TUMACÁCORI NATIONAL HISTORIC PARK

3 miles south of Tubac.

Father Kino established the Tumacacori Mission in 1791, but the Jesuits didn't build a church here until 60 years later. Walk through the mission ruins and visit the main attraction, the pretty Mission of San Jose de Tumacacori, built by the Franciscans around 1799–1803. The historic Anza Trail runs through the park.

GETTING HERE AND AROUND

Take Exit 29 off Interstate 19 and follow signs half a mile to the park (from Tucson, go under the highway to East Frontage Road and turn left).

EXPLORING

Tumacácori National Historic Park. Encompassing mission ruins, the church of San Jose de Tumacácori, and a portion of the Anza Historic Trail, Tumacácori National Historic Park became a national monument in 1908. Guided tours of the beautiful church and grounds are available daily October through March, and information on both the mission and the historic trail is available at the visitor center. A small museum displays some of the mission's artifacts, and sometimes fresh tortillas are made on a wood-fire stove in the courtyard. In addition to a costumed historical high mass held in October, creative educational programs, such as full-moon tours, bird walks, and a Junior Ranger Program, are offered January through March (call to check schedule). An annual fiesta the first weekend of December has arts and crafts and food booths. ✉ *1891 E. Frontage Rd., I–19, Exit 29, Tumacácori* ☎ *520/377–5060* 🌐 *www.nps.gov/tuma* 🎟 *$3* 🕒 *Daily 9–5.*

EN ROUTE

Santa Cruz Chili & Spice Co. Across the street from the Tumacácori National Historic Park, the Santa Cruz Spice Factory packs and sells 240 varieties of herbs and spices, including the owner's home-grown chili powders and pastes, if you want to take a taste of the Southwest home. A little museum, tasting area, and store are open Monday through Saturday. ✉ *1868 E. Frontage Rd., Tumacácori* ☎ *520/398–2591* 🌐 *www.santacruzchili.com* 🕒 *Closed Sun.*

WHERE TO STAY

$ RESORT

🏨 **Esplendor Resort at Rio Rico.** This secluded hotel and conference center that appeals to golfers has a historic (rather than hokey) Western feel, with vistas of open prairie and an elongated bar reminiscent of a Tombstone saloon. **Pros:** great golf and tennis; a sense of leaving the world behind; 15-minute drive to Mexico. **Cons:** somewhat isolated; golf and tennis are across the highway (shuttle bus provided). [$] *Rooms from: $99* ✉ *1069 Camino Caralampi, off I–19 at Rio Rico Rd., Rio Rico* ☎ *520/281–1901, 800/288–4746* 🌐 *www.esplendor-resort.com* 🛏 *179 rooms* 🍴 *No meals.*

8

SOUTHERN
ARIZONA

Visit Fodors.com for advice, updates, and bookings

WELCOME TO SOUTHERN ARIZONA

TOP REASONS TO GO

★ **Tour Kartchner Caverns:** The underground world of a living "wet" cave system is a rare and wonderful sensory experience. You'll see a multicolor limestone kingdom and probably feel "cave kiss" droplets grace your head; just *don't touch anything*.

★ **Hike in the Chiricahuas:** Stunning "upside-down" rock formations, flourishing wildlife, and relatively easy trails make for great hiking in this unspoiled region. The 3.4-mile Echo Canyon Loop Trail is a winner.

★ **Explore Bisbee:** Board the Queen Mine Train and venture into the life of a copper miner at the turn of the last century. Afterward, check out the narrow, hilly town's Victorian houses and thriving shops.

★ **Stargaze at Kitt Peak:** Clear skies and dry air provide ideal conditions for stargazing; the evening observation program, with top-notch telescopes and enthusiastic guides, is an excellent introduction to astronomy.

1 Southeast Arizona. Old West history, colorful limestone caverns, bizarre hoodoo formations, sweeping "Sky Islands," Arizona's wine country, rolling grasslands, a world-renowned birding paradise, and rustic ranch retreats create a perfect mix of historical adventure and outdoor recreation.

GETTING ORIENTED

Southern Arizona ranges from the searing deserts surrounding Organ Pipe Cactus National Monument and the town of Yuma in the southwest to the soaring "Sky Islands"—steep hills that rise from the desert floor into the clouds—and rolling grasslands in the southeast. Towns are few and far between in the southwestern corner of the state, where the desert and dry climate rule. In stark contrast, the varied terrain in the south-eastern region ranges from pine-forested mountains and cool canyons to desert grasslands and winding river valleys. A complex network of highways links the many communities situated in this part of the state, where the next town or attraction is just over the hill, making the decision on which way you want to go next the hardest part of traveling.

8

2 **Southwest Arizona.**
The historical Yuma Territorial Prison, a world-class observatory, national wildlife refuges, Colorado River recreation, and Organ Pipe Cactus National Monument keep visitors busy in this remote desert region.

EXPERIENCE THE WILD WEST

Arizona's identity was forged like horseshoes by cattle, copper, and the men who chased both. The "Old West" stretches as long as a cowboy's yarn and as broad as a 19th-century cattle drive. Follow the echoes of gunslingers like Wyatt Earp, or drink in majestic landscapes popularized on the silver screen.

Above: You can still ride a stagecoach in Tombstone. Top right: Western watchers will find Canyon de Chelly familiar. Lower right: Tours go deep into the Copper Queen Mine.

In 1862, when Arizona became a U.S. territory, it began to fill immediately with fortune-seekers. In towns like Bisbee (copper) and Tombstone (silver), the discovery of a single ore begot legendary boom-and-bust mining cycles. Precious metal brought miners, then speculators, real wealth, and services such as saloons and brothels. Just as quickly, the ore ran out, and envy, shoot-outs, and desolation followed. With the arrival of railroads in 1880, Arizona's stock grew from a few thousand to a million-plus in less than 20 years—but ranchers were also shortsighted and the "boom" subsided just as fast. Still, cowboy life is one of the most enduring icons of Americana.

TOURISM BONANZA

Movies like *Gunfight at the O.K. Corral* started a renaissance in many ghost towns, and the modern "boom" is tourism. Main Street's drinking and gambling establishments have given way to B&Bs (try **School House Inn** in Bisbee), historic bars (visit **Crystal Palace Saloon** in Tombstone), and boutiques (**55 Main Gallery** in Bisbee).

SOUTHERN ARIZONA WILD WEST ROAD TRIP

Start your Old West explorations in Tucson with a half day at the **Old Tucson Studios** and a stop at **Mission San Xavier del Bac**. Kids will love the simulated gunfights, rides, and stunt shows at the studios where *Gunsmoke* and *Bonanza* were filmed. Mom and Dad can channel the West in a more contemplative way inside the 18th-century mission, where the bad guys no doubt went for sanctuary or forgiveness.

Southeast Arizona may be the most dense and interesting corner in which to explore various aspects of the Old West. The Apache tribe, led by Cochise and later Geronimo, held out for decades against U.S. troops and settlers amid the 12 ranges of the Coronado National Forest, before surrendering in 1886. You can hike through the remains of the Butterfield stagecoach stop at Fort Bowie. Imagine warrior-tribes in the canyons and rock formations of the **Chiricahua National Monument,** where spotting jaguar, rare deer, and flora are treasures in their own right.

Also in the southeast, the colorful towns of Tombstone and Bisbee were centers of mining (silver and copper, respectively) and wealth, larger-than-life characters, and movie depictions that came with them. **Tombstone** is more touristy, but the historic Allen Street buildings and the re-creation of the gunfight at the O.K. Corral are so steeped in Old West history (Wyatt Earp and Doc Holliday walked away, but three of the notorious Clanton gang weren't so lucky) that it's worth a visit. More authentic experiences await in **Bisbee.** Don a hard hat and yellow rain slicker when you take the 75-minute underground tour of the **Copper Queen Mine,** or if you're prone to claustrophobia, stick to the **Bisbee Mining and Historical Museum,** which served as the company's offices.

ELSEWHERE IN ARIZONA

In north-central Arizona, **Jerome** and **Prescott** are two other boomtowns worth a half-day's exploration. Jerome was once known as the Billion Dollar Copper Camp, but its 15,000-person population dwindled to 50 before rebounding to today's 500 or so. Stop for a hearty burger in the **Haunted Hamburger/ Jerome Palace,** where the resident ghost purportedly hangs out upstairs. Thirty miles away, Prescott is home to the world's oldest rodeo during July's **Frontier Days** and has regular live music at the historic bars on **Whiskey Row.**

Thanks to Hollywood, the wide-open vistas of the West are some of the most recurring images of a bygone era. Fortunately for you, **Monument Valley** and **Canyon de Chelly** in northeast Arizona remain virtually unchanged from the way that cowboys and Native Americans experienced them in the 19th century.

8

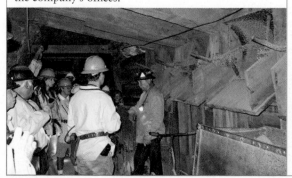

Updated by
Mara Levin

Southern Arizona can do little to escape its cliché-ridden image as a landscape of cow skulls, tumbleweeds, dried-up riverbeds, and mother lodes—but it doesn't need to. Abandoned mining towns, sleepy Western hamlets, rugged rock formations, and deep pine forests beckon visitors for birding, hiking, and horseback riding, as well as more tame adventures like wine-tasting, stargazing, and moseying down historic main streets. This diverse range of activities, along with the feel of stepping back in time, affords a rich and satisfying tour.

In 1540, 80 years before the pilgrims landed at Plymouth Rock, Spanish conquistador Don Francisco Vásquez de Coronado led one of Spain's largest expeditions from Mexico along the fertile San Pedro River valley, where the little towns of Benson and St. David are found today. They'd come north to seek the legendary Seven Cities of Cibola, where Native American pueblos were rumored to have doors of polished turquoise and streets of solid gold. The wealth of the region, however, lay in its rich veins of copper and silver, not tapped until more than 300 years after the Spanish marched on in disappointment. Once word of this cache spread, these parts of the West quickly became much wilder: fortune seekers who rushed in came face-to-face with the Chiricahua Apaches, led by Cochise and Geronimo, while Indian warriors battled encroaching settlers and the U.S. Cavalry was sent to protect them.

The western side of the state wasn't untouched by the search for mineral booty and the rage to plunder. Interest in going for the gold in California gave rise to the town of Yuma. The Colorado River had to be crossed to get to the West Coast, and Fort Yuma was established in part to protect the Anglo ferry business at a good fording point from Indian competitors. The Yuma Tribe lost that battle, but another group of Native Americans, the Tohono O'odham, fared better in this part of the state. Known for a long time as the Papago—or "bean eaters"—they were deeded a large portion of their ancestral homeland by the U.S. Bureau of Indian Affairs, and you'll traverse their vast reservation if you travel to Organ Pipe Cactus National Monument and Kitt Peak Observatory.

SOUTHERN ARIZONA PLANNER

WHEN TO GO

As you might expect, the desert areas are popular in winter, and the cooler mountain areas are more heavily visited in summer. If you're seeking outdoor adventure, spring and fall are the best times to visit this part of the state. The region is in full bloom by late March and early April, and spring and fall are the peaks of birding season.

FESTIVALS AND EVENTS

JANUARY **Wings Over Willcox.** This birding extravaganza the third week in January is highlighted by the morning flights of thousands of wintering sandhill cranes lifting off from the Willcox Playa. ☎ 520/384–2272 ⊕ *www. wingsoverwillcox.com.*

FEBRUARY **Cochise Cowboy Poetry and Music Gathering.** In Sierra Vista, this three-day festival in early February showcases Western culture, history, and folklore through poetry readings, storytelling, and musical performances. Most of the programs are held at Buena High School Performing Arts Center. ☎ 520/417–6960 ⊕ *www.cowboypoets.com.*

OCTOBER **The Rex Allen Days.** A rodeo, a country fair (turtle races, anyone?), and Western music and dance fill the first weekend of October each year in Willcox. Watch the parade through historic downtown on Saturday. Rodeo events are held at the Willcox Rodeo Arena, while the fair and evening concerts take place at Keiller Park and Willcox High School, respectively, both on Bisbee Avenue in downtown Willcox. ☎ 520/384–2272 ⊕ *www.rexallendays.org.*

Helldorado Days. The third weekend of October, history comes alive in Tombstone with gunfights in the streets, a parade, and an 1880s fashion show. ☎ 888/457–3929 ⊕ *www.tombstonechamber.com.*

PLANNING YOUR TIME

The diverse geography of the region and the driving distances between sights require that you strategize when planning your trip. With Tucson as a starting point, the rolling hills and grasslands of Sonoita and Patagonia are little more than an hour away, as are the underground marvels in Kartchner Caverns (to the southeast) and the starry skies above Kitt Peak Observatory (to the southwest). You can explore the Old West of Tombstone, Bisbee, and the surrounding ghost towns in one day, or more leisurely in two. If you're heading to the cactus-studded hillsides at Organ Pipe Cactus National Monument, leave yourself at least a full day to explore the monument and the nearby town of Ajo. A trek through the stunning Chiricahua rock formations calls for an overnight stay, since the area is a 2½-hour drive southeast of Tucson.

GETTING HERE AND AROUND

Tucson is the major starting point for exploring both the southwest region and the southeast corner of the state. Yuma's remote location on the California–Arizona border makes it a destination in itself, or a convenient halfway point on a road trip from Phoenix or Tucson to San Diego, California. While it can be reached on a lengthy three-hour drive from Tucson or Phoenix, Yuma is also easily accessed through Yuma International Airport.

CAR TRAVEL

A car is essential in southern Arizona. In fact, the best way to explore southeastern Arizona is on a leisurely road trip. The intricate network of highways in the San Pedro Valley provides looping access to the many scenic vistas and Old West communities, which makes the drive an integral part of the adventure. In stark contrast, a drive through the southwestern portion of the state is filled with long stretches of desert broken infrequently with tiny towns and intermittent gas stations. If you're heading west, pack a lunch, a few games, and plenty of music for entertainment along the way.

The best plan is to fly into Tucson, which is the hub of the area, or Phoenix, which has the most flights. You can rent a car from most national companies at the Tucson or Phoenix Airports, and several at Yuma International Airport.

TRAIN TRAVEL

Amtrak trains run three times a week from Tucson to Benson and Yuma.

RESTAURANTS

In southern Arizona cowboy fare is more common than haute cuisine. There are exceptions, though, especially in the wine region of Sonoita and in the trendy town of Bisbee, both popular for weekend outings from Tucson. And, as one would expect, Mexican food dominates menus.

HOTELS

There are plenty of chain hotels found throughout the southern region of Arizona, especially along the interstate highways, but why settle for boring basics in this beautiful and historic corner of the state? For the best experience, seek out an old-fashioned room in a historic hotel, a rustic casita at a working cattle ranch, or a spacious suite in a homey bed-and-breakfast. There are a few scattered dude ranches in the sweeping grasslands to the south. It's usually not hard to find a room any time of the year, but keep in mind that prices tend to go up in high season (winter and spring) and down in low season (summer through early fall). *Hotel reviews have been shortened. For full information, visit Fodors.com.*

WHAT IT COSTS				
	$	**$$**	**$$$**	**$$$$**
Restaurants	under $12	$12–$20	$21–$30	over $30
Hotels	under $121	$121–$175	$176–$250	over $250

Restaurant prices are the average cost of a main course at dinner or, if dinner is not served, at lunch. Hotel prices are the lowest cost of a standard double room in high season, excluding taxes and service charges.

SOUTHEAST ARIZONA

From the rugged mountain forests to the desert grasslands of Sierra Vista, the southeast corner of Arizona is one of the state's most scenic regions. Much of this area is part of Cochise County, named in 1881 in honor of the chief of the Chiricahua Apache. Cochise waged war against troops and settlers for 11 years, and was respected by Indians and non-Indians alike for his integrity and leadership. Today Cochise County is dotted with small towns, many of them smaller—and tamer— than they were in their heyday. Cochise County encompasses six, and part of the seventh, of the twelve mountain ranges that compose the 1.7-million-acre Coronado National Forest.

In the valleys between southeastern Arizona's jagged mountain ranges you'll discover the 19th-century charm of Bisbee—Queen of the Copper Camps. You can explore the eerie hoodoos and spires of Chiricahua National Monument and walk in the footsteps of the legendary Apaches, who valiantly stood against the U.S. Army until Geronimo's final surrender in 1886. This is also where you can travel through the grassy plains surrounding Sonoita and Elgin—the heart of Arizona's wine country.

A trip to this historically and ecologically important corner of the state will also take you to Fort Huachuca, the oldest continuously operating military installation in the Southwest; to southeastern Arizona's "Sky Islands," the lush microclimates in the Huachuca and Chiricahua mountains, where jaguars roam and migratory tropical birds flit through the canopy; and to historic mining and military towns, the tenacious survivors of the Old West—including Bisbee, Sierra Vista, and Tombstone.

TOMBSTONE

70 miles southeast of Tucson, 24 miles south of Benson via AZ 80, 28 miles northeast of Sierra Vista via AZ 90.

When prospector Ed Schieffelin headed out in 1877 to seek his fortune along the arid washes of San Pedro Valley, a patrolling soldier warned that all he'd find was his tombstone. Against all odds, his luck held out: he evaded bands of hostile Apaches, braved the harsh desert terrain, and eventually stumbled across a ledge of silver ore. The town of Tombstone was named after the soldier's offhand comment.

The rich silver lodes from the area's mines attracted a wide mix of fortune seekers ranging from prospectors to prostitutes and gamblers to gunmen. But as the riches continued to pour in, wealthy citizens began importing the best entertainment and culture that silver could purchase. Even though saloons and gambling halls made up two out of every three businesses on Allen Street, the town also claimed the Cochise County seat, a cultural center, and fancy French restaurants. By the early 1880s the notorious boomtown was touted as the most cultivated city west of the Mississippi.

In 1881 a shoot-out between the Earp brothers and the Clanton gang ended with three of the "cowboys" (Billy Clanton, and Tom and Frank McLaury) dead and two of the Earps (Virgil and Morgan) and Doc Holliday wounded. The infamous "gunfight at the O.K. Corral" and the ensuing feud between the Earp brothers and the Clanton gang firmly cemented Tombstone's place in the Wild West—even though the actual course of events is still debated by historians.

All in all, Tombstone's heyday lasted only a decade, but the colorful characters attached to the town's history live on—immortalized on the silver screen in such famous flicks as *Gunfight at the O.K. Corral*, *Tombstone*, and *Wyatt Earp*. The town's tourist industry parallels Hollywood hype. As a result, the main drag on Allen Street looks and feels like a movie set (even though most of the buildings are original), complete with gunning desperados, satin-bedecked saloon girls, and leather-clad cowboys. Today, the "Town Too Tough to Die" attracts a kitschy mix of rough-and-tumble bikers, European tourists, and pulp-fiction thrill seekers looking to walk the boardwalks of Tombstone's infamous past.

GETTING HERE AND AROUND
Start your tour of this tiny town and pick up a free map at the visitor center. As you drive into Tombstone on U.S. 80, historic Allen Street parallels the highway one block west. The visitor center sits in the middle, on the corner of Allen and 4th Street. Park along any side street or at one of the free lots on 6th Street.

ESSENTIALS
Visitor Information Tombstone Visitor Center ✉ *104 S. 4th St., at Allen St.* ☎ *520/457-3929* ⊕ *www.tombstonechamber.com* ☉ *Mon.–Thurs. 9–4, Fri.–Sun. 9–5.*

TOURS
Old Tombstone Tours. There's a self-guided walking tour, but the best way to get the lay of the land is to take the 15-minute stagecoach ride ($10) around downtown with Old Tombstone Tours. Drivers, dressed in cowboy attire, relate a condensed version of Tombstone's notorious past. The tour also passes by the Tombstone Courthouse and down Toughnut Street, once called Rotten Row because of the lawyers who lived there. ✉ *429 E. Allen St.* ☎ *520/457-3018* ⊕ *www.oldtombstonetours.com.*

EXPLORING
TOP ATTRACTIONS

FAMILY **O.K. Corral and Tombstone Historama.** Vincent Price narrates the dramatic version of the town's fascinating past in the Historama—a 26-minute multimedia presentation that provides a solid overview. At the adjoining, authentic **O.K. Corral,** a recorded voice-over details the town's famous shoot-out, while life-size figures of the gunfight's participants stand poised to shoot. A reenactment of the gunfight at the O.K. Corral is held daily at 2 pm. Photographer C. S. Fly, whose studio was next door to the corral, didn't record this bit of history, but Geronimo and his pursuers were among the historic figures he did capture with his camera. Many of his fascinating Old West images and his equipment may be viewed at the **Fly Exhibition Gallery & Studio.** ✉ *326 Allen St., between 3rd and 4th sts.* ☎ *520/457–3456* ⊕ *www.ok-corral.com* ▦ *Historama, O.K. Corral, and Fly Exhibition Gallery & Studio $6; gunfight reenactment $4 extra* ◷ *Daily 9–5, Historama every half hr 9:30–4:30.*

Rose Tree Inn Museum. Originally a boardinghouse for the Vizina Mining Company and later a popular hotel, the Rose Tree Inn Museum has 1880s period rooms and—its main attraction—a humongous rose tree (hence the name). Covering more than 8,600 square feet, the Lady

CLOSE UP

The Legend of Wyatt Earp and the O.K. Corral

Popularized in dime novels and on the silver screen, the legend of Wyatt Earp follows the American tradition of the tall tale. This larger-than-life hero of the Wild West is cloaked with romance and derring-do. Stripped of the glamour, though, Earp emerges as a man with a checkered past who switched from fugitive to lawman several times during his long life.

Born in 1848, Wyatt Berry Stapp Earp earned renown as the assistant city marshal of Dodge City. Wyatt and his brothers James, Virgil, and Morgan moved to Tombstone in 1879, and it was here that they, along with Wyatt's friend Doc Holliday, made their mark in history. Wyatt ran a gambling concession at the Oriental Saloon, and Virgil became Tombstone's city marshal. When trouble began to brew with the Clanton gang, Virgil recruited Wyatt and Morgan as deputy

policemen. The escalating animosity between the "cowboys" and the Earps peaked on October 26, 1881, at the O.K. Corral—a 30-second gunfight that left three of the Clanton gang dead and Morgan and Virgil wounded. Doc Holliday was grazed, but Wyatt walked away from the fight uninjured. And then the real trouble for the Earps began.

In December, Virgil was shot and crippled by unknown assailants, and on March 18, 1882, Morgan was shot to death in a pool hall. In retribution, Wyatt went on a bloody vendetta. After the smoke settled, the remaining "cowboys" were dead and Wyatt had left Tombstone for good. He made the rounds of mining camps in the West and up into Alaska, then settled in California. He died on January 13, 1929. His legend lives on in movies such as *Tombstone* and *Wyatt Earp.*

Banksia rose tree, planted by a homesick bride in 1885, is reported to be the largest of its kind in the world. The best time to see the tree is from April to May, when its tiny white roses bloom. Romantics can purchase a healthy clipping from the tree to plant in their own yards. The museum might not look like much from the outside, but the collectibles and tree make this one of the best places to visit in town. ⊠ *118 S. 4th St., at Toughnut St.* ☎ *520/457–3326* 🖭 *$5* ☉ *Daily 9–5.*

Tombstone Epitaph Museum. You can see the original printing presses for the town's newspaper and watch a video about the production process at the Tombstone Epitaph Museum. The newspaper was founded in 1880 by John P. Clum, a colorful character in his own right, and is still publishing today. You can purchase one of the newspaper's special editions—*The Life and Times of Wyatt Earp, The Life and Times of Doc Holliday,* or *Tombstone's Pioneering Prostitutes.* ⊠ *11 S. 5th St.* ☎ *520/457–2211* ⊕ *www.tombstoneepitaph.com* 🖭 *Free* ☉ *Daily 9:30–5.*

WORTH NOTING

The Bird Cage Theater. A Tombstone institution, known as the wildest, wickedest night spot between Basin Street and the Barbary Coast, the Bird Cage Theater is a former music hall where Enrico Caruso, Sarah Bernhardt, and Lillian Russell, among others, performed. It was also the site of the longest continuous poker game recorded: the game started when the Bird Cage opened in 1881 and lasted eight years, five months, and three days. Some of the better-known players included Diamond Jim Brady, Adolphus Busch (of brewery fame), and William Randolph Hearst's father. The cards were dealt round the clock; players had to give a 20-minute notice when they were planning to vacate their seats, because there was always a waiting list of at least 10 people ready to shell out $1,000 (the equivalent of about $30,000 today) to get in. In all, some $10 million changed hands.

When the mines closed in 1889, the Bird Cage was abandoned, but the building has remained in the hands of the same family, who threw nothing out. You can walk on the stage visited by some of the top traveling performers of the time, see the faro table once touched by the legendary gambler Doc Holliday, and pass by the hearse that carried Tombstone's deceased to Boot Hill. The basement, which served as an upscale bordello and gambling hall, still has all the original furnishings and fixtures intact, and you can see the personal belongings left behind by the ladies of the night when the mines closed and they, and their clients, headed for California. ⊠ *535 E. Allen St., at 6th St.* ☎ *520/457–3421* ⊕ *www.tombstonebirdcage.com* 🕮 *$10* ⊗ *Daily 9–6.*

Boot Hill Graveyard. This graveyard, where the victims of the O.K. Corral shoot-out are buried, is on the northwest corner of town, facing U.S. 80. Chinese names in one section of the "bone orchard" bear testament to the laundry and restaurant workers who came from San Francisco during the height of Tombstone's mining fever. One of the more amusing epitaphs at the cemetery, however, is engraved on the headstone of Wells Fargo agent Lester Moore; it poetically lists the cause of his untimely demise: "Here lies Lester Moore, four slugs from a .44, no les [sic], no more." If you're put off by the commercialism of the place—you enter through a gift shop that sells novelty items in the shape of tombstones—remember that Tombstone itself is the result of crass acquisition. ⊠ *U.S. 80* ☎ *520/457–3300* 🕮 *Free* ⊗ *Daily 8–dusk.*

Tombstone Courthouse State Park. For an introduction to the town's—and the area's—past, visit the Tombstone Courthouse State Historic Park. This redbrick 1882 county courthouse offers exhibits on the area's mining and ranching history and pioneer lifestyles; you can also see the restored 1904 courtroom and district attorney's office. The two-story building housed the Cochise County jail, a courtroom, and public offices until the county seat was moved to Bisbee in 1929. The stately building became the cornerstone of Tombstone's historic-preservation efforts in the 1950s, and was Arizona's first operational state park. Today you can relax with an outdoor lunch at the park's tree-shaded picnic tables. ⊠ *219 E. Toughnut St., at 3rd St.* ☎ *520/457–3311* ⊕ *www.azstateparks.com/Parks/TOCO* 🕮 *$5* ⊗ *Daily 9–5.*

Tombstone Western Heritage Museum. Aficionados of the Old West have most likely seen the photograph of Billy Clanton in his coffin, which was taken after his demise at the infamous gunfight at the O.K. Corral. But Steve Elliott, owner of the Tombstone Western Heritage Museum, offers another glimpse of this cowboy—one with his eyes wide open. The 5-inch-by-7-inch black-and-white photograph, taken by C. S. Fly

SOUTHERN ARIZONA BIRD-WATCHING

Southern Arizona is one of the best areas for bird-watching in the United States; nearly 500 species have been spotted here. To the east, birders flock to the Patagonia–Sonoita Creek and Ramsey Canyon preserves, the San Pedro Riparian National Conservation Area, the ponds and dry lakebeds south of Willcox, and the Portal–Cave Creek area in the Chiricahua Mountains near the New Mexico border. To the west, the Buenos Aires and Imperial national wildlife refuges are among the many places famed for their abundance of avian visitors. All in all, more than a quarter of the birds found in North America nest in the rich habitats provided by the secluded canyons and diverse microclimates of southern Arizona's "Sky Islands." Some of the most coveted avian species spotted in this birder's paradise include painted redstarts, elegant trogons, violet-crowned hummingbirds, northern goshawk, and sulphur-bellied flycatchers.

Ramsey Canyon, near Sierra Vista, holds the birding claim to fame as the "Hummingbird Capital of the United States." The proliferation of the colorful, winged wonders (14 species in all) is the focus of the Southwest Wings Birding and Nature Festival, held in August. Get up close and personal with these tiny birds at feeder stations in Miller's Canyon or by participating in guided walks and activities during Fiesta de las Aves in early May. For more information on birding sites and educational programs in the area, contact the **Southeastern Arizona Birding Observatory** (☎ *520/432–1388* 🌐 *www.sabo.org*); or pick up an Arizona birding trail guide for $3 at the **Tucson Audubon Nature Shop** (✉ *300 E. University Blvd., #120, Tucson* ☎ *520/629–0510* 🌐 *www.tucsonaudubon.org*) or at the visitor center in Bisbee.

in the 1880s, shows the Clantons, the McLaury brothers, and Billy Claiborne all saddled up and ready to ride. According to Elliott, it is the only known photograph of Billy Clanton taken while he was still among the living. Other relics of the Old West at the museum include 1880s dentist's tools, clay poker chips, historic photographs, vintage firearms, and a stagecoach strongbox. ✉ *517 Fremont St., at 6th St.* ☎ *520/457–3933* 🌐 *www.thetombstonemuseum.com* 🎟 *$7.50* 🕒 *Mon.–Sat. 10–5, Sun. 1–5.*

WHERE TO EAT AND STAY

$$ AMERICAN 🍴 **Crystal Palace Saloon.** If you're looking to wet your whistle or fill up on satisfying portions of steak, salmon, or pizza, stop by the Crystal Palace, where a beautiful mirrored mahogany bar, wrought-iron chandeliers, and tinwork ceilings date back to Tombstone's heyday. Locals come here on weekends to dance to live country-and-western music. Lunch and dinner are served daily. [$] *Average main: $12* ✉ *436 E. Allen St., at 5th St.* ☎ *520/457–3611* 🌐 *www.crystalpalacesaloon.com.*

$ AMERICAN FAMILY 🍴 **Longhorn Restaurant.** You won't find anything fancy at this noisy eatery across the street from Big Nose Kate's Saloon, but you will find generous helpings of basic American and Mexican food at decent prices. The menu covers everything from breakfast to dinner with such entrées as omelets, burgers, steaks, tacos, and enchiladas. The food is a little bland, but the rustic environment and easy accessibility keep this long-time establishment in the running. $\boxed{S}$ *Average main: $11* ✉ *501 E. Allen St.* ☎ *520/457–3405* ⊕ *www.bignosekates.info.*

$ — B&B/INN — 🎴 **Marie's Engaging Bed & Breakfast.** Filled with Western kitsch, curios, and family portraits, Marie's has the feel of a stay at Grandma's house without the obligation. **Pros:** friendly hosts; convenient location. **Cons:** two rooms in the main house share a bathroom. $\boxed{S}$ *Rooms from: $109* ✉ *101 N. 4th St.* ☎ *520/457–3831, 877/457–3831* ⊕ *www. mariesbandb.com* ⇄ *3 rooms, 1 with bath* ⏐❍⏐ *Breakfast.*

$ — HOTEL — 🎴 **The Tombstone Grand Hotel.** Nestled into a hill just outside town, this modern two-story property offsets basic rooms with spectacular views of the mountains and desert valley. **Pros:** clean; modern; pool and hot tub. **Cons:** longer walk (or three-minute drive) into town; no elevator (request a ground-floor room if you don't want to climb stairs). $\boxed{S}$ *Rooms from: $99* ✉ *580 W. Randolph Way* ☎ *520/457–9507* ⊕ *www.tombstonegrand.com* ⇄ *60 rooms* ⏐❍⏐ *Breakfast.*

NIGHTLIFE

Big Nose Kate's Saloon. This popular pub was once part of the original Grand Hotel, built in 1881. Saloon girls dressed in red-feather boas and dusters encourage visitors to get into the 1880s spirit. Occasionally an acoustic concert livens things up even more. ✉ *417 E. Allen St., between 4th and 5th sts.* ☎ *520/457–3107* ⊕ *www.bignosekates.info.*

SHOPPING

Several souvenir shops and old-time photo emporiums await in the kitschy collection of stores lining Allen Street.

Silver Hills Trading Co. This store offers everything from Native American jewelry to Southwestern and Old West souvenirs, including replica guns and Tombstone sheriff badges. ✉ *504 E. Allen St.* ☎ *520/457–3335* ⊕ *www.silverhillstrading.com.*

T. Miller's Tombstone Mercantile. Get into the spirit of the Old West by purchasing high-quality, 1880s-style clothing and jewelry, as well as Western art, cowboy hats, and spurs, at T. Miller's Tombstone Mercantile. Refuel for more shopping or shoot-outs with a root beer float from the on-site ice cream and sandwich shop. ✉ *530 E. Allen St.* ☎ *520/457–2405* ⊕ *www.tombstonemercantileco.com.*

BISBEE

FodorsChoice ★ *24 miles southeast of Tombstone on AZ 80.*

Like Tombstone, Bisbee was a mining boomtown, but its wealth was in copper, not silver, and its success continued much longer. The gnarled Mule Mountains aren't as impressive as some of the other mountain ranges in southern Arizona, but their rocky canyons concealed one of the richest mineral sites in the world.

Jack Dunn, a scout with Company C from Fort Huachuca chasing hostile Apaches in the area, first discovered an outcropping of rich ore here in 1877. By 1900 more than 20,000 people lived in the crowded canyons around the Bisbee mines. Phelps Dodge purchased all the major mines

8

A visit to Tombstone isn't complete without witnessing the re-created gunfight at the O.K. Corral.

by the Great Depression, and mining continued until 1975, when the mines were closed for good. In less than 100 years of mining, the area surrounding Bisbee yielded more than $6.1 billion of mineral wealth.

Once known as the Queen of the Copper Camps, Bisbee is no longer one of the biggest cities between New Orleans and San Francisco. It was rediscovered in the early 1980s by burned-out city dwellers, and the cool but scruffy vibe, hilly terrain, and Victorian architecture conjure up a sort of 1960s San Francisco scene. The locals are an interesting mix of retired miners and their families, aging hippie jewelry makers, and enterprising restaurateurs and boutique owners from all over the country.

GETTING HERE AND AROUND

If you want to head straight into town from U.S. 80, get off at the Brewery Gulch interchange. You can cross under the highway, taking Main, Commerce, or Brewery Gulch streets, all of which intersect at the large public parking lot. Most of the restaurants and shops are here. Or drive a half-mile south on U.S. 80 to the visitor center, housed in the Copper Queen Mine building, for up-to-date information on attractions, dining, lodging, and tours, before heading into town.

TOURS

Lavender Jeep Tours. Tom Mosier, a native of Bisbee, gives the Lavender Jeep Tours, ranging from a one-hour tour of greater Bisbee ($40) to a six-hour tour that includes neighboring ghost towns ($150). He regales locals and visitors with fascinating tales while winding through the hills of historic Bisbee and the surrounding region. ⊠ *Copper Queen Hotel, 11 Howell St.* ☎ *520/432–5369* ⊕ *www.lavenderjeeptours.com.*

Fodor's Choice **Southeastern Arizona Bird Observa-**
★ **tory.** This nonprofit organization offers guided birding tours, educational programs, and detailed information about birding in the region. Tours range from morning walks and evening "owl prowls" to one-week hummingbird trips. During the Fiesta de las Aves, the first

week in May, you can participate in multiple birding activities each day; sign up to observe a hummingbird banding session, where you can assist researchers. ☎ *520/432–1388* ⊕ *www.sabo.org.*

ESSENTIALS

Visitor Information Bisbee Visitors Center ⊠ *Copper Queen Mine Tour Building, 478 N. Dart Rd.* ☎ *520/432–3554, 866/224–7233* ⊕ *www.discoverbisbee. com* ⊙ *Weekdays 10–5, weekends 10–4.*

EXPLORING

TOP ATTRACTIONS

Bisbee Mining and Historical Museum. The redbrick structure this museum is housed in was built in 1897 to serve as the Copper Queen Consolidated Mining Offices. The rooms today are filled with colorful exhibits, photographs, and artifacts that offer a glimpse into the everyday life of Bisbee's early mining community. The exhibit "Bisbee: Urban Outpost on the Frontier" paints a fascinating portrait of how this "Shady Lady" of a mining town transformed into a true mini–urban center. Upstairs, the "Digging In" exhibit shows you everything you ever wanted to know about copper mining, including what it felt and sounded like in a mining car. This was the first rural museum in the United States to become a member of the Smithsonian Institution Affiliations Program, and it tells a story you can take with you as you wander through Bisbee's funky streets. ⊠ *5 Copper Queen Plaza* ☎ *520/432–7071* ⊕ *www. bisbeemuseum.org* 🖃 *$7.50* ⊙ *Daily 10–4.*

FAMILY **Copper Queen Mine Underground Tour.** For a lesson in mining history, take the Copper Queen Mine Underground Tour. The mine is less than ½ mile to the east of the Lavender Pit, across AZ 80 from downtown at the Brewery Gulch interchange. Tours are led by Bisbee's retired copper miners, who are wont to embellish their spiel with tales from their mining days. The 75-minute tours (you can't enter the mine at any other time) go into the shaft via a small open train, like those the miners rode when the mine was active. Before you climb aboard, you're outfitted in miner's garb—a yellow slicker and a hard hat with a light that runs off a battery pack. You may want to wear a sweater or light coat under your slicker, because temperatures inside are cool. You'll travel thousands of feet into the mine, up a grade of 30 feet (not down, as many visitors expect). Reservations are suggested. ⊠ *478 N. Dart Rd.* ☎ *520/432–2071, 866/432–2071* ⊕ *www.queenminetour.com* 🖃 *$13* ⊙ *Tours daily at 9, 10:30, noon, 2, and 3:30.*

Main Street. This hilly commercial thoroughfare is lined with appealing art galleries, antiques stores, crafts shops, boutiques, and restaurants—many in well-preserved, turn-of-the-20th-century brick buildings.

WORTH NOTING

Brewery Gulch. A short street running north–south, Brewery Gulch is adjacent to the Copper Queen Hotel. In the old days the brewery housed here allowed the dregs of the beer that was being brewed to flow down the street and into the gutter. Nowadays, this narrow road is home to Bisbee's nightlife.

Copper Queen Hotel. Built a century ago and still in operation, the Copper Queen Hotel is behind the Mining and Historical Museum and has hosted some famous people over the years. General John "Black Jack" Pershing, John Wayne, Theodore Roosevelt, and mining executives from all over the world made this their home away from home. Though the restaurant fare is basic, the outdoor bar area is a great spot for enjoying a margarita and for people-watching. The hotel also allegedly hosts three resident ghosts; the journal at the front desk contains descriptions by guests of their encounters. ✉ *11 Howell Ave.* ☎ *520/432–2216* 🌐 *www.copperqueen.com.*

Lavender Pit Mine. About ¼ mile after AZ 80 intersects with AZ 92, you can pull off the highway into a gravel parking lot, where a short, typewritten history of the Lavender Pit Mine is attached to the hurricane fence (Bisbee isn't big on formal exhibits). The hole left by the copper miners is huge, with piles of lavender-hue "tailings," or waste, creating mountains around it. Arizona's largest pit mine yielded some 94 million tons of copper ore before mining activity came to a halt.

WHERE TO EAT

$$ AMERICAN

🍴 **Bisbee's Table.** You might not expect diversity at a place with a reputation for having the best burger in town, but this restaurant delivers with salads, sandwiches, fajitas, pasta, salmon, steaks, and ribs. The dining room, built to resemble an old train depot, fills up fast on weekends. Its location directly across the street from the Mining Museum makes for a convenient meal. [$] *Average main: $15* ✉ *2 Copper Queen Plaza* ☎ *520/432–6788* 🌐 *www.bisbeegrille.com.*

$$ ITALIAN Fodor's Choice ★

🍴 **Café Roka.** This is the deserved darling of the hip Bisbee crowd. The constantly changing northern Italian–style evening menu is not extensive, but whatever you order—gulf shrimp tossed with lobster ravioli, roasted quail, New Zealand rack of lamb—will be wonderful. Portions are generous, and all entrées come with soup, salad, and sorbet. Exposed-brick walls and soft lighting form the backdrop for original artwork, and the 1875 bar harks back to Bisbee's glory days. Reservations are strongly advised. [$] *Average main: $20* ✉ *35 Main St.* ☎ *520/432–5153* 🌐 *www.caferoka.com* ⏲ *Closed Sun.–Tues. No lunch.*

WHERE TO STAY

$ HOTEL

🏨 **Canyon Rose Suites.** Steps from the heart of downtown, this all-suites inn includes seven pretty and spacious units of varying size, all with hardwood floors, 10-foot ceilings, and fully equipped kitchens. **Pros:** quiet, yet just off Main Street; well-equipped, attractive suites; easy parking behind building. **Cons:** no breakfast or common area; no elevator (guest rooms are on second floor). [$] *Rooms from: $99* ✉ 27

Subway St. ☎ *520/432–5098, 866/296–7673* 🌐 *www.canyonrose.com* 🛏 *7 suites* 🍴 *No meals.*

$ B&B/INN 🏨 **Letson Loft Hotel.** This beautifully restored boutique hotel is perched above the galleries and shops of Main Street and well appointed with upscale comforts. **Pros:** luxurious amenities; comfy, pillow-top mattresses. **Cons:** some noise from Main Street below; no elevator (all guest rooms are upstairs). [$] *Rooms from: $115* ✉ *26 Main St.* ☎ *520/432–3210, 877/432–3210* 🌐 *www.letsonlofthotel.com* 🛏 *8 rooms* 🍴 *Breakfast.*

$ B&B/INN Fodor's Choice ★ 🏨 **School House Inn.** Each of the rooms at this charming, 1918 schoolhouse-turned-B&B is brimming with character and themed in a different "subject"—history, music, library, reading, arithmetic, art, geography, and the principal's office—reflected in the décor. **Pros:** well-preserved property; exceedingly friendly hosts; hearty vegetarian breakfast. **Cons:** a mile walk or short drive into town. [$] *Rooms from: $89* ✉ *818 Tombstone Canyon Rd.* ☎ *520/432–2996, 800/537–4333* 🌐 *www.schoolhouseinnbb.com* 🛏 *6 rooms, 3 suites* 🍴 *Breakfast.*

$ RENTAL Fodor's Choice ★ 🏨 **Shady Dell Vintage Trailer Court.** For a blast to the past, stay in one of the funky vintage aluminum trailers at this trailer park south of town, where accommodations range from a 1952 10-foot homemade unit to a 1951 33-foot Royal Mansion. **Pros:** unique (how many vintage trailer-park hotels with a hip vibe are out there?); fun; cheap. **Cons:** walking to the public restrooms in the middle of the night. [$] *Rooms from: $87* ✉ *1 Old Douglas Rd.* ☎ *520/432–3567* 🌐 *www.theshadydell.com* 🛏 *10 trailers* 🕒 *Closed Dec. and Jan.* 🍴 *No meals.*

NIGHTLIFE

Once known for shady ladies and saloons, Brewery Gulch retains a few shadows of its rowdy past.

St. Elmo Bar. Established in 1902, St. Elmo Bar is decorated with an assortment of the past and present, including a 1922 official map of Cochise County that hangs next to a neon beer sign. Locals and tourists hang out here beginning at lunchtime. The jukebox plays during the week, but on weekends Buzz and the Soul Senders rock the house with rhythm and blues. ✉ *36 Brewery Ave.* ☎ *520/432–5578.*

Stock Exchange Saloon. Located in the historic Muheim building, the beautifully renovated Stock Exchange Saloon has a pool table, shuffleboard, and—on many nights—live music ranging from local jazz and blues to national acts. The 1914 stock board still hangs on the wall. ✉ *15 Brewery Ave.* ☎ *520/432–1333* 🌐 *www.stockexchangesaloon.com* 🕒 *Closed Mon.*

SHOPPING

55 Main Gallery. Artist studios, galleries, and boutiques in historic buildings line Main Street, which runs though Tombstone Canyon. 55 Main Gallery is one of several noteworthy art galleries selling contemporary work along the main drag. ✉ *55 Main St.* ☎ *520/432–4694.*

Belleza Gallery. This unusual gallery is owned and operated by Bisbee's Women's Transition Project, which aids homeless women and their children. Belleza features the artwork of local and national artists, as well as Adirondack chairs and birdhouses made by women receiving assistance from the program. The gallery's 50% commission goes directly into funding the Transition Project. ⊠ *27 Main St.* ☏ *520/432–5877* ⊕ *www. bellezagallery.org.*

Killer Bee Guy. A trip to Bisbee wouldn't be complete without a stop at the Killer Bee Guy, the shop of beekeeper Reed Booth, who has appeared on TV. You can sample his honey butters and mustards and pick up some killer honey recipes. ⊠ *20 Main St.* ☏ *877/227–9338* ⊕ *www.killerbeeguy.com.*

Old Bisbee Roasters. In Peddlers Alley, grab a free cup of freshly brewed espresso from Old Bisbee Roasters, then buy some equally fresh-roasted beans at their shop down the road. ⊠ *7 Naco Rd.* ☏ *866/432–5063* ⊕ *www.oldbisbeeroasters.com.*

Optimo Custom Panama Hatworks. Nationally renowned Optimo Custom Panama Hatworks is popular for its custom, handwoven Panama hats. It also sells works of beaver, cashmere, hare, and rabbit felt. ⊠ *47 Main St.* ☏ *520/432–4544, 888/346–3428* ⊕ *www.optimohatworks.com.*

SONOITA

55 miles west of Bisbee on AZ 90 to AZ 82, 34 miles southeast of Tucson on Interstate 10 to AZ 83, 57 miles west of Tombstone on AZ 82.

The grasslands surrounding modern-day Sonoita captured the attention of early Spanish explorers, including Father Eusebio Francisco Kino, who mapped and claimed the area in 1701. The Tuscan-like beauty of the rolling, often green hills framed by jutting mountain ranges has been noticed by Hollywood filmmakers. As you drive along AZ 83 and AZ 82 you might recognize the scenery from movies filmed here, including *Oklahoma* and *Tin Cup.*

Today this region is known for its family-run vineyards and wineries, as well as for its ranching history.

Sonoita's "town," at the junction of AZ 83 and AZ 82 (known by locals as "the crossroads"), consists of a few restaurants and shops, an inn and a gas station, but it's the nearby wineries that draw the crowds. There are often weekend events at the wineries, including live jazz concerts and the Blessing of the Vines in spring and the Harvest Festival in fall. Summer is also a good time to visit, when you can escape the heat of Tucson, sample some of Arizona's vintages, and chat with local vintners.

GETTING HERE AND AROUND

To explore the wineries of southern Arizona, head south on AZ 83 from Sonoita and then east on Elgin Road. Most of the growers are in and around the tiny village of Elgin, 9 miles southeast of Sonoita. The best times to visit the vineyards are Friday through Sunday, when most are open for tastings (though a few are open daily). To plot your course through Arizona's wine country, check out the Sonoita/Elgin Wine Trail map from Arizona Wine Growers Association.

ESSENTIALS

Winery Information Arizona Wine Growers Association ⊕ *www. arizonawine.org.*

ARIZONA WINERIES: A GRAPE ESCAPE

The soil and climate in the Santa Cruz Valley southeast of Tucson are ideal for growing grapes, even if "Arizona wine country" may sound odd. Wine grapes first took root in the region 400 years ago, when the Spanish missionaries planted the first vines of "mission" grapes for the production of sacramental wine. But it wasn't until the 1970s that the first commercial vinifera grapes were planted here as part of an agricultural experiment. The hardier vines, such as syrah, grenache, and malvasia, seem to tolerate the summer heat and retain good acidity.

Connoisseurs have debated the merits of the wines produced in this area since 1974, but if you want to decide for yourself, tour some of the region's wineries. **AZ Hops & Vines, Callaghan Vineyards, Dos Cabezas Wineworks, Flying Leap Vineyards, Lightning Ridge Cellars, Kief-Joshua Vineyards, Rancho Rossa Vineyards, Sonoita Vineyards, Village of Elgin Winery,** and **Wilhelm Family Vineyards** all have something to tantalize the taste buds. You can purchase a wine glass at the first tasting room you choose, then take it with you to any of the other wineries for a reduced tasting fee.

Farther east, vineyards are springing up around Willcox, and elsewhere in the state, vineyards south of Sedona along lower Oak Creek are garnering attention as well. ⇨ *See the listings in this chapter and Chapter 4, North-Central Arizona, for contact info.*

WINERIES

AZ Hops & Vines. With interesting varietals (try Zinnerpeace, a smooth and light zinfandel), a hip vibe, and bottomless bowls of Cheetos to accompany tastings, AZ Hops & Vines splashed onto the Sonoita wine-tour scene in 2012. Open Thursday 10–4 and Friday through Sunday 10–6, this spunky, family-friendly winery boasts outdoor seating and a petting zoo. ✉ *3450 AZ 82* ☎ *520/955–4249* ⊕ *www.azhopsandvines.com.*

Fodor's Choice
★ **Callaghan Vineyards.** Open Friday through Sunday 11–4, this vineyard produces some of the best wine in Arizona. Its Buena Suerte ("good luck" in Spanish) Cuvée is a favorite, and its 1996 fumé blanc is considered one of the top wines in the United States. ✉ *336 Elgin Rd., Elgin* ☎ *520/455–5322* ⊕ *www.callaghanvineyards.com.*

Dos Cabezas WineWorks. Award-winning reds and whites (some have been served at The White House) can be sampled Thursday through Sunday 10:30–4:30 at Dos Cabezas Wineworks, near the intersection of highways 82 and 83. You can taste all the wines and keep the glass for $15. ✉ *3248 AZ 82* ☎ *520/455–5141* ⊕ *www.doscabezaswinery.com.*

Flying Leap Vineyards. Open Wednesday through Sunday 11–4, Flying Leap Vineyards specializes in full-bodied red wines like grenache and graciano. The grapes—said to have a higher alcohol content and richer flavor because of the longer growing season—are grown on the vineyards around Sonoita and Willcox (where there is also a tasting room), and the wine is produced on site. ✉ *342 Elgin Rd., Elgin* ☎ *520/455–5499* ⊕ *www.flyingleapvineyards.com.*

8

Kief-Joshua Vineyards. Winemaker Kief Manning uses the traditional methods of open fermentation and barrel aging he learned in Australia. The winery is open daily from 11 to 5; tastings are $8 for 5 tastes and a souvenir glass (or $5 if you bring a glass). If you're here on a Sunday, Manning and his chef might dish up omelets with locally grown veggies to complement the wines produced from organically grown grapes. You can get a tour of the vineyards for $10 if you call ahead and schedule one. ⊠ *370 Elgin Rd., Elgin* ☎ *520/455-5582* ⊕ *www.kj-vineyards.com.*

Lightning Ridge Cellars. You might think you're in Italy when you visit Lightning Ridge Cellars, housed in a Tuscan-style building perched on a pretty hillside and open Friday through Sunday 11–4. The wide porch with Adirondack chairs and a bocce ball court invite you to linger awhile after sampling Italian varietals like their sangiovese and primitivo. ⊠ *2368 Hwy. 83, Elgin* ☎ *520/678-8220* ⊕ *www. lightningridgecellars.com.*

Rancho Rossa Vineyards. Known for its dry and fruity varietals, Rancho Rossa Vineyards offers tastings Friday through Sunday from 10:30 to 3:30. For $10, you'll get seven tastes and a glass (or $8 if you bring a glass). All of the fruit used to make the wines is estate-grown—something to brag about in these parts. Philanthropists as well as oenologists, they donate a portion of wine sales to local and national charities. They will give you a free, brief tour of the wine-making area if the winemaker is on site (inquire in advance). ⊠ *32 Cattle Ranch La., Elgin* ☎ *520/455-0700* ⊕ *www.ranchorossa.com.*

Sonoita Vineyards. This vineyard, known for its high-quality reds, offers tours and tastings daily 10–4. Originally planted in the early 1970s as an experiment by Dr. Gordon Dutt, former agriculture professor at the University of Arizona, this was the first commercial vineyard in Arizona. ⊠ *290 Elgin Canelo Rd., Elgin* ☎ *520/455-5893* ⊕ *www. sonoitavineyards.com.*

Village of Elgin Winery. Stop for tastings, offered daily 11 to 5 at Village of Elgin Winery, one of the largest producers of wines in the state and the home to Tombstone Red, which the winemaker claims is "great with scorpion, tarantula, and rattlesnake meat." You'll get a souvenir glass and 6 samples for $10 (or bring another winery's glass and pay $8). ⊠ *471 Elgin Rd., Elgin* ☎ *520/455-9309* ⊕ *www.elginwines.com.*

Wilhelm Family Vineyards. You can tour as well as taste at Wilhelm Family Vineyards, producers of seven red varietals, including a homegrown Syrah and tempranillo. Tastings, offered daily from 11 to 5, cost $10 for five samples and a keepsake glass (or $5 if you bring a glass from another local winery). Call ahead to schedule a tour ($25), which includes the tastings and a glass. ✉ *21 Mountain Ranch Dr., Elgin* ☎ *520/455–9291* 🌐 *www.wilhelmfamilyvineyards.com.*

WHERE TO EAT AND STAY

$$ AMERICAN 🍴 **Steak Out Restaurant & Saloon.** A frontier-style design and a weathered-wood exterior help to create the mood at this Western restaurant and bar known for its tasty margaritas and live country music played on weekend evenings. Built and owned by the family that operates the Sonoita Inn next door, the restaurant serves cowboy fare: mesquite-grilled steaks, ribs, chicken, and fish. [$] *Average main: $20* ✉ *3235 AZ 82* ☎ *520/455–5205* 🌐 *www.azsteakout.com* 🕐 *No lunch weekdays.*

$ B&B/INN 🏨 **Sonoita Inn.** The owner of this small hotel also owned the Triple Crown–winning racehorse Secretariat, and the inn, built to resemble a huge barn, celebrates the horse's career with photos, racing programs, and press clippings. **Pros:** cheery equestrian décor; walk to restaurants. **Cons:** some road noise. [$] *Rooms from: $109* ✉ *3243 AZ 82* ☎ *520/455–5935, 800/696–1006* 🌐 *www.sonoitainn.com* 🛏 *18 rooms* 🍽 *Breakfast.*

$$ B&B/INN 🏨 **The Walker Ranch.** If you've ever fantasized about living on a horse ranch, this B&B will be an easy place to settle into and a hard place to leave. **Pros:** attractive rooms and suites; tranquil setting. **Cons:** if you want breakfast, it costs extra. [$] *Rooms from: $120* ✉ *99 Curly Horse Rd.* ☎ *520/455–4631* 🌐 *www.thewalkerranch.com* 🛏 *6 rooms* 🍽 *No meals.*

SPORTS AND THE OUTDOORS

HORSEBACK RIDING

Arizona Horseback Experience. If you want to see the region from atop a trusty steed, Arizona Horseback Experience saddles 'em up for 3-hour, all-day, or overnight rides. You can opt for more or less challenging terrain—climbing mountains or loping along in lower elevations—within the Coronado National Forest. On the wine-tasting ride, travel via horse to a vineyard (but they can't make you drink); you'll even get a souvenir glass and bottle of wine. ✉ *16 Coyote Ct.* ☎ *520/455–5696* 🌐 *www.horsebackexperience.com.*

PATAGONIA

12 miles southwest of Sonoita via AZ 82, 18 miles northeast of Nogales via AZ 82.

Served by a spur of the Atchison, Topeka, and Santa Fe Railroad, Patagonia was a shipping center for cattle and ore. The town declined after the railroad departed in 1962, and the old depot is now the town hall. Today, with the migration of artists and health-conscious urban refugees here in recent years, art galleries, natural food stores, and yoga/Pilates studios coexist with real Western saloons in this tiny, tree-lined village in the Patagonia Mountains. The surrounding region is a prime birding destination, with more than 275 species of birds found around Sonoita Creek.

GETTING HERE AND AROUND

As you approach Patagonia on AZ 82 from either direction, the galleries and restaurants are either along the highway (called Naugle Avenue through town) or one block south on McKeown Avenue. There's plenty of street parking.

VISITOR INFORMATION

Patagonia Visitor Center/Patagon Bike Rental. At this storefront on Patagonia's small main drag, which the visitor center shares with Patagon Bike Rental, you can pick up free maps and information, and rent a mountain, road, or comfort bike to explore the region. Many of the old mining and forest roads attract cyclists looking for a little challenge and great vistas. ⊠ *305 McKeown Ave.* ☎ *520/394–0060, 888/794–0060* ⊕ *www.patagoniaaz.com* ☉ *Closed Sun.*

EXPLORING

Nature Conservancy Patagonia–Sonoita Creek Preserve. At the Nature Conservancy Patagonia–Sonoita Creek Preserve, 1,350 acres of cottonwood-willow riparian habitat are protected along the Patagonia–Sonoita Creek watershed. More than 275 bird species have been sighted here, along with white-tailed deer, javelina, coatimundi (raccoonlike animals native to the region), desert tortoise, and snakes. There's a self-guided nature trail, and guided walks are occasionally offered (call to inquire). Three concrete structures near an elevated berm of the Railroad Trail serve as reminders of the land's former use as a truck farm. The admission fee is good for seven days. ⊠ *Blue Haven Rd.* ✢ *To reach preserve from Patagonia, make right on 4th Ave.; at stop sign, turn left onto Blue Haven Rd.* ☎ *520/394–2400* ⊕ *www.nature.org/patagonia* ☒ *$6* ☉ *Apr.–Sept., Wed.–Sun. 6:30–4; Oct.–Mar., Wed.–Sun. 7:30–4.*

FAMILY **Patagonia Lake State Park.** Five miles south of town, this is the spot for water sports, birding, picnicking, and camping. Formed by the damming of Sonoita Creek, the 265-acre reservoir lures anglers with its largemouth bass, crappie, bluegill, and catfish; it's stocked with rainbow trout in the wintertime. You can rent rowboats, paddleboats, canoes, and fishing gear at the marina. Most swimmers head for Boulder Beach. The adjoining Sonoita Creek State Natural Area is home to giant cottonwoods, willows, sycamores, and mesquites; nesting black hawks; and endangered species. From mid-October to mid-April, rangers offer guided birding and discovery tours by pontoon boat ($5) on Saturday and Sunday at 9, 10:15, and 11:30 am (call visitor center to sign up); free guided bird walks are on Monday and Friday at 9 am (call first to check schedule). ⊠ *400 Lake Patagonia Rd.* ☎ *520/287–6965, 520/287–2791 for visitor center* ⊕ *www.azstateparks.com/Parks/PALA* ☒ *$10 per vehicle weekdays; $15 weekends* ☉ *Park daily (gates closed 10 pm–4 am); visitor center mid-Oct.–mid-Apr., Thurs.–Mon. 8:30–4.*

WHERE TO EAT

$ ✗**Gathering Grounds.** This colorful café and espresso bar, which also

CAFÉ doubles as a gallery featuring local artists, serves healthful breakfasts and soups, salads, and sandwiches through the late afternoon. Beverage choices include organic fair-trade coffees; ice cream, cakes, and cookies draw the local younger set. $ *Average main: $7* ⊠ *319 McKeown Ave.* ☎ *520/394–2009* ☾ *No dinner.*

$$ ✗ **Velvet Elvis Pizza Company.** There aren't too many places where you

PIZZA can enjoy a pizza heaped with organic veggies, a crisp salad of organic greens tossed with homemade dressing, freshly pressed juice (try the beet, apple, and lime concoction), organic wine, and microbrewed or imported beer while surrounded by images of Elvis *and* the Virgin Mary. Owner Cecilia San Miguel uses a 1930s dough recipe for the restaurant's delightful whole-wheat crust; daily specials such as Carne Adobada, tender roasted pork in a red chili sauce, and curried vegetable stew entice those who may seek a lower-carb alternative. $ *Average main: $12* ⊠ *292 Naugle Ave.* ☎ *520/394–2102* ⊕ *www. velvetelvispizza.com* ☾ *Closed Mon.–Wed.*

$ ✗ **Wagon Wheel Saloon.** The cowboy bar here, with its neon beer signs

AMERICAN and mounted moose head, has been around since the early 1950s. This is where every Stetson-wearing ranch hand in the area comes to listen to the country jukebox and down a longneck, maybe accompanied by some jalapeño poppers. The restaurant serves basic ribs, steaks, and burgers. $ *Average main: $9* ⊠ *400 W. Naugle Ave.* ☎ *520/394–2433.*

WHERE TO STAY

$$$$ 🏨 **Circle Z Ranch.** Rimmed by giant sycamore, ash, and cottonwood trees

ALL-INCLUSIVE and surrounded by the Patagonia–Sonoita Creek Preserve, this seasonal

FAMILY guest ranch with plenty of activities served as a setting in the movie *Red River* and in several episodes of *Gunsmoke*. **Pros:** excellent dude ranch experience in a lush (rather than desert) setting; friendly staff and guests; massage therapist on site. **Cons:** "all-inclusive" is pricey. $ *Rooms from: $400* ⊠ *1476 AZ 82, 4 miles southwest of town* ☎ *520/394– 2525, 888/854–2525* ⊕ *www.circlez.com* ⤴ *24 rooms* ☾ *Closed mid-May–Sept.* ◯| *All-inclusive.*

$$ 🏨 **Duquesne House Bed & Breakfast/Gallery.** Built as a miners' board-

B&B/INN inghouse at the turn of the 20th century, this adobe home has rooms painted in pastel Southwest colors, lovingly and whimsically detailed by a local artist, and decorated with hand-stitched quilts and Mexican folk art. **Pros:** quiet location only a couple of blocks from town; cheerful, contemporary interior. **Cons:** breakfast isn't served on weekdays (but rates are much lower). $ *Rooms from: $130* ⊠ *357 Duquesne Ave.* ☎ *520/394–2732* ⊕ *www.theduquesnehouse.com* ⤴ *4 suites* ▭ *No credit cards* ◯| *Breakfast.*

SHOPPING

Patagonia is quickly turning into a shopping destination in its own right. Unlike the trendy shops in nearby Tubac, the stores here have reasonable prices in addition to small-town charm.

Creative Spirit Artists Gallery. This gallery features a thoughtful selection of jewelry, paintings, photography, quilts, and pottery by more than 60 local artists. Wooden flutes are also sold here. ⊠ *317 McKeown Ave.* ☎ *520/394–2100* ⊕ *www.azcreativespirit.com.*

Global Arts Gallery. Everything from local art and antiques to Native American jewelry, Middle Eastern rugs, and exotic musical instruments

Bird-watchers flock to Ramsey Canyon Preserve for rare ecosystems where deserts meet mountains.

is showcased at Global Arts. ✉ *315 McKeown Ave.* ☎ *520/394–0077* ⊕ *www.globalartsgallery.com.*

FodorsChoice
★
High Spirits Flutes. You can peruse and purchase a selection of Native American-like flutes, created by Odell Borg, at his factory store. Not only beautiful, the flutes' five-note pentatonic scale makes them easy to learn to play. Call first to make sure someone is available to show you around. ✉ *714 Red Rock Ave., off Harshaw Rd.* ☎ *800/394–1523* ⊕ *www.highspirits.com.*

Mesquite Grove Gallery. Regina Medley, a talented local painter, weaver, and jewelry maker, markets her lovely wares here, along with the work of other regional artists. ✉ *371 McKeown Ave.* ☎ *520/400–7230* ⊕ *www.reginamedley.com.*

SIERRA VISTA

42 miles east of Patagonia, 70 miles southeast of Tucson, 30 miles southeast of Sonoita, via AZ 82 to AZ 90.

A characterless military town on the outskirts of Fort Huachuca, Sierra Vista is nonetheless a good base from which to explore the more scenic areas that surround it—and at 4,620 feet above sea level the whole area has a year-round temperate climate. There are quite a few fast-food and chain restaurants for your basic dining needs, and more than 1,100 rooms in area hotels, motels, and B&Bs offer shelter for the night.

Fort Huachuca, headquarters of the army's Global Information Systems Command, is the last of the great Western forts still in operation. It dates back to 1877, when the Buffalo Soldiers (yes, Bob Marley fans—*those* Buffalo Soldiers), the first all-black regiment in the U.S. forces, came to aid settlers battling invaders from Mexico, Indian tribes reluctant to give up their homelands, and assorted American desperadoes on the lam from the law back East.

GETTING HERE AND AROUND

The most direct route to Sierra Vista from Interstate 10 is a straight shot south on AZ 90 (about 30 miles). If you're not going to Fort Huachuca, take a left on the Route 90 bypass to reach the shopping centers, most of the chain motels, and the intersection of AZ 92, which takes you to Ramsey Canyon and Coronado National Memorial. If you're going to the fort, stay on AZ 90 and the fort will be on your right. From here, Fry Boulevard will lead you through town to the AZ 92.

EXPLORING

FAMILY **Coronado National Memorial.** Those driving to Coronado National Memorial, dedicated to Francisco Vásquez de Coronado, will see many of the same stunning vistas of Arizona and Mexico the conquistador saw when he trod this route in 1540 seeking the mythical Seven Cities of Cibola. Hikers come here for both the excellent views and the opportunity to walk the 1-mile Yaqui Trail, the southernmost leg of the 800-mile Arizona Trail, that ends at the Mexico border. The views are excellent atop the nearly 7,000-foot Coronado Peak; to get there you drive (or walk) a little more than 3 miles up a dirt road from the visitor center to Montezuma Pass Overlook, and then go another ½ mile on foot only. There's also Crest Trail, a difficult but rewarding 12-mile round trip to Miller Peak, the highest point in the Huachuca Mountains (9,466 feet).

Kids ages 5 to 12 can participate in the memorial's Junior Ranger program, explore Coronado Cave, and dress up in replica Spanish armor.

The turnoff for the monument is 16 miles south of Sierra Vista on AZ 92; the visitor center is 5 miles farther. ✉ *4101 E. Montezuma Canyon Rd., Hereford* ☎ *520/366–5515* ⊕ *www.nps.gov/coro* 🎫 *Free* ☉ *Visitor center daily 8–4.*

Fort Huachuca Museum. Three miles from the fort's main gate are the Fort Huachuca museums. The late-19th-century bachelor officers' quarters and the annex across the street provide a record of military life on the frontier. More often than not, you'll be sharing space with new cadets learning about the history of this far-flung outpost. Motion sensors activate odd little sound bites in the multimedia experience. Another half block south, the **U.S. Army Intelligence Museum** focuses on American intelligence operations from the Apache Scouts through Desert Storm. Code machines, codebooks, decoding devices, and other intelligence-gathering equipment are on display. Enter the main gate of Fort Huachuca on AZ 90, west of Sierra Vista. You need a driver's license or other photo identification to get on base. ■TIP→ **International visitors need to call at least 3 weeks in advance to arrange for a military escort.** ✉ *Grierson Ave. and Boyd St., off AZ 90, west of Sierra Vista, Fort Huachuca* ☎ *520/533–3638* ⊕ *www.huachucamuseum.com* 🎫 *Free* ☉ *Tues.–Sat. 9–4* ☉ *Closed Sun. and Mon.*

8

Fodor's Choice
★

Ramsey Canyon Preserve. Managed by the Nature Conservancy, Ramsey Canyon Preserve marks the convergence of two mountain and desert systems: this spot is the northernmost limit of the Sierra Madre and the southernmost limit of the Rockies, and it's at the edge of the Chihuahuan and Sonoran deserts. Visitors to this world-famous bird-watching hot spot train their binoculars skyward hoping to catch a glimpse of some of the preserve's most notable inhabitants. Painted redstarts nest, and 14 magnificent species of hummingbirds congregate here spring through autumn—the jewels of this pristine habitat. Even for nonbirders, the beauty of the canyon makes this a destination in its own right. The rare stream-fed, sycamore-maple riparian corridor provides a lush contrast to the desert highlands at the base of the mountains. Guided hikes begin at 9 am Monday, Thursday, and Saturday from March to October. Stop at the visitor center for maps and books on the area's natural history, flora, and fauna. Admission is good for seven days. ■TIP→ Due to wildfires in Arizona, call ahead before visiting. ⊠ 27 Ramsey Canyon Rd., Hereford ☎ 520/378–2785 ⊕ www.nature.org/arizona ☑ $6 ⊗ Thurs.–Mon. 8–5.

> **WORD OF MOUTH**
>
> "Ramsey Canyon is a nature preserve administered by the Nature Conservancy and is loaded with wildlife . . . especially hummingbirds . . . you're gonna love it there!!" –peterboy

OFF THE BEATEN PATH

San Pedro Riparian National Conservation Area. The San Pedro River, partially rerouted underground by an 1887 earthquake, may not look like much, but it sustains an impressive array of flora and fauna, and makes for great hiking and birding. To maintain this fragile creekside ecosystem, 56,000 acres along the river were designated a protected riparian area in 1988. More than 350 species of birds come here, as well as 82 mammal species and 45 reptiles and amphibians. Animals from long ago—including woolly mammoths and mastodons—also make their former presence here known through the area's massive fossil pits; in fact, many of the huge skeletons in Washington's Smithsonian Institute and New York's Museum of Natural History came from here. As evidenced by a number of small, unexcavated ruins, the migratory Indian tribes who passed through thousands of years later also found this valley hospitable, in part because of its many useful plants. Information, guided tours, books, and gifts are available from the volunteer staff at San Pedro House, a visitor center operated by Friends of the San Pedro River (⊕ www.sanpedroriver.org/wpfspr). ⊠ San Pedro House, 9800 E AZ 90 ☎ 520/508–4445, 520/439–6400 for Sierra Vista BLM Office ⊕ www.az.blm.gov ☑ Free ⊗ Visitor center daily 9:30–4:30, conservation area daily sunrise–sunset.

WHERE TO EAT AND STAY

$$
STEAKHOUSE

✕ **The Mesquite Tree.** Ask a local for the best restaurant in town, and you'll probably be directed to a chain restaurant near the shopping mall (folks tend to be literal in these parts); but if you're willing to drive a few miles south toward Ramsey Canyon, most agree that The Mesquite Tree towers above them all. This unassuming steakhouse turns out fish and chicken classics, like trout piccata and chicken florentine, just as consistently as its tasty ribeyes and T-bones. Generous entrées include a salad and choice of potato, rice, or veggies. *$ Average main: $20 ✉ 6398 S. AZ 92, Hereford ☎ 520/378–2758 🌐 www.mesquitetreesierravista.com ⏲ Closed Mon. No lunch.*

$$ B&B/INN Fodor's Choice ★ **Casa de San Pedro.** Bird-watchers are drawn to this contemporary hacienda-style B&B abutting the San Pedro Riparian National Conservation Area. **Pros:** gracious hosts; tranquil setting; midway between Bisbee and Sierra Vista. **Cons:** some may feel too isolated. *$ Rooms from: $169 ✉ 8933 S. Yell Lane, Hereford ☎ 520/366–1300, 888/257–2050 🌐 www.bedandbirds.com ⇨ 10 rooms, 1 suite 🍴 Breakfast.*

$ HOTEL **Garden Place Suites.** Though not technically suites, all the rooms at this convenient hotel have kitchenettes, sitting areas with pull-out sofa-beds, and king-size beds (the bedroom and sitting room are separated by a half-wall). **Pros:** pool and hot tub; free breakfast and happy-hour drinks and snacks; free Wi-Fi. **Cons:** bland décor. *$ Rooms from: $95 ✉ 100 N. Garden Ave., Sierra Vista ☎ 520/439–3300 🌐 www.gardenplacesuites.com ⇨ 96 rooms 🍴 Breakfast.*

$$ B&B/INN **Ramsey Canyon Inn Bed & Breakfast.** The Ramsey Canyon Preserve is an internationally renowned bird haven, and the nearby Ramsey Canyon Inn is a bird-watcher's delight. **Pros:** perfect base for birding and hiking; comfortable rooms. **Cons:** a little dull for nonbirders. *$ Rooms from: $150 ✉ 29 Ramsey Canyon Rd., Hereford ☎ 520/378–3010 🌐 www.ramseycanyoninn.com ⇨ 6 rooms, 2 suites 🍴 Breakfast.*

CHIRICAHUA NATIONAL MONUMENT

65 miles northeast of Sierra Vista on AZ 90 to Interstate 10 to AZ 186, 58 miles northeast of Douglas on U.S. 191 to AZ 181, 36 miles southeast of Willcox.

With its "upside-down" rock formations and abundant wildlife, the Chiricahua National Monument is well worth the two-hour drive from Tucson. You'll be rewarded with unique, stunning scenery and unspoiled wilderness for birding, hiking, and camping.

GETTING HERE AND AROUND

Though a little more remote than other sights in southeastern Arizona, Chiricahua National Monument is just over a half-hour drive from Willcox. You might combine a trip to this area with Willcox winetasting. The nearest gas stations are in Willcox or Sunizona, so be sure to fill your tank first.

EXPLORING

FAMILY Fodor's Choice ★ **Chiricahua National Monument.** Vast fields of desert grass are suddenly transformed into a landscape of forest, mountains, and striking rock formations as you enter the 12,000-acre Chiricahua National Monument. The Chiricahua Apache—who lived in the mountains for centuries and, led by Cochise and Geronimo, tried for 25 years to prevent white pioneers from settling here—dubbed it the Land of the Standing-Up Rocks. Enormous outcroppings of volcanic rock have been worn by erosion and fractured by uplift into strange pinnacles and spires. Because of the particular balance of sunshine and rain in the area, in April and May visitors will see brown, yellow, and red leaves coexisting with new green foliage. Summer in Chiricahua National Monument is exceptionally wet: July through September there are thunderstorms nearly every afternoon. Few other areas in the United States have such varied plant, bird, and animal life. Deer, coatimundi, peccaries, and lizards live among the aspen, ponderosa pine, Douglas fir, oak, and cypress trees—to name just a few.

Chiricahua National Monument is an excellent area for bird-watchers, and hikers have more than 17 miles of scenic trails. The admission fee is good for seven days. Hiking trail maps are available at the visitor center. The most popular and rewarding hike is the moderately easy **Echo Canyon Loop Trail.** This 3.4-mile path winds through cavelike grottos, brilliant rock formations, and a wooded canyon. Birds and other wildlife are abundant here. ✉ *AZ 181, 36 miles southeast of Willcox* ☎ *520/824–3560* 🌐 *www.nps.gov/chir* 🎟 *$5* 🕒 *Visitor center daily 8–4:30.*

WHERE TO STAY

Lodging is a bit of a challenge in this remote area. For those preferring to sleep indoors, the closest accommodations are about a half-hour drive, either north to one of several decent chain hotels in Willcox or to a B&B or guest ranch south of the monument. Within the monument there are 22 first-come, first-served campsites at Bonita Canyon Campground ($12). Some of the most beautiful and untouched camping areas in Arizona are nearby, in the Chiricahua Mountains. Backcountry campsites at Sunny Flat ($10) in the Cave Creek area, part of the Coronado National Forest (☎ *520/364–3468* 🌐 *www.fs.usda.gov/coronado*), have toilets and water.

$ B&B/INN 🏨 **Dreamcatcher Bed and Breakfast.** Plenty of wildlife, from deer to Mexican blue jays, roam this 27-acre property 11 miles from Chiricahua National Monument. **Pros:** excellent value; tranquil; convenient to Chiricahuas. **Cons:** isolated location. [$] *Rooms from: $92* ✉ *13097 S. AZ 181, Pearce* ☎ *520/824–3127* 🌐 *www.dreamcatcherbnb.com* 🛏 *3 rooms, 1 suite* 💳 *No credit cards* 🍴 *Breakfast.*

$ HOTEL 🏨 **Portal Peak Lodge.** This humble structure with a few nearby cottages on the eastern side of Chiricahua National Monument near the New Mexico border is notable less for its rooms (clean and pleasant but nondescript) than for its winged visitors: the elegant trogon, 14 types of hummingbird, and 10 species of owl are among the 330 varieties of birds that flock to nearby Cave Creek canyon. **Pros:** inexpensive; decks outside each room; on-site restaurant and store. **Cons:** very isolated setting; no king-size beds. [$] *Rooms from: $85* ✉ *2354 S. Rock House Rd., Portal* ☎ *520/558–2223* 🌐 *www.portalpeaklodge.com* 🛏 *16 rooms* 🍴 *No meals.*

$$$$ B&B/INN 🏨 **Sunglow Guest Ranch.** Named after the ghost town of Sunglow, the lodge consists of twelve casitas—some with connecting rooms to be configured for families—decked out in Southwestern style with fireplaces. **Pros:** very isolated (a great escape); many on-site activities (even massages). **Cons:** very isolated; it's a 30-minute drive to hike in the Chiricahuas. [$] *Rooms from: $299* ✉ *14066 S. Sunglow Rd., Pearce* ☎ *520/824–3334, 866/786–4569* 🌐 *www.sunglowranch.com* 🛏 *12 casitas* 🍴 *Some meals.*

CLOSE UP

Geronimo: No Bullet Shall Pass

The fearless Apache war shaman Geronimo, known among his people as "one who yawns," fought to the very last in the Apache Wars. His surrender to General Nelson Miles on September 5, 1886, marked the end of the Indian Wars in the West. Geronimo's fleetness in evading the massed troops of the U.S. Army and his legendary immunity to bullets made him the darling of sensationalistic journalists, and he became the most famous outlaw in America.

When the combined forces of the U.S. Army and Mexican troops failed to rout the powerful shaman from his territory straddling Arizona and Mexico, General Miles sent his officer Lieutenant Gatewood and relatives of Geronimo's renegade band of warriors to persuade Geronimo to parley with Miles near the mouth of Skeleton Canyon, at the edge of the Peloncillo Mountains. After several days of talks, Geronimo and his warriors agreed to the presented treaty and surrendered their arms.

Geronimo related the scene years later: "We stood between his troopers and my warriors. We placed a large stone on the blanket before us. Our treaty was made by this stone, as it was to last until the stone should crumble to dust; so we made the treaty, and bound each other with an oath." However, the political promises quickly unraveled, and the most feared among Apache medicine men spent his next 23 years in exile as a prisoner of war. He died on February 17, 1909, never having returned to his beloved homeland, and was buried in the Apache cemetery in Fort Sill, Oklahoma.

In 1934 a stone monument was built on State Route 80 in Apache, Arizona, as a reminder of Geronimo's surrender in 1886. The 16-foot-tall monument lies 10 miles northwest of the actual surrender site in Skeleton Canyon, where an unobtrusive sign and a pile of rocks mark the place where the last stone was cast.

8

FORT BOWIE NATIONAL HISTORICAL SITE

8 miles northwest of Chiricahua National Monument.

Fort Bowie was built in 1882 to protect this important travel route for wagon trains. Historic sites, including the fort ruins and the stagecoach stop, and sweeping mountain vistas are accessible by moderately easy trails.

GETTING HERE AND AROUND

From Chiricahua National Monument, take AZ 186 west (about a 30-minute drive); 5 miles north of the junction with AZ 181, signs direct you to an unpaved road leading to the fort. At the site's entrance there's a winding gravel road to the parking area, where a moderately challenging walking trail leads 1.5 miles to the visitor center and ruins. For those unable to hike to the visitor center, arrangements can be made to drive in (call ahead).

EXPLORING

Fort Bowie National Historical Site. It's a bit of an outing to get to the site of Arizona's last battle between Native Americans and U.S. troops in the Dos Cabezas (Two-Headed) Mountains, but history buffs will find it an interesting hike with the added benefit of high-desert scenic beauty. Once a focal point for military operations—the fort was built here because Apache Pass was an important travel route for Native Americans and wagon trains—it now serves as a reminder of the brutal clashes between the two cultures. The fort itself is virtually in ruins, but there's a small ranger-staffed visitor center with historical displays, restrooms, and books for sale.

A 1.5-mile historic trail, moderately easy but rocky in some areas, leads to the visitor center and ruins. Points of interest along the way include the remnants of an Apache *wickiup* (hut), the fort cemetery, Apache Springs (their water source), and the **Butterfield stage stop,** a crucial link in the journey from east to west in the mid-19th century that happened to be in the heart of Chiricahua Apache land. The alternate trail, looping back to the parking area, is higher and affords nice views of the ruins and surrounding hills. ✉ *3327 S. Old Fort Bowie Rd., 26 miles southeast of Willcox, Bowie* ☏ *520/847–2500* ⊕ *www.nps.gov/ fobo* ✉ *Free* ⊙ *Daily 8–4.*

WILLCOX

26 miles northwest of Fort Bowie National Historical Site on AZ 186.

The small town of Willcox, in the heart of Arizona ranching country, began in the late 1870s as a railroad construction camp called Maley. When the Southern Pacific Railroad line arrived in 1880, the town was renamed in honor of the highly regarded Fort Bowie commander, General Orlando B. Willcox. Once a major shipping center for cattle ranchers and mining companies, the town has preserved its rustic charm; the downtown area looks like an Old West movie set. An elevation of 4,167 feet means moderate summers and chilly winters, ideal for growing apples, and apple pie fans from as far away as Phoenix make pilgrimages to sample the harvest. The climate also seems favorable for growing grapes, and Willcox has sprouted several vineyards and tasting rooms in the last couple of years.

GETTING HERE AND AROUND

The small, historic downtown area of Willcox is just a few blocks south of Interstate 10 from Exit 340. Take Rex Allen Drive south, turn right on Haskell Avenue, then left on Maley Street and left onto Railroad Avenue for an authentic glimpse of southern Arizona circa 1912, including mercantile stores, banks, and the railroad depot. Museums, wine-tasting rooms, and a few restaurants are also here. To reach the visitor center and Apple Annie's country store, drive north from Interstate 10 Exit 340 on Fort Grant Road, and follow signs.

ESSENTIALS

Visitor Information Cochise Visitors Center/Willcox Chamber of Commerce ✉ *1500 N. Circle I Rd.* ☏ *520/384–2272, 800/200–2272* ⊕ *www. willcoxchamber.com.* **Willcox Wineries** ⊕ *www.willcoxwines.com.*

Remote Chiricahua National Monument is filled with dramatic "upside-down" or "standing-up" volcanic rock formations.

EXPLORING
TOP ATTRACTIONS

Apple Annie's Orchards. From August to October pick your own apples just outside town at Apple Annie's Orchards. Peaches are ready July through September; veggies ripen mid-summer through fall. Or stop at Apple Annie's in-town country store, next to the Cochise Visitors Center, for delicious homemade pies, fudge, and fruit butters. ⊠ *2081 W. Hardy Rd.* ☎ *520/384–2084* ⊕ *www.appleannies.com.*

Chiricahua Regional Museum and Research Center. Learn about the fierce Chiricahua Apaches and the fearless leaders Cochise and Geronimo at this research center, located in downtown Willcox. Other interesting tidbits about the area can be found in displays featuring the U.S. Cavalry, a nice collection of rocks and minerals, and relics of the famed Butterfield Overland Stage Route. One oddity the museum points out is that the memoirs of Civil War general Orlando Willcox, for whom the town was named, don't even mention a visit to Arizona. ⊠ *127 E. Maley St.* ☎ *520/384–3971* ⬚ *$2* ⊘ *Mon.–Sat. 10–4.*

FAMILY **Rex Allen Arizona Cowboy Museum.** This museum in Willcox's historic district is a tribute to Willcox's most famous native son, cowboy singer Rex Allen. He starred in several rather average "singing" cowboy movies during the 1940s and '50s for Republic Pictures, but he's probably most famous as the friendly voice that narrated Walt Disney nature films of the 1960s. Check out the glittery suits the star wore on tour—they'd do Liberace proud. ⊠ *150 N. Railroad Ave.* ☎ *520/384–4583* ⊕ *www. rexallenmuseum.org* ⬚ *$2* ⊘ *Mon. 10–1, Tues.–Sat. 10–4.*

WORTH NOTING

Willcox Commercial Store. Established in 1881, the Willcox Commercial Store, near the Rex Allen Cowboy Museum, is the oldest retail establishment in Arizona. Locals like to say that Geronimo used to shop here. Today it's a clothing and general store. ⊠ *180 N. Railroad Ave.* ☎ *520/384–2448.*

Willcox Playa. If you visit in winter, you can see some of the more than 10,000 sandhill cranes that roost at the Willcox Playa, a 37,000-acre area resembling a dry lake bed 10 miles south of Willcox. They migrate in late fall and head north to nesting sites in February, and bird-watchers migrate to Willcox the third week in January for the annual Wings over Willcox bird-watching event held in their honor. ⊠ *Kansas Settlement Rd., 3 miles south of AZ 186, Cochise.*

WHERE TO EAT AND STAY

$
MEXICAN

✕ **Salsa Fiesta Mexican Restaurant.** You can't miss the bright neon lights of this little restaurant, just south of Interstate 10 at Exit 340 in Willcox. The interior is cheerful and clean, with tables, chairs, and walls painted in a spicy medley of hot pink, purple, turquoise, green, and orange. The menu consists of Mexican standards, and the salsa bar runs the gamut from mild to superhot. There is a modest selection of domestic and Mexican beers, and takeout is available. $ *Average main: $8* ⊠ *1201 W. Rex Allen Dr.* ☎ *520/384–4233* ☉ *Closed Tues.*

$
HOTEL

▦ **Holiday Inn Express & Suites Willcox.** With mighty slim pickin's for a place to hang your hat in cowboy country, the new Holiday Inn Express with clean and well-furnished rooms and full breakfast buffet is a welcome addition. **Pros:** clean; comfortable; cheap. **Cons:** generic hotel off the highway. $ *Rooms from: $90* ⊠ *1251 N. Virginia Ave.* ☎ *520/384–3333* ⊕ *www.willcoxlodging.com* ⊷ *100 rooms* ⦿ *Breakfast.*

TEXAS CANYON

Fodor'sChoice
★

16 miles southwest of Willcox off Interstate 10.

A dramatic change of scenery along Interstate 10 will signal that you're entering Texas Canyon. The rock formations here are exceptional— huge boulders appear to be delicately balanced against each other.

GETTING HERE AND AROUND

Get off Interstate 10 at Exit 318, and then turn right onto Dragoon Road. The Amerind Foundation is a mile down on the left, and Triangle T Guest Ranch, with lodging and a restaurant, is next door.

EXPLORING

The Amerind Foundation. Texas Canyon is the home of the Amerind Foundation (a contraction of "American" and "Indian"), founded by amateur archaeologist William Fulton in 1937 to foster understanding about Native American cultures. The research facility and museum are housed in a Spanish colonial–style structure designed by noted Tucson architect H. M. Starkweather. The museum's rotating displays of archaeological materials, crafts, and photographs give an overview of Native American cultures of the Southwest and Mexico.

The adjacent Fulton–Hayden Memorial Art Gallery displays an assortment of art collected by William Fulton. Permanent exhibits include the work of Tohono O'odham women potters, an exquisite collection of Hopi kachina dolls, prized paintings by acclaimed Hopi artists, Pueblo pottery ranging from prehistoric pieces to modern ceramics, and archaeological exhibits on the Indian cultures of the prehistoric Southwest. The museum's gift shop has a superlative selection of Native American art, crafts, and jewelry. Beautiful picnic areas among the boulders can accomodate large and small groups. ⊠ *2100 N. Amerind Rd., 1 mile southeast of I–10, Exit 318, Dragoon* ☎ *520/586–3666* ⊕ *www. amerind.org* ⊠ *$8* ⊙ *Tues.–Sun. 10–4.*

WHERE TO STAY

$$
B&B/INN
⊞ **Cochise Stronghold Bed & Breakfast.** Nestled in the Dragoon Mountains and bordered on three sides by national forest land, Cochise Stronghold Bed & Breakfast beckons nature lovers and anyone seeking solitude in a beautiful setting. **Pros:** great breakfast; peace and quiet. **Cons:** remote location. $ *Rooms from: $129* ⊠ *2126 W. Windancer Trail, Pearce* ☎ *520/826–4141* ⊕ *www.cochisestrongholdbb.com* ⇌ *3 units* ⦿| *Breakfast.*

$$
B&B/INN
⊞ **Triangle T Guest Ranch.** Enjoy the romance of the Old West at this historic ranch on 160 acres of prime real estate in Texas Canyon. **Pros:** horseback riding (extra fee) and hiking trails; saloon with live Country-Western music; good base for exploring the region. **Cons:** isolated. $ *Rooms from: $159* ⊠ *4190 Dragoon Rd., at Exit 318 off I–10, Dragoon* ☎ *520/586–7533* ⊕ *www.triangletguestranch.com* ⇌ *11 casitas* ⦿| *Breakfast.*

BENSON

12 miles west of Texas Canyon, 50 miles southeast of Tucson via Interstate 10.

Back in its historic heyday as a Butterfield stagecoach station, and later as the hub of the Southern Pacific Railroad, Benson was just a place to stop on the way to somewhere else. Not much has changed, except that a few more visitors come through for a meal or to fill their gas tanks, following the 1974 discovery of a pristine cave beneath the Whetstone Mountains west of Benson, culminating 25 years later with the opening of Kartchner Caverns State Park, one of the most remarkable living cave systems in the world.

GETTING HERE AND AROUND

Amtrak runs trains from Tucson to the Benson depot three times a week. The Benson Visitor Center is inside the train depot on 4th Street, the main drag through this sleepy town. Benson Taxi offers transport services in the Benson area, as well as to Tombstone, Bisbee, and Kartchner Caverns, which lies a few miles west.

ESSENTIALS

Transportation Contacts Benson Taxi ☎ *520/586–1294.* **Benson Visitor Center** ⊠ *249 E. 4th St.* ☎ *520/586–4293* ⊕ *www.bensonvisitorcenter.com* ⊙ *Mon.–Fri. 9–5* ⊙ *Closed Sun..*

EXPLORING

The San Pedro Valley Arts and Historical Museum. Though the city is undergoing some modern development, you can see the story of Benson's past at this free museum open Tuesday through Saturday (but closed in August). Exhibits include a re-creation of an old-fashioned grocery store, a horse-drawn school bus, quilts, and railroad paraphernalia. On Saturday morning, you'll find an outdoor artisan market here; during summer months, local farmers join in selling their fruit and vegetables. ⊠ *180 S. San Pedro Ave., at E. 5th St.* ☎ *520/586–3070* ⊕ *www. bensonmuseum.com* ⧆ *Free* ☉ *Sept.–July, Tues.–Fri. 10–4, Sat. 10–2.*

Singing Wind Bookshop. As you pass Benson on Interstate 10, watch for Ocotillo Avenue, Exit 304. Take Ocotillo north about 2¼ miles, where a mailbox with a backward "SW" signals that you've come to the turnoff for Singing Wind Bookshop. Make a right at the mailbox onto Singing Wind Road and drive ½ mile to the shop. You might meet Winifred Bundy, who also runs the ranch. She knows just about every regional author around, so this unique bookshop-on-a-ranch has signed copies of books on almost any Southwestern topic. She doesn't take credit cards. ⊠ *700 W. Singing Wind Rd.* ☎ *520/586–2425* ☉ *Daily 9–5.*

WHERE TO EAT AND STAY

$

AMERICAN

✕ **Reb's Café.** For a more traditional take on Southwestern food—none of that newfangled "nouvelle" stuff—this unpretentious diner is of the cowboy variety. It serves Mexican food and a little Italian, but it really prides itself on steaks and hamburgers, and a darned good breakfast (served all day). Ⓢ *Average main: $7* ⊠ *1020 W. 4th St.* ☎ *520/586–3856.*

$

HOTEL

▦ **Comfort Inn Benson.** The closest lodging to Kartchner Caverns State Park, this modern motel sits just off Interstate 10 at the "Kartchner Corridor," a few miles west of Benson. **Pros:** clean; friendly; convenient location. **Cons:** just off the highway; not particularly serene or scenic. Ⓢ *Rooms from: $99* ⊠ *630 S. Village Loop* ☎ *520/586–8800* ⊕ *www. choicehotels.com* ⇥ *62 rooms* ⏀ *Breakfast.*

KARTCHNER CAVERNS STATE PARK

9 miles south of Benson on AZ 90.

Kartchner Caverns is a large and beautifully maintained cave system where visitors can walk through the fantastic stalactites and stalagmites while learning about the unique and fragile ecosystem. It's a wet, "live" cave, meaning that water still rises up from the surface to continually add to the multicolor calcium carbonate formations already visible. Amateur cavers discovered Kartchner Caverns in 1974, and it opened to the public in 1999.

GETTING HERE AND AROUND

From Exit 302 off Interstate 10, take AZ 90 for 9 miles.

EXPLORING

FAMILY

Fodor's Choice

★

Kartchner Caverns. The publicity that surrounded the official opening of Kartchner Caverns in November 1999 was in marked contrast to the secrecy that shrouded their discovery 25 years earlier and concealed

DID YOU KNOW?

Abandoned mining gear, like this ore loading chute, is all that remains of some of southern Arizona's former boomtowns. Copper, silver, and gold have all attracted miners at different times.

their existence for 14 years. The two young spelunkers, Gary Tenen and Randy Tufts, who stumbled into what is now considered one of the most spectacular cave systems anywhere, played a fundamental role in its protection and eventual development. Great precautions have been taken to protect the wet-cave system—which comprises 13,000 feet of passages and two chambers as long as football fields—from damage by light and dryness.

WORD OF MOUTH

"If you haven't been [to Kartchner Caverns], I don't think it matters which tour you do—Big Room or Rotunda/Throne Room—as long as you see the caverns, one or the other. They are absolutely amazing." –Birdie

The Discovery Center introduces visitors to the cave and its formations, and hour-long guided tours take small groups into the upper cave. Spectacular formations include the longest soda straw stalactite in the United States at 21 feet and 2 inches. The Big Room is viewed on a separate tour: it holds the world's most extensive formation of brushite moonmilk, the first reported occurrence of turnip shields, and the first noted occurrence of birdsnest needle formations. Other funky and fabulous formations include brilliant red flowstone, rippling multihued stalactites, delicate white helictites, translucent orange bacon, and expansive mud flats. It's also the nursery roost for female cave myotis bats April through September, during which time the lower cave is closed.

The total cavern size is 2.4 miles long, but the explored areas cover only 1,600 feet by 1,100 feet. The average relative humidity inside is 99%, so visitors are often graced with "cave kisses," water droplets from above. Because the climate outside the caves is so dry, it is estimated that if air got inside, it could deplete the moisture in only a few days, halting the growth of the speleothems that decorate its walls. To prevent this, there are 22 environmental monitoring stations that measure air and soil temperature, relative humidity, evaporation rates, air trace gases, and airflow inside the caverns. ■TIP→ Tour reservations are required, and should be made well in advance. If you're here and didn't make a reservation, go ahead and check: sometimes same-day reservations are available (call or arrive early in the day for these). Hiking trails, picnic areas, and campsites ($25 with hook-ups) are available on the park's 550 acres; and the Bat Cave Café, open daily, serves pizza, hot dogs, salads, and sandwiches. ⊠ AZ 90, 9 miles south of Exit 302 off I–10 ☏ 520/586–4100 for info, 520/586–2283 for tour reservations ⊕ www. azstateparks.com ⊠ Park admission $6 per vehicle up to 4 people, $2 each additional person (fees waived for cave tour ticket holders). Rotunda/Throne Room tour or Big Room tour $23. ⊙ Daily 8–6; cave tours daily 8–4, by reservation only.

SOUTHWEST ARIZONA

The turbulent history of the West is writ large in this now-sleepy part of Arizona. It's home to the Tohono O'odham Indian Reservation (the largest in the country after the Navajo Nation's) and towns such as Ajo—created (and almost undone) by the copper-mining industry—and

Nogales, along the U.S.–Mexico border. Yuma, abutting the California border, was a major crossing point of the Colorado River as far back as the time of the conquistadors.

These days people mostly travel *through* Sells, Ajo, and Yuma en route to the closest beaches. During the school year, especially on warm weekends and semester breaks, the 130-mile route from Tucson to Ajo is busy with traffic headed southwest to Puerto Penasco (Rocky Point), Mexico, the closest access to the sea for Arizonans. All summer long, Interstate 8 takes heat-weary Tucsonans and Phoenicians to San Diego, California, and Yuma is the midpoint.

Natural attractions are a lure in this starkly scenic region: Organ Pipe Cactus National Monument provides trails for desert hikers and birders, and Buenos Aires and Imperial wildlife refuges—homes to many unusual species—are important destinations for birders and other nature-watchers. Much of the time, however, your only companions will be the low-lying scrub and cactus, and the mesquite, ironwood, and palo verde trees.

BUENOS AIRES NATIONAL WILDLIFE REFUGE

66 miles southwest of Tucson.

Encircled by seven mountain ranges in the Altar Valley, remote Buenos Aires National Wildlife Refuge is the only place in the United States where the Sonoran-savanna grasslands that once pervaded this region can still be seen. The U.S. Fish and Wildlife Service oversees this 115,000-acre preserve, managing programs to restore native grasses and protect endangered species such as the masked bobwhite quail. Birding and wildlife-viewing are popular here.

GETTING HERE AND AROUND
From Tucson, take AZ 86 west 22 miles to AZ 286; go south 40 miles to milepost 8, and it's another 3 miles east to the preserve headquarters.

EXPLORING
Buenos Aires National Wildlife Refuge. Bird-watchers consider Buenos Aires National Wildlife Refuge unique because it's the only place in the United States where they can see a "grand slam" (four species) of quail: Montezuma quail, Gambel's quail, scaled quail, and masked bobwhite. If it rains, the 100-acre Aguirre Lake, 1½ miles north of the headquarters, attracts wading birds, shorebirds, and waterfowl—in all, more than 320 avian species have been spotted here. The quail share the turf with deer, coati, badgers, bobcats, and mountain lions. Touring options include a 10-mile auto tour through the area; nature trails; a 3.8-mile guided hike in Brown Canyon ($5; offered on second and fourth Saturdays—call to sign up); a boardwalk through the marshes at Arivaca Cienega; and a guided bird walk, also at Arivaca Cienega, on Saturday at 8 am November through April. Admission and guided bird walks are free; Brown Canyon hikes cost $5. Pick up maps at the visitor center. ✉ *AZ 286, at milepost 7.5, Sasabe ✛ Turn off Hwy. 286 at milepost 7.5, and drive into the refuge for 3 miles to arrive at Refuge Headquarters and Visitor Center.* ☎ *520/823–4251* ⊕ *www.fws.gov/*

8

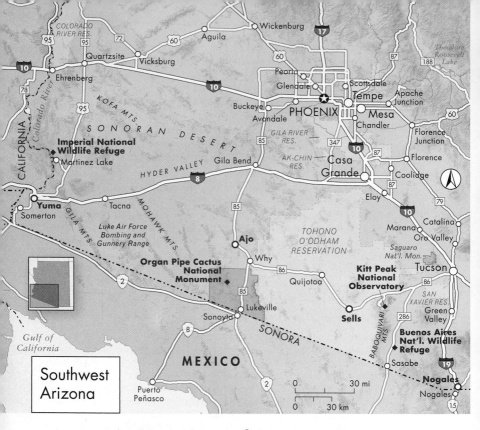

Southwest Arizona

refuge/buenos_aires ⌂ Free ☉ Visitor center Sept.–May, daily 7:30–4;
June–Aug., weekdays 7:30–4. Refuge open 24 hrs.

WHERE TO STAY

$$$$ ⌂ **Rancho de la Osa.** Set on 250 eucalyptus-shaded acres near the Mexi-
B&B/INN   can border and Buenos Aires preserve, this tranquil late 19th-century
ranch with adobe buildings offers guests activities such as cooking lessons, hiking, and guided history walks. **Pros:** good riding; good food
and extensive wine list; pretty setting. **Cons:** somewhat isolated for
those interested in touring the region. ⓢ *Rooms from: $279* ⌂ *41480
S. Sasabe Hwy., Sasabe* ☎ *520/823–4257* ⊕ *www.ranchodelaosa.com*
↪ *19 rooms* ⦿ *Some meals.*

KITT PEAK NATIONAL OBSERVATORY

*70 miles northwest of Buenos Aires National Wildlife Refuge on AZ
286 to AZ 86, 56 miles southwest of Tucson.*

Funded by the National Science Foundation and managed by a group
of more than 20 universities, Kitt Peak National Observatory is on
the Tohono O'odham Reservation. Kitt Peak scientists use the high-
powered telescopes here to conduct vital solar research and observe

BORDER TOWN SAFETY: NOGALES, MEXICO

Nogales used to draw tourists and locals, who would park on the American side and walk across the border. Though shopping bargains and cheap bars are enticing, safety issues have changed in recent years.

⚠ Drug-related violence in Mexico—especially near the U.S. border—has increased to the point that the U.S. government strongly discourages travel in and around Mexico border towns. Check ⊕ www.state.gov/travel for updates and details.

If you decide to cross, bring your passport, remain alert, and stay in the central area on Avenida Obregón, which begins a few blocks west of the border entrance and runs north–south.

distant galaxies; visitors can tour the facilities by day and view stellar happenings at the evening observation program.

GETTING HERE AND AROUND

To reach Kitt Peak from Tucson, take Interstate 10 to Interstate 19 south, and then AZ 86. After 44 miles on AZ 86, turn left at the AZ 386 junction and follow the winding mountain road 12 miles up to the observatory. In inclement weather, contact the highway department to confirm that the road is open. To get to Sells (for the nearest food and gas), from the base of the mountain, it's 20 miles west on AZ 86.

EXPLORING

Kitt Peak National Observatory. After much discussion back in the late 1950s, tribal leaders of the Tohono O'odham nation agreed to share a small section of their 4,400-square-mile reservation with the National Science Foundation to house sophisticated research telescopes. Among these is the McMath-Pierce, the world's largest solar telescope, which uses piped-in liquid coolant. From the visitors' gallery you can see into the telescope's light-path tunnel, which goes down hundreds of feet into the mountain.

The visitor center has exhibits on astronomy, information about the telescopes, and hour-long guided tours ($7.75 per person) that depart daily at 10, 11:30, and 1:30. Complimentary brochures enable you to take self-guided tours of the grounds, and there are picnic areas outside and below the observatory. The observatory sells snacks and drinks, which is good to know, because there are no restaurants (or gas stations, for that matter) within 20 miles of Kitt Peak. The observatory offers an outstanding nightly observing program ($49 per person); reservations are necessary. ⊠ *AZ 386, Pan Tak* ☎ *520/318–8726* ⊕ *www.noao.edu/kpno* 🖭 *Free; tours and observatory programs extra* ☉ *Visitor center daily 9–4.*

8

SELLS

32 miles southwest of Kitt Peak via AZ 386 to AZ 86.

The Tohono O'odham Reservation, the second largest in the United States, covers 4,400 square miles between Tucson and Ajo, stretching south to the Mexican border and north almost to the city of Casa Grande. To the south of Kitt Peak, the 7,730-foot Baboquivari Peak is considered sacred by the Tohono O'odham as the home of their deity, I'itoi ("elder brother"). Less than halfway between Tucson and Ajo, Sells—the tribal capital of the Tohono O'odham—is a good place to stop for gas or a soft drink. Much of the time there's little to see or do in Sells, but in winter an annual rodeo and fair attract thousands of Native American visitors.

GETTING HERE AND AROUND

If you're traveling east or west along AZ 86, take the exit for the Sells Hospital to explore this tiny town, which consists of a few stores, offices, and a school (about a half-mile from the highway). The Papago Cafe sits at the highway exit. To get into town, drive south past the hospital, and go over the bridge.

WHERE TO EAT

$ ✕ **Basha's Deli & Bakery.** At the Sells Shopping Center, the good-size
SOUTHWESTERN market Basha's Deli & Bakery can supply all the makings for a picnic.
$ *Average main: $7* ✉ *AZ 86* ☎ *520/383–2546.*

$ ✕ **Papago Cafe.** For traditional Indian and Mexican food like fry bread,
SOUTHWESTERN tacos, and chili, try the Papago Cafe, open weekdays breakfast through dinner, and Saturday for breakfast and lunch only. $ *Average main: $9* ✉ *AZ 86, near Chevron Station* ☎ *520/383–3510* ☉ *Closed Sun. No dinner Sat.*

AJO

90 miles northwest of Sells on AZ 86.

"Ajo" (pronounced *ah*-ho) is Spanish for garlic, and some say the town got its name from the wild garlic that grows in the area. Others claim the word is a bastardization of the Indian word *au-auho,* referring to red paint derived from a local pigment.

For many years Ajo, like Bisbee, was a thriving Phelps Dodge company town. Copper mining had been attempted in the area in the late 19th century, but it wasn't until the 1911 arrival of the Calumet & Arizona Mining Company that the region began to be developed profitably. Calumet and Phelps Dodge merged in 1935, and the huge pit mine produced millions of tons of copper until it closed in 1985. Nowadays Ajo is pretty sleepy; the town's population of 4,000 has a median age of 51, and most visitors are on their way to or from Rocky Point, Mexico. At the center of town is a sparkling white Spanish-style plaza. The shops and restaurants that line the plaza's covered arcade today are rather modest. Unlike Bisbee, Ajo hasn't yet drawn an artistic crowd—or the upscale boutiques and eateries that tend to follow. Chain stores and

Kitt Peak National Observatory is open to visitors during the day, but it's easy to enjoy the night sky here.

fast-food haven't made a beeline here either—you'll find only one Dairy Queen and a Pizza Hut in this remote desert hamlet.

GETTING HERE AND AROUND

As you drive into Ajo on AZ 85, you'll see the small historical plaza, with a few shops, a pharmacy, and a library, immediately on your right. After jogging west for several blocks and changing its name three times, the highway turns north again, becomes 2nd Avenue, and takes you out of town, past the Cabeza Prieta Wildlife Refuge and north to Gila Bend.

EXPLORING

Cabeza Prieta National Wildlife Refuge. This 860,000-acre national wildlife refuge, about 5 miles (a 10-minute drive) from Ajo, was established in 1939 as a preserve for endangered bighorn sheep and other Sonoran Desert wildlife, including the long-nosed bat and the Sonoran pronghorn deer, the fastest mammal in North America. People come here for hiking, photography, and primitive desert camping. A free permit, essentially a "hold-harmless" agreement, is required to enter, and only those with four-wheel-drive, high-clearance vehicles, or all-terrain vehicles—needed to traverse the rugged terrain—can obtain one from the refuge's visitor center, which is in Ajo, about a mile north of the downtown plaza. ⊠ *1611 N. 2nd Ave., at North St.* ☎ *520/387–6483* ⊕ *www.fws.gov/refuge/cabeza_prieta* ⊠ *Free* ⊙ *Visitor center weekdays 8–4, refuge daily dawn–dusk.*

New Cornelia Open Pit Mine Lookout Point. You get an expansive view of Ajo's ugly gash of an open-pit mine, almost 2 miles wide, from the New Cornelia Open Pit Mine Lookout Point. Some of the abandoned equipment remains in the pit, and mining operations are diagrammed at the volunteer-run visitors' center, where there's a 30-minute film about mining. The mine is always "open," but visitor's center hours are sporadic. The mine is about a mile southwest of the plaza; take La Mina Road or Estrella Road to Indian Village Road. ✉ *Indian Village Rd.* ☎ *520/387–7742* 🎟 *Free* 🕒 *Call for hrs.*

WHERE TO EAT AND STAY

$ SOUTHWESTERN 🍴 **100 Estrella.** It can be hard to decide which burger to order from the dozen or so on the menu here. In the mood for the popular bacon and avocado burger, the "bleu cheese," or the free-range bison burger? If you're brave enough for something spicier, try "Summer in Ajo"—a beef patty with jalapeños, green chiles, onions, and pepper jack cheese. Herbivores can find veggie burgers, organic veggie pizzas, and salads with tepary beans, a Native American legume loaded with protein, fiber, and flavor. The bar at this colorful eatery offers 10 beers on draft and a good selection of bottled brews. [$] *Average main: $9* ✉ *100 Estrella Ave.* ☎ *520/387–3110* 🕒 *Closed Sun., and Sat. Apr.–Dec.*

$ B&B/INN 🏨 **The Guest House Inn.** Built in 1925 to accommodate visiting Phelps Dodge VIPs, this lodging is a favorite for birders: guests can head out early to nearby Organ Pipe National Monument or just sit on the patio and watch the quail, cactus wrens, and other warblers that fly in to visit. **Pros:** pleasant hosts; well-preserved home. **Cons:** may be a little sedate for some. [$] *Rooms from: $89* ✉ *700 Guest House Rd.* ☎ *520/387–6133* 🌐 *www.guesthouseinn.biz* 🛏 *4 rooms* 🍽 *Breakfast.*

ORGAN PIPE CACTUS NATIONAL MONUMENT

32 miles southwest of Ajo on AZ 86 to AZ 85.

The largest habitat north of the border for organ-pipe cacti, the beautiful (multiarmed cousins of the saguaro) is off the beaten path, unless you're driving to Puerto Penasco, Mexico. But it's a worthwhile destination to view large groves of this desert flora, fairly common in Mexico but rare in the United States.

GETTING HERE

From Ajo, drive to Why and take AZ 85 south for 22 miles to reach the visitor center.

SAFETY AND PRECAUTIONS

Be aware that Organ Pipe has become an illegal-border-crossing hot spot. Migrant workers and drug traffickers cross from Mexico under the cover of darkness. At this writing, much of Puerto Blanco Drive is closed indefinitely to the public. A two-way road that only travels 5 of the 53 miles on Puerto Blanco Drive is open, but the rest of the road remains closed due to continuing concerns over its proximity to the U.S.–Mexico border. Even so, park officials emphasize that tourists only occasionally have been the victims of isolated property crimes—primarily theft of personal items from parked cars. Visitors are advised by rangers to keep valuables locked and out of plain view and not to initiate contact with groups of strangers whom they may encounter on hiking trails.

EXPLORING

Organ Pipe Cactus National Monument. This designated part of the Sonoran Desert preserves more than two dozen species of cacti, including the park's namesake, as well as other desert plants and animals. Because organ pipe cactus tend to grow on the warmer, usually south-facing, slopes, you'll get the best views of them by taking either the 21-mile scenic loop **Ajo Mountain Drive** (a winding, one-way dirt road) or **Puerto Blanco Drive,** a 53-mile, two-way dirt road, of which only the first 11 miles are currently open to the public. In an effort to limit the number of cars that traverse Puerto Blanco Drive, the monument requires drivers to obtain a free permit at the visitor center. Ranger-led tours and talks are offered January through March. A campground at the monument has 208 RV (no hookups) and tent sites ($12). Facilities include a dump station with potable water, showers, flush toilets, grills, and picnic tables. ✉ *10 Organ Pipe Dr., Ajo* ☎ *520/387–6849* ⊕ *www.nps. gov/orpi* ✉ *$8/vehicle* ☉ *Visitor center daily 8:30–4:30.*

YUMA

232 miles northwest of Organ Pipe Cactus National Monument, 170 miles northwest of Ajo.

Today many people think of Yuma as a convenient stop for gas and a meal between Phoenix or Tucson and San Diego. While this is surely true, the town boasts some historic sites and agricultural tours (Yuma is the lettuce capital of the U.S.) that may prompt you to pause here a bit longer.

It's difficult to imagine the lower Colorado River, now dammed and bridged, as either a barrier or a means of transportation, but until the early part of the 20th century this section of the great waterway was a force to contend with. Records show that since at least 1540 the Spanish were using Yuma (then the site of a Quechan Indian village) as a ford across a relatively shallow stretch of the Colorado.

Three centuries later, the advent of the shallow-draft steamboat made the settlement a point of entry for fortune-seekers heading through the Gulf of California to mining sites in eastern Arizona. Fort Yuma was established in 1850 to guard against Indian attacks, and by 1873 the town was a county seat, a U.S. port of entry, and an army depot.

During World War II, Yuma Proving Ground was used to train bomber pilots, and General Patton readied some of his desert war forces for battle at secret areas in the city. Many who served here during the war returned to Yuma to retire, and the city's population swells during the winter months with retirees from cold climates who park their homes on wheels at one of the many RV communities. One fact may explain this: according to National Weather Service statistics, Yuma is the sunniest city in the United States.

GETTING HERE AND AROUND

AZ 8 runs through Yuma, which is approximately halfway between Casa Grande and the California coast. Most of the interesting historic sites are at the north end of town. Stop in at the Yuma Convention and

Visitors Bureau, on the grounds of Quartermaster Depot State Park, and pick up a walking-tour guide to the historic downtown area. Yuma is accessible by a few commercial airlines: US Airways, recently merged with American Airlines, has direct flights to Yuma from Phoenix, and United Express flies nonstop from Los Angeles to Yuma.

Yuma City Cab has the best taxi service in Yuma.

Amtrak trains run three times a week from Tucson west to Yuma.

ESSENTIALS

Transportation Contacts Yuma City Cab ☏ *928/782–4444.* **Yuma train station** ✉ *281 Gila St.* ⊕ *www.amtrak.com.* **Yuma International Airport (YUM)** ☏ *928/726–5882* ⊕ *www.yumaairport.com.*

Visitor Information Yuma Convention and Visitors Bureau ✉ *201 N. 4th Ave., at Quartermaster Depot Park* ☏ *928/783–0071, 800/293–0071* ⊕ *www. visityuma.com* ☉ *Daily 9–5.*

TOURS

Yuma River Tours. You can take a boat ride up the Colorado with Yuma River Tours. Canoe, kayak, cruise on a stern-wheeler, or book 12- to 45-person jet-boat excursions through Smokey Knowlton, who has been exploring the area for more than 35 years. The jet-boat tours range from $48 to $95 and in length, from three to seven hours, while the three-hour sternwheeler cruises range from $48 for a lunch cruise to $63 for a sunset dinner cruise. Canoe and kayak tours are two- or three-day camping trips. ✉ *1920 Arizona Ave.* ☏ *928/783–4400* ⊕ *www.yumarivertours.com.*

EXPLORING

Sanguinetti House Museum. This adobe-style museum, run by the Arizona Historical Society, was built around 1870 by merchant E. F. Sanguinetti; it exhibits artifacts from Yuma's territorial days and details the military presence in the area. If you're dining at the Garden Café this makes for an interesting stop, but it's not worth a visit on its own, especially if you plan on visiting the more popular Quartermaster Depot State Historic Park. ✉ *240 S. Madison Ave.* ☏ *928/782–1841* ⊕ *www. arizonahistoricalsociety.org* ◫ *$3* ☉ *Tues.–Sat. 10–4.*

Yuma Quartermaster Depot State Historic Park. On the other side of the river from Fort Yuma, the Civil War–period quartermaster depot resupplied army posts to the north and east and served as a distribution point for steamboat freight headed overland to Arizona forts. The 1853 home of riverboat captain G. A. Johnson is the depot's earliest building and the centerpiece of Quartermaster Depot State Historic Park. The residence also served as a weather bureau and home for customs agents, among other functions, and the guided tour through the house provides a complete history. Also on display are antique surreys and more "modern" modes of transportation like a 1931 Model A Ford pickup. You can visit a re-creation of the Commanding Officer's Quarters, complete with period furnishings. The Yuma Visitors Bureau is also here. ✉ *201 N. 4th Ave., between 1st St. and I–8* ☏ *928/783–0071* ◫ *$2* ☉ *Daily 9–4:30. Closed Mon. June–Sept.*

FAMILY **Yuma Territorial Prison State Historic Park.** The most notorious tourist sight in town, Yuma Territorial Prison, now an Arizona state historic park, was built for the most part by the convicts who were incarcerated here from 1876 until 1909, when the prison outgrew its location. The hilly site on the Colorado River, chosen for security purposes, precluded further expansion.

Visitors gazing today at the tiny cells that held six inmates each, often in 115°F heat, are likely to be appalled, but the prison—dubbed the Country Club of the Colorado by locals—was considered a model of enlightenment by turn-of-the-20th-century standards: in an era when beatings were common, the only punishments meted out here were solitary confinement and assignment to a dark cell. The complex housed a hospital as well as Yuma's only public library, where the $0.25 that visitors paid for a prison tour financed the acquisition of new books.

The 3,069 prisoners who served time at what was then the territory's only prison included men and women from 21 different countries. They came from all social classes and were sent up for everything from armed robbery and murder to polygamy. R. L. McDonald, incarcerated for forgery, had been the superintendent of the Phoenix public school system. Chosen as the prison bookkeeper, he absconded with $130 of the inmates' money when he was released.

The mess hall opened as a museum in 1940, and the entire prison complex was designated a state historic park in 1961. ✉ *1 Prison Hill Rd., near Exit 1 off I–8* ☎ *928/783–4771* 🌐 *www.yumaprison.org* 🎟 *$6* 🕓 *June–Sept., Thurs.–Mon. 9–5; Oct.–May, daily 9–5.*

WHERE TO EAT

$ CAFÉ 🍴 **The Garden Café.** Before or after a visit to the Sanguinetti House Museum, this adjoining café is a good place to stop for breakfast or lunch. The charming dining spot features lush gardens and aviaries on the outdoor patio, historical photos on the walls, and a menu of homemade salads, soups, and sandwiches. Favorites include the quiche, served with homemade fruit bread, and the tortilla soup. Breakfasts are top-notch, too. One of the best times to visit is Sunday brunch—complete with carne asada, tortillas, potatoes, scrambled eggs, a layered ham-and-egg strata, breakfast meats, fruit, and dessert. [$] *Average main: $10* ✉ *250 S. Madison Ave.* ☎ *928/783–1491* 🌐 *www.gardencafeyuma.com* ✍ *Reservations not accepted* 🕓 *Closed Mon. and June–Sept. No dinner.*

$ MEXICAN 🍴 **La Fonda.** A Yuma institution, La Fonda opened as a tortilla factory in 1940, then added a colorful restaurant onto the original building in 1982; locals have been enjoying the carne asada, pollo asado, and chile rellenos here ever since. Only canola oil is used (not lard), and all the sauces and marinades are made fresh, as are the corn tortillas, which many say are the best in town. Save room for the homemade desserts—the flan and fried ice cream are fabulous. Open for breakfast (served all day), lunch, and early dinner, La Fonda closes at 8 so the employees can go home to their families. [$] *Average main: $9* ✉ *1095 S. 3rd Ave.* ☎ *928/783–6902* 🌐 *www.lafondarestaurantandtortillafactory.com* 🕓 *Closed Sun.*

Crested saguaros at Organ Pipe National Monument are found alongside the monument's namesake cacti and other succulent plants.

$ SOUTHWESTERN 🍴 **Lutes Casino.** Packed with locals at lunchtime, this large, funky restaurant and bar claims to be the oldest pool hall and domino parlor in Arizona. It's a great place for a burger and a brew. The "Especial" combines a cheeseburger and a hot dog and adds a generous dollop of Lutes's "special sauce." For dinner, dine early on weeknights: Monday through Thursday, it's shuttered by 8, and Sunday it closes at 6. [$] *Average main: $5* ✉ *221 S. Main St.* ☎ *928/782–2192* 🌐 *www.lutescasino.com.*

$$$ AMERICAN 🍴 **River City Grill.** This hip downtown restaurant is a favorite dining spot for locals and visitors. It gets a bit loud on weekend nights, but the camaraderie of diners is well worth it. Owners Nan and Tony Bain dish out a medley of flavors drawing on Mediterranean, Pacific Rim, Indian, and Caribbean influences. For starters you can sample everything from Vietnamese spring rolls to curried mussels. Entrées include pistachio-crusted salmon, rack of lamb, and a sizeable selection of vegetarian dishes like ricotta-and-spinach ravioli and coconut curry veggies. [$] *Average main: $22* ✉ *600 W. 3rd St.* ☎ *928/782–7988* 🌐 *www.rivercitygrillyuma.com* ⏲ *No lunch weekends.*

WHERE TO STAY

$ HOTEL 🏨 **Best Western Coronado Motor Hotel.** Built in 1938, this Spanish tile–roofed motor hotel has been well cared for and was where Bob Hope used to stay during World War II, when he entertained the gunnery troops training in Yuma. **Pros:** convenient location near AZ 8 and within a short walk from the historic downtown area; retro property; full breakfast at restaurant. **Cons:** some highway noise in rooms.

[$] *Rooms from: $99* ✉ *233 S. 4th Ave.* ☎ *928/783–4453, 800/528–1234* 🌐 *www.bestwestern.com* 🛏 *86 rooms* 🍴 *Breakfast.*

$ HOTEL 🏨 **Clarion Suites Yuma.** One wing of this sprawling hotel surrounds a well-manicured courtyard with a fountain; another faces the pool and Cabana Club, where the complimentary breakfast and happy-hour drinks are served. **Pros:** spacious suites; quiet. **Cons:** no restaurant. [$] *Rooms from: $89* ✉ *2600 S. 4th Ave.* ☎ *928/726–4830* 🌐 *www.clarionyuma.com* 🛏 *164 suites* 🍴 *Breakfast.*

$$ HOTEL 🏨 **Hilton Garden Inn Yuma-Pivot Point.** One of the newer hotels in town, the Hilton Garden Inn Yuma caters to families and business travelers equally, with well-equipped rooms, a pleasant pool area, and convenience to historic sights, the river park, and the highway. **Pros:** comfortable rooms; pool, hot tub, and gym; easy walk to historic Old Town area. **Cons:** generic property. [$] *Rooms from: $129* ✉ *310 N. Madison Ave.* ☎ *928/783–1500* 🌐 *www.yumapivotpoint.hgi.com* 🛏 *150 rooms* 🍴 *No meals.*

SHOPPING

Art studios, antiques shops, and specialty boutiques have taken advantage of downtown Yuma's face-lift. The town's largest shopping center, Yuma Palms, sits just to the east side of U.S. 8 (at the 16th Street exit).

Basket Creations/Bard Date Company. The retail outlet of the Bard Date Company is a great place to sample and purchase all grades of the high-fiber, fat-free fruit grown in this region, including delicious date shakes. ✉ *245 S. Main St.* ☎ *928/341–9966* 🌐 *www.barddate.com* ⏲ *Closed Sun.*

Colorado River Pottery. This shop in the heart of Yuma features handcrafted bowls, vases, and dishes. ✉ *67 W. 2nd St.* ☎ *928/343–0413* 🌐 *www.coloradoriverpottery.com* ⏲ *Closed Sun.*

Timeless Elegance. A favorite antiques shop of locals and visitors, Timeless Elegance carries an eclectic selection of furniture, jewelry, and knickknacks. Bring your heirlooms here to sell or be appraised. ✉ *315 S. Main St.* ☎ *928/329–6250* ⏲ *Closed Sun. and Mon.*

8

IMPERIAL NATIONAL WILDLIFE REFUGE

30 miles north of Yuma on U.S. 95.

Something of an anomaly, this 25,765-acre wildlife refuge created when the Imperial Dam was built is home both to marshy-river species and to creatures that inhabit the adjacent Sonoran desert—coyotes, bobcats, desert tortoises and bighorn sheep. Mostly, though, it's a major bird habitat, with waterfowl and shorebirds year-round, and masses of migrating flocks during spring and fall.

GETTING HERE AND AROUND

From Yuma, take U.S. 95 north and follow the signs to the refuge. It's about a 40-minute drive, and between January and March look for army paratroopers taking practice jumps as you pass the Yuma Proving Ground.

EXPLORING

FAMILY **Imperial National Wildlife Refuge.** A guided, volunteer-led tour is a good way to visit this wildlife refuge and birder's paradise. The peak seasons for bird-watching are spring and fall, when you can expect to see everything from pelicans and cormorants to Canada geese, snowy egrets, and some rarer species. Mid-October through May is the most pleasant time to visit, when it's cooler and the ever-present mosquitoes are least active.

Canoes can be rented at Martinez Lake Marina, 3½ miles southeast of the refuge headquarters. Kids especially enjoy the 1.3-mile Painted Desert Nature Trail, which winds through the different levels of the Sonoran Desert. From an observation tower at the visitor center you can see the river, as well as the fields where migrating birds like to feed. You can sign up for guided walks (including evening walks when the moon is full) November through March (call ahead). ⊠ *12812 Wildlife Way, Yuma* ☎ *928/783–3371* ⊕ *www.fws.gov/refuges* ✉ *Free* ☉ *Visitor center: Apr.–Oct., weekdays 7:30–4; Nov.–Mar., weekdays 7:30–4, weekends 9–4.*

NORTHWEST ARIZONA AND SOUTHEAST NEVADA

WELCOME TO NORTHWEST ARIZONA AND SOUTHEAST NEVADA

TOP REASONS TO GO

★ **Get wet:** Boating, fishing, and water adventure top the list of favorite activities on the cool Colorado River and the adjoining lakes of Havasu, Mohave, and Mead.

★ **Experience a slice of England:** Pass under on a boat or take a guided tour over London Bridge in Lake Havasu City.

★ **Drive the open road:** Take a road trip on legendary Route 66 and cruise the longest remaining stretch of the Mother Road from Seligman to Kingman.

★ **Take a walk on the wild side:** For Vegas-style gambling and glitz spend some quality play time in the twin riverside cities of Laughlin, Nevada, and Bullhead City, Arizona.

★ **Hike Hualapai:** Take a break from the desert and climb the cool climes of Hualapai Mountain Park—the highest point in western Arizona.

Laughlin, Nevada's casinos are just over the Colorado River.

1 **Northwest Arizona.** Take a drive down memory lane on the longest remaining stretch of historic Route 66—roll down the windows and watch the sweeping desert views pass you by. Along the way, check out the funky little ghost towns of Oatman and Chloride and make a splash in the cool blue waterways of Lakes Mohave, Mead, and Havasu.

2 **Southeast Nevada.** Laughlin attracts laid-back gamblers and elite entertainers looking for all of the glitz and glamour of Las Vegas without the high prices and large crowds. Take a quick jaunt into Nevada for a look at monumental Hoover Dam and a hand or two of black-jack in a riverside casino.

Rt. 66 is a classic American route for road trips.

GETTING ORIENTED

In the far northwestern corner of Arizona, the fast-growing communities of Lake Havasu and Laughlin/Bullhead City are good bases for outdoor recreation and gaming, respectively. Kingman, the Mohave County seat and a historic shipping center, is an ideal launch pad for exploring historic and quirky Route 66. The Colorado River flows out of the Grand Canyon to the north and then sweeps directly south, serving as the western border of the state of Arizona and supplying the lifeblood to the otherwise desolate desert region. Created from dams on the mighty Colorado River, Lakes Mead, Mohave, and Havasu provide a common link in the tristate area by offering some of the best water recreation around.

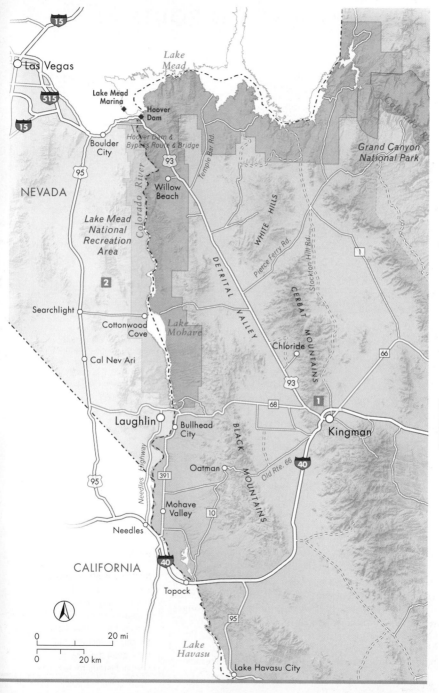

GET YOUR KICKS ON ROUTE 66

In 1938 the 2,400 miles of roadway connecting Chicago and Los Angeles was declared "continuously paved." U.S. Route 66 had been transformed from a ragged string of local lanes connecting isolated small towns into an "all-weather" highway that eased travel.

Just as the road crews changed what had been a string of rutty dirt roads into a paved roadbed, Route 66 changed the social landscape as communities adapted to the new road. The needs of travelers were met by new concepts, such as the gas station, the diner, and the motel. Nostalgic remnants from this retro road-tripping culture still exist along this stretch of the "Mother Road."

Most of old Route 66 has been replaced by the modern interstate system, but at Exit 139 from Interstate 40 you'll find yourself at the beginning of the longest remaining continuous stretch of the original Route 66. This 160-mile journey leads through Seligman, Peach Springs, Truxton, Valentine, Hackberry, Kingman, and Oatman, and on to the Colorado River near Topock.

Above: A convertible is perfect for exploring the historic route. Top right: Colorful signs abound on the "Mother Road." Lower right: Gas pumps from the time when Route 66 was a major highway.

BEST TIME TO GO

Although Route 66 is accessible year-round, spring and fall are the best times to explore roadside attractions or partake of nearby hikes.

FUN FACT

Route 66 is no longer an officially recognized U.S. highway—it hasn't appeared on maps or atlases since 1984, except for certain sections that have been designated as special historic routes.

BEST WAYS TO EXPLORE

SHOP FOR RETRO COLLECTIBLES IN OATMAN

The Leather Shop of Oatman. You can get in the spirit of the Old West with the leather jackets, Western gun holsters, and moccasins offered at this shop. ⊠ *162 Main St., Oatman* ☎ *928/768–3833.*

Main Street Emporium. This emporium offers a wide array of handcrafted items including Western-themed wall art, handwoven blankets, and cholla cactus candles. ⊠ *150 Main St., Oatman* ☎ *928/788–3298* ⊕ *www.main-st-emporium.com.*

Ore House. Browse through a nice selection of Indian jewelry, colorful gems, pottery, textiles, and Southwestern art at the Ore House. ⊠ *194 Main St., Oatman* ☎ *928/768–3839.*

SIGN HERE

One of the joys of exploring Route 66 is admiring the vintage signage along the way.

Delgadillo's Snow Cap Drive-in. In Seligman, you can stop here for a "small soda" and to view the old Coca-Cola and Burma Shave signs. In fact, the whole town is rife with old signs and cars. ⊠ *301 W. Chino Ave., Seligman* ☎ *928/422–3291.*

Hackberry General Store. At this store, which is both a shop and museum dedicated to Mother Road memorabilia, you can pose for pictures with vintage cars, kitschy signs, ancient gas pumps, and highway memorabilia while sipping a bottle of sarsaparilla. ⊠ *11255 E. AZ 66, Hackberry* ☎ *928/769–2605* ⊕ *www.hackberrygeneralstore.com.*

Wigwam Motel. In eastern Arizona, the parking lot of the Wigwam Motel—where the rooms are inside 30-foot-tall wood-and-concrete tepees—you'll see a vast collection of classic cars, from a '59 Chevy Impala to a '51 Studebaker Land Cruiser. ⊠ *811 W. Hopi Dr., Holbrook* ☎ *928/241–8413* ⊕ *www.sleepinawigwam.com.*

QUICK BITES

Oatman Hotel. This allegedly haunted landmark (there are no overight accommodations anymore) is on Oatman's main drag. Claims that Carole Lombard and Clark Gable honeymooned here have been debunked, but this quirky establishment contains a fun restaurant that's renowned for its juicy buffalo burgers and addictively filling "burro ears"—house-made potato chips served with tangy salsa. The rambling dining room has an astounding number of dollar bills plastered on its walls. ⊠ *181 Main St., Oatman* ☎ *928/768–4408.*

West Side Lilo's. An unassuming roadhouse along Route 66 in Seligman, West Side Lilo's is a must for well-prepared, hearty short-order cooking. The prodigious breakfast burritos, green-chile stew, hefty cheeseburgers, and massive cinnamon buns are a hit with regulars and tourists. One "slice" of the famous carrot cake is equal to three or four slices at most restaurants. ⊠ *415 W. AZ 66, Seligman* ☎ *928/422–5456.*

9

Updated by Andrew Collins and Michael Weatherford

Bisected by a dramatic stretch of the Colorado River, home to the longest unbroken section of old Route 66, and anchored at opposite ends by the plucky gaming town of Laughlin and the water-sports recreation hub of Lake Havasu City, northwestern Arizona and southeastern Nevada comprise a unique blend of deserts, mountains, and miles of shoreline. This sparsely populated region about midway between Las Vegas and Phoenix appeals strongly to road-trippers, who appreciate the wide-open roads and scenic byways through frozen-in-time hamlets, and boaters and kayakers enthralled with the basaltic canyons and dammed lakes in the Colorado River's path.

The defining feature of the region is the Colorado River, which affords visitors myriad opportunities to view local wildlife, Jet Ski, fish, and even rent houseboats. Since the late Pleistocene epoch when Paleo-Indians first set foot in the river that was once described as "too thick to drink and too thin to plow," the Colorado has been a blessing and a barrier. Prehistoric traders from the Pacific Coast crossed the river at Willow Beach on their way to trade shells for pelts with the Hopi Indians and other Pueblo tribes farther east. When gold was discovered in California in 1848, entrepreneurs built ferries up and down the river to accommodate the miners drawn to the area by what Cortez called "a disease of the heart for which the only cure is gold." Prosperity followed, particularly for Kingman.

Every spring the snowmelt of the Rocky Mountain watershed of the Colorado River rushed through high basaltic canyons like water through a garden hose and washed away crops and livestock. Harnessing such a powerful river required no ordinary dam. In 1935, notched into the steep and narrow confines of Black Canyon on the border separating

Arizona and Nevada, 726-foot-high Hoover Dam took control of the Colorado River and turned its power into electricity and its floodwaters into the largest man-made reservoir in the United States: Lake Mead. In 2010, the similarly dramatic Hoover Dam Bypass (also known as the Mike O'Callaghan–Pat Tillman Memorial Bridge) opened just south of the dam, vastly reducing the time it takes for automobiles to cross over the Colorado River.

NORTHWEST ARIZONA AND SOUTHEAST NEVADA PLANNER

WHEN TO GO

Unlike many destinations, the communities in northwestern Arizona don't have distinct high and low seasons. The arid climate and clear winter skies attract "snowbirds," retirees flocking south to escape the harsh northern climes. On the flip side, the hot, sunny summer months attract sports enthusiasts looking to cavort in the cool, blue waterways—despite searing temperatures that occasionally top 110°F.

Lake Havasu City plays host to hordes of college revelers during spring break in March, and Kingman fills up fast during the annual Route 66 Fun Run drive in May. Things simmer down a bit during the rest of spring as well as the fall months. Overall, expect fairly busy weekends during the summer months and sold-out rooms during sporting events and fishing tournaments.

Hualapai Mountain Park is the one part of northwestern Arizona that is high-altitude enough to get occasionally heavy snow in winter.

FESTIVALS AND EVENTS

LATE APRIL– EARLY MAY **Route 66 Fun Run.** This three-day event in early May is a 40-mile drive along the longest remaining section of the "Mother Road." ☏ *928/753–5001 ⊕ www.azrt66.com.*

SEPTEMBER **Andy Devine Days.** The festival honors the film and television actor with a parade and an impressive rodeo. ☏ *928/753–6106 ⊕ www. kingmanrodeoaz.com.*

OCTOBER **London Bridge Days.** Lake Havasu City heats up with a weeklong Renaissance festival, a parade, and British-themed contests. ☏ *928/453–8686 ⊕ www.golakehavasu.com.*

PLANNING YOUR TIME

Kingman is an ideal base for exploring Lake Mead National Recreation Area, the ghost towns of Oatman and Chloride, and the forested Hualapai Mountain Park. You'll need at least a day to enjoy water sports on Lake Mead, whereas an hour or two is enough to explore the funky little ghost towns. Visitors to Lake Havasu should spend a night or two to get a real sense of this recreation hub, although you can get a quick taste by making a day trip from Bullhead City.

Water activities dominate the scene here, but in a shorter visit you can check out London Bridge, go on a birding expedition at Havasu National Wildlife Refuge, or a foray into the quaint if touristy shops in English Village. Fans of gambling can just hop across the Colorado

River to Laughlin and spend hours or days reveling in the glitz and glitter. There are also casinos near Lake Havasu City, one on the Arizona side in Parker, an hour south, and the other easily reached across the lake in California.

■TIP→ Remember that Arizona, in the Mountain Time zone, doesn't observe Daylight Saving Time, but the neighboring states of Nevada and California, both in the Pacific Time zone, do. When scheduling interstate travel, double-check all times to avoid confusion and missed connections.

GETTING HERE AND AROUND
AIR TRAVEL
Kingman (IGM) has limited air service, with direct flights available on Great Lakes Airlines from Los Angeles. Laughlin-Bullhead City (IFP) is presently served only by charters, but has been lobbying for scheduled commercial service—stay tuned. Most visitors arriving by plane reach this part of the state after first flying into Las Vegas (two hours from Laughlin) or Phoenix (four hours from Kingman or Lake Havasu City) and renting a car.

CAR TRAVEL
Most visitors drive to this corner of the state—after all, Kingman is on the longest remaining stretch of Route 66. At first glance, the countryside can seem a bit stark and remote, but there are many surprises in this part of the world, including the strange-looking Joshua tree, the defining plant of the Mojave Desert. Historic Route 66 crosses east–west and curves north of Interstate 40, which provides the fastest path across the region. U.S. 93 is the main route for north–south travel. All of these roads are in excellent condition. On Interstate 40 high winds occasionally raise enough blowing dust to restrict visibility. In winter, ice may be present on Interstate 40 east of Kingman, as well as on sections of Route 66. Most of the county roads are improved dirt roads, but washboard sections bounce you around a bit, so take your time and drive no faster than prudence dictates. Beware that many maps and GPS devices show what appear to be viable dirt roads that may actually be unmaintained or even abandoned—stick with established routes. ■TIP→ Fuel up while you're in this part of Arizona—all grades of gasoline can be as much as $0.50 to $0.75 per gallon less in Kingman and Bullhead City than across the border in Nevada and California.

TRAIN TRAVEL
Kingman is the only city in this region served by Amtrak; the *Southwest Chief* stops in Kingman on its daily run between Los Angeles and Chicago (via Albuquerque).

RESTAURANTS
Dining in this remote corner of the state is quite casual, though also affordable. You're more likely to find a 1950s-inspired diner, a taqueria, or a family-owned café than a sophisticated, high-end eatery. For the most part you'll find home-cooked American and Southwestern favorites. The few higher-end dining options are in Lake Havasu and across the Colorado River in Laughlin's casinos, where steak houses proliferate.

HOTELS

Mid-price chain accommodations abound in Kingman and Lake Havasu, and to a lesser extent Bullhead City—though the casino resorts across the river in Laughlin are among the best values in the region. Lake Havasu City has a few somewhat upscale resorts, as does Laughlin, with its several glittery but reasonably priced gaming properties. Staying in a houseboat on Lake Havasu or Lake Mead puts a decidedly different twist on water recreation. These floating rooms with a view can be maneuvered into countless coves and inlets, allowing for peaceful solitude rarely found on the busy beaches and popular waterways. *Hotel reviews have been shortened. For full information, visit Fodors.com.*

WHAT IT COSTS				
	$	$$	$$$	$$$$
Restaurants	under $12	$12–$20	$21–$30	over $30
Hotels	under $141	$141–$175	$176–$250	over $250

Restaurant prices are the average cost of a main course at dinner or, if dinner is not served, at lunch. Hotel prices are the lowest cost of a standard double room in high season, excluding 10% tax.

NORTHWEST ARIZONA

Towns like Kingman hark back to the glory days of the old Route 66, and the ghost towns of Chloride and Oatman bear testament to the mining madness that once reigned in the region. Water-sports fans, or those who just want to laze on a houseboat, enjoy Lake Havasu, where you'll find the misplaced English icon, the London Bridge, and Lake Mead, one of the best fishing spots in the state.

9

KINGMAN

200 miles northwest of Phoenix, 149 miles west of Flagstaff via Interstate 40.

The highway past Kingman may seem desolate, and the city itself doesn't have a ton of attractions, but the mountains that surround the area offer outdoor activities in abundance, especially along the Colorado River. Water sports play a big part in the area's recreation because about 1,000 miles of freshwater shoreline lie within the county along the Colorado River and around Lakes Havasu, Mohave, and Mead—all of which are within a one-hour drive of this major stopping point for fishing and boating aficionados. And for those interested in the region's mineral wealth, the nearby "ghost" towns of Chloride and Oatman offer a glimpse of the Old West.

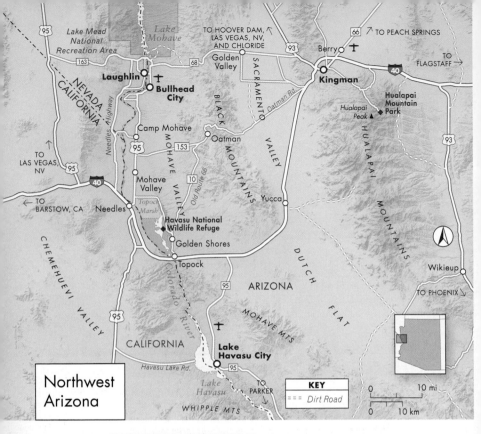

Northwest
Arizona

GETTING HERE AND AROUND

Most visitors to the region arrive by car, which is by far the best way
to explore Kingman and area sites. Additionally, Amtrak's *Southwest
Chief* stops daily in Kingman, and the town's small airport has regular
service on Great Lakes Airlines from Los Angeles.

ESSENTIALS

Transportation Contacts Kingman Cab ☎ *928/753–1222.*

EXPLORING

TOP ATTRACTIONS

Grand Canyon Ranch. Sprawling at the base of Spirit Mountain, this
historic 106,000-acre working cattle ranch about a 75-minute drive
from Kingman takes guests on an adventure to the Old West. Corriente
cattle still roam the hills and their cowboy caretakers guide horseback
tours and horse-drawn wagon rides through the rugged countryside.
Tap Duncan (a member of the Hole-in-the-Wall Gang) lived here, and
Andy Devine supposedly spent some time working here. The ranch now
offers rustic cabins, home-cooked meals, horseback riding, wagon rides,
and a helicopter tour of Grand Canyon West. Located just 14 miles
southwest of Grand Canyon West, the ranch is a popular stopping-off
point for day-trippers seeking spectacular canyon views in this remote
region. Call ahead to arrange your visit and obtain directions. Several

activities packages are available, with or without meal plans. ✉ *3750 E. Diamond Bar Ranch Rd., Meadview* ☎ *702/736–8787, 800/359–8727* ⊕ *www.grandcanyonranch.com* ⚓ *Reservations essential.*

Fodor's Choice
★
Hualapai Mountain Park. You haven't truly hiked in northwestern Arizona until you've hiked in Hualapai Mountain Park. A 15-mile drive from town up Hualapai Mountain Road leads to the park's more than 2,300 wooded acres, with 10 miles of developed and undeveloped hiking trails, picnic areas, ATV trails, rustic cabins ($50 to $135 per night), teepees ($35 per night), and RV (full hookups) and tent areas. Along the park's trail system you'll find a striking variety of plant life such as prickly pear cactus and Arizona walnut. Abundant species of birds and mammals such as the piñon jay and the Abert squirrel live here, and pristine stands of unmarred aspen mark the higher elevations. Any of the trails can be hiked in about three hours. The **Hayden Peak Trail** is a branch of a 16-mile trail system, which links with many other trails at a high elevation. The popular **Aspen Peak Trail** is shorter, 2 miles one-way. Keep in mind the terrain in the park ranges from 5,000 to 8,500 feet above sea level, and snow—sometimes heavy—is common in winter. ✉ *6250 Hualapai Mountain Rd.* ☎ *928/681–5700, 877/757–0915 for cabin reservations* ⊕ *www.mcparks.com* 🖅 *$7.*

OFF THE BEATEN PATH

Chloride. The ghost town of Chloride, Arizona's oldest silver-mining camp, takes its name from a type of silver ore mined here. During its heyday, from 1900 to 1920, some 60 mines operated in the area: silver, gold, lead, zinc, molybdenum, and even turquoise were mined here. Around 370 folks live in and around Chloride today; there's a restaurant, saloon, convenience store, two RV parks, and a smattering of old buildings.

Western artist Roy Purcell painted the large murals on the rocks on the east edge of town. Ten feet high and almost 30 feet across, they depict a goddess figure, intertwined snakes, and Eastern and Native American symbols. To reach the murals, follow signs from the east end of Highway 125 along the unpaved road—it's a slow, twisting drive best attempted with four-wheel drive. Outdoors enthusiasts can take advantage of the miles of hiking trails and explore the mineral-rich hills with excellent rockhounding opportunities.

Mock gunfights in the streets mark high noon on Saturday (only the first and third Saturdays in July and August). In late June the entire town turns out for Old Miner's Day—the biggest event of the year featuring a parade, bazaar, bake sale, and family-friendly contests (St. Patrick's Day is also a big to-do here).

The marked turnoff on Highway 125 for Chloride is about 12 miles north of Kingman on U.S. 93. For more information, contact the **Chloride Chamber of Commerce** (✉ *4940 Tennessee Ave., Chloride* ☎ *928/565–4251* ⊕ *www.chloridearizona.com*). ⚠ Give wide berth to abandoned mine entrances and shafts, which are often unstable and can cave in without warning. Experts believe there are more than 200,000 abandoned mines in Arizona, many in the rich mineral regions such as the one surrounding Chloride. ✉ *Chloride* ⊕ *www.chlorideaz.com.*

9

Northwest Arizona is full of interesting pit stops off Historic Route 66.

WORTH NOTING

Bonelli House. History buffs should check out the 1915 Bonelli House, an excellent example of Anglo-territorial architecture, featuring a facade of light-gray quarried stone and whitewashed wood accents, a very popular style in the early 1900s. It is one of more than 60 buildings in the Kingman business district listed on the National Register of Historic Places and contains period pieces including a large wall clock that was once the only clock in Kingman. ⊠ *430 E. Spring St.* ☎ *928/753–3175* ⊕ *www.mohavemuseum.org/bonel.html* ⊡ *$2* ⊙ *Weekdays 11–3.*

Kingman Railroad Museum. Developed by Kingman's active legion of railroad aficionados, the Whistler Stop Railroad Club, this museum is set inside the town's vintage 1907 Santa Fe Railroad depot and contains vintage model train layouts from the 1940s through the 1960s, plus additional memorabilia chronicling the region's rail history. ⊠ *400 E. Andy Devine Ave.* ☎ *928/718–1440* ⊕ *www.whistlestoprailroadclub. org* ⊡ *$2* ⊙ *Tues.–Sun. 9–5.*

Mohave Museum of History and Arts. This museum includes an Andy Devine room with memorabilia from Devine's Hollywood years and, incongruously, a portrait collection of every president and first lady. There's an exceptional library collection of research materials related to the region. There's also an exhibit of carved Kingman turquoise, displays on Native American art and artifacts, and a diorama depicting the mid-19th-century expedition of Lt. Edward Beale, who led his camel-cavalry unit to the area in search of a wagon road along the 35th parallel. You can follow the White Cliffs Trail from downtown to see the deep ruts cut into the desert floor by the wagons that came to

Kingman after Beale's time. ✉ *400 W. Beale St.* ☎ *928/753–3195* ⊕ *www.mohavemuseum.org* ✉ *$4, includes Historic Route 66 Museum and Bonelli House* ⊙ *Weekdays 9–5, Sat. 1–5.*

FAMILY **Powerhouse.** The Powerhouse building is a great first stop for visitors. The **Kingman Visitor Center** (☎ *928/753–6106 or 866/427–7866* ⊕ *www.gokingman.com*), in a converted 1907 electrical plant, has the usual brochures to acquaint you with local attractions. Pick up a walking-tour map, which highlights more than two-dozen historic sights, including Locomotive Park—home to the 1928 steam locomotive Engine No. 3759.

Inside the visitor center, the **Powerhouse Route 66 Museum** (☎ *928/753–9889* ✉ *$4, includes Bonelli House and Mohave Museum of History and Arts*) provides a nostalgic look at the evolution of the famous route that started as a footpath followed by prehistoric Indians and evolved into a length of pavement that reached from Chicago, Illinois, to Santa Monica, California. **Memory Lane,** also inside the Powerhouse, is a store crammed with kitschy souvenirs.

The first weekend of May each year, the Historic Route 66 Association of Arizona holds the three-day Route 66 Fun Run, a 40-mile drive that attracts classic car buffs. Admission to the Historic Route 66 Museum also includes a visit to the nearby Mohave Museum of History and Arts and the Bonelli House. ✉ *120 W. Rte. 66* ☎ *866/427–7866, 928/753–6106* ⊕ *www.gokingman.com* ⊙ *Daily 9–5.*

EN ROUTE

Traveling north from Kingman, keep an eye out for the strange-looking namesakes of the **Joshua Tree Forest** (*Yucca brevifolia*). This native of the dry Mojave Desert isn't a tree, but actually a member of the lily family. Standing as tall as 40 feet, the alien-looking plant can be recognized by its gangly limbs ending in dense clumps of dark green, bayonet-shape leaves. Mormon emigrants traveling through the area in the mid-19th century named the towering plants after the biblical figure Joshua. From February through March, Joshua trees bloom in clusters of creamy white blossoms. The trees don't branch until after they bloom, and, because they rely on perfect conditions to flower, they don't bloom every year—you're most likely to see blossoms following a rainy December or January.

ANDY DEVINE

Kingman's most famous citizen is Andy Devine (1905–77). The raspy-voiced Western character actor appeared in more than 400 films, most notably as the comic cowboy sidekick "Cookie" to Roy Rogers in 10 films. He also played "the Cheerful Soldier" in *The Red Badge of Courage* and was in several John Wayne flicks, including *The Man Who Shot Liberty Valance, Stagecoach,* and *Island in the Sky.* On the last weekend of September each year, Kingman celebrates its favorite son with the Andy Devine Days Rodeo (⊕ *www. kingmanrodeoaz.com*), parade, and community fair.

9

WHERE TO EAT AND STAY

$ **✕ El Palacio.** Set in a century-old building in the heart of Kingman's
MEXICAN historic downtown, this regional chain (there's also a location in Lake Havasu City) is a reliable choice for well-prepared Mexican favorites and Southwest specialties—and what many believe are the best chiles rellenos in the area. Other notable options include *machaca con huevos* (scrambled eggs with shredded beef and vegetables), carne asada tacos, *sopa del mar* (seafood stew with cilantro and lemon), and chicken mole poblano. A comprehensive drink menu includes a selection of Mexican beers, guava and banana margaritas, and fruity sangria. $ *Average main: $11 ⊠ 401 E. Andy Devine Ave. ☎ 928/718–0018 ⊕ www. epfamilyrestaurants.com.*

$ **✕ Mr. D'z Route 66 Diner.** This popular spot serves up road food with
AMERICAN a '50s flair for breakfast, lunch, and dinner. (Even Oprah and Gayle
FAMILY King stopped here on their cross-country adventure several years ago.) The jukebox spins favorites, and tributes to Elvis and Marilyn Monroe adorn the walls in this old-fashioned diner decked out in bright turquoise and hot pink. Expect low prices and large servings of your favorite burgers, milk shakes, and more substantial fare (chicken-fried steak, baby back ribs) at dinner, plus root beer made on the premises. $ *Average main: $10 ⊠ 105 E. Andy Devine Ave. ☎ 928/718–0066 ⊕ www.mrdzrt66diner.com.*

$ **✕ Redneck's Southern Pit BBQ.** Drop by this unassuming storefront eat-
BARBECUE ery in Kingman's historic downtown for tender, perfectly seasoned and smoked barbecue. Pulled pork sandwiches, Cajun-style andouille sausage platters, and sides of mac-and-cheese, baked beans, and chunky potato salad are favorites among the lunch crowd. At dinner, dig into hefty platters of juicy ribs or smoked bone-in chicken breasts. There's also an ice cream shop on premises—all the easier to enjoy that homemade peach cobbler à la mode. $ *Average main: $10 ⊠ 420 E. Beale St. ☎ 928/757–8227 ⊕ www.redneckssouthernpitbbq.com ⊗ Closed Sun. and Mon.*

$ **Best Western Plus–King's Inn & Suites.** Conveniently located at the inter-
HOTEL section of Interstate 40 and U.S. 93, this hotel has clean, spacious rooms and is a good base for visiting Hualapai Mountain Park, Laughlin, and the ghost towns of Chloride and Oatman. **Pros:** several restaurants are within walking distance; nicely kept rooms; hot breakfast included. **Cons:** traffic can be heard from the highway. $ *Rooms from: $89 ⊠ 2930 E. Andy Devine Ave. ☎ 928/753–6101, 800/750–6101 ⊕ www.bestwesternarizona.com ⋗ 101 rooms ‖◉‖ Breakfast.*

NIGHTLIFE

Fodor'sChoice **Cellar Door Wine Bar.** With more than 20 wines by the glass (priced with
★ a very reasonable markup) plus a noteworthy selection of imported and craft beers, this wine bar provides a sophisticated but low-key after-dark option in historic downtown Kingman. There's live music many evenings, and you can accompany your wine-sipping with a few well-prepared small plates, from cheese platters to bruschetta topped with tomatoes and mozzarella. There is also a retail wine shop here. ⊠ *414 E. Beale St. ☎ 928/753–3885 ⊕ www.the-cellar-door.com ⊗ Closed Sun.–Tues.*

EN
ROUTE
Oatman. A worthwhile if hokey stop between Kingman and Bullhead City, the ghost town of Oatman lies along old Route 66. It's a straight shot across the Mojave Desert valley for a while, but then the road narrows and winds precipitously for about 15 miles through the Black Mountains. Oatman's main street is right out of the Old West; scenes from a number of films, including *How the West Was Won,* were shot here. It still has a remote, old-time feel: many of the natives carry sidearms, and they're not acting. You can wander into one of the three saloons or visit the shabbily endearing **Oatman Hotel,** which now contains a restaurant but no longer rents overnight accommodations. Several times a day, resident actors entertain visitors with mock gunfights on the main drag.

More than 20 curio shops and eclectic boutiques line the length of Main Street. The burros that often come in from nearby hills and meander down the street, however, are the town's real draw. A couple of stores sell carrots to folks who want to feed these "wild" beasts, which at last count numbered about a dozen and which leave plenty of evidence of their visits in the form of "road apples"—so watch your step. For information about the town and its attractions, contact the **Oatman Chamber of Commerce** (☎ 928/768–6222 ⊕ *www.oatmangoldroad.org*).

LAKE HAVASU CITY

60 miles southwest of Kingman on Interstate 40 to AZ 95.

If there's an Arizona Riviera, this is it. Lake Havasu has more than 45 miles of lake shoreline—it's actually a dammed section of the Colorado River—and the area gets less than 4 inches of rain annually, which means it's almost always sunny. Spring, winter, and fall are the best times to visit; in summer, temperatures often exceed 100°F. You can rent everything from water skis to Jet Skis, small fishing boats to large houseboats. The lake area has about a dozen RV parks and campgrounds, more than 120 boat-in campsites, and hundreds of hotel and motel rooms. There are golf and tennis facilities, as well as fishing guides who'll help you find, and catch, the big ones. This city of about 53,000 has grown rapidly over the past couple of decades, and downtown has become steadily more upscale—at least compared with the rest of northwestern Arizona.

Learn about the purchase and reconstruction of London Bridge at the exhibit showcased at the Lake Havasu City Visitor Center, which is also a great place to pick up other information on area attractions.

GETTING HERE AND AROUND

You can explore downtown and the lakefront easily on foot, but most visitors arrive by car—the city lies about 25 miles south of Interstate 40 via AZ 95, and about 100 miles north of Interstate 10 via AZ 95. In town, call Amore Shuttle & Sedan Service for local taxi service. Aloha Airport Express offers service from Lake Havasu to several Laughlin casinos and then on to McCarran Airport in Las Vegas.

9

ESSENTIALS

Transportation Contacts Amore Shuttle & Sedan Service ☎ *928/854–7744* ⊕ *www.amoreshuttlelhc.com.* **Aloha Airport Express** ☎ *928/854–5253, 888/948–3427* ⊕ *www.azaloha.com.*

Visitor Information Lake Havasu City Visitor Center ✉ *422 English Village* ☎ *928/453–3444, 800/242–8278* ⊕ *www.golakehavasu.com.*

EXPLORING

TOP ATTRACTIONS

FodorśChoice
★
Havasu National Wildlife Refuge. Situated between Needles and Lake Havasu City, this spectacular 37,515-acre refuge is home to wintering Canada geese and other waterfowl, such as the snowy egret and the great blue heron. More than 315 species have been observed resting and nesting here. ✉ *Off Oatman-Topock Hwy., Exit 1 off I–40 at state border, then follow signs to refuge entrance, Topock* ☎ *760/326–3853* ⊕ *www.fws.gov/refuge/Havasu.*

FodorśChoice
★
London Bridge. Remember the old nursery rhyme "London Bridge Is Falling Down"? Well, it was. In 1968, after about 150 years of constant use, the 294-foot-long landmark was sinking into the Thames. When Lake Havasu City founder Robert McCullough heard about this predicament, he set about buying London Bridge, having it disassembled, shipped more than 5,000 miles to northwestern Arizona, and rebuilt, stone by stone. The bridge was reconstructed on mounds of sand and took three years to complete. When it was finished, a mile-long channel was dredged under the bridge and water was diverted from Lake Havasu through the Bridgewater Channel. Today, the entire city is centered on this unusual attraction. Walking tours are offered daily at 11 October through April; the cost is $5 per person, and reservations are required. These guided stroll leave from the east base of the bridge, where you'll find a colorful re-creation of an **English Village** that houses a few curio shops and restaurants and offers good views of the channel of cool blue water flowing under London Bridge. On the west side, you'll find a handful of more urbane restaurants as well as the hip **Heat Hotel.** ✉ *1550 London Bridge Rd.* ☎ *928/855–5655 for tours.*

WORTH NOTING

Bill Williams River National Wildlife Refuge. This 6,055-acre desert oasis contains the largest surviving cottonwood-willow woodland in the region. The refuge is a favorite byway of neotropical migratory birds such as the flashy vermilion flycatcher and the brilliant summer tanager. ✉ *60911 AZ 95, between mileposts 160 and 161, 23 miles south of Lake Havasu City* ☎ *928/667–4144* ⊕ *www.fws.gov/refuge/bill_williams_river.*

Lake Havasu Museum of History. This museum takes an in-depth look at the history of the region with exhibits on the Chemehuevi Indians, London Bridge, Parker Dam, the mining industry, and historic steamboat operation. ✉ *320 London Bridge Rd.* ☎ *928/854–4938* ⊕ *www. havasumuseum.com* ▨ *$5* ⊙ *Tues.–Sat. 10–4.*

OFF THE BEATEN PATH

'Ahakhav Tribal Preserve. The 1,253-acre preserve, which includes a 3½-acre park and 250 acres of aquatic habitat, is on the Colorado Indian Tribes Reservation and is a top spot in the area for bird-watching and hiking. Some 350 species of migratory and native birds live around the region or visit on their annual migrations. The best bird-watching is along the shoreline of the backwater area branching off the Colorado River. The 4.6-mile hiking trail has exercise stations along the way, and a trail extension will lead you to the tribal historical museum and gift shop. From AZ 95 in Parker, which is at the southern end of Lake Havasu, head west on Mohave Road for about 2 miles. When you reach the "Parker Indian Rodeo Association" sign, continue ½ mile farther and turn left at the "Tribal Preserve" sign at Rodeo Road. ✉ *Rodeo Rd., off of Mohave Rd. and AZ 95, Parker* ☎ *928/669–2664* 🌐 *www.crit-nsn.gov/crit_contents/tourism* 🕒 *Daily dawn–dusk.*

WHERE TO EAT

$$$ AMERICAN Fodor's Choice ★

🍴 **Cha-Bones.** Fiber-optic lighting, mod hanging lamps, and water sculptures create a contemporary vibe at this hip, elegant restaurant a short drive north of London Bridge. Superbly prepared steaks and seafood are the key draw, from 24-ounce porterhouse cuts to cioppino in a saffron-tomato broth, but also consider the barbecue ribs and linguine with chicken and poblano chiles. There's also an extensive tapas list, including yam fries with honey–key lime sauce and seared ahi, and a great selection of wine and cocktails. [$] *Average main: $22* ✉ *112 London Bridge Rd.* ☎ *928/854–5554* 🌐 *www.chabones.com.*

$ MEXICAN

🍴 **Chico's Tacos.** This always-hopping taqueria in the nondescript Basha's Shopping Center serves reliably good Mexican food. It's not fancy, but this clean and comfortable short-order joint turns out tasty tacos, enchiladas, flautas, burritos, and fajitas served with chicken, grilled fish, carne asada, and other meat and veggie options. Six different salsas at the salsa bar add a bit of spice to the mix. [$] *Average main: $6* ✉ *1641 N. McCulloch Blvd.* ☎ *928/680–7010.*

$$ MODERN AMERICAN Fodor's Choice ★

🍴 **College Street Brewhouse.** Although it's in a somewhat industrial area a short drive north of downtown, this lively, high-ceilinged restaurant and microbrewery with an enormous patio enjoys nice views of the lake. The craft beers, especially the crisp but balanced IPA and refreshing, unfiltered American wheat, are reason alone to stop by, but the kitchen also turns out consistently tasty, artfully presented comfort food that pairs well with the brews. Worthy starters include lump crab–stuffed fried avocados and green-chile mac-and-cheese. Entrées include hefty sandwiches (note the first-rate pastrami burger topped with cabbage chow-chow and Swiss cheese), pizzas, and several Cajun-influenced dishes, with scallop-and-shrimp jambalaya topping the list. [$] *Average main: $14* ✉ *1940 College Dr.* ☎ *928/854–2739* 🌐 *www.collegestreetbrewhouseandpub.com.*

$$ AMERICAN

🍴 **Juicy's River Café.** This downtown locals' favorite moved into a cheerful new space in 2014 and remains popular—it fills up fast, especially for breakfast. The chicken-fried steak with biscuits and eggs is legendary. The varied menu of lunch and dinner standards includes burgers with barbecue sauce, cheddar, and smoked bacon; meat loaf; pot roast Stroganoff; and homemade soups and desserts. Great service is paired with reasonable prices. [$] *Average main: $13* ✉ *42 S. Smoketree Ave.* ☎ *928/855–8429, 877/584–2970* 🌐 *www.juicysrivercafe.com* 🕒 *No dinner Sun. mid-Sept–May.; no dinner Sat.–Thurs. June–mid-Sept.*

$$ ITALIAN 🍴 **La Vita Dolce.** This informal, bustling, family-run restaurant with indoor and outdoor seating serves reliably tasty, straightforward Italian fare, from classic pastas and grills—spaghetti and meatballs, portobello-mushroom ravioli, veal piccata—and a small but creative selection of thin-crust pizzas. The Maui Waui with capicola ham, sweet pineapple, and marinara sauce is a local favorite. Appetizers are half off and beer and wine are discounted during the daily happy hour (3–6 pm). [$] *Average main: $15* ✉ *231 Swanson Ave.* ☎ *928/208–4138.*

$$$ AMERICAN 🍴 **Shugrue's.** This attractive space set on a bluff overlooking London Bridge has one of the best wine lists in town, plus consistently well-prepared steaks, seafood, and other traditional American and international dishes. Highlights include flat bread with Havarti cheese, portobello mushrooms, and olive-tomato tapenade for a starter and baked Dijon-garlic-crusted halibut with sea scallops and tomato concasse as a main course. Be sure to request a table with a bridge view. [$] *Average main: $24* ✉ *1425 McCulloch Blvd.* ☎ *928/453–1400* 🌐 *www.shugrues.com.*

WHERE TO STAY

$ RESORT 🏨 **Havasu Springs Resort.** On a low peninsula reaching into Lake Havasu, this moderately priced resort 15 miles north of Parker comprises four motel buildings, each with different attributes and many with expansive views of the water or desert. **Pros:** comprehensive dining and recreation; affordable; nice lakeside beachfront. **Cons:** the most economical rooms have dated furnishings; RV traffic; 30-minute drive from Lake Havasu City. [$] *Rooms from: $75* ✉ *2581 AZ 95, Parker* ☎ *928/667–3361* 🌐 *www.havasusprings.com* 🛏 *38 rooms, 4 suites, 3 apartments* 🍽 *No meals.*

$$ HOTEL Fodor's Choice ★ 🏨 **Heat Hotel.** The hip rooms at this sleek, angular-looking boutique hotel on the west side of London Bridge capture the see-and-be-seen playfulness of Vegas, making it a hit with well-heeled, stylish visitors. **Pros:** stylish and posh décor; steps from London Bridge and many restaurants; swanky bar and cabana area. **Cons:** might be a bit too trendy and modern for some tastes; bar and pool area can be a scene on weekends and during spring break; no restaurant on site. [$] *Rooms from: $169* ✉ *1420 McCulloch Blvd.* ☎ *928/854–2833, 888/898–4328* 🌐 *www.heathotel.com* 🛏 *17 rooms, 8 suites* 🍽 *No meals.*

$$ RESORT 🏨 **London Bridge Resort.** If you want to be close to the bridge, this hotel is a dependable choice with plenty to see and do on site. **Pros:** great views of London Bridge; suites come with sleeper sofas for extra guests; nightlife and business center. **Cons:** limited availability during the busy summer months; sales pressure from the resort's time-share options; rooms need renovating. [$] *Rooms from: $139* ✉ *1477 Queen's Bay* ☎ *866/331–9231, 928/855–0888* 🌐 *www.londonbridgeresort.com* 🛏 *4 studios, 72 1-bedroom suites, 46 2-bedroom suites* 🍽 *No meals.*

$$ RESORT FAMILY 🏨 **The Nautical Beachfront Resort.** This expansive waterfront resort on a scenic stretch of Thompson Bay is a favorite choice of families and sports enthusiasts. **Pros:** lots of recreation amenities on site; set on a beautiful and relatively quiet section of lakefront; spacious rooms.

On Lake Havasu, boaters combine recreation with a bit of English history as they pass under the London Bridge.

Cons: $20 daily resort fee; 20-minute walk to restaurants and shops at London Bridge. [$] *Rooms from: $169* ✉ *1000 McCulloch Blvd. N* ☎ *928/855–2141, 800/892–2141* 🌐 *www.nauticalinn.com* 🛏 *138 suites* 🍴 *No meals.*

9

NIGHTLIFE

Clubbing and barhopping are increasingly popular pastimes among visitors to Lake Havasu. Most of the top venues in town are located in hotels and restaurants, including Heat Hotel, College Street Brewhouse, and Cha-Bones. ⇨ *See Where to Eat and Where to Stay in Lake Havasu City for reviews.*

BlueWater Resort & Casino. A big nightlife draw around Lake Havasu is BlueWater Casino, 40 miles south in the town of Parker. The gaming area comprises 475 slot machines, plus blackjack, poker, and bingo, and it adjoins a full-service resort with a concert hall, bars, a movie theater, restaurants, a 164-slip marina, and a 200-room hotel. ✉ *11300 Resort Dr., Parker* ☎ *928/669–7777, 888/243–3360* 🌐 *www.bluewaterfun.com.*

Fodor's Choice ★ **Desert Bar.** Along a remote mining road in the Buckskin Mountains roughly midway between Lake Havasu City and Parker, the quirky Desert Bar, aka the Nellie E. Saloon, is one of the region's most fabled curiosities. It's only open on weekends and occasional holidays (from noon until sunset), from Labor Day through Memorial Day. This cash-only, solar-powered entertainment compound is a work in progress, comprising indoor and outdoor bars, a stage with live music throughout the day, a horseshoe pit, a covered footbridge, and a nondenominational church that's the occasional site of weddings. ✉ *Cienega Springs Rd.,* *off AZ 95, 5 miles south of Lake Havasu City (follow signs)* ⊕ *www.thedesertbar.com.*

Havasu Landing Resort and Casino. Just across the Colorado River from Lake Havasu, this small but lively casino and bar, which has live music most weekends, has become extremely popular thanks to the new ferry service that zooms passengers over from London Bridge between 6:45 am and midnight (until 2 am on Friday and Saturday). The cost is $2 round-trip per passenger, and the scenic ferry ride takes 17 minutes. You can also tie up your own boat at Havasua Landing's marina. The casino has 245 slots, plus blackjack and three-card poker tables. ⊠ *1 Main St., Havasu Lake, California* ☎ *760/858–4593, 800/307–3610* ⊕ *www.havasulanding.com.*

> ### LODGING ALTERNATIVE: HOUSEBOATS
>
> What houseboats lack in speed and maneuverability they make up for in comfort and shade. **Lake Havasu Houseboats** has some of the most luxurious boats on the lake and the crew makes certain that boaters get the best instruction and tips for their travel into cool blue waters. Boats sleep 10 or more and have sundecks, waterslides, kitchens, and plenty of other amenities. Expect to pay $850 to $2,600 per night during the summer high season—the longer you rent, the less costly it is per day. ⊠ *1000 McCulloch Blvd., Lake Havasu City* ☎ *800/843–9218* ⊕ *www.lakehavasuhouseboating.com*

SPORTS AND THE OUTDOORS

There's no white water on the Colorado River below Hoover Dam. Instead, the river and its lakes offer many opportunities to explore the gorges and marshes that line the shores. If you prefer to do it yourself, look into the canoe and kayak rentals available on Lakes Mead, Mohave, and Havasu. Raft adventures will take you through the Topock Gorge near Lake Havasu, or you can take a trip upriver from Willow Beach 12 miles to the base of Hoover Dam. Along the way, chances are good you'll see bighorn sheep moving along the steep basaltic cliffs, and depending on the season, you can view hundreds of different types of migrating birds.

BOAT TOURS

BlueWater Jet Boat Tours. From September through May, BlueWater Jet Boat Tours takes guests on a 2½-hour narrated trip up the Colorado River to Topock Gorge in the climate-controlled *Starship 2010.* Other tours run to Bill Williams Wildlife Refuge (3 hours) and around the lake's famed lighthouses (1½ hours). ⊠ *501 English Village* ☎ *928/855–7171* ⊕ *www.coloradoriverjetboattours.com* ⊡ *From $24* ☉ *Closed June–Aug.*

CANOEING

Jerkwater Canoe Co. Jerkwater offers three different one-day canoe trips, including exploratory excursions in Topock Gorge and Black Canyon. Multiday paddling trips along several scenic stretches of the Colorado River are also available. ⊠ *13003 Powell Lake Rd., Topock* ☎ *928/768–7753, 800/421–7803* ⊕ *www.jerkwatercanoe.com* ⊡ *From $41.*

Western Arizona Canoe & Kayak Outfitter (WACKO). This outfitter gets the outdoor adventure going with paddling trips of Topock Gorge, Lake Havasu, and Bill Williams Wildlife Refuge. ☎ *928/855–6414, 888/881–5038* ⊕ *www.azwacko.com* ✉ *From $25.*

KAYAKING

FAMILY **Desert River Outfitters.** Kayakers can choose between Davis Dam to Rotary Park half-day paddling trips along the Colorado River Heritage Trail ($35 per person) and all-day trips from Topock Gorge to the upper reaches of Lake Havasu ($50 per person). The full-day trips are for intermediate kayakers and are available only from mid-October to mid-April; the others are suitable for beginners and can be undertaken year-round. Some excursions are offered in the evening, by moonlight. ✉ *1034 AZ 95, Bullhead City* ☎ *888/529–2533* ⊕ *www. desertriveroutfitters.com* ✉ *From $35.*

GOLF

The Courses at London Bridge Golf Club. You can play on two beautifully laid-out 18-hole courses at this golf club set along the shore of Lake Havasu, with stunning views of the mountains. The Nassau course runs a bit shorter than Olde London, but both are similarly challenging, with tight fairways and demanding, relatively small greens on the former and ample bunkers and water hazards on the latter. ✉ *2400 Clubhouse Dr.* ☎ *928/855–2719* ⊕ *www.londonbridgegc.com* ✉ *$65* ⚲ *Nassau Course: 18 holes, 6140 yds, par 72. Olde London Course: 18 holes, 6466 yds, par 71.*

WATER SPORTS

When construction of Parker Dam was completed in 1938, the reservoir it created to supply water to Southern California and Arizona became Lake Havasu. The lake is a 45-mile-long playground for water sports of all kinds. Whether it's waterskiing, jet skiing, stand-up paddling, powerboating, houseboating, swimming, fishing, or you name it, if water is required, it's happening on Lake Havasu.

With a boat, you have more options: you can find a quiet, secluded cove or beach to swim or fish. If you have a need for speed, you can plane up and down the lake with or without a skier in tow.

Cattail Cove State Park. On the eastern shore of the lake 15 miles south of Lake Havasu City is 2,000-acre Cattail Cove State Park, a popular spot for fishing and boating (you can rent boats at the marina). There are 61 first-come, first-served campsites ($15–$26) with access to electricity and water, and public restrooms with showers. ✉ *AZ 95, 15 miles south of Lake Havasu* ☎ *928/855–1223* ⊕ *www.pr.state.az.us/parks/CACO* ✉ *$10/vehicle on weekdays, $15 on weekends* ☉ *Sunrise–10 pm.*

Lake Havasu State Park. Near the London Bridge, Lake Havasu State Park has an interpretive nature garden and a level 1¾-mile trail that's perfect for watching the sunset. With three boat ramps, extensive docking, electrical hookups, and about 45 first-come, first-served campsites ($30–$35 daily, including day-use fee), it's an extremely popular spot in summer. ✉ *699 London Bridge Rd.* ☎ *928/855–2784* ⊕ *www. pr.state.az.us/parks/LAHA* ✉ *$10/vehicle on weekdays, $15 on weekends* ☉ *Sunrise–10 pm.*

EQUIPMENT
AND RENTALS

If you don't have the equipment or the vessel necessary to enjoy your water sport, you can rent one from a number of reputable merchants.

Arizona WaterSports. You can rent Jet Skis, jet boats, ski boats, and pontoon boats here, as well as a variety of other water toys, from wakeboards to inner tubes, and off-road vehicle rentals. The company also has branches down at Parker Dam and at Blue Water Resort & Casino, in Parker. ⊠ *655 Kiowa Ave.* ☎ *928/453–5558, 800/393–5558* ⊕ *www.arizonawatersports.com.*

AZ Built Sports. In addition to renting motorboats, outrigger canoes, and kayaks—not to mention a wide variety of bikes—AZ Built Sports offers stand-up paddleboards, which have become an extremely popular way to play and exercise on the lake. ⊠ *191 Swanson Ave.* ☎ *928/505–8669* ⊕ *www.azbuiltsports.com.*

Sand Point Marina and RV Park. You can rent everything from Jet Skis to pontoon boats, by the day or by the week, at this park, which has a 104-slip marina, convenience store, and café. ⊠ *7952 S. Sandpoint Rd.* ☎ *928/855–0549* ⊕ *www.sandpointresort.com.*

SOUTHEAST NEVADA

Laughlin, Nevada, and Bullhead City, Arizona, are separated by a unique state line: the Colorado River. It's an interesting juxtaposition of cities, with the casino lights of Laughlin sparkling across the river from Bullhead City. Sixty miles upstream, just southeast of Las Vegas, Boulder City is prim, languid, and full of historic neighborhoods, small businesses, parks, greenbelts—and not a single casino. Over the hill from town, enormous Hoover Dam blocks the Colorado River as it enters Black Canyon. Backed up behind the dam is incongruous, deep-blue Lake Mead, the focal point of water-based recreation for southern Nevada and northwestern Arizona and the major water supplier to seven Southwest states. The lake is ringed by miles of rugged desert country. Less than half a mile downstream from the Hoover Dam and Lake Mead, another engineering marvel, a bridge spanning the river canyon and linking northwestern Arizona to southeastern Nevada, opened in fall 2010. It's dramatically reduced traffic across dam.

BULLHEAD CITY, ARIZONA, AND LAUGHLIN, NEVADA

35 miles west of Kingman via U.S. 93 to AZ 68.

Laughlin, Nevada, is separated from Arizona by the Colorado River. Its founder, Don Laughlin, bought an eight-room motel here in 1964 and basically built the town from scratch. By the early 1980s Laughlin's Riverside Hotel-Casino was drawing gamblers and river rats from northwestern Arizona, southeastern California, and even southern Nevada, and his success attracted other casino operators. Today Laughlin is the state's third major resort area, attracting more than 3 million visitors annually. The city fills up, especially in winter, with both retired travelers who spend at least part of winter in Arizona and a younger resort-loving crowd. The big picture windows overlooking the Colorado River

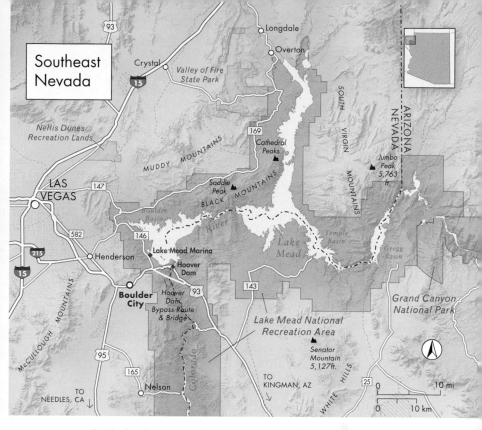

Southeast Nevada

lend a bright, airy, and open feeling unique to Laughlin casinos. Take a stroll along the river walk, then make the return trip by water taxi ($4 one-way, $20 all day). Boating, using Jet Skis, fishing, and plain old wading are other options for enjoying the water.

TIMING

The state of Nevada is in the Pacific Time zone, while Arizona is in the Mountain Time zone. Arizona doesn't observe Daylight Saving Time, however. As a result, in summer Nevada and Arizona observe the same hours.

GETTING HERE AND AROUND

To get to Laughlin from Kingman by car, follow U.S. 93 north for 3 miles, and then head west on AZ 68 for about 30 miles.

Mills Tours, River City Shuttle, and Tri State Shuttle offer regular service from McCarran International Airport to Laughlin/Bullhead City. Reservations for all shuttle services are required.

Lucky Cab & Limo Company of Nevada services Laughlin and Bullhead City. For another approach in getting from casino to casino in Laughlin, hop aboard a water taxi with River Passage. Fares can be purchased at the casino dock ticket booths.

EXPLORING

FAMILY **Colorado River Museum.** Across the Laughlin Bridge, ¼ mile to the north on the Arizona side of the river, the Colorado River Museum displays the rich past of the tristate region where Nevada, Arizona, and California converge. Earnest volunteers guide you through the haphazard array of artifacts from the Mojave Indian tribe and the gold rush era in nearby Oatman. There are also exhibits on the building of Davis Dam, 18th-century explorer Fr. Francisco Garces and the experimental use of camels in the area by a pre–Civil War U.S. Army. You can also kick back in the museum's video room and watch films of historical highlights. ✉ *2201 AZ 68, Bullhead City, Arizona* ☎ *928/754–3399* 🎟 *$2* 🕒 *Sept.–June, Tues.–Sat. 10–4.*

FAMILY **Searchlight Historic Museum.** Searchlight was once the biggest boomtown in southern Nevada, and some of its rich mining and railroad history is now compressed into a one-room museum inside the hamlet's community center. There is recorded narration, a recreated assayer's office, outdoor mining exhibit, and a display devoted to Clara Bow, the silent-screen star who lived near Searchlight after marrying screen cowboy Rex Bell. ✉ *200 Michael Wendell Way, Searchlight* ✥ *On the way to Laughlin from Las Vegas on U.S. 95, turn off at Cottonwood Cove Road, drive almost a mile to the end of town, and turn left on Michael Wendell Way* ☎ *702/297–1682* 🌐 *www.searchlighthistoricmuseum.org* 🎟 *Free* 🕒 *Weekdays 9–5, Sat. 9–1.*

WHERE TO EAT

$$$$ STEAKHOUSE 🍴 **The Range Steakhouse.** This counterpart to the Harrah's Las Vegas steakhouse of the same name is Laughlin's most prestigious dining room. Some menu items change seasonally to augment standards such as seafood pasta, ahi tuna, lamb chops, and a surf-and-turf platter. Riverfront views and an extensive wine list add to the elegant experience. [$] *Average main: $40* ✉ *Harrah's, 2900 S. Casino Dr.* ☎ *702/967–7999* 🌐 *www.harrahslaughlin.com* 🕒 *No lunch.*

$$$ STEAKHOUSE 🍴 **Saltgrass Steakhouse.** This kicked-back, Texas-style steakhouse serves up certified Angus beef, barbecued ribs, chicken, and seafood, rounded out by homemade soups, bread, and a generous selection of sides. [$] *Average main: $25* ✉ *Golden Nugget, 2300 S. Casino Dr.* ☎ *702/298–7153* 🌐 *www.saltgrass.com* 🕒 *No lunch weekdays.*

WHERE TO STAY

$ RESORT 🏨 **Edgewater Hotel Casino.** This 26-story hotel has a large casino with more than 1,000 machines and three restaurants, including a buffet that serves up weekend brunches and the Hickory Pit Steakhouse. **Pros:** central location on the river walk; mountain and river views; motorized scooters available for rental. **Cons:** Fees for Wi-Fi ($9.99 for 24 hours) and refrigerators ($10 per night); design doesn't fully exploit riverfront location; swimming pool gets crowded. [$] *Rooms from: $60* ✉ *2020 S. Casino Dr.* ☎ *702/298–2453, 800/677–4837* 🌐 *www.edgewater-casino.com* 🛏 *1,356 rooms* 🍽 *No meals.*

$ RESORT 🏨 **Golden Nugget Laughlin.** Although its casino is smaller than some of its Laughlin neighbors, this resort has a more upscale feel and is home to two chain restaurants as well as an exceptional steakhouse. **Pros:**

local nightlife scene at Gold Diggers; attached parking garage. **Cons:** limited room availability; the only no-smoking area is a detached area in the slot section of the casino. [$] *Rooms from: $65* ✉ *2300 S. Casino Dr.* ☎ *702/298–7111, 800/950–7700* 🌐 *www.goldennugget.com* 🛏 *300 rooms* 🍴 *No meals.*

$ RESORT 🏨 **Harrah's.** This is the classiest joint in Laughlin: it comes with a private sand beach and two casinos (one is no-smoking). **Pros:** separate family and adult towers and pools; smoking and no-smoking casinos; air-charter flights from all over the United States directly to resort for player card members. **Cons:** pools fill up fast; long lines for guest services; incidental fees for Wi-Fi ($10.95 for 24 hours). [$] *Rooms from: $60* ✉ *2900 S. Casino Dr.* ☎ *702/298–4600, 800/427–7247* 🌐 *www.harrahslaughlin.com* 🛏 *1,505 rooms* 🍴 *No meals.*

BOULDER CITY

78 miles north of Laughlin on NV 163 and U.S. 95, 76 miles northwest of Kingman on U.S. 93.

In the early 1930s Boulder City was built by the federal government to house 5,000 construction workers on the Hoover Dam project. A strict moral code was enforced to ensure timely completion of the dam, and to this day the model city is the only community in Nevada in which gambling is illegal. (Note that the two casinos at either end of Boulder City are just outside the city limits.) After the dam was completed, the town shrank but was kept alive by the management and maintenance crews of the dam and Lake Mead. Today it's a vibrant little Southwestern town.

GETTING HERE AND AROUND

It takes about 75 minutes via U.S. 93 to get from Kingman to Boulder City.

ESSENTIALS

Contacts **Boulder City Chamber of Commerce** ✉ *465 Nevada Way* ☎ *702/293–2034* 🌐 *www.bouldercitychamberofcommerce.com* 🕒 *Weekdays 9–5.*

9

EXPLORING

Boulder Dam Hotel. Be sure to stop at the Dutch Colonial style Boulder Dam Hotel, built in 1933. On the National Register of Historic Places, the 20-room bed-and-breakfast once was a favorite getaway for notables, including the man who became Pope Pius XII and actors Will Rogers, Bette Davis, and Shirley Temple. It's still a point of pride for Boulder City and the heart of Downtown. The guest rooms have been remodeled to stay competitive but retain a historic feel. ✉ *1305 Arizona St.* ☎ *702/293–3510* 🌐 *www.boulderdamhotel.com.*

Boulder City/Hoover Dam Museum. For its size this small museum inside the Boulder Dam Hotel is well done. It includes hands-on exhibits, oral histories, artifacts from the building of Hoover Dam, and a glimpse at what it was like for Great Depression-era families to pull up roots and settle in the rock and dust of the harsh Mojave Desert. ✉ *1305 Arizona St.* ☎ *702/294–1988* 🌐 *www.bcmha.org* 🎟 *$2* 🕒 *Mon.–Sat. 10–5.*

HOOVER DAM

8 miles northeast of Boulder City, 67 miles northwest of Kingman via U.S. 93.

GETTING HERE AND AROUND

Hoover Dam is about a 75-minute drive from Kingman via U.S. 93; it's about 15 minutes from Boulder City.

EXPLORING

FAMILY

Fodor$Choice

★

Hoover Dam. In 1928 Congress authorized $175 million for construction of a dam on the Colorado River to control destructive floods, provide a steady water supply to seven Colorado River Basin states, and generate electricity. Considered one of the seven wonders of the industrial world, art deco Hoover Dam is 726 feet high (the equivalent of a 70-story building) and 660 feet thick (more than the length of two football fields) at the base. Construction required 4.4 million cubic yards of concrete— enough to build a two-lane highway from San Francisco to New York. Originally referred to as Boulder Dam, the structure was later officially named Hoover Dam in recognition of President Herbert Hoover's role in the project. Look for artist Oskar Hansen's plaza sculptures, which include the 30-foot-tall *Winged Figures of the Republic* (the statues and terrazzo floor patterns were copied at the new Smith Center for the Performing Arts in Downtown Las Vegas).

The tour itself is a tradition that dates back to 1937, and you can still see the old box office on top of the dam. But now the ticketed tours originate in the modern visitor center, with two choices of tour. The cheaper, most popular one is the **Powerplant Tour**, which starts every 15 minutes or so. It's a half-hour, guided tour that includes a short film and then a 537-foot elevator ride to two points of interest: a less-than-overwhelming view of a diversion tunnel, and the more impressive eight-story room housing still-functional power generators. Self-paced exhibits follow the guided portion, with good interactive museum exhibits and a great indoor/outdoor patio view of the dam from the river side. The more extensive **Hoover Dam Tour** includes everything on the Powerplant Tour but limits the group size to 20 and spends more time inside the dam, including a peek through the air vents. Tours run from 9 to 5 in the winter and 9 to 6 in the summer. Visitors for both tours submit to security screening comparable to that of an airport. January and February are the slowest months, and mornings generally are less busy. The top of the dam is open to pedestrians and vehicles, but you have to remain in your vehicle after sundown. The new bypass bridge is the way to and from Arizona. Those willing to pass a security checkpoint (with inspections at the discretion of officers) can still drive over the dam for sightseeing, but cannot continue into Arizona; you have to turn around and come back after the road dead-ends at a scenic lookout (with a snack bar and store) on the Arizona side. ■TIP→ The dam's High Scaler Café is fine for a cold drink or an ice-cream cone, and the outdoor café tables even have misters. But you can improve upon the $9 burger by having lunch in Boulder City instead. ⊠ U.S. 93, east of Boulder City ☎ 702/494–2517, 866/730–9097 ⊕ www.usbr.gov/lc/ hooverdam ⊠ Powerplant Tour $15, Hoover Dam Tour $30, visitor *center only $10; garage parking $10 (free parking on Arizona-side surface lots) ⊙ Daily 9–5 ☞ Security, road, and Hoover Dam crossing info: 888/248–1259.*

SPORTS AND THE OUTDOORS
RAFTING

Black Canyon, just below Hoover Dam, is the place for river running near Las Vegas. You can launch a raft here on the Colorado River year-round. On the Arizona side, the 11-mile run to Willow Beach, with its vertical canyon walls, bighorn sheep on the slopes, and feeder streams and waterfalls coming off the bluffs, is reminiscent of rafting the Grand Canyon. The water flows at roughly 5 miles per hour, but some rapids, eddies, and whirlpools can cause difficulties, as can headwinds, especially for inexperienced rafters.

If you want to go paddling in Black Canyon on your own, you need to make mandatory arrangements with one of the registered outfitters. They provide permits ($12) and the National Park Service entrance fee ($5) as well as launch and retrieval services (the road in and out is in a security zone for the dam). You can get a list of outfitters at ☎ 702/294–1414, or go to the paddle-craft and rafting-tours section on the Bureau of Land Management's website (⊕ *www.usbr.gov/lc/hooverdam*).

Black Canyon/Willow Beach River Adventures. If you're interested in seeing the canyon on large motor-assisted rafts, Black Canyon/Willow Beach River Adventures is a group excursion launching most mornings from the Hoover Dam Lodge (formerly Hacienda Casino and Hotel). You only get wet if you want to, and a picnic lunch on the river bank is included. The trip is $92 for adults, or $35 for a half-hour "post card" tour. ✉ *Depart from Hacienda Casino and Hotel, U.S. 93, Boulder City* ☎ *800/455–3490* ⊕ *www.blackcanyonadventures.com.*

LAKE MEAD

About 4 miles from Hoover Dam on U.S. 93, 67 miles northwest of Kingman.

GETTING HERE AND AROUND

From Hoover Dam, travel west on U.S. 93 to the intersection with Lakeshore Drive to reach Alan Bible Visitors Center, which reopened in early 2013 with a new welcome film and exhibits after two years and nearly $3 million in renovations. It's open Wednesday to Sunday 9 to 4:30. Call ☎ 702/293–8990 for more information.

ESSENTIALS

Alan Bible Visitors Center. The information center for Lake Mead had a 2013 facelift, complete with a new hi-def film about the lake narrated by Stockard Channing. It's just past the Lake Mead turn-off from AZ 93, before you get to the pay booth for park entry. (A second visitor center in downtown Boulder City, at 601 Nevada Way, is open weekdays, so there's one open every day of the week.) ☎ 702/293–8990 ⊕ *www.nps.gov/lake* ⊙ *Wed.–Sun. 9–4:30.*

EXPLORING

Lake Mead. Lake Mead, which is actually the Colorado River backed up behind Hoover Dam, is the nation's largest man-made reservoir: it covers 225 square miles, is 110 miles long, and has an irregular shoreline that extends for 550 miles. You can get information about the lake's history, ecology, recreational opportunities, and the accommodations available along its shore at the Alan Bible Visitors Center. People come to Lake Mead primarily for boating, but a few areas or shoreline are cultivated for swimming: **Boulder Beach** is the closest to Las Vegas, only a mile or so from the visitor center.

Angling and house boating are favorite pastimes; marinas strung along the Nevada shore rent houseboats, personal watercraft, and ski boats. At least 1 million fish are harvested from the lake every year including the popular striped and largemouth bass. It's stocked with rainbow trout on a weekly basis from late October to March. You can fish here 24 hours a day, year-round (except for posted closings). You must have a fishing license from either Nevada or Arizona (details are on the National Park Service website), and if you plan to catch and keep trout, a separate trout stamp is required. Willow Beach is a favorite for anglers looking to catch rainbow trout; Cathedral Cove and Katherine are good for bass fishing. Divers can explore the murk beneath, including the remains of a B-29 Superfortress, which crashed into the Overton Arm of the lake in 1948. Other activities abound, including waterskiing, sailboarding, canoeing, kayaking, and snorkeling. ⊠ *601 Nevada Way, Boulder City* ☎ *702/293–8990* ⊕ *www.nps.gov/lake* ⊠ *$10 per vehicle, good for 7 days; lake-use fees $16 1st vessel, good for 7 days. Annual pass is $30 per vehicle or per vessel.*

SPORTS AND THE OUTDOORS

BOATING

Lake Mead Marina. Lake Mead Marina, at Hemenway Harbor near Hoover Dam, has a general store, rentals, and a floating restaurant, the Harbor House Cafe. It's the closest marina to the public beach, Boulder Beach. The marina was moved in 2008 due to dropping water levels but has stayed put since. Boat rentals and personal watercraft are available through the **Las Vegas Boat Harbor** (☎ *702/293–1191 or 877/765–3745*). ⊠ *490 Horsepower Cove Rd., Boulder City* ☎ *702/293–1191* ⊕ *www.boatinglakemead.com.*

CRUISES

Lake Mead Cruises. At Lake Mead Cruises you can board the 300-passenger *Desert Princess,* an authentic Mississippi-style paddle wheeler that plies a portion of the lake, offering views of Hoover Dam and ancient rock formations such as an extinct volcano called Fortification Hill; brunch and dinner cruises are available seasonally. Ninety-minute sightseeing cruises occur year-round. ⊠ *Hemenway Boat Harbor near*

9

Boulder Beach ☎ *702/293–6180* ⊕ *www.lakemeadcruises.com* 🎫 *From $26; advance ticketing online.*

SCUBA DIVING AND SNORKELING

The creation of Lake Mead flooded a huge expanse of land, and, as a result, sights of the deep abound for scuba diving. Wishing Well Cove has steep canyon drop-offs, caves, and clear water. Castle Cliffs and Virgin Basin both have expansive views of white gypsum reefs and submerged sandstone formations. In summer Lake Mead is like a bathtub, reaching 85°F on the surface and staying at about 80°F down to 50 feet below the surface. Divers can actually wear bathing suits rather than wet suits to do some of the shallower dives. But visibility— which averages 30 feet to 35 feet overall—is much better in the winter months before the late-spring surface-algae bloom obscures some of the deeper attractions from snorkelers. Be aware that Lake Mead's level has dropped because of low snowfall in the Rockies. This has had some effect on diving conditions.

Outfitters Dive Into Fun ✉ *50 N. Gibson Rd., Ste. 170, Henderson* ☎ *702/479–7900* ⊕ *www.diveintofun.com.*

TRAVEL SMART ARIZONA

GETTING HERE AND AROUND

Most visitors to Arizona arrive either by car via one of the main east–west interstates, Interstate 40 or 10/8, or by air into the state's major airport in Phoenix. (Smaller but still significant numbers fly into Tucson.) Most visitors who arrive by air rent cars; public transportation is limited and limiting, and this vast state is ideally suited for car touring. The state's highways are well maintained, have minimal congestion outside of Phoenix, and have high speed limits (up to 75 mph on interstates); so traveling even significant distances by car isn't a great challenge, and the scenery throughout most of the state is stunning.

▌ AIR TRAVEL

Despite its high passenger volume, lines at the check-in counters and security checkpoints at Phoenix Sky Harbor are usually brisk and efficient, although during busy periods (spring break, holiday weekends, and so on) you should anticipate longer waits and arrive at the airport 30 to 60 minutes earlier than you would otherwise. Because Phoenix is a hub for Southwest and American Airlines (as a result of its recent merger with US Airways), it has direct flights to most major U.S. cities and a number of international destinations elsewhere in North America (Calgary, Cancún, Edmonton, Guadalajara, Mexico City, Puerto Vallarta, Toronto, Vancouver, and San José, Costa Rica, among them), as well as nonstop service to London on British Airways.

Sample flying times from major cities are: one hour from Los Angeles, three hours from Chicago, and five hours from New York City. Keep in mind that several destinations have only seasonal nonstop service from Phoenix (usually from mid-autumn through mid-spring).

AIRPORTS

Major gateways to Arizona include Phoenix Sky Harbor International (PHX), about 3 miles southeast of Phoenix city center, and Tucson International Airport (TUS), about 8½ miles south of the central business area.

Phoenix Sky Harbor International Airport is one of the busiest airports in the world for takeoffs and landings but rarely suffers from congestion or lengthy lines. Its spacious, modern terminals are easily navigable, with plenty of dining options as well as free Wi-Fi. Sky Harbor's three passenger terminals are connected by the free Sky Train, which runs regularly throughout the day and also links to the rental car center and the 44th St./Washington METRO Light Rail station.

Tucson International Airport has one terminal that has a smattering of restaurants and free Wi-Fi. Although it services far fewer passengers per day than Sky Harbor, it does offer nonstop flights to a number of major metropolitan areas around the western half of the country (Atlanta is the only eastern city with direct service).

Airport Information Phoenix Sky Harbor International ☎ *602/273-3300* ⊕ *www.phxskyharbor.com.* **Tucson International Airport** ☎ *520/573-8100* ⊕ *www.flytucsonairport.com.*

FLIGHTS

Phoenix is a hub for Southwest Airlines and American Airlines, due to its recent merger with US Airways. These carriers offer direct flights in and out of Phoenix to most of the country's larger metro areas; Southwest also has direct flights from Tucson to Chicago, Denver, Las Vegas, Los Angeles, and San Diego, and American Airlines has numerous daily connections between Tucson and Phoenix. The nation's other major airlines also fly into Phoenix and have a few flights into Tucson as well.

Among the smaller carriers, Alaska Airlines has direct service from Phoenix and Tucson to Portland and Seattle. Frontier connects Phoenix with Denver. Hawaiian Airlines flies from Phoenix to Hawaii. JetBlue has service from Phoenix to Boston and New York. Sun Country Airlines has seasonal service from Phoenix to Minneapolis. Canada's WestJet connects Phoenix directly with most major cities in western Canada. Low-cost carrier Spirit Airlines arrived in Phoenix in late 2013, adding direct service to Denver, Chicago, and Minneapolis. Another newcomer is discount Mexican airline Volaris, which flies from Phoenix to Mexico City and Guadalajara.

Within Arizona, American Airlines flies from Phoenix to Flagstaff and Yuma. Great Lakes Airlines flies connects a number of smaller Arizona cities (Kingman, Page, Show Low, Prescott) with Phoenix, Los Angeles, Denver, Las Vegas, and a few other smaller airports around the Southwest—sometimes one or two connections are required. Scenic Airlines flies from Las Vegas to the Grand Canyon.

Airline Contacts Alaska Airlines
🖃 800/252-7522 ⊕ www.alaskaair.com.
American Airlines 🖃 800/433-7300 ⊕ www.aa.com. **Delta Airlines** 🖃 800/221-1212 ⊕ www.delta.com. **jetBlue** 🖃 800/538-2583 ⊕ www.jetblue.com. **Southwest Airlines** 🖃 800/435-9792 ⊕ www.southwest.com. **United Airlines** 🖃 800/864-8331 ⊕ www.united.com.

Smaller Airlines Frontier Airlines
🖃 800/432-1359 ⊕ www.flyfrontier.com. **Great Lakes Airlines** 🖃 800/554-5111 ⊕ www.greatlakesav.com. **Hawaiian Airlines** 🖃 800/367-5320 ⊕ www.hawaiianair.com. **Scenic Airlines** 🖃 855/235-9422 ⊕ www.scenic.com. **Spirit Airlines** 🖃 801/401-2200 ⊕ www.spirit.com. **Sun Country Airlines** 🖃 800/359-6786 ⊕ www.suncountry.com. **Volaris** 🖃 866/988-3527 ⊕ www.volaris.com. **WestJet** 🖃 888/937-8538 ⊕ www.westjet.com.

▌CAR TRAVEL

A car is a necessity in Arizona, as even bigger cities are challenging to get around in using public transportation. Distances are considerable, but you can make excellent time on long stretches of interstate and other four-lane highways with speed limits of up to 75 mph (even rural two-lane highways often have speed limits of 65 mph). In cities, freeway limits are between 55 mph and 65 mph. If you venture off major thoroughfares, slow down. Many rural roadways have no shoulders; on many twisting and turning mountain roads speed limits dip to 25 mph, and police officers often patrol heavily near entrances to small town centers, where speed limits drop precipitously. For the most part, the scenery you'll take in while driving makes road-tripping worth the time and effort.

At some point you'll probably pass through one or more of the state's 22 Native American reservations. Roads and other areas within reservation boundaries are under the jurisdiction of reservation police and governed by separate rules and regulations. Observe all signs, and respect Native Americans' privacy. Be careful not to hit any animals, which often wander onto the roads; the fines can be very high.

Note that in Phoenix certain lanes on interstates are restricted to carpools and multioccupant vehicles. Seat belts are required at all times. Tickets can be given for failing to comply. Driving with a blood-alcohol level higher than 0.08 will result in arrest and seizure of your driver's license. Fines are severe. Radar detectors are legal in Arizona, as is driving while talking on handheld phones—but note that texting while driving is illegal in Phoenix and Tucson, and state police do pull drivers over for both talking and texting on mobile phones, citing the state law that you are driving at a "speed not reasonable and prudent." Law enforcement argue that any speed is not reasonable and prudent when you're using a mobile device, because drivers need to pay full attention to their driving.

Always strap children under age five into approved child-safety seats. In Arizona children must wear seat belts regardless of where they're seated. In Arizona you may turn right at a red light after stopping if there's no oncoming traffic.

Information Arizona Department of Public Safety ☎ *602/223–2000* ⊕ *www.azdps.gov.*

Arizona Department of Transportation ☎ *511 for Arizona road info from within the state, 888/411–7623 for Arizona road info from outside state* ⊕ *www.az511.com.*

GASOLINE
Gas stations, many of them open 24 hours, are widely available in larger towns and cities and along interstates. However, you'll encounter some mighty lonely and long stretches of highway in certain remote sections of Arizona; in these areas it's not uncommon to travel 50 or 60 miles between service stations. It's prudent to play it safe when exploring the far-flung corners of the state and keep your tank at least half full. Gas prices in Arizona are slightly higher than the national average but generally lower than in neighboring Nevada and California.

PARKING
Parking is plentiful and either free or very inexpensive in most Arizona towns, even Phoenix and Tucson. During very busy times, however, such as holidays, parking in smaller popular places like Sedona, Flagstaff, Scottsdale, and Bisbee can prove a little challenging.

ROAD CONDITIONS
The highways in Arizona are well maintained, but there are some natural conditions to keep in mind.

Desert heat. Vehicles and passengers should be well equipped for searing summer heat in the low desert. If you're planning to drive through the desert, make sure you're well stocked with radiator coolant, and carry plenty of water, a good spare tire, a jack, a cell phone, and emergency supplies. If you get stranded, stay with your vehicle and wait for help to arrive.

Dust storms. Dust storms are common on the highways and interstates that traverse the open desert (Interstate 10 statewide, and Interstate 8 between Casa Grande and Yuma). These usually occur from May to mid-September, causing extremely low visibility. They also occur occasionally in northeastern Arizona around the Navajo and Hopi regions. If you're on the highway, pull as far off the road as possible, turn on your headlights to stay visible, and wait for the storm to subside.

Flash floods. Warnings about flash floods shouldn't be taken lightly. Sudden downpours send torrents of water racing into low-lying areas so dry that they're unable to absorb such a huge quantity of water quickly. The result can be powerful walls of water suddenly descending upon these low-lying areas, devastating anything in their paths. If you see rain clouds or thunderstorms coming, stay away from dry riverbeds (also called arroyos or washes). If you find yourself in one, get out quickly. If you're with a car in a long gully, leave your car and climb out of the gully. You simply won't be able to outdrive a speeding wave. The idea is to get to higher ground immediately when it rains. Major highways are mostly flood-proof, but some smaller roads dip through washes; most roads that traverse these low-lying areas will have flood warning signs, which should be seriously heeded during rainstorms. Washes filled with water shouldn't be crossed unless you can see the bottom. By all means, don't camp in these areas at any time, interesting as they may seem.

Fragile desert life. The dry and easily desecrated desert floor takes centuries to overcome human damage. Consequently, it's illegal for four-wheel-drive and all-terrain vehicles and motorcycles to travel off established roadways.

Winter snow and ice. First-timers to Arizona sometimes doubt the intensity and prevalence of icy and snowy winter weather in the state's higher elevations: the Interstate 40 corridor, Grand Canyon region, north-central and northeastern Arizona, as well as some high-elevation communities in eastern Arizona. It's not uncommon for Phoenix to enjoy dry weather and temperatures in the 50s and 60s, while Flagstaff—just 140 miles north—is getting heavy snow and high winds. Facilities at the North Rim of the Grand Canyon are closed from mid-October through mid-May, and the road to the North Rim usually closes by or before December 1. Always check on weather conditions before planning trips to northern and eastern Arizona from late fall through mid-spring.

ROADSIDE EMERGENCIES

In the event of a roadside emergency, call 911. Depending on the location, either the state police or the county sheriff's department will respond. Call the city or village police department if you encounter trouble within the limits of a municipality. Native American reservations have tribal police headquarters, and rangers assist travelers within U.S. Forest Service boundaries.

Information Automobile Association (*AAA*). ☎ *800/222-4357* ⊕ *www.aaa.com.*

CAR RENTAL

Car-rental rates in Phoenix typically begin around $28 a day or $140 a week for an economy car with air-conditioning, automatic transmission, and unlimited mileage—rates vary according to supply and demand, tending to be lower in summer and often dramatically higher in winter. This doesn't include taxes and fees on car rentals, which can range from about 15% to 50%, depending on pickup location. The base tax rate at Sky Harbor Airport is about 30%. When you add the daily fees (which are about $6 or more a day), taxes and fees can add up to almost half the cost of the car rental. Taxes outside the airport are typically around 25% or less.

Check the Internet or local papers for discounts and deals. Local rental agencies also frequently offer lower rates.

Most agencies in Arizona won't rent to you if you're under the age of 21, and several major agencies won't rent to anyone under 25.

In Arizona the car-rental agency's insurance is primary; therefore, the company must pay for damage to third parties up to a preset legal limit, beyond which your own liability insurance kicks in.

Major Rental Agencies Alamo ☎ *877/222-9075* ⊕ *www.alamo.com.* **Avis** ☎ *800/633-3469* ⊕ *www.avis.com.* **Budget** ☎ *800/218-7992* ⊕ *www.budget.com.* **Hertz** ☎ *800/654-3131* ⊕ *www.hertz.com.* **National Car Rental** ☎ *877/222-9058* ⊕ *www.nationalcar.com.*

▌ TRAIN TRAVEL

Amtrak's *Southwest Chief* operates daily between Los Angeles and Chicago, stopping in Needles, California (near the Arizona border), Kingman, Williams Junction (from which bus transfers are available to the scenic Grand Canyon Railway), Flagstaff, Winslow, and Gallup, New Mexico (near the Arizona border). The *Sunset Limited* travels three times each week between Los Angeles and New Orleans, with stops at Yuma, Maricopa (about 25 miles south of Phoenix), Tucson, and Benson. There's a connecting bus (a three-hour trip) between Flagstaff and Phoenix.

Train Information Amtrak ☎ *800/872-7245* ⊕ *www.amtrak.com.*

ESSENTIALS

■ ACCOMMODATIONS

Arizona's hotels and motels run the gamut from world-class resorts to budget chains and from historic inns, bed-and-breakfasts, and mountain lodges to dude ranches, campgrounds, houseboat rentals, and RV parks. Make reservations well in advance for the high season—winter in the desert and summer in the high country. A few areas, such as Sedona and the Grand Canyon's South Rim, stay relatively busy year-round, so book as soon as you can. Tremendous bargains can be found off-season, especially in the Phoenix and Tucson areas in summer, when even the most exclusive establishments may cut their rates by half or more.

Phoenix and Tucson have the most variety of accommodations in the state, with Flagstaff offering the largest number in the northern part of the state. Lodgings in Sedona and in some of the smaller, more exclusive desert communities can be pricey, but there are inexpensive chains in or near just about every resort-oriented destination. That said, even the budget chains in these areas can have rates in at least the upper double-digits.

The Grand Canyon area is relatively pricey, but camping, cabins, and dorm-style resorts on or near the national park grounds offer lower rates. ■TIP→ If you plan to stay at the Grand Canyon, make lodging reservations as far as a year in advance—especially if you're looking to visit in summer. You might have a more relaxing visit, and find better prices, in one of the gateway cities: Tusayan, Williams, and Flagstaff to the south, and Jacob Lake, Fredonia, and Kanab, Utah, to the north. Of all of these, Flagstaff has the best variety of lodging options in all price ranges.

After booking, get confirmation in writing and have a copy handy when you check in. Be sure you understand the hotel's cancellation policy. Some places allow you to cancel without any kind of penalty—even if you prepaid to secure a discounted rate—if you cancel at least 24 hours in advance. Others require you to cancel a week in advance or penalize you the cost of one night. Small inns and B&Bs are most likely to require you to cancel far in advance. Most hotels allow children under a certain age to stay in their parents' room at no extra charge, but others charge for them as extra adults; find out the cutoff age for discounts.

Our local writers vet every hotel to recommend the best overnights in each price category, from budget to expensive. Unless otherwise specified, you can expect private bath, phone, and TV in your room. *For expanded reviews, facilities, and current deals, visit Fodors.com. Prices in the reviews are the lowest cost of a standard double room in high season.*

BED-AND-BREAKFASTS

Arizona is one of the better destinations in the country when it comes to B&Bs. You'll find luxurious Spanish colonial–style compounds and restored Victorian inns in the more upscale destinations, such as Tucson, Sedona, Flagstaff, and Prescott, as well as less fancy lodges virtually everywhere. Check with the Arizona Association of Bed and Breakfast Inns for details on its roughly 30 members throughout the state. The Arizona Trails Travel Service also has an extensive list of B&Bs and other lodgings, and can also help with vacation packages, guided tours, and golf vacations. Arizona-based Mi Casa Su Casa offers properties in a range of styles, from adobe haciendas in areas like Sedona and Tucson to pine cabins in the White Mountains. More general booking services like BedandBreakfast.com, BBonline.com, and BnBFinder.com also have quite a few Arizona listings, with BedandBreakfast.com leading the pack.

Reservation Services Arizona Association of Bed and Breakfast Inns ☎ *520/760–4200* ⊕ *www.arizona-bed-breakfast.com.* **Arizona Trails Travel Services** ☎ *480/837–4284, 888/799–4284* ⊕ *www.arizonatrails.com.* **Bed & Breakfast Inns Online** ☎ *800/215–7365* ⊕ *www.bbonline.com.* **BedandBreakfast.com** ☎ *512/322–2710* ⊕ *www.bedandbreakfast. com.* **BnBFinder.com** ☎ *888/469–6663* ⊕ *www.bnbfinder.com.* **Mi Casa Su Casa** ☎ *480/990–0682, 800/456–0682* ⊕ *www. azres.com.*

DUDE–GUEST RANCHES

Guest ranches afford visitors a close encounter with down-home cooking, activities, and culture. Most of the properties are situated around Tucson and Wickenburg, northwest of Phoenix. Some are resort-style compounds where guests are pampered, whereas smaller, family-run ranches expect *everyone* to join in the chores. Horseback riding and other outdoor recreational activities are emphasized. Many dude ranches are closed in summer. The Arizona Dude Ranch Association provides names and addresses of member ranches and their facilities and policies.

Information Arizona Dude Ranch Association ☎ *520/823-4277* ⊕ *www.azdra.com.*

■ COMMUNICATIONS

INTERNET

As in all major U.S. cities, high-speed Internet and Wi-Fi connections are ubiquitous at hotels throughout the state, even in remote areas (sometimes at high-end resorts or business hotels, especially in big cities, there's a fee of $5 to $15 per day, though free Wi-Fi is increasingly becoming the norm). There are also typically free connections at cafés (including Starbucks), restaurants, and other businesses.

■ EATING OUT

Two distinct cultures—Native American and Sonoran—have had the greatest influence on native Arizona cuisine.

Chiles, beans, corn, tortillas, and squash are common ingredients for those restaurants that specialize in regional cuisine (cactus is just as tasty but less common). Mom-and-pop taquerias are abundant, especially in the southern part of the state. In Phoenix, Tucson, Sedona, Flagstaff, and increasingly Bisbee, Prescott, Lake Havasu City, and a growing number of smaller communities, you'll find hip, intriguing restaurants specializing in contemporary American and Southwestern cuisine—often with an emphasis on local produce and meats—as well as some excellent purveyors of Asian cuisine, with Thai, Chinese, Vietnamese, and Japanese leading the way. *Prices in the reviews are the average cost of a main course at dinner or, if dinner is not served, at lunch.*

RESERVATIONS AND DRESS

Regardless of where you are, it's a good idea to make a reservation if you can. In some places (top resort restaurants in Scottsdale and Tucson, for example) it's expected. We only mention them specifically when reservations are essential (as in, there's no other way you'll get a table) or when they're not accepted. (Large parties should always call ahead to check the reservations policy.) We mention dress only when men are required to wear a jacket or a jacket and tie, which is rare in the casual Southwest, although you may want to dress smartly at a few upscale, cosmopolitan spots in Phoenix, Scottsdale, and Tucson.

Online reservation services, such as OpenTable, make it easy to book a table before you even leave home.

Contacts OpenTable ⊕ *www.opentable.com.*

WINES, BEER, AND SPIRITS

Although Arizona isn't typically associated with viticulture, the region southeast of Tucson, stretching to the Mexico border, has several microclimates ideal for wine growing. The iron- and calcium-rich soil is similar to that of the Burgundy region in France, and, combined with the temperate weather and lower-key atmosphere, has enticed several independent and family-run wineries to open in the past few decades in the Elgin, Sonoita, and Nogales areas, with a somewhat more nascent but increasingly respected crop of them having developed north of Phoenix, around Sedona and Verde Valley. Microbreweries are another fast-growing presence in Arizona, with a number of good ones in Phoenix, Tucson, Sedona, and Flagstaff, and other notables in Lake Havasu City, Prescott, Bisbee, and a few other towns.

In Arizona you must be 21 to buy alcohol. Bars and liquor stores are open daily, including Sunday, but must stop selling alcohol at 2 am. Smoking is prohibited in bars and restaurants that serve food. You'll find beer, wine, and alcohol at most supermarkets. Possession and consumption of alcoholic beverages is illegal on Native American reservations.

Contact Arizona Craft Brewers Guild ⊕ *www.azbrewguild.com.* **Arizona Wine Growers Association** ☎ *623/236–2338* ⊕ *www.arizonawine.org.*

❚ HEALTH

ANIMAL BITES

Wherever you're walking in desert areas, particularly between April and October, keep a lookout for rattlesnakes. You're likely not to have any problems if you maintain distance from snakes that you see—they can strike only half of their length, so a 6-foot clearance should allow you to remain unharmed, especially if you don't provoke them. If you're bitten by a rattler, don't panic. Get to a hospital within two to three hours of the bite. Try to keep the area that has been bitten below heart level, and stay calm, as increased heart rate can spread venom more quickly. Keep in mind that 30% to 40% of bites are dry bites, where the snake uses no venom (still, get thee to a hospital). Avoid night hikes without rangers, when snakes are on the prowl and less visible.

Scorpions and Gila monsters are less of a concern, since they strike only when provoked. To avoid scorpion encounters, look before touching: never place your hands where you can't see, such as under rocks and in holes. Likewise, if you move a rock to sit down, make sure that scorpions haven't been exposed. Campers should shake out shoes in the morning, since scorpions like warm, moist places. If you're bitten, see a ranger about symptoms that may develop. Chances are good that you won't need to go to a hospital. Children are a different case, however: scorpion stings can be fatal for them. Always try to keep an eye on what they may be getting their hands into to avoid the scorpion's sting.

Gila monsters are relatively rare and bites are even rarer, but bear in mind that the reptiles are most active between April and June. Should a member of your party be bitten, it's most important to release the Gila monster's jaws as soon as possible to minimize the amount of venom released. This can usually be achieved with a stick, an open flame, or immersion of the animal in water.

DEHYDRATION

This underestimated danger can be serious, especially considering that one of the first major symptoms is the inability to swallow. It may be the easiest hazard to avoid, however; simply drink every 10–15 minutes, up to a gallon of water per day when outside in summer, and keep well hydrated other times of year, too, as even cool winter days can be very dry.

HYPOTHERMIA

Temperatures in Arizona can vary widely from day to night—as much as 40°F. Be sure to bring enough warm clothing for hiking and camping, along with wet-weather gear. It's always a good idea to pack an extra set of clothes in a large, waterproof plastic bag that would stay dry in any situation. Exposure to the degree that body temperature dips below 95°F produces the following symptoms: chills, tiredness, then uncontrollable shivering and irrational behavior, with the victim not always recognizing that he or she is cold. If someone in your party is suffering from any of these symptoms, wrap him or her in blankets and/or a warm sleeping bag immediately and try to keep him or her awake. The fastest way to raise body temperature is through skin-to-skin contact in a sleeping bag. Drinking warm liquids also helps.

SUN EXPOSURE

Wear a hat and sunglasses and put on sunblock to protect against the burning Arizona sun. And watch out for heatstroke. Symptoms include headache, dizziness, and fatigue, which can turn into convulsions and unconsciousness and can lead to death. If someone in your party develops any of these conditions, have one person seek emergency help while others move the victim into the shade and wrap him or her in wet clothing (is a stream nearby?) to cool down.

▌ HOURS OF OPERATION

Most museums in Arizona's larger cities are open daily. A few are closed Monday, and hours may vary between May and September (off-season in the major tourist centers of Phoenix and Tucson). Call ahead when planning a visit to lesser-known museums or attractions, whose hours may vary considerably. Major attractions are open daily.

Most smaller retail stores are open 10–6, although big-box stores and small businesses tend to stay open until 9 or 10. Those in less-populated areas are likely to have shorter hours and may be closed or have shorter hours on Sunday.

▌ MONEY

ITEM	AVERAGE COST
Cup of Coffee	$2.50
Glass of Wine	$7
Glass of Beer	$4
Sandwich	$6
1-Mile Taxi Ride in Phoenix	$7
Museum Admission	$10

Prices throughout this guide are given for adults. Substantially reduced fees are almost always available for children, students, and senior citizens.

▌ PACKING

Pack casual clothing and resort wear for a trip to Arizona. Stay cool in cotton fabrics and light colors. T-shirts, polo shirts, sundresses, and lightweight shorts, trousers, skirts, and blouses are useful year-round in all but the higher-elevation parts of the state, where cooler temperatures mandate warmer garb. Bring sun hats, swimsuits, sandals, and sunscreen—essential warm-weather items. Bring a sweater and a warm jacket in winter, necessary November through April in the high country—anywhere around Flagstaff and in the White Mountains. And don't forget jeans and sneakers or sturdy walking shoes year-round.

SHIPPING SPORTING EQUIPMENT

If you're driving here, lugging your gear isn't much of a hassle. But travelers arriving by plane may find hauling bags of clubs, mountain bikes, and skis a bit daunting. Luggage Forward specializes in shipping gear. The service isn't cheap, but it's highly reliable and convenient.

Contact Luggage Forward ☎ 866/416–7447 ⊕ www.luggageforward.com.

▮ SAFETY

Arizona's track record in terms of crime is not unlike that of other U.S. states, if a little higher than average in Phoenix and Tucson. In these big cities you should take the same precautions you would anywhere—be aware of what's going on around you, stick to well-lighted and populous areas, and quickly move away from any situation or people that might be threatening.

▮**TIP➔** Check the U.S. government travel advisory before you plan a trip to the Mexico border towns. Visitors should take extra precautions.

Contacts Transportation Security Administration (TSA). ☎ 866/289–9673 ⊕ www.tsa. gov. **U.S. Department of State** ⊕ travel.state. gov.

▮ TAXES

Arizona state sales tax (called a transaction privilege tax), which applies to all purchases except food in grocery stores, is 5.6%. However, individual counties and municipalities then add their own sales taxes, which add another few percentage points, making giving some cities in the state among the highest sales taxes in the country, including Tucson (9.1%) and Phoenix (8.3%). Sales taxes don't apply on Indian reservations.

▮ TIME

Arizona is in the Mountain Time zone, but neighboring California and Nevada are in the Pacific Time zone. Arizona doesn't use Daylight Saving Time, though, and as a result, from spring through fall Arizona observes the same hours as Nevada and California and is an hour behind Utah and New Mexico. ▮**TIP➔ The Navajo Nation** does observe Daylight Saving Time, so it's always the same time on Navajo territory as in Mountain Time zone areas outside Arizona. Timeanddate.com can help you figure out the correct time anywhere.

Information Timeanddate.com ⊕ www. timeanddate.com/worldclock.

▮ TIPPING

The customary tip for taxi drivers is 15%–20%, with a minimum of $2. Bellhops are usually given $1–$2 per bag. Hotel maids should be tipped $2 per day of your stay. A doorman who hails a cab can be tipped $1–$2. You should also tip your hotel concierge for services rendered; the size of the tip depends on the difficulty of your request, as well as the quality of the concierge's work. For an ordinary dinner reservation or tour arrangements, $3–$5 should do; if the concierge scores seats at a popular restaurant or show or performs unusual services (getting your laptop repaired, finding a good pet-sitter, etc.), $10 or more is appropriate.

Waiters should be tipped 15%–20%, though at higher-end restaurants a solid 20% is more the norm. Many restaurants add a gratuity to the bill for parties of six or more. Ask what the percentage is if the menu or bill doesn't state it. Tip $1 per drink you order at the bar, though if at an upscale establishment, those $15 martinis warrant a $2 tip.

▮ TOURS

ARCHAEOLOGY

Archaeological Conservancy. This esteemed organization offers a number of multiday tours covering significant sites around the country, including one or two Southwest trips each year that may involve sites in Arizona. Additionally, the conservancy oversees and offers visits to a pair of archaeological preserves in Arizona, Sherwood Ranch Pueblo in Apache County, and Mission Guevavi in Santa Cruz County. ☎ 505/266–1540 ⊕ www.

archaeologicalconservancy.org ✉ *From $1,995.*

Crow Canyon Archaeological Center. Based in southwestern Colorado, this teaching and research center has a few different trips that touch on portions of Arizona; most last six or seven days. Trip agendas vary year to year, but they have included Carrizo Mountain Country hikes, Hopi kachina and silver-jewelry workshops, backcountry archaeology in Canyon de Chelly, and the study of Ancient Peoples of Arizona. ☎ *970/565–8975, 800/422–8975* ⊕ *www.crowcanyon.org* ✉ *From $3,000.*

BICYCLING

A number of companies offer extensive bike tours that cover parts of the Southwest. ■ **TIP→ Most airlines accommodate bikes as luggage, provided they're dismantled and boxed.**

AOA Adventures. This Scottsdale-based outfitter offers a variety of bike trips throughout the state, including half-day and multiday mountain-biking rides through the Sonoran desert and road-biking tours of Scottsdale and metro Phoenix as well as other parts of the state. ☎ *480/945–2881, 866/455–1601* ⊕ *www. aoa-adventures.com* ✉ *From $115.*

Bicycle Adventures. This Washington-based company offers a very popular six-day bike excursion, the Cactus Classic Bike Tour, through Tucson's Saguaro National Park and down through Tombstone and Bisbee. Lodgings each night are at high-end resorts and hotels throughout the region. ☎ *800/443–6060, 425/250–5540* ⊕ *www.bicycleadventures.com* ✉ *From $2,895.*

Magpie Cycling. Although specializing in tours around southeastern Utah, this Moab-based outfitter does have some exciting multiday mountain-biking trips around the North Rim of the Grand Canyon and covering parts of Lake Powell and the surrouding Navajo Nation. ☎ *800/ 546–4245* ⊕ *www.magpieadventures.com* ✉ *From $1,175.*

GOLF

Golfpac. This company specializing in custom golf-vacation planning arranges trips all over the world, with Phoenix, Scottsdale, and Tucson being among its most popular destinations. ☎ *888/848–8941, 407/260–2288* ⊕ *www.golfpactravel.com* ✉ *From $172.*

HIKING

AOA Adventures. This reliable company based in Scottsdale offers multiday and half-day hiking (as well as kayaking and rafting) excursions through some of the state's most dramatic scenery, from the Grand Canyon to Havasupai. ☎ *480/945–2881, 866/455–1601* ⊕ *www. aoa-adventures.com* ✉ *From $95.*

Just Roughin' It Adventure Company. The knowledgeable, enthusiastic guides at this Chandler-based outfitter offer myriad day and multiday hikes all around the state, with the Grand Canyon being a major focus. Try everything from ambitious rim-to-rim treks to shorter jaunts to Indian Garden and along the iconic Hermit Trail. Other guided hikes around the state cover some of the stunning mountains and canyons around Phoenix. Rock-climbing trips are also available. ☎ *480/857–2477, 877/399–2477* ⊕ *www.justroughinit.com* ✉ *From $70.*

Timberline Adventures. This Colorado-based company has multiday hiking tours in the Grand Canyon as well as in Chiricahua National Monument and the Sonoran Desert near Tucson. ☎ *303/368–4418, 800/417–2453* ⊕ *www.timbertours.com* ✉ *From $2,445.*

NATIVE AMERICAN HISTORY

Native American Journeys. You can explore a number of parts of the state important to indigenous peoples—Sedona, the Grand Canyon, Hopi Country, Antelope Canyon, Canyon de Chelly, Monument Valley—on walking, float-trip, and Jeep tours offered by this first-rate company. ☎ *928/284–4735* ⊕ *www.nativeamericanjourneys.com* ✉ *From $79.*

NATURAL HISTORY

Naturalist Journeys. Tours by this Arizona-based outfitter emphasize birding and geology, and venture into southeastern Arizona as well as the Grand Canyon region. ☎ 520/558–1146, 866/900–1146 ⊕ www.naturalistjourneys.com ✉ From $1,895.

Off the Beaten Path. Founded in 1986, this company offers a variety of tours in northern Arizona and elsewhere in the Southwest, including a six-night tour covering the Grand Canyon and Zion National Park (in southern Utah), a six-night tour of the Four Corners region (including Monument Valley), and a six-night Puebloan Mystery tour exploring Canyon de Chelly and New Mexico's Chaco Canyon. ☎ 406/586–1311, 800/445–2995 ⊕ www.offthebeatenpath.com ✉ From $2,595.

Victor Emanuel Nature Tours (VENT Birding Tours). This excellent, world-renowned tour operator that emphasizes birdwatching has been going strong since 1976, offering four or five different multiday tours throughout the year across Arizona. ☎ 512/328–5221, 800/328–8368 ⊕ www.ventbird.com ✉ From $2,195.

RIVER-RAFTING

Rafting on the Colorado River through the Grand Canyon is a once-in-a-lifetime experience for many who try it. Numerous reliable companies offer rafting tours through the canyon, including Action Whitewater Adventures, OARS, Western River Expeditions, and Wilderness River Adventures.

Action Whitewater Adventures. This company, founded in 1955, leads several different three- and six-day rafting itineraries through the Grand Canyon. ☎ 801/375–4111, 800/453–1482 ⊕ www.riverguide.com ✉ From $1,175.

OARS. This California-based company is highly respected for its rafting adventures through the Grand Canyon, which last from 5 to 18 days. ☎ 209/736–4677,

800/346–6277 ⊕ www.oars.com ✉ From $2,374.

Western River Expeditions. This Utah-based company's three-, four-, six-, and seven-day rafting trips through the Grand Canyon are geared to all ability levels, with the shorter adventures best for beginners. ☎ 801/942–6669, 866/904–1160 ⊕ www.westernriver.com ✉ From $1,265.

Wilderness River Adventures. Based in Page and part of the respected Aramark Parks and Destinations brand, this rafting company has trips both through the Grand Canyon and from Moab, Utah, through Cataract Canyon to Lake Powell on the Arizona border. Both motorized and paddle options are available. ☎ 800/992–8022 ⊕ www.riveradventures.com ✉ From $1,135.

▮ VISITOR INFORMATION

For local tourism information, see specific chapters and towns. Many of Arizona's Native American reservations have websites and helpful information. Some require permits for visiting certain areas.

Visitor Information Arizona Office of Tourism ☎ 602/364–3700, 866/275–5816 ⊕ www.arizonaguide.com.

Native American Contacts Arizona Commission of Indian Affairs ☎ 602/542–4426 ⊕ www.azcia.gov/tribes_of_arizona. *asp.* **Discover Navajo** ☎ 928/871–6436

⊕ *www.discovernavajo.com.* **Gila River Indian Community** ☎ *520/562-9715* ⊕ *www. gilariver.org.* **Hopi Tribe** ☎ *928/283-4500* ⊕ *www.hopiartstrail.com.* **Salt River Pima-Maricopa Indian Community** ☎ *480/362-7740* ⊕ *www.srpmic-nsn.gov.* **Tohono O'odham Nation** ☎ *520/383-0211* ⊕ *www. tonation-nsn.gov.* **White Mountain Apache Nation** ☎ *928/369-2036* ⊕ *www.wmat.nsn.us.*

ONLINE RESOURCES

Information of particular interest to outdoorsy types can be found on the website for Arizona State Parks, which administers 30 properties around the state. The site for the National Park Service has links to 26 Arizona parks, monuments, and other properties operated by the NPS, including Grand Canyon, Saguaro, and Petrified Forest national parks. The Great Outdoor Recreation Page (GORP) is another font of information for hikers, skiers, and the like.

There's a handful of excellent general-interest sites related to travel in Arizona.

A good bet is the *Arizona Republic*–sponsored ⊕ *azcentral.com*, which provides news, reviews, and travel information on the entire state, with a particular emphasis on Phoenix. Alternative newsweeklies are another helpful resource, among them the Phoenix *New Times*. For the southern part of the state, look for *Tucson Weekly*. In Flagstaff and north-central Arizona, check out Flagstaff Live! ⊕ *GayArizona. com* lists gay-friendly accommodations, nightlife, and other businesses around the state.

Contacts Arizona State Parks ☎ *602/542-4174, 800/285-3703* ⊕ *www.azstateparks. com.* **AzCentral.com** ⊕ *www.azcentral. com.* **Flagstaff Live!** ⊕ *www.flaglive.com.* **GayArizona.com** ⊕ *www.gayarizona.com.* **Great Outdoor Recreation Page (GORP)** ⊕ *www.gorp.com.* **National Park Service** ☎ *202/208-3818* ⊕ *www.nps.gov.* **Phoenix New Times** ⊕ *www.phoenixnewtimes.com.* **Tucson Weekly** ⊕ *www.tucsonweekly.com.*

INDEX

PHOTO CREDITS

Front cover: Ed Callaert [Description: Organ Pipe Cactus National Monument]. 1, Kerrick James. 2-3 Kerrick Jones. 5, Christophe Testi/Shutterstock. Chapter 1: Experience Arizona: 8-9, gary718/ Shutterstock. 10, Wilde Meyer Gallery. 11 (left and right), Metropolitan Tucson Convention & Visitors Bureau. 14 (top left), National Park Service. 14(bottom left), Mike Norton/Shutterstock. 14 (right) and 15 (left and top center), Kerrick James. 15 (top right), Katrina Brown/Shutterstock. 15 (bottom right), Daniel Gratton/Shutterstock. 16, Kerrick James. 17 and 18, Metropolitan Tucson Convention & Visitors Bureau. 19 (left), luchschen/Shutterstock. 19 (right), Paul Markow/Rancho de los Caballeros. 20, Royal Palms Resort and Spa. 22, Jeffrey Kramer, Fodors.com member. 24, Royal Palms Resort and Spa. 28-29, Adventurephoto/age fotostock. 30, julius fekete/Shutterstock. 32 (top), Jim West/age fotostock. 32 (bottom), Peter Mukherjee/iStockphoto. 33, NPS. 34 (top), iShootPhotos, LLC/iStockphoto. 34 (bottom), Kenneth Bosma/Flickr. 35, James Metcalf/iStockphoto. 36 (top), Tom Grundy/Shutterstock. 36 (bottom), Anton Foltin/Shutterstock. 37, Anton Foltin/Shutterstock. 38 (left), Frank Leung/iStockphoto. 38 (top center), IPK Photography/Shutterstock. 38 (bottom center), Dominic Sherony/wikipedia. org. 38 (top right), gary yim/Shutterstock. 38 (bottom right), Steve Byland/Shutterstock. 39 (top left), Mike Norton/Shutterstock. 39 (bottom left), EuToch/Shutterstock. 39 (top center), Nina B/Shutterstock. 39 (bottom center), robert van beets/iStockphoto. 39 (right), Walter Siegmund/wikipedia.org. 40 (left), Ashok Rodrigues/iStockphoto. 40 (top right), Daryl Faust/Shutterstock. 40 (bottom right), Eric Foltz/iStockphoto. Chapter 2: Phoenix, Scottsdale and Tempe: 41, Kerrick James. 42, John C. Russell/ Four Seasons Hotels & Resorts. 43, Barbara Kraft/Four Seasons Hotels & Resorts. 44, Royal Palms Resort and Spa. 45 (top), Sanctuary on Camelback Mountain, Scottsdale. 45 (bottom), InterContinental Hotels Group. 46, Starwood Hotels & Resorts.47 (top), David Peeters/iStockphoto. 47 (bottom), The Boulders Resort & Golden Door Spa. 48, Paul Markow/ Rancho de los Caballeros. 54 and 63, Kerrick James. 74, Royal Palms Resort and Spa. 98, Kerrick James. 100, Stuart Pearce/age fotostock. 116, JW Marriott Desert Ridge Resort. 127 and 130, Kerrick James. Chapter 3: Grand Canyon National Park: 133 and 135 (top and bottom), National Park Service. 136, Nickolay Stanev/Shutterstock. 148, poutnik/Shutterstock. 152, National Park Service. 165, Kerrick James. 170, Mark Lellouch/National Park Service. 172–73, Christophe Testi/Shutterstock. 174, Anton Foltin/Shutterstock. 175, Geir Olav Lyngfjell/Shutterstock. 176 (top and bottom) and 177 (top), Kerrick James. 177 (bottom), NPS. 178, Mark Lellouch/NPS. 179, Kerrick James. 184, Kerrick James. Chapter 4: North-Central Arizona: 187, Kerrick James. 188, Tom Grundy/Shutterstock. 189 (top), sochigirl/Shutterstock. 189 (bottom), Tom Grundy/Shutterstock. 190, David M. Schrader/Shutterstock. 207, Zack Frank/Shutterstock. 210, Kerrick James. 221 and 224, Kerrick James. 227, Lindy Drew. 239, Kerrick James. 240, LouLouPhotos/ Shutterstock. Chapter 5: Northeast Arizona: 249, Kerrick James. 250 (left), Sourav and Joyeeta Chowdhury/Shutterstock. 250 (right), Katrina Brown/Shutterstock. 251 (top and bottom), Aramark Parks & Destinations. 252, Sylvain Grandadam/age fotostock. 253 (top), Library of Congress Prints and Photographs Division. 253 (bottom), SuperStock/age fotostock. 254, Frank Staub/ age fotostock. 255, Wolfgang Staudt/Wikimedia Commons. 256, Robcsee/Shutterstock. 266-67, 272, 284, 291, 294-295, and 297, Kerrick James.302, CAN BALCIOGLU/Shutterstock. Chapter 6: Eastern Arizona: 305, Kerrick James. 306, George Burba/Shutterstock. 307 (top), Mike Norton/ Shutterstock. 307 (bottom), Zack Frank/Shutterstock. 308, Jeffrey M. Frank/Shutterstock. 314, Raymond Forbes/ age fotostock. 323, 329, 335, and 337, Kerrick James. 340, Sebastien Burel/Shutterstock. Chapter 7: Tucson: 343, 344, and 345 (top and bottom), Metropolitan Tucson Convention & Visitors Bureau. 346, Metropolitan Tucson Convention & Visitors Bureau. 358, Kerrick James. 374, Metropolitan Tucson Convention & Visitors Bureau. 385, 392, Metropolitan Tucson Convention & Visitors Bureau. 398, Phil Coleman. Chapter 8: Southern Arizona: 417, Kerrick James. 418 (top), Kevin Cole/wikipedia.org. 418 (bottom), Mark Godfrey/The Nature Conservancy. 419 (top and bottom). Metropolitan Tucson Convention & Visitors Bureau. 420, Walter Bibikow/age fotostock. 421 (top), Nickolay Stanev/iStockphoto. 421 (bottom), Jlahorn/wikipedia.org. 422, Metropolitan Tucson Convention & Visitors Bureau. 432, Kerrick James. 442, Mark Godfrey/The Nature Conservancy. 449, wikipedia.org. 453, Kerrick James. 459, Metropolitan Tucson Convention & Visitors Bureau. 464, Kerrick James. Chapter 9: Northwest Arizona and Southeast Nevada: 467, Kerrick James. 468 (left), cloki/Shutterstock. 468 (right), Bruce Grubbs/ Shutterstock. 470, Heeb Christian/age fotostock. 471 (top) Kerrick James. 471 (bottom), jader alto/ age fotostock. 472, Kerrick James. 478, Rolf Hicker Photography/Alamy. 485 and 494, Kerrick James. Back cover (from left to right): Dave Morgan ileximage/iStockphoto; Kerrick James; Wikimedia Commons [Creative Commons Attribution-Share Alike 3.0 Unported license]. Spine: Steven Allan/iStockphoto. About Our Writers: All photos are courtesy of the writers except for the following: Andrew Collins, courtesy of Fernando Nocedal; Mara Levin, courtesy of Shelley Shelton.

NOTES

NOTES

NOTES

NOTES

NOTES

NOTES

ABOUT OUR WRITERS

 Andrew Collins, a former Fodor's editor, updated the Northeast Arizona, Northwest Arizona and Southeast Nevada, and Travel Smart sections of the book. A resident of Oregon who travels several times annually to the Southwest, he has authored more than a dozen guidebooks and produces the website ⊕ *GayTravel. About.com.* He also writes a syndicated monthly travel column, writes about restaurants for *Four Seasons Magazine* and travel for *New Mexico* magazine, teaches food writing and travel writing for Gotham Writers' Workshop, and has contributed to *Travel & Leisure, Sunset,* and dozens of other periodicals.

 Tucson, Grand Canyon, North-Central, and Southern Arizona updater **Mara Levin** divides her time between travel writing, traveling, and social work. A native of California, Mara now lives in Tucson, where the grass may not be greener but the mountains, tranquility, and ... of desert life have their own ...

 A Phoenix-based freelance writer and editor, **Elise Riley** left her native Arizona to report for newspapers across the country. She quickly learned that no place had Mexican food like the Valley, and eventually found the way back to her favorite salsas and enchiladas. Today she appreciates the striking desert sunsets more than she did in her childhood, and eagerly awaits the next out-of-state visitor she can take on a tour of her favorite local restaurants. For the 2015 edition, Elise updated the Experience; Phoenix, Scottsdale, and Tempe; and Eastern Arizona sections.

 Michael Weatherford updated parts of the Southeast Nevada section of this guide. He's lived in Las Vegas since 1987, is the author of *Cult Vegas— The Weirdest! The Wildest! The Swingin'est Town on Earth,* and, as the entertainment reporter for the *Las Vegas Review-Journal,* sees all the shows.